CINCINNATI
OBSERVED

Urban Life and Urban Landscape Series
Zane L. Miller and Henry D. Shapiro, General Editors

CINCINNATI OBSERVED

Architecture and History

John Clubbe

A Sandstone Book

Ohio State University Press
Columbus

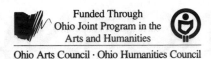

Funded Through
Ohio Joint Program in the
Arts and Humanities

Ohio Arts Council · Ohio Humanities Council

This book was published with the support of the Ohio Joint Program in the Arts and Humanities.

Library of Congress Cataloging-in-Publication Data
Clubbe, John.
    Cincinnati observed: architecture and history / John Clubbe.
      p. cm.—(Urban life and urban landscape series)
    "A Sandstone book."
    Includes bibliographical references and index.
    ISBN 0–8142–0512–7 (cloth: alk. paper).—ISBN 0–8142–0514–3
(pbk.: alk. paper)
      1. Architecture—Ohio—Cincinnati. 2. Cincinnati (Ohio)
—Buildings, structures, etc. I. Title. II. Series.
NA735.C5C58 1991
720' .9771'79—dc20   91–7446
                                               CIP

Text design by Hunter Graphics.
Type set in Times Roman by Graphic Composition, Athens, GA.
Printed by Edwards Brothers, Ann Arbor, MI.

The paper in this book meets the guidelines for permanence and durability of the Committee on Production Guidelines for Book Longevity of the Council on Library Resources.⊗

Printed in the U.S.A.

9 8 7 6 5 4 3 2 1

to Judy

Contents

Attractiveness of Cincinnati—walking tours—scope and range of tours—
organization of this book—maps—the urban experience—author's
background—acknowledgments.

Introduction: Stalking the City *3*

Portrait of a city—characteristics of Cincinnati—American vs. European
cities—Cincinnati a city of tradition—the Mapplethorpe controversy—visual
qualities of Cincinnati—"reading" a city—the pleasures of perception—
walking a city—urban surprises.

Chapter 1.
Fountain Square *11*

Tyler Davidson Fountain—Henry Probasco's vision—the pleasures of
water—history of Fountain Square—public places—Fountain Square
today—Dubois and other towers—Carew Tower—traffic poles—the Carew
Arcade and its history—Netherland Plaza—origins and characteristics of Art
Deco—Palm Court and Hall of Mirrors—the Carew observation deck—the
"living map" of Cincinnati—the Basin—downtown Cincinnati then and
now—transformation in the 1960s—Cincinnati's grid—history of the grid—
Philadelphia as model—what Cincinnati does to the grid—urban haze—
panoramas to north, east, south, and west—outline of this book—
skywalks—the Westin atrium—modern atria—Contemporary Arts Center—
a stroll along the skywalks.

Maps

Foreword

John Clubbe, a native of New York City and now a professor of English Literature at the University of Kentucky, in Lexington, has lived, like many peripatetic academics, in many cities. But more importantly he is an indefatigable explorer of cities in America, Britain, and continental Europe, and a voracious reader of the literature of cities, including past and present travel accounts as well as novels, poems, histories, plans, memoirs, diaries, and guidebooks. From Lexington he has launched repeated forays into Cincinnati. Goaded by an unflagging curiosity, he has tramped the city's streets, alleys, hills, riverfront, and neighborhoods, snooped through the interiors of its buildings, evaluated its architecture, savored its varied cityscapes, and measured its social, political, and cultural ambience. To these adventures he has brought vast knowledge and a store of insight, wisdom, and wit, which he uses in this book to put what *he* has seen in a comparative perspective that casts our understanding of American and European cities in the light of Western culture generally.

The result is an extraordinary production—consistent in tone, charming in manner, engaging and interesting throughout. We find embedded in the tours not only descriptions of places, things, and people, but also a host of brief essays—on alleys in Europe and America, including a lament that Cincinnati has not made more of its legacy of these delightful breaks in the downtown grid of streets; on the nineteenth-century French origins of English and American resistance to apartments as somehow conducive to immorality, especially adultery; on coal smoke in cities, and how some nineteenth-century English and Americans loved it for its visual and artistic effects and the pleasant associations it summoned; on viewing the skyline (a word, he informs us, that entered the language in the 1890s, together with *skyscraper*) not only from various stations but also while zipping down an expressway, the only such piece we know, and one that may inspire a new mode and genre of urban landscape "analysis." He also showers us with quotable quotes from eminent people and celebrities, including Ada Louise Huxtable, Charles Dickens, Frances Trollope, Ralph Waldo Emerson, Henry David Thoreau, Lafcadio Hearn, August Heckscher, and Cincinnati's own Doris Day, to cite just a few. He even gives us the name of "Cincinnati's most cheerful waitress," and her place of employment, so you can look her up sometime.

We have often talked vaguely about and longed for a book on the history of the city (any city, but Cincinnati in particular) which one could WALK as well as READ, and this book is close to what we had in mind.

It does not begin at the beginning, the way history books usually do, and does not tell us how great oaks from little acorns grow, the way history books usually do. It starts where we are and uses the *now,* conceived as the product of historical processes (including human decision making), to illumine the past and those same processes. Thus in the chapter on the Cincinnati Art Museum (chapter 12) we hear about the history of museums as civic institutions and about the history of museum architecture (*monumental,* to remind us of something) as a variation on the history of civic architecture, about the history of art collecting and therefore about the history of taste, about the history of museum practice (interior design, display, curatorship), and about the history of museum collecting policies or practices and the financial support for museums *as well as* about the history of art, the provenance of paintings, the relationship of paintings in one museum to paintings in other museums. In addition, he makes occasional connections between the plastic and the literary arts, and suggests other such connections—between, for example, the vogue for portraiture and concepts of individualism, between genre painting and genre writing—that we may not have noticed without Clubbe's hints.

Beyond this the book has the capacity to help locals see and acknowledge design as a set of choices, and human history, including urban history, as a series of choices. For "outsiders," even if they never visit Cincinnati, this volume as "case study" provides the esthetic and political distance necessary for the perception of their own places also as the product of human choices, and thereby will help them to see the possibility of good and humane design in their own places. It will make that lesson more forcefully for Cincinnatians, including ex-residents. For them, as for us, much of this material—not only the scenes but also some of the words, some of the emphases, some of the observations—will be familiar. But much of it is unfamiliar, even to us who have made the history, life, and landscape of Cincinnati our special business. We read the unfamiliar with interest, and wonder why we have never noticed what Clubbe notices, have never discovered what Clubbe has discovered. More important, we read the unfamiliar as if we have seen what he is talking about. It doesn't matter that we have never been there before Clubbe takes us. We are there now, and sometimes we like and sometimes we dislike what he enables us to see.

The focus of this book, then, is on the "urban experience" rather than on "urban history," for it is the experience of the city and especially the experience of *perceiving* the city that Clubbe wishes to convey and to prompt us to practice and think about. Walking along a path may be pleasant, and the exercise stimulating, but we must all be taught to see.

Clubbe does not say that, but he knows it. In a letter to us he places this book "within a long tradition . . . that began with Aristotle and goes down to the present of, say, Jane Jacobs or Georgina Masson or the earlier James Morris, via Wordsworth, Dickens, Dreiser, Howells, Bellow . . . ," the "urban appreciators, you might call them, most (not all) lovers of cities or, if not (Wordsworth, for example), fascinated by them." They sought, like Clubbe, as he puts it, "to respond *imaginatively* to the city." So he regards professional urban historians as "the new kids on the block," whose discipline dates from the 1950s. "You," Clubbe told us, have the "union cards, the jobs, the professional organizations, but we—the urban appreciators—are out there too, pounding the pavements, looking around, trying to seize and understand the life flowing by that we (most of us, anyway) love. Cities are too big to belong to any one discipline."

So they are, and we suggest that you take these walking tours with this learned and eloquent guide. But the book is also written to be read at leisure, from front to back, or by skipping at random from chapter to chapter, or even within chapters. It lacks the condensed style of most guides, and is purposely discursive and intimate, and properly didactic. Like the city itself, it is full of surprises. It entertains as it leads and teaches. And it is compelling not as the delineator of *the* culture of the city but in its exuberant willingness to participate in the ancient and persisting debate over the cultures of cities and what they might be made to become, if we choose.

Zane L. Miller
Henry D. Shapiro

Preface

Cincinnati is one of the oldest cities west of the Alleghenies; from the 1820s to about 1860, it was also the largest. Beautifully sited on a series of large bends of the Ohio River, it offers an impressive diversity of public and private buildings, including America's largest remaining collection of Italianate architecture. Its downtown is vital, its cultural institutions are impressive and well supported, and it has, arguably, several of the loveliest suburbs of any American city. Cincinnati has long beguiled visitors. Charles Dickens, sharply critical of much that he observed in the America of the 1840s, singled it out as "a beautiful city; cheerful, thriving, animated." In 1933 Winston Churchill spoke of Cincinnati as "the most beautiful of the inland cities of the Union."

Cincinnati Observed takes the form of walking tours. My portrait focuses on the city's architecture and history; its cultural traditions; its literary, artistic, and musical life; and its urban and suburban ambience. Cincinnati's hills demarcate it into sharply defined areas that facilitate the organization of tours. A few days suffice to sample significant parts of the city on foot. Like any painter of portraits, I have of course been selective. No single person, or even team of observers, can hope to comprehend a city fully. The best that we can hope for are glimpses, for insights that illumine the whole. So, rather than put together a compendium of all the interesting sights of Cincinnati, I pick and choose and, in regard to what I include, try to say *why* I find it interesting. Cincinnati has (by one count) forty-nine neighborhoods and forty-six suburbs. I make no attempt to cover all or even most of them. Seven bridges connect Cincinnati with northern Kentucky, itself an attractive area to explore, but except for discussion in chapter 6 I have omitted detailed consideration of it. Focusing on fewer things has resulted in a still formidable, but more manageable, volume. The gain in coherence will compensate, I trust, for the loss of inclusiveness.

Through its sequence of tours this book offers a detailed reading of the cityscape. I begin with Cincinnati's heart, Fountain Square. Chapters 2 through 8 cover downtown, the riverfront, and Over-the-Rhine. Pre-Civil War Cincinnati was largely contained within the Basin. (From the air central Cincinnati and northern

Kentucky, encircled by hills, appear to be nestled in a gigantic basin bisected by the Ohio River—hence the designation.) After the Civil War, the city expanded onto its hills. I consider in chapters 9 through 11 three of the hilltop suburbs—Mount Auburn, Clifton, and Mount Adams—that are of historic, architectural, and topographical distinction. Cincinnatians live in a series of contiguous villages and identify as much with these smaller communities as with the larger urban entity. Examining the development of the smaller enclaves enables us to obtain different perspectives on the city. Chapter 12, on the Cincinnati Art Museum, considers the city's artistic heritage in relation to its growth and history. The final chapter takes in major landmarks and institutions beyond the central area—among them Union Terminal, Spring Grove Cemetery, and the Cincinnati Zoo—as well as two outlying suburbs, Glendale and Mariemont.

My perspective on Cincinnati derives from my own experience of the city—my particular beat, so to speak. I have focused on the Cincinnati I know—and like—best. The result is a book that is at times discursive and intimate, but not, I think, idiosyncratic. The tours, except for chapter 13, are designed as walking tours. Even this last chapter, though it requires vehicular transportation, remains in essence a walking tour. To get to know a city well there is no substitute for using one's feet. Walking is a passion of mine, and this book is largely about the city that can be walked.

Organization is the essence of any book. One person's way of depicting a city differs from the next's. I interpret more than I describe, though I often describe. Within the area I cover I tell you where you should go and what you should see. Occasionally I even suggest where you might eat. "Good food and good buildings," Ada Louise Huxtable once (rightly) observed, "are natural allies and related pleasures." Two centuries before, Dr. Samuel Johnson was more blunt: "I look upon it that he who does not mind his belly will hardly mind anything else." Gustatory landmarks are as much a part of the urban scene as any other. We shall not neglect them, transitory as they often are. I have made every tour roughly circular: it ends at or near where it began. I have also tried to keep the walks to a manageable length. None, I hope, exceeds a long morning or afternoon. If that sounds too forbidding, take part of a tour one day, the rest on another. Before walking any chapter consult the list of opening times at the back of the book. There you will also find a bibliography to guide further reading.

Tours can be taken independently or in conjunction with one another. For the convenience of those with limited time, I have conceived the first six chapters as a unit. The hardy sightseer may be able to manage chapters 1 through 3 in one full day; similarly, chapters 4 through 6. These "core chapters" offer a comprehensive introduction to Cincinnati's downtown and waterfront. They start either at or within a few minutes walk of Fountain Square. Those with more than a few days can pick and choose among other tours. Chapters 7 and 8, covering Over-the-Rhine, may be taken together, one in the morning, one in the afternoon. Whenever possible, I have tried to correlate paired tours. Thus chapter 8 begins near where chapter 7 ends. Similarly, chapters 9 and 10, Mount Auburn and Clifton, form a pair. Clifton is easily reached by bus from where the Mount Auburn tour ends. Chapter 11, Mount

Adams/Eden Park, ends near the Cincinnati Art Museum (chapter 12). Chapter 13 requires a car for the complete circuit. You *can* encompass it in one extremely full day, but you may prefer to visit the points of interest individually or undertake them as separate expeditions.

Being oriented in a city begins with maps. Each chapter includes a map of the area covered with the tour route indicated. These maps should be adequate for most purposes, though if you plan to use this book extensively, I recommend three others. *Metropolitan Cincinnati* (H. M. Gousha Co.) serves nicely for general orientation. One side represents the Greater Cincinnati area; the reverse renders clearly the city center's street grid. Cincinnati's grid, oriented on roughly north-south and east-west axes, facilitates the giving of directions. *Metropolitan Cincinnati* includes the terrain covered in ten chapters (1–8, 11, 13) and a large portion of that in chapter 9. It does not cover Clifton (chapter 10) or the Cincinnati Art Museum, which will supply you with a floor plan. For the second map I recommend either the Geographia *Greater Cincinnati Street Atlas* or the Hagstrom *Greater Cincinnati Atlas,* particularly if you wish to move beyond the central area. Each comes in the form of looseleaf books, with the city and vicinity divided into sections; each has an index of streets. I have used both extensively, and the differences between them are negligible. An advantage in having both, at least for the serious Cincinnati explorer, is that each is platted differently. Thus it may be easier to cover a particular area using one instead of the other, not because the map in one is intrinsically better than that in the other, but because the area covered is more easily followed on one map than on the other.

The locations of selected major tour items appear on the accompanying maps in the order that we encounter them. They also appear in **boldface** at their main point of discussion in the text. Other items of interest, though not shown on the maps, are also boldfaced in the text as they occur. Take along binoculars if you can. They will enhance your pleasure in picking out detail in the vistas from the Carew Tower or from Mount Adams, to say nothing of bringing into focus the pelicans on the Central Trust Tower, the elves atop the Rothenberg School, and, especially perhaps, the extraordinary mosaics in Union Terminal. And don't forget good walking shoes.

I have designed *Cincinnati Observed* for anyone who wishes to know more about Cincinnati, its architecture, its history, and its cultural life. Since visitors will use this book, I have tried to keep their needs in mind. It is designed for long-term as well as short-term visitors; for native Cincinnatians, curious about their city; for the armchair traveler, whether visitor or native; and for the walker of cities seeking guidance where to go and what to look for. It is also designed for lovers of cities, actual or would-be. Explore one individual deeply enough, Emerson claimed, and truths about all individuals emerge. Similarly with cities. Although my focus is on Cincinnati, my subject is the urban experience. Intended as a field book, *Cincinnati Observed* is presented as a continuous narrative. I hope you will find reading it an enjoyable experience.

Since I am not by birth or residence a Cincinnatian, my perspective lacks the intimacy of a life lived within the city. I am a former New Yorker, privileged to have been raised and educated in midmost Manhattan, that most spectacular of urban

wonderlands. In Cincinnati I contemplate a smaller city, one that in odd, often unexpected, ways reminds me of my hometown. Since 1976 I have resided in Lexington, Kentucky, a much smaller city in a rural state, from which I look upon
Cincinnati as a regional metropolis. Before moving to Kentucky I had a ten-year
stint in Durham, North Carolina. Between New York and Lexington, I have lived,
for periods from six months to over a year, in Paris, Münster, Rome, London, and
Cambridge, Massachusetts. Cities have fascinated me since childhood, and these
earlier urban experiences have no doubt shaped my response to Cincinnati.

Immediacy and personal involvement in the life of a city are valuable but not
everything. One advantage in approaching a subject as a relative outsider is that you
are not bound by accepted truisms or to conventional postures. The best book on
London that I know—*London: The Unique City* (1934)—is by a Dane, Steen Eiler
Rasmussen, who never lived in London for more than one month a year. The most
perceptive visitor Florence has ever had, according to Eve Borsook, was Hippolyte
Taine, who stayed in the city eight days. Between James Boswell's first meeting
with Samuel Johnson in 1763 and Johnson's death in 1784, Boswell was in Johnson's company only about 300 days. Like Rasmussen and Taine, Boswell made
every day count. Out of his hoarded hours in Johnson's company he wrote his *Life
of Johnson,* arguably the best biography in English. Weekends are when I enjoy
Cincinnati's company. Though I intend no comparison between this endeavor and
Boswell's (or Rasmussen's or Taine's), I too have tried to make my days count.

This book derives as much from personal experience as from academic study.
Where academic, it is academic in an unusual way. The contemporary discourses of
academic specialization have increasingly left knowledge fragmented and techno-
cratic. Scholars in the humanities rarely risk writing on subjects outside their own
disciplines. Since a major city is the most complex of man's achievements, no single
discipline can pretend to encompass it entirely. My own training is in English literature, with a specialty in the nineteenth century. For this book, however, I have
mostly drawn upon other disciplines—among them architectural history, urban
studies, landscape design, aesthetic theory, and art history—in none of which do I
claim professional competence. Specialists will no doubt smile at my errors, my
innocent assumptions, my crudities of thought. But in the nature of the undertaking
they may be inevitable. Believing in the need to interrelate humanistic knowledge,
I have written a book that falls into no easily definable category. That may be its
weakness. It may also be its strength.

Acknowledging kindnesses received in preparing a book is always a happy
task. A great many people have contributed though no one of them is to be held
responsible for statements I make. If I have not cited here all who have helped, I
must mention a few: Felix F. Bere, Robert J. Duffy, and Charlotte T. ("Tommie")
Birdsell of Cincinnati's City Planning Department; Frances Crotty, Gregory Thorp,
Cecil Scott, and Gibson Yungblut, all devoted to Union Terminal; Bob Wimberg,
an aficionado of Cincinnati's urban past like no other, who has been generous of his
time in introducing Cincinnatians (and me) to the city through his excellent Saturday walking tours; Humbert S. Nelli, the University of Kentucky's urban historian,

who has counselled wisely and well; Steve and Melissa Abshire, who have in ways they may not be aware of helped make my time in Cincinnati particularly pleasant; Robert Hemenway, former chairman of the English Department at the University of Kentucky, who arranged a reduced teaching load for 1985–1986 that enabled me to progress more rapidly; Kevin Kiernan, who followed him, for a similar gift of time in the spring of 1989. Walt Foreman and Armando Prats, the Department's resident experts on WordStar, came to my rescue on more than one occasion when I was floundering amidst its complexities. Gyula Pauer, director of the University's Cartography Laboratory, prepared the excellent maps; Robert Hemenway, now Chancellor of the University of Kentucky, and Kevin Kiernan were instrumental in finding funds to pay for them. Harry Gilbert and Dan Hodge, past and present librarians of the University's School of Architecture, made extraordinary efforts answering queries. The Ohio State University Press's official readers, Zane L. Miller and Henry D. Shapiro, have been unusually sympathetic to my ways of looking at Cincinnati. At the Press itself I have had the good fortune to work with Alex Holzman and Victoria Althoff, both of whom have expertly smoothed the metamorphosis of manuscript into book. I particularly wish to thank the joint committee of the Ohio Humanities Council and the Ohio Arts Council for a generous grant that allowed the inclusion of additional photographs by J. Miles Wolf. J. Chewning gave good advice on historical photographs. Unless stated otherwise, the photographs are mine.

Over the years I have spent many happy hours and made many fortunate purchases in Cincinnati's secondhand bookshops. Among those who have generously shared with me their knowledge of Cincinnati and of bibliopoly are Jim Fallon and Dick Baringhaus of the Ohio Book Store; John Coleman of Acres of Books; Sam Jenike and Phil Metz of The Dust Jacket; Stanley Duttenhofer and Russ Speidel of Duttenhofer's; Carolyn Downing of Significant Books; Dan Nagle of T & S Books (Covington); and Tom Brengelman of The Bookstore.

I wish to thank those who graciously read individual chapters of my manuscript, or parts thereof. They include Ted Eversole, Cissie Dore Hill, J. Chewning, Marjorie Meanwell, Karl Raitz, and Charles Westheimer; Jan Weigel, Katharine Hanna, and Ruth Meyer, who commented usefully on my pages on the Taft Museum; Jane Durrell, who did the same in even greater detail for my chapter on the Cincinnati Art Museum; Sallie R. Wadsworth, who had many good observations to make on my Introduction and on the first six chapters; Allen Bernard, who sharpened my awareness of Mount Adams; and David Ehrlinger who, in conversation and through correspondence, honed my understanding of the development of the Cincinnati Zoo. More generally, Deborah Schwabach has illuminated urban life for me.

Revisions were accomplished during my tenure in 1989–1990 as a Visiting Scholar at Harvard, where I benefited from conversations with James S. Ackerman, Sarah Allaback, Alex Krieger, Neil Levine, and Dan Aaron, the last a Cincinnati aficionado of half a century's standing. Neil Levine kindly provided me with a forum to try out my ideas about Cincinnati, as did John and Judith Dowling, masters of Leverett House. To the camaraderie of Leverett's Senior Common Room I owe many fruitful interchanges, and for making possible this privilege, among a bounty of other courtesies, I am grateful to Elizabeth and Jerome Buckley. During this Cambridge year Jill Rubenstein in far-away Cincinnati, in addition to keeping me posted on local developments, generously took time to read my manuscript and to make useful suggestions. In helping with proofs and the index, Joan Blythe took precious hours away from her own research to render invaluable assistance.

My greatest long-term obligations are three. To Richard D. Altick, Regents Professor Emeritus at The Ohio State University, I am again indebted, as so often in the past, for invaluable guidance. His customarily acute critique of three chapters of my manuscript proved immensely beneficial; in addition, I owe much to the model of travel writing that is his *To Be in England* and to his epistolary encouragement of my work at all times. Patrick Snadon, formerly of the University of Kentucky, taught me to regard buildings within an embracing humanistic perspective and has patiently honed whatever innate sensibility for architecture I may have. Patrick read several chapters and together we walked several more—Over-the-Rhine II, Mount Auburn, Clifton. His comments, written and oral, have been invaluable. I owe an immense personal debt, expressed in the dedication, to Judith M. Wiza. She often accompanied me on my walks about Cincinnati, listened patiently to my notions about cities, and gave me the benefit of her own insights. Throughout she has been, in every way, a cheering and sustaining presence.

Writers on other cities have influenced my conception of Cincinnati. These include, on New York, Jane Jacobs and Gerard R. Wolfe; on London, Steen Eiler Rasmussen, David Piper, and Simon Jenkins; on Paris, Vincent Cronin and John Russell; on Rome, Georgina Masson; on Venice, Hugh Honour and James (Jan) Morris; on Cincinnati, Harry Graff and the other authors of the 1943 WPA guide; and, on urban life generally, Mark Girouard, Donald J. Olsen, and William H. Whyte. It was Jane Jacobs, in particular, who years ago in that staggering book, *The Death and Life of Great American Cities,* opened my eyes to the urban environment. Her subject is really about learning to see and understanding what one sees. She conceptualized for me elements of urban life that I had long felt. Thanks to her, I could now begin to grasp them in my own terms.

Cincinnati itself, through its gentle beauty and its vital cultural life, has stimulated my work greatly. Indeed, the city has been as much lived as studied. I have walked its streets in all seasons, in grim January snowstorms with below-zero temperatures and under muggy August skies with temperature and humidity both topping ninety. In these walks I have experienced numerous little, nameless, but remembered, acts of kindness. Cincinnati is, in my experience of it, a good place to be. I have enjoyed exploring the city as much as I have enjoyed writing about it. Whatever else this book does or does not do, I hope it gives readers a sense of that pleasure.

Cincinnati Observed

Introduction: Stalking the City

"WHAT," Thoreau asks in *Walden,* "does architecture amount to in the experience of the mass of men?" A fair question, and one that I attempt to answer in regard to Cincinnati in the following pages. The range of a city's architecture determines its essential outward character. Architecture is more than mere construction. It is a cultural endeavor, one that gains significance from its historical and social context. The buildings a city erects express its history, its values, its tastes. To understand Cincinnati's architecture is to begin to understand the city itself. Thus my main purpose will be to introduce you to some of Cincinnati's most interesting buildings, in different styles and from different eras, in order to allow you, in an organized manner, to discover the city on your own.

A portrait such as this looks not just at standard sights but at those hardly known, not just at landmarks but also at the anonymous buildings that provide the basic scenery of urban life, at the "ordinary" things—lampposts, cast-iron storefronts, street signs—that constitute the texture of the streetscape. In their very ordinariness we may find historic eloquence. Descriptions of buildings usually take up questions of style and taste. The year that often follows the first mention of a building is its date of completion. Accounts of structures tend to engage a historic dimension, to move outward to the larger community that is the city, and to see the city within a national and even an international context.

I have tried to seize Cincinnati at a particular moment in its history. Every city is always in a state of flux, every portrait of it at least slightly out of date. This book went to press late in 1990, but in any event a city always keeps one step ahead of its chronicler. A book on it must be an interim report, for a city is an organic whole, not a static work of art, and, like other organic wholes, is constantly evolving. Although a portrait of a city need not dwell on its vanished buildings, I do occasionally discuss one that had a powerful presence in the city's urban fabric or has left a powerful memory, either of itself or as the source of other buildings. For Cincinnati two such buildings, once neighbors on Vine St., are Isaiah Rogers' Burnet House (1850) and Henry Hobson Richardson's Chamber of Commerce Building (1889). The Burnet House influenced every subsequent Cincinnati hotel, the Chamber of

3

Commerce, a number of the city's massive Romanesque structures. Other buildings, like the Albee and Palace theaters downtown, more recent losses, are still mourned.

Cincinnati offers much that makes an urban environment fulfilling. Certain cities need to be savored, not rushed through. Cincinnati is one of them. Cumulatively it satisfies, for more than most cities, even some much older, it retains its architectural past. A city's buildings anchor it to time and place. "In the city," Lewis Mumford once observed, "time becomes visible." In other words, architecture is the primary visual manifestation of the stages in a city's history, a "dialogue across time," as Vincent Scully calls it. Properly understood, architecture is history itself: history palpable, visible, layered. A city's older buildings allow us truly to visualize the past for they are, in a very real sense, time capsules. The values they embody—identity, scale, complexity, style, intimacy—have accrued through several centuries of civilization.

Though Cincinnati's centuries are but two, in the annals of American cities two centuries is a long time. New York, founded in 1609, may have fewer buildings dating before 1850 than Cincinnati, founded in 1788. In part, this is because after the Civil War Cincinnati grew at a more measured pace than other major American metropolises. It never experienced the phenomenal growth in absolute numbers that Chicago did in the last decades of the nineteenth century or Detroit in the first decades of the twentieth. Even today most larger American cities are so caught up in the frenzy of the diurnal round that the touchstones of the past disappear virtually unnoticed. For good or for ill, things happened—and happen—more slowly in Cincinnati. A major benefit of this slower growth is that more older buildings, the tangible evidence of its past, have survived into the present. The relative stability Cincinnati offers, with its familiar landmarks and associations, also helps bind together the city's inhabitants.

A sense of place plays a profound, if largely unconscious, part in the emotional makeup of most people. If we can recognize, develop, and cultivate our sense of place in relation to other kinds of awareness, we surely give our lives greater meaning and interest. "One's own landscape," wrote John Burroughs in 1873, "comes in time to be a sort of outlying part of oneself." Appreciation of the built environment enhances our appreciation of life. The common memories Cincinnatians share of places they know enable them to feel satisfaction in their environment. Cincinnati, a hospitable city, is also a proud one. For this pride Cincinnatians have, as Dickens commented in 1842, "good reason." They are citizens of no mean city.

Americans care less about their cities than Europeans about theirs. Certainly we spend less money on them. Yet much in our urban heritage needs no apology. Our nineteenth-century buildings rival Europe's best; those of the twentieth often surpass them. Oddly, Cincinnati retains more of its nineteenth-century urban fabric than most European cities not bombed in World War II. It looks more "European" than many a European city today. Yet it is also that unexpected anomaly: a modern, well-run American city, vital and flourishing.

Most major European cities have inspired excellent books. Most major American cities, with the exception of New York, Chicago, San Francisco, and perhaps Boston and Los Angeles, have not. They have not in part because Americans (including many who should know better) think their own cities less interesting, less "historic," less worthy of studying or visiting than European cities. Few of those who travel thousands of miles to Europe or the Far East, who return laden with slides and superlatives, are aware of what their hometowns offer—or what surprises lie an hour's drive away. If Americans think of travel in America, it is to New York or to San Francisco, to Niagara Falls or to the Grand Canyon. "The realization is growing," Ada Louise Huxtable has written, "that . . . there is a whole world of architecture between New York and San Francisco and beyond Charleston and Savannah, lost in the shadow of the Chicago skyscrapers. It has been there all along, but the tendency has been to write it off and out of the history books." Cincinnati is part of that lost world. Americans persistently underrate the attractiveness and cultural richness of their own land. I limit myself to one further example. In his standard *History of Art* H. W. Janson speaks of the Great Serpent Mound, fifty miles east of Cincinnati, as an "extraordinary work of landscape architecture, as mysterious and moving in its way as Stonehenge." Most who have seen both the Great Serpent Mound and Stonehenge are likely to agree with Janson. But more Americans, I suspect—perhaps even more Cincinnatians—have visited Stonehenge.

By neglecting the cultural and visual resources of their country Americans do it an injustice, one that European visitors, agape over our museums, our landscapes, and our architecture, note with amazement. Travel to any major midwestern metropolis—Cleveland, Pittsburgh, Indianapolis, Toledo, Detroit, St. Louis, Minneapolis, Kansas City—and you will be hard put to find an up-to-date study of the city, or, for that matter, any decent book at all on it. In Europe the situation is otherwise. Every major city there boasts a plethora of books of varying degrees of complexity, from the massively detailed to the spectacularly pictorial. Eventually, as Americans become more aware of their urban heritage, our cities will gain the studies they deserve. But few exist now. I have prepared this book in the hope of providing such a study for Cincinnati.

The historians who often accuse Americans of trying to disown their past have not visited Cincinnati. It is a city where traditions die hard, where change comes slowly. One recent commentator asserts that "Cincinnati has never quite recovered from Mrs. Trollope's visit nor from its reputation as a tradition-bound town." He may well be right. Frances Trollope, who lived in Cincinnati from 1828 to 1830, left in her satiric portrait, *Domestic Manners of the Americans* (1832), an unforgettable image of a frontier town where pigs ran wild in the streets. A few decades later, Mark Twain allegedly opined, "When the end of the world comes, I want to be in Cincinnati—it is always ten years behind the times." In this century, *Time* magazine in 1948, covering the opening of the Terrace Plaza (now Hilton) Hotel, called the city "dowdy."

Today Cincinnati, if no longer dowdy, remains a conservative town, a town so safe it can legitimately be accused of dullness. Randall Katz cites an early Humphrey Bogart film in which Bogey, before taking on the bad guys, sends his girlfriend to Cincinnati "to keep her out of harm's way." For Katz the episode is "an example of the tendency in American literature and popular culture to depict Cincinnati as the last place in the universe where anything important, good or bad, is likely to happen to anybody." In other words, life in Cincinnati has a stalagmitic quality, which appears to put it outside our own experience. The city positively glories in its "safe" reputation; it is described in an official publication, presumably without irony, as "staid to the point of prudishness, solid to the point of petrifaction." The city regularly votes Republican in state, national, and many local elections. A 1986 article in the ultraconservative *Cincinnati Enquirer* spoke of Cincinnati as "the city that bans smoking in public places, the city so concerned about pigeon droppings that it once hired a man to shoot the pesky birds early in the mornings when no one was around, the city that fights pornography at every opportunity." Indeed, Cincinnati does not have a red-light district. (Those interested in such pleasures have traditionally driven across the Ohio River to Newport, Kentucky.) There are no adult bookstores, peep shows, nude dancing clubs, or X-rated videos. Newsstands do not carry *Penthouse* or *Hustler,* whose publisher, Larry Flynt, the city successfully prosecuted. You looked in vain on your TV for the *Playboy* channel.

Cincinnati's distaste for what some of its citizens consider pornography took an ugly turn in April 1990. The Contemporary Arts Center had agreed to show a traveling exhibit of photographs by Robert Mapplethorpe, a controversial modern photographer. Of the 175 images, five depicted homoerotic subjects, two nude or seminude children. The exhibit had caused problems elsewhere. The previous summer, the National Endowment for the Arts had drawn severe criticism for awarding it a grant and Washington's Corcoran Gallery had cancelled its showing. How to present such a hot potato in conservative Cincinnati? The Contemporary Arts Center compromised by hanging the disputed photographs in a room of their own—a policy that, as the poet Byron said once in another context, "saves, of course, the trouble of an index." (The titular hero of his great poem *Don Juan* rejoiced when he found that in a volume of his favorite classical authors all the prurient passages had been conveniently tucked away in an appendix.) But the compromise didn't work.

The center immediately became an easy target for local antipornography groups, who protested that the appearance of the Mapplethorpe photographs defamed the Queen City. Demonstrations and counterdemonstrations followed. The controversy polarized the city. Would "Banned in Boston" be succeeded by "Censored in Cincinnati"? Simon Leis, Hamilton County's sheriff, hoped so. He called the works "criminally obscene" even before the show opened. After the opening, Leis, backed by a small army of city police, swooped down upon the center, and on April 7th had it and its director Dennis Barrie indicted for allegedly pandering obscenity. For ninety minutes Leis closed the exhibit to videotape the offending photographs.

Tensions flared. Many Cincinnatians, outraged, denied the city had a right to censor art. In the end the photographs remained up, all of them. But for weeks the controversy brought the city an avalanche of negative publicity, from an Art Buchwald column to almost daily articles in the *New York Times,* which in the process once again aired the image of Cincinnati as a straight-arrow conservative bastion and antipornography stronghold. Unfortunately, few outside the city realized that the image had become outdated. Six citizens in ten, a poll taken at the height of the controversy revealed, thought the Mapplethorpe photographs had a right to be shown. And they were. The exhibit lasted out its Cincinnati run. People supported it with their feet. It drew 4000 on opening night, nearly three times as many as any other opening in the center's fifty-one year history. Lines went around the block, and the show set an attendance record. In October 1990 a jury of eight Cincinnatians acquitted Barrie and the center of all charges. Not bad for a city allegedly tradition-bound.

Cincinnati has progressed in other ways, too. Reverence for the past and hesitance to innovate comprise only part of the story. Cincinnati looks forward as well as backward. Its list of "firsts" is impressive. It was the first city its size to adopt (in 1925) a comprehensive development plan. It followed that plan with three others, one in 1948, another in 1964, the most recent in 1982. This last, the *Cincinnati 2000 Plan,* currently guides its policies and is updated at intervals. All these plans are models of their kind. Downtown development has on the whole worked well. Older buildings have often been preserved; newer ones, if architecturally uninspired, have usually been compatible. Losses there have been, and mistakes there have been, but the downtown today is still alive and still safe. The riverfront has been attractively redone and opened to the public. The expressways that disfigure most American cities disfigure Cincinnati less. They also move traffic in and out of the city center efficiently—which expressways all too often fail to do. I could go on, but trust I have made my point: new and old, backward-looking and forward-looking combine to advantage in Cincinnati.

Cincinnati presents strong, positive visual images. More than most cities, it engages the eye. Visitors past and present have invariably commented with pleasure on its sinuous river and its curvaceous hills. As we walk along, we look around, out, and up. Vistas abound. Unusual perspectives—a Victorian mansion silhouetted against a hilltop, the skyline glimpsed down an alley—appear by surprise. Architecture speaks a language accessible to the eye. The mind may not understand all that the eye sees but the important thing is to look for ourselves and to try to understand something of what we see. Awareness of history and tradition, of building styles and landscape design, gives depth and reverberation to what the eye perceives. Occasionally—always a happy moment—sight may become insight. As the poet Gerard Manley Hopkins once put it, "These things, these things were here and but the beholder Wanting." With its buildings and its streetscapes, its river and its hills, its vistas and its perspectives, Cincinnati rarely fails to offer the beholder a visual challenge. At its best its landscapes can become, as Hopkins implies, symbolic and poetic. Nor are they accidental landscapes. Urban history no less than human history involves choice. Every city is the result of conscious choice, or rather of thousands of conscious choices made over the course of its history. No matter how haphazard parts of Cincinnati's cityscape may appear, it reflects the work of some hand or eye. Sometimes it is worth pausing, as we shall do occasionally, to ponder why things are as they are.

Cincinnati Observed is also about perception, about how we see things. Most of us go through life blind. Trees, flowers, birds, clouds, the phenomena of the natural landscape: we are aware that they are there, true, but how many of us can identify or discuss intelligently what we see? The urban landscape fares even less well than the natural. A major city is the largest of manmade objects, enormously complex and constantly evolving, yet much that we see, with time and will and patience, can be understood. We look at buildings and streets, if we look at all, uncomprehendingly. Before we can understand, we must realize that there is something to understand. This portrait attempts to make you aware of the Cincinnati cityscape by "reading" it, reading it in much the same way that we read a complex book, that is, by analyzing its component parts in the hope, ever elusive, that we may understand something of its meaning. To read is to interpret. If we learn to read a city better—to understand how it started out, how it has changed, why it now looks the way it does—much that appears incoherent in it becomes intelligible.

"To see takes time," once said Georgia O'Keeffe. It also takes work. "Hard looking," the art historian Kenneth Clark has written, involves "an effort of will which can scarcely be distinguished from heightened perception." In *The Other Half,* the second volume of his autobiography, Clark expressed his amazement over how "astonishingly observant of detail" was the art critic Bernard Berenson. "Things came as a fresh revelation to him every time he saw them. 'Where were my eyes yesterday?' he used to say." Sight, or the heightened perception that comes from it, was equally important for the novelist Joseph Conrad. His aim, he once asserted, was "before all, to make you *see.*" Equally, my aim has been to make you, whether visitor or native, look hard at sights familiar and unfamiliar in Cincinnati, in short "to make you *see.*" Emerson said of Thoreau that he "saw as with microscope, heard as with ear trumpet, and his memory was a photographic register of all that he saw and heard." And the elder Pliny, in the first century A.D., observed that the true instrument of observation was not the eye but the mind. Perception is a word that nicely bridges, on the one hand, a sensory alertness, and, on the other, a fullness of understanding. The chances are good that you will discover that even vision less keen than Thoreau's will delight the mind no less than it will delight the eye.

A sociologist will write one kind of book about a city, a businessman another, an urban historian a third, an architect a fourth. Those who live in a city relate to it differently from those who do not. Every Cincinnatian has opinions about the city. Some people are more conscious, or more articulate, about them than others. Downtowners perceive a different cityscape than suburbanites; the view from the interstate differs from that from the sidewalk. If a city has streets and buildings, it also has flavor and tone. I try to render a sense of Cincinnati's flavor and tone, of the city as a whole as well as of its parts, of its human as well as of its urban character. I also try to isolate the qualities that make Cincinnati distinctive. We are students of life before we become students of history or of architecture or whatever. More than being about architecture or history, this book is about how one responds to the urban experience. It is meant as an exercise in imaginative perception.

As well as in the physical structure of its buildings or in the minds of its inhabitants, a city lives in the words of the visitors who have described it over time. Among the many notable travelers who have passed through Cincinnati are Frances Trollope, Alexis de Toqueville, Harriet Martineau, Charles Dickens, Francis Parkman, Walt Whitman, Moritz Busch, and Lafcadio Hearn. Some who came to visit stayed a while: Mrs. Trollope over two years, Lafcadio Hearn nearly eight. Curious about Cincinnati, the great new metropolis of the West, these travelers afford us a perspective unobtainable from residents. The familiar to the resident is unfamiliar to the traveler. By inducing us to view the familiar in a different way, travelers convert us from our fixed modes of experience. In short, they give us new eyes.

A question we may ask in regard to any city is, is it walkable? Few, after all, are the North American cities that we can walk extensively and with pleasure. Is Cincinnati one of them? Does it provide variety and delight to the walker of its streets? Observers often described pre-Civil War Cincinnati as "the most compact city in America." Locked in its Basin, its hills preventing easy expansion, it possessed geographical compactness. Nineteenth-century Cincinnati was indeed an eminently walkable city, one where people went everywhere on foot. However great the decline in pedestrianism from that century to this, Cincinnati remains a walking city. Since I believe that most people are born with some capacity for urban enjoyment, I focus on the walking city and combine in this book what are, for me, the two great pleasures of walking and savoring the urban landscape.

Why walk?—and why walk in a city? Fair questions, both. Abstract knowledge about a subject or place is, let us admit, no substitute for practical acquaintance. Much of the meaningful knowledge in our lives derives from personal experience; much of our human enjoyment rests on physical contact with the world around us. This enjoyment can take many forms. Walking gives us a personal relationship to the environment, one that we cannot acquire in any other way. I do not mean to belittle the automobile. In the twentieth century it has caused an immense enlargement in the possibilities of enjoying life. But this gain has brought with it a concomitant loss, and to appreciate a city best we must walk it. Walking allows us the leisure to study buildings, to savor the streetscape, to think about the past and present city. Look hard at what you see, respond to it, feel the overall impression it leaves upon you, analyze the details. Study the city with your legs, draw its portrait with your eyes. Walking heightens your awareness of its tangible, physical reality. Walking takes you back through time. "Walking," writes Alfred Kazin, "I always knew how I felt by the music in my head." "Places do things to people," John Russell has observed, and "new kinds of places do new kinds of things to them." Walking the city we discover, or rediscover, an environment that should always retain its capacity to surprise.

"A pedestrian is a man in danger of his life; a walker is a man in possession of his soul." So writes David McCord in his splendid *About Boston*. To walk well in the city, for McCord, "requires all the cunning of a talented woodsman." Put another way, the urban walker must become a Sherlock Holmes, seeking out things to see, the clues that, cumulatively, will form his or her portrait of the city. In this book I tell you about some of the things you will come upon in your walks; I point out what I find attractive (and unattractive) about Cincinnati, and indicate why. Every time I take an extended walk in the city I anticipate a visual feast: vistas, façades, windows, doorways, shop fronts. No less do I appreciate the reassuring and familiar church, park, or palazzo. But only the unexpected will turn an ordinary walk into an unforgettable experience. Every time I stalk the city I also anticipate the unexpected—a Victorian house newly painted, a hitherto unnoticed cast-iron storefront by a firm I had not heard of, a cat perched atop a brick wall, a friend not seen for a year and a half. I am never disappointed.

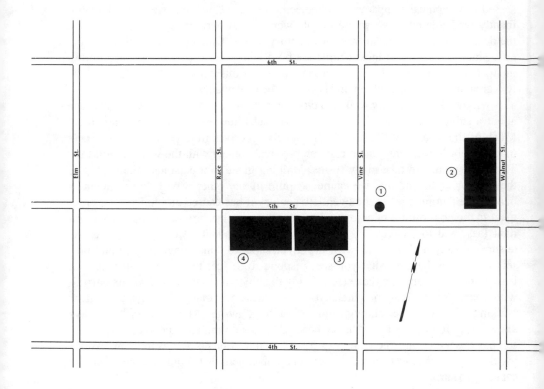

FOUNTAIN SQUARE

1. Tyler Davidson Fountain
2. DuBois Tower
3. Carew Tower
4. Netherland Plaza Hotel

1

Fountain Square

Fountain Square, at 5th and Vine streets, is Cincinnati's chief public place. It is its hub, its heart, its symbol, the knot that ties the city together. It has all the essential ingredients: a large open area, a central location, a fountain, moving water. People when downtown gravitate toward Fountain Square. Some use it as a short-cut, others to meet friends; children romp while parents or grandparents look on. Still others feed the pigeons or loll about or make casual conversation. Office work-ers eat their lunches on its benches. Tourists, camera-laden, parade by. It is this human congress that makes Fountain Square come alive, and within its precincts people-watching becomes an art.

Asolare, a useful Italian verb meaning to sit in the sun and do nothing, nicely describes those caught within the **Tyler Davidson Fountain**'s magnetic field. Many people go out of their way to look at the fountain and to hear its waters. Some who come to look and hear stay longer than they had anticipated. Many people are smil-ing. No surprise about that, for being in Fountain Square is a cheering experience. Even when we are not there, we enjoy it vicariously. If we contemplate the square and its fountain in our mind's eye, our image of it, our knowledge that it is there, affords us delight. It rests and recharges us. Whether or not we realize it, it is Foun-tain Square that holds together our conception of Cincinnati's downtown. However far into the boondocks the suburbs may stretch, no one questions downtown's pri-macy as the city's center or Fountain Square's as the center's center.

Water drips from the fingers of the *Genius of Water* atop the candelabra-shaped Tyler Davidson Fountain. Her outstretched arms invoke a liquid blessing on those who gaze up at her. The sound of falling water will always attract passersby. It is a restful, "white" sound that masks the street's intermittent honks and clangs, direct-ing auditory and visual attention away from the nearby bustle. Without our quite realizing it, the sound of water ties together the diverse impressions that make up our experience of Fountain Square. When the fountain is turned off, the spell is broken. Fountain Square seems nowhere as pleasant—or as tranquil—a place.

A Nuremberg sculptor, August von Kreling, designed the fountain in the

The Genius of Water, Tyler Davidson Fountain. The fountain, originally dedicated in 1871, was rededicated in 1971 when Fountain Square largely assumed its present form. Made in Munich, the Tyler Davidson Fountain serves as a focal point both for Fountain Square and for Cincinnati itself. It has become the city's most durable symbol.

1840s. His unusual scheme included none of the gods and goddesses of classical mythology that traditionally adorned fountains: no Neptune, no tritons, no nereids. Instead, his scheme embodied in realistic form the actual benefits that water brings to man. Von Kreling could not find a patron to undertake his unorthodox fountain, however, and for twenty years his design languished in the files of the Royal Foundry in Munich.

Enter Henry Probasco, prominent Cincinnati businessman and a partner in the Tyler Davidson Hardware Company. Probasco had come from Connecticut to Cincinnati in 1835, at the age of fifteen. Davidson took him into his business, the two men became close friends, and in 1840 Probasco became a partner and married Davidson's half-sister, Julia Carrington. After Davidson died in 1865, Probasco wished to commemorate his friend with a suitable public memorial. He and Davidson had considered a fountain before Davidson's death, even before the Civil War.

Touring Europe in 1866, Probasco stopped at the Royal Foundry, where the director, Ferdinand von Miller, showed him the fountain designs on file. All of them depicted scenes from mythology, presumably with tritons and nereids. None satisfied Probasco, who began to think about a stained-glass window instead. Then von Miller recalled von Kreling's unexecuted design. Because it rendered the tangible benefits of water rather than mythological scenes, Probasco immediately found it appealing. In May 1867 he offered the fountain to the city of Cincinnati if the city would agree to maintain it. The city accepted his offer. A bronze model was made and sent to Cincinnati in 1869 (it is on display in the Cincinnati Art Museum). In 1870 von Miller, assisted by his younger son, also named Ferdinand, had the fountain cast from old bronze cannon. The next year young Ferdinand came to Cincinnati to superintend the fountain's installation. It turned out to be a formidable undertaking, for to supply sufficient water pressure for the fountain the city had to install a special storage tank on Mount Auburn.

On October 6, 1871, before a crowd estimated at 20,000 but perhaps twice that, Henry Probasco officially presented the Tyler Davidson Fountain to the city. "Water," he declared in his dedicatory speech, "is not only beautiful in nature and useful in art, but it is rich with meaning in the teachings of religion. It is . . . a symbol of purity and life in the soul." Probasco appears not only to have had a mystical rapport with water but, wanting his fountain to have tangible benefit for the people, he had the very American idea of having it dispense water that was iced for drinking. Beneath the fountain he installed two thousand feet of coiled pipe surrounded by ice. Thus the turtle, goose, dolphin, and viper at the fountain's base— all designed by the younger Ferdinand von Miller—once served a more than decorative purpose: attached to each was a communal drinking cup. American practicality!

The four groups below the *Genius of Water* depict the benefits water provides for humanity. A man seeks rain to extinguish the fire destroying his house; a young woman offers water to an aged man; a farmer leaning on his plow watches the water revive his fields; a mother leads her child to bathe, or rather, the child leads the mother. This female figure, perhaps the fountain's most admired sculpture, nicely complements the *Genius of Water*. Rumor has it that the notorious Lola Montez— courtesan, international glamor girl, and in the 1840s consort of the Bavarian monarch Ludwig I—served as von Kreling's model. If true, Lola's presence would be the single risqué touch in this most moral, most Teutonic work of art. Adorning the fountain's shaft are four bas reliefs representing humanity's practical use of water: navigation, milling, fishing, and power. Navigation, on the north side, depicts a steamboat chugging along, while in the foreground (perhaps a fanciful rendering of Cincinnati's Public Landing) a family group waves farewell. Figures of children designed by the younger Ferdinand von Miller occupy the corner niches of the pedestal. A girl adorns herself with a string of pearls; a warmly clad boy puts on an ice skate; a girl listens to the sea roar in a shell; and a boy triumphantly holds up a crayfish he has netted. These children suggest the pleasures of water.

But perhaps the fountain's most dazzling sculpture, one never twice the same, is the water emanating from its many orifices. The water's ever-changing movement offers constant visual pleasure as it reflects light: luminous when still, brilliant when agitated, sparkling when falling. The water shoots up, gurgles, splashes, drips, plops, splats. It is the city's voice. The spectacle holds us entranced, perhaps because the sight and sound of water—even water domesticated in a city fountain— stir elemental feelings within us. In winter the fountain, its waters stilled, becomes magical in another way. Tiny white lights cascade down from the *Genius of Water*'s outstretched hands, encircling the fountain and the trees on the square like soft floating snowflakes.

A curving pavement of stone blocks fans out, chrysanthemum-like, from the fountain. The pavement inclines gently inwards, with the fountain, deliberately and effectively off center, at the plaza's lowest point. It draws you like a magnet into its orbit; it is difficult not to walk toward it. Once there, it is pleasant to sit, to look, to listen, to reflect—and to linger. Just as the *Genius of Water* appears to answer the prayers of those who implore her, so we may extend a blessing to the two men, Henry Probasco and Tyler Davidson, whose enduring friendship the fountain commemorates. In the pleasure the fountain has given many over the decades, the city has indeed been blessed by them and by their gift.

The Tyler Davidson Fountain is at once realistic and idealistic, practical and poetic. Symbolizing water, the "old bronze candlestick" (as Lafcadio Hearn once called it) has come to symbolize a city on the water, a city that has long lived in a symbiotic relationship with the Ohio River. Steamboats and the people and commerce they brought have been its life. Today, though barges and towboats have supplanted the steamboats, the Ohio remains vital to Cincinnati.

For nearly a hundred years the fountain stood in a narrow raised esplanade straddling 5th from Vine to Walnut Streets. Designed by William Tinsley, the architect of Probasco's Clifton castle, the esplanade was roughly like a flattened ellipse in form. Sixteen lampposts encircled it. Always much loved by Cincinnatians, the fountain, with traffic roaring by on both sides, became increasingly difficult of access. Originally it faced east, toward Europe, from which have come so many of Cincinnati's citizens. With the redoing of Fountain Square in the late 1960s, the fountain was realigned to face west, and now recalls the time when the city was the chief stepping-off point for immigrants heading in this direction. In honor of its centennial, the fountain underwent major restoration and repair work by the Karka-doulias brothers. Today, though no longer dispensing iced water, the Tyler Davidson Fountain remains more than ever the beloved focal point of Cincinnati's urban life. It is also a focal point in another way. Like the obelisks, columns, and triumphal arches in Rome and Paris, the fountain acts as a vertical, visual terminus to the 5th St. approach to the square from the west.

Our initial impression of Fountain Square is of the fountain itself. Only gradually do we become aware of the square. Many European cities have such a central public place: Venice's Piazza San Marco, Brussels' Grand-Place, and London's Trafalgar Square come quickly to mind. Citizens in the Middle Ages crowded into the public place to hear news, meet friends, and attend events. The public place came

Fountain Square, ca. 1910. Before its remodeling in the late 1960s, the original "square" was a rectangular plaza, curved at the ends, on which the Tyler Davidson Fountain stood facing east. On the redesigned square the fountain faces west. The photograph looks east. The large French Second Empire building with flags rising from its crested mansard roof is the old U.S. Post Office and Courthouse, completed in 1885. The present U.S. Post Office and Courthouse (1939) now occupies the spot. Courtesy of the Cincinnati Historical Society.

to focus and express civic life; rarely was it used for commercial activities. In ways hardly understood but deeply felt the public place helped to hold the community together. This need for community continues in modern times. "We need public places," writes Spiro Kostof, "to enjoy the unplanned intimacy of civil society and to celebrate that sense of belonging to a broad community." Originally planned in the nineteenth century and completely redone a hundred years later, Cincinnati's Fountain Square reflects American urban design at its best. Edmund Bacon, a leading city planner, termed the new Fountain Square "the most successful public square in America." For William H. Whyte, perhaps the keenest-eyed of contemporary observers of the modern American city, it is simply "the finest square in the country."

Not every city has an effective central place. In Paris, the Place de la Concorde was obviously intended as a great *place,* but although it offers fabulous perspectives it has become a pedestrian's nightmare. You risk your life dodging traffic to get to

Fountain Square, Oktoberfest 1990. Oktoberfest, supported by the city's large Germanic population, takes place on a weekend in mid-September. Cincinnatians munch on brats and metts as they listen to vernacular Teutonic music. The square also serves as the venue for numerous other planned activities over the year.

its center. Bostonians from Oliver Wendell Holmes on like to think of themselves as living at the hub of the universe, but if the town *has* an actual hub one cannot find it. San Francisco's Union Square is splendidly sited, ringed with hotels and upscale shops, but is some distance from the city's business core. Manhattan has at least one spectacular public place—Grand Army Plaza on 5th Avenue between 58th and 59th—but few regard it as the city's center.

Fountain Square is a twentieth-century American evocation of a European piazza. We may enter it from almost any point in the compass. It is within the city yet apart, public yet private. Walls along most of its western and southern axes cut it off from the street. But where there are steps, they are low, easy, and inviting. We are almost pulled up them. The plaza itself is spacious, yet compact. Different levels break it up. We have a choice of places to sit, both public and semiprivate. The walls afford good vantage points for people-watching. The trick seems to be to arrange all the parts of a plaza so that people can see them and use them, yet retain spots that give a feeling of privacy. Fountain Square has done this with reasonable success. Different flowers bloom at different seasons, and in summer hardwoods offer shade. The public place changes in its function from hour to hour. It rarely stands still to be photographed. Except in deepest winter, Fountain Square is the center for numerous planned activities—among them the Public Library's annual book sale. During lunch hour of any weekday we may encounter zoo animals, a contest, or bands playing. A granite stage and proscenium north of the fountain serve as the setting for Summer Sounds on the Square, a series of Monday evening band concerts. Designed as "sculpture," the stage is not, as sculpture, an unqualified success. A gift to the city, it is well intentioned, but its looming presence does not improve the plaza. Nor was it really necessary. But its bulk hardly detracts from the square's overall effect of spaciousness. Few American cities have so appealing, so comfortable, or so useful a center as Fountain Square.

At the southwest corner (Vine and 5th streets) stands a single flower stand, circa 1890, designed by one of Cincinnati's best-known architects, James W. Mc-Laughlin. The old Fifth Street market, chiefly dilapidated butchers' stalls, had occupied the square's site since 1827. The city appropriated the land on February 4, 1870, and on same day tore down the stalls in forty-three minutes. To maintain the myth that the site remains a market, flowers are offered for sale one day a year. Just beyond, on Vine, horsedrawn carriages, for two or for twenty, wait to take you on a tour of downtown.

On the flagpole hang several flags: the American, then (usually) Ohio's, then Cincinnati's, and finally that of the Society of the Cincinnati. The city's flag has three wavy dark blue stripes on a white background. Within a stylized red laurel wreath we read Cincinnati's motto, *Juncta Juvant*. The Latin means "Things when joined aid each other," or, more simply, "Strength through Union." In our walks we shall often discover these words on public buildings.

Last on the pole often hangs the flag of the Society of the Cincinnati. A plaque near the pole's base tells us that the Society derives its name from Cincinnatus, a fifth-century B.C. Roman, part historical figure, mostly legend. His countrymen, threatened with invasion, asked him to lead their defense. A delegation found him working his land. Livy records that he put down his plough, took up his sword, assumed dictatorial powers, led his countrymen to victory, and returned to his farm—all within sixteen days. After the American Revolution a number of army officers who shared Alexander Hamilton's Federalist principles formed an association dedicated to upholding what they believed should be the ideals of the young Republic. Conceiving of no better model than the self-sacrificing Roman, they named themselves the Society of the Cincinnati. The Society developed a reputation for being strongly aristocratic and Federalist. Thomas Jefferson, an ardent democrat, feared the organization would become a seedbed for a hereditary American aristocracy. A Society member, General Arthur St. Clair, renamed the fledgling frontier outpost after the Society, not Cincinnatus. (The older regional pronunciation "Cincinnata," fostered by John Cleves Symmes as early as 1791, is still occasionally heard.) Even so, the legend of the Roman hero has particular aptness for Cincinnati. *Juncta Juvant,* "Strength through Union," echoes Rome's rallying together to defend itself, implying that a city's communal life must be animated by a spirit of cooperation. Throughout Cincinnati's more than two hundred years of history, its citizens have often contributed generously to advance the communal well-being.

The buildings surrounding Fountain Square, all dating from this century, constitute a mix of ages, styles, shapes, and colors. Except for the Carew Tower none represents a major architectural achievement. Their very insipidity sets off not only the square but also the fountain's Victorian intricacy. The *Genius of Water* rises against the soaring vertical lines of the thirty-one story DuBois Tower/Fifth Third Center (1970). The edifice was named DuBois because of DuBois Chemicals, the largest division of the Chemed Corporation, and later Fifth Third because of the merger in 1908, one of many, of the Fifth National and Third National banks. The combined banks adopted this unusual, if perfectly logical, name.

The **DuBois Tower** is a typical International style skyscraper of the kind that has come to dominate most downtown skylines. Designed by Harrison and Abramowitz of New York, the building resembles in its contours Manhattan's U.N. Secretariat. (Harrison is Wallace K. Harrison, who coordinated the Secretariat's design.) An elongated rectangular box, elegant and spare, it looks best, like many of its contemporaries, when seen by itself, a thing apart from its environment. The vocabulary for the International style was developed for freestanding structures. Buildings that stand alone tend to disrupt the cityscape, yet, as an integral part of the layout of the Fountain Square block and meant to be encountered on all sides, the DuBois Tower does relate to its surroundings. It can legitimately stand alone. Unfortunately, like most International style buildings, it is virtually dead at ground level. Although characterless and derivative in design, excellent materials went into its making, for example, the vertical limestone panels. The DuBois Tower possesses its own sober integrity, a quality one might term quintessentially Cincinnatian.

Across 5th St. stand the Star Bank Center and the Westin Hotel (1981), two buildings looking too much like one. If neither strikes us as particularly imaginative, neither draws our attention away from Fountain Square. Indeed, the city restricted the Westin's height so that it would cast less of a shadow on the square. Visually, the Westin functions as much as a sculptural backdrop as a building. Once the Albee Theater (1927), designed by leading theater architect Thomas Lamb, stood on this site. Its magnificent Palladian arch we shall discover resurrected, three blocks west, in the south façade of the Convention Center.

The city has long intended that on the half block due west of Fountain Square be built the late twentieth-century kingpin of Cincinnati's skyline. For a decade, developers and architectural schemes have come and gone. The most recent plan called for a forty-eight story tower that, at 648 feet, would have been Cincinnati's tallest. Developed by the Galbreath Company of Columbus and designed by Helmut Jahn, a leading modernist architect whose structures have aroused considerable controversy in Chicago, Fountain Square West (as this on-again, off-again project is now called) was as dramatic in its contours as Galbreath's earlier ventures—the Dubois Tower and the Star Bank/Westin complex—were bland. But this plan too has collapsed.

At 574 feet the forty-eight story **Carew Tower** (1930), designed by Walter W. Ahlschlager of Chicago with the assistance of Delano & Aldritch of New York, currently remains Cincinnati's tallest skyscraper. Ahlschlager did a number of buildings in his native city, including the Sheraton-Chicago Hotel (1929), but nothing he did there works as well as this one in Cincinnati. A skeletal steel frame supports the Carew's exterior "curtain" walls, that is, non-load bearing. Limestone facing covers the lower floors, then for most of the building's height a variegated tawny brick predominates. When the sun strikes the façade, the copper facing near the top

Carew Tower. Since 1930 the city's tallest building, the Carew Tower is also of great architectural interest. It and the adjoining Netherland Plaza Hotel constitute one of the nation's finest Art Deco ensembles. The observation deck on the Carew's 49th floor provides a splendid panorama of Cincinnati and offers an excellent visual introduction to the tours in this book.

dazzles the eye. The Carew Tower is roughly contemporaneous with Manhattan's major Art Deco skyscrapers: the Fred E. French (1927), Chrysler (1930), and Empire State (1931) buildings, and Rockefeller Center (begun 1932). Whereas the Empire State and the Chrysler taper to an elegant spire, the Carew, like the French Building and the Rockefeller Tower, culminates in a flat roof.

Starrett Brothers and Eken, the New York construction company responsible for the Empire State Building completed the steel framework for the Carew and the adjoining Netherland Plaza in sixty-one days, the buildings themselves in less than nine months. The New York and Cincinnati buildings look alike in uncanny ways. New York City passed a law in 1916 requiring its new skyscrapers to have setbacks to allow sufficient light and air to filter down to the city streets below. This restriction led to the wedding-cake style, buildings getting narrower as they grew higher, the hallmark of skyscraper architecture between the wars. Cincinnati's *Official City Plan* of 1925 endorsed comparable zoning restrictions for its highrises. The Carew's carefully worked out series of setbacks gives the building a three-dimensional quality, distantly akin to that of an elongated Babylonian ziggurat or a stepped Mayan pyramid. The setbacks allow more light to reach Fountain Square. Because of them the Carew has only 360,000 feet of floor space, less than several recent buildings half its height.

As we walk toward the Carew, we see a number of multipurpose **traffic poles**. These went up early in the 1970s in an effort to reduce the amount of street furniture that disfigures most city streets. The poles appear in various forms and sizes throughout the downtown. Three eighteen-foot high steel tubes make up the basic unit. Add-on items include a boom projecting over the street with traffic lights or directional signals and a thirty-two foot mast that fits into the curbside leg to support street lights and luminaires. Creatively designed banners announcing coming events in the Greater Cincinnati area hang from the poles; they add color as well as impart information. At their base are trash receptacles or newspaper vending machines. The traffic poles not only help give an interrelated physical harmony to downtown but also solve a major structural problem of a dense urban area: how to get information to pedestrians and motorists economically without cluttering the cityscape. Their lean design—to my mind, a stroke of genius—has drawn national attention and won several awards. Along with the redesigned Fountain Square and the new buildings, the multipurpose poles contribute to downtown's sparkle.

The Carew Tower forms part of a larger complex, built by Thomas Emery's Sons (now Emery Realty, Inc.), a firm that has probably given the city more important buildings than any other. The complex includes a hotel, the adjoining Netherland Plaza (1931) and an arcade running through both buildings; it originally included an automated garage and a major department store. Conceived in the flush days of the late 1920s, the Carew-Netherland Plaza complex was completed in the early years of the Depression. Accurately described by John Emery in 1929 as a "city within a city," it set a national standard for urban development, anticipating Rockefeller Center as a fully mixed-use structure by several years. In their day, the Carew and the Netherland were the last word in modernity. They remain among Cincinnati's major urban monuments, its single greatest piece of urban real estate and for over sixty years the centerpiece of its skyline.

On the Carew's ground floor, the black granite sets off the bronze window frames while a stylized eagle delimits the first setback on the fifth floor. A band features a pattern of "C," for Joseph Thomas Carew, the nineteenth-century Cincinnati merchant prince whose Mabley & Carew Building stood on this site and from whom the building derives its name. The Mabley & Carew department store remained in the building until 1963. Before entering the Carew Tower arcade from Vine St., look above the entrance at the Art Deco bas reliefs. They embody the theme of work. One sandalled male nude wields a spade, another a hammer. On the plaque between them the sun rises over the rounded hills, revealing two sheaves of wheat. This scene draws upon that on the Great Seal of Ohio, the difference being that on the seal one sheaf consists of seventeen arrows (Ohio became the nation's seventeenth state). The bronze medallions around the entrance focus on transportation. Horses and covered wagons, steamboats and funnel-topped locomotives, tractors and 1920s airplanes portray pioneer progress and conquest of the frontier.

We enter the arcade. Its central portion rises two stories. Originally, the upper level also had shops and, with the recent remodeling, has them again. Stylized pilasters in black and gold, favorite Art Deco colors, accentuate the arcade's verticality. At either end compositions of Rookwood tiles reveal bold geometric floral patterns in primary colors, adding a local touch to a basically New York skyscraper. Against the golden-hued ceiling, which echoes the floor pattern, bulbs shielded by diamond-shaped metal strips give off indirect light. The Carew arcade maintains a tradition, for a forty-foot high, glass-roofed, two-story arcade formed part of the Hotel Emery (1877), which stood on this site, from Vine to Race streets. In 1990–1991 the arcade was renovated; it has been tied to the Tower Place development at 4th and Race streets.

Commercial arcades are in their present reincarnations essentially nineteenth-century phenomena. The first, opened in 1784 in the Palais-Royal in Paris, enjoyed immense success. It soon became a legendary place for an urban, emancipated society to promenade, to see and be seen. Numerous other arcades—actually *passages,* i.e., shops on either side of a toplit, enclosed arcade—followed in Paris after the turn of the nineteenth century. Imitations spread across Europe. Several of those in London, among them the Piccadilly and Princes St. arcades, continue to flourish, as does the Palais-Royal. At their best, center-city arcades allow unhampered pedestrian activity at ground level.

Near the Carew's elevator bank we descend to the lower arcade. Here we find the Art Deco styling hardly altered. The bronze window frames, wall sconces, ventilator grilles, the elegant birds incised on the elevator doors: all remain intact. The design on the elevator doors here differs from that on the level above. We return to the upper level via the stairs at the other end, then walk a few feet further on. A passageway on the right takes us to the 5th St. foyer of the **Netherland Plaza**.

We are in what is probably America's finest Art Deco hotel, one whose scale and opulence owe much to the heady optimism of the late 1920s. When the Netherland Plaza opened, contemporaries marveled at its fantastic interiors. This truly "grand hotel," one of the last of its kind before the Depression caused the breed to become extinct, represents the culminating expression of the American dream of democratizing old world opulence and luxury. Actually, the "grand hotel" is largely an invention of nineteenth-century America. Isaiah Rogers, the "father" of the

American hotel, designed Boston's Tremont House (1829), New York's Astor House (1836)—and, after moving to Cincinnati, the city's famed Burnet House (1850), built on a scale hitherto unknown. Like the Netherland, the Burnet House contained shops and provided varied services. Awed Europeans called these grandiose new hotels "American hotels." *Imperial Palace* is the name of Arnold Bennett's fascinating novel (1931) about the international grand hotel. The Netherland Plaza once was—and has again become—an "imperial palace."

Influenced by the jazz culture of the 1920s and its movie palaces—creations whose decor seemed to come out of the *Arabian Nights*—hotels became stage sets in which Americans could live out their fantasies. The Netherland Plaza's Art Deco magnificence rivals that of New York's better-known Waldorf-Astoria. During 1982–1983 the hotel underwent a twenty-eight million dollar restoration that reduced the number of rooms from one thousand to six hundred and twenty and returned its interior spaces to an approximation of their former splendor. Occasional details—kitschy carpets, awkward banquettes—strike false notes, but they are few. What you see around you is not exactly what the first patrons of the hotel saw but rather an imaginative re-creation, not restoration, by modern designers that reflects contemporary taste yet remains essentially faithful to the spirit of Art Deco.

The Art Deco style gained impetus—and its name—from the 1925 Paris *Exposition internationale des arts décoratifs et industriels modernes*. The style caught on almost immediately in this country and in the interwar years became the preferred style for the decoration of urban highrises. One can see why. It has jazzy lines, it uses traditional materials in ways that startle, yet its abundant historical echoes reassure those offended by the International style's austere look. Art Deco ornamentation consists usually of low relief geometrical designs that take the form of parallel straight lines, zigzags, chevrons, and stylized floral motifs. Often these designs purport to reflect Egyptian, Classical, even Babylonian influences as transformed or modified by French Art Deco designers. In the United States, the ancient civilizations of Mexico and Peru, relatively near at hand, offered designers an alternative to the attractive novelties spawned by the Paris exposition. Thus in American Art Deco buildings Mayan, Aztec, and Indian motifs jostle Egyptian and Classical. This ornamentation stresses the natural world and the life of humanity through the centuries. Thematically, it approaches the universal.

The Netherland's decoration has a richness and sophistication, but also a unity, matched by few hotels in the land. All aspects of the design are interrelated: lighting, lettering, railings, carpets, wall ornaments, ceiling plasterwork. To create a building of this magnitude and quality, architects, engineers, mural artists, sculptors, carpet weavers, and diverse other craftspeople and artisans had to collaborate closely. Ornament is what Art Deco is about, and the style achieves its effect by combining diverse materials. On the outside, we saw stone, marble, brick, terra cotta, and copper; on the inside, we see scagliola, glass, rosewood paneling, and a variety of metals, chiefly brass and nickel-silver. Much of the Netherland Plaza's decoration—for example, the motifs on its balcony railings, grilles, doors, elevators, walls, ceilings—comes directly from the catalogue of the 1925 Paris Exposition. Borrowing from here and from there, the decoration deserves a prize for eclecticism, fascinating to gape at if elusive to analyze. Its profusion and lushness dazzle us as we walk through the hotel's public areas. On each visit we will notice something new. Never will it be economically feasible to do again such total design of rooms and public spaces. Art Deco was, it now seems likely, the last great period for the decorative arts.

In the street-level foyer brass *torchères* shaped like obelisks and lit from within guard the way. Such freestanding column lamps provide indirect illumination by aiming light at the floor or ceiling. Those here reveal a French Art Deco interpretation of Egyptian motifs. Indirect lighting constitutes one of Art Deco's lasting contributions to design. Torchères work best at low light levels. Keeping a room slightly dark not only contrasts materials and colors but also imparts to it a sense of mystery, an atmosphere of magic. Think of guests entering this hotel during the Depression, gazing at the torchères, and, as they climbed up to the lobby, experiencing step by step this evocative fantasy world.

We go up the main stairs to the first landing. On the ceiling twenty-four gazelles surround an off-center compass. Divided into two groups, they symbolize the hours. Gazelles reappear frequently in the decoration. The words "Bienvenu aux voyageurs" remind us of Art Deco's French derivation. Surprise constitutes a major characteristic of Art Deco, and we experience it everywhere in these interiors. The extraordinarily complex sequence of spaces creates pure architectural theater; drama is also very much an Art Deco feature. Standing on the landing, we have commenced a journey on a deliberately conceived narrative path: up the stairs to the low-ceilinged lobby, then into the high-ceilinged Palm Court. Another flight, and we have reached the mezzanine with its astonishing perspectives. Still more stairs before we finally reach the climax, though not the end, of our journey in the fabulous Hall of Mirrors. Vistas open up unexpectedly: we experience a low, then a lofty, ceiling. A vertical room succeeds a horizontal, itself succeeded by a horizontal; axes change with bewildering frequency. We are in a spatial environment; as we walk about, we constantly view the interior spaces and the bewitching objects in them from different angles. The chandelier above our head, for example, we shall also see from the top of the stairs, from the Palm Court, from the entrance to the Continental Room, and—arguably the best view of all—from the mezzanine.

In the low-ceilinged lobby, we note the sage green frieze of flowers, the richly colored scagliola (a compound of marble chips in plaster) on the walls, and the rare Brazilian rosewood paneling. Visible from the balcony at the lobby's far end is the Carew Arcade. In the main corridor, the flowers of the frieze metamorphose into lotus leaves, an Egyptian motif that in various manifestations is omnipresent.

From the lobby we go up more steps to the mezzanine, where we gain an overall view of the vast **Palm Court**. It is Cincinnati's most elegant place to meet for a drink or conversation, and is a good place to enjoy a nocturne or some Gershwin on the grand piano while we rest our feet. Originally a sitting room off the lobby, the Palm Court now functions as an entertainment and dining area that includes the gourmet restaurant, Orchids. A deliberate contrast in height to the lobby and foyer, the Palm Court yet retains intimacy with clusters of wing-backed chairs.

The Palm Court combines Egyptian motifs with French. The heavy piers and massive proportions suggest the weight and solidity of Egyptian architecture. Egyptian themes had an extraordinary vogue after 1922, the year Howard Carter discovered, in the most dramatic archaeological find of the century, the unravaged tomb of the young pharaoh Tutankhamen. Its contents caused a tremendous sensation. Egyptian motifs immediately influenced fashions in clothes and furnishings, and much in the Netherland Plaza's decoration reveals indebtedness to King Tut. The Palm Court also reflects French influence. The murals that curl up the walls onto the ceiling recall the light, airy world depicted by eighteenth-century French masters such as Watteau, Boucher, and Fragonard. They suggest the *douceure de vivre* of the prerevolutionary France of Louis XV and XVI. Unabashedly elitist in theme, they recreate a never-never land of aristocratic indulgence in which courtiers idled away the hours in lush gardens. If *you* stayed in this hotel, they imply, you too could escape into such a fantasy world.

Ancient Egypt and French Rococo offer a contrast in extremes: one suggests permanence and weight, the other transience and frivolity. At the far end of the Palm Court are intriguing web-footed sea horses. Out of their heads arise, unicorn-like, lotus leaf crowns of light. Here Egyptian and French motifs mesh in a spectacular Art Deco fantasy. Beyond, the sea horses guard a fountain crowned by a huge ram's head. Both fountain and quadrupeds came from Cincinnati's famed Rookwood Pottery.

Another flight up and we stand before the **Hall of Mirrors.** The name of this two-story ballroom deliberately echoes that of the *Galerie des Glaces,* the main reception hall in Louis XIV's Versailles. The *Galerie's* mirrors suggest a world of illusion, and it often served as a model for 1920s American movie palaces and hotel interiors. Like the Netherland's other public spaces, the Hall of Mirrors suffers from a *horror vacui:* very few spaces in it are not profusely decorated. Its mirrored arches pick up on those of its Versailles namesake. The scagliola pilasters mimic dark green draperies in their upper portions. The balustrade consists of Art Deco's two basic metals, bronze and nickel-silver, prized because they simulate gold and silver. Hermaphroditic pipers dance on the medallions. The ceiling's recessed lighting, no less than the indirect lighting of the walls, brings out the Hall's muted colors and subtle forms. At the Bachelor's Cotillion Cincinnati debutantes in elegant gowns and long white gloves make their bow to society here. We climb the stairs leading to the balcony to admire Tom Backer's *Downtown Cincinnati at Night,* six twenty-one-foot-high panels in luminous paint.

We return to the mezzanine overlooking the Palm Court. From there we make our way past the elevators to the Hall of Apollo. Its ceiling mural represents the Sun God—an allusion to Louis XIV, the "Sun King"—taking his chariot on its daily journey across the heavens. A retreating but absentminded Diana readies an arrow at her brother. Here we gain a closer view of the extraordinary ram's head fountain, shaped, like both the Carew and the Netherland Plaza, roughly in the form of a Babylonian ziggurat. Vines hang down from the ram's horns, his eyes are closed, and water drools off his tongue. He has to be at peace with himself and the world.

Water, like the sun, symbolizes life, strength, and freedom: favorite Art Deco themes. The adjoining Continental Room was formerly the hotel's main dining area; ice-skating shows entertained guests at lunch. Today's grown-up children fondly recall magical moments here. The two chandeliers are twins to that above the entrance stairs; the charming murals represent the four seasons. Again, we find the ubiquitous *trompe l'oeil* marble pilasters of green drapery. We return to the lobby, then take the stairs opposite the reception desk down to the Carew arcade. Once in the arcade we head for the Carew Tower's elevator bank.

Two elevators and a flight of stairs later we emerge onto the highest vantage point in Cincinnati: the Carew's **observation deck**. From the fairyland world of the Netherland Plaza we have ascended nearly six hundred feet above ground level and are now higher than the surrounding hills. We have left Cincinnati's grandest sequence of interior spaces; now we contemplate its most spectacular panorama. An open environment replaces a closed one. The contrast is bracing. And there is contrast of another kind. The observation deck, like that atop the Empire State Building, is open to the elements. In the newer towers—Manhattan's World Trade Center, Chicago's Sears Building, Boston's Hancock Tower—it is not. We experience the view, sanitized, in a glassed-in cage and climate-controlled environment. Reflections, even unwashed windows, further erode visual immediacy. Here our ceiling is the sky. The observation deck offers an unsurpassed vantage point from which to enjoy a bird's-eye view of Cincinnati. Although we have lost the rich detail of the urban texture, distance clears the field of vision. Here sounds reach us faintly; below, people appear lilliputian; the immediate, particular, seemingly disordered continuum of life is far away. But only apparently. As we step back from the city, we sense something of the unity and order that underlies its bustling disarray. We begin to put our diverse impressions together within an overall perspective. We grasp the scene, if not as a whole, at least with an illusion of wholeness.

Harriet Martineau, who visited Cincinnati in 1835, said that whenever in an unfamiliar city she went at once to the highest point in the neighborhood from which she could see the city stretched out below her as a "living map." Admittedly, when Martineau wrote, cities could be visually encompassed from a relatively limited height. The upward and outward explosion of urban boundaries in most American cities did not occur until the later nineteenth century. Four years before Martineau's visit, Victor Hugo published his novel *Notre-Dame de Paris,* where in the chapter "A Bird's-eye View of Paris" he claimed, with pardonable exaggeration, that the principal "beauty" of Notre-Dame Cathedral was "the view of Paris as it then [in 1482] appeared from the summit of the towers." A century after Martineau and Hugo, Winston Churchill echoed them both. "Whenever I come to a new city," wrote Churchill in 1933, "I always make haste to climb the tallest building in it and examine the whole scene from this eagle's nest. They are wonderful, these bird's-eye views; each one gives an impression of its own which lies in the memory like a well-known picture." Admittedly, Martineau and Hugo wrote before the airplane made aerial perspectives easily available (Churchill before air travel became common for civilian use), but their advice still holds good. A bird's-eye view offers us a *point de départ* from which to survey the larger picture, to let it lie "in the memory." Such views can teach us much about a city that we cannot easily learn otherwise. Churchill, who found Cincinnati the "most beautiful" of America's inland metropolises, enjoyed the setting sun from his suite in the Netherland. "From the tower of its unsurpassed hotel the city spreads far and wide its pageant of crimson, purple, and gold, laced by silver streams that are great rivers." We, too, may find the view enthralling but we shall also examine what we see closely and in detail. Space has freed the eye. It can also educate it.

As we gaze around the horizon from our perch atop the Carew, we slowly translate the message of the landscape into the language of topography and history, into the "living map" that Harriet Martineau spoke of. We gain, first of all, an awareness of Cincinnati's shape. Before us lie ranges of hills to the east, north, and west. South across the Ohio River we see another range. In effect, we are in the middle of a large shallow bowl, a natural amphitheater. Within these encircling hills, in the area known as the Basin, lies a series of terraces. Ninety-seven feet above the mean water level of the Ohio, and well above the flood plain, Cincinnati's present downtown stands on the highest of these terraces. The city is splendidly sited. Not every metropolis is so blessed. Columbus, Ohio, and Indianapolis are not; New York and San Francisco are.

It is Cincinnati's circle of hills, bisected by the sinuous Ohio, that constitutes its topographical distinction. Hills and houses together illustrate beautifully the possibilities of cooperation between nature and art. Even Mrs. Trollope, that famous traveler, so caustic about much that she saw here, thought Cincinnati "finely situated." Pondering the hills before us, we may gauge something of the influence they have had upon the city's development. Hills, though they provide views, can constrict a city's growth. Since the hills are often too steep to build upon, a large part of Cincinnati—some thirty percent of the land area—remains covered with trees. I have sometimes wondered if the hills have also inhibited the psychological growth of Cincinnatians. In Manhattan the eye looks out on all sides upon water, in Chicago it ranges without hindrance over Lake Michigan or contemplates the endless prairie, even in hilly San Francisco the eye catches glimpses of the distant ocean or bay. But in Cincinnati, curled up in its hills, the eye contemplates an enclosed, locked-in environment. Do the city's hills foster inward rather than outward looking?

"Men, thinly scattered," Samuel Johnson told Boswell in 1773, "make a shift, but a bad shift, without many things. . . . It is being concentrated which produces high convenience." What made London an exciting place for Johnson, a passionate lover of cities, was its human concentration. Until the middle of the last century cities lacked effective transportation systems. With horizontal (and vertical) movement restricted to normal pedestrian range, even populous cities like Johnson's London were perforce compact cities, walking cities. Most urban life was managed over an area within a one- or two-mile radius from the center. In nineteenth-century Cincinnati walking was the usual means for getting around the Basin. After the Civil

War, urban transportation systems developed but even with them walking remained for many—and certainly for the poor—the primary means of locomotion.

Downtown Cincinnati today encompasses a smaller area than it did a hundred years ago. Old maps of the city indicate a downtown sprawling east and west and built up, except for the Public Landing where the steamboats docked, virtually to the river bank. Until well into the nineteenth century the city's topography kept it confined within the Basin. So steep were its hills that horses could not pull loaded wagons or streetcars up them. Cincinnati's hills compressed it into one of the most compact, most densely populated of major American cities. In 1870 only Manhattan rivalled in density its 32,000 inhabitants per square mile. By the Civil War Cincinnati was bursting. Between 1860 and 1870 its population grew by 55,000, and people began moving out to the hilltops. Only the establishment in the 1870s of the inclined railways up the hills and the development of an electric streetcar system after 1888 made the hilltops practicable for intensive settlement.

Today, **interstates** ring the center city on three sides. Presumably the last of the major transportation systems to be superimposed upon the Cincinnati landscape, they are incontestably its single most important manmade feature. Along with the hills and the Ohio River, they influence the ways the city works. As once did the hills, their presence restricts downtown's expansion. Fortunately, interstates have not been for Cincinnati the unmitigated disaster they have been for some cities. None, for example, slices through the central business district. Furthermore, they are at or below ground level, thus there is less of them to see—and hear. In addition, the interstates solved downtown's traffic problems by permitting easy entrance and evacuation, thus helping its survival in the 1960s and 1970s. In Cincinnati, they may even have helped to preserve the downtown's compactness. True, I-75 (completed 1964) and I-71 (completed 1974) demolished neighborhoods to the east and west. Ft. Washington Way (also 1964) below 3rd St. demarcates the downtown's southern border. The Stadium, Coliseum, and Yeatman's Cove Park replaced riverfront streets, houses, and factories. But by containing sprawl the interstates compressed the downtown into renewed vitality. Most American cities with successful downtowns, such as San Francisco, Boston, and Manhattan, lack space to expand because the surrounding water limits available land. The Ohio River formed Cincinnati's original boundary; the hills eventually became another. The interstates, by serving as edges or "walls" around the central core, further define downtown's boundaries east, west, and south. River, hills, and interstates give the city one of the most clearly demarcated downtowns of any American metropolis, one that offers distinct visual images.

Small in area compared with cities its size and age, Cincinnati's downtown did not always manifest its present vitality. The city's 1948 *Metropolitan Master Plan* concentrated on the suburbs. Downtown was left to develop, or not to develop, as it pleased. For a decade nothing much happened. The beginning of the 1960s found the city with a downtown in disarray and without a strategy to arrest decline. The riverfront consisted of decaying warehouses and railroad tracks; businesses abandoned the core; Fountain Square became sleazy; few souls ventured downtown at night or on weekends. People increasingly noted the downtown's lifelessness. Numerous FOR RENT signs dotted shop and office building windows. Ten years later, downtown Cincinnati had made an about-face, achieving one of the most successful renewal programs in the country. The FOR RENT signs had largely vanished, and have not reappeared.

How did this transformation come about? It began in 1962 when voters approved a tripartite package that encompassed a central riverfront development, a downtown reconstruction program, and a convention hall. Three efforts in previous years to revitalize the city center had failed. One proposal, by Victor Gruen Associates, had called for a totally malled downtown with streets closed to traffic and large parking garages ringing the center core. Gruen's plan lacked widespread public support, however, and voters rejected it. But in June 1962 they approved the redevelopment package for downtown or, in the jargon of planning, the Central Business District (CBD). A Working Review Committee of eighteen, composed of representatives from city council, the city planning department, and the business community was set up. It brought in three outside planning consultants: Baltimore architect Archibald Rogers, transportation consultants Alan M. Voorhees and Associates, and economic consultants Hammer and Co. Rogers became de facto commander-in-chief. Mark Upson, a recently retired Procter & Gamble executive, served ably as chairman of the Working Review Committee; Peter Kory, later to become Cincinnati's Director of Urban Development, served equally ably as its secretary.

All elements in the community participated in the planning and decision making. The plan, evolutionary rather than revolutionary, gained approval in stages. It called for the redevelopment of twelve blocks or partial blocks in the center city. By starting its rebuilding later than most cities, Cincinnati benefited from their mistakes. It never attempted to raze its core and rebuild on the rubble. And the plan, in operation by 1963, worked. Block by block, the core was rebuilt almost exactly according to plan. Fountain Square, which sits atop a huge multilevel garage, was completed in 1969. The DuBois Tower followed a year later. The surrounding twelve-block core gained 2,000,000 square feet of new office space. And on October 16, 1971, a hundred years and ten days after its original installation, the Tyler Davidson Fountain was rededicated.

Since then the downtown has witnessed much new construction. Not large in extent, downtown yet has more life in it than does Los Angeles', on the demographic charts a far vaster metropolis. And Cincinnati is more of a city, more "urban" in the ways that count: density, coherence, a focused cultural life. One can walk across the downtown, east to west, in fifteen minutes; south to north, in ten. The construction of Tower Place and the renovation of the Carew arcade are well advanced; the new arts center appears set. Other developments will occur. They should reinforce downtown's primacy as the commercial and entertainment center.

Cincinnati lacks only a large residential population downtown, but this is a major lack. "I know of no great and beautiful city," writes Lawrence Halprin,

"where people do not live close to the core. For the whole quality of a city's life—
its personality and its image—is set by its inhabitants." In recent years the downtown residential situation in Cincinnati has become livelier. Several apartment
buildings have gone up or been renovated, and developers have converted older
commercial structures to residential use. Loft apartments in downtown Cincinnati
are few, however, because city and state codes make conversion of urban warehouses difficult. In sum, an increasing number of people like the convenience of
downtown living. Recent figures show about 2800 downtown housing units for
somewhat less than 4000 residents; the *Cincinnati 2000 Plan,* adopted in 1982,
projects about 6000 housing units with 10,000 people. Political priorities, however,
still favor downtown office buildings.

Looking down from the Carew Tower's observatory deck, we discover that Cincinnati, like most American cities, has a **gridiron street plan.** The grid has advantages. One is that it is easy to locate oneself in it and to get around. Although canted
about nine degrees to the northwest, Cincinnati's downtown grid lies sufficiently on
a north-south axis to facilitate orientation. We basically go with the grain of the
grid. The Basin's slightly off-center grid also has benefits not available to the rest of
the city, which is on a true north-south axis. Since downtown's north-south avenues
point nine degrees northwest, their eastern sides catch the midday light earlier than
they would otherwise; the southern sides of the east-west cross streets get additional
light in late afternoon.

The orthogonal grid goes back to the beginnings of urban life. Egyptian cities
used it five thousand years ago. Roman cities, many begun as army camps, also
followed this pattern. A number of the great cities of China, Beijing among them,
were planned along rectilinear lines; even Chinese villages are gridded. The commercial interests that plan and dominate most cities prefer a grid because it facilitates trade and communication. The grid was adopted early in this country. It
maximizes commercial frontage. Rectangular lots are easy to lay out, easy to sell.
"Strait-sided and right-angled houses," asserted the commissioners who planned
Manhattan's grid in 1811, "are the most cheap to build and the most convenient to
live in." The grid also appealed to the American colonists because its undiscriminat-
ing pattern appeared egalitarian. The new cities of the trans-Appalachian West received a repetitive schematic geometry that usually ignored their varying
topography. Only in a few American cities—Washington, for example, and nearer
Cincinnati, Detroit and Indianapolis—do squares, diagonals, and radial axes mod-
ify the grid. Several mid-nineteenth-century advocates of the picturesque—Andrew
Jackson Downing, Calvert Vaux, Frederick Law Olmsted—advocated curvilinear
layouts. For them the grid denied the sense of working with the shape of the land,
its curving rivers, its rolling hills. Downing, Vaux, and Olmsted had considerable
impact on urban park systems and on suburban development, but not on cities. Nor
does the grid differentiate between streets that carry through-traffic and quiet residential streets. It does move traffic; as an environment for living it may be less
successful. Most American city planners remained tied to the grid until the City
Beautiful movement of the 1890s.

Because the grid showed so little respect for varied terrain, it prevented many American cities from acquiring distinctive visual images. Not all grids produced the same effect, however. Some result in a boring landscape, others function quite magically. "Almost always when man's will dominates over nature, the grid is boring," David Lewis has observed, "But when nature fights back, when a river slices through a grid, forcing it to leap across on delicate bridges, when hills heave and warp, . . . then the grid is at its richest and best." The Ohio River is of course Cincinnati's main street. A winding river and hills everywhere can create problems, however. Lynn Narlesky advises newcomers to Cincinnati that the city "is not based on a grid you can figure out, so don't bother. If you're pointed downhill, you're headed downtown. Therefore, when you want to go home, just drive uphill and you'll be there. Whenever you see water, turn around or you'll be in Kentucky." It's that easy.

Israel Ludlow laid out Cincinnati on a grid, six blocks facing the river, seven moving away from it. As model he used the plan of Philadelphia, the American city most influential and most emulated in the trans-Appalachian West. Philadelphia's downtown streets running off the Delaware River are, Market St. excepted, relatively narrow. Thus Cincinnati does not have the wide streets of other midwestern metropolises. Broadway, as its name indicates, is a partial exception. (Central Parkway, discussed subsequently, is a twentieth-century development.) Even the arboreal names of Cincinnati streets running off the Ohio—Sycamore, Walnut, Vine, Elm, Plum—duplicate or recall those in the City of Brotherly Love. Quakers named streets for trees and numbers to avoid "man-worship." Even though Cincinnati's simplified plan lacks Philadelphia's squares and radial axes, the young metropolis impressed many. "How beautiful this city is," remarked Gideon Burton, an early visitor to Cincinnati, "how much like Philadelphia."

The meandering Ohio River, along with the undulating hills, hardly gives Cincinnati's grid a chance to impose boredom. When nothing draws the eye to the end of a grid's streets we can have a visually dull city. But in Cincinnati something does draw the eye. Usually that something is a green hill, and usually buildings are perched on the hill. As we walk around the downtown, our eyes often come to rest against the city's hills. The view refreshes them. That in Cincinnati we constantly have to look up lends excitement to downtown walks. In effect, the city's topography forever bends the grid out of shape. A number of streets in the Basin do strange things as they approach the hills. Streets cannot climb a thirty degree slope. So some go left or right, some curl or bend, others come to a dead stop—often to resume, as if it were nothing unusual, sometimes even retaining the same name, at the top of the hill. The grid applied with some sensitivity or happy accident? The latter, I'm afraid, but it hardly matters. A city needs visual drama. The Ohio River provides one kind. The ever-changing backdrop of Cincinnati's hills, by interrupting the grid in unpredictable ways, provides another.

Even downtown, Cincinnati's is not an unvarying grid. Some downtown streets jog to left and right, 5th St., for example. Let us temporarily overcome our terror of heights and look down upon 5th from the Carew observation deck. As we follow it east, we see that if it continued straight it would run right into the Tyler Davidson Fountain. Visual drama again. Court St., five blocks north, has several jogs and at one point widens considerably before abutting the Hamilton County Courthouse. More visual drama. These jogs frequently come about because of the position of nineteenth-century street markets. Many of Over-the-Rhine's east-west thorough-fares jog left or right or cease after a few blocks. Skywalks and alleys, we shall discover, further alleviate what H. W. S. Cleveland in 1873 called "the endless repetition of the grid."

Cincinnati's streets are narrower than in comparable midwestern cities. By and large, this works to the good. Dayton's Main St. seems to take half an hour to cross, but with the exception of Central Parkway, Cincinnati doesn't have wide lifeless boulevards functioning as barriers, dividing the life on one side of the street from the life on the other, neighborhood from neighborhood. Nor can narrow streets function well as racetracks. City blocks, many of them modest 400-foot squares, and usually bisected by alleys in both directions, are neither too large nor too long. The scale is intimate. We quickly get to the end of one block, then have a choice of routes by which to continue. Whereas Manhattan's long rectangular blocks (as Jane Jacobs has pointed out) separate inhabitants living on one cross street from those on the streets on either side, Cincinnati's short square blocks facilitate communication—and walking, though perhaps at the expense of block identity.

The view from the Carew Tower extends for miles in all directions. Not always was it so clear. For over a century, only on the crispest winter day could people make out buildings in the Basin. Nineteenth-century photographs invariably show a white pall hanging over downtown. (The word "smog" did not gain general currency until the 1950s.) This mantle of smoke reminded Alexander Mackay, an English traveler of 1847, of the English manufacturing districts. In 1872 the astronomical observatory on Mount Adams had to be moved four miles farther east from the hazy downtown to Mount Lookout. "Cincinnati is built at the bottom of a funnel," wrote Max O'Rell, a Frenchmen, in 1891, "from which rise hundreds of chimneys vomiting fire and smoke. From the neighboring heights, the city looks like a huge furnace, and so it is, a furnace of industry and activity." For O'Rell, the city called to mind Glasgow. "Soot, ashes, and sulfurous gases arising from the combustion of bituminous coal in houses, public buildings, factories, steamboats, and locomotives," urban historian Carl Condit (himself Cincinnati-born) has observed, "gave Cincinnati the reputation of having the most concentrated atmospheric pollution in the world." Not until the 1950s, when the city passed legislation limiting the burning of soft bituminous coal, did the pall of smoke disappear. Today, except in muggy weather, Cincinnati's Basin remains relatively smoke free.

We have been looking about us and thinking in general terms. Presumably we are no longer quite so bewildered by the labyrinth of streets, bridges, roofs, towers, spires, and steeples. Now that our eyes are steady enough to examine this tumultuous assortment in detail, let us begin to pick out individual elements in the cityscape below. What we see of Cincinnati from the Carew Tower is basically what we shall explore on foot in the chapters that follow, so I enumerate here a few of the buildings and sights we shall encounter subsequently. We begin by facing north, the entrance to the observation deck at our backs. Our eyes follow Vine St., the city's longest, most sinuous north-south axis. Undergoing numerous identity changes as it snakes its way into the suburbs, Vine St. officially divides east from west. The plum-colored Cincinnati Commerce Center stands on the northeast corner of 6th and Vine. On the next block, the Federated Building's trapezoidal sheath of white aluminum, its corners serrated in a sleek corporate version of a sawtooth pattern, appears to good advantage. Beyond it to the right is the rectangular Kroger Building. Vine St. now enters a district of nineteenth-century three- and four-story red-brick buildings interspersed with spires. This is Over-the-Rhine, largely settled after 1830 by Germans from the Rhineland and southwest Germany. Music Hall, towered and pinnacled, rises beyond (and to the left of) the Federated Building.

The houses above the hills extending across the northern horizon are in Fairview. Scanning from the left (left of the television towers), we discern the campanile of St. Monica's Church and the massive Jacobean tower of Hughes High School. Barely visible are bits of several buildings belonging to the University of Cincinnati, among them the steeple of McMicken Hall. Nearby are the twin spires of St. George's Church.

Adjacent to Fairview is Mount Auburn, oldest of the hilltop suburbs. The cupola of Christ Hospital is a familiar landmark to many Cincinnatians. Halfway up the hill, just above the I-71 expressway, the imposing white mansion is Pendleton house (1870), once the home of Senator George Pendleton, author of the first federal civil service bill. Higher up, the large modern building of red brick and tinted glass houses Great American Broadcasting Co.

Across I-71 is Mount Adams. The Cincinnati Art Museum, its companile breaking the sky, stands on a hill, in line with the DuBois Tower and the Art Deco *Times-Star* (now Burke) Building downtown. Left of the museum, the Grand Baldwin Building also sports a campanile; below it is the former Museum of Natural History building. The museum's white dome contains a planetarium. The picturesque houses of Mount Adams cling to the hillside. Linking two hills is the great arch of the Ida Street Bridge. Atop Mount Adams is the former Holy Cross Monastery, now offices; at the far right, the Church of the Immaculate Conception anchors the panorama.

We are now looking east, or upriver. Directly below us lies Fountain Square. Along 5th St. past the DuBois Tower is the Chiquita Center. It has virtually the same color, shape, and ribbon window pattern as the Cincinnati Commerce Center at 6th and Vine streets. Behind Chiquita Center, hardly visible, is one of the two pyramidal towers of the new Procter & Gamble headquarters. Continuing clockwise, we come upon the Central Trust Center, its corners indented in white travertine marble. To its right are Atrium I and II, stepped rather than indented, yet stylistically related to the Center. The oasis of green between the Central Trust Center and Atrium I and II is Lytle Park. Beyond it we make out the yellow parabolic arches of the Daniel Carter Beard Bridge, locally known as the "Big Mac." Bellevue and Dayton lie distant on the Kentucky shore. Two other metal bridges closer in link Cincinnati with Newport, Kentucky. On the near side of the Ohio are the Coliseum, shaped like a sardine can, and the Stadium, a flying saucer come to roost. Actually, the Stadium is shaped like the Colosseum in Rome, whereas Cincinnati's Coliseum is shaped more like a Roman stadium. Several walkways connect downtown with the Stadium-Coliseum complex. On the far shore the Licking River, dividing Newport from Covington, empties into the Ohio River.

We are now facing almost due south. Directly before us rises in gleaming white terra cotta the thirty-four story Central Trust Tower. From here we gain the best view of the miniature classical temple atop its pyramidal crown, whose copper has acquired the green patina of exposure. Pyramid and temple fancifully re-create the tomb of King Mausolus, from which we derived *mausoleum*, at Halicarnassus (in modern Turkey), one of the Seven Wonders of the ancient world. Once the lower-lying land beyond the Central Trust Tower teemed with commercial buildings, warehouses, and habitations. When the Ohio River flooded, as it frequently did, this land lay under water. Now it consists largely of parking lots. With the Ohio better behaved than in the past, the city envisages eventually developing the area, known as Riverfront West and at present wastefully under-used, for commercial and residential use.

Across the Ohio River is Covington, largest of the northern Kentucky cities. An apartment highrise, unfortunately situated, partially obscures the splendid Basilica of the Assumption, modeled upon Notre Dame in Paris and St.-Denis. Closer in, we discern the twin verdigris towers of Mother of God Church. On the other side of the I-75 expressway rise the hills of Covington's Devou Park. Downriver lie the communities of Ludlow and Bromley.

When we explore the waterfront we shall look more closely at the bridges spanning the Ohio but for orientation purposes I name them here. From east to west, they are the yellow-arched Daniel Carter Beard (or I-471) Bridge, the Louisville & Nashville Bridge, the Central Bridge, the Roebling Suspension Bridge (with its mighty stone towers), the Clay Wade Bailey and Chesapeake & Ohio bridges (the two looking like one, the first for vehicular traffic, the other for trains), and the double-decked Brent Spence Bridge (over which run I-71 and I-75). Visible further downriver is the Cincinnati Southern Bridge, for trains only.

We have moved around to the west. The Ohio River gleams in the distance. This was presumably the view at sunset that so impressed Winston Churchill. Price Hill hugs the river across the Millcreek Valley. Directly below us rises the thirty-one story Netherland Plaza. Beyond it is the Hyatt Hotel in salmon-colored brick; its copper-tinted ribbon windows reflect surrounding structures. To its right, the twin towers of another hotel, the Clarion; behind it, the low-lying Convention Center. I-75 runs through what is left of the West End, a residential area of gutted, decaying, and restored nineteenth-century houses, one of Cincinnati's main entry neighborhoods for over a century. Halfway across the Millcreek Valley rises the huge half-dome of Union Terminal (1933). Close in, at the edge of downtown stands the massive City Hall (1893), Richardsonian Romanesque in style. To its left, barely visible behind the Art Deco telephone building and its sterile modern addition, we discover the steeple of St. Peter-in-Chains Cathedral and the twin minarets of the Isaac M. Wise Temple. Closer in we may discern, if we look hard, the octagonal dome of the former Shillito (now Lazarus) department store.

Before descending from the Carew observation deck, it will be useful, with the panoramas before us still fresh in mind, to indicate what lies ahead in our explorations of the city. The next chapter will take us through the downtown that lies west of Fountain Square; chapter 3 tours the downtown that lies east. Chapter 4 goes, from west to east, the length of 4th St., the city's chief commercial artery. It ends at Lytle Park which, together with the Taft Museum (not visible from the Carew deck), forms the subject of the fifth chapter. Chapter 6 takes us along the historic riverfront, now redone and once again a focus of Cincinnati's urban life. We cross the Roebling Bridge, explore Covington's riverside district, and (if we like) cruise up the Ohio, an experience that will orient us in regard to this river that has played so vital a role in Cincinnati's history. Chapters 7 and 8 explore the historic Over-the-Rhine district to the north. As we walk along streets that have changed little in a hundred years, we gain a vivid sense of the nineteenth-century city that hovers on the edge of the twentieth-century city.

Chapters 9 through 11 cover the nearby hilltop suburbs. Chapter 9 tours Mount Auburn, whose main street includes several splendid Italianate houses. In one of them grew up President and Chief Justice William Howard Taft, the best-known member of a distinguished Cincinnati clan and one of four presidents associated with the city. In chapter 10 we wander along the streets of Clifton, further north, to admire a succession of magnificent Victorian mansions. Chapter 11 takes us to the narrow, precipitous streets of Mount Adams, from which panoramas open up over downtown, the Ohio River, and the Kentucky hills. This tour includes a stroll through Eden Park and a stop at the Krohn Conservatory. Chapter 12 completes our sequence of core tours with a visit to the Cincinnati Art Museum. The concluding chapter, best done by car, takes in landmarks beyond the central area.

The vistas seen from the Carew Tower have given us an overall sense of Cincinnati. We now return to Fountain Square to complete this tour with a promenade along the city's **skywalks**.

"Skywalks"—how the name smacks of *hubris,* the overweening (and fatal) pride of the heroes of Greek drama. Eighteen feet above street level, the skywalks wander through department stores and hotel lobbies, by specialty shops and restaurants, between alleys and across streets. One hooks up to the Convention Center. If the urge to shop is upon you now is the time, for we go by or into a number of the downtown emporiums. The skywalks are open to all and remain open (Sundays excepted) even when the buildings through which they pass are closed. In an era when downtowns in America deteriorated and urban crime soared, Cincinnati built its skywalks and trusted (for the most part rightly) its citizens to respect them and their city.

Elevated pedestrian walkways are not in themselves new. The idea of separating foot from vehicular traffic goes back at least to Leonardo da Vinci. It was, for ex-

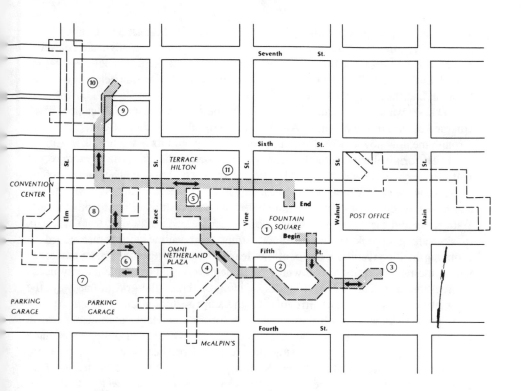

SKYWALKS

1. Tyler Davidson Fountain
2. Westin Hotel
3. Contemporary Arts Center
4. Carew Tower
5. *Traveler's Column*
   (Pomodoro Sculpture)

6. Saks
7. Hyatt
8. Clarion
9. Cincinnati Athletic Club
10. Lazarus
11. 525 Vine (Ameritrust Center)

ample, an integral part of Olmsted and Vaux's plan for Manhattan's Central Park. Le Corbusier, the twentieth-century French modernist architect, advocated elevated paths in this century for his *Ville Contemporaine* and later for his *Ville Radieuse*, though Le Corbusier had the vehicular traffic above, the pedestrian below—a dreadful idea, and the reverse of Cincinnati's system.

The skywalks have added a new dimension to Cincinnati's urban life. They emerged as part of the dream of Archibald Rogers, the Baltimore architect who put through the downtown redevelopment plan. The city built its first skywalk in August 1971. The original ones, though covered, were open to the air; those of more recent vintage are enclosed and, as needs be, heated or air conditioned. They allow people to walk, without descending to street level, to most places in the city's heart. Car and bus (and pedestrian) traffic operate below without disturbance or inconvenience. With stairs and escalators at strategic points, people can easily shift from sidewalk to skywalk and back again. In effect, streets and walkways together afford us shopping-mall convenience (without the deadening homogeneity of most malls) set within the rich diversity of a downtown. To achieve visual excitement a city needs to crack its grid. The hills surrounding Cincinnati crack the grid in one way; the skywalks crack it in another. Irregularity and surprise lurk at this grid's heart. Superimposing skywalks upon the grid makes for a completely different pattern; in effect, two cities compete for the same piece of turf. The danger of course is that a downtown, streets and skywalks together, can support just so many shops. Skywalks in other cities—Baltimore and Minneapolis, for example—have had a mixed success. But in Cincinnati the irregular skywalks appear to mesh well with the regular grid. FOR RENT signs rarely appear on either level. The skywalks have become a strengthening element in the downtown's texture. "Life attracts life," urban historian Jane Jacobs once wrote. That Cincinnati's downtown life, once in a perilous state, now appears reasonably healthy can in part be attributed to its success with the skywalks.

This superimposed pedestrian network, irregular and humane, was created with plenty of wayward human touches: windings and curves, nooks and crannies, alternation of indoor and outdoor. We come to expect the unexpected: unanticipated encounters with, or surprising perspectives on, familiar landmarks. The skywalks also make it easier for us to examine the decorative elements on many buildings. Much sculptural ornament is so placed that it is virtually invisible. "Architecture," believed John Ruskin, "is the art of ornamenting buildings." Ornament gladdened Ruskin's soul; it may gladden ours too. The nineteenth century regarded architecture as morally uplifting. We discover that it is also physically uplifting: we have to crane our necks to look up. Every so often we should think about raising our eyes for an architectural break. What we see in downtown Cincinnati will rarely disappoint us.

Being above ground, Cincinnati's skywalks avoid the disorientation of the underground concourses that I have experienced in Toronto and Montreal. When we lack aboveground landmarks or the sun's orientation, we often get lost, at least I do. On the Cincinnati skywalks we can usually figure out where we are. Familiar downtown buildings and street scenes, though often viewed from unexpected angles, orient us. In addition, near most entrances to the skywalk system we find maps either on plaques or on freestanding cubes. Skywalk routes in brightly painted colors are superimposed over the downtown grid in white. So don't fear to lose your way. You may, of course, but a glance at a map should quickly orient you.

We join the system at Fountain Square. Climbing the steps east of the Tyler Davidson Fountain, we cross 5th St. and enter the Westin Hotel. The **atrium,** a glass-covered expanse supported by a trellis-like system of metal struts, offers light and trees, yet remains unfocused. Too little happens in too large an area. The ground the atrium encloses, actually public land, was to have become an integral element of Fountain Square, the city's "living room." But the city failed to specify *how* the space was to be used. The developer decided not to develop and, in effect, thumbed his nose at the city. The atrium has no public benches and its emptiness does not encourage dawdling. What could have become an indoor complement to Fountain Square, for Cincinnati what Quincy Market is for Boston, has remained as it began: an empty space.

Atria, like arcades, are both an old and a new phenomenon. In recent years they have opened up the core of many office buildings. "The atrium has been revived twice since it was first born in the Roman house," has observed Cheryl Kent, on whom I draw for this paragraph. In antiquity the atrium was open to the elements; modern atria are not. Glass structures such as the Crystal Palace (1851) in London are its progenitors. The first revival of atria occurred at the end of the last century. Several Chicago buildings by Burnham and Root feature them. The Rookery (1886), subsequently remodeled by Frank Lloyd Wright in 1905, is one. The second revival of atria occurred in the late 1960s. The Ford Foundation Building (1967) on Manhattan's 42nd St., designed by Kevin Roche and John Dinkeloo, and in Atlanta, the Hyatt Regency (1968), designed by Edwards and Portman, are the seminal structures that have influenced many subsequent atria, including those in Water Tower Place (1976) and the State of Illinois Center (1984), both in Chicago. Today, atria come in all sizes and shapes. On this tour, two interesting atria still before us are those in the Hyatt and in the 525 Building.

From the Westin's atrium we veer left, cross Walnut and find ourselves at the top of an escalator overlooking a treelined arcade that leads to the Formica Building. To our left is the entrance to the **Contemporary Arts Center**. Founded in 1939 as the Cincinnati Modern Art Society, the center is (after Boston's) the second oldest institution of its kind in the country. It changed its name in 1953 and, after a peripatetic existence, in 1970 finally settled in this space. Dedicated to displaying avant-garde visual works, the center also offers lectures and programs in music, dance, photography, architecture, and film. Its goal since its founding has been to present modern art adequately in conservative Cincinnati, not the easiest town in which to develop a taste for, say, melting (plastic) popsicles. Maintaining no permanent collection, the center defines itself as a museum of ideas, not of objects.

Exhibits (there are usually several going on at once) change every few months. Only an Alexander Calder mobile of 1947 remains on permanent display. This delicate creation of painted steel above the entrance doorway risks being overlooked. Like other Calder mobiles, it possesses harmony and beauty of design and a graceful movement. Calder uses primary colors and elemental shapes in ways that recall the organic, abstracted compositions of Joan Miró and Jean Arp. (In the Cincinnati Art Museum we may juxtapose another Calder mobile with a mural by Miró.) The shallow-domed room beyond the entrance has an oculus to let in light. It echoes Rome's Pantheon, a favorite building of Harry Weese, the architect responsible for the center and the adjacent Formica Building. The spacious exhibit rooms display the art objects well. Floor-to-ceiling windows projecting over 5th St. provide unexpected perspectives on downtown buildings. Actually, the windows become an extension of the center, for in looking through them we experience in effect huge wall paintings—three-dimensional, alive, and ever-changing—of the city.

As we reenter the skywalk system, we gain sight of another urban vista: the lacework fire escapes of the Mercantile and Tri-State buildings above us. We return to the Westin's atrium, cross the bridge over Vine St. into the Carew Tower. As we cross the bridge over 5th St., we must not miss the elongated, finned Art Deco "coach" lamps on the Netherland Plaza's façade. Such coach lamps were a sign of hospitality; today, more ornamental than illuminative, we often discover them before hotels. Soon we find ourselves in an open space, largest in the skywalk system, with benches and an outdoor sculpture. *Traveler's Column* (1967), a vertical bronze fountain set in a circular base, is by Arnaldo Pomodoro. The skywalk here, oldest in the system, is undergoing major change in line with the Fountain Square West development.

We now bear left, cross Race St., and enter the Fifth & Race Tower Arcade. At the first intersection, we turn left again toward Saks (1984). After crossing 5th St., we turn left once more, not forgetting as we do to look up through the curved glass roof at the Netherland Plaza silhouetted against the sky. After perhaps browsing in Saks, we then enter the atrium of the Hyatt (1984), the building by RTKL, Archibald Rogers's firm, instrumental in redesigning much of downtown in the late 1960s. Enticing sofas offer rest for the weary; the fountain's splashing, muffled by its glass cage, relaxes. This atrium, smaller than the Westin's, works better. Palms in oversized planters, art works, and muted colors create an intimate atmosphere.

We return to the Race Tower Arcade, turn left at the intersection into the lobby—a gloomy place—of the Clarion (1970, 1977). Then we take a hard right following indicators to Lazarus, another of the city's downtown emporiums. On the way, we look at the artworks affixed to the side of the Cincinnati Athletic Club, founded in 1853 and formerly the Cincinnati Gymnasium and Athletic Club (CGAC appears on the four medallions above the façade arches). This splendid Renaissance Revival palazzo has salmon-colored brick, a rusticated stone base, and rock-faced masonry. The plaque reproduces an article on the building's inauguration from the *Cincinnati Enquirer* of May 16, 1902.

Lazarus, originally the John Shillito Co., has been for over a century one of Cincinnati's premier department stores. We retrace our steps and return to the intersection with the Pomodoro sculpture. From there we pass through the imposing seven-story atrium of the 525 Vine Building (1985), now the Ameritrust Center, by Michael Moose of Glaser & Myers. The subdued colors are part of its postmodern decoration, a style owing much to Art Deco. This atrium strikes me as fashionable high camp. The balconies, cantilevered out like the interior of a ziggurat, lead the eye to a ceiling ornament that incorporates a geometrical flower medallion.

Crossing 5th St., we find ourselves once again in Fountain Square.

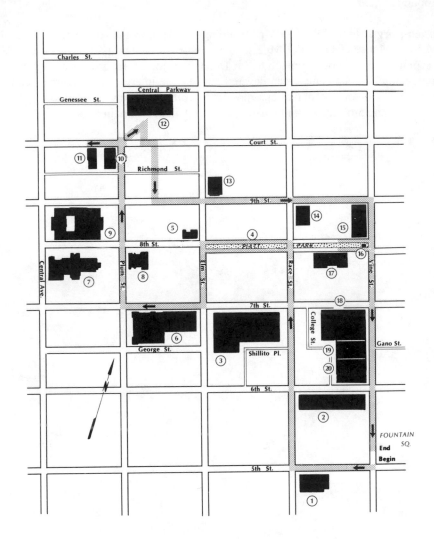

DOWNTOWN—WEST OF VINE

1. Netherland Plaza
2. Terrace Hilton
3. Lazarus
4. Piatt Park
5. Norfolk Apartments
6. Cincinnati Telephone Building
7. St. Peter-in-Chains Cathedral
8. Isaac M. Wise Temple
9. City Hall
10. Lloyd Library

11. Fire Museum
12. Court Street Center
13. Crosley Square
14. Phoenix Club
15. 2 Garfield Place
16. James Garfield Statue
17. Doctors Building
18. Federated Building
19. 617 Vine (*Enquirer* Building)
20. Cincinnatian Hotel

2

Downtown—West of Vine

THIS tour takes us by a number of downtown Cincinnati's major buildings. They are in a gallimaufry of architectural styles: the Terrace Hilton (Modern Movement), St. Peter-in-Chains (Greek Revival), the Isaac M. Wise Temple (Moorish Revival), City Hall (Romanesque Revival), the Doctors Building (skyscraper Gothic), and the Cincinnatian Hotel (Second Empire exterior, postmodern interior). We pass a library housing one of the world's outstanding collections of pharmaceutical books, we visit a fire museum that commemorates one of the nation's first professional fire departments, we may even sample a local speciality—Cincinnati chili.

We begin at Fountain Square. As we head west along 5th St., we see above the entrance to the Netherland Plaza two flared hexagonal lamps. Before them sits Shiva, Hindu god of destruction and procreation: a particularly apt deity for American cities. We shall encounter Shiva again, this time with extra sets of arms, in the Cincinnati Art Museum. We turn right on Race St. and walk north to the **Terrace Hilton** (1948). Like the Netherland Plaza, this nineteen-story structure was built by the Emery interests. Until 1965, when the Emerys sold it to the Hilton chain, it was known as the Terrace Plaza. Designed by Skidmore, Owings, & Merrill, the Terrace Plaza was the first major building to rise after World War II in downtown Cincinnati. The seven windowless floors, a monolithic pedestal for the tower above, once held two department stores, Bond's on Vine, and Penney's on Race. The hotel lobby is on the eighth floor, on which is also the terrace that gives the hotel its name. In winter it once converted to an ice skating rink, in summer it is still used for dining.

In its day, the Terrace Hilton set the pace in hotel design as much as had, twenty years before, its bigger cousin, the Netherland Plaza. Room design included multifunctional furniture, with a bed that came out of the wall and a desk that converted to a bar or luggage rack. Everything in the hotel—including ashtrays designed by Rookwood Pottery—was custom made. Even the unusual idea of beginning the hotel on the eighth floor was part of the overall plan: not only the tower's height but the setback protected guests from street noise. Various remodelings have taken their toll. Both the lower lobby and the eighth-floor lobby have been redesigned and the rooms redone.

Architectural historians have acclaimed the Terrace Hilton as one of America's pioneer Modern Movement buildings. Cincinnati architectural critic Jayne Merkel deems the Terrace Hilton "historically significant because it is one of a very few hotels built in that rigorous style." Well and good. We may certainly appreciate the building's tradition-breaking qualities. Only small, token Modern Movement structures had appeared in the United States by the 1930s. We may laud the Emerys' courage in taking on the daring design of Skidmore, Owings, and Merrill, then a relatively new firm that had never before done a hotel. How the structure must have startled when first it towered above its nineteenth- and early twentieth-century neighbors! After forty years it still looks like no other Cincinnati building. Yet even if we concede its pioneer design, we must still contemplate a blank wall seven stories high. And where the windows begin, little holds the eye. The building appears at best a mixed success. Only the elongated Roman brick saves it. Brick is a traditional building material infrequently used in modern highrises. The brick here, a warm red and laid like tile with the vertical joints aligned, looks attractively different.

Until 1965 the Terrace Hilton's **Gourmet Room,** its twentieth-story circular restaurant, housed a huge curved, vividly colored mural commissioned from the Spanish painter Joan Miró. The mural occupied the back wall; the remaining 270 degrees of window space offered splendid views over the city. Besides the Miró, the hotel had a fanciful Saul Steinberg mural depicting Cincinnati, and a Calder mobile. Before the Emery firm sold the hotel it generously gave all three artworks to the Cincinnati Art Museum.

Sixth St. from Vine to Central held from 1826 to 1959 a huge market that included a block of flower stalls. Though the market is gone, the older structures on the street's north side allow us to gain a partial sense of the nineteenth-century commercial city. Before Kathman's Shoe Repair hangs a huge highbuttoned shoe; until recently an equally huge cod hung nearby. Old prints of Cincinnati reveal a profusion of placards, signs, and billboards. A German visitor, Moritz Busch, observed in 1851 "enormous rifles advertising the gun shop, great golden mortars advertising the physician and the apothecary, monstrous boots advertising the footwear artist. . . . Great plows . . . greet the farmer as a customer at 3,000 paces." In the 1870s Lafcadio Hearn revelled in Cincinnati's variety of signs, many couched in dubious spellings. Murray Seasongood, growing up on west 8th St. in the 1880s, recalls seeing "red-and-white leech's striped barber poles; erect wooden Indians for tobacconists; two large glass globes or urns, one green and the other purple, and a mortar and pestle, for Martin & Heister at Seventh and Elm as well as other druggists . . . ; a swinging pendant boot and shoe representing makers and sellers of footwear; and a large gilt framed pair of eyeglasses for the optician."

Sign painting was once an important activity. Many prominent nineteenth-century American artists, such as Worthington Whittredge, Godfrey Frankenstein, and Henry Farny in Cincinnati, began their artistic careers as sign painters. In England, in the previous century, William Hogarth had painted signs. A hundred years

"Cape Cod." Such colorful, self-explanatory street signs are fast vanishing from the Cincinnati scene. "Cape Cod" went in 1988, but farther along the street the boot touting Kathman's Shoe Repair remains.

ago, downtown Cincinnati was an artist's paradise; the 1880 *Williams Directory* listed twenty-eight sign painters. Since many people were illiterate or semiliterate, shop signs served to identify goods. They were also a colorful element in the streetscape. The gradual disappearance of these signs has resulted in a visual impoverishment of which few are aware. Like other picturesque features, the signs had their inconvenient side: they creaked horribly in the wind, they dripped upon passersby, they even fell down without warning. Still, surviving signs in other cities are often treasured. The most beloved object in Boston may be the famous 227-gallon kettle that hangs from the Sears Block near City Hall Plaza. Today, with buildings shaped like derbies or hot dogs, this kind of folk art has gone mad. What we see in Las Vegas, as Robert Venturi has reminded us, is merely the "strip" of most American cities writ large. But even those visually deadened by our omnipresent commercialism should find Kathman's boot on 6th St. charming. Losing signs can be almost as significant as losing buildings. May this relic of an older era—and other hardy survivors elsewhere in Cincinnati—long continue to adorn the cityscape!

Race St. has undergone a mild facelift: sidewalks widened and indented, pavement gussied up, trees planted. A gaggle of sidewalk merchants peddle cheap goods. Lazarus occupies the block's west side, from Shillito Rikes Place to 7th St. The city's oldest department store, it began in 1830 when John Shillito and a partner opened a dry goods enterprise on Main St. The John S. Shillito Company became after a 1982 merger Shillito Rikes. (The earlier name is still visible above the Race St. entrance; at the entrance on 7th it appears in an irresistible undulating band.) Although the Lazarus clan of Columbus has owned the store since 1928, not until 1986 did Shillito's become known as Lazarus. When this building opened in 1878, it housed under one roof the largest department store in the country. During the 1930s, the Race and 7th street façades received a smooth Art Deco limestone facing. The motifs, I'm told, are Mayan.

Prominent Cincinnati architect James W. McLaughlin designed the original 1878 structure. The present Art Deco exterior conceals a pioneer building. From Shillito Rikes Place we may still glimpse McLaughlin's original façade. Although most architectural historians designate Chicago as the birthplace of the Commercial style, Winston Weisman has shown conclusively that Chicago's First Leiter Building (1879), designed by William Le Baron Jenney and often considered the groundbreaking commercial building of its day, in fact drew its inspiration from McLaughlin's Shillito store. Its internal iron skeleton preceded First Leiter's. The interior, modelled after that of Paris's famed department store *Le Bon Marché* (1869), once boasted a multistoried arcaded atrium 120 feet high, capped by a glass dome sixty feet across. In the 1930s the Fire Department requested Shillito's to fill in the atrium for safety reasons. But the dome is still there, visible, as we saw, from the Carew observation deck.

Seven nineteenth-century commercial buildings occupy the north side of the Race to Vine block. Few alterations above the shop level disfigure them; the tallest of the seven retains its splendid cornice with anthemions. Near the Vine St. end must be Cincinnati's narrowest building, its two windows a lovely exercise in the mode known as neo-Grec. In bibliographic circles it would be designated a slim tome. The **Leeds Building** (1894), on the northeast corner of Race & 7th streets, typifies the commercial Renaissance Revival architecture of its day, with its terra cotta-and-brick façade, huge round-arched openings, and squat look. It is, in effect, a stretched-out Italian palazzo. If we look carefully at the façade on Race, we discover that (as often with the downtown highrises) it is joined near the center. So closely matched are the façades that the addition must have gone up soon after the original. Across the street is 707 Race (1910) with an incised and interlaced façade of limestone and concrete. It exhibits a later phase of the turn-of-the-century Renaissance Revival, one influenced by the Chicago School. The Movies Repertory Cinema at 719 Race St. is a mecca for Cincinnati's enthusiasts of foreign, independent, and overlooked Hollywood films.

Piatt Park extends two blocks along 8th St., to the east and west of Race. The

Piatt brothers, John H. and Benjamin M., donated the land in 1817 "for a market space," but no market ever stood here. Instead, the land became the city's first park. Named for James Garfield, our twentieth president, in 1882, it was renamed Piatt in 1940, though the surrounding road surface remains—to everyone's confusion— Garfield Place. With Covenant-First Presbyterian closing the park's western end and behind it the soaring minarets of the Wise Temple, the classical steeple of St. Peter's Cathedral, and the massive tower of City Hall, we have one of the great urban set-pieces of the midwest.

The park long served the city's street people as a watering hole, though water was not what was drunk here. In some ways, such a use is a good thing. Many of those who have quit the race for this world's honors have an integrity all their own. Further, as Ian Nairn, the English architectural critic, has argued, a public area "without bums has something very wrong with it, because the bums know instinctively what we have to learn so laboriously and with so much effort—that is, whether a place feels right." Piatt Park obviously feels, or felt, right to Cincinnati's down and out. But not everyone finds undesirables (as town planners call them) a good thing. What to do? A solution was to make the park attractive to everyone else. The city fathers had such a goal in mind. They wished to make Piatt Park the focal point for a residential district, with upper-income housing, both medium-rise and townhouses, to sprout here and on surrounding blocks. The highrise apartment building between Race and Elm streets dates from 1969; 2 Garfield Place, on Vine, from 1982. Thus far they are the only sprouts. To encourage pedestrian use the city renovated the park, put in honey locusts, granite borders, raised flower beds with shrubs, ivy, a wider promenade, arches, and fountains on either side of the Race St. intersection. Garfield Place may eventually be closed to traffic. Both park and place have the potential to focus one of the city's most livable urban spaces. But presently few people sit on the benches.

General William Henry Harrison looms over Piatt Park's western end. Harrison was the United States's ninth president and the first from Ohio. Dedicated in 1896, this equestrian statue is the work of Louis T. Rebisso (1837–1899). Italian-born but resident in Cincinnati, Rebisso is best known for his equestrian statues of General McPherson in McPherson Square, Washington, and of General Grant in Chicago's Lincoln Park. He captures Harrison in his military days and renders him younger, more vigorous than when he assumed the presidency. That his horse has one foot raised indicates that Harrison was wounded in battle. Vandals have thrice stolen his sword. Equestrians have long delighted in pointing out that the sculptor neglected to provide the general with a saddle.

Harrison is an important figure in Cincinnati history. He came to Ohio in November 1791 as an eighteen-year-old ensign in the U.S. Army and later served as General Anthony Wayne's aide-de-camp. After Wayne's victory at Fallen Timbers in 1794 Harrison stayed on, and in 1795 married Anna Tuthill Symmes, second daughter of John Cleves Symmes, who once owned all the land between the two Miami rivers. After resigning from the army, Harrison was appointed secretary of the Northwest Territory. Made governor of the Indiana Territory in 1800, he negotiated numerous treaties with the Indians. His moment of glory came in October

1811, at Tippecanoe, when he defeated an Indian confederation led by the fearsome warrior Tecumseh. Commander of the Army of the Northwest during the War of 1812, Harrison vanquished a force of British and Indians at the Battle of the Thames, at which Tecumseh fell. In 1814 Harrison, having again resigned from the army, returned to North Bend (downriver from Cincinnati) to work his 2000-acre farm. A popular hero, he remained well liked in the Cincinnati area. He served in the Ohio House of Representatives and Senate, briefly as minister to Colombia in 1828, and in the 1830s held civic posts in city and county government.

In 1840 Harrison ran for president. His candidacy symbolized the recognition that Cincinnati had arrived on the national scene; already by 1840 Ohio had become the Union's third largest state. Harrison's opponent, New York's dapper Martin Van Buren, allegedly depicted the Ohioan as a "backwoodsman" who "drinks hard cider" and whose mother "still lives in a log cabin." The contest soon became known as the "Log Cabin and Hard Cider" campaign. Whig backers of "Old Tippecanoe" turned the taunts to advantage. They pretended that this educated and moderately wealthy farmer really *was* a rough pioneer who lived in a log cabin and drank hard cider. Log cabins assumed new dignity; hard cider suddenly became a national beverage. This carnival brouhaha along with the deliberate use of deception marked the beginning of modern political campaigning. Harrison won the election and assumed the presidency in March 1841, aged sixty-eight. While delivering his one hour and forty-minute inaugural address in a pouring rain, he caught pneumonia and, one month later, died in office. At North Bend, an imposing granite monument commemorates his burial place. His grandson, Benjamin Harrison, also became president.

Directly in front of the Harrison statue, giving the park a focal point, lies **Covenant-First Presbyterian Church** (1875). The original congregation, one of the oldest in Ohio, was founded in October 1790. Like many other Cincinnati churches, Covenant-First Presbyterian came about (as its name indicates) through a merger of several historic parishes. Covenant itself swallowed Second, Fifth, and Central Presbyterian. In 1934 First Presbyterian, the city's oldest congregation (which earlier had absorbed Reformed Presbyterian and West Liberty Presbyterian) gave up its 4th St. property to unite with Covenant. Now with only 215 members, Covenant is one of the few surviving houses of worship in the downtown. The English-derived Gothic Revival design we owe to the architect William Walter, possibly assisted by William Stewart. Towers of different shape and height create an asymmetrical façade. The limestone tracery around the portals nicely accentuates the vertical thrust.

The **Norfolk** (1891), on the northwest corner of 8th and Elm streets, is also (as indicated above the front entrance) known as the Waldo. It is one of downtown's potential Cinderellas. "An imposing building unsurpassed by any apartment house in the city," wrote D. J. Kenny in his 1893 guide to Cincinnati. Few would agree with Kenny today. But architecturally the Norfolk constitutes a wondrously sophisticated eclectic mix: French Second Empire mansard roof, Tudor arches, clusters of pressed brick colonnettes, a rusticated rock-faced pink and gray granite base, and a splendid Romanesque-arched entrance. Once the Norfolk offered some of the city's finest flats: large rooms, excellent light, wood mantels, parlors finished in cherry, a

private hall with floor of imported tile, exceptionally thick ceilings and walls between apartments. I have not been inside, but with its exterior recently cleaned, the
Norfolk would appear to be a prime candidate for a showcase interior rehabilitation.

In the 1880s and 1890s the brothers Thomas J. and John J. Emery erected in
Cincinnati more than a score of apartment houses including the Norfolk. The names
they chose for the first four—Lorraine, Lombardy, Brittany, Saxony—evidence
their love for the great regions of Europe. The Saxony and Brittany we come upon
later in this walk; the Lombardy, most magnificent of all though now in a parlous
state, we pass in chapter 4. Of these five buildings, four still stand. Only one is in
good condition today, but merely their continued presence in downtown Cincinnati
testifies to the city's measured growth since the nineteenth century's close. Buildings that a faster growing city would long ago have torn down often survive here.

Izzy's restaurant (819 Elm St.) occupies the lower floor of an Italianate Victorian rowhouse. Its kosher corned beef and pastrami sandwiches deserve their city-
wide renown. In 1901 Israel Kadetz opened the original Izzy's on Central Avenue;
when the building succumbed to urban renewal, Izzy's moved here. Still family-
owned, the restaurant has since opened several branches, including one on Main St.
and, to cheer displaced Cincinnatians, others in Columbus and Dayton. A meal at
Izzy's involves savoring the raucous atmosphere no less than the tasty food. Afterwards, you tell the cashier what you had, pay, and depart—and that's that.

We turn down Elm to 7th St. Until March 1988 a wall painting by Tom Stroh-
maier adorned an older building razed for the Garfield Place project. It depicted a
grinning King Kong, known as Kosherilla, against a skewed version of the city's
skyline. Kosherilla, creature of legend, travelled from coast to coast ravaging Kosher delicatessens. Did he swipe the pickle in his hand from Joe's New York Deli
below? Scattered about the center city, with a few beyond, are a fast-diminishing
number of other wall paintings. Local artists created the paintings either for the
nonprofit community project called Urban Walls, sponsored in the early 1970s by
Cincinnati's Carl Solway Gallery, or (like this one) done as a spinoff from that project. Unlike the equally fast-disappearing store signs, the wall paintings are more
artistic than utilitarian. They add color, brightness, and a sense of the unexpected to
our visual experience of the cityscape. The paintings also help camouflage the city's
wounds.

On the southwest corner of 7th and Elm streets we face the twelve-story **Cincinnati Telephone Building** (1931). Spectacular copper-and-bronze lamps stand
guard before the entrances. The alternating telephones and headsets lining the second floor frieze are symbolic as well as ornamental. In 1930 Cincinnati Bell began
conversion to dial service. The decoration anticipates the change, not completed
until 1952: telephones are more prominent than headsets. Note the stylized Art Deco
lettering, "Elm Street/Seventh Street," with "A.D. 1930" (the year construction began) in marble below. The bas relief above the entrance on Elm, difficult to make
out, includes Benjamin Franklin, who puts in another appearance, as a printer, on
the *Times-Star* Building across town. Harry Hake of Hake & Kuck designed the
telephone building. Its austere classicism bears a family resemblance to Hake's Masonic Temple, the Taft Theater (both in chapter 3), and Fourth & Race Tower (chap-

Kosherilla (1974–1987), formerly near the northeast corner of Elm and 7th. An offspring of the "Urban Walls" project, *Kosherilla* was one of a number of intriguing wall paintings that appeared in downtown Cincinnati during the 1970s. As buildings fall, the paintings vanish. *Kosherilla,* whom many Cincinnatians remember with affection, appropriately loomed over Joe's Deli.

ter 4). In all, dressed limestone remains the favored façade covering. The building's flat roof, the 1943 WPA guide noted, would permit adding twelve more stories. But when the time came to expand, Cincinnati Bell built the intimidating, windowless (on three sides) monolith (1975) next door—also by the Hake firm—New Brutalistic in shape if not in materials (the inevitable concrete blocks are here disguised by being set in mortar). Utilities tend to go for blank walls, and the walls deaden the cityscape. Even though the lack of windows is explained by the building being a long-distance switching center, its floor space occupied by equipment, attractive it is not. We walk to Plum St.

Visible to the south, straddling the Elm to Plum block, is the city's **Convention Center** (1967), by Hake and Hake. In 1985 it was renamed after Dr. Albert Sabin, discoverer (through his research in Cincinnati) of an effective oral vaccine against polio. The 1987 rebuilding and addition, on both sides of Plum St., not only increased floor space from 161,000 sq. ft. to 301,000 but vastly improved the Center's appearance. The sequence of gables complements the Albee arch (discussed in chapter 4) facing Plum to the south.

At Plum and 8th streets we come upon the city's finest aggregate of architectural treasures: St. Peter-in-Chains Cathedral (1845), the Isaac M. Wise Temple (1866), and City Hall (1893).

St. Peter-in-Chains Cathedral derives its name from a huge painting, given to the diocese in the 1830s and attributed to Murillo, that long hung above the cathedral's altar. Until 1938, when St. Monica's in Fairview supplanted it, St. Peter's served as the diocesan cathedral. After the 1952–1957 restoration it again became the cathedral. Archbishop John B. Purcell (1800–1883), who headed the Cincinnati diocese for five decades (it became an archdiocese in 1850), wanted his new cathedral in the "Grecian style of architecture." Purcell, a colorful figure in the city's early history, had come to America from Ireland at eighteen. Edward Fenwick, Cincinnati's first bishop, had died of cholera in 1832, and Purcell succeeded him the following year. In 1838 he visited Europe, including England and Ireland, and memories of Dublin's St. George and, even more, of London's St. Martin-in-the-Fields must have influenced his choosing the "Grecian style" for St. Peter's.

The cathedral is the work of Henry Walter, the architect principally responsible for the Ohio state capitol in Columbus. (His son William designed the Covenant-First Presbyterian Church we have just passed.) For the cathedral Walter adapted elements of various Greek buildings into an original design. St. Peter's begins as a Greek temple only a shade smaller in scale than the Parthenon. Massive Corinthian columns, without bases, serve as a hexastyle entrance portico. Instead of the usual triangular pediment, Walter designed an entablature of receding moldings. The column capitals, composed of acanthus leaves topped by tall narrow leaves instead of the usual volutes, derive from Athens's Tower of the Winds, as reproduced in that Bible of Greek Revival architects, Stuart and Revett's *Antiquities of Athens* (four volumes published between 1762 and 1816). When St. Peter's was dedicated in November 1845, it still lacked part of its portico and spire; the interior also remained unfinished. Work continued until 1855.

Most nineteenth-century visitors found St. Peter's the most impressive church in Cincinnati. Charles Cist, the city's chief civic booster at midcentury, deemed it "the finest building in the west." Moritz Busch, the acerbic German, found it, however, "an unforgivable insult to good taste, . . . a shameless ravaging of good marble!" Busch, like many Europeans, judged American architecture by Old World standards and found it wanting. Few since Busch have found St. Peter's exterior wanting. He objected particularly to the "white tasteless tower," to my mind St. Peter's architectural glory. It is modelled upon the steeples Sir Christopher Wren placed on the London parish churches he designed after the Great Fire of 1666; it also owes a debt to the tower designed by James Gibbs for St. Martin-in-the-Fields, itself influenced by Wren. St. Peter's spire rises from a square base in a series of octagons. Such a design is called a *broach spire*. Like the Wren steeples and St. Martin's, this spire also achieves, despite its classical forms and its use of the classical orders, the effect of Gothic verticality.

It is **Lafcadio Hearn** who makes St. Peter's tower come alive for us. Arriving in Cincinnati in 1869 as a penniless nineteen-year-old, young Hearn called the city home for seven years. He gradually became a newspaperman of unusual determination and energy. In articles for the *Enquirer,* and later for the *Commercial,* he chronicled the city's life, particularly the life of its poor and downtrodden. Short sketches and travel pieces emerged as significant literary forms in the 1870s, and Hearn, along with Mrs. Trollope, remains the most pungent observer the Cincinnati scene has ever had. In our walks around the city we shall often encounter his ghost.

In 1876, to commemorate Archbishop Purcell's Golden Jubilee in the priesthood, decorations were placed atop St. Peter's cross. Three experienced steeplejacks undertook the job of taking them down. Hearn covered the story. The assignment included climbing the steeple. "Steeple Climbers" narrates his climb through the steeple's interior. He presents himself as the terrified novice of the party. Gas jets fitfully illumine green mold on the walls. As Hearn climbs, the "solemn pulsations" of the steeple's clock (since removed) become gradually louder. His beating heart echoes its ticking. One hundred-fifty feet above terra firma the party scrambles out onto a ledge; for the remainder of the ascent they will use a rope ladder. Fortified by a shot of whiskey, Hearn begins to climb the swinging ladder. We agonize with him as, rung by rung, level by level, he pulls himself up. His terror he compares to a waking nightmare. The story captures his anxiety and universalizes it: we share his fear as it becomes ours. Finally, Hearn reaches the top, 221 feet above ground. Passersby below, their "faces upturned to the cross," look lilliputian: "even with a small opera glass it was difficult to distinguish faces." He does not linger over the view because, blind in one eye and with imperfect sight in the other, he probably saw little of the scene below that nonetheless he describes vividly. Hearn's best work, brief sketches like "Steeple Climbers," uncannily conveys the intensity of a single focus: here his fear of heights. He wisely chooses to describe, not the view, but the terror of the ascent. No one who reads his graphic narrative will ever again look in the same way at St. Peter's spire gleaming peacefully in the sun.

Church authorities in 1952 commissioned a major restoration of St. Peter's. Edward J. Schulte was supervising architect. The floor was removed, the old foundation strengthened, and the church extended to Central Avenue. Transepts, of uneven size and beginning approximately where the old rear wall ended, were added to the north and south. Unusual (to say the least) in Greek Revival churches, they scarcely enhance the building. Stone tracery filled in the nave windows. The spire was rebuilt, the granite stairs in front of the church were added, as was the wall facing the street. Also new are the esplanade lamps. An austere *St. Peter-in-Chains* looms above the entrance to the north transept. This bronze by Dayton sculptor Robert Koepnick radiates integrity.

We enter St. Peter's through the narthex covered in black marble. Bronze doors guard the entrances to the nave. The plan vaguely resembles a Roman basilica;

within, Roman Corinthian columns with gilt capitals support the coffered ceiling. Carl Zimmerman, a Cincinnati artist, created murals of the Stations of the Cross. Reputedly in imitation of Greek black-figure and red-figure vases, they look, to this eye, more like a Mexican-Egyptian hybrid. The interior comes across as debased Art Deco, a monstrous *bouillabaisse* of Roman and Greek motifs. It is too rectilinear and too angular, too opulent and—after thirty years—too new looking. The discrepancy between the austere exterior and the decadent interior jars the viewer. "Where once was drab plaster," says a church brochure issued after the restoration, "there is now lustrous Imperial Black marble and shimmering gold." Would that the drab plaster remained, to cover up this tasteless exercise in vulgar ostentation. Only the modern window behind the baptismal font, done in an abstract pattern of stone crosses meant to recall chain links, offers a note of relief: its lustrous English crown glass scintillates in a kaleidoscope of deep blues and reds. But stained glass hardly suits a Greek Revival church.

Facing St. Peter's is the Temple Bene Yeshurun (1866), a structure no less historic and, architecturally, even more significant. Designed by James Keys Wilson, a native Cincinnatian, Bene Yeshurun is usually designated the Isaac M. **Wise Temple** after Cincinnati's famous rabbi, or, more simply, the Plum Street Temple.

The Wise Temple combines Romanesque, Gothic, Byzantine, and Moorish motifs. Moorish, or Moresque, may predominate. "A Moorish design alludes to the Near East and the roots of Judaism," asserts John Tauramac, "so as a style it is a natural for a religion without an architectural heritage of its own." Early nineteenth-century Romanticism fostered an Oriental vogue, in part through its rediscovery of the Near East via the voyages of Byron and Chateaubriand, the paintings of Delacroix and Ingres, and, significantly for Judaism, the novels of Benjamin Disraeli. Disraeli, who visited the Holy Land in 1830–1831, published two years later *The Wondrous Tale of Alroy,* a novel set in Jerusalem, Baghdad, and Hamadan, in which the Temple of Jerusalem appears to the hero in a dream.

Indirectly, this revived European interest in the Orient led to the building in Cincinnati of the first Moorish temple in America. The intricate surface ornament and slender, minaret-like spires impart to the Wise Temple an exotic Near Eastern flavor. An early engraving even reveals pinnacles soaring up from the minarets and the domes. The façade carving, floral designs in low relief, suggests arabesques. The Temple's design deliberately alludes to the Alhambra in Granada, the architectural summit of Moorish civilization, commemorated by Washington Irving in his *Tales from the Alhambra* (1832). St. Peter's and the Wise Temple: from Wren's London to Granada's Alhambra in one architectural and visual leap! Nineteenth-century Revival styles certainly make strange bedfellows. Wise himself, who termed the temple's architecture "Byzantine," wished it to recall the Golden Age of Moorish Spain, when Jews lived peacefully with their Christian and Moslem neighbors and their culture thrived.

As the temple reflects the Moorish Revival, so it also reflects the Gothic. In one sense, its Moorish design represents a Jewish response to the Gothic style that everywhere triumphed in mid-nineteenth-century ecclesiastical architecture; in another, the Temple partakes in that same Gothic Revival—appropriately, for its con-

Isaac M. Wise Temple. A blend of Moorish and Gothic and
much more, the temple (1866) presents a majestic façade to
Plum St. Its architect was James Keys Wilson. Isaac Mayer
Wise was the main force behind the development of Reform
Judaism in America.

gregation, like Wise himself, was German-born, and Germany no less than America
had wholeheartedly embraced the Gothic style for ecclesiastical buildings. Wilson,
the architect, had assisted James Renwick on Manhattan's Gothic Grace Church and
usually himself worked in the Gothic style. Of his few surviving works in Cincinnati—among them the Shoenberger house in Clifton (chapter 10), the administration building, gatehouse, and Dexter Mausoleum in Spring Grove Cemetery
(chapter 13), and a villa in East Walnut Hills—only the McAlpin's building on 4th
St. is not an unabashedly Gothic creation.

Oriental and Gothic counterpoint each other on the façade. The three portals,
corresponding to the divisions of the oblong basilican plan, are Gothic in concept.

However, their treatment is Oriental, for a decorative rectangular frame (a familiar device of Moslem, particularly Moslem Indian, architecture) encloses each portal. The main portal is set within a huge recessed Gothic arch. The rose windows above the portals also point to Gothic precedent. Contrasts between brick and stone constantly enliven the façade. How this world-class building came to be boxed in on two sides by an unsightly, neon-lit parking structure must make an interesting story.

Within the temple is the city's single most arresting interior space, its most elaborate, vibrant, and colorful. Not normally open to the public, it is well worth making an attempt to see. Delicate iron columns hold up sequences of hemispheric domes, thirteen in all; five large ones are in the nave, eight smaller ones in the transepts and aisles. The domes recall the synthesis of Byzantine-Romanesque architectural traditions, of East and West, that is Venice's St. Mark's. Yet the nave has Gothic arches and, at the clerestory level, Gothic windows. Above the ark a rose window displays the two tablets of the Law. Walls and ceilings, in patterns that may owe something to Owen Jones's influential *Grammar of Ornament* (1856), are hand-painted stencil designs. Reds, yellows, oranges, browns dazzle in a polychromatic tour de force. Every square inch appears covered, not with figures as in a Christian church but with geometrical forms, arabesques, calligraphy. Moorish and Hebrew ideas of decoration are not unlike. Islam banned the appearance of human figures in religious art: God had created man, it was sacrilegious for man to create God. There is also another reason: Yahweh had told the Jews to worship the invisible God and to refrain from the creation of idols.

Basement exhibit cases recount the history of the congregation, based since 1976 in Amberley Village, with an intervening stop in Avondale. One man dominates its history: **Isaac Mayer Wise**, one of the great figures of American Jewry, who served the congregation as rabbi from 1854 until his death in 1900. Though not the founder of Reform Judaism, he was the chief force behind it. Under his guidance Cincinnati functioned as the cradle for this relatively young and now major branch of Judaism. Hebrew Union College (1875) in Clifton, the oldest rabbinical seminary in the United States, owes its existence to Wise. Prior to its founding, American rabbis had to go to Europe for their training. Wise also established in 1854 *The Israelite* (after 1874 the *American Israelite*), once a national newspaper, still the oldest continuously published Jewish-American newspaper in America. In 1873, along with another major Reform rabbi, Max Lilienthal of Bene Israel, he organized the Union of American Hebrew Congregations. Such nineteenth-century Jewish leaders as Wise and Lilienthal believed that Cincinnati was on the way to becoming the center of American Jewry. Wise's son Isador, asked to write the chapter on Jewish life for Goss's 1912 *History of Cincinnati*, began: "Cincinnati is the pioneer city of the west; so far as the Jews are concerned, she is the pioneer city of the world. To the long-suffering children of Israel she is indeed the 'Queen City.' . . . The relations of the Jews of Cincinnati to their fellow citizens were always peculiarly pleasant, cordial, mutually forebearing." Though this idyllic picture blurs reality somewhat, anti-Semitism never became as severe here as in many other communities.

Across the street is **City Hall** (1893). Designed in the Richardsonian Roman-

City Hall. Designed by the city's premier architect, Samuel
Hannaford, City Hall (1893) is Cincinnati's grandest state-
ment in the Richardsonian Romanesque style. At the bot-
tom left of the photograph are two columns of the Greek
Revival St. Peter-in-Chains Cathedral. Courtesy of J. Miles
Wolf.

esque style by the distinguished local architect Samuel Hannaford, the building
owes much to H. H. Richardson's Allegheny County Courthouse (1884–1888) in
Pittsburgh. In numerous cities downstream from Pittsburgh, Cincinnati among
them, architects patterned courthouses and public buildings after this structure.
Hannaford, in addition, had a local model: Richardson's own Chamber of Commerce Building (1889) that stood at 4th and Vine streets until 1911. "The power of
Richardson's forms," writes architectural historian Vincent Scully, "gave a demonstration of unmatched confidence to those architects who most closely followed and
understood him, and that confidence was in three things: in continuity, in permanence, and in the power of a building to embody a heroic attitude." Cincinnati's City

Hall amply reflects these qualities. The city's flag, with its motto *Juncta Juvant* ("Strength through Union"), flies before the building. The exaggerated roughness of City Hall's massive rock-faced granite walls radiates strength. Probably the city's best civic example of the Richardsonian style, City Hall remains a bold, powerful building.

Samuel Hannaford was born in 1835 in Devonshire, England. In 1844 his family came to the United States. After receiving his architectural training in Cincinnati under William Hamilton, he opened a practice as architect here in 1857 in collaboration with Edwin Anderson, a partnership that continued until about 1870. In 1887 his sons Harvey and Charles became full partners in what had become, by late Victorian times, the city's most prominent architectural firm. Before his retirement about 1896 this important and prolific architect had designed more than four hundred structures in Ohio, Kentucky, and Indiana. The diversity of his Cincinnati commissions indicates a mastery of the eclectic styles then prevalent. His extant structures include works as different as Music Hall, the Cincinnati Workhouse, the Observatory in Mount Lookout, College Hill's Town Hall, and the Probasco Fountain in Clifton. Later works by the firm include the Hamilton County Memorial Building (1905) and the *Times-Star* Building (1931).

City Hall contrasts markedly with St. Peter's and the Wise Temple in style, color, and texture. St. Peter's is in smooth Dayton limestone, the temple in warm orange brick, and City Hall in brown and beige stone. The building displays a mix of textures equally diverse: rusticated rock-faced granite on the ground floor, sandstone on those above, slates on the roof. The arches and lintels are of different stone from the walls; often they protrude to catch the sun's shadows. The depth of the window reveals, or openings, along with the breadth and height of the roof planes, reinforces our sense of the building's weight and mass. We think its walls thicker, its dimensions larger, than they are. By making the windows smaller at each level the architect achieved an illusion of height. Similarly with the roof slates: larger at the bottom, smaller toward the top. Again, the effect is to make the building look taller. Unlike St. Peter's and the Wise Temple, City Hall is deliberately asymmetrical. The tower, positioned on a corner, lumbers heavenward with the heavy burden of city government. Even though the façade facing Plum St. appears roughly symmetrical, its window pattern differs on either side. On the 8th St. entrance, that with A.D. 1888 on it, we observe on the right a squat column, on the left a pilaster. Asymmetry can go no further.

We go in the Plum St. entrance, whose interlocking decorative carving recalls Louis Sullivan's work. Inside, we find ourselves under a forest of arches. With the exception of the ceiling mural directly above the main entrance, an elaborate allegory, replastering of ceilings and walls has obscured the original murals and stencilling by Charles Pedretti of F. Pedretti & Sons. As we climb the stairs, we encounter a sequence of stained glass windows. In *The Queen of the West* at the first landing, a young, handsome Cincinnatus stands to the Queen's left, the poet Longfellow, white-haired and bearded, to her right. Mercury rests below the Queen. We read the famous lines—famous in Cincinnati if nowhere else—from Longfellow's poem "Catawba Wine":

> The Queen of the West
> In her garlands dressed
> On the banks of the Beautiful River.

The Queen herself, flanked by apple trees and buckeyes, looks a little bored with the proceedings. Cincinnati received its appellation "The Queen City" well before Longfellow wrote. A newspaper article of January 21, 1831, referred to the city thus. (Since 1984 the city's business interests have downplayed "The Queen City" in favor of "The Blue Chip City," which both narrows and lessens the connotations.) Windows on the right of the Queen depict *Agriculture and Pastoral Life* and *Liberty and Peace*; windows on the left, *Labor and Education* and *Industry and Abundance*. The juxtapositions indicate nineteenth-century values. On the next landing are five other windows, the central one devoted to the renaming of Cincinnati by General Arthur St. Clair. The Latin inscription reads *"Omnia relinquit servare rem publicam,"* or "he left all to serve the republic." *Republic* means, literally, "the public good." The third landing depicts the Roman delegation going to Cincinnatus as he ploughs his fields.

Opposite the mural is the Council Chamber, where the city council meets to foster the public good. Four ceiling frescoes by Charles Pedretti—said to depict the seals of the nation, state, county, and city—have been recently rediscovered. For inspiration a miniscule *Spirit of Cincinnatus* stands to the right of the podium. What could—and should—be one of Cincinnati's finest interior spaces is instead, with a linoleum floor and junk-shop furniture, one of its tattiest.

The muckraking journalist Lincoln Steffens published his classic *Shame of the Cities* in 1904. When he visited Cincinnati the next year, he was so appalled by what he found that in a piece for *McClure's* he called the city the "worst-governed" in America. No one was surprised, at least no Cincinnatian. The Fabian Socialist Beatrice Webb, passing through the city in 1898, found City Hall "crowded with loafers of all classes, with here and there an old official haunting the corridors and awaiting dismissal. . . . We watched the proceedings [of City Council]: an indifferent-looking set of men, decent enough but not capable." Like most metropolises then, Cincinnati had widespread graft, electoral fraud, and its "boss," George B. Cox, who had run the city for nearly twenty years. The Cox years were marked by a per capita debt that in 1900 was among the nation's largest, high taxes, and often ineffective public services. Although Cox retired in 1912, for a decade more his henchmen Rudolph K. ("Rud") Hynicka and August Herrmann kept the city under control.

Not until the mid 1920s did a group of reform-minded civic leaders topple the remnants of the Cox machine. The reformers put through fundamental changes in the city government, among them, a charter and proportional representation on the city council. They founded a new organization, the **Charter party,** that remains to this day a force in city politics. A local political party, with no ties to state and federal parties, can take positions and campaign for issues evaded by Republican and Democratic organizations. Historically, the Charter movement remains an important civic phenomenon of the post-World War I decade. The reformers also instituted the position of city manager—Cincinnati was the first large city to adopt this form of government. It is the city manager, responsible only to the council, who oversees the daily running of the governmental apparatus. The nine candidates who receive the most votes in a municipal election form the city council, which until 1987 chose one from among itself as mayor for a one- or two-year term. That year an amendment to the city's charter made the top vote-getter in the council mayor for the next two years. Murray Seasongood, first of the reform mayors (1926–1930), is but one of many distinguished Cincinnatians who have served on the council and as mayor. From having one of the worst local governments in the country, Cincinnati achieved one of the best. In 1956 the authors of *The Exploding Metropolis,* put together by the editors of *Fortune,* declared Cincinnati "the best-run big city in the United States." But what has long worked well may now work less well. Cincinnati in recent years has lacked leadership. The city manager does not have a power base and the mayor plays a largely ceremonial role. It is a nice irony that whereas City Hall went up in the heyday of the Cox machine, the governing body of this relatively smoothly functioning metropolis presently operates in the grubbiest of surroundings.

The **Lloyd Library,** a block north of City Hall on Elm St., moved to this building, the third to house its collections, in 1971. Nondescript architecturally, it contains some 200,000 volumes, including the largest collection of pharmacopoeias and of Eclectic medical books in the world, the latter dealing with the use of plant extracts as remedies for illnesses. The library also holds major collections in more than sixty languages of books in botany, mycology, plant chemistry, pharmacy, and allied fields. In pharmacognosy it ranks first in the country. Among its rare tomes is the first pharmaceutical book set in type: *Mesue: Vulgare Della Consolatione de le Medecine Simplici Solutive,* published in Venice in 1493. The Lloyd brothers, whose personal libraries formed the basis of the present holdings, put together much of their collection just before and after World War I. They knew the right people at a time when collectors could more easily acquire rare books at affordable prices.

There were three Lloyd brothers: John Uri, Curtis Gates, and Nelson Ashley. John Uri (1849–1936) was the eldest and best known. Any list of distinguished Cincinnatians has to include this most remarkable man. He authored a number of books in pharmacy and chemistry (several of them long standard texts), held professorships at different times in two Cincinnati institutions, and was a leader in pharmaceutical education and experimentation. The U.S. Patent Office holds fifteen patents in his name. Although born in New York, he grew up in the fields and forests near Florence, Kentucky, a village a few miles south of Cincinnati. His chief teachers were his parents. Apprenticed at fifteen to a Cincinnati druggist, for whom he worked backbreaking hours for two years, young Lloyd then apprenticed himself to another druggist, George Egers; subsequently he joined a drug manufacturing company that became, in time, the Lloyd Brothers pharmaceutical company. Curtis Gates, the second brother, a pharmacist turned mycologist, collected and described thousands of mycological specimens, i.e., fungi, from all over the world. It was he who in the early 1920s impressed upon his brothers the need to endow the library so that it might carry on after their lifetimes and even after their company's lifetime. In 1940 he sent on long-term loan his herbarium of flowering plants, comprising over 29,000 sheets, to the University of Cincinnati's Department of Botany. The third brother, Nelson Ashley, a pharmacist turned businessman, ran the company, paid the bills, and saw to it that the library lacked nothing. He sent agents to Europe to buy rare books, long runs of scientific serials, and even complete collections.

John Uri Lloyd wielded an indefatigable pen. Between his scientific works and his nearly 5,000 professional papers, he wrote novels re-creating the northern Kentucky scene. *Stringtown on the Pike* (1900), the most famous of these local color tales, depicts rural life during the Civil War and Reconstruction. Lloyd based many of its characters on local residents, and several landmarks he described are still recognizable. So that he might get his dialect correct, he prepared an extensive glossary that a friend who lived in the area checked for him. *Stringtown on the Pike* became a national bestseller; after three months 50,000 copies were in print. But Lloyd's most interesting novel was his first, *Etidorhpa: Or, The End of the Earth* (1895). Written at about the same time as such speculative fictions as Edward Bellamy's *Looking Backward, 2000–1887,* W. D. Howells's *A Traveller from Altruria,* and Ignatius Donnelly's *Caesar's Column, Etidorhpa* recounts a trip through the center of the earth. The work of a visionary and deeply imaginative man, it blends scientific with metaphysical speculation. A utopian novel, startlingly illustrated, it would be classified today as science fiction. Although dealing with alchemy, chemistry, philosophy, metaphysics, morals, biology, and sociology, it is, surprisingly perhaps, the most readable of Lloyd's works. *Etidorhpa,* "Aphrodite" spelled backwards, ran to eighteen editions and underwent translation into seven languages.

Around the corner from the Lloyd Library, on Court St., is the **Cincinnati Fire Museum.** Harry Hake, whose Art Deco Telephone Building we looked at earlier, designed this Renaissance Revival building in 1906–1907. Hake, as Hannaford before him in the 1860s and 1870s, designed firehouses on contract with the city, mostly in Renaissance styles, in the early 1900s. A staunch Republican, he was well rewarded with commissions for his support. The façade, reflecting Venetian influences, has carefully wrought detail, muted colors, wide bands, and an elaborate bracketed cornice. A series of arches cumulatively forms an arcade. Almost as intricate is the rear façade, which, unusually, also has a door. Within are walls of white-glazed brick and a pressed tin ceiling; an ornate spiral staircase links the floors. Inside and out, the building has been sensitively restored by Cincinnati architect Bruce Goetzman.

The Fire Museum opened at this location in 1980. One of the most comprehensive museums of its kind, it well repays a visit. Exhibits, arranged chronologically, are clearly organized and presented. To get a feeling for firefighting, open the gate near the entrance and slide down the pole. (Stairs exist for the faint of heart.) Begin your tour with the film "Fire, fire!" The basement focuses on the bucket brigades when every householder had to furnish two two-and-a-half gallon leather buckets (leather buckets were lighter than wooden) and every male between sixteen and fifty had to help with firefighting. By 1810 the village had its first volunteer company. It needed it, for fires frequently broke out in the crammed-together wooden houses.

The main floor exhibits informatively present the development of firefighting equipment during the last hundred years. Return to the basement to learn about the modern fire department—Cincinnati's consistently rates as one of the nation's best—and about fire safety. If a fire buff, try on a fireman's helmet.

The volunteer fire companies that replaced the bucket brigades had a colorful history. Often they reflected the city's social and ethnic fragmentation. German and Irish immigrants, as well as westward-traveling Americans, often did not know a soul when they landed in Cincinnati. Joining a volunteer fire company gained them a set of friends. Prominent citizens also served as volunteers. Firemen often became local heroes; the fancy outfits they wore in parades reflected the pride they felt in their companies. By the early 1850s rivalry between companies began to get out of hand. On June 7, 1850, several companies rioted; in 1851 and 1852 frequent brawls occurred among companies. Then even more than now violence was endemic to American life. A company called out to a burning building might spend less time fighting the fire than battling competing companies.

A growing city needed a better system. Two developments precipitated a change: the building of a practical fire engine in 1852, and the decision the next year to establish a salaried professional fire department. The volunteers opposed both the fire engine and the professional department. At this point Miles Greenwood, local entrepreneur, civic leader, and fire volunteer, agreed to head the company that operated the steam-powered machine. Greenwood, a lantern-jawed industrialist aptly nicknamed "Ajax," had by 1850 become virtually sole owner of the Eagle Iron Works, largest in the West. Designed by A. B. Latta, in conjunction with Abel Shawk, the engine was named (after a councilman) "Uncle Joe Ross." The ordinance creating a professional department passed on March 27, 1853. At the first fire for which "Uncle Joe Ross" was brought into commission, the expected battle between the company using the steam-engine and the volunteer companies opposed to professionalism and mechanism failed to materialize. Progress carried the day. A committee headed by Greenwood surveyed firefighting methods throughout the United States. New Orleans used horses to pull its apparatus, New York had steam fire engines, Boston paid its personnel, but it was Cincinnati's distinction to combine into a single system all three elements. 444 paid fireman replaced the 1800 volunteers. If not (as local partisans have sometimes claimed) the first professional fire department, Cincinnati created a totally new system that had far-reaching effect on the development of American firefighting.

Exhibiting the steam fire engine to a committee from Baltimore, Greenwood noted two points of its superiority over the volunteer companies: it never got drunk, and it never threw brickbats. Its only fault, he said, was that it couldn't vote. Obviously a man of sense, Greenwood subsequently became the Fire Department's first Chief Engineer. One result of the professionalization, he reported in 1854, was that the engine houses ceased serving as "nurseries where the youths of the city are trained up in vice, vulgarity, and debauchery; and where licentiousness holds her nightly revel." No longer did battles between rival companies shatter the Sabbath calm. For the next sixty years, until 1913 when motorized trucks and pumpers were introduced, the department served as a model for other urban American fire companies. As usual the city that proudly boasted it could make anything rose to the occasion. For decades Cincinnati was the major center for the manufacture of fire engines. Ahrens-Fox, which had bought out Latta's steam engine and which after 1869 made its own horse-drawn steam pumpers, subsequently produced, from 1922 until the company's dissolution thirty years later, high-quality motorized fire equipment.

The **Court Street Center** (1918; 1985) occupies the Plum-to-Elm block between Court St. and Central Parkway. Formerly the building housed the French Bauer Ice Cream Co. Turning a World War I vintage factory into modern offices posed a nice challenge in adaptive re-use. Here the challenge has been superbly met. The building's exterior has been stuccoed and painted plum. Upper-story windows are fashioned from gold, blue-green and silver reflective glass; their lines create a three-dimensional effect. The façade hints at the atrium within. Like a ziggurat seen from the inside, the atrium has a floor of imitation Italian marble, a panoply of fluted columns, and a cool postmodern violet-and-plum color scheme. The effect is deliberately theatrical. My reservations about the Court Street Center have less to do with the building than with its wasteful use of land. The building occupies a fraction of its lot; the rest of an entire city block is given over to parking. Excessive space for ground-level parking detracts from center-city urban density. It is good that a developer has turned a decaying, long-empty structure into attractive offices and that he has made an effort at landscaping. But a downtown needs density, and this building, which would look more at home in a suburban office park, wastes space.

The south side of 9th St., between Plum and Elm, returns us to the Victorian residential city. Several townhouses, with largely unaltered exteriors, have undergone interior renovation. The restored stone façades of 213 and 215 (ca. 1877) present delicately incised curvilinear and rectilinear decoration.

Crosley Square (1922), at 9th and Elm streets, is Classical Revival in style. Designed by Harry Hake as an Elks lodge, the building for many years after 1942 housed WLW, one of the pioneering radio stations of the 1920s. When WLW in 1928 expanded to 50,000 watts, it gained a reputation as "the *Nation's* Station." Operating at 500,000 watts from 1934 to 1939, it was the most powerful broadcasting system in the world. So strong was WLW's signal in the Cincinnati area that people heard it coming out of faucets, milking machines, and barbed wire fences. From the beginning the station earned a reputation as a broadcasting innovator. It early rejected mere record playing in favor of live shows, and regularly sent scouts to New York to see whether any of Manhattan's offerings might pass muster in the Queen City. It helped to launch Doris Day (a Cincinnati native), it gave initial voice to Rosemary and Betty Clooney, and it aired such notables as Andy Williams, Red Barber, the McGuire Sisters, Fats Waller, and Red Skelton. For twenty-five years from 1942, first on radio, after 1949 on WLW-TV (which remains in the building), the station sponsored a hugely popular weekday noon to one-thirty talk-variety show, the "50/50 Club," presided over by Ruth Lyons, a kind of midwestern Arthur Godfrey. (Though Ruth Lyons retired in 1967, the Ruth Lyons Children's Christmas Fund still provides toys in area hospitals for children.) The "Bob Braun Show" succeeded

Ruth Lyons. Not until 1984, when the station cancelled it, did daily local programming (news excepted) entirely disappear.

No chronicle of WLW can overlook "Moon River." Most of the romancing engaged in by young men and women of ardent disposition in the late 1930s and 1940s throughout the eastern half of the United States had as its indispensable background (beginning about the midnight hour) WLW's program of dreamy organ music. Interspersed with it were readings of appropriate poetry entitled—the words overflow with romantic connotations—"Moon River." Fans listened breathlessly as Peter Grant recited "Down the river of a thousand yesterdays / Flow the bright waters of Moon River. . . ." Few of the program's devotees appear to remember what pieces were played or what poems recited, but the two in conjunction enhanced a generation's amorous propensities. "Moon River," as much a part of the 1930s as the Big Bands, remains to many a cherished memory.

Powel Crosley, Jr. (1886–1961), another of the city's great men, had founded WLW in March 1922. Intrigued by his son's crystal set, Crosley had begun to manufacture inexpensive radios in 1921. What better way to sell more radios than by giving customers a station to listen to? An entrepreneur of genius, Crosley was also a tinkerer, an inventor, and a dreamer. One gadget he did not invent but in 1931 shrewdly bought the patent for was shelves on refrigerator *doors*. The Shelvador was born! Today Crosley is best remembered for the tiny car named after him, an American version of the Volkswagen bug. First available in 1939 but put aside during the war effort, the Crosley stayed in production from 1946 to 1952. It had its best year in 1947–1948, with 30,000 sold, the same year the Volkswagen was introduced into the United States. But most postwar Americans liked their cars big and had cheap gas to power them, so the Crosley, which retailed for less than $1000 and sipped gas, failed to catch on.

Crosley Square heralds another nineteenth-century block. Italianate and Greek Revival townhouses, a number rehabilitated in the 1980s, stand cheek-by-jowl on 9th between Elm and Race streets. At 133, across from Crosley Square, two couchant **lions** adorn the area stoops. Couchant, rampant, guardant, peering down upon us from a cornice or hanging on a wall like some kind of hunting trophy from the British Raj, lions appear everywhere in downtown Cincinnati. Indeed, the city's buildings flaunt a veritable menagerie of metal, stone, and terra cotta beasts. Lions are the most ubiquitous denizens, but we encounter a menagerie of other creatures as well. In western iconography the lion is omnipresent: he haunts Assyrian palaces, Roman cities, medieval churches, and Baroque squares. *Felix leo* may turn up at any elevation and on almost any kind of building or ornamental medium. If someone decides to compile a Cincinnati bestiary, lions should have a chapter to themselves.

Boss Cox lived for a time at 115 West 9th St. The Emery brothers put up the two apartment buildings at the intersection of 9th and Race: the six-story Brittany (1885), recently restored, and the five-story Saxony (1891). Samuel Hannaford & Sons designed both. Like the Norfolk (and the Lombardy of chapter 4), the Brittany and Saxony offered stylish "flat" accommodations to turn-of-the-century downtown residents.

On the southeast corner of 9th and Race streets is the former **Phoenix Club.**

Designed by Samuel Hannaford, Cincinnati's finest Italian Renaissance palazzo would not look out of place in Florence. On the façade, boasting downtown's most elaborate terra cotta work, we make out the building's date, "1893." Tiffany stained glass panels adorn the marble stair hall. Founded in 1856, the Phoenix Club provided programs in the arts, music, and literature (in German until 1881) for the city's German-Jewish elite, who were often excluded from other clubs.

By the late nineteenth century America's industrial might had achieved international impact. Entrepreneurs put up buildings exuding confidence and prosperity. Art historians speak of the several decades before World War I as the American Renaissance. The architecture of this period was often inspired by, or in reaction to, uninhibited capitalism. It was also inspired by a desire to bring European standards of culture and visual organization to American cities. Fifty years earlier America's public buildings harked back to Greek gods and Roman senators. The mercantile age of the post-Civil War era required an architecture of its own. Victorian merchants on both sides of the Atlantic delighted in comparing themselves to Renaissance merchant princes. The Phoenix Club would not have shamed a Medici. The first warehouse resembling an Italian palazzo went up in Manchester, England, in 1839. It was meant to impress, and it did. The style caught on. A building such as the Phoenix Club celebrates capitalist enterprise publicly and privately: publicly because onlookers were expected to gape at it, privately because it accepted only a chosen few. Cleaned in 1985 of a century's soot and restored within, the Phoenix Club has risen again, this time as a center for conferences, receptions, and banquets. Within is an excellent gourmet restaurant, the Phoenix, in a luxurious setting. The building is once more among the city's treasures.

Attached to the Phoenix, on Garfield Place, is the **Cincinnati Club** (1924). Frederick W. Garber and Clifford B. Woodward designed this restrained, ten-story neoclassical edifice. With its initial cornice above the fourth floor, the Cincinnati Club nods to the Phoenix as it stretches from a palazzo to a highrise. Both buildings have the majestic *piano nobile,* or second story, characteristic of the Italian palazzo. The Cincinnati Club spun off from the popular Business Men's Club in 1892 and folded in 1990. Within, the building has among an array of spectacular spaces a gymnasium, billiard room, bowling alley, Turkish baths, and a reading room. The two buildings reopened in 1985 as the **Piatt Park Center,** with the Cincinnati Club retaining the Center's second and third floors.

We walk back to 9th and continue east one block to Vine St. before turning south down Vine alongside **2 Garfield Place** (1982), a chic residential highrise for short-term business visitors. The balcony railings in red trim create a playful effect. Notice how the building's coloration changes every few stories: the dark gray at the base gradually lightens in shade—in homage to the sun?—as the building rises. Across the street is the Public Library (which I discuss in the next chapter); the 1982 addition occupies the site of Cincinnati's last burlesque house, the Gayety. A bronze statue of **James Garfield,** designed by Cincinnati sculptor Charles Niehaus and unveiled in 1887, dominates the eastern entrance to Piatt Park. With papers in hand, coat flying, the to-be assassinated president declaims to an audience of indifferent pigeons. Garfield, along with Harrison at the park's other end, has the dubious distinction of having served the shortest presidential term.

On Piatt Park's north side we face the concrete Butterfield Senior Center (1976), designed by David Lee Smith. It is more imaginative than most exercises in cold concrete. The style is New Brutalism, an architectural descendant of Le Corbusier's *béton brut*. The adjoining stone-faced building, now part of the Center, went up in 1862 as a townhouse for Marcus Fechheimer. New building and old, stone and poured concrete, mesh awkwardly. The **Fechheimer mansion**, one of Samuel Hannaford's early commissions, sports an imposing Renaissance Revival façade. Its symmetrical lines derive from Renaissance principles of unity and proportion. Pilasters framing the pedimented windows help maintain the balance. Behind the windows are built-in walnut shutters; in front, attractive cast-iron railings connect carved stone pillars. Sir Charles Barry had initiated this domestic, palazzo-style architecture in London with his Travellers' Club (1832) and Reform Club (1841). For many years after 1937 the Fechheimer mansion served as headquarters for the Cuvier Press Club, founded in 1871. This male preserve once relaxed its membership regulations to admit a woman: the shapely and much-married Lillian Russell, toast of the Gay Nineties, whose theme song was "Come Down, My Evenin' Star."

Across from Piatt Park is the **Doctors Building** (1923), 19 Garfield Place. Designed by Tietig & Lee, it long provided a convenient base for downtown physicians and dentists. The terra cotta Tudor Gothic façade is more exuberantly Gothic, particularly in its upper reaches, than any other in Cincinnati. Why a Gothic highrise? Cass Gilbert's Woolworth Building (1913) in Manhattan aroused tremendous interest not only because of its record-breaking height but also for its French Gothic ornamentation of crockets, ogee arches, and tracery. Gothic now became an accepted mode for the historicist skyscraper. Form could even follow function: Gothic was, after all, a "vertical" design for a vertical building type. Hood and Howells's Gothic design won the controversial 1925 competition for the Chicago Tribune Tower. In the saga of the Gothic skyscraper Cincinnati's Doctors Building, a mere eight stories, constitutes a lively local footnote.

East along 7th, between Vine and Walnut streets, once glittered Cincinnati's Broadway. Theaters here provided several generations of Cincinnatians with entertainment. The neoclassical George B. Cox (1921), on the corner nearest us, offered legitimate drama; on the far corner, now occupied by an office building (1989), stood the Capitol, torn down in 1972. Between the Cox and the Capitol was the brownstone Shubert. Its building, put up in 1848 as the city's first YMCA, was converted to a theater in 1921 and knocked down in 1976. Under its ornate ceiling the Theatre Guild put on legitimate drama. The Shubert subsequently provided lighter fare, including vaudeville and film. "Every Friday," recalls Doris Day in her autobiography, "my mother and I would go downtown and . . . see a show at one of the big downtown houses, the Shubert or the Albee. . . . After the film they had a stage show, and a Hollywood star would often put in a personal appearance. That's how I fell in love with Betty Grable."

Now, instead of theaters humming with playgoers, we see vacant lots, nadirs of downtown self esteem. **Parking lots** are a kind of nonarchitecture. They constitute the worst blight on the American cityscape since the railroad yards—and rarely did the railroads penetrate the city center. The Housing Act of 1949 initiated the process, and the Interstate Highway Act of 1956 moved it along. The government's aim was to clean up decaying American cities. The bulldozer method of urban renewal of the late 1950s and 1960s disrupted city cores and greatly increased the number of downtown parking lots. It was analogous to surgery in which the operation is hailed as a success, but the patient dies. Knocking down buildings without intending to replace them constitutes in effect a kind of deliberate vandalism. Parking lots sap urban vitality. Fortunately in 1987 the city began to limit downtown lots by mandating garages for unused land. The ground-level lots that remain do not have to be eyesores. Here as elsewhere landscaping is possible.

The ten-story **Provident Bank Building** (1909) dominates the southeast corner of 7th and Vine streets. Harry Hake designed it in a commercial Renaissance Revival style. Although the bank long ago relocated its main office three blocks south, the "P" on the cartouches below the cornice still announces the original proprietor. Beside the cartouches, other Renaissance influences include segmental arches with pronounced keystones and white limestone set off against red brick. In 1926 Hake designed the five-bay addition on the left, virtually indistinguishable from the 1909 building, except that the central bay is slightly off center.

If we were to walk down Ruth Lyons Lane, to the Provident Building's left, we would come upon a brick warehouse with pyramidal turrets at either end. This unusual building (1860), its existence unsuspected by most Cincinnatians, housed the Lodge St. Synagogue, used by the Orthodox congregation Shearith Israel. This congregation broke away from the liberal Bene Israel, Cincinnati's first Jewish Congregation, founded in 1824.

The **Federated Building** (1978), gleaming in its glass-and-aluminum sheath, houses the headquarters of Federated Department Stores, long one of the largest of the department store chains. Before being taken over in 1988 by Campeau Corporation of Toronto, Federated owned stores in thirty states, including such well-known establishments as Abraham & Strauss and Bloomingdale's in New York, Filene's in Boston, and Lazarus in Cincinnati. Campeau was forced to relinquish control of his empire early in 1990. For decades Federated was run by the Lazarus clan, originally from Columbus. Its most spectacular member was Fred J. Lazarus, Jr., who in 1928 planned the purchase of Shillito's at 7th and Race streets. During the early 1930s, Fred, Jr., noted that *Le Printemps* in Paris arranged dresses by size, not price. He brought the idea home, changed the layout of the Columbus store, and revolutionized American merchandising. Perhaps his greatest coup occurred in 1939 when he persuaded Franklin D. Roosevelt to alter Thanksgiving from the fourth Thursday in November to the third. A longer shopping season helped national prosperity, claimed Fred Jr., and only incidentally Federated. (When designating Thanksgiving a legal federal holiday in 1941 Congress returned it to the fourth Thursday.) Fred Jr. came to work each day until 1972, the year before he died at the age of eighty-eight. The last Lazarus associated with the company in a major position retired in 1984. Even so, the family's direct control over their empire outlasted that of nearly all the other great department store names.

Rogers, Taliaferro, Kostritsky, and Lamb, now RTKL, Inc., designed this International style building (this is the same Rogers who oversaw the downtown redevelopment plan). The twin indentations near the building's top echo the rear façade's sawtooth pattern, visible from the Carew Tower's observation deck. Before Federated's main entrance stands Louise Nevelson's *Sky Landscape II* (1979). Born in Russia, Nevelson (1900–1988) is an important American sculptor who has had her works placed in major American cities and museums, including the Cincinnati Art Museum. Designed to incorporate patterns of sun and shadow, *Sky Landscape II* stands on the building's north side—where the sun rarely shines. We have insufficient room to step back and gain a perspective on it. Cramped in its awkward site, the work deserves better.

The Federated Building houses a downtown branch of **Skyline Chili.** Those who associate chili with Texas and the Southwest will find—to their surprise—that Cincinnati abounds in chili parlors. In the early 1920s a Macedonian immigrant named Athanas Kiradjieff opened a restaurant called the Empress. One day onto a bed of plain spaghetti he heaped chili, cheese, onions and kidney beans in layers. Cincinnati chili was born! It is distinguished from Tex-Mex chili by its ingredients and by the way it is served. If served "two-way," the spaghetti is topped with chili; if "three-way," the most popular choice, it is topped with chili and grated yellow cheese; if "four-way," diced white onions are added; if "five-way," kidney beans as well. Local connoisseurs deem a "coney" (from Coney Island), a hot dog smothered with chili, onions, and grated cheese, to be *the* accompaniment. Though chili may not be everyone's favorite dish, Cincinnati chili—less hot and spicy than the Texas variety and invariably served with oyster crackers—is well worth a try. After all, food is an important element in our celebration of urban life. Whenever in a new city, we will wish to seek out its specialties—crabcakes in Baltimore, baked beans and scrod in Boston, deep dish pizza in Chicago, po' boys in New Orleans, sour dough bread in San Francisco, cheese steak sandwiches in Philadelphia—and chili in Cincinnati.

Skyline Chili originated in 1949 in a Price Hill restaurant owned by a Greek family, the Lambrinides. The restaurant caught on, a franchise opened downtown, and in 1990 there were more than seventy in six states, including a far-flung outpost in the restored Union Station in Washington, D.C. That year *Washingtonian* magazine dubbed its fare the "best chili in town." Skyline, still owned by the Lambrinides, makes its chili in a commissary in Reading; like its chief competitors, Gold Star and Empress, it boasts its "secret" blend of spices. Each chain has its devotees, who argue violently regarding the respective merits of their favorite, and over a hundred other establishments in the area concoct their own. Although irreverent outsiders may wonder what Cincinnati chili has to do with what the rest of the country calls chili, many Cincinnatians consider it the gastronomic equivalent of Fountain Square.

In his now classic essay "Eating in Cincinnati" (1974) Calvin Trillin, the *New Yorker*'s food critic, noted that "Cincinnati eaters take it for granted that the basic way to serve chili is on spaghetti, just as they take it for granted that the other ways to serve it go up to a five-way . . . . and that the people who do the serving are Greeks. . . . There are probably people in Cincinnati who reach maturity without realizing that Mexicans eat anything called chili, in the same way that there are probably young men from Nevada who have to be drafted and sent to an out-of-state Army camp before they realize that all laundromats are not equipped with slot machines." Cincinnati chili can be addictive. A few years ago I remember reading in the *Enquirer* about one Matt Daniels, a Cincinnati high school football star, who went off to play for the University of Pittsburgh, a major powerhouse. Homesick, Daniels returned after a year. "I missed Skyline too much," he sighed. "You can't get a Three-Way anywhere in Pittsburgh." The incident amused me when I read it. I know better now.

The **617 Vine Building** (1928, restored 1982) has a majestic symmetrical façade that at night is dramatically lit. The fine bronzework of the ground-level shops has been restored. Art Deco bas reliefs interrupt the dressed limestone façade. Beneath the stone balcony crouched figures peer down.

The lower floors of 617 Vine house the offices of the *Cincinnati Enquirer.* The year 1841 is the generally accepted date for the founding of the city's longest surviving daily. In 1843 it became a morning paper exclusively; its Sunday edition, the nation's fifth oldest, began in 1848. Sunday blue laws long delayed the arrival of Sunday editions. Many denounced them when they first appeared; some newsdealers refused to handle them. Today, the *Enquirer*'s Sunday edition is the oldest that survives. The paper, in the Gannett chain since 1982, is Cincinnati's only morning daily.

On the northwest corner of 6th and Vine streets stands the **Cincinnatian Hotel** (1882; redone 1987), originally the Palace. Samuel Hannaford designed this eight-story structure, once the city's tallest, though now dwarfed by new highrises. It is downtown's finest remaining large-scale building in the French Second Empire style. Thomas Emery, who commissioned the Palace, wanted it to compete against more expensive hotels. "As long as the sun shines," he promised, "the Palace will be a two-dollar hotel." Stephen Birmingham (from whom I take this anecdote) notes that, when built, the Palace had—standard for the time—only one public toilet and bathroom per floor. Fortunately, the hotel has been preserved. Its survival typifies downtown Cincinnati's fortunate mix of old and new. In 1987, rebuilt from top to bottom, it reopened as a European-style luxury establishment. Except at the lower levels the exterior remains largely unaltered; the interior, however, with neon and recessed lighting to supplement a skylight, is postmodern with a vengeance. The developer missed a chance to recreate a period interior, like the Netherland Plaza's, distinctive of its time and place. The Cincinnatian enables us to consider the evolution of hotel design over a century. Within a few blocks we have seen hotels dating from 1882 to 1984 (the Hyatt), with in between the Netherland Plaza (1931), Terrace Hilton (1948), and Clarion (1970, 1977). In decor Cincinnati's oldest hotel is its newest.

On the other side of Vine St., the **Cincinnati Commerce Center** (1984) stands on the site of the Palace Theater. Following the Albee on Fountain Square, the Palace was the last to go of Cincinnati's gigantic downtown theaters. Such theaters still exist in Indianapolis and Columbus (housing in each city the symphony orchestra) but no longer in Cincinnati. Their absence is a major loss. The Palace's replacement, the Cincinnati Commerce Center, is unsympathetic to its urban context. Indeed, set behind a multilevel plaza on 6th and offering an uninteresting façade to Vine, it is antiurban. The plaza has the public sculpture—Clement Meadmore's *Open End* (1984)—now deemed obligatory before every new highrise. Made up of large twisted bronze beams, this work has not endeared itself to Cincinnatians. In fact, for a time it was actually a menace as people kept banging their heads against it until finally a curb was built. Within the center's atrium is a welcome counterpoint: *Open Spaces,* a playful, multipart composition of glittering and undulating vanes by the Japanese artist Michio Ihara.

We walk a block further south, past 525 Vine with its imaginative window pattern, and Fountain Square again lies before us.

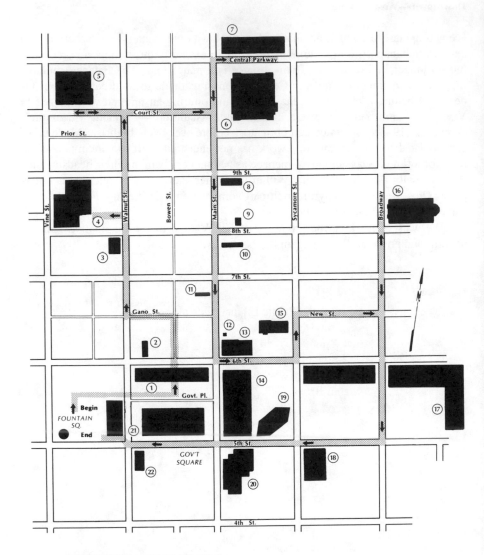

DOWNTOWN—EAST OF VINE

1. 580 Building
2. The Maisonette
3. St. Louis Church
4. Public Library
5. Kroger Building
6. Hamilton County Courthouse
7. Alms & Doepke Building
8. Second National Bank
9. Arnold's
10. Ohio Book Store
11. Acres of Books
12. Izzy's
13. Gwynne Building
14. Federal Building
15. St. Francis Xavier
16. Burke Building
   (800 Broadway/*Post & Times-Star* Building)
17. Procter & Gamble Towers
18. Taft Theater
19. Chiquita Center
20. Central Trust Center
21. U.S. Post Office and Courthouse
22. Tri-State Building

3

Downtown—East of Vine

T HIS tour also begins at Fountain Square. We shall visit several of the nineteenth-
century commercial districts that a hundred years ago formed the city's core.
We shall walk by (and into) the Public Library, then along Court St., one of Cincinnati's oldest commercial thoroughfares, to the Hamilton County Courthouse. Where
now is Central Parkway once flowed the Miami and Erie Canal. We walk down
Main, another nineteenth-century commercial street, wander into downtown's eastern fringe to Broadway. Cincinnati's historic Public Landing originally stretched
along the Ohio River from Broadway to Main St. Gradually, as the city grew inland,
its center shifted westward and Broadway came to demarcate the downtown's eastern boundary. We return along 5th St., whose new buildings, including Procter &
Gamble's corporate headquarters, appear to herald a reawakening of this long dor-
mant area.

North of Fountain Square we ascend the skywalk and head east toward Walnut
St. Few downtown edifices offer more varied façades than does the **580 Building**
(1972), on the southeast corner of 6th and Walnut streets and stretching to Main. We
see one side from the skywalk over Walnut. Rogers, Taliaferro, Kostritsky & Lamb
designed the 580 in conjunction with Harry Hake, Jr., son of the Harry Hake whose
telephone building and fire station we passed in the previous tour. Rogers is the
Archibald Rogers who was largely responsible for the redesigned Fountain Square;
his firm also did the Federated Building.

The 580 is the downtown highrise for which we have the greatest difficulty
getting a strong visual image. Its southern façade is of brown brick, its northern
largely of smoked glass; eastern and western walls combine brick and glass. No less
varied are the building's elevations and projections. Once in the well-lit atrium, look
back through the glass roof to discover the wittiest of Cincinnati's wall paintings: a
man on a scaffold painting a wall! By Wayne Dunne, this painting is a spinoff from
the original Urban Walls project. Past the staircase on the left, the Central Trust
Bank occupies a second-level atrium designed to take advantage of the skywalk. We
enter the bank from here rather than from the street. Natural light floods the atrium.
Three tiers of executive offices overlook the main floor. Instead of the paneling and

marble traditional in banking decor, we find bright colors, theater lights, mirrors, graphics—even a conventional window looking out over 6th St. Money can be fun!

We descend the staircase at the atrium's left to emerge on 6th between Walnut and Main streets, opposite what is, in effect, Cincinnati's **Restaurant Row**, a gourmet landmark known to the cognoscenti. Downtown's entertainment facilities have clustered on the block between Vine and Main, and 6th and 7th streets. Bars and restaurants for every taste and pocketbook abound here. On 6th, wedged between fast-food establishments, are the Samurai, Giacomo's, La Normandie, and the Maisonette. An arts center is destined for the western half of the block bounded by Walnut and Main, 6th to 7th. Current plans call for a 2500-seat theater, another smaller theater, and exhibit space for the Cincinnati Art Museum and other arts organizations.

Cincinnati deserves its reputation as a city that likes its food. For its population, it has more restaurants and bars than any city in the country except San Francisco. Quality does not yield to quantity. Second again to San Francisco, Cincinnati has far more three-, four-, and five-star restaurants than any other American city its size, more than a much larger city like Philadelphia and about as many as Chicago. Fine restaurants come about in a city because people feel comfortable there and want to enjoy good food. "Great is the beauty of its situation," wrote Montaigne, about 1580, in regard to Paris, "but above all incomparably great because so many of the pleasures of life are to be found there." We may also find the pleasures of life in Cincinnati. The **Maisonette,** serving food that ranks with any in the land, is only the best known of the city's many excellent restaurants. Founded in 1949 by the Comisar family, one of Cincinnati's several restaurant dynasties (the Comisars also own La Normandie next door), the Maisonette moved into its present location in 1966. Every year since 1964 it has been one of the very few restaurants to garner the coveted Mobil five-star award. The Maisonette deserves its reputation. The Lucullan feast that you will be served here will not be inexpensive, but it will be worth what you pay for it.

Directly before us is Bowen St., one of Cincinnati's innumerable **alleys.** Alleys running north-south and east-west split most downtown blocks. Along with the hills that interrupt the grid and the skywalks that ignore it, the city's network of midblock alleys further mitigates the charmless monotony of the grid. Like the skywalks, the alleys provide alternate routes from building to building, street to street: skywalks do it one way, alleys another. Like the skywalks, too, the alleys could become (some of them, anyway) open-air arcades. Alleys give the grid unexpected intimacy. To be sure, they themselves form part of the grid, but such is their narrowness (and their paving bricks and cobblestones) that few vehicles willingly enter them. Nowadays pedestrians have them pretty much to themselves. Downtowners use them as shortcuts, but to many who pass them they remain unheralded and unknown. This was not always the case. Growing up in Over-the-Rhine around World War I, George M. Henzel recalls a time when Cincinnati's alleys were more used. On nonmarket days hucksters with horse and wagon hawked their wares from the alleys; so did the ice men, who in winter metamorphosed into sellers of coal. Garbage collectors traveled the alleys once a week "in open metal wagons drawn by mules." Alleys ceased to be necessary adjuncts to middle-class neighborhoods when servantless neighborhoods became the norm and large refrigerators and deep freezes permitted once-a-week shopping at the supermarket.

The redoubtable Mrs. Trollope in 1830 expectedly found Cincinnati's alleys to be "horrible abominations." They will become worse, she predicted, "with every passing year." They haven't, but they haven't become much better either. Certainly they are not the attractive, intimate corridors that we find in many European and in a few American cities, among them, New Orleans, Boston, and even Philadelphia, from whose grid Cincinnati borrowed its north-south alleys, and which has nicely tidied up a number of its own center-city alleys. "No right-minded Bostonian," observes Walter Muir Whitehill, "would dream of walking along a street if he could by any chance cut through an alley headed even approximately in the direction he is going." That statement suggests the distance Cincinnati has to go. So does this comment by Nelson Algren, a writer who wallowed in Chicago's seamy side but who felt passion for his city: "You will never truly love it till you can love its alleys too."

Cincinnati wants to spruce up its midtown alleys to encourage foot traffic. At present the alleys lack appeal. Some are dark, some dirty, some too little traveled for pedestrians to feel secure in them. Some stink. Others have quietly disappeared. "Gradually over the years," Jayne Merkel has pointed out, "the dimensions of the city blocks have multiplied as the old alleys that divided them into two or four equal parts have been obliterated, covered by second level walkways, or absorbed into new buildings." The skywalks, she notes, not only filled alleys but "cast shadows over sidewalks and diverted pedestrians away from them." Above 6th St., however, the situation is different: the alleys remain, though underused and often dilapidated. Those that pass muster offer a variety of urban pleasures: humanly scaled structures, a sense of the quaint, quiet (we are away from the traffic), olfactory delights, including potent, often mouth watering aromas emanating from restaurant exhaust vents. In summer the temperature drops ten degrees from the adjoining streets. So for the city to develop the alleys makes good economic sense. More people traversing the alleys would induce more entertainment businesses to locate on them. It would make good esthetic and visual sense, too, since the alleys offer us unexpected, often dramatic, views of the cityscape. They offer as well changes of pace and scale that can contribute to the varied and intimate pleasures afforded by urban life. Eliminate fear, stink, and, where possible, vehicular traffic, and walking the alleys should add an intimate and pleasurable dimension to downtown excursions. Even unimproved, the alleys provide an element of surprise in our experience of the city.

Bowen St., splitting the Walnut to Main block, shows what one unsightly alley can become: an inviting pedestrian walkway with restaurants and stores opening off it and with charming period lights set in a pavement of interlocking trefoil blocks. One Bowen Place, an ex-warehouse fronting two alleys, has been attractively modernized and a restaurant installed at ground level. We turn left at the first cross street, Gano, and emerge on Walnut. If we continued on Gano another half block, we would encounter Ruth Lyons Lane. On Gano is the **Barn Rib Pit,** full of 1940s memorabilia, including on the walls black-and-white photos of Ida Lupino, Rita Hayworth, and Gloria DeHaviland caught in unflinching smiles. "Movie stars," the waitress tells you, "looked more natural back then." If Mark Twain could return to Cincinnati today, he would find the Rib Pit a place where time indeed had stopped. It also serves superb ribs. "I love to see Harry eat ribs," Calvin Trillin recorded of one customer's delight. "He just inhales those ribs. You look at him and he's just glowin'." The city, incidentally, has named its alleys more imaginatively than its major thoroughfares. Whereas its north-south street names hardly differ from those of many other American cities, deriving (presumably via Philadelphia) from the trees early settlers found growing locally, the alleys recall prominent Cincinnatians. Bowen and Gano were two of the city's versatile settlers, whereas Ruth Lyons's talk show on WLW-TV in the 1950s and 1960s made her a household name. We proceed up Walnut St.

On the southwest corner of 8th and Walnut streets stands the headquarters building (1929) for Cincinnati's Roman Catholic archdiocese. The bell tower, narrow round-arched windows, and the indented crenellations of the parapet indicate Florentine influence. Within is **St. Louis Church.** The church interior, Byzantine-Romanesque in style, possesses somber dignity. We may note particularly the fine carving of the capitals and the intradoses in between.

At 110 East 8th (1889) is another of Cincinnati's numerous restored firehouses. The building served for over thirty years as the headquarters of the Underwriters Salvage Corps of Cincinnati. One of the first conversions, done in 1980, it now functions as a small office building. Other firehouses have become restaurants, schools, recreation centers, shops, apartments, one (as we have seen) a fire museum. Jones & Speer, the architectural firm responsible for this conversion, has its offices on E. 12th in, of course, a converted firehouse.

Next door is the **Citadel** (1905), designed by the Hannaford firm. Tourelles rise from its machicolated and crenellated parapet. The intertwined insignia of an "S" and a cross, bolted to the façade, and the "S" and "A" above the door, indicate that the building once served as local headquarters for the Salvation Army. The Salvation Army began in London in the early 1860s. In 1885 it set up its first Cincinnati mission in Bucktown, a slum neighborhood on the city's east side, largely populated by blacks and Irish-Catholics. The city's reputation as a hard-drinking, rough river port led the Army to view it as an especial challenge. Commander Evangeline Booth, daughter of the organization's founder, General William Booth, laid the cornerstone. From such bastions the Army sallied forth to make (as we read in the spandrels above the entrance) "the world for God." The Army's present more workaday headquarters is on Central Parkway a few blocks north.

The **Public Library** of Cincinnati and Hamilton County takes up the block bounded by Walnut and Vine, and 8th and 9th streets. The original building (1955), designed by Woodie Garber, occupies the area bordering 8th. It replaced an earlier structure, a block or so south on Vine, that began life as Handy's Opera House (1869). James W. McLaughlin was its architect. When Handy went bankrupt in 1870, his opera house became the city's library. The library system itself goes back to 1853.

The 1982 addition (designed by Architekton) through which we enter blends almost imperceptibly with the 1955 building. The addition's brick pattern is com-

Cincinnati waterfront in 1848. Depicting the city on a quiet Sunday, this is the third of eight panels from a famous daguerrotype series made in 1848. Charles Fontayne and William S. Porter took the photographs from a vantage point in Newport. A large-scale reproduction of the complete series hangs over the lending desk of the Public Library. In this panel the twin Gothic spires of Christ Church on 4th St., erected in 1835 and demolished in the early 1950s, loom over the city. Just to their left we make out the dome of Frances Trollope's famous Bazaar. Courtesy of the Public Library of Cincinnati and Hamilton County.

mon bond, not the original's Flemish bond: a concession no doubt to spiraling construction costs. Built on the open-plan concept, the library has an atrium rising the height of the building. Potted trees surround us, ivy cascades down from the balconies, and light floods the scene. We have a sense of space, of height, of breadth. Yet intimacy is not lost, for if we wish to read or browse, inviting nooks beckon us. More than a visual delight, the building serves as flagship for one of the nation's premier library systems. Whereas Cincinnati currently ranks twenty-sixth in metropolitan area size in the nation, the Public Library's four-million volume collection ranks an impressive eighth in total number of volumes, fourth in number of volumes per capita, and—a statistic to be proud of—first in number of volumes borrowed per person. Seeing people walk out of the Library arms filled with books makes dry statistics come alive.

Over the lending desk hang huge blowups of eight daguerrotypes of Cincinnati's waterfront in 1848. They were taken from Newport, Kentucky, by Charles Fontayne and William S. Porter. A brochure available at the desk identifies buildings and steamboats. The photographs, of great historical value, portray much of early Cincinnati clearly, accurately, and in detail. They are worth our study, for in chapter 6 we will walk along the waterfront. Although it has changed greatly, the Ohio River

remains the defining element of Cincinnati's landscape. The city's hills, here virtually denuded of trees, we shall discover reforested. When Fontayne and Porter took
these photographs, the river stood at low water and the waterfront was unusually
still. Given the long exposure required for daguerrotypes, a quiet period was necessary. Cincinnati history sleuths have studied the photographs intensively, checked
the docking times of the steamboats visible, looked up the construction history of
incomplete buildings, and pinpointed the time of exposure to the early afternoon of
Sunday, September 24th, 1848.

We may take a moment to relax in the garden (1955, reestablished in 1983), an
oasis of quiet within the city's bustle. Stone and water have been used for symbolic
effect. Massive boulders are grouped around the pond, in which are placed smaller
stones and from which a single jet of water shoots up. Sparrows come to drink and
bathe; pedestrians wander or sit amid bushes and flower beds. An entire landscape
is implied in a small space. The economy of design recalls a Japanese garden. The
serpentine wall facing 8th St. echoes that fronting the Ohio River in Yeatman's Cove
Park. Both echo the curving lines of the garden walls that Thomas Jefferson designed for faculty houses on the University of Virginia campus.

Opposite the Library is **Walnut Towers** (1929). With its stone base and discreet
Tudor ogee arches, it reveals a more abbreviated Gothic detailing than the Doctors
Building on Piatt Park. Venetian influence accounts for the crisscrossing brickwork
(called "diapering" or "diaper work") of the upper stories. Now converted to apart-
ments for the low and moderate income elderly, Walnut Towers formerly housed the
YWCA. Begun in 1868 and the nation's fifth oldest, it retains facilities within.

At Court and Vine streets stands the **Kroger Building** (1959). Kroger has long
had a presence in this area. In 1893 Bernard Henry Kroger (he assumed the name
"Barney" in his early twenties) opened his seventeenth Great Western Tea Co. store
at 37 East Court, just across the street; the next year the company changed its name
to the B. H. Kroger Co. Born in 1860, Kroger opened his first store in 1883 with
$372 in hard-earned savings. When he died in 1938, he had fulfilled the rags-to-
riches saga of so many self-made men of his era and had become one of the city's
major philanthropists. The company has long had a history of innovation. It was the
first grocery chain to operate its own bakery and to install meat markets in its stores.
Today, largely based in the Midwest, it is America's largest supermarket chain.

The Kroger Building (1960), the city's first International style tower, remains
its least successful. Why does this building not appeal? A major factor is that its
height leaves it startlingly out of scale with its three- and four-story neighbors. Not
only is the tower set back from the street, it sits atop a windowless garage. Admittedly, the brown brick base (part of the 1980 remodeling) makes a timid gesture
toward the older structures in height and scale. But blank walls greet the eye at
ground level. Furthermore, the structure's steel-and-glass sheath blends ill with its
neighbors' brick and stone. Until 1980 the façade alternated square blue and white
panels in a strikingly discordant rhythm. Another factor is the lack of ornament.
The city's Art Deco buildings—the Carew Tower, for instance—have ornament at
their base and near the top. Despite their height, this ornamentation ties them to a
nineteenth-century tradition, lending them scale, both at close range and from a

Interior of Kroger's main store at 5th & Main. The photograph reveals turn-of-the-century food displays and prices. The meats are prominently displayed in the front of the shop. Pressed metal ceilings like this one, often made by local firms, were once common in Cincinnati stores and restaurants. Courtesy of the Cincinnati Historical Society.

distance. The Kroger lacks ornament and has an unarticulated top. It is antiurban; in fact, it is antihuman.

The block's south side does retain its human scale. Downtown Cincinnati looked much like this a hundred years ago. Only one narrow slash for a parking lot mars an extraordinarily intact row of historic structures. The buildings, from three to five stories high, share a number of materials and stylistic features: brick and stone; cast-iron storefronts; double-hung windows with a regular pattern of window openings; and prominent, pressed-metal cornices (several removed). The Greek Revival structures go back to the 1840s and 1850s. 21–23 East Court, three stories and modestly proportioned, probably dates from the 1850s. Its façade, however, subsequently had added to it window moldings and a bracketed Italianate cornice. Taller buildings on the block, from 1860 to 1885, are definitely Italianate in style. The finest of these is 17–19 East Court; its warm brownstone reminds me of Manhattan townhouses, though of lighter hue. Windows with both circular and rectangular hood moldings (the latter called *label moldings*) lead to six oculi, elaborate decorative work, and a stylish balustrade. Stop in at **Avril's,** number 33. Photographs of old delivery wagons hang on the back wall. Since 1890 (at this location since the 1930s), Avril's has made its own varieties of sausage as well as unusual local

Cincinnati-German specialties like goetta, a largely pork and oats concoction with onions, herbs, and spices. Fried, it emerges as a breakfast dish comparable to Pennsylvania Dutch scrapple.

Tuesday and Thursday mornings (days when Findlay Market is closed) a bustling produce market enlivens the south side of Court St. With the opening of the Miami and Erie Canal in 1827 Court St. began to prosper. The arrival of merchants and dealers caused property values to soar. In 1829 the city built the first market here; a later structure of 1850 was condemned in 1912, torn down about 1915. Today only temporary stalls are set up. In 1988 the parking area was turned into a miniature pedestrian esplanade, with a metal skeleton on both the Vine and Walnut street ends. The bell overlooking Walnut actually chimes the hours—and calls customers to market. We see distinctive street posts and lamps, newly paved streets and sidewalks, benches and trees. Fortunately, this unobtrusive prettifying has enhanced, not detracted from, the *gemütlichkeit* conveyed by the street's older structures.

Across Walnut, 117–121 Court St., with splendid carved stone entrances, has been attractively restored. To the east, Court St. abuts against the **Hamilton County Courthouse.** The first courthouse here, in 1819, gave the street its name. This neoclassical colossus, completed in 1919, imposes with its Ionic columns, rusticated base, and seven entrances. The fourth courthouse on the site, it suggests, as it was meant to suggest, the law's weight and majesty. Within the lobby a time-worn statue—time-worn because it stood in Lincoln Park until moved to make way for Union Terminal—honors Captain John J. Desmond. Desmond was shot while leading the militia against the mob during the infamous **Courthouse riots of 1884.** The statue calls to mind the three worst days in Cincinnati's history.

The 1880s proved difficult for the city as for the nation. The decade recorded a dramatic rise in lawlessness and a fifty percent increase in the number of prison inmates. Cincinnatians read of numerous grisly crimes, axe killings, even murders for the purpose of selling bodies to the Medical College of Ohio. The city, opined Congressman Benjamin Butterworth, seemed "doomed to perdition." Newspapers, by printing all the lurid details, fanned the flames of popular discontent. By the spring of 1884 twenty-two convicted murderers sat in the county jail; others had been set free or convicted on lesser charges by lenient judges and juries. Cincinnatians became impatient with what they rightly perceived as an increasing mockery of justice.

On Christmas eve of 1883 two youths, Wilhelm Berner, a German immigrant, and Joseph Palmer, a mulatto, brutally murdered their employer, William Kirk, a horse trader, for his bankroll. Palmer, tried separately, was hanged. On March 24, 1884, a jury found Berner guilty only of manslaughter. A group of citizens called a meeting on March 28 at Music Hall to discuss what they could do about crime. More than 10,000 irate Cincinnatians showed up. After the meeting, someone yelled, "To the jail! Come on! Follow me and hang Berner!" The crowd, growing as it went, stormed toward the jail, then as now behind the courthouse. One group broke in, but was met by Sheriff Morton L. Hawkins who told them he had already dispatched Berner to the state penitentiary at Columbus. Disbelieving rioters tried to break into

1884 Courthouse riots. The photograph shows state militia behind hastily constructed barricades defending the city jail against an aroused mob of Cincinnatians, who thought housed within was Wilhelm Berner, a notorious murderer. Undefended by the troops, however, was the nearby Courthouse, which the mob entered and burned. Courtesy of the Cincinnati Historical Society.

the cells of other murderers. The police and fire departments joined the fray. They had nearly succeeded in clearing the jail when shots rang out. A seventeen-year old boy slumped dead. The militia arrived, lost its cool, and started firing. The enraged mob continued the battle until three A.M. By the time the violence ended, five persons had died, including a policeman. Fifty had been wounded.

The following evening, March 29, another mob formed. Many had weapons. Armed militia barricaded the jail with barrels, wagons, and mattresses. Sheriff Hawkins decided to leave the nearby courthouse undefended. The crowd charged the barricade and exchanged gunfire with the militia. Casualties mounted. Unperceived, a group stole into the courthouse, piled up furniture, and set it ablaze with kerosene. Soon the entire building was on fire. Silhouetted against the flames, an exultant street huckster stood on the first-floor balcony calling for bids on "the temple of justice"—a moment Henry Farny captured graphically in an illustration for *Harper's Weekly*. The scene, as Cincinnati historian Charles Greve later wrote, "would have done justice to the worst days of the French Revolution." At this point Captain Desmond met his death. As he led a detachment of militia to protect the courthouse, a rioter shot at him, killing him instantly. The mob prevented fire wagons from reaching the inferno. By morning the courthouse, in part designed in 1851 by famed architect Isaiah Rogers, had burned to its foundations. More rioting occurred on March 30 before the demonstrations finally ended. At least fifty-six persons died (the number varies with the source), two hundred suffered serious injuries, hundreds more were wounded, and decades of priceless court records were destroyed.

Across Central Parkway is the vast **Alms & Doepke Building.** A composition altogether more imaginative than the courthouse, it now houses juvenile and criminal courts. In 1865 Frederick H. Alms, with his brother William and William F. Doepke, founded the department store that bore their names. The original store was several blocks further north on Main St. In 1878 Alms & Doepke moved into the first of its buildings here; eventually it occupied the entire city block. Its "building" actually consists of several structures from different times. Samuel Hannaford designed that at the northwest end (1888), Daniel Burnham Associates that at the east end (1912). The store closed in 1953; the tasteless ground-level modernization, dating from 1960, remains. A major tidying up in 1985, with exterior repainting on three sides, has returned the building to a semblance of its original appearance.

On the traffic island on Central Parkway between the courthouse and the Alms & Doepke Building a time-worn plaque hangs suspended between two stanchions. It commemorates the two main routes early military expeditions took leaving Cincinnati for forays into southwest Ohio. Generals Clark and Harmar went east, along present Reading Road; Generals St. Clair and Wayne went west, following the Millcreek Valley north, along present Central Parkway. In 1794 Wayne soundly defeated an Indian confederation at Fallen Timbers, a victory that opened up the Northwest Territory.

No plaque here (there is one, easily overlooked, at Central Parkway and 14th St.) commemorates another major transportation artery, the **Miami and Erie Canal.** The canal followed Wayne's route, now Central Parkway, curling northwards past crowded tenements and factories, around the city's hills, then into the countryside. Southeastwards, it went from here down present Eggleston Avenue in ten locks, completed in 1834, to the Ohio River. A twenty-year undertaking, the canal involved enormous cost. In 1827 the first boats left for Middletown, by 1829 they reached Dayton, and by 1845 the canal extended 244 miles to Toledo on Lake Erie. For several decades the Miami and Erie Canal (its name after 1849) served as a main avenue for Cincinnati's commerce. The canal network supplemented and extended the great river highways. Production had long been hampered by the unsatisfactory New Orleans market, where Cincinnati merchants sometimes had to dispose of goods at a sacrifice; and the cost of reaching markets at Philadelphia and Baltimore was considerable. With the canal the New York market was within range. Traffic in Ohio reached a peak in 1851, when tolls recorded their highest figure. But the railroads, developed almost concurrently, were cheaper, faster, more direct, and did not freeze in winter. Ultimately they proved too stiff a competition.

Of the Ohio canals, the Miami and Erie clung the most tenaciously to life. Even after being supplanted in the 1850s as the primary transportation mode, the colorful canal boats, pulled by mules or horses, retained until the 1890s a place in the state's economy. When their days of usefulness ended, they lined the banks, rotting. The canal in Cincinnati became an eyesore. Its waters putrid and rank—Archbishop

Miami and Erie Canal, ca. 1916. A trolley crosses one of the many bridges over the canal, here seen in its last, quiet days. In 1919 it was filled in. Central Parkway now occupies the site. The denuded hillside in the distance is Mount Adams, crowned by the campanile of the now-disused Holy Cross monastery (1901). The highrise to right center is the Second National Bank Building (1908). Courtesy of the Cincinnati Historical Society.

Moeller referred to it as "this cesspool in our midst"—the canal was rimmed with decaying factories and slums. Boys swam in its waters in summer, skated on its surface in winter. But in 1919 the city filled in the canal, and Cincinnati lost its "Rhine." The canal soon became the stuff of legend. Many male Cincinnatians dug deep into their boyhoods to recall daring escapades on or in it.

Nor does a plaque commemorate Cincinnati's **subway tunnel.** Only an unobtrusive air shaft cover, one block west of where we stand, between Main and Walnut streets, indicates its existence. The shaft leads to a tunnel, built over six decades ago by the city in the former bed of the Miami and Erie Canal. The tunnel would have been the first section of a sixteen-mile loop encircling the city. One of Cincinnati's perennial "what-ifs" concerns its subway that never was. Voters first put up the money for it in 1916 when they overwhelmingly approved a $6.1 million bond issue. In the early 1920s the remnants of the corrupt Cox machine spent the money building the tunnel and acquiring rights-of-way. In 1924, however, a reform group took over the city government and work stopped temporarily. Three years later the

Building the subway. Post-World War I Cincinnati thought
it needed a subway. Begun in 1919, work continued until
1926, when the project was abandoned. The subway ran
underground in the excavated bed of the former Miami and
Erie Canal, now Central Parkway. The rear façade of Music
Hall is visible on the right, though today it lacks its turret.
The tunnels still exist. This photograph is dated October
1920. Courtesy of the University of Cincinnati Libraries.

city shelved the subway permanently—not, however, before workers had excavated
two-and-a-half miles of tunnel. What Carl Condit has called "the most expensive
tragicomedy in municipal history" was over.

To finish the subway would have required an additional ten million dollars, and
no one quite knew whether a subway would even be needed. Also, by the 1920s
Henry Ford's Model T had captured the imagination of Americans as an easy means
of getting around. Then came the Depression, and most construction stopped. After
World War II the city, economically stable but with its population contracting,
turned its energies elsewhere. In 1966 the $6.1 million bond issue was finally paid
off; with interest, it had cost the city thirteen million. With downtown's renewed
vitality, talk of completing the subway—touted as a light-rail system in the *Cincinnati 2000 Plan*—has occasionally revived. The route proposed would begin in the
suburbs, make use of the already existing tunnel, then cut down Walnut, stop at
Court St., 5th St., and the Stadium, and eventually cross the river to Covington.

Underground Cincinnati remains officially off limits, and I offer no tour of it here. Periodic reports surface of intrepid bands who enter the tunnel, even traverse it from one end to the other. Beginning approximately where we stand, the tunnel heads west, then curves north behind Music Hall before ending below Central Parkway near Marshall Ave. (The twin entrances, blocked by steel doors, are still visible when traveling southbound on I-75.) If of imaginative bent, we may thrill to the thought of the catacombs in Rome or the majestic Gothic arches in London's Victorian sewers, or we may empathize with Jean Valjean in Hugo's *Les Misérables* as he evades Inspector Javert in the Paris *égouts*. But an expedition into underground Cincinnati is a more workaday affair. If the thought of a huge tunnel meandering its way under the city stirs the imagination, the reality is otherwise. The tunnel's cement walls are slick with mold. Adventurers step gingerly along railroad ties marking the path of imaginary trains. They come upon incomplete train platforms, civil defense rations stockpiled in the 1950s (when the city converted a section of the tunnel into a bomb shelter), half-finished toilets, even a working telephone. But if you are entranced by the prospect of urban spelunking, the subway tunnel *is* there.

We return to Main St. and walk south. Main is the last lively street in the downtown's eastern half. James H. Booty, visiting the city in 1859, described Main St. as the city's "great business highway." Until the Civil War (when Walnut became as important) Main, particularly between 3rd and 6th streets, was Cincinnati's chief retailing axis. For a century and a half, it has also connected the business district with the courthouse. Not coincidentally, the street still has on it a number of bookstores and stationers.

From Court to 6th streets, Main also retains a splendid collection of nineteenth- and early twentieth-century commercial buildings. 925 Main is a four-story, stone-faced Italianate building with incised decoration. Double hood moldings over the central bay vary at each level, and the building tops out in an elaborate pressed metal cornice with tiny frieze windows. The neo-Georgian structure (1928) at 125 East 9th has a far different roofline: urns surmounting a balustrade. Splendid limestone elephant heads guard the entrance; an eagle hovers over the door. What *do* these beasts portend? If our political imaginations are working, we should come up with the answer; if not, a plaque tells us that the building once housed Cincinnati's Republican organization.

Looming above its neighbors at 9th and Main streets is the **Second National Bank Building** (1908). A dentilled cornice with splendid lions crowns the building. The two massive Tuscan columns of the lower façade were meant to impress upon observers the power of money—and the stability of the institution guarding it. This lower façade, like those of many older banks, derives, at least indirectly, from the fifth century B.C. Treasury of the Athenians at Delphi; more directly, it derives from the Second Bank of the United States (1818–1824) in Philadelphia. This bank, designed by William Strickland, was one of America's first pure Greek Revival public buildings, the one that established the Greek Revival style in this country. How different is the Central Trust Bank before us from the Central Trust in the 580 Building that we saw at the beginning of this tour. If the colorful graphics of the bank in the 580 Building seemed to say "money can be fun," the bank before us replies, "Yes, but your money is safe here."

East down 8th St., we sight an awning with a large "A." The "A" stands for **Arnold's.** Arnold's began in 1861 when Simon Arnold, a maker of billiard tables, bought half of this building. The first floor he turned into a tavern. Arnold's, which remained in the family until 1976 and has been owned since by Jim Tarbell, is the city's oldest continuously operating eatery. It offers good food amid a casual ambience; evenings there may be music or poetry readings. The third floor houses the offices of the Cincinnati Folk Arts Society, which among its diverse activities sponsors concerts of traditional music.

Like Izzy's, Arnold's is a Cincinnati institution, probably the city's closest equivalent in atmosphere to an English pub. Arnold's now consists of two Greek Revival townhouses joined together. Such "vernacular" townhouses are distinguished by relatively small scale (usually two stories), simply detailed openings, six over six window panes, a row of dentils under the cornice, and a lack of fancy decoration. Originally, the left-hand entrance, now disused, was reserved for ladies. Upstairs dining rooms retain the intimacy of the townhouse floor plan. Alvin Harlow in *The Serene Cincinnatians* of 1951 cited Arnold's as one of the city's many establishments that had existed for several generations without major change. A bathtub in one of the second-floor dining rooms remained, Harlow noted, "because once that was the family bathroom, and some thread of aversion to change gives it permanence. Even the patrons do not object to it, seeming to regard it as a part of the eternal scheme of the universe." The bathtub, Tarbell conjectures, could have been used in the Depression to make bathtub gin. It remains.

Across from Arnold's is the **Aurora** (1910), the first building in this commercial district designed mainly for housing. The Aurora has four oriel windows and one of downtown's most elegant cast- and wrought-iron fire escapes. Even the shop fronts appear little changed. Architectural details, as in contemporaneous apartment houses on San Francisco's Nob Hill, stand out by being painted in different colors, cheerful but inauthentic. The colors force you to notice the details. Around the corner at 726 Main (1916), where the Ohio Book Store is, we see above the ground floor the seal of the University of Cincinnati. The University built the building, along with that at 646 Main (1913), for investment purposes.

Housed within the **Ohio Book Store** are five stories of secondhand books, including the area's largest collection of material on Cincinnati and the Ohio Valley. Together with **Acres of Books** (at 633 Main), the Ohio Book Store serves as the downtown port of call for those searching after out-of-print books. A city can be judged by its buildings, its museums, its cultural or sports facilities; it can also be judged by its bookstores, secondhand no less than new. Secondhand bookstores help preserve and make available the written heritage of mankind. Even in today's technological world, we rely upon the written word to transmit most of what is worth knowing. The Ohio Book Store and Acres of Books, along with the five other secondhand bookstores in the Cincinnati area, constitute one of the city's most valuable, and least recognized, cultural resources.

An uninterrupted sequence of late nineteenth-century commercial structures

Main St., 600 block. This block presents a virtually intact row of late nineteenth-century commercial buildings. Main St., the city's chief commercial thoroughfare before the Civil War, retains its importance today as the primary route between the business district and the courthouse.

lines the west side of Main between 6th and 7th streets. At 626 is the Bay Horse Cafe (1870s) with an interesting twentieth-century sign. Here before World War I, the authors of the 1943 WPA guide recalled, no doubt in a wistful mood, "the bartender shook your gin fizz for 30 minutes before serving." The building is an excellent (and virtually unaltered) example of Italianate architecture. It retains its original cast-iron rope-turned columns, window moldings vary at each level, and an impressive cornice crowns the façade. In the 1880s Main St. north of 6th became a wholesale center; new structures went up as high as six stories. The Fort Washington Hotel (1897), at 621 Main, its decorative brickwork in the Queen Anne style, was originally an office building. In 1927, as part of a trend toward rooming houses in the district, it became a hotel. Like the Dennison up the street, it provides single rooms chiefly for the elderly poor. Cincinnati Art Galleries at 635 Main offers an excellent selection of artworks deriving from this area.

A number of buildings on Main St. have **cast-iron fronts.** During the 1850s and 1860s cast iron became popular nationally for commercial structures. It allowed more window space to let in light and to display goods. The cast-iron frame, a structural innovation comparable in appeal to the balloon frame developed several decades before, combined lightness, openness, adaptability, and speed of construction. And it was attractive: the original builders and owners of iron structures designed and painted them to look like stone. Rising above the sea of Federal and Greek Revival structures that constituted the city at midcentury, they provided dramatic contrasts to their understated neighbors in height, detailing, color, and style. But cast-iron buildings, originally thought fireproof, turned out to be as vulnerable as others. Interiors—flooring, joists, beams, staircases—were often of combustible wood; though cast iron did not itself burn, the shock of water from firemen's hoses often cracked it. The great Chicago blaze of 1871, which destroyed much of the city, marked the beginning of the end of cast iron's great popularity though builders in Cincinnati and elsewhere continued to use it for more than two decades longer. The development in the 1870s and 1880s of the steel skeleton, with its greater tensile strength, permitted buildings of far greater height.

Cincinnati may even have pioneered in cast iron. Most architectural historians consider James Bogardus in New York to have put up the United States's oldest surviving cast-iron building, though by no means the oldest in point of time, Manhattan's Laing Stores (1849). But *The Builder* (London) of September 25, 1847, citing the Cincinnati *Daily Commercial* of July 27, 1847, reported "a block of three-story buildings . . . in the course of erection in Cincinnati, the entire fronts of which are of cast iron." We hear no more of these buildings and they may never have been built. Turpin C. Bannister, in a 1956 article in the *Journal of the Society of Architectural Historians,* cites in support of Cincinnati's claim, however, the evidence of Miles Greenwood. Greenwood, the driving force behind the establishment of Cincinnati's professional fire department, asserted that his Eagle foundry had been turning out cast-iron fronts since 1843. "While no contemporary corroboration or executed examples have thus far been found," Bannister concludes, "Greenwood's reputation for probity and his interest in fire prevention and incombustible construction make his claim highly credible." Whatever the status of Cincinnati's role as a cast-iron pioneer, the city, both downtown and even more in Over-the-Rhine, still has numerous cast-iron buildings. Chicago, for example, does not have a single full-sized iron front left, whereas New York has between 250 and 300, more than any other city according to Edmund V. Gillon, Jr. Scattered about the Basin rather than concentrated like those in SoHo in Lower Manhattan, Cincinnati's cast-iron structures lack the detailed attention—and publicity—that Gillon has given Manhattan's. Remarkably intact is that at 654 Main, now housing Cianciolo Grocers. The buxom female figures gracing the fourth floor remind us that cast iron had other than strictly utilitarian uses.

At 610 Main we come upon a small Art Deco building (1945) designed by Hake and Kuck for Caproni's Restaurant. Pegasus races across the cornice. The building now houses the eastside **Izzy's,** a more capacious, if less colorful, version of the establishment on Elm. Here, as across town, waitresses yell in orders and do not issue checks. You simply tell the cashier what you had. If we miss the human compression, the communal tables, the raucous shouting back and forth of the Elm St. locale, no less ample here are the corned beef and pastrami specialties.

The **Gwynne Building** (1914), at 6th and Main streets, was designed by a well-known New York architect, Ernest Flagg. Flagg had previously done both the "Little

Cast-iron goddess. One of two late nineteenth-century cast-iron figures adorning 654 Main St. Features and head-gear—possibly a crown—deliberately evoke classical statuary. In 1848 Hiram Powers's famous statue *The Greek Slave* caused a sensation in Cincinnati with its sentimental eroticism. Puritans objected violently to its nudity. To forestall alarm these figures are presented as deities or queens.

Singer Building" (1904) at Broadway and Prince in Manhattan, also twelve stories, and the forty-seven story Singer Tower (1908), in the financial district, briefly the tallest building in the world. Some architectural historians consider the Little Singer the first true skyscraper with an obvious curtain wall. The Singer Tower, when taken down in 1967–1968, had the dubious distinction of being the tallest building ever dismantled. Comparable in height and façade treatment to Flagg's Little Singer Building, the Gwynne is Cincinnati's most highly ornamented highrise. Its exuberant façade may owe a debt to Louis Sullivan, an American architect known for his mastery of ornamental detail. It certainly owes its wonderful arches to Flagg's training at France's Ecole des Beaux Arts. Graduates of that famous institution often

Gwynne Building. One of Cincinnati's most distinguished commercial buildings, the Gwynne Building (1914) was designed by Ernest Flagg. The campanile draws upon Italian models. Visible are the filigree metalwork and attenuated columns of the casement windows, as well as awnings over windows. Before air conditioning became common around 1960, awnings graced most older office buildings. Garlanded oxen appear above the ninth-floor corners. Courtesy of the Cincinnati Historical Society.

displayed a fondness for large round arches. Flagg adored them. A huge arch dominates the façade of his first Singer building, a torrent of arches cascaded down the second, and arches define the Gwynne's façade.

Filigree metalwork and attenuated columns frame the Gwynne's huge casement windows. Turn-of-the-century office buildings once had generous awnings, as contemporary photographs attest, to protect workers within from the sun's rays. The Gwynne is very much a family affair. Note the alternating "G" and "V" (for "Gwynne" and "Vanderbilt") on balcony grilles: Alice Gwynne Vanderbilt thus dedicated the building to her father, Abraham E. Gwynne of Cincinnati. Flagg's cousin, Alice Claypoole Gwynne, had married Cornelius Vanderbilt II, who, aware of Flagg's abilities, offered to pay his expenses to attend the Ecole des Beaux Arts. Flagg subsequently designed other structures for the Vanderbilt interests. Elegant brackets sustain the delicate cornice, under which we discern brightly colored mosaic panels. A campanile-like tower crowns the Gwynne, another of its many debts, along with the metalwork, the arches, and the mosaics, to the Italian Renaissance. All this sumptuous decoration reflects the Beaux Arts attitude toward the prestige office building.

Garlanded heads of disconsolate oxen protrude above the ninth-floor corners. I'm not sure what purpose oxen serve on the façade of a structure long associated with Procter & Gamble, a company known for products once made from hogs. P & G, as it is known locally, leased the building from 1914 before purchasing it in 1935 for its company headquarters, which it remained until 1956. The Gwynne does, however, occupy the site where in 1837 William Procter, soapmaker, and James Gamble, candlemaker, who had married sisters, first went into business together, renting an earlier building from David Gwynne, father of Abraham. Whatever the oxen may symbolize, they add a welcome domestic component to downtown's menagerie.

One creature no longer evident on Main St., however, is the **hog.** In the three decades before the Civil War, slaughtering hogs and curing pork was Cincinnati's most visible industry. The hog was the chief livestock on the Ohio frontier, corn the chief crop. "Let your corn walk to market" went the catch phrase. The first slaughterhouse in Cincinnati opened in 1810; by the early 1820s pork-packing had begun to boom. Pigs were and are the all-purpose animal. In addition to being entirely edible, from toes to tail, they provide bristles for brushes, hides for shoes and gloves, lard for candles and (later) soap. Thus their presence fostered related industries. In the days before refrigeration, slaughtering and curing were done from November through February. Henry Farny in a famous illustration for *Harper's* depicted, stage by stage, the carefully controlled production process. In developing the continuously moving assembly line for his Model T in 1912–1913, Henry Ford learned from the "dis-assembling" techniques of Cincinnati's pork-packing industry, which, according to his grandson, he had seen during a visit in the early 1900s. By 1835 Cincinnati had become America's chief meat-packing center, the nation's "pork-shop"; by 1848 it processed half a million hogs annually. Hams from the Queen City, consumed nationwide, went to fashionable homes and hotels, restaurants, even to the White House. But in the 1850s, as new rail routes east opened up, Cincinnati began to lose its dominance. By the outbreak of the Civil War, though still the city's second largest industry, pork-packing had been overtaken by Chicago.

Cincinnati's devotion to the hog exacted a price. Any stroller down Main St. before the Civil War knew what that price was. Not only were hogs processed in Cincinnati but bands of them roamed the streets. By the late 1820s the city had paved its chief thoroughfares with limestone blocks; the porous stone resisted water poorly, however, and gradually disintegrated. Worse, citizens made little effort to keep the streets clear of animal droppings and garbage. Though clean animals, pigs like dirt and are content to eat garbage. Protected by law in Cincinnati, they were allowed to consume whatever suited their palates. Thus, keeping the streets clean, they became a civic necessity, an unofficial sanitation department, the initial line of defense, so to speak, against filth. The law even required citizens to throw refuse, not at the side of the street, but in the middle where the hogs could more easily dispose of it. Efficient sanitation removal lay decades in the future. Meanwhile, the hogs, bristling with self-pride, walked the streets snouts high. Daring youngsters— even a son of the Rev. Dr. Lyman Beecher—honed their bareback riding skills on them. Cincinnatians, used to porcine ways, tolerated them. Less forgiving were travelers from abroad.

Few were the visitors to Cincinnati before 1860 who did not deplore the risks the ubiquitous hogs posed to their sartorial dignity. "If I determined upon a walk up Main-street," lamented Frances Trollope in a famous passage of her *Domestic Manners of the Americans* (1832), "the chances were five hundred to one against my reaching the shady side without brushing by a snout fresh dripping from the kennel." Typical was the response of Mrs. Houston, an English traveler of 1849. Cincinnati she found to be "literally speaking *a city of pigs* . . . a monster piggery" where "grunts and . . . squeals meet you at every moment." Instead of the Queen City, Cincinnati was named, at least by those jealous of her renown, "Porkopolis." Moritz Busch, the German traveler who would not be pleased, even termed natives "Porkopolitaners." After the Civil War, when Cincinnati fielded America's first professional baseball team, the Red Stockings, it was inevitable that with a president, Josiah L. Keck, who was himself a pork packer, that local wits would also dub it the "Porkopolitans."

The phenomenon of metropolitan piggery was not unusual in mid-nineteenth century America. Hogs foraged in the streets of many American cities, including New York. Other cities called various scavengers to the task: turkey buzzards patrolled Charleston's streets and elsewhere in the South goats and geese did the job. In New York Charles Dickens admired the hogs' "perfect self-possession and self-reliance, and immovable composure." One Manhattan wag penned this jingle:

> A question 'tis, and mooted strong
>   Between the citizens and the swine,
> To which the streets do most belong,
>   Of this most glorious city.

Cincinnati's vast pork-packing industry aggravated the hog problem locally. By the

1850s so numerous were these four-legged scavengers that whenever they came to number 6000 the city rounded them up to sell at auction. Although then disappearing from New York, the hogs hung on longer in Cincinnati. Nicholas A. Woods, the London *Times*'s correspondent accompanying the Prince of Wales on his American tour in September 1860, though he praised Cincinnati's appearance in general, questioned the presence of so many hogs: "the very gutters are congested with them, as a sort of dull monotony of pigs is visible everywhere." This outburst prompted the editor of the Cincinnati *Commercial* to retort that in the past month he hadn't seen more than ten hogs roaming loose. Perhaps as a result of the royal visit, the city in December 1860 instigated a drive to clear swine from the streets.

Before leaving Main St., we penetrate the bland exterior of the John Weld Peck Federal Building (1964) between 5th and 6th streets, a creation of Harry Hake, Jr. On the lobby's back wall is a delightful mosaic of wildlife. Charles Harper, a Cincinnati artist known for his animal paintings, created this two-part mural of one-inch square Cambridge tiles. Multicolored and cheerful, it depicts, quite wonderfully, American mammals, insects, birds, reptiles, fish—but no hogs!

Catholic activity in Cincinnati has long centered on Sycamore St. between 6th and 7th. The first frame church was moved here from Liberty in 1826, the first school founded shortly afterwards. **St. Francis Xavier** (1861), designed by Anthony and Louis Piket, once formed part of a complex that included a high school and an elementary school. The high school took over the St. Xavier College buildings in 1920 when the college became a university and moved to its new campus on Victory Parkway. Xavier had opened on October 7, 1831, the Northwest Territory's first Catholic institution of higher learning. Ten years before, the Roman Catholic diocese of Ohio had been created, and in the 1820s, Edward Fenwick, its first bishop, purchased this property. Only the church now remains. A fire in 1882 destroyed the original slender Gothic spire; the present stone-faced tower, designed by Louis Piket, has a lower, more rounded form than Piket originally intended. Inside, the building's vertical aspect is emphasized by other Gothic elements, notably clustered columns, tall windows, pointed arches, even confessionals.

Opposite St. Francis Xavier is the **Krippendorf Building** (1888). This rambling seven-story commercial structure in the Romanesque Revival style, one of a number of comparable buildings downtown, was also designed by Louis Piket. Originally it housed Krippendorf, Dittmann & Co., a maker of women's shoes. The building further testifies to H. H. Richardson's powerful grip on American architecture in the 1880s and 1890s. With their massive dimensions, rough-hewn textures, and thick masonry-bearing walls, Richardson's buildings conveyed an image of solidity and strength that appealed to American businessmen. Like City Hall, the Krippendorf is one of the several local progeny that drew upon Richardson's Chamber of Commerce. Stone beltcourses separate the Krippendorf's floors; the windows, like those of City Hall, get progressively smaller as the building rises, giving viewers the illusion that it stands taller than it does. Below the cornice "squeezed" arches overlap one another. From here we follow the narrow New St. east to Broadway and then walk a block north. On either side of the 7th St. and Broadway intersection the city has created a small park, minuscule spaces that bring grace and beauty to downtown.

The **Times-Star Building,** at 800 Broadway, a sixteen-story limestone building of 1931, was designed by Samuel Hannaford and Sons. With its extended base, the building has more floor space than first appears. We need to examine this Art Deco masterpiece both from afar and close up. Numerous setbacks stress verticality, as do window lines and the bronze spandrels. Note in ground-level spandrels the intertwined "T" and "S." Formerly the building housed the *Times-Star,* later the *Post* and *Times-Star.*

To describe 800 Broadway in all its intricacy would require a chapter in itself. Huge statues project from the tower's upper corners. Does not the bewigged jurist (southwest corner) looking down at us have an uncharacteristically beatific visage? These statues allegedly represent four essential characteristics of a 1930s newspaper: Truth, Patriotism, Progress, and Speed. Which one our jurist is I shall let you decide. No less improbably benign is the laurelled figure, Dante presumably, Patriotism presumably, facing southeast. The huge eagle below the flag appeared on the *Times-Star* masthead. Numerous bas reliefs are embedded in the walls. Gazing across at each other from the third story corners facing Broadway are Franklin and Gutenberg. Caxton hovers around the corner from Gutenberg, Elzevier from Franklin. Famous printers all, they symbolize the progress of their trade—and, by extension, of learning. The arched entrance serves as an intricately decorated frontispiece, appropriate in so literate a building. The bronze grille depicts printers and other artists going about their tasks.

No less intricate is the lobby decoration. From the geometric, polychromed marbled floor (reminiscent of American Indian designs) to the bellicose eagles in the ceiling, few spaces have been left undecorated. Gazelles cavort madly across the radiator grilles. Printers' marks adorn the balcony; no-nonsense females, the elevator doors. Right of the front entrance a plaque honors Charles Phelps Taft; on the left, another honors his wife, Anna Sinton Taft: "Her whole heart was wrapped up in the future of Cincinnati." Supported by his father-in-law David Sinton, Taft bought the *Times* and the *Evening Star* separately in 1879 and the next year merged them. He was editor in chief, at least nominally, of the *Times-Star* from 1880 until his death in 1929. After Taft's death, his nephew, Hulbert Taft, took over the editorial helm. John Gunther once characterized Hulbert as the most conservative man in America. Publisher and paper were, needless to say, unfailingly Republican in national elections.

The *Post,* begun as *The Penny Paper* in 1881, became part of the Scripps chain that year and in 1890 received its present name. Priding itself on political independence, the *Post* made a reputation exposing municipal corruption. In 1958, after Hulbert Taft's retirement, the *Post* bought the *Times-Star,* which ceased publication as an independent newspaper. In 1979, having consolidated its printing operation with the *Enquirer,* the *Post* moved out of 800 Broadway. The owner since 1984, Burke Marketing Services, Inc., a Cincinnati-based marketing research firm, has sensitively restored the building.

East of Broadway, between 6th and 7th streets, now consists largely of ware-

Bewigged jurist, 800 Broadway. Cincinnati's older buildings often sport interesting statuary and decorative work.
This figure smiles blandly down upon the city from his
perch.

houses and parking lots. In the nineteenth century this area, known as **Bucktown,**
with its mixed population of blacks and whites, ranked along with the riverfront as
the rowdiest of Cincinnati's inner-city neighborhoods. The seamy life there mixed
with the smells of the Miami and Erie Canal, which ran down present Eggleston
Avenue, and of the Deer Creek slaughterhouses. The authors of the 1943 WPA
guide described the situation thus: "Here lived the lowest whites and blacks—
pimps, prostitutes, thieves, rag pickers, levee hands and their mistresses, and white
women with colored lovers—in a buttery, evil fellowship. The decayed shacks and
foul odors of this wretched bottom were no worse than the inhabitants, who stole,
fought, made love, and got drunk with unfailing regularity."

In the 1870s Lafcadio Hearn sought out in Bucktown those whose lives the
official histories had forgotten. He exposed the human misery and brutality that
existed behind the façade of Bucktown's vice. In "Some Pictures of Poverty" he
described its "picturesque wretchedness." Hearn, who could evoke buildings and

people with Dickensian intensity, hardly yields in his account of Bucktown's totter-
ing hovels to Dickens's description in *Bleak House* of the London slum dwellings in
Tom-All-Alone's. Like Dickens, he intends a correlation between the bizarre shapes
and appearances of buildings and the equally bizarre shapes and appearances of the
people who live in them. As a chronicler of Cincinnati's urban scene, Hearn in his
minor key is Dickens, Dostoevsky, and Gissing rolled into one.

No less vividly than places does Hearn evoke Bucktown's inhabitants. An ancient Negro couple, both past eighty, reminisce about when they first met on a Virginia plantation sixty years ago; a woman of part Indian descent, bereft of family,
remembers the face of her mother who had died when she was a child; another
woman shows him the last cherished letter from her son gone to the Far West—it is
postmarked "1849." He just misses a Negro woman, 117 years old, who recalled
Africa's tropical landscape and who "was accustomed to speak of Washington." As
he moves from one haunting encounter to another, Hearn names no one—except the
landlord, whom he names three times. The tragedy of one human soul is the tragedy
of all. A scene unrolls in "the second story of a sooty house, perched on the ragged
edge of Eggleston Avenue Hill." "Sixteen years in bed," said the overseer of the man
they find there, his "limbs and body . . . swollen by disease to a monstrous size."
Below a drunken woman screams curses as she beats her child furiously. Such
"grisly and spectral" visions haunt Hearn's mind with "nightmare tenacity." "Bucktown is nothing if not seen by gaslight," he writes in "Pariah People"; "then it presents a most striking effect of fantastic *chiar'scuro.*" In Hearn's painterly technique
light and dark alternate to render a world dreamlike, yet intensely real. Although
occasionally stilted and literary, his prose even after more than a century resonates
with anguish become eloquent.

Two blocks further south, on the northwest corner of Broadway and 5th St.,
stood until 1974 the Wesley Chapel (1831), a simple Georgian structure based on
John Wesley's own chapel at 47, City Road, London. When built, the Wesley
Chapel was Cincinnati's largest building. Its 1200 seats provided the most com-
modious assembly hall in the trans-Appalachian West. Here in 1841 William
Henry Harrison's funeral service took place; four years later, John Quincy
Adams addressed Cincinnatians here on the virtues of supporting an astronomical
observatory.

Now this block and that across Broadway are filled by the Procter & Gamble
complex. No American company approaches its dominant position in the consumer
marketplace. Among its 200 products are such familiar brand names as Ivory
soap (since 1878); the company remains the largest soap manufacturer in the
world. In the 1950s it developed new products—Crest toothpaste, Duncan Hines
cake mix, Folgers coffee. The company takes pride that 97 percent of American
households use its products. For many years it had the largest advertising budget
of any U.S. company; it is the soap behind (too many) soap operas, a genre it invented; and it is Cincinnati's biggest firm, one associated with the city since 1837.
Yet in its hometown this corporate giant has kept a consistently low profile. It
downplays publicity about itself, preferring instead to cultivate an image as a con-

Procter & Gamble Towers. A major example of postmodern architecture, the towers (1985) have received widespread recognition for their design. The architects are Kohn Pedersen Fox. In the foreground George Sugarman's multicolored steel sculpture *The Story of Cincinnati* insinuates itself gracefully in the pool before the Chiquita Center and acts as a foil to the towers.

servative, very smooth organization run efficiently and somewhat anonymously. Its headquarters building serves as an appropriate corporate symbol. The new towers reflect its wish to maintain an understated—but powerful—presence in Cincinnati.

Most people respond vigorously to the **Procter & Gamble Towers** (1985), designed by Kohn Pederson Fox Associates of New York. Either they strongly like or strongly dislike them. Few take a middle ground. I admit to being among the few. In style, the Towers are postmodern, that is, designed in one of the related modes that succeeded the International style. The International style, or Modern Movement, came into being in 1919 with Walter Gropius's Bauhaus in Germany, but it did not really catch on in the United States until after World War II. In Cincinnati, the Terrace Hilton is early International style, the Kroger unsuccessful, and the DuBois Tower representative. Many highrises today are still built to International style formulas, for example the Cincinnati Commerce Center at Vine and 6th, and its fraternal twin Chiquita Center, nearby at 5th and Sycamore streets. Both buildings, however, nod toward postmodernism. The International style prided itself on a cool look. "Less is more" claimed Mies van der Rohe, its most accomplished practitioner in skyscraper design. It shunned decoration or reference to previous historical periods or styles. An elitist style, it succeeds best when handled by talented architects.

Pluralism characterizes today's architecture. Postmodern architects comprise a more diverse lot than modernists, less concerned about what is "right" or "wrong," united only in rejecting the previous generation of modernists, though even there not entirely. Although their buildings retain modernism's cool look, they include contrast, variety, symbolism, historical echoes ("quotations" from the past), and whatever ornament budgets allow. Eclecticism is given free rein. The new Procter & Gamble Towers, in 1987 one of three office buildings in the world to receive an award from the American Institute of Architects, is regarded as one of postmodernism's major triumphs.

To construct a powerful building that does not overly call attention to itself represents a civilized urban gesture on the company's part. With their tapered, stainless steel crowns, the seventeen-story, octagonal Towers have an unmistakable silhouette, virtually the same from all directions. They work well with surrounding buildings and with the overall cityscape. The six-story L-shaped base also fits in sympathetically, both in height and form, with the neighborhood's older buildings. Cincinnati's skyline begins low on the edges and rises to a peak in the Carew Tower. A very tall building at the edge of downtown would have dramatically thrown off the skyline's symmetry. P & G acted in the city's interest as well as in its own.

Specifically, Kohn Pederson Fox designed the Towers to be compatible with the adjoining twelve-story building (now called the Central Building). Designed by Voorhees, Walker, Smith, and Smith and completed in 1956, it was subtly extended (to the east) in 1971. The new towers adopt the older building's window pattern, upper-level marble colonnade, and facing of Bedford limestone. To the last it added pilasters of white marble and the little square plaques that appear to be a postmodern trademark. Façade windows look into, not offices, but exterior circulating corridors: thus we see no shades or blinds.

The octagonal pyramids of the Towers intentionally echo downtown's other pyramidal structures. These include the *Times-Star* Building, Cincinnati Gas & Electric, the Central Trust Tower, even the Federated Building. The Towers's many setbacks also echo earlier structures; their extended base counterpoints that of the *Times-Star* building. Such echoes remind us how much postmodernism owes to Art Deco. Classical in their understated proportions and dignified restraint, the Towers look to the past no less than to the future.

Perched above the entrances is P & G's logo of the man in the moon surrounded by thirteen stars. (A larger version adorns the 1956 building.) Developed by 1851 and a registered trademark since 1882, the logo has undergone an at least eight-stage evolution. Its present form dates from 1932. In recent years the logo has undergone hard times. The moonies adopted it in the 1960s; twenty years later superstitious folk linked it—and P & G—to Satanism. Not even Ann Landers could reassure them. In May 1985, after receiving 12,000 calls in two months, the publicity-conscious company eliminated the logo from its products, retaining it, however, on corporate letterheads. Even today, fundamentalist sects periodically call for the boycott of Tide and other P & G products, proving once more that the facts seldom get in the way of a good rumor.

Procter & Gamble's **garden** aligns the complex toward Fountain Square. A pergola of cast concrete pylons topped with a redwood trellis, in summer covered with wisteria, defines the space. Within the pergola are laid out formal, geometric green areas and parterres. Modest fountains and pools serve as focal points. If only in sheer acreage, the ensemble is impressive.

The complex comes into its own as a visual element within the cityscape. We approach it from 5th St., and all of a sudden—there it is. The Towers serve as a focus to the long vista developed by the lines of the garden. The 1956 building directs the eye to them. Silhouetted against the sky, the Towers anchor the eastern skyline. I-71 and Mount Adams will prevent anything being built behind them. From the east, the Towers serve as a gateway to downtown. As we descend I-71's great curve toward the city, before the roadway disappears under Lytle Park, the Towers present an unforgettable image, particularly at dusk, when they are silhouetted against the setting sun. Even more spectacular is the view from the 6th St./Downtown exit ramp off Columbia Parkway. We appear to circle the Towers, then head straight into them, before veering off at the very last moment.

Citygoers like to have their eyes engaged by the urban scene. They like to see other people. A downtown needs density both of buildings and of population. What contribution, we may ask, does the P & G complex make to Cincinnati's downtown? If diversity of structure and imaginative use of space foster a downtown's health, has P & G developed its acreage wisely? Let us admit that the Towers have an unusual, though not particularly imaginative, design. They do not dominate the cityscape, and, visually, they anchor the eastern downtown. Many new highrises, modernist and postmodern alike, disrupt the cityscape, but the P & G Towers do not. In short, they address the humanistic and esthetic dimensions of Cincinnati. All this is to the good. But if esthetically a modest success, the Towers, to my mind, add little visual excitement to downtown. Neither engaging the eye at close hand nor challenging us, they work best from afar. We gaze, we admire, we walk away. The cool colors and abstract patterns come across as impersonal, even sterile. I find the Towers convincing intellectually but not emotionally. Particularly on a gray day, the complex fails to come to life. Gray buildings for a gray eminence? The effect, however grand, is lifeless. Monuments at the end of vistas, the Towers as urban structures fail on a human level.

Even the garden, pleasant to look at and admirable on its own terms, leaves a disconcerting effect. At first it had a hard-edged, formal quality. Like any landscape, though, as the plantings matured, it began to appear less stark. But the garden is also disconcerting in a more serious way. Like the Towers, it is in the downtown but not of it. On weekends, the allées are discreetly chained off, as if P & G wished to say, "you may admire but we request that you do not enter." We are in a company garden, not a public place. The distinction is important. Although open to all during business hours, no one will mistake this corporate cloister for a park or a place to assemble like Fountain Square. If allowed to stroll under the pergolas, we do so as invited guests. With its allées and parterres, its undeviating symmetry and its carefully contrived effects, the P & G enclave radiates an aloofness that I find disturbing. It reminds me of Versailles, as if the Sun King had deigned to plop down in Cincinnati a townhouse amidst his manicured grounds.

Across 5th St., between Broadway and Sycamore, is the **Masonic Temple** (1928). Designed by Harry Hake and Charles Kuck in Hake's restrained neoclassical style, this imposing limestone structure appears aloof and forbidding and, like other masonic temples of its vintage, more than a little dull. The upper-level colonnade seems an afterthought; the few windows offer no clue to the mysteries within. Exterior decoration is sparse; a single anthemion crowns the roofline.

Next door, the **Taft Theater,** also 1928 and also by Hake and Kuck, has equally restrained decoration. It is one of downtown's few remaining large public auditoriums. Named for Charles Phelps Taft, who helped finance it, the theater, like the temple, derives in style from the 1920s Roman Revival. The 2500-seat auditorium—grand, austere, little remodeled since construction—has much painted decoration, vaguely Pompeian in style. It retains its old wooden telephone booths. Today, Broadway shows on tour use the Taft, as does, for two weeks each year, Children's Theatre of Cincinnati.

Harry Hake strikes me as Cincinnati's answer to Washington's John Russell Pope. Pope designed many of the capital's public buildings between world wars I and II. Ada Louise Huxtable, the former architecture critic for the *New York Times*, once labeled him the "King of the Correct Classicists." Characteristic of Pope's "architecture of inhumanism" was, Huxtable claimed, "a depersonalized magnificence," a "dry Olympian grandeur." What is wrong with many of Washington's public buildings—their monochromatic coloring, their aridity of design, their aloofness and grandiosity—is precisely what is wrong with some of Cincinnati's, including the Masonic Temple and the Taft Theater.

Except during business hours, downtown east of Main St. lacks sustaining life. The area has few shops, restaurants, small businesses—in short, few signs of other than corporate life. The cityscape consists of parking lots, garages, warehouses— and the new corporate towers. "Just east of Main Street north of Fifth," observed the authors of the wartime WPA guide, "the downtown district loses its characteristic busyness." So it was in 1943, so it is today. Walk this area during other than business hours and you walk a ghost town. A vacuum has sucked the life out of the sidewalks. "Nothing so devitalizes a street," the architectural historian William Jordy has remarked, as "an excessive number of buildings discreetly dedicated to maintaining a 'corporate image.'" In terms of revitalizing Cincinnati, the corporate renaissance of eastern downtown has limitations as well as benefits. If Cincinnati is a long way from acquiring the spectacular but arid downtown cityscape of Houston, the city's highrises do not generate life other than during business hours. Few make any effort at all to engage the eye at street level. Without variety of function and humanity of scale, the cityscape loses its vitality. P & G's presence may stimulate development, but unless other kinds of activity arise—shops, residences, restaurants—this part of downtown will remain dead.

Chiquita Center (1984), on the northwest corner of 5th and Sycamore streets, typifies the Cincinnati highrise of the early 1980s. It began life under the rubric of Columbia Plaza but gained its present name, not to the happiness of all its other tenants, with the arrival of Chiquita Brands in 1987. Freestanding columns, or *pilotis*, leave the ground level open. First used by Le Corbusier for the Swiss Pavilion (1932) in Paris's Cité Universitaire, the *pilotis* allow a free public zone at ground level. They became the model for a multitude of postwar buildings in America. Above ground level, the Chiquita Center's design is unimaginative. It is a highrise, not a proud tower. The building's top, lit at night, acts as the city's weather vane: when a bright green, the next day will be clear and sunny; when blue, cloudy and/ or raining; bright orange is a severe weather warning. Behind the building a tiered, colorfully landscaped area offers steps on which to sit and eat lunch. Paid for by the city, it hooks into the skywalk system. In front, enlivening the raised esplanade, is an extraordinary fountain.

Winding in and out of the fountain is George Sugarman's multicolored steel sculpture, *The Story of Cincinnati*. This gaudy composition of wavy bands may suggest the city's rising from the banks of the Ohio River. Or again it may not. In regard to another of Sugarman's creations, *Baltimore Federal*, this one before a U.S. district court in Baltimore and (to my eye, at least) rather similar to Cincinnati's, a museum director opined that the ribbon forms suggested the continuity of the law. In like vein, we may regard this *jeu d'esprit* as a giant bouquet of colorful metal water-flowers or as leaves of a tropical fruit. However we interpret it (and we need not interpret it at all), Sugarman's sculpture with its freewheeling undulations and riotous primary colors—reds, blues, and greens—certainly does thumb its nose at the formal symmetry across Sycamore.

On the southeast corner, before the Central Trust Center, stands another sculpture, George Rickey's kinetic *Two Rectangles: Vertical Gyratory II*. Alexander Calder, the pioneer kinetic sculptor, based his works on natural forms. Rickey, however, does not. These scuffed steel panels, installed in 1979, respond to whatever breeze wafts by. Motor-driven devices within kinetic sculptures often create a standardized or syncopated movement. Rickey's sculptures depend solely on natural elements, usually (as here) wind. At one moment the moving panels appear a leaden gray, the next a luminous silver. As the artist undoubtedly planned, the movement is slightly disconcerting. Who expects to see so large, so seemingly solid, an object moving about?

In recent decades there has occurred in most large metropolitan downtowns an explosion of monumental outdoor art. *Monument* means "to bring to mind," and both the Sugarman and Rickey sculptures form part of Cincinnati's contribution to making people think about art. These works were commissioned under a city regulation that requires the inclusion of public art in or before new buildings downtown. Unlike most other kinds of art, **public sculptures** regularly impinge upon our daily urban experience. They are a three-dimensional aspect of the functioning city scene. Sculpture is evocative in a way that paintings are not. We can walk around a sculpture, we can (in many cases) feel its texture in our fingertips. No form of art is more pervasive today: more people experience sculpture in city streets than they do paintings in museums or galleries. Once Victorian sculpture, with its calculated stage effects, served as an ideal accent for city spaces. Its success often depended as much on its architectural setting as on its representational or historical attributes. The *Genius of Water,* Cincinnati's quintessential Victorian sculpture, superb unto itself, perfectly focuses the public place that is Fountain Square. So, too, do the monuments to Garfield and Harrison in Piatt Park: they look to advantage both in themselves and as complements to their settings. Even the carefully molded and detailed pedestals, or plinths, of Victorian statues contribute significantly to their public effect. Such venerations in bronze (or elsewhere in stone) lend nobility to the urban landscape. They represent, as Edmund Wilson once wrote, "the desire of human beings to transcend human limitations." One might even wish for more such monuments: not just of men and not just of presidents, but of artists, writers, musicians, scientists, thinkers, explorers of the world and of the mind.

Today, it seems, every new highrise in Cincinnati sports before it the obligatory sculpture. This public art maintains the tradition of earlier Art Deco buildings like the *Times-Star,* and, before them, turn-of-the-century Beaux Arts edifices like Memorial Hall (chapter 8). Such statues as these buildings sport were admonitory lessons, or "examples," in civics. The durability of the material, whether stone or bronze, carried with it the conviction or hope that the lessons would be lasting. No one would claim that these statues are great art. Yet in direct and unmistakable ways they exert a compelling visual impact. Whereas the older buildings incorporated sculpture into their façades, today's highrises reserve an area, usually in front, for an art work often specifically designed ("site specific") for it. Older sculpture was deliberately representational and often educational; modern sculpture is (often) abstract and nondidactic. There are exceptions of course; two of them, Andrew Leicester's and Barna von Sartory's sculptures, both in Bicentennial Commons at Sawyer Point, we consider in chapter 6. But many modern sculptors, like many modern architects, have little use for familiar historical styles or for the storytelling aspects of decoration. We appreciate their works for the beauty of the geometric elements rather than for evocations of natural forms or history. Such sculpture, it must be said, often appears to have little or no public meaning. Except as objects of curiosity, or derision, they rarely engage the attention of passersby.

So what justification can we find for these sculptures? Their presence on the scene, some argue, helps develop an esthetic sense. If we become more aware of the juxtaposition of things—the forms of sculpture, say, in relation to the forms of buildings—we may begin to appreciate the cityscape more, to notice its odd, unexpected harmonies. And if we respond to outdoor sculpture, who knows?—we may even develop a liking for contemporary sculpture and art in museums. Certainly we cannot return to the old heroic representational sculpture, the sculpture of declaiming presidents and larger-than-life generals. No one today would advocate a work like the Lincoln Memorial, not only because individuals of Lincoln's stature appear to be fewer but also because notions about art have changed. Such sculpture as the Garfield and Harrison statues in Piatt Park or Daniel Chester French's giant seated figure of Lincoln in Washington emerged because people believed in the values that those individuals (and the society at large) embodied, or at least regarded as ideal. Today such belief is lacking. Art, for better or worse, reflects an age's beliefs, or lack of them, and we live in a skeptical age, one disillusioned with its public figures, an age of the antihero. So abstract sculpture is what we shall find in front of Cincinnati's highrises. It has merits of its own, not the least of which is that the works themselves, the Sugarman and the Rickey, for example, are often good fun. And they validate the concept of the city as an open museum.

Looking south down Main St. from 5th, we catch sight of the Art Deco **Cincinnati Gas & Electric Building:** its carved stone balconies, its setbacks, its cornices, its pyramidal tower (lit at night a delicate gold, white, and green), its bas reliefs and its sculptures. Huge eagles support the urns below the tower. The decoration, less exuberant than that of the *Times-Star,* nonetheless shares a kinship with it. John Russell Pope—Washington's austere classicist—designed this exterior.

Ahead on 5th St., dominating Government Square, looms the **U.S. Post Office and Courthouse** (1939). A surprising nine stories high (count them at the back), this structure rivals in dullness the Federal Building (1964) across Main St. These two monoliths, along with the Hamilton County Courthouse (1919), four blocks north at Court and Main streets, offer us a brief, though instructive, lesson in governmental architecture. Several decades apart in construction, they form a sequence that reveals the changing, yet unchanging, nature of the "classical" governmental style. In architecture the federal government has not set the pace: its notions regarding style lag even behind those of the general public. The Hamilton County Courthouse of 1919 has a full-blown classical façade, with columns fully disengaged. By the late 1930s, when the Post Office was built, governmental façades had become (as Lois Craig has observed) "simplified, their classical ornaments turning angular and disappearing into the masonry, their walls becoming more planar and their window openings shallow and anonymous. What resulted was a gaunt, underfed, 'starved' classicism." Exterior surfaces became continuous and unembellished. This minimal classicism, a variant of Art Deco, is sometimes termed classical moderne, or PWA moderne. "Flattened, sterilized, and abstracted forms" of buildings such as the Post Office mark, believes the architectural historian Vincent Scully, "the last phase of the Beaux-Arts in America." After World War II, the Modern Movement's influence diluted the classical tradition even further. Except by its form and size, the 1964 Federal Building is virtually unrecognizable as classical.

A century ago, a gigantic Victorian Post Office and Federal Building (1874–1885) occupied this site. Government architect Alfred B. Mullett (who attended Farmers' College in College Hill, a Cincinnati suburb) was responsible for the initial design; Samuel Hannaford was supervising architect. In appearance this splendid French Renaissance chateau, long a Cincinnati landmark, was comparable to Washington's still-standing Executive Office Building (originally the State, War, and Navy Building). The Pavillon Denon of the New Louvre, the archetype of the grandiose Second Empire style in America, provided the model for both the Washington and Cincinnati buildings.

The attractive **bus concourse** (1978) on the square's north side offers sheltered waiting areas made of glass, metal, and stone. They even appear to be designed more for the comfort of people than for the display of advertising. Curvilinear below and rectilinear above, the shelters maintain the pyramidal motif that we have come to recognize as characteristic of Cincinnati. Lighting bollards, trash receptacles, paving blocks designating bus paths: all contribute to the harmony of effect. We even see, on a direct axis, the Tyler Davidson Fountain. A century ago, instead of buses, big hay wagons filled the area. Today buses leave from Government Square to most parts of the city and its suburbs; maps on kiosks indicate routes. Cincinnati's Metro (as the system is called) deserves its excellent reputation for maintaining schedule. In 1985 the American Public Transit Association rated the Metro the best system in the country.

Our final piece of public sculpture on this tour is the twenty-seven-foot high *Metrobot* (as it is known) standing in front of the Contemporary Arts Center. The center commissioned it from Korean-born artist, Nam June Paik, a sculptor and video artist who specializes in creating works from TV sets. Unveiled in October 1988, *Metrobot,* a congeries of television-like cubes, has a neon smile, a pulsating violet heart, and no doubt a cheerful soul. The creature tells time, promotes the center's current exhibits via the video screens, and displays ads on a left "arm" that is a programmable electronic sign. It has a sense of civic responsibility, too, for built into the back of its left knee is a most unusual public telephone. Of the sculptures we have seen, this one appears to have it all: it instructs, it says something about our age, it is semiabstract yet recognizably in the robot tradition, and it is lots of fun.

The **Tri-State Building** (1902), on the southeast corner of Walnut and 5th streets, was built for the Cincinnati Traction Company (thus the building's earlier name as the Traction Building) which ran the city's streetcar system. Designed by Daniel Burnham Associates, a Chicago architectural firm whose work we will encounter several times on 4th St., it is one of Cincinnati's more attractive turn-of-the-century highrises. Tri-State, resembling a classical column, is also tri-partite and tri-colored: pink granite at the "base," multishaded red brick in the "shaft," gray-beige stone for the top or "capital." Particularly masterful are the elaborate brick patterns.

One block more, and we again find ourselves at Fountain Square.

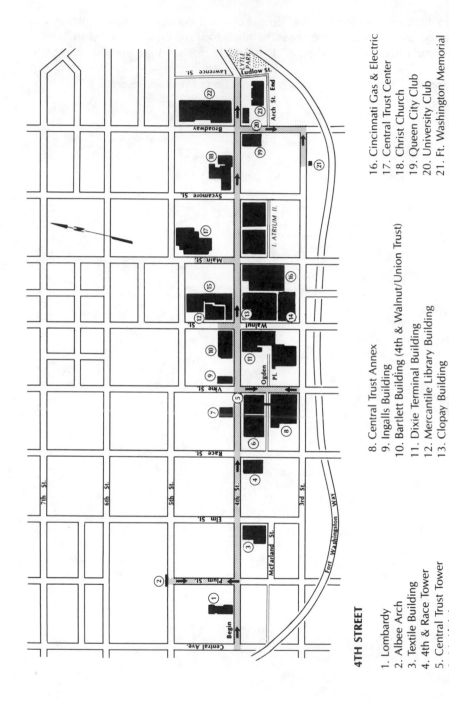

4TH STREET

1. Lombardy
2. Albee Arch
3. Textile Building
4. 4th & Race Tower
5. Central Trust Tower
6. McAlpin's
7. Gidding-Jenny
8. Central Trust Annex
9. Ingalls Building
10. Bartlett Building (4th & Walnut/Union Trust)
11. Dixie Terminal Building
12. Mercantile Library Building
13. Clopay Building
14. 312 Walnut
15. Formica Building—Contemporary Arts Center
16. Cincinnati Gas & Electric
17. Central Trust Center
18. Christ Church
19. Queen City Club
20. University Club
21. Ft. Washington Memorial
22. Western-Southern Complex
23. Guilford School

4th Street

4

EVERY street, from the meanest alley to the grandest boulevard, has its particular character. It comes from somewhere, it goes somewhere else; it has movement, it has direction. Usually a street's character changes over its length, often many times. At 4th St. and Central Ave., where this tour begins, we contemplate a cluster of late nineteenth-century commercial and apartment buildings. Fourth St. gradually becomes the city's major shopping, commercial, and financial thoroughfare, then resumes a more modest scale before terminating in the oasis of green that is Lytle Park. Bounded by interstates at either extremity, 4th is almost exactly one mile long. We traverse it from its western end to its eastern.

Fourth St. originally lay on the village outskirts. Then as 3rd St. assumed dominant commercial prominence in the early nineteenth century, 4th became a prestigious residential address. After mid-century the street supported a variety of activities: elegant townhouses there still were, but now also hotels, churches, department stores, educational institutions. "Pre-eminently the fashionable street of the city," D. J. Kenny called it in his 1875 guide to Cincinnati. Inevitably, the carriage-trade shops took over, though even now a few (converted) townhouses survive. After 1900 a burst of highrise construction, prompted by major banks moving up from 3rd to join the department stores, transformed 4th St. into the city's business and financial district. The street's central blocks, as we see them today, resulted from the building that took place between 1900 and 1913. In the early 1980s another wave of highrise construction rolled over Cincinnati, again a response to economic forces. But most of the new buildings went up on 5th St., not 4th. In the early 1990s the city's most recent tall buildings are rising on 3rd.

Of Cincinnati's downtown streets, only 4th partakes (somewhat) of the nature of a Manhattan canyon with long shadows and the reverberating clang of automobiles. Buildings front directly onto the sidewalk, giving the street a big-city feel. Though Cincinnati has no "grand" avenue like New York's Fifth Avenue or Chicago's North Michigan, the "Magnificent Mile," in 4th it has a street of genuine urban distinction. On weekdays at least, it generates the kind of authority that characterizes a great street.

Try to take this tour on a weekday, for then you will experience the bustle of Cincinnati's downtown life. On weekdays you can also enter the lobbies of many buildings. Some are closed on Saturday, almost all on Sundays and holidays. In order to see the buildings better, we will find ourselves moving from one side of the street to the other. The sidewalk on 4th's south side, between Central Ave. and Plum St., has been rejuvenated with alternating paving brick and cement. It is forested with Moraine Locusts, a tree that, along with the Little Leaf Lindens that we observe elsewhere downtown, does well in an intensely developed urban environment.

At the corner of Central Avenue and 4th we discover one of Cincinnati's **wall paintings.** Nine paintings (of ten commissioned) by local artists went up around downtown between 1971 and 1973 as part of the community project entitled Urban Walls, Cincinnati, sponsored by the Carl Solway Gallery (314 West 4th); other wall paintings were produced with Solway's advice and assistance. This one (designed by Margaret Wenstrup) has an abstract pattern, its convolutions perhaps reflecting Ft. Washington Way, the traffic distributor that here bends round the southwest corner of downtown and whose roar we hear. "Urban walls ask people to react," John A. Chewning, the project's historian, has written, "perhaps for the first time in their lives, to the intrusion of design in their environment. Urban walls ask people to look up from the sidewalk and keep looking up. Maybe they will see more—upper stories of buildings, architectural curiosities, city sky."

On the other side of 4th and Central is the four-story **Wells' Building** (1865; remodeled 1876, 1985). The Ionic pilasters framing the entrance lead the eye up to an unusual pedimented cornice. A mansard roof tops this Italianate structure. The building is clad in orange-red brick. What brownstone is to Manhattan or *pietra serena* to Florence or greystone to Montreal, orange-red brick is to Cincinnati, at least to the nineteenth-century city. And, unlike these somber colored materials, Cincinnati's brick is warm and cheerful, even on dullish days. We shall often encounter this pumpkin-colored brick in our excursions around the older city. Whereas the limestone lintels of the Wells' Building and of other Cincinnati edifices usually derive from quarries in eastern Ohio or south-central Indiana, its older brick, soft and porous but attractive in its coloration, came from kilns along the nearby Millcreek Valley. The orange reflects the soil content from which it is made.

Fourth St. between Central Avenue and Plum St. is one of the two chief remaining bits of downtown with a group of late nineteenth-century commercial and high-density residential buildings. The block is listed on the National Register of Historic Places. In 1985 the city planning commission made a daring proposal to turn most of 4th St. into a new kind of historic district. Rather than try to preserve every structure, the proposal would mesh new development with historic buildings. The ordinance establishing a Fourth Street Historic District, from Central Ave. to Race St., passed City Council in April 1986. It protected as "local landmarks" about fifty buildings, about half built before 1885. But the Council, bowing to pressure from business interests, excepted by a five-to-four vote twelve of 4th's major buildings. Though none of the twelve lies under immediate threat, without the protection of the city's tough preservation statutes their ultimate survival may well be problematic.

Several buildings that we see before us hum with new life: art galleries occupy the ground floor, refurbished apartments the upper levels. A number of galleries occupy space on the north side of the street, several in the same building. This block, if not exactly Greenwich Village or SoHo, provides the city with a modest contemporary arts presence.

Alterations in commercial structures occur most frequently on the ground floor. Even on this level, however, nineteenth-century elements often survive. Number 340, for example, retains its fine oak doorway. The gallery to the right still has its original cast iron façade: the decorative ironwork below the window remains intact. Number 330, the **Biltmore Building** (ca. 1880), the block's tallest structure, began life as the Henrietta Apartments. Although its ground-level façade has undergone alteration, the incised curvilinear design in the stonework still entertains the eye. The wrought-iron balcony and fire escape railings are superb. Everywhere on this block old and new exist in (usually) appealing conjunction.

Number 322 is the **Lombardy** (1881). Thomas Emery's Sons commissioned this seven-story apartment building from Samuel Hannaford. It caught on immediately. An early tenant, occupant of flat 25, was the rising young attorney William Howard Taft, who lived here until his marriage in 1886. Today, this building, vacant since 1976 and long neglected, hangs on tenuously to life. Even in its decrepit state, its Renaissance Revival façade of cut sandstone offers an architectural cornucopia: incised decoration, ornate brackets supporting an elaborate pressed-metal cornice, the whole topped by a spectacular pediment dormer. The interior, which we cannot enter, has marble floors and one of the city's first passenger elevators. If restored inside and out, the Lombardy would dominate the block.

The idea of apartments, or **"flats"** as they were originally called, is a relatively new one in Western society. (The word *flat* arose because, instead of the up-and-down of houses, the entire living area was on one level.) To meet the enormous population pressures on them, nineteenth-century cities had to accommodate more and more people—this at a time before efficient transportation had brought the suburbs within easy reach. Nineteenth-century urban life gradually separated living and labor. Residences over shop or office became rarer. Apartment buildings reflected this separation. The first apartment houses specifically designed as "flats" went up in Paris in the 1850s. Class-conscious Londoners resisted the idea until the 1870s. If well-to-do, they reasoned, you had a house. Why live horizontally in a flat when you could live vertically in your own home?

Flats also caught on slowly in the United States. Apartment houses (i.e., for the middle class, as opposed to tenements for the poor) appeared in New York after 1870, in Chicago a few years later. "French" flats they were sometimes called, or "Parisian" flats, perhaps to suggest continental glamor, perhaps also, as Mark Girouard conjectures, to "free the buildings of any associations with tenements." Eventually they became known as "apartments," also a French word (*appartement*) in origin. Hardly less than the English, blue-blooded Americans took slowly to the idea that they could share with unknown others sudden, unexpected intimacy in public stairs and hallways—and in the newfangled elevators—and still remain respectable. In *The Age of Innocence* (1920), set in 1870s New York, Edith Wharton records society's wonder before the decision of Mrs. Manson Mingott, a venerable society dowager, to live on one floor of her townhouse. Visitors were "startled and fascinated by the foreignness of this arrangement, which recalled scenes in French fiction, and architectural incentives to immorality such as the simple American had never dreamed of. That was how women with lovers lived in the wicked old societies, in apartments with all the rooms on one floor, and all the indecent propinquities that their novels described." A one-floor apartment created, in effect, "the stage-setting of adultery." To attract a proper clientele, therefore, flats in the New World had to imply respectability. They also had to offer the last word in urban amenities. The Lombardy's five-room units provided such luxuries as private baths and full kitchens.

Cincinnati's Lombardy went up in 1881, two years before New York's oldest surviving apartment building, The Grammercy; in its sumptuous living spaces, the Lombardy anticipates the fabulous Dakota (1884) on Manhattan's Central Park West. But living closely together has rarely appealed to Americans. The vogue for these luxurious apartment buildings was as brief in Cincinnati as it was in most other American cities. The middle class followed the wealthy—and the streetcar—into the suburbs. In the 1920s Cincinnati witnessed a revival of interest in large apartment buildings, but few have gone up since.

314 West 4th (1883), Renaissance Revival like the Lombardy, has simpler detailing and touches of the rectilinear neo-Grec style. Occupying the first level is the Carl Solway Gallery, sponsor of Urban Walls and for the past quarter of a century a vital link between local collectors of modern art and the New York art scene.

We arrive at Plum St. The building at **4th & Plum** (1921), on the southeast corner, underwent conversion to apartments in 1980. Two stories were added on, recessed balconies installed, and a pool was put in on the top floor. The building once served as headquarters for the Gibson Art Company, now Gibson Greeting Cards; in 1959 it began twenty-one years as a municipal garage. A walkway links 4th & Plum to the red-brick extension of the former Cincinnati Gas-Light & Coke Building (1870), designed by James McLaughlin. Recently the company's former headquarters building, on the southwest corner, has also undergone conversion. Converting commercial buildings into apartments has given downtown a needed influx of new residents. Anywhere downtown lies within a ten-minute walk.

Note the **street furniture.** Just in from the southwest corner of 4th and Plum Streets are several antique cast-iron bishop's crook lampposts. Their shafts reveal fluting, acanthus-leaf motifs, and other ornamentation; the "crook" above sports the traditional curlicue known as a *feuille rinceau,* French for curling or scrolled leaf, or arabesque. Over the street looms a modern multipurpose pole. Once, different light standards meant different kinds of light. The older lampposts gave out light that was soft, yellow, picturesque, and insufficient; the newer, light that was harsh, white, glaring, and ample. Now the difference is less evident. Whereas the lamppost represents the survival of the old city, the pole symbolizes the new. The pole is undoubtedly more functional and efficient, but the lamppost possesses charming decorative detail that today's street furniture often lacks. Old and new coexisting together suggests that a vibrant downtown needs both. As a visual bonus, look down at the sidewalk (still on the southwest corner) at a whimsical circular mosaic (1988) of intertwining animals—a black wolf, a brown snake's head, a large red deer—by Jan Marx Knoop. The mosaic, entitled *In This Together,* is an ecological statement but also a reminder that in our city walks we should look down as well as up and around.

Blocking the vista to the north is the Albert B. Sabin **Convention Center** (1966; 1987). Convention centers are, by their nature, big and dull. Normally they present completely blank walls to the city around them. They lack windows because those who hire them want to be able to control interior lighting in displaying their wares. Making a two-block long building humane, or even interesting, is the toughest possible challenge for an architect, but CRSS of Houston rose to the challenge. Extensive remodeling, using black and rose granite, transformed the awkward modernist design of 1966 into a successful postmodern composition, with stylized classical motifs, awash in trendy purple and browns. A modest triumph!

Incorporated into the 5th St. façade is the monumental white marble Palladian **Albee arch.** Once it adorned the Albee Theatre (1927), formerly on Fountain Square, razed in March 1977. Thomas W. Lamb, the leading theater architect of the day, designed the Albee. Seating 3500 and Cincinnati's finest theater in size and in luxury of decor, it offered both movies and stage shows. Lamb also designed Manhattan's Strand (1914) and Rivoli (1917) and Boston's Savoy (1928). A huge Palladian arch was his hallmark. Unlike many fragments saved with local hurrahs that subsequently turn out to be disappointments when set up elsewhere, this arch, spare and majestic, looks splendid in its new location.

Until 1989, when it was knocked down, a building to the east of the arch sported the most risqué of Cincinnati's wall paintings: eight scenes relating the progress of a bedroom encounter between a man and a woman that ends in an embrace. The last of the original set of Urban Walls, this work by Thomas B. Smith was completed in the summer of 1973. When the painting first became shabby, the building's owner wanted to cover it over. The resulting uproar forced him to reconsider. This supposedly staid city never fails to surprise!

Midway up the next block (no. 221), we come upon a Queen Anne commercial building (1881). Designed by Edwin Anderson, it has a cut stone façade and an ornate gabled center bay. Although the ground-floor modernization is unsatisfactory and several roofline anthemions have disappeared, the building largely retains its structural integrity. It now houses Contemporary Galleries, which has kept the old stairways and, on the top floor, most of the old lights.

On the corner stands the imposing twelve-story **Textile Building** (1905; 1985). This Renaissance Revival structure reveals Chicago school influence in its triple-bay windows. For decades the Textile Building housed under one roof a number of clothing-related industries. Its ornament is nothing if not large-scaled: wide terra cotta bands, gigantic cartouches below the top floor, and a mighty cornice. The architect was Gustav W. Drach; Glaser & Myers handled the excellent 1985 restoration. Montgomery Schuyler, America's most distinguished architectural critic of

Albee Arch, Sabin Convention Center. This majestic Palladian arch originally formed part of the façade of the Albee
Theater (1927) on Fountain Square. The theater was demolished in 1977 and the arch installed here ten years later.

the time, deplored the building's "unaffected ugliness and bare utilitarianism. . . .
The cornice projecting above the eighth story . . . is a futile sacrifice to the graces."
If the graces disdained this sacrifice, I do not. Such bold profiling was necessary for
the building to stand out in Cincinnati's sooty atmosphere. Most of what we think
of as Victorian gloom is twentieth-century grime. Until older buildings are cleaned,
it takes a considerable effort of imagination to envisage their original appearance.
The classical-style structures of "The White City," the 1893 Columbian Exposition
in Chicago, prompted light-colored buildings to sprout across the United States.
Twentieth-century highrises abandoned Victorian red brick and Richardsonian Romanesque's dark browns in favor of white and gray tones. The Textile Building must
be one of Cincinnati's latest-built edifices to flaunt its dazzling multicolored bricks
and orange terra cotta bands.

Urban Wall. This most risqué of the "Urban Walls" paintings shows a woman moving, step by tentative step, toward an embrace with a man. The building it adorned, on 5th St. near Elm, was torn down in 1989 for a hotel that has not been built.

In the middle of the Elm to Vine St. block we find three High Victorian Italianate buildings. Two have lost their cornices; that on the left (1876) gives the impression of being three, but the regularity of its window design and cornice line indicates it is actually one. Pigalls, now a popular upscale café, occupies a three-story structure (ca. 1830), originally Greek Revival, now heavily altered with labeled window molds and crowned by a crenellated parapet.

Prior to the early 1980s downtown Cincinnati underwent two major construction booms: one after the turn of the century, the other in the late 1920s. The Textile Building went up during the first boom, the **Fourth & Race Tower** (1927), at 105 West 4th, during the second. This elegant oyster-colored structure was designed by Tietig and Lee in association with Hake and Kuck. It is in a demure neoclassical style, appealing in its simplicity, that derives via English Palladianism from the Italian Renaissance. Originally occupied by the Federal Reserve Bank of Cleveland, the building housed on its *piano nobile,* or second floor, the Cincinnati Chamber of Commerce. Above the entrance and windows are cast-bronze griffins holding up chests. In 1985, when the marble and limestone façade underwent a scrubbing, the griffins emerged as if new-born from sixty years of soot and urban pollution. Griffins, mythological beasts, have the head, wings, and forelegs of an eagle and the rear quarters of a lion. Frequently pictured as guardians of goldmines, they eventually came to represent trade and security: thus their symbolic appropriateness for the Chamber of Commerce. The lobby reflects pre-Depression opulence: elaborate chandeliers hang from the copper and gilt ceiling. The bank area, traditional as that in the 580 Building (chapter 3) was untraditional, has solid walnut paneling and elaborate rosettes in its coffered ceiling.

So badly designed is the parking garage (1960, by Raymond Loewy) across the street that it interrupts the sidewalk flow. Favoring automobile ramps over sidewalks does the pedestrian public a disservice: it reverses what should be the city's priorities. Tucked into the garage's eastern end is Closson's, founded by A. Burton Closson, Jr., in 1866 and the oldest furniture and decorative arts gallery west of New York, one of the oldest in the United States. In 1883 Closson's sponsored a major exhibit of young Cincinnati artists, the "Duveneck boys," after Frank Duveneck, the premier painter to emerge from the Cincinnati area. Closson's second-floor art gallery regularly puts on interesting shows. Period and contemporary art nudge each other in unexpected juxtaposition.

East up 4th St., the thirty-four story **Central Trust Tower** (1913) dominates the view. Buildings in the blocks before it rise toward its pyramidal peak. The Central Trust Tower, known until 1964 as the Union Central Building, was Cincinnati's response to the early wave of gigantic skyscrapers. When completed, it stood the tallest building outside New York City, fifth tallest in the world. Cass Gilbert designed it in collaboration with the Cincinnati firm of Garber & Woodward, whose first major commission it was and whose work we shall encounter frequently along 4th. In its dazzling white terra cotta and its tower rising from a larger base, the Central Trust Tower recalls Manhattan's Woolworth Building, also by Gilbert. Even the date of completion, 1913, corresponds. The light-weight, fire-resistant white terra cotta in both glistens to this day. Terra cotta is self-cleaning, which explains the Central Trust Tower's remarkable brightness. Both structures top out in a pyramidal form. Whereas the Woolworth has French Gothic ornament, the Central Trust combines Classical with Renaissance.

The Woolworth Building we may admire from City Hall Park across Broadway; the Central Trust Tower, more difficult to gain a perspective on, we see best from 4th St. or from Ft. Washington Way. It looks good both at a distance and close up. As the Woolworth Building was the world's tallest before the Chrysler Building briefly surpassed it in 1929, so the Central Trust Tower ranked as Cincinnati's tallest, and the tallest structure west of the Hudson, until the Carew Tower's completion in 1930. It culminated downtown's first wave of expansion, the Carew the second. A skyscraper, Louis Sullivan wrote in 1896, "must be every inch a proud and soaring thing." His own were not, but buildings in the twentieth century began to soar. Soar the Central Trust did and does. For nearly two decades no other structure challenged its height. The Central Trust remains one of Cincinnati's luminous buildings, one that expands our conception of what a skyscraper can be.

Cass Gilbert, like many architects trained in the New York office of McKim, Mead, & White, then the United States's most prestigious architectural firm, viewed the skyscraper in terms of a classical column composed of base, shaft, and capital. The model for the Central Trust, as for many other turn-of-the-century American

Central Trust Tower. The view is from 4th & Race looking east. Once the tallest building west of the Hudson, the Central Trust is exactly contemporaneous with Manhattan's Woolworth Building and was designed by the same architect, Cass Gilbert. Its gleaming white terra cotta dazzles as brightly today as when first unveiled in 1913. The upper structure is Gilbert's imaginative rendering of the tomb of Mausolus, one of the Seven Wonders of the ancient world. The skywalk in this recent photograph connected two department stores, McAlpins on the right and Pogue's (latterly L. S. Ayres) on the left. The Pogue's building has since been torn down. A new skywalk will connect Tower Place, its replacement (scheduled for 1991 completion), with McAlpin's.

skyscrapers, was the freestanding campanile of Venice's St. Mark's. The campanile was itself based on a classical column. A building's elevations, Sullivan had argued, should roughly correspond to a column's dimensions. Many early skyscrapers like this one have a three- or four-story "base" that relates it to people on the street. The "shaft," the main part of the building, leads the eye to a clearly demarcated "capital" of several stories that culminates in a cornice.

The Central Trust Tower follows this basic pattern, but then becomes fanciful. After the cornice three further stages rise up like an elaborate wedding cake. The Carew observation deck offers the best view of this elaborate superstructure. The first stage presents a four-sided façade of four massive columns with two pilasters at each end (the technical term for this arrangement is *tetrastyle in antis*). Above the columns sits an extravaganza of a pyramid, which, in turn, culminates in a miniature temple (that conceals the smokestack). As noted earlier, this superstructure replicates, imaginatively, reconstruction drawings of the fourth-century B.C. Mausoleum at Halicarnassus. Old photographs reveal that originally the Central Trust's superstructure sprouted finials at several levels and that the miniature temple had a sharply raked pediment. Both finials and pediment would have further accented the building's upward sweep. Evenings, a golden light floods this spectacular upper structure.

Between Race and Vine streets we are in department store territory. Until April 1988 L. S. Ayres occupied four buildings (1878, 1888, 1902, 1914) on the street's north side. Its closing left Cincinnati with only two full-service department stores downtown, McAlpin's and Lazarus: not what it ought to be, but two more than Toledo and Detroit. Until 1983 the H. and S. Pogue Co. occupied this space. Henry and Samuel Pogue had founded the original dry goods store in 1863. In the 1930s Pogue's expanded into the adjoining Carew Tower, then thirty years later leapt across the Carew's arcade. Planned to open on this site in 1991 is a three-story urban mall, Tower Place, a collection of upscale shops with a glass atrium. Across the street is the jewelry store **Newstedt-Loring Andrews,** designed (ca. 1875) by James W. McLaughlin and remodeled (1930) by Garber and Woodward. The firm, a 1965 merger, goes back to 1805. The 1875 building looked medieval; the decoration of metal and glazed tiles, in an interlocking pattern, suggests Arts and Crafts influence, as do the building materials. So oversized a cornice, so diminutive a building! The full-façade three-story bay window, along with the overbearing cornice, makes Newstedt-Loring Andrews a most unusual commercial structure.

Next door, **McAlpin's,** the city's second oldest department store, occupies three adjoining structures. Ellis, McAlpin & Co., a dry goods firm originally, began in 1852; in 1880 George Washington McAlpin became sole proprietor; when he died ten years later his brother William assumed control. Designed by major Cincinnati architects, the McAlpin's buildings are more interesting than at first they may appear. James McLaughlin erected that on the left in 1858 for the John S. Shillito Co., James Keys Wilson that in the center in 1873 as showrooms for Mitchell and Rammelsberg, one of the largest furniture companies in the United States. (McLaughlin, we remember, later did the pioneering Shillito's building on Race; Wilson designed the Wise Temple.) Both buildings are in Renaissance Revival commercial styles. In

1878, after Shillito's had left for its larger quarters at 7th and Race streets, Mc-Alpin's moved into the Shillito store, then in 1901 took over the adjoining building. The third structure, architect unknown, has musical motifs on its façade and dates from 1903. Although the lower stories of all three have been brutalized, their upper stories retain traces of their original form under the paint. Above the second floor of the second building we spot a lady wearing pearls. The famous sidewalk clock dates from 1901. Among Cincinnati's department-store dynasties McAlpin's, not locally owned since 1916, is the only name to survive.

We return to 4th St.'s north side. **Gidding-Jenny** (1880s; remodeled in 1907 and 1965) has an elaborate cast-iron façade with inlaid polychromed Rookwood tiles. The original building was redesigned by noted New York architect Frank Mills Andrews. Appropriately, a shop that sells fashionable women's clothing boasts the street's most stunning exterior. John D. Wareham, a leading Rookwood artist, designed the fruit and floral bouquets. On either side of the huge cartouche appears a lady in headdress. Indian motifs combine with Art Nouveau exuberance to produce a feast for the eye. Adjoining is the **Herschede Building** (ca. 1860), Renaissance Revival, from which curious heads peer down from keystones.

On the northwest corner is the **German National Bank Building** designed in 1904 by Rapp, Zettel, and Rapp in a pure Beaux Arts style. Cincinnati has few examples of this style, which takes its name from Paris's Ecole des Beaux Arts. The structure began as the German National Bank, changed its name in 1917 to Lincoln, and now houses a branch of Ameritrust. Its splendid arches are best seen from Vine St. The building's line of descent goes back initially to Richard Morris Hunt's Lenox Library (1877) in Manhattan, ultimately to Henri Labrouste's Bibliothèque Sainte-Geneviève (1850) in Paris. All three buildings have huge Roman thermal windows, roundels between the windows, and a second cornice line bisecting them.

We may now admire the Central Trust Tower from close up. Cream-colored marble facing, deeply rusticated, covers the first three floors. The façade is that of an Italian Renaissance palazzo. The rustication continues, less pronounced, on the terra cotta walls rising from the base. This pattern is virtually identical to that created by Michelozzo for the Palazzo Medici (1460) in Florence. The Central Trust's second story maintains such huge proportions because it was designed to house the Chamber of Commerce. The *piano nobile* of Italian palazzi was often reserved for public functions. Cass Gilbert maintained that use here. Scroll-like acanthus leaves ornament the entrance on 4th St. Further up, on each of two cartouches a mother pelican feeds a nest of little ones. Why? Until 1964 the building served as the home office for the Union Central Life Insurance Company. Founded in 1867 by the Methodist Church, it often used Methodist preachers as agents. Early Christians viewed the pelican as an image of Christ: as He sacrificed Himself for man's salvation, so in legend did the pelican pierce its breast to give blood to its young so that they might live. The pelicans on the façade in effect admonish us to buy insurance to protect our own young.

Where now stands the Central Trust Tower once stood the **Chamber of Com-**

4th St., looking east from in front of McAlpin's, 1990. In the far distance we make out the Parish House of Christ Church. Preceding it up 4th St. on the left are the Gidding-Jenny Building, the Herschede Building, the Ingalls Building, the Fourth National Bank Building, and the Bartlett Building. The clock before McAlpin's was installed in 1901.

merce Building (1888–1889). A late work of H. H. Richardson, the building went up after the architect's death in 1886. This granite Teutonic castle in the architect's massive Romanesque style had tapered corner towers and a high peaked roof. Although the 1904 Baedeker's guide rated the Chamber of Commerce "perhaps the finest building in the city," most architectural historians do not rank it among Richardson's more innovative works. The still-standing Flour and Grain Exchange Building (1889–1892) in Boston by Richardson's successor firm, Shepley, Rutan, and Coolidge, gives some idea of what Cincinnati's Chamber of Commerce looked like. On the night of January 10, 1911, a grease fire in its upper stories got out of control and this allegedly fireproof building burned. Though its walls still stood, it was judged irreparable.

The eagles that once perched on the dormer windows of the Chamber of Commerce Building now flank Eden Park Drive on either side of the Melan Arch Bridge

4th St., the same view, looking east in 1907. The north side of this portion of 4th was substantially complete by 1907. The imposing Third National Bank Building, with its three-story Ionic columns, has been replaced by an extension of Gidding-Jenny, then J. M. Gidding & Co. The western five bays of the Bartlett Building, originally the Union Savings Bank (1901), were added in 1914. On the south side of the street until 1911, where the Central Trust Tower now stands, was the massive Chamber of Commerce Building. Across Vine St. stood the brand new Sinton Hotel. Courtesy of the Cincinnati Historical Society.

(chapter 12). Assorted fragments of its limestone façade long rested in Miami Heights, near the Indiana border, for eventual use in building an astronomical observatory. That did not happen. In the mid-1980s architecture students at the University of Cincinnati recovered a few of the fragments, made them into a sculptural composition, and set them up in the south end of Burnet Woods. Those interested in architectural lineage should keep in mind that the massive proportions, rough-hewn masonry, and distinct roofline of Richardson's Chamber of Commerce exerted a tremendous influence on numerous Cincinnati buildings, residential no less than public. Among the latter are City Hall, the Krippendorf Building, the original Cin-

Pelican feeding its chicks, Central Trust Tower. The pelican
in legend pierced its breast to provide food for its young.
In Christian tradition this act symbolizes Christ's sacrifice
for His flock. The icon is appropriate for a building that
once housed the Union Central Life Insurance Company,
founded by Methodists.

cinnati Art Museum, and a number of the city's public schools put up in the 1890s.
I wonder, too, if its huge pyramidal roof—a dominant feature of the skyline for over
twenty years—influenced the erection of other pyramidal Cincinnati buildings.

    We walk down Vine toward 3rd St. The Central Trust's seven-story Annex,
connected to the main building by a hyphen (two hyphens actually) was originally
intended to rise much higher. Inside the front door a plaque commemorates an Indian mound located here, destroyed by 1802; Judge Burnet's estate (on this site for

Chamber of Commerce (1888–1911). The only work in Cincinnati (and a largely posthumous one at that) by the nationally famous Boston architect, Henry Hobson Richardson. It burned in 1911. Two years later the Central Trust Tower went up on the site. Courtesy of the Cincinnati Historical Society.

the next twenty years); and the **Burnet House** (1850–1926), a famed hostelry and one of the Cincinnati buildings I would most like to have seen.

When Jacob Burnet arrived in Cincinnati in 1796, he found a village of 500 souls lodged in log cabins. In 1853, when he died, Cincinnati's leading citizen, the city boasted a huge, six-story domed structure that many thought the finest hotel in the land. Here stayed visiting celebrities: Clay, Webster, and Douglas; the Prince of Wales (Edward VII to be); the singer Jenny Lind; the failed revolutionary Louis Kossuth; thespians Edwin Booth and Sarah Bernhardt. Here Abraham Lincoln, with Generals Grant and Sherman, formulated plans for southern campaigns.

Isaiah Rogers, one of America's leading architects, designed the Burnet House. Often referred to as the father of the modern hotel, Rogers inaugurated an age of spectacular hotels in this country. Before coming to Cincinnati he had put up Boston's Tremont House (1829) and New York's Astor House (1836), establishments without parallel abroad and which Europeans regarded as the epitome of luxury.

Burnet House, 1850s. The Burnet House (1850), shown here in an early engraving in which it still had its dome, survived on the northwestern corner of 3rd & Vine until 1926. It was torn down for the Central Trust Annex. Designed by Isaiah Rogers, the Burnet House was one of the most imposing hotels in America and enjoyed considerable contemporary renown. Courtesy of the Cincinnati Historical Society.

"From the early days of the 19th century, hotels were social centers," Daniel J. Boorstin has observed. "In the period of most rapid urban growth, it was not by churches or government buildings but by hotels that cities judged themselves and expected others to judge them." The Burnet House achieved a vast contemporary renown. The *Illustrated London News,* not given to overpraising America, hailed it as "one of the most magnificent buildings of the kind in the Union." "The best Hotel I ever saw," opined Nathaniel Hawthorne's good friend H. A. Bright. Another visitor found it "more like a royal palace than anything else."

The Burnet House's **3rd St.** location reminds us that the city's center has gradually shifted, not only away from the Ohio River, but north and west. For most of Cincinnati's history 3rd St. divided downtown from the boisterous waterfront. Even more absolutely does Ft. Washington Way mark that division today. With 3rd's entire south side demolished for this traffic artery, the north side long projected a rather forlorn appearance. Early in the nineteenth century elegant Federal and Greek Revival houses lined the street. By mid-century it had become the city's financial center. Most insurance companies had offices on 3rd. Kenny's 1875 city guide called 3rd St. "the most important business street in the city." But when the Burnet House closed in 1926, 3rd had long since yielded primacy to 4th St. as the city's chief commercial artery. This dowdy thoroughfare now housed only lesser mercantile establishments. Today, with its buildings enjoying a river view and much new con-

Burnet House, early 1900s. The streets are relatively quiet in this turn-of-the-century photograph. Now over fifty years old, the Burnet House has lost its dome but gained an additional story and cornice line. Looming behind the Burnet House is Richardson's Chamber of
Commerce, which burned in 1911. Visible across 4th St. is the German National Bank,
erected in 1904. Courtesy of the Cincinnati Historical Society.

struction underway, 3rd is undergoing a major renaissance. With the Ohio River
again becoming Cincinnati's "main street," 3rd has become Cincinnati's most visible east-west axis.

We return to 4th and Vine streets. Every history of architecture mentions the
Ingalls Building on the northeast corner. Melville Ezra Ingalls, railroad tycoon and
banker, put up this sixteen-story structure (now called the ACI Building) in 1902–
1903. Instrumental in Cincinnati's development as a rail center, Ingalls formed in
1884 the Cincinnati, Indianapolis, St. Louis, and Chicago Railway Company, officially advertised and popularly known as the Big Four. By 1889 he had become a
Vanderbilt lieutenant and, as such, chief executive officer of a gigantic railroad complex. His civic activities in Cincinnati include chairing several of the industrial expositions and a thirty-year tenure, from 1884 to 1914, as president of the board of
trustees of the Cincinnati Art Museum. Beatrice Webb described him in 1898 as
"the best type of American corporation official—a kindly-natured man with broad
statesmanlike views. He is open-minded to new ideas, but shrewdly aware of the
ends *he* wishes to promote, namely the prosperity of the Big Four and his own
personal power."

In 1902 Ingalls declared his intention "to erect an everlasting monument to
Cincinnati; her progress and enterprise." The Ingalls Building, designed by Cincin-

Ingalls Building, 1904. This photograph shows the newly
completed Ingalls Building (1902–1903). It was taken from
the roof of the Burnet House; the granite walls of the Chamber of Commerce Building stand out on the left. On the far
right we discern the steel skeleton of the 4th National Bank
Building, completed in 1905. The Sinton Hotel rose out of
the pit in the foreground in 1907. The Provident Tower occupies the site today. Courtesy of the Cincinnati Historical
Society.

nati architects Alfred O. Elzner and George M. Anderson, was the first highrise of
reinforced concrete. The Ferro-Concrete Construction Company, organized in 1901
by William P. Anderson, Jr., and Tylor Field, put it up. Henry H. Hooper was engineer in charge. A plaque on the right side of the 4th St. entrance commemorates the
building's distinction as a pioneer.

The first skyscrapers of the 1880s and 1890s had been built on steel frames. In
1902 no one had constructed a concrete building more than half the Ingalls Building's height. Many persons thought that a tall building poured into concrete molds,
even reinforced with metal bars, must soon topple of its own weight. One Cincinnati
newspaperman, hoping to scoop his colleagues, stayed up all night to watch the
Ingalls fall down. Vermont marble (now somewhat corroded) faces the first three
stories; above that, wire anchors fix the wall facing of glazed buff-colored brick to

the concrete. Although the Ingalls Building has not fallen, some of its bricks have, for here and there we discern lighter-colored replacements. The Ingalls Building revolutionized the construction industry. In the late twentieth century at least half the new highrises built use reinforced concrete.

The glass and brick **Provident Tower** (1967) across the street was originally intended to rise much higher. Downtown Cincinnati has few glass structures. Glass does not harmonize well with the city's prevailing stone and brick. Cincinnati has always had a solid look. In 1841 James Silk Buckingham noted that it had "more buildings built of stone, and much fewer of wood, than in the Eastern seaboard cities." Within the Provident Tower are the offices of the American Financial Corporation (AFC), a major holding company. Owned by Cincinnati's most prominent financier, Carl H. Lindner, Jr., AFC in recent years has pursued an aggressive policy of expansion. In 1987 it acquired United Brands, a major U.S. meat packer and processor whose main line of business is property and casualty insurance; its Chiquita division is the world's largest supplier of bananas. In 1987 AFC also acquired Penn Central, which, no longer in railroads, now focuses on telecommunications, electronics, defense, and energy.

On the site of the Provident Tower stood the **Sinton Hotel** (1907), designed by Frank Mill Andrews, architect of Gidding-Jenny. The Sinton was, for a generation, the city's most stylish hotel. An imposing French Second Empire building, it was built like the Ingalls Building of reinforced concrete. Above its classical detailing rose a magnificent mansard roof. Four Rookwood panels executed for the Sinton's Grand Café now grace the Cincinnati Art Museum's Terrace Court Restaurant.

Before the Sinton, **Pike's Opera House** occupied the site. In 1851 Jenny Lind, the "Swedish Nightingale," toured the country under the auspices of P. T. Barnum. Everywhere she went she captured the hearts of Americans. Her five performances in Cincinnati, April 14–22, were great successes. So smitten by her singing was Samuel N. Pike, a wealthy distiller, that in 1859 he built an opera house so that she would have a place to sing in Cincinnati worthy of her. Holding three thousand people, Pike's had thirteen entrances and a black-and-white marble lobby. Touring operatic and dramatic companies considered it the best house west of the Alleghenies. In 1860 the young Adelina Patti sang here: in 1862 Wendell Phillips, the fiery abolitionist, raised a storm lecturing on "Slavery and the War"; and on April 17, 1865, the actor Junius Brutus Booth, brother of John Wilkes, heard here the news of Lincoln's assassination—and slipped quietly out of the city. Pike's burned the next year. In 1867 Pike had the house rebuilt in slightly less opulent fashion but as a concert hall, seating 1600; Isaiah Rogers & Son designed it. In 1871 Pike's again became, slightly enlarged, an opera house. For a generation more, until it burned for the second time in 1903, it was one of Cincinnati's showplaces and a center of its cultural life.

The **Fourth National Bank Building** (1905), on the north side of the street, is the last built of four early twentieth-century downtown skyscrapers in Cincinnati designed by the famous Chicago firm headed by Daniel H. Burnham. Oddly, the most recent is in appearance the most old-fashioned. It reflects the early twentieth-century convention of festooning office buildings, against which the International style would later react so strongly. Burnham here returned to Beaux Arts classicism. In design this building is akin to his Tri-State on 5th and Walnut streets. The colorful façade has imposing Tuscan columns of pink granite at the "base" (stories one to three), yellow and red brick horizontal bands in its "shaft" (stories four to nine), and a terra cotta "capital" (stories ten to twelve) with beguiling details. This intricate scheme is vertical-horizontal-vertical. The middle section's horizontal bands effectively balance the top and bottom. Ostensibly in the classical style traditionally favored by banks, the building explodes in lines, colors, and textures that are most unclassical. The entrance, redone in Art Deco geometric patterns, is unmarred (except by proximity) by the colorful, yet dreadful, protrusion on the right.

The eighteen-story **Bartlett Building** (1901) on Walnut St. anchors the block. Like highrises everywhere, it changes its name with each new owner. Until 1985, when bought by the Bartlett Company, it was known as the Fourth and Walnut Building. It began life as the Union Trust Building. Paid for by Jacob Schmidlapp, this structure was dedicated on New Year's Day of 1901. For his new bank building Schmidlapp hired a "prestige" architect, Daniel Burnham, coauthor of the master plan for the 1893 World's Columbian Exposition in Chicago and then at the height of his fame. More of an organizer than an original creator of architecture—Frank Lloyd Wright once called him an "impressario"—Burnham worked with the best designers, and around the turn of the century his firm produced a number of buildings in the East and Midwest. The five most westerly bays of the Union Trust, also by the Burnham firm, were added in 1914; they sharply diminish the building's original vertical emphasis. This highly symmetrical structure has tripartite Chicago-style windows. Unlike most Chicago-style windows (where the large central pane does not open), these actually open in all three sections. Schmidlapp, the builder, was one of the city's leading entrepreneurs. He made his fortune in whisky, then organized the Union Savings Bank and Trust Company. Subsequently, he developed low-cost housing in Cincinnati for the poor, including the black poor, much of which still stands. His Model Homes Co., founded in 1911, gained nationwide recognition. The foundation he established still does good work in the city.

The Union Trust began the boom that, for more than seventy-five years, made 4th St. the city's financial center. In 1890 at least fifteen banks had addresses on 3rd. For another decade it remained the hub of Cincinnati's commercial activity. The Union Trust Building not only changed downtown's look, it changed its character. In the years before World War I downtown underwent a metamorphosis. From a mixed neighborhood of residences, apartments, rooming houses, schools, churches, markets, and manufacturing plants, it became a more uniform place dominated by banks, office buildings, and large department stores. Within six years of the Union Trust's arrival in 1901, four more banks had put up headquarters on 4th. Two also chose Burnham as their architect. In addition to the Union Trust and the Fourth National Bank Building, he designed the Tri-State and the Clopay Building—the latter catty-cornered from the Union Trust—which we shall consider shortly. The 4th St. we know today thus resulted from fundamental changes in the community's economic life. "The new skyscrapers," Compton Allyn has pointed out, "not only provided badly needed office space but also made an unmistakable visual statement of the increased role of financial institutions in the local community." There had always been rivalries between cities, but in the early twentieth century they grew more intense. A city's buildings were (and are) symbols of its standing in the urban community; they also made (and make) statements about its economic wellbeing. Cincinnati's rash of turn-of-the-century highrises indicated its determination to stand tall among the nation's cities.

The Union Trust Building was Cincinnati's first skyscraper. We may define a *skyscraper* as a building, usually with a steel skeleton, exceeding five stories. The word itself began to be used in this sense in the 1880s, and in 1891 the *American Slang Dictionary* defined it as "a very tall building, such as now are being built in Chicago." Originally, sailors in the eighteenth century had used the word to describe a sailing ship's topmost canvas. *Skyscraper* spawned *skyline,* first used later in the 1890s, to describe the new image of downtown created by the skyscrapers. The debut of the passenger elevator around 1870 made upper stories accessible without coronary mishap. With this achievement, the race for verticality was on. The other major breakthrough was the skeletal steel frame. Until the mid 1890s the massive masonry walls needed to support a tall building had limited height. Now buildings began to soar. The skeletal steel frame along with reinforced concrete (used in the Ingalls Building) represented major technological breakthroughs. Chicago architects developed many of these new techniques, and skyscrapers designed by them went up in cities across the land. *Highrise,* an Americanism, first began to afflict ears in the 1950s. Whether skyscraper or highrise, tall buildings have a strong claim to be regarded as an indigenous American building type.

Across the street is the **Dixie Terminal Building** (1921), Renaissance Revival in style. One of its shop fronts holds the downtown branch of **Graeter's,** a family-run ice cream and pastry concern (since 1871) with a rabid local following. Colorful Rookwood tiles surround the huge, slightly off-center arched entrance; signature pieces, "Rookwood" on them, appear at the bottom of the central posts. The grandiose lobby, the finest interior space on 4th St., is in the form of a Roman barrel vault. The picture window at the far end, actually a relatively recent alteration, draws us irresistibly to it for its view of the Stadium and the Roebling (Suspension) Bridge. Inset bronze eagles, worn down over the decades by human feet, adorn the marble floor. Off the arcade above, with its balustraded balconies, is the Cincinnati Stock Exchange, the smallest of the nation's five regional stock exchanges. The ceiling decoration, Adamesque in inspiration, is a subtle composition in marine, gold, ivory, and royal blue. It is well worth climbing the stairs to admire its detail. On the fanciful medallions a *putto,* or boy, rides a grasshopper, caresses a swan, catches a horse, spears a fish, rides a chariot pulled by rabbits, yawns at the sunrise, and holds a turtle by the tail. On several medallions he hammers away at the bust of an unknown individual. What can be happening? Rumor has it that the face caricatures the building's architects, Garber and Woodward, and their attorney Henry Lynch.

Descending to the lobby's lower level, we discover the Dixie Terminal's ostensible *raison d'être*: it once functioned as the major gateway for streetcar (and, after 1936, bus) transportation from northern Kentucky and the South. To this day buses have their own access ramp to the Roebling Bridge. The concourse does not appear to have changed since it opened except that the turnstiles are now disused. As a transportation hub, the Dixie Terminal is as obsolete as the city's Lunken Airport or Union Terminal. Greyhound and Trailways long ago abandoned it for modern facilities on the downtown's eastern edge. But like the old airport and railway station Dixie Terminal continues, in its modest way, to serve the city's needs—here as the terminus for TANK (Transit Authority of Northern Kentucky) buses.

The **Mercantile Library Building** (1902), just in from the northeast corner of 4th and Walnut streets and designed by Joseph Steinkamp, still houses the library that gave the building its name. Behind the round-arched windows of what seems to be the top (twelfth) floor, but is actually the eleventh, lies the reading room. (The twelfth-floor windows peek out from between the cornice's massive brackets.) Before entering, look at the entrance: the top left spandrel has a partially unfurled scroll, the top right an open book—apposite emblems for a building housing Cincinnati's oldest existing library.

When the Young Men's Mercantile Library Association came into being in 1835, Cincinnati, then a city of 28,000, had no public library. The Association was the first institution of its kind west of the Alleghenies. Joining it enabled those who were "not rich or members of the clergy" to keep up with the latest books and periodicals. Since its founding the Association has inhabited several structures on this site. In 1845, by a timely loan to the proprietor of its building, it obtained a lease "for a term of 10,000 years, renewable forever, free of charge, and secure and harmless against assessments and taxes." Alphonso Taft, Taft scion, drew up this fabulous document. When its last building was torn down, the Association reserved for itself—on the same terms!—the eleventh floor of this one. Membership, which began with forty-five, rose in the 1850s past the 3000 mark; today, although membership is under 1000, the Association survives (and prospers) as a downtown reading club, with scores of newspapers and magazines, and luncheons at which members meet writers. Although the 200,000 volumes of the Mercantile Library— it dropped "young" and "men" from its name earlier in this century—include a number of rare editions, it now specializes in recent books.

The Mercantile Library is one of the city's numerous nineteenth-century cultural institutions that has survived into the late twentieth century. Many prominent speakers have addressed its membership, including local luminaries Salmon P. Chase and Ormsby McKnight Mitchel; former Cincinnatians Henry Ward Beecher and Harriet Beecher Stowe; Ralph Waldo Emerson, Wendell Phillips, Edward Everett, and Bret Harte. From England came Thackeray and Galsworthy. Thackeray, who used the Library as a mail drop during his 1856 American tour, lectured to audiences "large and brilliant." At a luncheon not too long ago, a brother and sister, long Mercantile members, were asked if they came often to these affairs. "We missed Galsworthy," they said briskly, "but we've heard everyone since." Galsworthy last came to tea in 1930.

If we take the special elevator to the eleventh floor, we emerge into a nineteenth-century setting and atmosphere. J. Mozier's statue *Silence,* a toga-clad woman holding a finger to her lips, greets us as she has greeted members since 1856. Light pours in through the rounded windows; the high ceiling gives a sense of space. Artifacts from the library's Victorian past fill the room: Gothic mirrors, ancient wooden bookcases and reading stands (to which books would once have been fastened), Rookwood vases, faded photographs of nineteenth-century scenes, an eclectic collection of plaster busts of the disparate great, along with one in marble of Washington by Hiram Powers. Older tomes give off a slightly musty odor. Whenever the Library moved, along with the books came the bric-a-brac. A wooden phone booth stands next to the staircase. The staircase itself, it will be noted, winds to the ceiling and goes—nowhere. Why? It came with the 10,000-year lease. The metal shelves behind the desk hold the bulk of the collection; scenes of ancient Rome hang in front of the stacks; also behind the desk stands open a massive nineteenth-century safe with painted flowers on its doors. Even the pendulum of the clock appears to oscillate slowly. We seem to have entered a world where time has stopped. Yet time has not stopped. The newest books are at members' disposal upon publication. And library membership includes the unusual benefit of having books requested mailed anywhere.

We return to 4th and Walnut streets. From the southwest corner we can see all four Burnham buildings. Two we have passed on this tour; the third is the Tri-State at 5th and Walnut. The fourth, the **Clopay Building** (1904; restored 1984), is across the street. The unusual name came from an amalgamation of "clothes" and "paper," company products. Known until 1981 as the First National Bank Building, the Clopay arose as part of Cincinnati's turn-of-the-century construction boom. Burnham's firm designed this building, the city's finest in the Chicago style, to emphasize functional simplicity without irrelevant ornamentation. For seven stories, beginning at the fourth, a slightly convex projecting bay window not only emphasizes the building's verticality but softens its linear severity. On the Walnut side Burnham thrice repeated this undulation. The Clopay owes something to Burnham and Root's Monadnock Building (1889–1891) in Chicago, even more to Burnham and Co.'s Railway Exchange Building (1903–1904), also in Chicago, exactly contemporaneous with the Cincinnati structure. The Clopay's undulation strikes me as both more delicate and more restrained than that of the Railway Exchange.

We walk down Walnut St. toward the river. Before the advent of Ft. Washington Way, Cincinnatians looking south down most north-south streets could enjoy a river view. Now they can't. At 3rd St. we look back at the Clopay and Dixie Terminal buildings, whose rear façades present a plain brick exterior unadorned by decoration and without cornice. Why do these (and other) buildings on 4th's south side face *away* from the river?

Nineteenth-century photographs of Cincinnati reveal a **smoke-filled city,** a Los Angeles in miniature. Steamboats, burning coal after midcentury, belched forth clouds of smoke; riverfront factories and trains added to the miasma. "The smokiest city in the world," Charles Mackay, an English visitor, called it in 1858, "far murkier than London." "A winter month could go by when we couldn't see the sun," Daniel Ransohoff recalls of the 1930s. "The culprit was soft coal smoke. Over the Basin area, smog settled like a dense cloud, making breathing unbearable for long periods. In addition to this, industrial vapors emanated from the mills, shops, refineries, and, particularly, the tanneries." The hills rimming Cincinnati's Basin prevented the

Smog over Cincinnati. Rookwood Pottery on Mount Adams dominates the foreground. In 1858, Charles Mackay called Cincinnati "the smokiest city in the world." Soft (bituminous) coal smoke often covered the city and diminished visibility. Legislation in the 1950s forbade burning bituminous coal. Courtesy of the Cincinnati Historical Society.

smoke from blowing away. So the downtown early turned its back not only upon the riverfront but upon the Ohio River itself.

Most Cincinnatians of a previous century looked upon the smoke as inevitable. Some even liked it. It is we, in retrospect, who are appalled. People of past times often liked a city's smoke because of the pleasant associations it could summon up. "I love the very smoke of London," wrote Charles Lamb, "because it has been the medium most familiar to my vision." London's smoke was not "offensive" to Benjamin Robert Haydon, painter and diarist, but a "sublime canopy that shrouds the City of the World." Dickens in *Bleak House* (1853) spoke of it as "the London ivy." For visitors the smell of coal smoke, whether London's or Cincinnati's, defined the experience of being in that city.

"There are," said Frank Duveneck, "atmospheric effects to be found in Cincinnati that few cities afford." He was not being facetious. Actually, Duveneck was among the first painters to see the beauty within America's new industrial metropolises. He responded to his home town most in its smoke and grime. Relishing Cincinnati's brooding skies and blurred outlines, he seized the city in its variegated moods. While Duveneck painted Cincinnati, Monet and Whistler painted London. Who can forget Monet's serial paintings of Westminster Bridge or Whistler's of the Thames at dusk? They have unalterably shaped our image of the nineteenth-century

city. Until the late 1950s London had fogs so thick that pedestrians could not see
street lights. Like Cincinnati, it enacted legislation restricting the burning of bituminous coal. However spectacular the visual and artistic results, no one would wish
a return to the conditions that produced such extraordinary atmospheric effects.

It can take time for citizens of a river city to develop an esthetic regard for their
river. Not until about 1460 did Florentines begin to appreciate the Arno flowing
before their city; suddenly it became a favorite subject for painters. In 1822 the
young Thomas Cole, fresh from England, wandered down the Ohio River from
February to August in search of commissions as a portrait painter. The beauty he
perceived in the scenery moved him deeply and determined him to focus on landscape painting. In 1823 he went back east to Pittsburgh, then to Philadelphia, and
in 1825 to New York, before settling in Catskill on the Hudson. Cole founded and
was the chief glory of the Hudson River School of painting. He and his contemporaries called for an art and a literature that consecrated American scenes. Their
paintings offer lessons in the power of river scenery to move artists; they gained for
the Hudson fame in the world beyond its valley. The Ohio River is not as dramatic
in its landscapes as the wasp-waisted Hudson, but every nineteenth-century traveler
who went down it praised its variegated beauty. More than three times as long as the
Hudson, the Ohio is for most of its length a thoroughly satisfying stream to contemplate. If, instead of settling on the Hudson, Cole had returned to the Ohio and found
divinity in *its* landscapes, not only might the history of landscape painting in America have been different but also the history of the Ohio River itself—and our sense
of its esthetic qualities.

Only in recent decades have Cincinnatians rediscovered the esthetic pleasure of
living alongside their great river, though it has yet inspired few major paintings or
photographs of distinction. (Even the postcards available of this most photogenic
city and its river are a disgrace.) Downtown's newer buildings, like the Hyatt and
312 Walnut, have been designed to take advantage of whatever river view they possess—and to be seen from the Ohio. Facing the river, they enhance the visual attractiveness of the city.

312 Walnut (1990) is one of the new postmodern highrises that not only faces
but unequivocally addresses the Ohio. Seen to advantage from the Roebling Bridge,
this thirty-two story edifice leaves no doubt of its intent to monopolize the riverine
skyline. Its various colors and forms—a taut glass cylinder appears encased within
a traditional rectangular stone cube—make it an intriguing structure to contemplate
from any angle. Unlike the Provident Tower, the glass is reflective. Clouds float by
on it. From a distance, depending on the light, the glass can appear white or black
or most shades in between. Third St.'s tallest building and the center of the city's
river skyline, 312 Walnut, by its distinctive presence and shape, gives Cincinnati an
unmistakable front door. Two blocks west will rise 312 Elm, a twin-towered complex to be built in stages. A block east will be Queen City Square, with three towers
proposed. By the time all this construction takes place Third may have again become Cincinnati's glamour street.

We return to 4th St. Harry Weese designed the elegant **Formica Building**
(1970), on the northeast corner of 4th and Walnut streets, along with the adjoining

Contemporary Arts Center on 5th St. Windows of bronze-tinted glass are set within a façade of travertine marble. Entering the building's arcade, we come upon an unusual fountain sculpture. Water slides gently down its copper panels, at the bottom of which we see etched a fanciful rendition of the city's skyline from Price Hill to beyond Mount Adams. Above is a street map of the corresponding area. Past the sculpture the bright, well-designed arcade, lined with weeping figs, leads to the Contemporary Arts Center (chapter 1) and 5th St. Worth a careful look on the right-hand side is Terry Brown's imaginative design for the Contemporary Arts Center bookstore. To my mind, the Formica's rear façade, visible through the arcade roof, is its most interesting. Few notice it.

Across 4th St., at 310–314, three buildings restored in 1987 date back to circa 1870. The center structure housed the Holland Pen Co., makers of gold-tipped fountain pens; the three together are sometimes called the Holland Pen group. Their elegant façades (all of different brick) and mansard roofs with dormers transport us back to another era, when 4th St. was Cincinnati's most stylish commercial thoroughfare.

Garber & Woodward designed the **Cincinnati Gas & Electric Building** (1930; south addition, 1954) in collaboration with John Russell Pope. Its Classical Revival style draws upon Art Deco motifs. Huge Doric columns assert their presence at ground level. A plaque by the main door informs us that William Moody, the first child born in Cincinnati, came into the world here on March 17, 1790. Moody, who died in Cincinnati eighty-eight years later in 1878, witnessed the city's evolution from frontier village to western metropolis. Since 1945 young and old have delighted in the electric train exhibit every Christmas season, reputedly the largest "O" gauge model railroad in the world.

South down Main St. stand five newly renovated late nineteenth-century commercial structures. They went up within fifteen years on either side of 1878. Fortunately, these holdouts from the past have survived. Between the modern Atrium I and Riverfront Stadium, they function as a welcome if slightly incongruous presence in the cityscape.

We return to 4th St. and look north toward 5th at the elegant sheath of travertine marble that is the **Central Trust Center** (1979). Its stepped appearance makes it seem many faceted and many angled. The lines change their configuration from different perspectives. Particularly successful are the wide windows, recessed at the ends to achieve a beveled effect. The Central Trust Center is not meant to fit within an established cityscape. Self-conscious and aloof, this most chic of Cincinnati's recent highrises stands apart. Its garage on 4th St. is compatible with the main building. The architect, Richard Keating of the Houston office of Skidmore, Owings, and Merrill, sensibly allowed for commercial frontage (Wendy's). Adjoining it and stretching from 4th to 5th is a thirty-story tower (1991), the **Chemed Center,** that, a dozen years younger, looks older than the Central Trust Center. Its setbacks at different levels hark back to 1920s Art Deco skyscrapers, whereas the fenestration of its central tower echoes the tripartite windows of the turn-of-the-century Chicago school.

Skidmore also designed the fraternal twins **Atrium I** (1982) **and II** (1984), though these were done by the Chicago office. The multisided tower, folded and faceted, became for a while a trademark of this enduringly modernist firm. The

Terrace Hilton is an example of its earlier work in Cincinnati. Stylistically related to the Central Trust Center, Atrium I and II succeed less well. "One building is architecture," the British planner Gordon Cullen once said; "two buildings is townscape." These two crowd their sites. Compared to the Center's travertine, their poured-concrete façades look scrubby. Preferably we should look at these twins as part of the skyline, for they work better from the riverfront than close up as individual entities. They work best of all in conjunction with the Central Trust Center. The three buildings, stepping inward, complete themselves at an imagined point in the sky.

A curled corner façade, its windows *chamfered,* that is, cut on a diagonal, is Atrium I's most notable feature. Both buildings are stepped; both rise from south to north; Atrium II, taller, also rises from east to west. An annex—a third building actually—rises south along Sycamore. A fountain dominates Atrium I's lobby. Imperceptibly we move into the (stepped!) atrium between the buildings that gives the complex its name. Another fountain, gentler, features jets, a sequence of waterfalls, and stylized tiles depicting vegetation done by the Spring Street Pottery, an Over-the-Rhine firm. Sound connects the buildings. From the atrium a skywalk, appropriately pyramided, takes us to Riverfront Plaza.

4th St. was once a street of churches. Only **Christ Church** (Episcopalian) is left. The present building (1957) replaced a red-brick edifice of 1835, modelled upon London's now largely destroyed St. Dunstan's. It was one of America's earliest "Gothick" Revival churches. Old prints and photographs reveal it to have been an eyecatching structure. But internal decay led in the late 1940s to plans for a new building. Eliel Saarinen, originally designated the architect, prepared a modernistic design, the church committee balked, Saarinen died in 1950, and son Eero refused to consider a traditional structure. Too bad, for what went up instead is nondescript. The 1982 remodeling, lean and spare in its white austerity, retained the old structure's stained glass, including six signed Tiffany windows.

Reached from the main building is the St. Paul or Centennial Chapel (1917) commemorating the centennial of the congregation's founding. It also contains good glass as well a Rubens *Holy Family,* a gift from Mary M. Emery, the city's premier benefactress. Another of her gifts, the Parish House (1899; largely rebuilt in 1909), with its crocketed pinnacles, hints at the original church's appearance. It was also meant to be a community center for the inner-city poor and downtown office workers. Before it is one of the city's ubiquitous Murdock water fountains, made locally, that appear to function (amazingly) in winter as well as in summer. Opposite, a rowhouse reminds us that in the mid-nineteenth century 4th St. was largely residential. Originally Greek Revival, it has gained Italianate stonework and hood moldings along with a recessed panelled entrance.

Probably the most lastingly influential of Cincinnati's major civic organizations is the **Queen City Club,** established in 1874 by Joseph Longworth and friends. Harry Hake designed the present building (1927), on the southwest corner of 4th St. and Broadway, in a subdued English Renaissance style. Four Art Deco medallions give the bland façade, rigid and restrained, a little life. The two on 4th symbolize industry and commerce; on Broadway, art and agriculture. Within hangs a fine collection of Cincinnati art.

In *Babbitt* (1922) Sinclair Lewis portrays, satirically but affectionately, a representative American businessman striving for the good of his city, "Zenith." Although several cities have a claim to be the original of Zenith, Cincinnati has by far the best. Lewis had a *pied à terre* in the Queen City Club, then in its first clubhouse at 7th and Elm streets, for a stretch in 1921, and he found his time here "very useful." Taking extensive notes on the city and the people he met, he let his experiences here shape the novel's background.

Across Broadway Italianate and Second Empire vie with each other in the red-painted **University Club** (1880). This stretch of Broadway was once a fashionable Victorian neighborhood. The University Club, originally two private houses, has a distinctive mansard roof, oriel windows, and terra cotta panels on which romp swirling dragons. Further French influence appears in the *mascarons,* or grotesque sculpted heads (that on 4th red-eyed!), at the culminating point of the doorway arches. Next door, twin porticos with composite columns balance the stone façade of the **Academy of Medicine** (ca. 1850), which has occupied this six-bayed building since 1960. Founded in 1857, the Academy was the twelfth medical society organized in Cincinnati, an indication of the fragmented, often disputatious state of the medical establishment in the nineteenth century. Formerly C. C. Pierce, president of the U.S. Mail Lines, lived here. The adjoining Italianate three-bayed townhouse, the Nolan, Keeler and Stiles house (ca. 1865), has stylized Corinthian pilasters, topped by a floriated gable with odd little globes.

Next door is the **Second District Police Station** (1910). Two colossal Ionic columns dominate its symmetrical façade. The English bond brickwork (a row of stretchers alternating with a row of headers) is unusual for a Beaux Arts structure but not for a Georgian Revival, and this building partakes of both styles. The black and red brickwork gives it a lively staccato look. Cornice work includes various classical decorative motifs, including Greek key patterns, bay leaf garlands, dentils, and egg-and-dart moldings. Lion's heads peer down from the window keystones. Bundles of spears, or *fasces,* greet the viewer at the base and suggest an enthusiasm for authority. The façade's imperious air, together with the enveloping decoration, make for a fluid, dynamic building.

We continue down Broadway to 3rd St., cross over, and walk a half-block west to the **Ft. Washington Memorial,** unmistakable as a miniature blockhouse. Fort Washington occupied a site roughly 300 feet northeast of this monument, where the (easterly) Western-Southern parking garage and the Guilford School now stand. In October 1952, excavating for the garage, diggers uncovered the fort's powder magazine, built out of timbers from dismantled flatboats. Erected in 1789–1790 as the main western outpost against the British and the Indians, Ft. Washington was strategically located on high ground opposite the mouth of the Licking River. From here General "Mad Anthony" Wayne set forth in 1793 in the memorable campaign climaxed in 1794 by the Battle of Fallen Timbers, on the Maumee River not far from present-day Toledo. Wayne's stunning victory, accomplished in a forty-five minute battle, broke Indian power in the Northwest Territory. The Treaty of Greenville following in 1795 made Ohio safe for settlers. Ft. Washington stood until 1808 when, the need for it having disappeared, the army dismantled it. Four years before, the garrison had moved across the river to new barracks in Newport.

1788, the year of Cincinnati's founding, also witnessed the founding of two other settlements between the Miami and Little Miami rivers. Columbia was about five miles upriver; North Bend, about ten miles downriver. The three outposts vied for colonists—and preeminence. Which one of the three would dominate the region? The establishment here of Ft. Washington assured the hegemony of Cincinnati. It would grow as the other villages would not. Released by the military's presence from having to guard the outpost against Indians, the first Cincinnatians could turn to making a city. The advantages of a site for the most part above the floodplain proved even more evident as the city began to grow.

A block west of Ft. Washington stood Mrs. Frances Trollope's famous **Bazaar.** Erected by Seneca Palmer in 1828–1829, the Bazaar must rank as the most unusual building ever seen in Cincinnati. *Bazaar* conjures up an image of a hodgepodge of architectural styles—Greek, Moorish, Egyptian, Gothic—all of which went into its design. Shortly after her arrival in Cincinnati, Mrs. Trollope visited her compatriot, William Bullock, who was planning to turn his estate across the river in Ludlow, Kentucky, into the ideal city of "Hygeia." Bullock had been the proprietor of the Egyptian Hall (1812) in London, a neo-Egyptian monstrosity, and, as Clay Lancaster has pointed out, similarities exist between that building and Mrs. Trollope's. The Bazaar, as later the Wise Temple on Plum, drew inspiration from Romantic Orientalism. In temperament a Romantic, Mrs. Trollope steeped herself in the exotic verse tales of Lord Byron and Thomas Moore. The result was, as Donald Smalley observes, "*The Giaour* and *Lalla Rookh* mixed with a good deal of sheer personal whimsy and frozen into brick and stone." Architecturally, the Bazaar was the Brighton Pavilion and Neuschwanstein rolled into one, miniaturized, and dropped into the raw American West.

Every traveler who came through Cincinnati loosed a witticism at the Bazaar. No one viewed it, asserted Timothy Flint, "without wonder and a good humored laugh." For Harriet Martineau the Bazaar with its "Gothic windows, Grecian pillars, and . . . Turkish dome" was "the great deformity of the city." Captain Marryat, conceding its architectural variety, opined that "the order under which it must be classed is the preposterous." Locals dubbed it "Trollope's Folly." No less varied than its architecture were its intended uses. In addition to exotic goods (exotic at least for frontier Cincinnati), this exotic structure contained a coffee house, an ice cream parlor, exhibition galleries, and a grand ballroom. (Robert A. M. Stern would find in this building the origins of the department store.) Unfortunately, Mrs. Trollope had more imagination than capital, and to pay workmen she had to sell her Bazaar before completion. It was patronized, if insufficiently, by Cincinnati's "Corinthians," its ultrafashionables. The Bazaar's subsequent history was checkered. By the mid-1860s, noted Moncure D. Conway, it had lodged successively "a dancing school, an eclectic medical college, and a hydropathic establishment, had become a female medical college; it was the home of varieties of dreamers and reformers until it housed convalescent Federal soldiers during the civil war." Such diversity of use indicates the diversity of life spawned by a dynamic nineteenth-century city. After the war the Bazaar became for a while a house of prostitution before being torn down in 1881.

Mrs. Trollope abandoned Cincinnati in 1830 to go back to England. There she

Frances Trollope's Bazaar. Erected in 1828–1829 in a
hodgepodge of architectural styles—Greek, Moorish,
Egyptian, Gothic—this "folly" was the city's most unusual
building. It briefly housed the bazaar that Frances Trollope
hoped would recoup the family fortunes. After the enterprise failed, Mrs. Trollope abandoned Cincinnati in 1830.
The building was torn down in 1881. Courtesy of the Cincinnati Historical Society.

published her petulant but shrewd *Domestic Manners of the Americans* (1832), one
of the most notorious books ever written about this country—and this city. It is also
one of the wittiest. In it Mrs. Trollope did not spare Cincinnatians their cultural and
civic deficiencies. "Mrs. Trollope came," observed Thomas Hamilton, "and a zone
of light has ever since encircled Cincinnati. Its inhabitants are no longer a race
unknown to fame." But if she put the city on the map, she saddled it with a negative
image—a dubious legacy, and one from which it has yet to recover completely.

Ft. Washington Way necessitated destroying the historic Audubon and Drake
houses. The peripatetic **John James Audubon** (1785–1851) lived at 414 E. 3rd St.
for seven months in 1820. Daniel Drake hired him as a taxidermist at the Western
Museum, founded by him and a precursor to the present Museum of Natural History.
In Cincinnati Audubon received public praise as a wildlife artist. From here, at age
thirty-five, he embarked on the first of his journeys to discover every species of bird
on the continent. They led him to become one of the greatest of naturalists, the
author of *The Birds of America* (1827–1838).

Nearby at 429 E. 3rd St. was **Daniel Drake**'s own residence. Deservedly known as the "Benjamin Franklin of the West," Drake (1785–1852) possessed seemingly inexhaustible energies. He made his mark as physician, medical pioneer, writer, teacher, civic reformer, lover of books and libraries, and founder (and projector) of social institutions, medical schools not least. No citizen of this city ever exhibited a wider range of interests than he did or left his mark on so many areas of its life. "He started nearly everything in Cincinnati," declared the eminent physician William Osler, with pardonable exaggeration, "that is good and has lasted." Influenced by Philadelphia and its cultural life, Drake envisioned a new American Enlightenment in which the West, Cincinnati at its head, would lead the nation. His *Notices concerning Cincinnati* (1810) and *Natural and Statistical View, or Picture of Cincinnati and the Miami Country* (1815), solid exercises in descriptive geography, touted the city's virtues.

Returning to 4th St., we encounter the **Western-Southern Life Insurance** complex (1916–1961). The temple-like corner structure (1916), one of Hake and Kuck's neoclassical exercises in Roman grandeur, replaced Edmund Dexter's splendid Italianate residence, where (it is claimed) Dickens and the Prince of Wales had visited. The Western-Southern's 4th St. façade flaunts eight massive Ionic columns. The entablature decoration is enlivened by the Greek key motif; nonstop anthemions crown the cornice. Appropriately Ohio's largest insurance concern conveys an image of stability, yet neither this building nor its others quite come to life. After the race riots of June 12–18, 1967, the company covered the windows of the 1916 building with steel plates strong enough to withstand rifle fire. They blind the façade.

Across the street is the **Guilford School** (1914), designed by Garber and Woodward. Once a neighborhood school, it has since 1973 served handicapped students from all over the city. Its name memorializes Nathan Guilford, who in 1825 proposed legislation to support Ohio's first public schools through property taxes and who later served in Cincinnati as superintendent of schools. The Italian Renaissance façade, well proportioned, has elaborate patterned brickwork and terra cotta decoration. Two entrances, originally one for boys and one for girls, nicely balance the building, as do the two roof terraces. The terraces formerly served as playgrounds for the children in this inner-city school, once at the center of a poor, overcrowded district. High on the façade a cartouche depicts Ft. Washington. A cherub surmounts the cartouche, presumably to remind us that Providence kept a benevolent eye on the fledgling settlement. A plaque informs us that **Stephen Foster** lived here at the home of Mrs. Jane Griffin, when 4th was a tree-shaded residential street, from 1846 to 1850. Foster was working for a steamboat firm. Later his daughter remembered that he spoke of these formative years as "the happiest in his life." Possibly he wrote "Oh! Susanna" here; certainly he published his early songs in Cincinnati.

Around the corner on Arch St. are three Greek Revival houses, the central one with curved Italianate hood molds. They return us to the mid-nineteenth century city. The star tie rods visible on number 425's side wall prevent the exterior walls from bowing out. Above our heads the campanile of the Guilford School conceals, as do most twentieth-century campaniles, the smokestack.

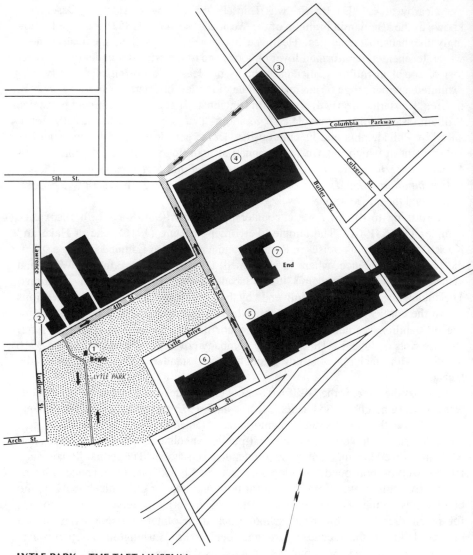

LYTLE PARK—THE TAFT MUSEUM

1. Barnard's *Lincoln—the Man*
2. Literary Club
3. Edwards Manufacturing Building
4. R. L. Polk Building
5. American Book Company Building
6. Anna Louise Inn
7. Taft Museum

Lytle Park—The Taft Museum

WE front, at the east end of 4th St., the green sward of Lytle Park. Directly before us stands George Grey Barnard's larger-than-life statue, *Lincoln—the Man*. A central walkway leads the eye to the beautifully proportioned Federal mansion that houses the Taft Museum. Spring through autumn floral displays brighten the walkway. Beyond, on Mount Adams, looms the Church of the Immaculate Conception.

In 1910 William Howard Taft, a Cincinnatian, president from 1908 to 1912, revived plans for a memorial to Lincoln in Potomac Park, Washington. That same year Charles Phelps Taft, William Howard's older half-brother, awarded George Grey Barnard a commission to create a statue of Lincoln for Lytle Park. "He has done some wonderfully strong things, and we are hoping that he will produce a great work of art," Charles wrote the president. The bronze statue, when unveiled and dedicated in 1917, caused a furor. Robert Todd Lincoln, the president's son, found it "uncouth"; he thought "it did his father great injustice." Replicas, originally destined for London and Paris, made their way instead to Louisville and Manchester. Lincoln stands before us, not on the formal plinth usual for statues of presidents (think of those in Piatt Park for Garfield and Harrison), but on a granite boulder, rough hewn, low to the ground. The granite suggests his rock-like strength in times of crisis. In placing Lincoln so that we look less up to him than *at* him, Barnard makes a statement about the president's accessibility, even about his vulnerability. With the passing of time, we may admire more readily the unflinching integrity of his vision of Lincoln, more meditative, less heroic than Daniel Chester French's memorial statue in Washington. No other representation of Lincoln I know renders his rough-hewn honesty, his troubled grandeur of soul, so uncompromisingly. He stands before us, gaunt, unsmiling, weary, hair tousled, unbearded, tie askew, vest ill-fitting, big handed, big footed, the reflective eyes fixed on eternity. Barnard did indeed, as Charles Taft hoped, produce "a great work of art."

Twelve plaques affixed to the curved brick wall on the park's south side recount the history of **Lytle Park.** The land on which we stand, originally hardwood forest,

George Grey Barnard, *Lincoln—the Man*. Guarding the entrance to Lytle Park, this once-controversial statue portrays
a rough-hewn Lincoln, appealingly human rather than
grandly heroic.

became successively cleared ground, a peach orchard, then the elegant, semirural
estate of William Lytle, one of Cincinnati's first settlers and the Northwest Territory's first surveyor general. About 1810, a decade before Martin Baum built a mansion in wood now known as the Taft Museum, Lytle built here a mansion in brick.
His grandson, William H. Lytle, born in 1826, died, a Civil War general, at Chickamauga on September 20, 1863. In Spring Grove Cemetery we shall see the family
tomb.

The "Golden Age" of Lytle Park occurred in the pre-Civil War decades. Community and business leaders gathered in the Lytle home and in Martin Baum's mansion, owned after 1830 by Nicholas Longworth. After the Civil War they largely
abandoned their downtown residences to erect great houses on the nearby hills. In
1905 the city bought the Lytle house, tore it down, and in 1907 turned its grounds
into a public play area. Mike Mullen, the local councilman, was the prime mover
behind the park, a civic necessity (as was the Guilford School to our right) for the

poor, densely populated area, teeming with immigrants, between where we stand and the river. The Bottoms, as it was called, was a thriving neighborhood during the first third of the century. Roy Rogers grew up here. In the 1960s when the building of I-71 threatened to destroy Lytle Park, public protest forced the expressway underground. Completely rebuilt above it, the park emerged in 1971 larger than before. The view to the southwest remains largely uncluttered; ·it gives the park abundant light and a sense of openness. The rededication on November 11, 1972, was marked by the unveiling of the newly refurbished Lincoln statue. Henry James once described small parks as "quiet interspaces" that function in a city as "breathing-spaces" do in conversation. Fortunately Cincinnatians rallied in time to save this particular interspace. In 1976 the Lytle Park area became Cincinnati's first historic district to gain admittance to the National Register.

A heterogeneous mix of buildings rings Lytle Park, yet old and new blend harmoniously. Charles Phelps and Anna Sinton Taft, who in the early twentieth century owned most of the land around the park, wished to foster the area's diversity: educational, cultural, residential, and commercial. They paid for the Anna Louise Inn, sponsored the Phelps Townhouse, and installed the Literary Club in its present quarters. Lytle Park became (and remains) a distinctive neighborhood. Earlier, with its mansions on either side of the Taft house and its row houses on the north side of 4th St., Lytle Park projected an ambience somewhat comparable to Manhattan's Grammercy Park. It still remains a residential island of calm within, yet detached from, the bustling city.

The two-story, Federal style building (ca. 1820) at 500 E. 4th houses the **Literary Club.** It has Flemish bond brickwork; added later were the Greek Revival doorway and portico. Founded in 1849, the Literary Club is the oldest surviving organization of its kind west of the Alleghenies. Founding members included Ainsworth Spofford, future Librarian of Congress, and Stanley Matthews, later-to-be United States senator and Supreme Court justice. Subsequently, Salmon P. Chase, Rutherford B. Hayes, and William Howard Taft joined. Members always composed a diverse lot. Before the Civil War the club roster included three of the country's four leading Hegelians: Johann B. Stallo, August Willich, and Moncure D. Conway. The Club did not seek for its membership the homogeneity of national origins, religion, social background, or financial affluence that doomed other Cincinnati social organizations with such restrictions.

Before the Literary Club secured these premises in 1930 it had thirteen different addresses. That year Anna Sinton Taft offered it this house on a ninety-nine year lease, renewable forever, at an annual rent of one hundred dollars. Within hangs a fine collection of paintings and drawings by Cincinnati artist (and member) Henry Farny. Club membership, which began with twenty-five, has been limited since 1875 to one hundred males. Every Monday evening from September to June members meet to hear a paper. Nonmembers do not read papers, though distinguished guests—among them Mark Twain, Oscar Wilde, Booker T. Washington, Israel Zangwill, William J. Mayo, Robert Frost, and Amos Alonzo Stagg—have attended meetings or spoken informally.

Next door is the Georgian Revival **Phelps Townhouse** (1926)—"Phelps" was the maiden name of Charles Phelps Taft's mother. Designed by Garber and Wood-ward, this apartment building was until quite recently one of Cincinnati's rare down-town highrises devoted to residential use. Cincinnati, its citizens traditionally valuing home ownership, has fewer large apartment buildings than do most other cities its size. This one would not look out of place on Manhattan's Park Avenue.

550 E. 4th (1970), the adjacent four-story red brick apartment building, re-places a row of Greek Revival townhouses torn down in 1967 to make way for I-71. The Western-Southern Insurance Co., which had paid for the slab over Lytle Park, also sponsored this complex. Designed in a modern idiom by Harry Hake and Part-ners, 550 was required to maintain the scale and basic proportions of the destroyed townhouses. Architects around 1970 began to pay increasing attention to older, sur-rounding structures. 550 dominates neither the Taft Museum nor Lytle Park itself. Its mansard roof and the projecting brickwork echo the Literary Club's twin chim-neys. The design achieves a subtle harmony of red and black: red bricks predomi-nate, but interspersed within them are darker ones. Black are the window surrounds, the balcony railings, the roof tile, even the fencing in front. From Pike St.—named not after Samuel N., twice builder of Pike's Opera House, but Zebulon S., early western explorer—we gain another view of this stylish complex. Modernity, alas, has gone too far with astroturf walkways!

We cross Pike, then 5th St., then descend the stairs to observe at close hand the trapezoidal **Edwards Manufacturing Building** (ca. 1905). Part of a former sheet-metal factory, the Edwards Building is one of the area's few surviving reminders of its industrial past. Until 1987 it housed a premier Italian restaurant. The interior renovation had shown imaginative re-use of an older structure; the former board room, richly panelled in walnut, became the main dining room. The Edwards Build-ing's narrow main façade, Ionic columns bestriding the entrance stairs, is Beaux Arts classical. What looks like chiselled stonework is actually terra cotta.

During the first half of the nineteenth century this area, known as the **Deer Creek Valley,** was filled with slaughterhouses for Cincinnati's burgeoning pork-packing industry. It adjoined Bucktown. "Deer Creek, pretty as its name is," Harriet Martineau noted in 1835, "is little more than the channel through which their blood runs away." In fact, Deer Creek was commonly referred to as "Bloody Run" or "Butcher's Hollow." The creek now flows in a culvert under I-71. The city has am-bitious plans to make the Deer Creek Valley into a forecourt for Sawyer Point Park; Eggleston Esplanade, newly landscaped and renamed, is to become a grand boulevard.

We return to Pike St. Dwarfing the adjacent Taft Museum is the stone-faced **R. L. Polk Building** (1905) by Dittoe and Wisenall. Recently, side façades were imaginatively painted in a postmodern geometric color scheme. Until the early 1980s the A. H. Pugh Printing Company was at this location. On January 1, 1836, Achilles Pugh, a Quaker, began publishing James G. Birney's *Philanthropist,* an important Ohio abolitionist journal. Birney was a former plantation owner from Alabama. Cincinnati, with its largely Southern market and its crucial trade connec-tion with New Orleans, had in its population far more anti-abolitionists than aboli-tionists. Twice, on July, 30, 1836, and again in 1841, anti-abolitionist mobs, which included in them a number of the city's prominent citizens, partially destroyed Pugh's press. Each time Pugh quickly had the *Philanthropist* back on the streets. Although Birney left for the East in 1837, the *Philanthropist* continued until 1847, one of the state's longest-running abolitionist papers.

On the Taft Museum's south side we come upon the former headquarters of the **American Book Company.** Through its classical lines and proportions this Renaissance Revival structure (1904) radiates a quiet harmony. In 1976 plans to convert the building into condominiums fell through; in 1981 it was lovingly redone into offices. Corner quoins of darker brick complement the mellow salmon-colored façade brick; the tinted mortar complements both. On the frieze metopes we discern an open book, "AB" on one page, "Co" on the other; in between, a torch symbolizes learning. The floor mosaic between the double doors duplicates this logo. The torch is a thoroughly appropriate symbol: for over three decades after 1890 the American Book Company published the McGuffey *Readers*.

In the 1830s William Holmes McGuffey (1800–1873), while a professor at Miami University, Oxford, Ohio, developed an enormously influential series of reading books for children. The first and second *Readers* appeared in 1836, the third and fourth the next year, the fifth (written by William's brother Alexander) in 1844. Their success was sudden and startling. The **McGuffey** *Readers* disseminated the three "R's" to millions of schoolchildren, particularly in the Mid- and Far West. In the process they inculcated in them the virtues of honesty, kindness, promptness, and truthfulness. With a strong emphasis on moral and ethical principles, the *Readers* presented a code of ethics that rewarded goodness and punished evil. Their useful information, their moralistic bent, and the passages they included from the classics of English and American literature helped shape the developing American consciousness. The *Readers* also taught several generations of boys and girls the virtue of reading *aloud.* They are more demanding than modern textbooks; the *Second Reader,* for example, is at today's seventh grade level. That their greatest success came outside of New England indicates that in theme and subject matter they fitted well the needs of the egalitarian, frontier West. Written by a western author, published in the West by a western firm, the *Readers* were stamped with the idealism and expansive spirit of the frontier.

For three-quarters of a century various Cincinnati firms brought out edition after edition of these ever more widely celebrated and disseminated schoolbooks. Sales reached their peak in the 1880s after Henry Farny illustrated the 1879 edition. By 1920, when the last major edition was published, someone estimated that 122 million of McGuffey's books had been sold and that, on the average, ten people had read each copy. In recent years the *Readers* have experienced a revival in popularity, particularly in smaller communities; 217,000 copies were sold in 1983. Such enduring popularity was, and remains, a phenomenon unmatched in the annals of education. That these readers came out of Cincinnati, along with many other books in the nineteenth century, in German as well as in English, reminds us that throughout most of the century this city, with over a dozen firms active in the book trade, was the largest publishing center in America west of the Alleghenies.

Across the street the **Anna Louise Inn** (1909; enlarged 1920) offers inexpensive lodgings for working and elderly women. Established by Anna Sinton Taft and named after one of her daughters, the Inn is run by the Cincinnati Union Bethel. Earlier her father David Sinton had endowed the Union Bethel, one of the city's oldest charitable organizations and still in existence, with a princely gift of $100,000. The Union Bethel was established in 1830 to provide relief and social activities for rivermen and those who lived near the riverfront. This Georgian Revival structure maintains the scale of other buildings around Lytle Park. Nearby is the neo-Tudor (or "Jacobethan") Earls Building (1919), at first a residence for the rector of Christ Church a few blocks away; the modern extension of 1953–1954 accords well with the original structure.

Most cities Cincinnati's size would consider themselves fortunate to have one institution of the quality of its Art Museum. But like New York, London, Washington, and Boston, Cincinnati has two art museums with major collections of Old Masters: one official, one a "house" museum. New York has its Metropolitan and Frick, London its National Gallery and Wallace, Washington its National Gallery and Phillips, Boston its Museum of Fine Art and Gardner—and Cincinnati its Art Museum and Taft. The **Taft Museum** was given to the citizens of Cincinnati by its last owners, who formed the collection and in whose home it remains on display. Like the other house museums, the Taft holds especial favor among those who find large public establishments daunting. It also appeals because its treasures are set out in the long-inhabited rooms of a private house. And since the Taft is relatively small, the collection is, if not absorbed, at least glimpsed in the course of a visit.

Quite apart from the artifacts within, the Taft possesses exceptional interest as a building. 1820, thought to be its date of construction, puts it among Cincinnati's earliest structures. The architect is unknown. That it was built along lines suggestive of the White House led many to attribute it to the White House's architect, James Hoban; others have seen in its lines the hand of Benjamin Henry Latrobe, the leading architect of the day. Neither attribution is now accepted. In 1820 America boasted few professional architects. Most likely, like other buildings of its era, the Taft was erected by a competent local carpenter-builder.

What is indubitable is that the house is a major example of Federal architecture. The central portion held the formal rooms and (at the rear) the music room; the lower wings (perhaps added a decade or so later), the dining room and bedrooms. The double entrance door, altered in Victorian times to a recessed hall, has been returned to its Federal form, with an elliptical fanlight and sidelights. Above the door is a majestic two-story portico with four Tuscan columns (a variant of Doric). Oval frieze windows appear on either side of the central unit; a row of dentils and a row of block modillions go around the entire house. A high basement, extending the width of the façade, becomes a full story in the rear because of the land's downward slope.

Federal architects, Thomas Jefferson among them, favored siting a house on an eminence so that from the front it appeared one story high, whereas in the rear it opened out to two. There is much of Jefferson in this house, within as well as without. A central block with a classical portico before it and balanced by wings was the

The Taft Museum. Erected in 1819–1820, Cincinnati's finest Federal residence fronts Lytle Park. It now houses one of the country's best small fine art collections.

formula developed by the great Renaissance architect, Andrea Palladio. Many later architects in England and America have spun variations on Palladio, among them Robert Adam in England and, in America, Jefferson, as Monticello makes clear. The Taft Museum thus stands at the end of a long tradition. "Homewood" (1801–1803), a rural Palladian villa now on the Johns Hopkins campus in Baltimore, formerly attributed to William Thornton and now thought to have been designed by its owner, Charles Carroll, Jr., may be its closest American cousin. So skillfully presented is the Taft that it appears to have the authentic air of a great eighteenth-century house. We contemplate a country seat set in the heart of downtown Cincinnati.

Martin Baum (1765–1831), its first owner, was born in Hagerstown, Maryland, of German descent (or, in another tradition, in Hagenau, Alsace). In the mid-1790s he came to Cincinnati via Connecticut. Beginning with a general store, Baum eventually became the city's first merchant prince. In 1803 he secured a charter for his Miami Exporting Co., a pioneer bank; in 1810 he built an iron foundry, the first in the West, and about the same time a sugar refinery and a steam mill. He also dabbled in real estate here and elsewhere in Ohio. Interested in his city and twice its mayor,

Robert Duncanson, *Nicholas Longworth*. One of the city's
major landowners, Longworth was also one of its most eccentric citizens. From 1830 to 1863 he lived in Belmont, as
the Taft Museum was formerly called, and made it a cultural center. He patronized a number of local artists, including Duncanson, a mulatto, now recognized as a significant
American painter. Courtesy of the Cincinnati Art Museum.

he helped organize the Western Museum, several schools, a subscription library, and
the Society for the Promotion of Agriculture, Manufacturing, and the Domestic
Economy. On September 1, 1812, he purchased the site of the Taft house from
Daniel Symmes; he waited seven years before building "Belmont," as he called his
elegant dwelling. He may not have lived long in it. Financial reverses in the Panic
of 1819 forced him to deed the house in 1825, in payment of a debt, to the Bank of
the United States.

For a few years Belmont was leased to a "female Seminary." Then in 1829
Nicholas Longworth acquired the property. Probably at this time he added the two
wings to gain needed space for his family. Longworth (1783–1863) had floated

down the Ohio River in a flatboat about 1800, studied law with Judge Jacob Burnet, and by 1807 had a flourishing practice. Accepting land in lieu of legal fees, he rapidly acquired large real estate holdings. About 1820 he ceased his legal practice to devote his energies to managing his properties and to developing his avocation for horticulture and viticulture. Gradually and shrewdly he accumulated enormous land holdings in and around Cincinnati. On these he built the city's largest fortune. When he died in 1863 at seventy-nine, his estate was valued at the then phenomenal sum of fifteen million dollars.

Generous to some, a penny pincher to others, Croesus yet Maecenas, firm in his views but tolerant of others', Longworth alternatively amazed and puzzled his contemporaries. He combined phenomenal luck with scientific curiosity, "You couldn't throw that man into the Ohio River," remarked John Adlum, the developer of the Catawba vine, "without his coming to the surface, a rare species of fish in one hand and a fresh-water pearl in the other." The artist Lily Martin Spencer, in a letter to her mother of 1841, described him as "a little bit of an ugly man. . . . His manners are extremely rough and almost coarse, but his shrewd eyes and plain manner hide a very strong mind and generous heart." "The wealthiest citizen of Cincinnati," exclaimed Moritz Busch, who found him fascinating, "he is at the same time the oddest of its eccentrics." Every Monday morning Longworth offered to those that wished them three to eight hundred ten-cent loaves of bread. Not an outright abolitionist, he yet detested slavery and in 1844 helped establish an orphanage for black children. Known for his oddities of dress and manners, he usually spoke of himself in the third person, most frequently as "Old Longworth." Once a tall stranger from Illinois came to Cincinnati to try a case. Finding time on his hands, he decided to visit the well-known grounds of Belmont. Mistaking Longworth for a gardener, he asked to be shown around and was. Only afterwards did Longworth reveal his identity—and Abraham Lincoln his.

No one in Cincinnati offered more spectacular hospitality than Longworth. Over the years he made Belmont the acknowledged social and cultural capital of Ohio. "The party at this house was the largest and most elegant of any I attended in Cincinnati," wrote the English polymath Harriet Martineau in 1835. "The spirit and superiority of the conversation were worthy of the people assembled." Longworth also loyally supported the arts in Cincinnati by encouraging and aiding, among other painters, the above-mentioned Lily Martin Spencer (America's first major woman painter), Alexander Helwig Wyant, Thomas Buchanan Read, and William Henry Powell. The two figures with whom he is most closely associated, however, are the sculptor Hiram Powers and the black artist Robert Duncanson. Powers he sent to Washington for further artistic training, eventually to Florence; Duncanson he commissioned to paint the murals in his entrance hall. Powers's marble sculpture and Duncanson's oil painting of their common benefactor we shall see in the Cincinnati Art Museum.

Along with the house, Longworth acquired the land behind it, including most of Mount Adams, which he gradually turned into a series of terraced vineyards. In the previous decades, German immigrants had begun planting Cincinnati's hillsides with grape vines. **Wine** had been produced in the Ohio Valley at the Swiss settlement of Vevay in Indiana as early as 1801. Longworth started his first vineyard in 1823; two years later, John Adlum sent him cuttings from Catawba vines. In time Longworth became a skilled viticulturalist. Already by 1828 his dry Catawba found favor among Cincinnati's Germans. But not with Frances Trollope, who deemed Longworth's best "miserable stuff," nor with the British traveler, Thomas Hamilton, who said (in 1833) that it tasted "more like sour cider." But two decades later Moritz Busch, our critical yet discerning German, conceded—high praise indeed from such a source—that Longworth's wine was "not simply to be scorned." In 1842 Longworth reinvented, quite by accident, champagne or, as he always called it, "Sparkling Catawba." Marketed as Golden Wedding Champagne, it was especially popular with Americans. Charles Mackay, another British traveler, pronounced it the equal of France's.

Longworth's interest in viticulture had a humanitarian as well as an economic motive. Wine drinking, he believed, had a less deleterious effect on people than the then ubiquitous hard liquor. In bringing Catawba to "public notice," he declared, "I have rendered my country a greater service than I would have done, had I paid off the National debt." Gradually the wines of the "Western Bacchus" (as Mackay called him in 1858) gained national renown, even inspiring Longfellow to a tribute in verse, "Catawba Wine," apparently written upon receipt of a gift of Longworth's wine. It had, the poet exclaimed, a "divine" taste, "dulcet, delicious, and dreamy." The fourth stanza could only conclude: "For richest and best / Is the wine of the West, / That grows by the Beautiful River."

"The day is not distant," Longworth had predicted in 1845, "when the Ohio Valley will rival the Rhine in the quantity and quality of this wine." By 1850 Cincinnati, shipping 120,000 gallons of wine annually, had become the center of a prosperous wine-growing region. Largely as a result of Longworth's encouragement, the cultivation of the grape spread throughout the Midwest. Winemaking reached a peak during the following decade when the Ohio River became known as "the Rhine of North America." By 1859 Ohio, producing 570,000 gallons a year, more than a third of the national total, had become the premier wine state. Within a twenty-mile radius of Cincinnati there were two thousand acres of productive vineyards. Few visitors to Cincinnati failed to seek out Longworth's famous cellars under Sycamore St. But encroaching settlement of the hillsides and spreading blight (black rot and mildew) in the vines weakened the wine industry. In the mid 1860s it declined and died. Today, after over a century of virtual abstinence, wine growing has returned in a small way to the Ohio Valley.

In 1871 David Sinton bought Belmont. One of many Scots-Irish who emigrated to the New World, Sinton arrived in Cincinnati in 1847. He developed interests in iron, railroads, natural gas, and real estate, built the Grand Opera House, and in 1900 died one of the city's richest men. The Sinton Hotel was named after him. When his only child Anna (born 1852) married Charles Phelps Taft in 1873, Belmont again shone as a center of culture.

The Tafts became discerning collectors of art. From 1902 to about 1911 they acquired by purchase at home and abroad one of the Midwest's finest art collections, one that also indexes collecting taste during that decade, and one of the few midwestern collections not to go east. Appreciating the value of their residence as a historic and architectural landmark and wishing to keep their art collection intact, the Tafts decided to present both to the citizens of Cincinnati. Accordingly in 1927 they announced that they would give the house, the land on which it stood, the art collection it contained, and the sum of one million dollars if others would contribute two and one-half million. The city accepted their generous offer. The additional amount was subscribed, and the historic mansion and its art collection were turned over to the newly formed Cincinnati Institute of Fine Arts. Upon Anna Sinton Taft's death in 1931, two years after her husband's, she bequeathed an additional million for restoring the Taft house to an approximation of its original Federal state. Furniture, mantels, and light fixtures of the period were hunted down and installed, or good reproductions made; the Duncanson murals on the walls uncovered; the ceiling decorations of acanthus leaves and eagles restored. On November 29, 1932, the Taft Museum was formally dedicated. In 1973 the Baum-Taft house was placed on the National Register.

The **Cincinnati Institute of Fine Arts** came into being "to further the musical and artistic education and culture of the people of Cincinnati and . . . to support schools of art, music and drama, art museums, symphony orchestras and other similar activities." The Tafts wished to ensure Cincinnati's renown as a center of culture. And in this they succeeded. "There is no reason," they observed in their letter to the Institute, "if intelligent direction is given to the natural interest and ability of the people, why Cincinnati should not be recognized as one of the greatest centers of art and music in the United States and in the world. In Europe, cities have secured more renown from their pre-eminence in this field than from their size and material development, and the residents of such cities have lived a happier and more varied life than those which relied alone on industrial development for their position." The Tafts's vision remains a valid one. "Men come together in cities to live," Aristotle claimed 2,300 years ago; "they remain there in order to live the good life." This is still true. The Muses are, after all, city folk. The Cincinnati Institute of Fine Arts makes possible "a happier and more varied life" for the citizens of this city. Since 1949 the Institute has sponsored the Fine Arts Fund, which helps support not only the Taft but also the Art Museum, the city's orchestra, ballet, and opera, the May Festival, the Playhouse in the Park, and the Contemporary Arts Center.

The 600 or so objects listed in the Taft's current catalogue (a new one announced for 1992 will revaluate the status of many works) may seem small for a major museum, most of which access more than that number in a single year. Yet the collection is of impressive artistic quality, and the effect it leaves is often overwhelming. Holdings of paintings are strongest in the seventeenth-century Dutch school, British portraitists of the eighteenth century, and in works of the Barbizon school. Landscapes and portraits hold pride of place. Several of these paintings rank among the great works of Western art.

The Tafts believed that the decorative arts no less than painting and sculpture merited attention. "Decorative" seems to imply a lesser importance, but the distinction between the so-called "fine" arts (chiefly painting and sculpture) and the "decorative" arts is, after all, a modern prejudice. By giving a sense of how people lived at different times, the decorative arts can make a period come to life as fully as paintings and sculptures. The Tafts collected in this field with the same enthusiasm that they collected paintings. The museum houses major collections of Italian Renaissance majolica, jewelry, and rock-crystal carvings; French Renaissance painted enamels; rare seventeenth- and eighteenth-century watches; and approximately two hundred Chinese porcelains of the K'ang Hsi, Yung Chêng and Ch'ien Lung periods. Many of the museum's Renaissance artifacts, for example, are small in size and easily overlooked on a first visit. But size deterred neither collectors of the Italian Renaissance like Lorenzo de' Medici nor collectors of the American Renaissance like the Tafts from appreciating their beauty. Anyone who visits this museum only to look at the paintings misses many of its greatest treasures.

We go past the Victorian gateposts to enter through the north wing, added by David Sinton about 1890, that now serves as the museum entrance. The elaborate, five-part Federal mantelpiece before us is the first of many, all finely carved, all different; its sunburst motif is particularly resplendent. The Chinese porcelain jars on the mantel offer a foretaste of the superb oriental artifacts to come.

Left of the stairway a passage leads to a room that often displays temporary exhibits. We can usually visit the Taft's garden. Walled in by the Polk and American Book Co. buildings, the garden, laid out in 1947–49 by Henry Fletcher Kenney, a leading landscape architect whose work we often encounter in the Cincinnati area, is based on French models. Since the Tafts had never laid out a formal garden, Kenny recreated an imaginary garden meant to evoke the early nineteenth century. The classical lines of its paths, set off by well-trimmed shrubs, complement the house's rear façade. On the garden terrace you can sit and rest. Below the garden (where now runs Eggleston Esplanade) once flowed the Miami Canal; beyond looms Columbia Parkway; above, the townhouses on Mount Adams cling precariously to the hillside. From the garden we can peer into the courtyard of the former American Book Co., the brick pavement in basketweave pattern. We also notice the building's campanile, virtually invisible from the street.

We ascend to the museum's second floor. The first room on the left often has temporary exhibits. The Taft Museum is currently revaluating its holdings for the forthcoming catalogue. Even though works here move around less than in large institutions like the Cincinnati Art Museum, they may not always be where I say they are. In the hallway hangs one of the Taft's major masterpieces, the sixteenth-century Flemish tapestry *The Adoration of the Magi,* its detailing exquisite, its colors delicate and muted. It is housed in a magnificent period frame.

Turner's *The Trout Stream,* the leaden skies taut with tension, dominates the room opposite. The Taft's Turner collection, two oils and ten watercolors, enables us to follow the artist's evolution in outline. *The Trout Stream,* an early work in somber colors, never leaves us in doubt regarding its subject. Turner appears here less an innovator than an inheritor of an earlier landscape tradition. Yet already the turbulent sky looks forward to later canvases. The subject of one of the brightly painted Italian majolica dishes in the cabinet is the death of Palinurus, Aeneas's steersman in the *Aeneid.* Nearby hangs John Singer Sargent's masterful portrait of Robert Louis Stevenson, meditative, relaxed, cigarette in hand. George Morland delightfully renders children gathering apples. Ingres portrays the solidly bourgeois

Mlle Jeanne Gonin. We should not miss *View near Rouen* by the wonderful and too short-lived R. P. Bonington.

The artistic treasures that surround us may cause us, momentarily at least, to neglect the rooms themselves. That would be a pity. They create a splendid setting in which to display the art works. Most of the furniture, drapery, and rugs, not original to the house, reflect Cincinnati taste during the nineteenth century's second and third decades, at least as specialists understood such matters in 1932. The interiors are in the French Empire style, modelled upon that of Imperial Rome, that came into being during Napoleon's rule. As Jefferson's influence (itself inspired by French and Italian models) stands behind the house's architecture, so Napoleon's lyres and eagles adorn its interior. Colors popular in the Federal period—reds, violets, yellows—have been employed. Let no one doubt the brightness, the boldness even, of Federal color schemes! The eyecatching carpets, conceived by the former museum designer within the past two decades, are based on those in the Empress Josephine's mansion at Malmaison, outside Paris. They often pick up motifs in the rooms they adorn. That in the room containing *The Trout Stream* explodes in lavender, rose, gold, turquoise, and black. New Brussels carpets, woven in England and based on a pattern drawn around 1800–1815, are projected for the lobby, staircase, and hallways. The museum purchased an excellent collection of Duncan Phyfe furniture, including several mahogany horsehair sofas. The curtains, single- and double-swagged, have elegant circle or star-shaped tiebacks. They also follow French models. The Sheffield silver doorknobs, the period wallpapers, the wall lamps and chandeliers adapt original designs. All elements in the decoration work together in a tasteful way. Such is the harmony of the Taft's interiors that we feel we have stepped not so much into a museum as into an elegant home.

Old London Bridge, in the Long Hall around the corner and formerly attributed to Turner, now appears to be someone's copy after a sketch by Turner. Yet it is a colorful and assured composition. River craft occupy the foreground; baskets of fish lie about. The haze, more Venetian than English, envelops the background, blurring vistas.

The first room off the Long Hall contains seventeenth-century Dutch scenes including *The Music Lesson* by Pieter de Hooch. (Another music lesson, this one by Gerard ter Borch, hangs in the Art Museum.) Aert van der Neer's *Landscape with Figures* complements his *Winter Landscape* in the Art Museum. Jacob van Ruisdael is represented by a moody street scene, and we find characteristically earthy works by Steen, van Ostade (*A Carpenter's Shop*), and ter Borch (*The Sleeping Soldier*), this last masterful in the verisimilitude of its textures: feathers, satin, armor, velvet.

Turner's late *Europa and the Bull* hangs in the second room along the Long Hall. Foreground and background merge in a great blaze of yellow and blue light. Without the caption we would be hard put to determine the painting's subject. Earth, air, water, and fire engage in a cosmic strife that dwarfs Europa's rape by Zeus disguised as a bull. The sun bathes the scene in a symphony of primary colors that suggests indifference to the struggle to take place. This room also exhibits Turner watercolors in rotation, several of Swiss and Italian scenes. These luminous sketches capture the European landscape before railroads had cut ugly swaths through it. Turner was an inveterate traveler. Inspired by Byron's poetry, he followed in the poet's wake across Europe. The watercolors reveal another facet of Turner's genius, one even more suited to his talent than oil.

In this same room we may easily overlook an exquisite Gothic ivory of French origin, *The Virgin of Saint Denis* (ca. 1260–1280). She stands in *contrapposto,* body curving, her smile as mysterious as the Mona Lisa's. It would be difficult to imagine a more delicate or subtle rendering of feminine beauty. Here also we find the Taft's most important Limoges enamel, a fifteenth-century triptych. The central panel depicts the Crucifixion, those on either side St. James and St. Catherine of Alexandria. Two sixteenth-century French miniature enamel portraits in splendid period frames evince impressive psychological penetration.

In the next room hang portraits of elegant women by eighteenth-century British artists: Raeburn, Reynolds, Hoppner, and Gainsborough. The Scot Raeburn caught Jane Fraser-Tytler in a haunting, evocative mood. Over the mantel hangs Gainsborough's pensive Maria Walpole, Duchess of Gloucester. A pair of vases in *sang-de-boeuf* glaze, a rich red produced from copper, set off this portrait. Display cases hold exquisite K'ang Hsi porcelains in *claire-de-lune* and peach-bloom glaze. *Claire-de-lune,* literally "moonlight" blue, is an exquisite pale blue; peach bloom, a soft red shading to green. Collectors prize porcelains in peach bloom highly, those in *claire-de-lune* (rarer still) even more highly. Porcelains in both glazes were probably destined for Imperial use. They possess a classic perfection of form and surface texture as well as of color. A bowl in rice-grain pattern, intricate and delicate, sits on the center table. The Tafts collected Qing porcelain chiefly of the seventeenth and eighteenth centuries. Their holdings are world class and we find examples in several rooms.

The room on the other side of the foyer holds Rembrandt's *Man Leaning on a Sill.* So sad-eyed is his gaze that the painting could pass for a self-portrait. Actually, experts now think it was done by an eighteenth-century imitator of Rembrandt; the adjacent *Portrait of an Elderly Woman* is thought to be by a seventeenth-century follower. In *Portrait of a Young Man,* authentically Rembrandt's, the artist catches the young burgher in the act of rising to extend his hand—to his wife hundreds of miles away in the Metropolitan Museum. His forced smile appears to imply that he has more important business to attend to. By having the hand cut diagonally across the canvas and the body bent, Rembrandt responds to Baroque ideas of energy, motion, and drama. Both the Museum's "Goyas" have recently been reattributed to nineteenth-century followers of Goya. *Queen María Louisa* looks down from over the mantel. Hard eyed, her smile fixed, intolerant, suspicious: the artist captures it all, including the Hope Diamond around her neck. Vulgar and ostentatious, Maria Louisa knew who she was and what she wanted. The painting is taken from a royal family portrait in the Prado. A friend of Goya's, the young bullfighter *Joaquin Costillares* offers a contrast: a popular idol, he has frank eyes but a petulant mouth.

Whistler's *At the Piano* (1858–1859), one of the artist's early masterpieces, also hangs in this room. A portrait of his half-sister Deborah and her daughter, it is even more a study in black and white. This tranquil domestic subject, understated in its muted colors, both looks back to Velázquez and foreshadows major paintings of Whistler's later years, including *Arrangement in Grey and Black, No. 1: The Artist's Mother* and *No. 2: Thomas Carlyle. At the Piano,* one of the few works here not included in the original bequest of 1927, was given to the museum by the Tafts's two daughters, along with other works, in 1962.

Plump, genial *William Howard Taft* by Joaquin Sorolla imposes his good nature upon the elongated (bed)room that follows. It was from the portico of his half-brother's house that on July 28, 1908, Taft accepted the Republican nomination for president. This portrait dates from the following year. Constant Troyon's *Cattle at the Watering Place* is one of several bucolic landscapes in the collection. Among the limpid Corots is *Le Soir,* pretty, yet timeless. Its homage to the evening finds frequent echo in paintings by the Barbizon School, a mid-nineteenth century group of landscape painters (the name derives from the village of Barbizon, southeast of Paris). Nineteen works by these artists—Troyon, Millet, Daubigny, Dupré, Rousseau, even (to a degree) Corot—found their way into the Taft collection. (The museum has no Impressionist paintings, for when the Tafts did their buying at the turn of the century the Impressionists had not achieved the astonishing celebrity later to be theirs.) Once enormously popular, the Barbizon painters subsequently went through decades of critical disfavor before again coming into their own. Imbued with a spiritual dimension often lacking in the Impressionists, these artists sought to capture elemental aspects of man and of nature. They lovingly depict the French countryside; they render its settings and probe its moods; they value the homely toil of those who live on the land.

Across the Long Hall is the former dining room, extended by Mrs. Taft to its present length in 1910. The ceiling plasterwork has a delicate, two-dimensional quality indebted to Robert Adam's work. A display case holds the Tafts's splendid collection of seventeenth- and eighteenth-century gold and enamelled English and European watches. My preference among the Corots here, the haunting *Souvenir de Riva,* catches the Lago di Garda as dusk falls. Corot universalizes the moment to any lake, any dusk. Usually photographs try to imitate paintings; here Corot appears to imitate contemporary daguerrotypes, in which leaf movement during the necessarily long exposure times often left the trees looking blurred. The majestic *Evening on the Oise* by Daubigny, an artist sometimes called "the poet of the river," captures a moment of utter peace. Soft yellow light bathing the horizon gives the scene an aura of timelessness. Daubigny had a special raft built from which to paint the river. Galsworthy, who passed through Cincinnati several times near the end of his life, calls this painting, in *Swan Song* (1928), "a very fine landscape." He does not exaggerate.

The little room adjoining holds another Daubigny river scene, equally mellow. Blue-and-white porcelain of the K'ang Hsi period (1662–1722), with underglazed cobalt blue decoration, fills the wall cabinet. This hard paste K'ang Hsi ware ranks among the summits of Chinese porcelain. The cobalt is as intense and luminous today as it was three centuries ago. "Crackling," the tiny lines on some pieces, is often intentionally induced. A large network is called "ice crackle"; a tiny circular network, "fish roe crackle." On some items in this case the cracks are hand painted to symbolize the "breaking-up" of winter; the prunus blossom symbolizes the coming of spring.

In the hallway is Anton Mauve's aptly named *Changing Pasture* (aptly because the sheep change direction depending on which side of the painting we stand). Immensely popular in America as a painter of sheep, Mauve was a member of the Hague School, active from circa. 1870–1900, a Dutch equivalent to the Barbizon School, from which it drew inspiration. Its members worked chiefly in landscape and in genre scenes. In the Taft we also see major works of this school by Josef Israëls, its artistic leader, and the Maris brothers, all masters of atmospheric painting in this land of moist air and muted colors.

All is symmetry in the music room. Two magnificent chandeliers balance two fireplaces. In earlier times dancers could have raised the lower sections of the ballroom's six triple-hung sash windows, or French windows, and walked unimpeded onto the balcony, there to enjoy the cool evening air. Jefferson first introduced French windows into the United States at Monticello. In 1873 Charles Phelps Taft and Anna Sinton were married in this room. On several Sunday afternoons in winter the museum offers chamber music concerts here.

On one side of Gainsborough's portrait of the *Tomkinson Boys* hangs Frans Hals's portrait of a too-satisfied young man, on the other the mischievous-eyed young woman who was his wife. Both are exceptionally fine renderings, among the best that Hals ever did. At the other end of the room Hals captures a fleeting moment of disdain in *Portrait of a Man (Michiel de Wael?)*. Adjoining, Gainsborough's *Landscape with Figures and Cattle* reminds us how much lovers of landscape lost by the artist's financial need to paint portraits instead of the rural scenes he loved. Above the mantels are Raimundo de Madrazo's renderings of Charles Phelps and Anna Sinton Taft.

Robert Duncanson painted the four picturesque foyer murals. Another four are in the Long Hall. In the 1931–1932 restoration they were rediscovered under layers of wallpaper. Duncanson (1821–1872), his father a Scots-Canadian, his mother a freed mulatto, spent much of his life in Cincinnati. Nicholas Longworth appreciated his talent (more impressive as a landscapist than as a portraitist) and about 1848 commissioned these imaginary landscapes from him. It was an important commission for Duncanson, for he went on in the 1850s to a series of achieved masterpieces. Sometime after Longworth's death in 1863, these murals were covered with a patterned Victorian wallpaper, but not before they had been carefully protected by a coat of varnish.

The murals reflect Duncanson's romantic conception of landscape. Hudson River artists—Allston, Durand, Cole—depict intricate details against a broadly painted background; the small figures are dwarfed by the vast landscape. These artists found inspiration in the classic European landscape tradition, Poussin in particular, Claude even more. Duncanson saw paintings by the Hudson River school in local collections and drew upon them in creating these murals. The murals, it has recently been pointed out, also imitate scenes on fashionable French and English wallpaper designs, themselves imitations of paintings. Instead of paying for expensive wallpaper, Longworth commissioned murals—and probably saved money. Duncanson cleverly painted the shadows on the trompe l'oeil rococo frames to suggest light coming through the door panes.

In the Long Hall Frank Duveneck's *Cobbler's Apprentice*, cigar in hand, coolly blows out a wisp of smoke. Born in Covington in 1848, Duveneck studied after 1870 in Munich, then a leading art center. There he picked up the German school's

Frank Duveneck, *The Cobbler's Apprentice*. Painted in Munich in the 1870s, this is the most famous painting by one of the major artists identified with the Cincinnati area. Courtesy of the Taft Museum.

somber palette and inclination toward realism, and there in 1877 he painted this picture. Although Duveneck's canvases are "northern" in their muted colors, realistic subjects, and impeccable finish, they also reflect Manet, Velázquez, and Hals—especially Hals, whose reputation reemerged in the late nineteenth century after a two-hundred-year eclipse. Like Van Gogh and Monet, Duveneck sought to recapture Hals's vibrant expressionistic technique. Opposite *The Cobbler's Apprentice* hangs a major work by Henry Farny, *The Song of the Talking Wire*. A puzzled, inquisitive Plains Indian leans against a telegraph pole trying to pierce the mystery of the "singing wires." He does not quite grasp that it signals the end of his way of life. Farny, who drew illustrations for *Harper's Weekly* and for the McGuffey *Readers,* also traveled extensively in the Far West and remains best known for his Indian scenes. In the Cincinnati Art Museum we shall encounter other works by Duncanson, Duveneck, and Farny, but few more interesting than those we see here.

RIVERFRONT

1. Lytle Park
2. 1 Lytle Place
3. Concourse Fountains
4. Yeatman's Cove Park
5. *Westward*
6. Central Bridge
7. Public Landing
8. *Showboat Majestic*
9. Coliseum
10. Riverfront Stadium
11. John A. Roebling Bridge
12. *Mike Fink*
13. George Rogers Clark Memorial F
14. Carneal House
15. Laidley House
16. Shinkle Row
17. B B Riverboats, Inc. Dock
18. L.& N. Bridge
19. Bicentennial Commons
    at Sawyer Point
20. *Cincinnati Gateway* Sculpture
21. *Law and Society*

Riverfront

FOR five chapters we have nudged the Ohio River. Occasionally we may even have glimpsed it. Now we go to it. Of all areas of Cincinnati, the riverfront has in recent decades experienced the greatest change. The streets and sights described in the 1943 WPA guide have been virtually obliterated. Today we see before us, in effect, a new creation, one still evolving. The *Cincinnati 2000 Plan* projects significant further development. Yet the Ohio River remains, linking Cincinnati's historic past to its vital present. We begin our tour at Lytle Park. To the south the Ewart Simpkinson Bridge, above I-71, leads to Yeatman's Cove Park.

1 Lytle Place (1980) is a spare, roughly textured structure in striated or "corduroy" concrete, a stylistic device much favored by Paul Rudolph, a leading modern architect. Inset and (on the river side) cantilevered balconies provide spectacular views. 1 Lytle Place is the first of several highrise apartment buildings, first envisaged in the 1948 *Master Plan,* destined for this area. I hope it is the last. I question the wisdom of erecting such a tall building, or any tall buildings, between the business district and the river. Granted, 1 Lytle Place provides views for those fortunate enough to live in it; yet so out of scale is it with everything else, particularly with the buildings surrounding Lytle Park, that its presence jars. After all, only a tiny proportion of Cincinnati's land area adjoins the river. The use of this strip for activities neither public nor water connected is questionable. The building not only has no relationship to its river environment but blocks our view of the Ohio from the city. We cannot assign precise monetary values to views. Their value is intangible. We often know best what a view is worth when we no longer have it.

Insinuating ourselves through a passageway alongside 1 Lytle Place, we emerge unexpectedly upon the flowing exuberance of the **Concourse Fountains** (1976). "No swimming" a sign says, and indeed no swimming is possible in a pool a foot deep. But on warm summer days waders plash about enjoying the jets of water that shoot down on them. The fountain is dedicated to David Sinton; the reflecting pool below was donated in memory of Hulbert Taft, who for decades was in charge of the family paper, the *Times-Star,* and worked valiantly for the city's good.

Concourse Fountains, Yeatman's Cove Park. A favorite place for young and not-so-young to frolic in summer.

Cities often define themselves, at least initially, by a dominant symbol. Venice has its St. Mark's Square, Florence its great dome by Brunelleschi, Pisa its Leaning Tower, Berlin its Brandenburg Gate, Athens its Parthenon, even Las Vegas its Fremont Street. A few large cities have several dominant symbols: New York the Statue of Liberty and Empire State, Paris the Eiffel Tower and Arc de Triomphe, London Big Ben and St. Paul's. These symbols are the most visible and distinctive features these cities have. A city without a dominant symbol is difficult to visualize. We think of such cities less and, unconsciously perhaps, think less of them. But when we come upon a dominant, recognizable symbol, in reality or in imagination, we often experience a deep, soul-tingling thrill. The symbol encapsulates for us that city's essence.

Cincinnati has several symbols—the Roebling Bridge, the Carew Tower, the Tyler Davidson Fountain—but none dominates. In 1948 St. Louis held a national competition for a riverfront symbol. Eero Saarinen won the competition with the 630-foot high stainless-steel Gateway Arch (completed in 1965). When planning Yeatman's Cove Park, the city fathers sought a symbol. Cincinnati's waterfront fountain, though visually less spectacular than St. Louis's arch, succeeds as well in human terms. In its diverse organization and population, its nooks and crannies, this multilevel fountain serves as a paradigm of the city itself. It is a paradise for the young and not-so-young—and for people watchers. Its exits and entrances, steps on which to sit and steps on which to get soaked, towers that exude water and towers

Cincinnati skyline, from Concourse Fountains. Two new towers anchor this view of the skyline, the 312 Walnut Building (1990) at the left and the Chemed Center (1991) on the right. The middle of the photograph is dominated by the fraternal twins, Atrium I and II. Behind Atrium I is the Carew Tower. Peeping out from behind 312 Walnut is the Central Trust Tower.

that shoot it out, provide innumerable places to explore, to play in, and in which to hide.

Before descending to Yeatman's Cove Park, we pause to contemplate the Cincinnati **skyline.** In our walks we shall come upon an abundance of vantage points, some well known, some unexpected, from which to view this cluster of skyward-soaring structures. The land rises sharply from the river to form the plateau extending several hundred yards inland on which we stand. Between 3rd and 4th streets the land again rises sharply, remaining relatively flat until it approaches the base of the encircling hills. Although downtown buildings begin on 3rd St., the taller ones are on the higher ground of 4th and 5th—set, in effect, upon a pedestal. Scanning from right to left, we move from the twin octagonal towers of the Procter & Gamble complex across the skyline to 312 Walnut, with the Central Trust Tower half hidden behind it. Cincinnati's Basin faces toward the sun, and the southern exposure allows optimum light to fall on the buildings at all seasons. Over the course of the day the play of light and shade gradually changes.

At night the vista is more spectacular still. With tall buildings we think first about daytime views, but increasingly cities define their image of downtown by its appearance at night. Television newscasts, to give viewers a sense of immediate orientation, often open with a nighttime aerial panorama of the city. A number of Cincinnati's tall buildings, among them Cincinnati Gas & Electric and the Central Trust and Carew towers, are floodlit. In Cincinnati as in most American cities the lighted buildings are the great skyscrapers of the 1920s and 30s; the elongated rectangles of the subsequent International style do not light well. Today the older buildings convey an image of enchantment as well as of commerce, and much of the current silvery or golden lighting is designed to make them look even more fantasy-like. With the lights placed on the setbacks—ideal podiums from which to beam rays upwards—we have little sense of where the illumination comes from. Close up, the lighting may be virtually impossible to see, but from afar the floodlit skyscrapers appear untouchable, mysterious, magical.

Most cities offer a disappointing collection of highrises. Few appear designed specifically for the urban landscape in which they are located. Many of them, like 1 Lytle Place, could have sprouted anywhere. Towers tend to work best when massed or in clusters, as in Manhattan or San Francisco; worst when they are isolated from each other, as in London or Louisville. Towers tend to work best when they are of different styles. Virtually every tall building on the Boston skyline—except the Art Deco Custom House Tower—has a flat top. This induces monotony. The Cincinnati skyline is unusual in that it is one of the few urban skylines that, in part at least, has been deliberately planned. Architects have designed several recent buildings to be viewed within the overall perspective. The newer structures echo the pyramidal or stepped appearance of the city's earlier Art Deco edifices. The P & G Towers, the *Times-Star,* Cincinnati Gas & Electric, the Central Trust Tower actually culminate in pyramids or in pyramid-like structures; Atrium I and II and the Central Trust Center have a deliberately stepped appearance. Lower-scaled structures to east and west build to the taller center. The buildings—pyramidal, stepped, even flat topped—climax in the Carew Tower, which itself pyramidal, stepped, and flat topped is the apex of a pyramidal skyline.

Cincinnati has one of the most visible skylines of any American metropolis. Unlike some urban dwellers elsewhere, Cincinnatians have exceptional opportunities to view their skyline. It arises at the center of a natural topographic bowl; we may admire its contours from the four points of the compass. The hills that ring the city, north and south, upriver and downriver, offer a choice of vantage points. From all of them the skyline is the city's cynosure. Whereas we enjoy Manhattan's skyline most readily from outside the island—from New Jersey, Staten Island, Brooklyn, best of all from the moveable feast of a boat ride—we enjoy Cincinnati's without having to leave the city.

Cincinnati's buildings are composed chiefly of stone, terra cotta, brick, marble, granite, concrete—materials that convey an impression of solidity and permanence. There are few tall metal buildings and only two (partially) glass towers, the Provident Bank Tower and 312 Walnut. In instant cities like Houston, the newer buildings dominate the scene; in Cincinnati, the older and newer work together. The city's slower growth has meant that recent constructions do not constantly alter the character and outline of its silhouette. The French rightly call their most significant buildings *monuments historiques.* Historical monuments, or landmarks, can enrich our lives greatly. In Cincinnati the long presence of its two signpost buildings, the stately Carew and the more flamboyant Central Trust, enables us to maintain a sense of relationship and continuity with the cityscape. The Central Trust is the city's most prominent "pyramid"; it and the tapered Carew, directly behind it, maintain the visual dominance of downtown. Together, they serve as visual icons and as such are important in focusing our image of the city. With their high recognition factor, the Central Trust and Carew are graphic symbols that have become civic emblems. Visible from miles away, by day and by night, these unmistakable landmarks impress their familiar contours upon our imagination. The character of a city depends upon the survival of vestiges from the past. Like its historic buildings from the nineteenth century and even the old shop signs, Cincinnati's long-established landmark towers deepen the city's historical dimension, however unconscious people may be of it, and lend it dignity. The Central Trust and the Carew provide emotional satisfaction, even security, in a world of dislocation and change. Like the hills and the river, we experience them every day, often in different ways. They are sources of identity as well as of pleasure. They are there, and so are we.

The skyline not only changes with the vantage point and the time of the day, it offers an altogether different effect when viewed driving along **Ft. Washington Way.** This distribution system of freeways, connectors, feeders, and exit ramps gives access to the central business district. People, as Kevin Lynch has pointed out, know a city from the paths they follow, and Americans increasingly follow the paths of the freeway. Freeways enable us to experience the city in ways entirely new from our forebearers. No longer are we limited to static images. The car's kinetic trajectory leaves us with a palimpsest of ever-changing, overlapping images, one superimposed upon the other, like a movie run in slow motion. These images, perhaps because of their very transience, may remain all the more vivid in the mind's eye.

Built in the 1960s and fortunately depressed throughout most of its length, Ft. Washington Way has the feel of a Rube Goldberg creation. The uninitiated cannot but find it bewildering; even veterans undergo repeated (mis)adventures before mastering its intricacies. Ollie M. James, the longtime *Enquirer* columnist, once compared it to "a near-sighted octopus eating spaghetti." Be assured that Ft. Washington Way does make sense, much of it anyway, but driving this sunken racetrack the first time or alone you had better keep your eye on the road. Navigating its lanes at busy times requires the concentration normally given to shooting whitewater rapids. Trying to avoid traffic hightailing it toward ramps swerving in every direction tests the reflexes. But if someone else is at the wheel, then experience to the full the shifting geometry of the cityscape: the fleeting glimpses of individual buildings, the changing perspectives on the overall skyline, the ever-moving composition of space and form. Speed no less than space frees the eye. We glimpse the backs of buildings we looked at on 4th St. but now we find ourselves unconcerned with detail, liberated from architectural closeups by the fast lane. The elements come together and fall apart, compose and recompose, as we race along. The experience, whether terrifying or exhilarating or both, leaves a lasting impression.

Expressways can add a vibrant new dimension to our urban lives. As with our pedestrian motion, we need to think about the quality of our high-speed motion through a city. Hurtling along an expressway, we respond to a series of constantly changing impressions moving by like frames in a film. Expressways not only open up great panoramic views but afford us, in effect, new vistas of experience. Expressways can also embody qualities of a work of art. They can be among the most beautiful structures of our age, not only when seen in aerial photos—where their curves and cloverleafs stand out dramatically against the landscape—but in the images they provide as we ride them. Ft. Washington Way is not beautiful, however. It strikes me as awkwardly designed: redundant, confusing, even hazardous. But the approaches to Cincinnati, those from the east in particular, can be exhilarating. The descent toward the city from I-71, with the skyline silhouetted against the setting sun, is unforgettable. A ride on the 6th St. ramp off Columbia Parkway (such a ride concludes this book) allows multiple perspectives on the spectacular profile of the Procter & Gamble Towers. The design of this ramp impresses me as brilliant, virtually a new form of urban sculpture for motion.

Everyone will come to have his or her favorite view of the skyline. Mine remains that by which I first experienced it, years ago, driving up on I-75 from the south. Descending toward the Ohio I knew to be near, I suddenly caught a fleeting glimpse of an impressive mass of buildings fronting the river. The buildings quickly passed in review from east to west, then disappeared from sight, only to reemerge a few seconds later. Now the skyline appeared whole and it stayed in view. To this day, my first sight of Cincinnati from I-75 remains ineradicable. Interstate construction in 1990 eliminated a bend and altered the view—the city no longer disappears momentarily from sight. Even so, every time I approach the city via this route I relive my initial delight.

The city we remember most vividly is often the city we first see. The first view of Cincinnati most early settlers and travelers had was from the Ohio River. After floating hundreds of miles through often pristine forest, they rounded the bend at Mount Adams and there it was: a bustling metropolis in the midst of apparent wilderness. The experience never failed to amaze. Visitors to Cincinnati also arrived by wagon and canal boat, even on foot, and subsequently via the city's five passenger train terminals. After 1933, many enjoyed their first perspective on the city from the portals of Union Terminal. Even before Union Terminal opened, the automobile had become a major means of transportation. Today, along with the airplane, it is the major mode of entry into the city, and even most air travelers approach the city via the I-75 route described above. "We tend to slide into cities today," writes Lawrence Halprin, "as if the encounter was not worthy of great theater. . . . The approach to the great city should be celebrated as a dramatic event." Halprin cites San Francisco and Jerusalem as two cities in which the initial view "is a breath-taking and emotional event." He might also have cited Cincinnati.

At the base of the Concourse Fountains we take the left-hand path toward the river. **Yeatman's Cove Park,** dedicated in 1976, encompasses Cincinnati's oldest, most historic ground. Nearby the first boatload of pioneers disembarked on December 28, 1788. Five years later, at the northeast corner of Front and Sycamore streets, Griffin Yeatman opened a tavern. This two-and-a-half story log structure, stretching one hundred feet along Sycamore, was the community's first center, serving as post office, ballroom, and all-purpose meeting place. In the 1970s responsible civic leadership, federal grants, and enlightened private enterprise brought Yeatman's Cove

Serpentine Wall, Yeatman's Cove Park. This undulating esplanade is ideal for river watching. The Coliseum is in the middle distance, Riverfront Stadium behind it, the Central Bridge to the left.

Park into being. The result is impressive. Walkways wind over grounds that are attractively landscaped; lighting is built into bollards or placed on tubular poles; trash receptacles disguised as ships' air funnels give the park a nautical air that ties it to the river. Less successful is the fixed seating of which there is too much. Fixed seats limit choice; for casual sitting, William H. Whyte reminds us, they are inflexible and can be socially uncomfortable. Unfortunately, too, these modernistic benches and chairs also vie with each other in providing a bruising perch.

We do better choosing a spot on the **Serpentine Wall** that fronts the Ohio. The Wall has already become a Cincinnati landmark. The undulating design mirrors the river's course as it snakes its way past the city. Practical as well as esthetic, the Wall provides flood protection. Part of it even doubles as an outdoor amphitheater.

Opposite the Serpentine Wall is Newport, Kentucky. Clearly visible is the clock tower of A. C. Nash's grandiose 1884 Courthouse. Before it stands the stone spire of St. Paul's Episcopal Church. Left, we see the Louisville & Nashville Bridge (1872; 1897). The original span, built for the railroad, is the second oldest of Cincinnati's bridges. Later, a separate span went up for vehicles and pedestrians. After the Civil War Cincinnati found itself handicapped because it lacked direct rail access to its traditional southern markets. The city began to lose ground to its commercial rival, Louisville, positioned on the Ohio's other side. With the L & N Bridge, along with the Cincinnati Southern Bridge downriver, the city regained a competitive edge.

Beyond the L & N is the **Daniel Carter Beard Bridge.** It derives its name from

Daniel Carter Beard, born in Cincinnati and for a time a Covington resident, who founded the Sons of Daniel Boone in 1905, which five years later merged with the Boy Scouts of America. Opened in 1977, this bridge is the most graceful of the newer spans. Its parabolic arches, unfortunately painted a golden yellow, have led Cincinnatians to dub it affectionately (if unimaginatively) the "Big Mac" Bridge. Past the abandoned pylons, or ice piers, off the Serpentine Wall we sight, moored to the opposite shore, the furthest upriver of a flotilla of floating restaurants. The initial restaurant, "The Islands," a pink confection flaunting modernistic lines and Art Deco windows, moored here in 1983; four years later it floated down to Louisville. Its replacement was the "Newport Beach," also pink, also gone. The success of "The Islands" spawned the other restaurants we see on Newport's Riverboat Row.

Near the main walkway in Yeatman's Cove Park a bronze triptych records significant moments in Cincinnati's history, from 1788 to the Civil War. It focuses on the Ohio's role in the city's destiny, for its history and that of Cincinnati intertwine at every point. Past the triptych, David von Schlegell's sculpture *Westward* (1980) commemorates the movement across the land. The sculpture's precarious tilt when seen head on or from the rear may hint at the perils involved in migrating westward, traditionally the direction of hope in America. The piece is more reassuringly contemplated from where we stand.

Over time cities on a body of water evolve ceremonies, festivals, even sports events centering around it. Venice's annual wedding of herself to the sea is the most famous and long-lived of these ceremonies. Cincinnati's celebration of its water heritage hardly goes back further than the creation of Yeatman's Cove Park. Today the city sponsors numerous activities that center upon its waterfront. The most boisterous is Riverfest, begun in 1977 and intended to celebrate Cincinnati's relationship with the Ohio. It takes place each year on the Labor Day weekend, now draws 500,000 people to both sides of the river, and culminates in a spectacular display of fireworks and laser beams.

The Serpentine Wall is also a good place from which to contemplate the **Ohio River.** I find its steps, almost deserted on a Sunday morning, an ideal spot to read the papers, soak up the sun, and savor the river scene. A river, Emerson said in "Nature," provides "a perpetual gala, and boasts each month a new ornament." I like this river's steady, unhurried flow. I like the deep laryngeal sound of its towboat horns and the roar of their powerful engines. Rivers and their sounds can evoke long-buried memories. As a child growing up in Manhattan, I remember the deep bass of freighters' horns as they chugged up the East River to the swirling, treacherous currents of Hell Gate. Looking upon the Ohio, I feel as if I have come home.

"It is well to have some water in your neighborhood," wrote Emerson's friend Thoreau in *Walden*, "to give buoyancy to and float the earth." Mankind must have an innate preference for water in the landscape. Watching the Ohio River we experience the enduring contrast between liquid and solid; we participate in the eternal dialogue between river and sky. We respond to the river's varying moods: its early morning mists, the vapors rising like an exhalation; its whitecaps churning in a high wind; its twilight calm. Stone and water, we realize, do not go out of fashion. Nor do riparian pleasures pall.

Cities and rivers enjoy a relationship that goes back to the beginnings of civilization. From its founding Cincinnati has mingled its identity with its river. The Ohio flows for 981 miles from Pittsburgh to Cairo, Illinois, but it also flows from century to century. Like the city before which it passes, the river represents a continuum, related both to past and future. For most of the nineteenth century, and to a greater degree than we may realize in the twentieth, the Ohio was—and remains—Cincinnati's artery of life.

A river may even offer a poetic parallel to human life. Like a human being, a river acts and communicates. It embodies beginning, being, changing, flowing forward, and ending. We think on its meaning; we may partake of its movement. Watching this river we ponder the passing of time from 1788, when Cincinnati was founded, through its more than two centuries of existence. Although as much a part of time and change as we are, the Ohio River gives the impression—at least to our scurrying human senses—of having always been there. It is a symbol of permanence as well as of impermanence. (Actually, the Ohio is relatively recent in its present bed; in geological time it is not much more than a rivulet in the sand, one that may disappear with the next wave.) Flowing from the past through the present into the future, the river unites our lives with the humanity that has populated the site of Cincinnati. "Time present and time past / Are both perhaps present in time future, / And time future contained in time past." So T. S. Eliot begins his *Four Quartets*. "The river is within us." It reminds us of our place in time.

Most American cities, unlike their counterparts in Europe, have cut themselves off from their water. People find it difficult to get to the waterfront or to walk alongside it. Highways, docks, decayed factories, railroad yards, the detritus of an industrial past block access. For all of Chicago's magnificent lake and park frontage, how often do we actually get close to Lake Michigan? In Cleveland are we even aware of Lake Erie? Except when sighted from a freeway or a highrise, how often at Louisville is the Ohio River in evidence?—or the Connecticut at Hartford? But in Cincinnati the Ohio focuses the city. It is less the distance from open country that counts than the distance from the Ohio.

Most water frontages can, with help and care, survive the cruellest abuse. In recent decades, St. Louis has successfully opened up its riverfront, Boston has one of the most continuously accessible (and used) waterfronts in the country, New Orleans allows us to walk more of its Mississippi frontage than before. Even Manhattan's riverfront, accessible to the public at few points, often in direct competition with peripheral highway traffic, is now being developed more sensitively, at Battery Park City, for example. As early as 1907, the Kessler plan for Cincinnati's park system noted with regret "that in the past no attention has been paid to the matter of rescuing river front property within the city." It concluded that "for the present at least the reclamation of that river front seems out of the question." After letting its waterfront stagnate for six more decades, with Yeatman's Cove Park Cincinnati made a good start in reclaiming it. Such a venture reflected the city's new attitude toward its most marvelous natural amenity. Bicentennial Commons at Sawyer Point, upriver from the Louisville & Nashville Bridge, opens up more river frontage for public use. Other American cities have preserved their waterfronts. Ten miles of lakefront on either side of Chicago's Loop, much of it formerly industrial, became

1884 flood. The 1884 flood rose to 71 feet 4 inches, the highest level then recorded. Cincinnatians moved about lower Walnut Street by boat. Courtesy of the Cincinnati Historical Society.

public parks early in this century. Farther north on Lake Michigan, Milwaukee also has virtually open shore frontage. Although these achievements remain exceptional in the annals of American cities, they indicate the direction for Cincinnati to go. The Ohio River itself is being cleaned up. The fish have come back, and some species can be eaten; boating has become increasingly popular; perhaps one day Cincinnatians will again be able to swim safely in its waters. Perhaps one day they will also be able to walk along the Ohio's banks for long stretches, as Londoners do the Thames and, even more happily, Parisians the quays along the Seine.

Cincinnati has not always found it easy to come to terms with its river. T. S. Eliot, who grew up in St. Louis, which has the Mississippi in its front yard, speaks in *Four Quartets* of the river, any river, as a "strong brown god—sullen, untamed and intractable." The Ohio had some bad habits: in winter it overflowed its banks, in summer it dried up at inconvenient moments. There were reasons, then, to cite Eliot again, why "the brown god is almost forgotten / By the dwellers in cities." The Ohio's normal level is about twenty-six feet. Flood stage is fifty-two feet, and many years the Ohio exceeds it. On December 17, 1847, it crested at sixty-four feet, one of the highest recorded floods up to that time. Riverfront stores and offices were under water; navigation was suspended. By the following September the Ohio had fallen to its lowest point in twenty years. River traffic virtually ceased. Most years low water closed the Ohio at Cincinnati for a hundred days. In 1883, when the water level dropped to twenty-three inches, people waded across from Cincinnati to Covington. Although the Ohio has not been entirely cured of its bad habits, their consequences have become less severe. A sequence of fifty wicket **dams,** begun in 1910 by the Army Corps of Engineers and completed in 1929, ensured a minimum river depth of nine feet. Fixed concrete dams began in 1954 (in 1990 fourteen were in place) to replace the earlier ones. They increased the depth to twenty-five feet. In effect, the body of water we view before Cincinnati is less a river than a ninety-seven mile pool that allows year-round shipping. The Meldahl dam marks the upstream limit; the Markland, the downstream. Even though the Ohio River no longer dries up, it sometimes still overflows. Contrary to popular belief, the dams do not guarantee against a flood. But the flood control reservoirs and dams on the Ohio's tributaries, along with the levees and floodwalls on the Ohio itself, make floods less likely. They are no longer annual events.

We walk downriver toward the Public Landing. Overhead we hear the whine of traffic crossing the steel grid of the **Central Bridge** (1891). Connecting the city with Newport, it was the last span built across the Ohio at Cincinnati for nearly seventy years. Intended for vehicles and pedestrians, it is more simply designed than the L & N, for it did not have to bear heavily loaded trains. With its wrought-iron filigree embellishments set upon steel cantilever trusses, it is one of the river's more decorative spans. Increasing maintenance costs have apparently doomed the Central. Another bridge, downriver from the Roebling Bridge, is scheduled to replace it in the 1990s. Although three bridges presently connect Covington with Cincinnati, Covington officials believe that the Clay Wade Bailey and Brent Spence bridges do not provide adequate access to Covington's downtown and that the Roebling does not offer sufficiently easy access from Cincinnati's center.

Bits of the **Public Landing's** cobblestone paving remain. In summer sports enthusiasts crowd the landing to launch their pleasure boats. From here steamboats left for Coney Island, Cincinnati's fabled amusement park nine miles upriver. For several decades the second *Island Queen* (1925), the most famous of the Coney Island steamboats, made five round trips daily during summer months. Its five decks could accommodate 4000 passengers. As the paddlewheeler steamed upstream, its calliope merrily played "Take me out to the Ball Game" or "Daisy, Daisy." The *Island Queen* burned at a Pittsburgh wharf in September 1947, but its berth in the remembrances of a generation of Cincinnatians is secure. "Going up the beautiful, winding Ohio on the *Island Queen,*" Doris Day recalls in her autobiography, was "one of the dreamy memories of my youth."

Docked at the Public Landing since 1969 is the *Showboat Majestic.* This "last of the original floating palaces" (a plaque on board informs us) was built in 1923. One of the most recent showboats built, it is now listed on the National Register of Historic Places. Owned by the city since 1967, the *Majestic* illustrates the continuity of the city's river heritage. The first showboats appeared on the Cincinnati riverfront in 1831. Gustavus Wolfing describes an early entrepreneur in an 1835

Showboat Majestic. Each summer since 1969 the *Showboat Majestic* (1923) offers a medley of dramatic fare. Showboats in the nineteenth century were a frequent and welcome sight on the inland waterways. Permanently docked at the Public Landing, the *Showboat Majestic* is now the only showboat in existence. Across the Ohio the Licking River emerges from Kentucky. To the right are the fine mansions of Covington's Riverside district.

letter: "A smart fellow bought himself a boat, remodeled it into a theater, and gives performances on the Ohio River. Everybody is attracted by this novel idea, and he makes plenty of money. Being on the river, the city can collect no taxes from him." For the nearly three decades before the Civil War, showboat performances were a part of life along the inland rivers. A steam calliope, its sound carrying over the countryside ten miles or more, announced the showboat's arrival. Townsmen closed up shops, farmers left their ploughs, to gather at the dock. *Ten Nights in a Bar Room, Honest Hearts, Triss of the Rockies* thrilled the crowds at these small-town landings. In *Huckleberry Finn* (1884) Huck and Jim witness a travesty of Shakespeare "for men only" by Twain's memorable charlatans, the King and the Duke. The performance reflects Twain's own riverboat days in the late 1850s, a time when the showboat tradition had reached its lowest ebb. The revival—and the beginning of showboating's golden era—began in 1878 when Augustus Byron French launched his first boat from the foot of Lawrence St. in Cincinnati. Each summer the *Showboat Majestic* maintains this fine river tradition by presenting comedies and musicals. Although current shows are not carbon copies of the earlier melodramas, no one will accuse them of taxing their audience's intellectual resources. Until 1965 the *Majestic* made stops up and down the river but it now lies permanently moored in Cincinnati, the last survivor of the original showboats.

Flatboat and two keelboats. Early pioneers floated down the Ohio in flatboats, which on arrival were often broken up for shelter. Keelboats enabled a primitive commerce to develop on the inland waterways. Some keelboats had sails, but rivermen, pushing the boat forward with poles, provided the primary source of propulsion.

Cincinnati's Public Landing is a major historic site of the old Northwest Territory. For a hundred years the city's life centered around this stretch of riverfront, which then ran from Main St. to Broadway. Over two hundred years ago Cincinnati began as a tiny frontier outpost on the big bend of the Ohio River. Those who chose its site chose well. At the 470-mile point on the Ohio, Cincinnati is almost equidistant between Pittsburgh, where the river begins, and Cairo, where it flows into the Mississippi. Within this central location, it is also equidistant from Limestone (as Maysville was then called), an important jumping-off point for the populous Bluegrass region centered around Lexington, and Louisville, strategically located at the Falls of the Ohio. Cincinnati also lies opposite the mouth of the Licking River, a navigable stream that served as another gateway to the South. And it is located at the northernmost point at which the Ohio penetrates into the rich farmland of what was then the Northwest Territory. Settlers could float down to Cincinnati by flatboat, then proceed overland to Indiana and Illinois. A river offers people a way into a city—and a way out of it. Cincinnati quickly became a main provision point for settlers coming from the East. Many who stopped in the lively young city stayed.

Early settlers set off from Pittsburgh on **flatboats** that drifted downstream at three-and-a-half miles an hour. The flatboats were of varying sizes and shapes, from twenty to one hundred feet in length, twelve to twenty feet wide. Of simple (often shoddy) construction, flat bottomed and square at the ends, they were managed by a single large oar and were barely watertight enough for a single voyage. Settlers arriving at their destination either broke the boats up to build their first cabins or sold them for lumber. Others poled rafts down the current. On board was the family cow, chickens, grandma's rocking chair, and baby in the cradle. "Hi-o, away we go, floating down the O-hi-o," sang thousands of immigrants. Flatboats, even rafts, were still to be sighted along the Ohio as late as the 1870s. We may even consider the flatboats ancestors of the barges we find on the river today.

Virtually contemporaneous with the flatboats were the **keelboats.** Fifty to seventy feet long with a fifteen- to eighteen-foot beam, they had a retractable keel, sometimes a sail, and could be poled or towed upstream. Keelboats allowed a primitive form of river trade to develop. By 1815 perhaps some 300 of them plied the Ohio. They dominated the river's commerce until the 1820s. The coming of the steamboat doomed these colorful craft and the equally colorful men who navigated them. Like the flatboats, the keelboats were slow to disappear. Although **steamboats** took over commerce on the main streams, keelboats continued to work the side rivers.

In 1811 the steamboat *New Orleans* set out from Pittsburgh, passed by Cincinnati, and reached the destination for which it was named in January 1812. It did not, however, return to the Ohio. Other steamboats followed. In 1815 the *Enterprise* descended from Louisville to New Orleans. The year after, the *Washington* went from Brownsville on the Monongahela to New Orleans; the next spring it made a historic run upstream, reaching Louisville in twenty-five days. In the beginning steamboats were a curiosity. To Europeans that is what they remained. "These Western vessels are foreign to all the ideas we are accustomed to entertain of boats," exclaimed Charles Dickens in 1842. "I hardly know what to liken them to or how to describe them. . . . Except that they are in the water, and display a couple of paddle-boxes, they might be intended . . . to perform some unknown service, high and dry, upon a mountain top." Curiosities or not, these craft marked the beginning of a revolution in transportation that fundamentally changed the economic life of the Middle West and South. Though developed in the East, the steamboat had particular importance for the West. By allowing goods and people to come upstream easily, steamboats inaugurated a vast expansion of passenger and commercial traffic. Now that steam had proven it could master the willful rivers, Pittsburgh and Cincinnati shipyards clamored with activity. The *Vesta,* the first locally built craft, was launched in 1816. Eighty of the first three hundred made for the western rivers were constructed in Cincinnati. The *Washington,* with its flat-bottomed hull, shallow draft, and high-pressure, wood-burning boilers, first approximated what became the standard design. Future steamboats were modelled upon it. Big or small, steamboats were invariably painted white. Their life expectancy was short, rarely more than three or four years. Collisions, snags in the river, or their own exploding engines, doomed them. The most spectacular explosion in front of the city occurred on April 25, 1838, as the *Moselle,* a so-called "Brag Boat" and Cincinnati's pride, raced a competitor. All four of its boilers, overheated, blew up. Charred bodies crashed through the roofs of Cincinnati. The captain was hurled across the Ohio into Kentucky. The ship split and sank. In all, 136 perished.

During the first half of the nineteenth century the Ohio River became America's main "road" west, Cincinnati the main western entrepôt. Steamboat traffic made Cincinnati for a generation, from the mid-1820s to the mid-1850s, the West's boom-town, the nation's fastest-growing city. Many years arrivals and departures at the Public Landing exceeded 5000. The peak year, with 8000, was 1852. Mid-nineteenth century photographs reveal steamboats stacked three and four deep the length of the Public Landing. "A notable place," Mrs. Trollope described it in about 1830, "extending for more than a quarter of a mile." Twenty years later Moritz Busch found the Public Landing "covered with all sorts of bales, goods, and barrels, and . . . crowded with carts, porters, sailors, merchants, and departing and arriving travelers. It is, so to speak, the face of the city, and at the same time the entrance to the beehive that it resembles." Though in a northern state, Cincinnati has always looked south and west for its trading ventures. Carrying goods and passengers up and down the Ohio, the Mississippi, and their many tributaries, the steamboat helped Cincinnati become America's major inland port. The inland cities had land-ings instead of piers, but these freshwater extensions of an ocean-borne commerce were otherwise hardly less maritime than their coastal counterparts. With thirty thousand miles of river "coast" with which to trade, this city developed a commerce as extensive as if it had been placed on the shores of the Mediterranean or Atlantic. Cincinnati, thought Horace Greeley in 1851, was "destined to become the focus and market for the grandest circle of manufacturing thrift on the continent." By 1860 the city had risen to seventh in population, and third in manufactures, among the coun-try's urban centers.

As the steamboat traffic flourished, the waterfront area thrived. Stores, facto-ries, rooming houses, pork-packing facilities stood cheek-by-jowl. Front St., along the river just north of where Mehring Way runs today, was for half a century the city's busiest thoroughfare. Cincinnati became notorious for its wide open water-front. For most of its history the Public Landing was the center of a rough-and-tumble area. Life on the levee, as the waterfront was then dubbed, was (to recall Hobbes) "poor, nasty, brutish, and short." Whites, blacks, and mulattoes lived in squalid tenements along now obliterated and forgotten streets like Rat Row and Sausage Row. Before the Civil War most roustabouts and levee folk were white. In July 1862, when jobs were scarce, Irish levee workers drove blacks—who were underbidding them—off the docks and boats. Days of rioting followed. By the 1870's two-thirds or more of the roustabouts were black. The river did not discrim-inate. In high water it flooded the dwellings of all, black or white, who lived near its banks.

Lafcadio Hearn provides a graphic depiction of **levee life.** As a young news-paper reporter in the 1870s, Hearn described sympathetically the sights, the smells, the hard existence of the men who "ran on the river" and their women. He chroni-cled the tragedies of the downtrodden and depressed; he noted acts of unexpected generosity among them; he visited dancing halls and got to know their habitués; he talked to officers Knox and Brazil who patrolled the area; and he compiled one of the first collections of levee folk songs. Stephen Foster had earlier drawn inspiration from levee life. But whereas Foster softened and sentimentalized the songs he heard, Hearn took them down as he heard them.

House by house Hearn investigated Sausage Row and Rat Row. Sausage Row, which ran from Broadway to Ludlow, was largely black; on Rat Row, from Walnut to Main, lived "white tramps and roustabouts." The latter, asserted Hearn, was "a locality eminently unfavorable to reportorial enterprise. . . . Desperate and drunken levee hands and dusky-skinned, tigerish, half-famished courtesans, who mingle in groups at the entrance of the villainous looking grog-holes, that look out upon the river front, shouted forth blasphemies and abominations upon the item-hunter as he hurried by." Hearn did more than titillate middle-class readers by his accounts of slumming: with compassion but without condescension he endeavored to understand the degradation before his eyes. The "lights and shadows" of levee life, he wrote, "are alike characterized by a half savage simplicity; its happiness or misery is almost purely animal; its pleasures are wholly of the hour, neither enhanced nor lessened by anticipations of the morrow." This transience Hearn epitomized in "Dolly: An Idyll of the Levee," which tells of a beautiful mulatto girl who sacrifices herself and dies for a faithless lover.

When Hearn wrote in the 1870s, steamboat traffic had begun to decline. The canal trade had drawn off traffic from the Ohio after 1835. The railroads, which carried goods anywhere their tracks ran, further siphoned off the river's commerce. After the Civil War the once lively waterfront gradually became quieter. As floods drove businesses away from the river, the hub of the city gradually shifted north. The riverfront decayed. Each major flood left its quota of abandoned buildings. The mountainous ice-jams of 1918, crushing many boats, administered river life a crippling blow. The disastrous 1937 flood gave it its coup de grâce. The decrepit structures still stood, but their days were numbered.

After World War II Cincinnati decided to make a clean sweep of its waterfront. Ft. Washington Way, Riverfront Stadium and Coliseum, Yeatman's Cove Park emerged from the city's far-sighted 1948 *Metropolitan Master Plan*. This was followed by the 1964 *Plan for Downtown Cincinnati*. In the 1960s the standard approach to **urban redevelopment** was to wipe out all existing structures and build a totally new environment that had virtually no relationship to what was there before. This is what happened in Cincinnati. Almost all of its waterfront succumbed to the wrecker's ball. With hindsight, we may regret that the city flattened so much. Every older citizen will have his or her laments over what has been lost. Nothing comparable to Laclede's Landing in St. Louis, with its concentration of refurbished historic buildings now filled with restaurants and shops, is now possible in Cincinnati, though here and there we may still come upon waterfront warehouses with interesting possibilities for restoration. But change of some kind was clearly necessary. So instead of decaying structures, we have a spruced-up Public Landing, the Stadium-*cum*-Coliseum complex, Yeatman's Cove, and 1 Lytle Place, with other buildings to come. The view of the city from the river has changed dramatically.

Whatever the loss in color and historic structures, today's sanitized riverfront is clean and pleasant to walk through. Most preservationists will concede that retaining too many obsolescent buildings can put the future in a straitjacket. On the whole, I find the waterfront development well conceived, certainly a vast improvement over the dreary scene that preceded it. The redevelopment has enabled Cincinnatians to begin to rediscover the river that is their inheritance. What the waterfront presently lacks most is people. Except when events bring them to the Stadium or

1918 ice jam. Mountainous ice jams crushed the *Cincinnati* and other boats moored at the Public Landing. Courtesy of the Cincinnati Historical Society.

Coliseum, or on special occasions like Riverfest, the riverfront has few people-oriented things to do. Only on summer weekends does Yeatman's Cove Park attract more than a few strollers. Sawyer Point, easier of access and offering more opportunities for play, has begun to draw crowds. But in light of its potential, the waterfront is as yet imperfectly integrated into Cincinnati's urban life.

The Ohio remains vital to the city's economy. Unlike the Potomac before Washington, the Charles in Boston, or even the Hudson, it remains a hard-working river. In recent decades river traffic, though no longer transported by steamboats, has greatly increased. Powerful tugs called *towboats* push rows of huge barges. A number of shipping lines service the city, which has become the country's largest inland coal port. In fact, about two-thirds of the freight carried on the Ohio River at this time consists of energy-producing commodities—coal, coke, and petroleum. Nowadays three times as much tonnage passes on the Ohio before Cincinnati as goes through the Panama Canal. Weather forecasts give the river's water level as a regular feature. Even steamboats have made a modest comeback. The *Delta Queen,* built in Scotland in 1926, assembled in Sacramento, and once destined for the scrap heap, now plies the Ohio and Mississippi on a regular schedule, as does its bigger, more streamlined cousin, the *Mississippi Queen* (1976). On the rare occasions when we find one of them berthed at the Public Landing we glimpse a past when steamboats were a common sight.

Where once were no **bridges,** seven now span the Ohio River at Cincinnati. All of them belong to Kentucky. A 1784 pact resulted in Kentucky's border being drawn, not at the more usual midstream, but at the low-water mark of the Ohio's northern shore. Although recent legal decisions have given Ohio and Indiana a slightly greater share of the river, most of it still lies within Kentucky's boundary.

Looming before us downriver is the Covington-Cincinnati Suspension Bridge, since 1983 designated the John A. Roebling Bridge. It is one of the city's most famous landmarks. We walk toward it following the Riverwalk that opened as part of the 1988 bicentennial celebrations. **Riverwalk** consists of four miles of a distinctly marked path along both shores of the Ohio. Circular ceramic pavement insets, with a green and blue pattern of waves, appear on walkways at regular intervals. We shall follow them for much of this tour. Connecting Cincinnati, Covington, and Newport, Riverwalk enables pedestrians to savor and appreciate the Ohio River more easily than before. Beginning at Sawyer Point, it proceeds through Yeatman's Cove Park, crosses the river over the Roebling Bridge, then meanders along the Covington waterfront, goes across to Newport on the 4th Street Bridge, and returns to Cincinnati—and Yeatman's Cove—via the Central Bridge, which towers over the Public Landing. Along this route we will encounter statues and plaques explaining historic sites and personages. But this is to anticipate. First, the circles take us up the steps to the concrete plaza connecting the Coliseum and the Stadium.

Although it *is* possible to walk along the sidewalk that parallels the railroad tracks, the view from the plaza above is better. In regard to allowing pedestrians access to the river, the riverfront here strikes me as awkwardly designed. The stadium, for one, squats too closely to the river. A chance was missed, for the time being at least, to include an attractive, uninterrupted promenade-*cum*-bike path from one end of the Cincinnati riverfront to the other. And what a walk it would be, at least on the Cincinnati side, the side of the deep water channel, where for most of the year we stand on a platform about twenty-five feet above the river's normal level. A tended walkway, cleared in part of view-obstructing scrub and trees, would provide an unequalled natural and visual resource. And since Ft. Washington Way has been built further inland, walkers would not have to cope with the traffic din that can make comparable urban walks elsewhere an aural nightmare.

From the plaza we look across the Ohio to the mouth of the Licking River. Metalphoto plaques affixed to a nearby overlook tell of the changing river craft and detail their role in today's shipping. They identify the kind of ships we are likely to see. Visible to the left of the Licking is the Newport Barracks monument, a sawed-off pyramid. In 1809 the barracks replaced Ft. Washington on the Cincinnati side of the river. Here troops trained for the War of 1812 and the Civil War. After the barracks experienced repeated floodings, the Army in 1897 erected a new facility in Ft. Thomas, in the highlands above Newport. To the right of the Licking are the historic houses of Covington's Riverside district.

The plaza on which we stand contains Cincinnati's central riverfront. The pink, yellow, and gray granite blocks we find along plaza walkways were salvaged from the Public Landing. Behind us is the privately owned **Coliseum** (1975), seating 17,000. Originally built with professional hockey's (now defunct) Cincinnati Stingers in mind, it is now used for fairs, exhibits, the circus, rodeos, sports events (basketball, chiefly), and concerts of popular music.

Ahead of us looms the municipally owned **Riverfront Stadium** (1970) designed by Heery & Heery of Atlanta. It has become one of Cincinnati's icons, appropriately for so sports-loving a city. Such a huge mass makes its presence felt visually. From the river or from Kentucky, the stadium appears to sit atop its multi-level parking platform like an oversized spaceship. It also interrupts our view of the city's skyline. Initially, debate raged over whether to build the stadium here or outside the center city. The decision, hotly contested but in my view correct, was to build here. If the downtown has been compromised visually, urbanistically it has not been. Quite the contrary: on game days, when thousands of people fill the streets leading to the stadium, downtown gains new dynamism. As in Pittsburgh and St. Louis, a stadium close to downtown reinforces the life at the center.

Home to the baseball Reds and the football Bengals, the stadium was completed as part of the waterfront development. It seats 56,600 (60,300 for football) and can function even should the river level rise higher than the astroturf playing field. An elaborate, continuously operating underground drainage system pumps away ground water. Massive floodgates protect ground-level entrances so that water cannot inundate the playing field.

This stadium replaced Crosley Field (1911), originally Redland Field, at Findlay St. and Western Avenue in Cincinnati's West End. It was renamed Crosley after Powel Crosley, Jr., bought control of the Reds in February 1934. During the great flood in January 1937 the playing field lay submerged under twenty-one feet of water. Crosley could hold, if crammed, almost 37,000 (more than Boston's still-active Fenway Park). One of baseball's oldest stadiums, Crosley Field inspired rabid devotion from those who frequented it. Fans left the closely packed city, passed through the gates of Crosley Field, and beheld a wide expanse of rich green turf. It was an intimate ballpark, where fans sat close to the field and made their presence felt. Players could recognize—and hear—individual fans; fans in turn could see players sweating in the summer sun. Attending a game at Crosley Field (as at Fenway Park today) was as much a sociological as a baseball experience. The blue collar male fans who occupied the bleachers were (as they are still at Fenway) the most knowledgeable, if least genteel, of spectators. The entire community identified itself with the players and with the team's fortunes. Now Crosley Field has become a ballpark of the memory. Still, we should not overly idealize this particular "field of dreams." In *Ball Four* Jim Bouton cites one player's recollections of Crosley Field and Cincinnati in the 1960s: "horseshit park, horseshit clubhouse, horseshit hotel, lots of movies, nice place to eat after the game, tough town to get laid in."

"The fierce loyalty of fans to the old parks indicates that they prefer the former," writes John Pastier, "and also prefer age and history to newness." This is true, and not true. Top annual attendance at Crosley Field was 1,125,000; at Riverfront Stadium the Reds in 1976 drew 2,630,000. Although fans may well have preferred Crosley Field, they come to the team's new home in greater numbers. After World War II, Pastier points out, new stadiums profoundly changed the nature of our responses to baseball games.

Wrecking balls knocked down a number of the older stadiums including Ebbetts Field in Brooklyn and the Polo Grounds in Manhattan. Until about 1960, visiting fans and players could unfailingly tell where they were from the shape of the stadium. Today, they can't always be sure. The older parks were urbane artifacts shaped by their sites. . . . Recent stadiums, both in-town and suburban, are discrete objects divorced from any context. . . . The classic parks were personal and intimate, both because they tended to be smaller and because their straight-sided shapes, small foul areas, and interior columns put seats much closer to the action. . . . Spectator involvement was much higher than in the mega-stadiums of the past 20 years, most of which were also designed for football in rounded compromise shapes that serve neither sport well.

Cincinnati's new stadium admittedly compromises both baseball and football. Its oval shape and huge size mean that baseball fans sit much further away from the action than they sat at Crosley Field. The stadium lacks intimacy; its design, though functional, is undistinguished. The bland design suggests derivation from the same architectural tradition that brought us the shopping mall. The field is mostly plastic grass. There are, needless to say, no bleachers. Those assigned to the glassed-in and air-conditioned press box are cut off from the crack of bats and the roar of fans. From within we rarely see any Cincinnati buildings. It is hard to tell Riverfront Stadium apart from virtually identical new stadiums in St. Louis, Pittsburgh, and Philadelphia. In none does one get a sense of place. Yet Riverfront Stadium does seem to serve Cincinnati baseball and football fans well enough. The city certainly needed a new facility if it wished to have professional football, for which Crosley Field was inadequate. Cincinnati, the second smallest city represented in the major leagues, probably cannot afford separate stadiums for both professional baseball and football. And the stadium sits, not twenty miles away at an interstate junction, but squarely on the city's historic riverfront. It adjoins downtown, whose vitality it both supports and strengthens. And it came about, like so many improvements in this city, through cooperation between public and private sectors. Other successful joint initiatives include collaboration to revitalize downtown, to raise standards of public school education, and to rebuild the city's ageing infrastructure. If the stadium lacks intimacy, it strikes me, all things given, as a reasonable success.

Cincinnatians support their teams avidly. If in this book I give more space to the city's cultural traditions than to its sports scene, it is because the latter is so well documented elsewhere. The Cincinnati sports scene is remarkably varied and rich, particularly in baseball, where historians, with considerable justification, speak of Cincinnati as "the cradle of baseball." Cincinnati guards its baseball pride with certain traditions. For decades the Reds opened their season on an April Monday, one day before the other National League teams, in acknowledgment of their long baseball roots. In recent years, they have begun the season an hour ahead of other teams.

Founded in 1869, the **Reds** (from Red Stockings) are baseball's oldest professional team. Paying players spelled doom to the gentleman amateurs who had hitherto dominated the game. For a time the Red Stockings were even known, in allusion to Cincinnati's former renown as America's meat-packing center, as the Porkopolitans. During the 1869 season the team, its players the pick of the nation, went undefeated—a record hardly likely to be challenged—when it won sixty-four games and tied one. Most games it won by exotic scores; 49–16 was not unusual, one hapless team succumbed 103–8, and only in one game did the Red Stockings score fewer than fifteen runs. (In 1870 the team slipped, losing six games.) The extraordinary performance of the 1869 Red Stockings was a major stimulus in fostering public interest in the game. Indirectly, it led to the founding of the National League in 1876. On May 23, 1935, the Reds became the first major league team to play a night game, winning (under 616 floodlights) 2–1 against the Phillies. Larry McPhail, then general manager, introduced to baseball beer, usherettes, brass bands, fireworks, and clowns. Recent teams by and large reflect the town's conservative mores and eschewal of flamboyance: players, for example, can't sport moustaches or beards.

In the late 1950s the Reds were famed for the prowess of their hitters: their 221 homeruns in 1956 tied the still-standing National League record. From 1970 to 1976 the Big Red Machine dominated the league, winning five National League West championships, four pennants, and world championships in 1975 and 1976 when the team elicited comparisons to the Yankees of the Babe Ruth era.

The 1975 World Series against the Boston Red Sox, ultimately won by the Reds in the final inning of the seventh and last game, is regarded by baseball aficionados as just possibly the best ever played. The sixth game of that Series—won by the Sox in Fenway Park in the twelfth inning—ranks as a summit of disciplined excellence on the part of both teams. The seventh game was won four runs to three, with the Reds scoring the deciding run in the ninth inning. The next year the Reds swept the Pittsburgh Pirates for the National League pennant, then took the Yankees in four for the World Series. So convincing was their demonstration of skill and power that Roger Angell, who covers baseball for *The New Yorker,* opined after it was over that the Reds "must now be compared seriously with the two or three paramount clubs of the last half-century."

Another National League West championship came in 1990 and, after winning four games to two over Pittsburgh, the Reds had themselves another National League pennant. The World Series pitted a young Cincinnati team against the Oakland A's, generally considered baseball's dominant team. Oakland had just swept the Boston Red Sox in four games; most observers expected Cincinnati to fall as quickly. But it was Cincinnati, in one of the most stunning upsets in baseball history, that swept Oakland in four. Pandemonium broke out in Fountain Square after the last out as Reds fans hurried to the city's center to celebrate, many with brooms in hand (most of which were confiscated by police) to indicate a "sweep." One banner read "Oakland Weeps, Cincinnati Sweeps."

The Reds have spawned their heroes. The most enduring—and controversial—has been **Peter Edward Rose,** a local boy from the West Side, whose legendary career began in 1963. Pete Rose's finest sustained performance was his forty-four game hitting streak, a National League record, in 1978. On September 11, 1985, he achieved baseball immortality when he stroked hit number 4192 (a sharp single to left center) and thereby broke Ty Cobb's record for total number of hits. The previous year he had been named the team's player-manager. Second St. was renamed Pete Rose Way. But Rose's persistent gambling, including apparently bets on his own team, lead to his downfall. On August 24, 1989, baseball commissioner A. Bartlett Giamatti banned Pete Rose from baseball for life.

The football **Bengals** (the name derives from the Cincinnati Zoo's famous white tigers) arrived in 1970. A white tiger cub serves as mascot. It in effect tells opponents that they are playing less at Riverfront Stadium than in what is called (during winning streaks at least) "The Jungle." Tiger outfits appear in the stands; fans paint their faces with orange and black stripes. The new kid on the block, the Bengals managed game but losing Super Bowl appearances in 1982 and 1989.

From the stadium plaza we enjoy a fine perspective on the **John A. Roebling Bridge.** It is that rare creation: a work of man that enhances rather than detracts from the work of nature. Its design is a superb study in contrast. The massive towers—just *how* massive we discover as we approach—support a delicately arched roadway. A tension is established between the towers and the filigree of tightly strung cables emanating from them.

The idea of a bridge linking Cincinnati and Covington goes back to the early settlers. After the advent of the steamboat caused Cincinnati to expand rapidly, talk about spanning the Ohio River increased. In 1839 Lexington businessmen, resentful at being cut off from the lucrative river trade, drummed up considerable interest for a bridge that would allow a rail connection to Cincinnati. Nothing came of their efforts, however. In 1846 a group of Covington merchants formed the Covington and Cincinnati Bridge Company and invited John Augustus Roebling to Cincinnati. Roebling, born in Mühlhausen, Germany, in 1806 and splendidly educated at the Royal Polytechnic Institute in Berlin, had come to this country in 1830 to found a utopian agricultural community in Saxonburg, Pennsylvania. His restless genius tired of socialist monotony in less than a year, however, so he turned to engineering—and bridge building. He designed several spans, including, in 1855, a spectacular railroad bridge across the Niagara River just below the Falls.

The Ohio posed an even greater challenge. No one had ever bridged so wide a river. Roebling's first design (1846) had a massive pier on either shore, an even more massive pier in the middle. A battery of objections, chiefly from those whose business depended on the river traffic, soon emerged. Steamboat owners feared that at high water their boats would be unable to pass under the bridge; others thought that the central pier would affect currents and create sandbars. The absurdity of this fear—at least in hindsight—can be attested by looking at Cincinnati's other bridges, all of which have piers smack in the river. None has had a deleterious effect on the river or excessively hinders its traffic, though today's rivermen, descending the Ohio at high water with a full complement of loaded barges, still find shooting Cincinnati's seven spans a nervy proposition. Nonetheless, such was the clamor that Roebling redesigned the bridge to eliminate the central pier. Even then, the steamship and ferry interests did not give up. In 1849 they managed, as a last-ditch resort, to have the bridge's Ohio charter forbid it from lining up with any Cincinnati street. Covington's grid, laid out in 1815, deliberately lined up with Cincinnati's. Now the bridge could not line up with either. For an engineer Roebling had a fine esthetic sense. He lamented the mischief of not having the bridge in line with the street grids. It deprived Cincinnati, he wrote, of one of "the finest and most magnificent avenues on this continent."

The John A. Roebling Suspension Bridge, 1870s. Additional trusswork and cables, put in to strengthen the bridge in 1895–1896, have somewhat altered the bridge's graceful appearance. Courtesy of the Cincinnati Historical Society.

Seven more years passed in uncertainty. Finally, in 1856 the bridge company elected to its board Amos Shinkle, an energetic Covington coal merchant, whose presence galvanized the group into action. Construction, under Roebling's direction, began on the towers. But the 1856–1857 winter proved one of the worst on record, the Panic of 1857 froze money, the Irish laborers walked off the job (to be replaced—at Roebling's insistence—by Germans), and with the onset of the Civil War all work ceased. In September 1862 news of a Confederate army advancing upon Cincinnati caused consternation in the city. A pontoon bridge, erected in thirty hours, allowed 70,000 men quickly to cross the river and to take up positions along the Kentucky hills. Although the expected battle did not take place, the closeness of the escape made people appreciate the necessity of a bridge. Work began again in earnest. Late in 1866 the bridge was finally completed. "It is the highest thing in the country," wrote Roebling's son, Washington; "the towers are so high a person's neck aches looking up at them." On December 1, the bridge's informal opening day, 46,000 crossed it; on December 2, its official opening day, 120,000—about half the population of Cincinnati. On New Year's Day of 1867 the longest suspension bridge in the world was formally opened to vehicular traffic.

On the whole, the bridge has aged well. Streetcar tracks laid on its deck made necessary a second set of cables in 1895–1896, recognizable because they are anchored much further inland than the first. Although they detract from the bridge's elegant lines, they doubled its strength. In the process, however, the towers lost their

The 1937 Ohio River flood. The water level reached nearly 80 feet in the worst flood in the city's recorded history. The Roebling Bridge was the only bridge across the Ohio that remained open. Sandbags provide access to the roadbed on the Covington side in the foreground. Courtesy of the Cincinnati Historical Society.

balustrade and their elegant tourelles, the latter replaced by rounded pier caps, disfiguring bulbous protrusions now painted silver. Current plans call for the restoration of the tourelles. In 1916–1918 the bridge's entrances were extended and raised. In the mid-1950s its wooden roadway, increasingly oil soaked from traffic, burst into flames once too often. The state of Kentucky bought out the bridge company, took up the wood, and replaced it with a steel grid. Thus the Roebling Bridge became another of Cincinnati's singing spans. In 1976 the bridge was painted blue in honor of America's bicentennial; not coincidentally, blue is the color of the University of Kentucky. Few people notice that while the fifty-star American flag flies from the pier closest to Ohio, from that across the river flies a thirteen-star flag. In 1984, as a result of a dedicated campaign, the bridge gained a spectacular tiara of lights. The Roebling's finest hour occurred in the great flood of 1937, when, thanks to its high roadbed at both ends, it was the only Cincinnati bridge—in fact, the only bridge across the Ohio between Steubenville and Cairo—to remain open. Across it went trucks bringing needed food supplies to Kentucky.

Walking across the Roebling Bridge. Walkways on either side of the bridge provide stunning views of the Ohio River and its craft as well as of Cincinnati and Covington.

John Roebling went on to design the Brooklyn Bridge, completed long after his death by his son Washington in 1883. The Roebling Bridge is smaller than the Brooklyn Bridge, less long from tower to tower (1057 feet to 1595 feet), and less tall (the towers rise 230 feet above the water, those of the Brooklyn Bridge 271 feet). Whereas the towers of the Brooklyn Bridge have twin Gothic arches, the Roebling's have a single round arch. As opposed to the New York bridge's present six lanes, the Roebling Bridge has but two. But technologically it may be the more important, for the problems Roebling faced in constructing it enabled him to design its larger cousin. The Brooklyn Bridge refines, but does not depart from, techniques learned through his work on the Cincinnati bridge. Fittingly, in 1983 the Suspension Bridge was renamed for the engineer who designed it, who built it, and who remains one of America's largely unsung heroes. That year the bridge was also designated a National Historic Civil Engineering Landmark. Along with its more famous cousin, the Roebling Bridge stands as one of the most elegant and progressive statements of nineteenth-century American civilization.

I strongly recommend a walk across the Roebling Bridge. Several of Cincinnati's older spans have pedestrian walkways; unfortunately the newer ones do not. Even of those that do, none provides a more satisfying experience than does crossing the Roebling Bridge. It is one of those rare bridges designed to make pedestrians not feel inferior to vehicles. Besides, for the lover of bridges driving across will not do. We simply cannot appreciate a bridge from a fast-moving automobile. Bridge designers perversely delight in placing guard rails so exactly at eye level that car travelers sometimes cannot even glimpse the body of water they are traversing. No doubt this is a deliberate, perhaps even a wise, policy, one designed to reduce accidents. Still, to savor a bridge and the vistas it offers walk it we must. Only in so doing can we experience it fully as an expression of the human spirit and as a work of subtle beauty. The Roebling Bridge is both.

From the stadium plaza we follow the automobile exit ramp down to the bridge and then cross over to the walkway on its other (downriver) side. (Riverwalk goes down the ramp to ground level, then climbs the stairs adjoining the bridge to put us on the upriver side. The tour route avoids a climb down and then up.) On the nearby Cincinnati shore we look upon a dreary vista of parking lots, interrupted here and there by a warehouse or produce distribution center. The city's 1948 *Metropolitan Master Plan* spoke of this area as the city's "front yard." It has been a front yard long left untended. The *Cincinnati 2000 Plan* envisions the area as the future site of Riverfront West, a mixed-use development scheduled to rise in the 1990s. Apartment buildings, commercial structures, stores, hotels, will be built here, the whole—we may hope—on a scale that will not detract from the downtown skyline. The older warehouses that remain will be (or have been) rehabilitated. Walkways across Ft. Washington Way will connect Riverfront West with the central business district. According to the *Cincinnati 2000 Plan,* the development of Riverfront West along with further activity along Riverfront East (the land upriver from the Coliseum) will cause the waterfront to regain "its prominence as the origin of the city and the direction of future growth of the downtown." So hope (and have hoped) the planners. We shall see.

We walk to the first tower. Petroleum in the tower's beige Buena Vista sandstone enables it to resist the corrosive effects of water. Above our heads bands of white Dayton limestone, the same material used for St. Peter-in-Chains, slant inwards. We proceed to the middle of the bridge.

Downriver, we see the Chesapeake & Ohio Railway Bridge (1888) and the Clay Wade Bailey Bridge (1974), one bridge actually two. The latter span replaced an earlier one taken down in 1970. Bailey was a salty *Kentucky Post* newspaperman who covered for forty-six years the Kentucky legislature in Frankfort. Barely visible behind the C & O Bridge is the double-decked Brent Spence Bridge (1963), over which run I-71 and I-75. Spence, a Newport native and sixteen-term congressman to the U.S. House of Representatives (a Kentucky record), often fought to preserve the Ohio from pollution. Out of sight is the Cincinnati Southern Railway Bridge (1877; 1922). Although the riverscape, more industrial than upriver, retains much of interest, it is at present virtually impossible to walk along the bank very far on either side.

On the Covington side we gaze upon a concrete floodwall that further downriver becomes a grass levee. Behind the floodwall sits RiverCenter, a multimillion dollar development (1990), with an eighteen-story Kentucky National Bank and an Embassy Suites Hotel, both sitting atop garages. It is as if the skyscrapers of Cincinnati had begun to seed themselves across the Ohio. Situated in the river before the floodwall is **Covington Landing,** an essentially three-part floating barge complex. Shooting jets of water sixty feet into the air, a fountain heralds the festivity within.

Nearest the Roebling Bridge is *The Spirit of America,* a 262-foot long replica of the *J. M. White,* an 1878 Mississippi River sidewheeler. Among a bevy of pleasure spots, Belle's RiverSaloon offers a Gay Nineties atmosphere in a fanciful but credible re-creation of a riverboat interior. Connected to the *J. M.White* is a two-level structure, The Wharf, housing a medley of restaurants, bars, shops, and fast-food outlets. Other restaurants, a small theater, and the floating docks of BB Riverboats, Inc. complete Covington Landing.

For those not tempted by the apparently nonstop entertainment and food, there is good pedestrian access, particularly to The Wharf, from which visitors enjoy panoramas of the river scene and the Cincinnati skyline. This pleasure we shall forgo until after we have walked through Covington's Riverside district. The city envisages further development downriver by the Brent Spence (I-75) Bridge. An extension of Riverwalk will connect it to Covington Landing.

Covington and Newport realize that their undeveloped riverbank constitutes a major commercial and urban resource. Whether the two cities also realize that the riverfront also constitutes a major esthetic and landscape resource—and deserves preservation as such—is less evident. Cincinnati, by choosing parks over restaurants, has thus far shown more sensitivity to the river and to the public good. The Ohio is a broad highway, but it is a highway all the same. A riverine "strip" would be no less offensive than a roadside one, and far more visible.

After crossing the Roebling Bridge, we go left on 2nd St. and down the hill on Greenup St. to Riverside Terrace. In front of us is the *Mike Fink,* built in 1926 as the *John W. Hubbard,* a sternwheeler that towed Texaco oil barges on the Mississippi. Subsequently it towed coal on the Ohio, before opening in 1968 as a floating restaurant. The last ship of its design, it is on the National Register. Mike Fink was the roughest and toughest of all the rivermen. A former Indian fighter, this keelboat captain, "half-horse and half-alligator," became even in his lifetime (he died in 1823) a living legend. Known on the Ohio as the "Snapping Turtle" and on the Mississippi as the "Snag," Mike Fink worked both until steamboat competition drove him still further west.

On or near Riverside Terrace, where we stand, **seven bronze figures** by local sculptors recall significant individuals in the history of the Cincinnati area and of the Ohio River. They include John Roebling, bridge builder, captured in a Promethean, if probably uncharacteristic, pose. On the plaque to our left we make out the 1846 design for his bridge, that with the central pier in the middle of the Ohio. Other worthies include Simon Kenton, famed trailblazer and Indian fighter, less well known than Daniel Boone but of comparable stature, and Mary Greene (1868–1949), the only licensed woman riverboat captain. Both are in George Rogers Clark Park. Further along the walkway, sitting on a park bench, is James Bradley, a black who enrolled in Cincinnati's Lane Seminary in 1834 and became instrumental in the abolitionist movement and in the Underground Railroad. At the far end we encounter Little Turtle (1752–1812), the great chief of the Miamis, and John James Audubon, who resided in Cincinnati in 1820 and recorded in his diary that he sketched cliff swallows at the mouth of the Licking. Finally, on 3rd St. is Daniel Carter Beard, one of the founders of the Boy Scouts of America. All the statues—except that of James Bradley, who sits on the bench—are ten percent larger than life. All of them, like most of the rest of northern Kentucky, look toward Cincinnati.

By the 1850s elegant villas and rowhouses had begun to replace the riverfront's original rowhouses. Two stone-fronted double houses, 225–227 and 229–231 Riverside Terrace, survive from the earlier period. Severe and beautifully proportioned, they are pure Greek Revival. Their compactness also reminds us how densely settled the riverfront was in antebellum days. Note the delicate cast- and wrought-iron fence before 229–231. Cast-iron fences became very popular in America after 1830; generally, the heavier their design, the later the period.

After the intersection with Garrard St. is the **George Rogers Clark Memorial Park.** Here in 1780 and 1782 Clark gathered his forces for expeditions across the Ohio River against the Shawnees. In warm weather the Kohlbrand Fountain (1982), a battered capital poised on a columnar base, gently gurgles. A plaque behind it marks the site of the Thomas Kennedy house: cabin in 1791, stone house in 1801, demolished in 1909. Kennedy's 200-acre farm encompassed what is now downtown Covington. In 1792 he opened a ferry between Covington and Cincinnati. Early ferries were hand-rowed skiffs; later Kennedy used flatboats, barges, horse-powered paddle-wheelers, and, after 1830, steamboats. This area, at the confluence of the Ohio and Licking rivers, became known as "The Point." Kennedy's house soon doubled as a tavern. Travelers from the Bluegrass stopped here before venturing across the Ohio. In 1814 Thomas D. Carneal and John S. and Richard M. Gano, after persuading Kennedy to part with 150 of his acres, platted the city of Covington.

We walk upriver along Riverside Terrace. Benches, with cast-iron scrollwork on arms and supports, are attractively designed; the light poles, equally new, look "historic." Covington's antebellum mansions offer a visual contrast to Cincinnati's skyscrapers: South against North, Confederate against Yankee, even nineteenth century against twentieth.

Covington and **Newport** go back almost as far as Cincinnati. Lacking Cincinnati's superb site, they grew more slowly. All the same, thanks to the Queen City's dynamic expansion before the Civil War, Covington and Newport had by 1860 become Kentucky's second and third cities, outdistanced only by Louisville. In that year, Covington, named for General Leonard Covington, who died in the War of 1812, had 16,471 inhabitants, one tenth Cincinnati's population; Newport, named after Captain Christopher Newport, English mariner who, in attempting to colonize Virginia, was wrecked off the Bermudas in 1609, followed with 10,046 inhabitants. Covington's street grid lines up with Cincinnati's downtown grid. If we were to stand at, say, Scott and 5th streets in Covington and look north, we would have the illusion that Cincinnati's skyscrapers continue Covington's business district. The two cities appear one.

Covington and Newport boomed after the Civil War. The Suspension Bridge reduced traveling time between Covington and Cincinnati to a few minutes. Soon other bridges spanned the Ohio, and in 1874 one went across the Licking, connecting Covington with Newport. The 1904 Baedeker dismissed Covington and Newport as "two uninteresting cities in Kentucky, which need not detain the stranger." Even for antebellum days, this statement has questionable validity; for the period after, none whatsoever. Both cities have a colorful history; their nineteenth-century residential, commercial, and industrial architecture rivals Cincinnati's. The industrial boom continued until the Depression. In the 1920s and 1930s Newport, in addition, established a spectacular reputation for gambling, vice, and prostitution. It was considered the Las Vegas of the Midwest, a small-town hub for organized crime, "Cincinnati's Playground." Newport remained a wide-open town until the Kefauver hearings of 1950 led to crackdowns. (Monmouth St., though a shadow of its former self, is still the closest the Cincinnati area comes to having a red-light district.) As recently as 1950, Covington still ranked as Kentucky's second city; with a 1990 population of 43,264 it is now fourth. Growth in both cities, with little room for expansion, has since slackened.

Close to Cincinnati in minutes and miles, Covington and Newport are also visually close. The Ohio's banks—the northern with its skyscrapers, the southern with its nineteenth-century mansions—complement each other. Though the river separates, it no longer, with its many bridges, divides. Increasingly, Covington and Newport, indeed all the northern Kentucky communities, see themselves as integral elements within a larger metropolitan area.

In the 1960s, when Cincinnati experienced a downtown boom, few buildings rose in Covington and Newport. In part, this is because newer, more affluent communities elsewhere in northern Kentucky hem in Covington and Newport, limiting growth. With the I-275 beltway only eight miles from downtown Cincinnati, compared to the twenty-mile radius on the Ohio side, the northern Kentucky cities farther inland have prospered. In addition, the nearness of Greater Cincinnati Airport, which is in northern Kentucky, and the expansion of its main carrier, Delta Airlines, which has made Cincinnati a regional hub, have further stimulated growth inland. In recent years, however, Covington and Newport have experienced growth of other kinds. As middle-class housing close to Cincinnati's downtown has become more expensive and harder to find, Ohioans have discovered the benefits of living across the river. Covington and Newport are now even more than before bedroom communities for Cincinnati. Whereas the 1970s witnessed Cincinnati's redevelopment of its waterfront, the 1980s marked Covington and Newport's rediscovery of theirs.

320 Riverside Terrace, just past George Rogers Clark Park, is a double house built before 1860. Curvilinear Italianate window molds incompletely cover rectilinear Greek Revival stone lintels. On the park side a cast-iron portico ascends in grapevine arabesques, giving the house a New Orleans air. Complementing the wooden porch on the other side, the portico gives this symmetrical house an asymmetrical effect. An ornate cast- and wrought-iron fence predates the portico. Like most houses along Riverside Terrace, 320 has been divided into apartments.

321, beautifully set on its dais of dryrock, was built about 1916 for the painter and architect Charles McLaughlin. A brick walkway in a herringbone pattern curls up to the entrance. It leads the eye to a portico of four paneled box pillars à la Mt.

Vernon. With floor-to-ceiling windows, a two-story veranda, and a fanlight on the second floor, this Georgian Revival house recalls, in its large scale and generous proportions, a Southern plantation.

327, also built before 1860, began as a three-bay Greek Revival townhouse. The obligatory Italianate touches soon followed. Look for the rectilinear doorway behind the rounded Florentine entrance. The hood molds are of metal painted to look like stone. Note the ornamented double brackets, the attractive two-level inset veranda on the east side, and the foot scraper built into the front steps.

The double chimneys of 403–405 (1856) give it a distinctly Greek Revival side profile. Like most houses here, this one has been remodelled and added to. The original porches, destroyed by a flood, were partially restored in 1952; the present front porch dates only from 1981. Next door, 412–414 (ca. 1860) presents a twentieth-century Georgian Revival façade: balustraded balconies, Ionic columns at ground level, Corinthian above. A tiny fan window peeks out from under the gable. This markedly Palladian façade is almost prissily symmetrical.

At the bend was Kennedy's ferry, which crossed from here to the Public Landing. We walk up Shelby St. Just before number 109, on the alley, we peek into an shaded pocket garden with a fountain, reminiscent of hidden nooks in the French Quarter. Down the mews-like alley a number of coach houses have metamorphosed into apartments. Across Shelby, the Colonial Revival townhouses (1986) are appropriately scaled infill.

We return along 2nd St. 412, known in recent years as **"Mimosa"** from the tree in the front yard, began as an imposing Tuscan villa (1853–1855) erected by Thomas Porter. In 1861 Dannel J. Fallis, a banker, bought the house. In 1900 his daughter Harriet Rodgers vastly enlarged the Italianate core into a Colonial Revival blockbuster. The house lost its tower but gained a tetrastyle (four-column) portico with Corinthian cast-plaster capitals. Supervising this work was Elzner and Anderson, the Cincinnati architectural firm responsible for the pioneering concrete-frame Ingalls building at 4th and Vine streets. Mimosa, which has a river façade also, always faced 2nd St. Three stories high and comprising twenty-two rooms, it is northern Kentucky's largest mansion. Reputedly it is haunted by Harriet Rodgers's daughter, May Lovell, who died in 1950.

The interior is well worth a visit. It contains a fine collection of period furniture and architectural elements, both from the 1850s and from the turn of the century. The 1850s parlor, virtually unaltered, retains its original mantels; from this time also date the chandeliers with their etched and cut-glass globes. The leading national firms of Belter, Meeks, and Baudouine made the laminated Rococo Revival furniture. *In situ* are circa 1900 gas fixtures and the electrical lighting system, including carbon filament light bulbs. On display are a collection of older lamps, including gasoliers, girandoles, astral, and argand lamps. We leave by the back door in order to admire the interesting rear façade, perhaps glimpsed already from Riverside Terrace.

Opposite, at 405 2nd, is the **Carneal house** (ca. 1820). Federal in style, its architect unknown, it has long been considered one of Kentucky's finest mansions. Officially it should be the Gano-Southgate house: for John S. Gano, who, with his

Carneal house, Covington. This beautifully proportioned Federal mansion (ca. 1820) is among Kentucky's most distinguished residences. Trees along the street have grown up since this photograph was taken and now partially block the view of the house.

brother and Thomas D. Carneal, first platted Covington in 1814 and for whom the house was more likely built; and for V. N. Southgate, whose family long lived here. The salmon brick attractively contrasts with the stone bands. Four decorated stone panels beneath the cornice balance the façade. The fussy acorn-drop brackets are a Victorian addition. With its clustered columns and sunburst motif, the entrance looks like a mantelpiece. Within, a mantelpiece replicates it.

The plan of the Carneal house derives from that of the Villa Fornaro in Andrea Palladio's *Four Books of Architecture*. Its front façade imitates the Villa Fornaro's rear façade. The inset or recessed portico is called a portico *in antis*, that is, the columns are set within rather than without the structure. This most unusual feature was taken from Palladio's brilliant design. The columns are Ionic at ground level, Corinthian above. The architect has included Gothic touches, for example, pointed-arch windows with switch-pane tracery. The arches, protruding slightly at the lower level, are recessed at the upper. A provincial adaptation of a classic Palladian design, the Carneal house possesses unmistakable subtlety. Simplicity, we realize, can derive from carefully wrought complexity. We will see no finer residential façade in our walks.

Opposite is the **Laidley house** (ca. 1865), Italianate with a Second Empire mansard roof. W. J. Lowry was the first owner. For almost a century Frederick A. Laidley, salt merchant, steamboat captain, and owner of the White Packet Line, inhabited the house, as did his descendants after him. Stone Florentine molds enclose the recessed entrance, elaborately paneled in walnut. The house is a symphony of round arches: the front door's double arches play off against the single arch of the entrance fanlight and the windows of the right bay; in turn, these arches are echoed by the triple-arched left bay and the double-arched window above it. With its excellent proportions, immaculate appearance, and glowing orange-red brick, the Laidley house never fails to please.

Across Kennedy St., 326 2nd, a huge Second Empire creation sometimes called the **Lovell-Graziani house,** went up from 1877 to 1886. When built, the tower stood higher by two stories. Uninterrupted quoins delimit the projecting central bay as well as the main façade. The mansard roof of polychromed slates is original. Cast-iron Corinthian columns support the porch. The squarish stone window molds emphasize the house's rectilinearity. 322, next door, is early twentieth-century Georgian Revival. Between it and 326 we discover a charming carriage house with a roundel under the gable. Across 2nd St. the large-scale Georgian structure was once the W. M. Booth Memorial Hospital (1926), which moved to Florence, Kentucky, in 1979. Its former building, now containing apartments, occupies the site where Amos Shinkle, chief mover behind the Suspension Bridge, built his "castle" in 1869. Donated to the Salvation Army in 1913, Shinkle's house was demolished for the hospital.

On the northeast corner of the intersection of 2nd and Garrard streets is the Kennedy house (ca. 1847), not that of Thomas Kennedy, whose house was located just to the northeast, but a residence, now called Southgate Hall, he built for his daughter Nancy. Across 2nd, 202 Garrard is a well-maintained two-story Italianate townhouse. The Italianate townhouse opposite, at 201, dates from the early 1850s. Its New Orleans style cast-iron porch has the attractive grapevine motif seen below at 321 Riverside Terrace; the front gate culminates in a honeysuckle pattern. On the northwest corner of 2nd and Garrard streets stretch seven beautifully proportioned, three-bay Renaissance Revival row houses (1877–1886) with pedimented entrances. From their onetime owner, Amos Shinkle, they are known as the Shinkle Row.

Downriver from the Roebling Bridge lies the dock for **BB Riverboats, Inc.** If you plan to take a cruise along the Ohio now, proceed west along East 2nd St. past the bridge. East 2nd becomes RiverCenter Boulevard. The entrance to Covington Landing is on Madison. Bear right through the floodwall, then left to the BB dock. If not planning to take a cruise at this time, skip to p. 189.

I enthusiastically recommend an afternoon or evening cruise along the Ohio River. (For departure times call 1–606–261–8500.) Nothing else quite gives a feeling for this body of water that has played and continues to play so important a role in Cincinnati's history. The boats themselves, with their paddlewheels and pronounced smokestacks, are small-scale recreations of the steamboats that once plied the Ohio. To see them cruising on the Ohio adds a picturesque note to the river scene. On board we gain one of the best views of the Cincinnati skyline. The buildings appear to grow out of the forest, as in a real sense they have.

Once on our way, the boat passes quickly under the Roebling Bridge. Looking up, we experience a dramatic perspective on the bridge. It is auditory as well as visual. Like the Central Bridge, the Roebling is one of Cincinnati's singing spans.

Cincinnati skyline, from RiverCenter. From here we see the skyline to good advantage. In the foreground a towboat pushes the *Captain Ben,* one of the larger of BB Riverboats' flotilla of excursion craft.

The steel grid gives off a high-pitched whine as it meets revolving auto tires, a sound evocative of millions of swarming bees. The *Mike Fink* and the riverside mansions immediately come into view, then the mouth of the Licking River, itself a picturesque stream. The Licking inspired Cincinnati's first name of "Losantiville." The fey intelligence of John Filson, surveyor, mapmaker, adventurer, and early historian of Kentucky, coined this anagram in August 1788. L—os—anti—ville, a kind of verbal conglomerate, means (in reverse order) town opposite the mouth of the Licking (*os* is Latin for mouth). Before we raise our eyebrows at Filson's ingenuity, we must remember that after the Revolutionary War English names were out of favor; and Indian names, particularly on the raw frontier, often carried painful associations. Losantiville underscores the Licking's significance in the selection of the new settlement's site. Filson promptly disappeared into the wilderness, tomahawked, it was thought, by Indians. His dreadful name lasted little more than a year. General Arthur St. Clair, soon after his arrival at Ft. Washington in January 1790, renamed the fledgling settlement after the Society of the Cincinnati. No one will question that "Cincinnati," though difficult to spell (even by people who should know better), improves upon "Losantiville."

We go under the Central Bridge, then the Daniel Carter Beard Bridge, both connecting Newport to Cincinnati. Between them is Riverfront Place, Newport's contribution to riverside development. Bellevue, then Dayton, come into sight. Hidden in the hills above lies the elegant residential community of Ft. Thomas. Unlike Cincinnati, the lower-lying towns on the Kentucky side built levees for their protection after the 1937 flood and, in effect, cut themselves off from the river, at least until recently. Covington hides itself behind a concrete wall, completed in 1955; Newport and Dayton have constructed less obtrusive sloped, grass-covered levees.

Newport's levee, completed in 1951, protects the city from a flood up to the 83-foot mark, three feet higher than the highest recorded level. For the most part along the Ohio, concrete floodwalls are found downtown, levees where the real estate costs less. Buildings, when seen from the river over the levees, appear to begin at upper stories. On board this motorized platform we are virtually at water level. As the boat's prow cleaves the water, meeting the current head on, we realize how much the river is itself a thing of motion, and defined by its motion.

All the while we enjoy stunning perspectives on the Cincinnati skyline. We again appreciate the variegated textures, materials, colors, and shapes of the buildings, the different eras and styles of architecture they embody. Below, the Serpentine Wall, flattened by perspective, looks less sinuous than when we stood on it. After the downtown skyscrapers recede into the distance, the green slopes of Mount Adams appear. Highland Towers, an apartment building, arises near where the hill's incline once ended. Five of Cincinnati's hills once had inclines, or inclined railways, that conveyed pedestrians, and on all but one, streetcars, up and down their steep slopes. Crowning Mount Adams is the former monastery of the Holy Cross, now offices. Soon we observe the Gothic lines of the Church of the Immaculate Conception. Hugging the hillside is the modern apartment complex "The Cloisters." In wood and on stilts, it accords well with Mount Adams's older structures. Beyond it we discern the tip of the Art Museum's campanile; below rises the chimney of the Pumping Station. Every so often a break in the green canopy reveals the concrete retaining wall of Columbia Parkway, the city's main artery upriver. Above Eden Park's forest of green Samuel Hannaford's red-brick water tower (1894) juts into the sky. Adjoining it is St. James in the Park (1989), one of several new condo towers built or planned along the river.

Below was once the separate village of Fulton, a densely populated one-street community that stretched from the Cincinnati corporate line two-and-a-half miles upstream to Columbia. The Cincinnati area was long a major manufacturer of steamboats, and most of them were made in Fulton. Here where the river channel ran close to shore were once shipyards, drydocks, lumber yards, and iron foundries. Cincinnati was second only to Pittsburgh as a center for steamboat building. From 1816 to 1880 it made 900 new steamboats; thousands more were repaired and refitted here. In 1847, for example, Fulton turned out thirty-four steamboats, four steamships, two barges, and one brig. This boat building activity reminds us again that for most of its history Ohio has been, in effect, a major maritime, or rather, riverine, state. After the Civil War the boat-building industry also laid the groundwork, by providing the skills and artisans, for the city's big machine tool industry.

This river journey enables us to gain still another perspective on Cincinnati, to appreciate its magnificent natural site and to conceptualize the city in relation to its dominant features: its hills and its river. A number of the landmarks we see from the water we can visit on foot, but we now view them from the river and in relation to one another. Though for most of its length the Ohio extends about 1800 feet or a third of a mile across, in the Cincinnati area it is usually two-thirds that, barely 1200 feet. The distance seems right. People standing on one bank discern buildings and people on the other. Intimacy, though removed, is not lost. This closeness keeps the human scale. As we cruise upstream, the distance from the boat to the shores is halved. The life on the banks appears closer still. On huge rivers, the Mississippi, the St. Lawrence, and most of the Hudson, the experience we have is less intimate. The river in effect acts as a barrier between the two shores. The Mississippi divides absolutely; the Ohio, relatively. It is not without significance that Covington and Newport are healthier and more vital communities than East St. Louis and Algiers, those opposite St. Louis and New Orleans. Even the Ohio, by Louisville for example, sprawls out to lose the hills that usually rim its banks.

The Ohio is particularly sinuous around Cincinnati. We hardly realize as the boat chugs along that the river makes a great "S" sweep through the city and that we are constantly turning. Eighteenth-century estheticians, including the painter William Hogarth, based the "line of grace" on the female figure and found it to be serpentine, intricate, varied, and, above all, universally observed in nature. Human beings take pleasure in "winding walks and serpentine rivers," Hogarth believed, indeed in all forms made up of curving lines. Curves reflect the limitless variety found in life itself; perhaps for this reason human beings find curved paths more inviting than straight. We do not know what lies at the end of a curve, so we keep going to find out. The view upstream (and downstream) changes constantly. As the boat rounds the Ohio's lazy bends, we find our sense of expectancy heightening: we wonder what will come next into sight. We experience a tension between the known and the unknown. "Pursuing is the business of our lives," wrote Hogarth; it "is implanted in our natures. . . . Intricacy of form . . . *leads the eye a wanton kind of chace.*" We become enamored of the pursuit. In the process, we experience a kind of happy sadness, happy because the chase provides excitement, sad because ultimately it cannot satisfy us. Our curiosity is constantly gratified, but never satiated. Our great expectations come to nought—or do they? The Ohio's perspectives work their spell upon us unawares. A river is a mysterious being.

The **hills,** three or four hundred feet high, rise close to shore on the Ohio side; in Kentucky they may be a mile or so inland. They invite the eye to look up at them; they enhance our sense of intimacy with the landscape. These gently rolling hills may also recall Hogarthian curves. At least one early Cincinnati poet compared the hills to the "breasts of recumbent goddesses." And indeed we may consider the hills as emblems of satisfaction and fulfillment, breast-like, rounded and complete, full to touch and eye. Together with the river that flows between them, they constitute our strongest visual memory of the city. In 1835 Harriet Martineau recalled Cincinnati's "sunny and shadowy hills, advancing and retiring, . . . the rich bottoms always answering on the one shore to the group of hills on the other." Gentle curves in a landscape suggest peaceful harmony. In the Rockies or the Swiss Alps the shapes clash diagonally. Instead of peace, we experience a feeling of grand beauty, of fearful severity. But Cincinnati's hills rarely stir us by their drama; rather, they afford us a sense of tranquillity, of nature in harmony with itself. The vista invariably recedes into a wide horizon that provides its own quiet satisfaction.

Scarcely a decade previous, Timothy Flint recalled in 1826, "by far the greatest proportion of the course of the Ohio was through a forest." Its banks, he thought, were "destined shortly to become almost a continued village." J. P. Foote remembered that the hills early in the nineteenth century "formed a border of such surpassing beauty, around the plain on which Cincinnati stood, as to cause us, who remember them in their beauty, almost to regret the progress of improvement which has taken from us what it can never restore." Fortunately, time has proven Flint and Foote wrong. To a surprising degree the pastoral landscape they observed has returned. On the Cincinnati side, once our gaze has soared above the bank, we still see the hills of shining green that the pioneers saw. Like fallen snow, the green unifies the landscape. Oddly, the low-lying, less populated Kentucky shore appears far more built up than the hilly Ohio shore. We can understand why seventeenth-century French explorers translated Ohio (from the Iroquois) as "la belle rivière." For Harriet Martineau, the Ohio's shores were so beautiful that she "could not bear to lose a single glimpse between the hills." Even the acerbic Mrs. Trollope referred to "the ever lovely Ohio." For her it lacked only the occasional ruined abbey or feudal castle. The critical Dickens, though affected by the loneliness of "solitudes . . . unbroken by any sign of human life or trace of human footstep," deemed the Ohio "a fine broad river always."

If today Cincinnati's hills are clad in verdant raiment, for over a century they were bare-breasted. Photographs, from the famous 1848 panorama of the city's waterfront down to those taken in the 1940s, reveal slopes denuded of trees. The hills were not a pretty sight. The 1907 Kessler plan for Cincinnati's parks spoke of "the now very prominent, barren and ugly hillsides skirting Mount Auburn and extending into Mount Adams." The barrenness continued upriver. Cutting timber for log cabins, fuel, steamboats, and shipbuilding, clearing land for houses—these activities had quickly stripped the hills. For several decades after 1830 Nicholas Longworth and other vintners covered the eastern hills with vineyards. Although this experiment in viticulture failed after the Civil War, little systematic reforestation of the hills took place afterwards. The strong sculpture of their underlying forms stood revealed. In recent decades nature has reasserted itself. No longer are the recumbent goddesses scantily clad, as is appropriate for so decorous a city as Cincinnati. The green canopy we admire today must not appear too different from the virgin hardwood forest the pioneers came upon. Magnificent mansions line the crest of the hills but rarely do they interrupt our view of the green from the river. Except for the occasional wayward highrise, we can almost imagine the hills uninhabited. This landscape remains a thing of beauty.

Close to the riverbank is the red-painted, Gothic **St. Rose of Lima Church** (1869). Steamboat captains used its spire as a landmark and after 1890 set their watches by its four-sided clock. On the church's rear wall, facing the river, a white line indicates the Ohio's major recorded floods. The highwater mark of the 1937 flood came to just under eighty feet; that of 1884, the next worst, to seventy-one and three-quarters. Just beyond is the city's Main Pumping Station (1907). Where the hills end is Alms Park. Below it lies the village of Columbia. Contemporaneous in its founding with Cincinnati, it moved here in 1815 from the floodplain to the east. It hardly appears to have grown much since then. Out of sight on the flat area before

Mount Washington, the next range of hills, is Lunken Airport, the original site of Columbia. Before Greater Cincinnati Airport was developed after World War II Lunken was the city's main air terminal.

At this point the boat usually begins its return journey. Moving downstream, we now follow the usual route of pioneers and travelers who arrived in Cincinnati during the first half of the nineteenth century. As they rounded the bend past Mount Adams they found, much to their surprise, a metropolis in the wilderness. They did not see what we see 150 years later but, with an effort of the historical imagination, perhaps we can recapture something of the excitement of their initial discovery.

The boat tour is now over. Our next stop is Bicentennial Commons at Sawyer Point. We shall return to Cincinnati via Newport. From the BB dock we proceed to 2nd and Garrard streets, where we rejoin Riverwalk, and proceed north on Garrard. Just before 3rd St., at 215 Garrard, an Italianate townhouse (ca. 1860), built by Amos Shinkle, has a superb cast-iron veranda and fence. In 1986 the building and its carriage house were restored as a bed-and-breakfast facility. Left on 3rd is the boyhood home of Daniel Carter Beard, with an accompanying statue of an aged Beard and a scout. Riverwalk at this writing has been completed no further, so we shall improvise an interesting if less than perfect route. First we go back to Garrard, then one block further south, then left on the 4th St. Bridge across the Licking River. Where the roadway bifurcates on the other side, we turn left and take the second path in the public housing. It divides after fifty feet. We take the right fork and scramble up the grass levee, slippery when wet, and head right, following the path at the top until we arrive at the confluence of the Licking and Ohio rivers. We now overlook the Newport Barracks Monument.

Before us stretches a 180-degree **view.** To our left is John Roebling's span; across the Ohio, the Stadium; behind it, the Cincinnati skyline; upriver, Mount Adams. Spanning the Ohio, the Central, Louisville & Nashville, and Daniel Carter Beard bridges are superimposed on each other like huge outdoor sculptures. Even though the buildings are no more and bridges interrupt the perspective on both ends of the panorama, the view of the Cincinnati waterfront before us is very much that depicted in the Public Library's photographs taken from Newport in 1848. Actually, the photographs were taken from a roof top about four blocks upriver from where we stand.

In 1844 James Wickes Taylor described the scene before us from a comparable vantage point in the Newport hills: "The view of Cincinnati—its landing—the river with its graceful curves—the magnificent amphitheater which the valley forms with the hills in all directions that enclose it, all was a landscape, which I would walk much farther to look upon. The breeze was cool and refreshing—we threw ourselves on the springing turf—chatted—lounged—and gazed with a most delicious *abandon.*" Whatever the changes that have taken place, the river and the hills remain. The view today, if less bucolic than the one Taylor enjoyed, is no less splendid.

A vista should, according to Kevin Lynch, provide us with genuine "emotional delight." "Space and breadth of view" are, in his view, fundamental needs in our lives. The "wide visual sweep" of the city lying before us does indeed satisfy our sense of space. It also satisfies us emotionally.

After we have gazed upon the scene below "with a most delicious *abandon,*" we descend the levee. The 1848 panorama is affixed to the wall fronting the Newport Barracks Monument. It is part of a series of metalphoto plaques showing changes in the skyline from that time to this. Other plaques discuss the floodwalls, the three great Ohio River floods, and the military's presence here and in Ft. Thomas. We head along the roadway toward the Central Bridge and go through the entrance cut in the levee. This puts us on Columbia St. We walk into the TraveLodge parking lot and out the other end, then left onto the bridge walkway. After crossing the Ohio we ascend the steps by the Coliseum onto the plaza, then walk a short distance to the stairs that we originally climbed from the Public Landing. Once on the Public Landing, we traverse Yeatman's Cove Park to Sawyer Point.

The three huge brick arches before us look like a viaduct from the Roman Campagna that has beached itself on the Ohio's shores. The arches, newly restored, formed part of the rail approach to the **Louisville & Nashville Bridge;** to support loaded freight trains they had to be huge. The L & N's piers are composed of dressed limestone ashlar up to the highwater line, of local freestone above it; the distance between the piers of the channel span is 418 feet. The adjacent highway bridge, Cincinnati's most decorative span, has remarkably intact wrought-iron embellishments. Instead of going under the arches into Sawyer Point, we detour to the left and climb up onto the bridge overlook. There, in addition to a splendid view over the park, we find a number of metalphoto plaques descriptive and illustrative of the steamboats, the attempts to bridge the Ohio, and the early history of Cincinnati. Granite pavement inserts indicate the inland waterways in 1850, the railway network in 1900, the Northwest Territory in 1787, and the Ohio River.

The bridge overlook leads onto the bridge itself. We have already crossed two of Cincinnati's spans, and I do not insist upon a third. The walkway here runs in between the railway and the automotive paths, an unusual effect visually, somewhat comparable to that most spectacular of bridge walks, that across John Roebling's Brooklyn Bridge.

The overlook allows us to survey **Sawyer Point Park,** or as it was rechristened in 1988, Bicentennial Commons at Sawyer Point, twenty-two acres of reclaimed land along the Ohio dedicated on June 4, 1988. Formerly a scrap metal processing operation occupied the site. Sawyer Point memorializes one of Cincinnati's best-known citizens and benefactors, former Secretary of Commerce, Charles Sawyer. Before us on a pedestal of pink granite stands a large-scale bronze statue, *The Spirit of Cincinnatus.* The Cincinnatus Association, a local reform-minded civic group, commissioned it for the city's bicentennial from Eleftherious Karkadoulias, a local sculptor known for his restoration of the Tyler Davidson and Hyde Park fountains. Lucius Quinctius Cincinnatus holds in his right hand a *fasces,* or bundle of rods with an axe blade projecting from them, a symbol of Roman authority; in his left, he holds a primitive plough.

Beyond the statue our eyes take in the Procter & Gamble Performance Pavilion. Ahead, flags snap and fly in the breezes off the river. To their left, at the park's edge, we make out Andrew Leicester's Cincinnati Gateway Sculpture. Above it, the picture windows of Mount Adams townhouses peer down upon us, wide eyed. The city intends that the park—and the formerly industrial Deer Creek Valley behind it—become an urban showcase. Once grimy Eggleston Avenue has metamorphosed into an attractive, treelined boulevard, now given an upscale name, Eggleston Esplanade. The remaining warehouses and factories below Mount Adams, along with an old firehouse, could have become, if rehabilitated, Cincinnati's version of San Francisco's Ghirardelli Square. Probably the original waterfront restoration, Ghirardelli Square involved turning an old chocolate factory and adjoining buildings into an imaginative series of spaces full of shops and restaurants; outside are multilevel courtyards, fountains, and benches. Brought into being over a six-year period from 1962 to 1968, this pioneer "festival marketplace" led to the transformation of the San Francisco waterfront. Cincinnati, by encouraging a comparable development, could have created a wonderful support system for Sawyer Point. The whole complex was worth saving, but only the old firehouse remains and is to become a gourmet restaurant. Sawyer Point itself is a well-conceived and sensitively planned landscape, designed for use by lots of people, yet with a sequence of diverse spaces and greenery setting off the public areas. We shall explore Sawyer Point in a roughly clockwise direction.

First we descend the steps and go under the L & N Bridge's huge arches. Glaser Associates designed the attractive **Procter & Gamble Performance Pavilion** (1987). The lawn holds up to 5000. The facility is suitable for symphony and pop concerts as well as smaller musical events, plays, dance performances, and magic shows. Hovering cloudlike above the stage is an acoustically engineered removable tentlike structure made of white waterproof polyester, supported by two fifty-foot masts. Intended to be "invisible," the pavilion fits unobtrusively into the landscape. A curved earthberm, or hill, serves as its rear wall. Such earthberms are used near other park structures to divide one activity from another.

Directly opposite the stage facing north is Sawyer Point's most talked-about feature: Andrew Leicester's gigantic "environmental sculpture," officially the *Cincinnati Gateway Sculpture*. Leicester, a Briton based in Minnesota, created a work that is neither a statue nor an abstract modern sculpture. Jayne Merkel has compared it to "the Ishtar Gate from ancient Babylon, which had tall colorful walls with pictures imbedded in them." The nearly 250-foot long by 50-foot wide sculpture resembles a large serpentine mound symbolic of the Mound Builder culture, which thrived here before the arrival of European settlers. The entire sculpture depicts in eighteen sections or "stories" Cincinnati's history from geologic time down through historic time, including its settlement and growth as an Ohio River community. The city chose Leicester's sculpture over other proposals because it embodied a sense of place: it offers, in fact, a delightful child's-eye view of the Cincinnati universe.

Before the sculpture, and a part of it, stands a 115-foot tower. It playfully indicates the levels of Cincinnati's three major floods, including the eighty-foot level of

Gateway Sculpture and Flying Pig. This vast composition (1988) in Sawyer Point Park assumes new forms from every angle. Here we look down a miniature Ohio River as it winds along the top of what is meant to simulate an Ohio Indian mound. The famous flying pigs, one of which is seen here in closeup, appear to be shot out of steamboat smokestacks. The pigs are meant to recall Cincinnati's nineteenth-century fame (or notoriety) as "Porkopolis," when the city was the nation's meatpacking center. The wings suggest that the pig aspires to rise above its earthly state and fate. While the sculpture was being erected, some citizens thought these pigs an inappropriate symbol for the city. Good sense prevailed, however, and the pigs remain. Gateway photograph courtesy of J. Miles Wolf.

1937. A tree branch marks the one-hundred-foot level; at the top sits a miniature Noah's ark—which Cincinnatians will certainly need should the Ohio ever rise so high. Not all the sculpture's historical echoes are so playful. The tunnel before us, clad in attractive multicolored brick, replicates accurately and to scale a canal lock from the Miami and Erie Canal, which terminated here. On its right wall markers designate stops between Lake Erie and Cincinnati. The left wall alludes to Cincinnati's "seven hills." The tunnel also serves a very practical purpose, being the main walking entrance into the park from Eggleston Esplanade.

We walk through the tunnel and turn left. A plaque explains the symbolism behind the eighteen historical components of Leicester's sculpture. The captions afford us a quick review of Ohio Valley history. "History can be fun and refreshing," the plaque concludes, but it may provide too much of a good thing. Remember what you can but do enjoy the rest. We recross the tunnel entrance to look upon the adjoining brick wall. Fountain head masks spew out water in summer and sky masks (facing up on either side of the tunnel) reflect the ancient Indian cultures that long inhabited southwestern Ohio. Fossils and artifacts are also set in the brick wall. Continuing along, we climb the steps at the sculpture's east end. The undulating stairway railing recalls the famous Great Serpent Mound fifty miles east of Cincinnati, a major work of art in its own right. We stand on top of a berm that also recalls the mound. A big pyramid with a little one atop it perhaps alludes to Pittsburgh's Golden Triangle with Point State Park at the juncture of the Allegheny and Monongahela rivers. The Ohio River, which begins there, is unusual among major streams in that it begins virtually full grown, a mighty stream at birth. A miniature Ohio River, an actual rivulet, meanders from one end of the mound to the other. Solid bronze markers indicate the twenty dams and locks as well as altitude above sea level from Pittsburgh to Cairo, Illinois, the latter fancifully symbolized by a metal pyramid in the river. Cincinnati is exactly at the midpoint, on the bridge—its elaborate metalwork pays homage to the Roebling Bridge—above the entrance tunnel. We look up.

"The time has come," says the Walrus in Lewis Carroll's *Through the Looking-Glass*, "to talk of many things: / Of shoes—and ships—and sealing wax— / Of cabbages—and kings— / And why the sea is boiling hot— / And whether pigs have wings." Straight above our heads are four bronze pigs. They stand atop four columns. And they do have wings. For a while no one in Cincinnati talked about anything else but the Winged Pigs of Porkopolis. Actually the columns are riverboat smokestacks, and the pigs, presumably snorting wildly, appear to be blasted out from fiery boilers below. Though a small element in a complex work, the pigs have easily been the most controversial. Many wished them removed. Detractors, recalling the winged horse Pegasus of Greek mythology, dubbed the sculpture "Pigasus." Leicester's work, here as elsewhere consciously ironic, is not for those lacking in humor. For a time the pigs' survival appeared doubtful. Cincinnati's City Council, fearing the pigs would detract from the city's Blue Chip image and enhance its porcine one, debated their fate hotly. But good sense prevailed and the pigs remained, an echo both humorous and historical. They commemorate, after all, the meat-packing industry that led to Cincinnati's long-infamous nickname of Porkopolis. Why do they fly? Because nineteenth-century Porkopolitans dreamed of building a great and beautiful metropolis that would also be a renowned center of culture. The winged pigs reflect this aspiration.

We descend the stairs by the tunnel entrance, turn right, and go back through the tunnel. Ahead of us is the Daniel Carter Beard Bridge. Directly underneath the bridge, in an open space between the north- and south-bound lanes, is another sculpture, Barna von Sartory's *Law and Society* (1972). It is as simple as Leicester's is complex. The Cincinnati Bar Association commissioned this thirty-five ton work, a private gift from Charles Sawyer, to mark its hundredth anniversary. When revealed to the public in 1972, *Law and Society* kicked up a storm of outrage. Some likened it to the ruins of Stonehenge. Its detractors, very much in the majority, dubbed it "The Rock." Public art in Cincinnati, some said, was set back a decade. Over the years *Law and Society* has led an amazingly peripatetic existence. Sawyer intended it to stand in front of the steps of the Hamilton County Courthouse. However, it was originally sited on Fountain Square south of the DuBois Tower. Then it was exiled to the bus concourse across the street. In the early 1980s it migrated to an attractive paved semicircular plaza at what is now the main entrance to Sawyer Point. When that space was chosen for Leicester's work, it was moved to its present location. *Law and Society* relates well to the bridge's gigantic concrete supports. The circular freestanding luminaires surrounding it, even the trash receptacles, also echo the bridge supports.

The form of *Law and Society* is post and lintel—with a vengeance. Post and lintel, a basic mode of architecture going back to the Egyptians, suggests stability and permanence. Von Sartory intended the block of Indiana limestone to symbolize society, the (stainless!) steel pillars the intellect, that is, human accomplishments— in particular, the law. The rock is organic, the steel manmade. By his choice of materials, von Sartory represents society as monolithic, the law as solid and immutable. Modern, or rather, postmodern public sculpture can have, as we have seen in Leicester's work, a didactic as well as an esthetic effect. It can speak to our civilization and to the condition of our culture. It can be serious or humorous; it can criticize as well as commemorate. Here the intention appears to have been more didactic than esthetic. The sculpture makes a statement about the law's relationship to society: agree or disagree, the statement is unequivocal. Those who regard *both* law and society as mutable, organic, rooted in human fallibility, constantly evolving, may find *Law and Society* flawed in its symbolism. Though such a work might legitimately embody strength and suggest permanence, it might also remind us that in this pluralistic society of ours human beings, and the laws they make, are prone to error.

Past *Law and Society* is a delightful **playground** with slides that I find hard to resist. "Playground" is the word I grew up with; actually, this facility is termed an "adventure play area." There is a difference. The first thing we notice is the rubberized surface, in feel not unlike a Japanese tatami, no doubt to cushion falls from the jungle gyms. This innovative and imaginative complex includes a cluster of equipment designed to strengthen muscles. It also includes access for handicapped children. Adults wishing to avoid a trip to the beach can indulge in the sand volleyball courts.

Further along on the right, we come upon the limestone foundations of the former **Front Street Pumping Station;** a small amphitheater faces the wall. Although the Pumping Station occupies the site of Cincinnati's first waterworks of 1819, the stone walls we see date largely from 1862–1872. The Pumping Station supplied the Mount Adams reservoirs. The Ohio River's increasing pollution near Cincinnati dictated its closing, however, and the construction in 1907–1908 of the Cincinnati Waterworks upriver in California, Ohio.

Past the Pumping Station ruins is the Skating Pavilion, with a dual skating surface for ice skating in winter and roller skating in summer. The structure farthest upriver is the Boat House, containing the Cincinnati Rowing Center. One of only five such facilities in the United States and the only one not on the coasts, the Boat House provides world-class facilities for men and women training for Olympic rowing and paddling events. On the second and third levels the Montgomery Inn dispenses its ever-popular ribs to an enthusiastic clientele. Cincinnatians who take their ribs seriously—and many do—are well served here.

From the Boat House we return along the river. Riverwalk, which we follow, has several overlooks upon the Ohio, including a fishing pier just past the Pumping Station. Granite inserts on the pier identify Ohio River fish. In front of it we discover the beginning of a **Geologic Time Line.** Granite inserts embedded in the pavement of the first 1600 feet of Riverwalk depict, in texts and images, the 450 million years of the Ohio River Basin and the life—plants, fish, and dinosaurs—that has inhabited it. Each insert represents a million years. We follow the path, passing three more overlooks, as it curves above and along the river bank. How delightful to walk the river in so pleasing an environment! "It is most desirable from the standpoint of visual enjoyment and recreation," wrote the authors of the 1925 *Official Plan of the City of Cincinnati,* "that the city should gradually acquire enough land along the Ohio River to at least give a continuous promenade or pleasure drive from Eden Park to Columbia." That goal remains as desirable today as it was in 1925. No one will accuse Cincinnati of rushing things. But the pleasure we have had in walking the river on this tour reminds us that further opening of the riverfront remains a goal worth pursuing. As we amble along the Time Line, it is sobering to reflect upon how relatively brief a period humans have inhabited the Ohio Valley. The 5500 years of recorded history take up only the last three-eighths of an inch, signalled by an aluminum band. Cincinnati's brief two-hundred year history would be no wider than a pin. Once again the river reminds us how small a chink we are in the enormity of time.

Sawyer Point has provided an experience both educational and enjoyable. After we have savored the park's astonishing variety of amusements, activities, facilities, vistas, and public sculptures, we make out way back to Lytle Park—and downtown—most easily via Yeatman's Cove Park and the Concourse Fountains.

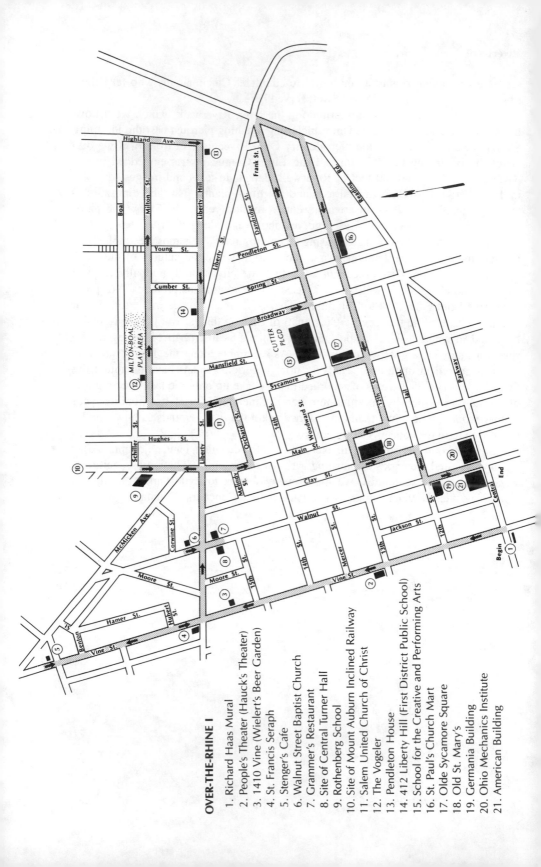

OVER-THE-RHINE I

1. Richard Haas Mural
2. People's Theater (Hauck's Theater)
3. 1410 Vine (Wielert's Beer Garden)
4. St. Francis Seraph
5. Stenger's Cafe
6. Walnut Street Baptist Church
7. Grammer's Restaurant
8. Site of Central Turner Hall
9. Rothenberg School
10. Site of Mount Auburn Inclined Railway
11. Salem United Church of Christ
12. The Vogeler
13. Pendleton House
14. 412 Liberty Hill (First District Public School)
15. School for the Creative and Performing Arts
16. St. Paul's Church Mart
17. Olde Sycamore Square
18. Old St. Mary's
19. Germania Building
20. Ohio Mechanics Institute
21. American Building

7

Over-the-Rhine I

"ÜBER dem Rhein," Over-the-Rhine—the name connotes both the river and a country, Germany. Cincinnati's "Rhine," the Miami and Erie Canal, flowed, and subsequently stagnated, where Central Parkway now runs. Many of the district's original inhabitants emigrated from Germany—chiefly from the Rhineland, Baden-Württemberg, and Bavaria—in the three or four decades after 1830. Other immigrant groups also clustered in Over-the-Rhine, including Irish and (later) Italian; but Germans predominated. In 1851, out of Over-the-Rhine's population of 19,000, Germans constituted 13,000, or about 60 percent. As Over-the-Rhine's population grew over the next half-century, that percentage declined. Native-born Americans and other nationalities came to constitute more than half the population. Yet the Germans stamped Over-the-Rhine, creating an ethnic enclave that, with its own architecture, language, and lifestyle, became a corner of the *Vaterland* transplanted to the New World.

In its distinctive ambience, we may compare Over-the-Rhine to New Orleans's French Quarter, New York's Greenwich Village, Washington's Georgetown, Philadelphia's Society Hill, even to Boston's Beacon Hill. Except for Over-the-Rhine, each of these districts now constitutes a focal point of its city, a source of its urban pride. They were all slums once. Society Hill, for example, long the most rundown area in Philadelphia, is now the most exclusive. If such comparisons risk blurring what is unique about the location, physiognomy, and history of each district, or no longer hold true, at least they should remind us that in Over-the-Rhine lies Cincinnati's chief claim to urban distinction. The neighborhood is unique in the Midwest. Today the whole area is on the National Register.

This, the first of two tours devoted to Over-the-Rhine, explores Vine St., the district's spinal cord, and the streets east of Vine. We pass several of the city's remaining monuments to its Germanic cultural traditions. Many are defunct, a few survive, others have been transformed into new uses. Among buildings still standing are Wielert's Beer Garden, Grammer's Restaurant, the Salem Church, St. Paul's, St. Mary's, and the Germania Building. The second tour explores the area west of Vine: Findlay Market, the former breweries, Washington Park, and Music

Hall. Both tours go beyond Over-the-Rhine's recognized boundaries. In this tour we climb Liberty Hill, actually part of Mount Auburn; in the second tour, we enter the West End to look at the Dayton St. mansions and, subsequently, those in the Betts-Longworth Historic District. This tour begins at Vine St. and Central Parkway; it ends, one block east, at Walnut St. and Central Parkway.

Over-the-Rhine *was* different. Anyone who crossed the canal, observed D. J. Kenny in his 1875 guide to Cincinnati, found

> himself in another atmosphere—in a foreign land, as it were. . . . The visitor leaves behind him at almost a single step the rigidity of the American, the everlasting hurry and worry of the insatiate race for wealth, . . . and enters at once into the borders of a people more readily happy, more readily contented, more easily pleased, far more closely wedded to music and the dance, to the song, and life in the bright open air. . . . The people are German; their faces are German; their manners and customs are German; their very gossip is German. They dance the German waltz as none but Germans can; they cook their food by German recipes, and sit long over their foaming beer.

A century and more later, nostalgic descriptions such as Kenny's make it easy for us to become sentimental about Over-the-Rhine, to see life in the nineteenth-century *Königinstadt* through a golden haze. Yet contemporary visitors often echo Kenny's depiction of a Teutonic Eden, *Germania in parvo*. Urban arcadia Over-the-Rhine may never have been, but it did possess qualities of community that often seem sadly lacking in urban life today. Edward Dicey, an English traveler visiting Cincinnati in 1862, found a German city transplanted to the shores of the Ohio:

> . . . the women, with their squat, stout figures, their dull blue eyes, and fair flaxen hair, sit knitting at their doors, dressed in the stuffed woolen petticoats of German fashion. The men have still the woolen jackets, the blue worsted pantaloons, and the low-crowned hats one knows so well in Bavaria and the Tyrol. There are *"Bier Gartens,"* *"Restaurations,"* and *"Tanz Saale [Säle],"* on every side.

Over-the-Rhine today consists of 110 blocks of nineteenth-century housing. It is bounded on the west and south by Central Parkway, on the north by McMicken Ave., on the east by Reading Road. With the largest single grouping of nineteenth-century Italianate urban buildings in the United States, it acts as a foil to the twentieth-century downtown. Even in the last century, visitors found the streetscape north of the canal different from that south. In contrast to downtown's "huge five-or-six story buildings with gigantic signs," A. B. Lakier, a Russian visitor of 1857, discovered in Over-the-Rhine's streets "small two-story houses intermingled with gardens. This in its own way is just like one of the small German towns with its inhabitants of modest wants, invariable steins of beer, and tobacco pipes." The burghers tended the potted plants on the window sills, cultivated tiny garden plots in the evenings after work, and every Wednesday and Saturday during the warm months whitewashed the front steps of their brick rowhouses.

Today seventy percent of Over-the-Rhine's surviving buildings are either sub-standard or vacant, twenty-eight percent livable but need repairs, and a bare two percent in good condition. Even more dramatic than the decline in housing stock has been the decline in population. The district's present population hovers under

10,000; as recently as 1950 it was nearly 32,000. Of course Cincinnati itself has lost population over this period, though its rate of decline has been much slower. In 1870, probably the peak period, Over-the-Rhine's population was 60,000. With 32,000 people per square mile, Cincinnati's population density approached Manhattan's. In 1870 the city had 216,000 inhabitants, of which 136,000 were native born. Of the nearly 80,000 of foreign birth, nearly 50,000 were German. By 1890 the German stock in Cincinnati reached its zenith. But as the century waned the Germans moved to the hilltops. Largely abandoning their old neighborhood, they distributed themselves over the city. Whereas metropolises comparable in their development to Cincinnati, such as Pittsburgh, St. Louis, Chicago, have retained ethnic enclaves, the Queen City has not.

Individually, Over-the-Rhine's buildings were, and are, often remarkable; collectively, they create the essence of the period and the spirit of the district. Neither monuments nor masterpieces, more "street" or "vernacular" architecture than "landmarks," they constitute a modest but nonetheless vital part of the city's fabric. What Ada Louise Huxtable has written regarding Manhattan's early nineteenth-century buildings applies with equal aptness to Cincinnati's far larger collection of buildings put up a generation or two later: "Their value is contrast, character, visual and emotional change of pace, a sudden sense of intimacy, scale, all evocative of the qualities of another century and way of life. They provide the impression of a city 'in depth,' the richness of past and present side by side."

Even today, Over-the-Rhine retains a homogenous physical presence in its compact blocks, its housing stock, the pervasive orange-red brick, and in the height and size of its streetscape. These low-scale structures, rarely more than four or five stories, usually two or three, afford us a pleasure different from that of skyscrapers: the pleasure of intimacy. They are based on a human scale that, however unconsciously, paid attention to human needs. When I walk in Over-the-Rhine, I experience a sense of spaciousness, a feeling that I am in a bowl of light. In an environment of small-scale buildings, surrounded by light and with the sky visible, we feel more in control of our circumstances.

In America, we tend to fence off historical features in the landscape in a preserve called History. We permit the public to look over the fence and to admire; sometimes we invite it in. But in Over-the-Rhine the *entire* district is historic. Significant as are its individual structures, Over-the-Rhine's distinction lies less in them than it does in the ensemble. The ensemble's coherence is a pleasure to contemplate, and is also a resource not to be overlooked. In this tour and the next I discuss specific buildings, but it is the overall cityscape that steals the show. We shall understand why one observer called Over-the-Rhine "Cincinnati's, and possibly America's, most architecturally distinguished slum."

Nineteenth-century Cincinnati was a walking city. Inhabitants and visitors alike, like every urban generation before our own, walked. Walkers in Over-the-Rhine a century ago encountered streets of small, well-kept houses. It began as a neighborhood for the poor in the 1830s when the city was in the middle of its first great development boom and population explosion. Though most Over-the-Rhine families lived in modest circumstances, few faced abject poverty. George M. Henzel, growing up in Over-the-Rhine during World War I, remembers that twenty-three children lived in the four flats of his tenement. Over-the-Rhine remains a neighborhood for the poor, to be sure, but its present inhabitants live at a much lower density than those a century ago. Crowding, that great nineteenth-century urban evil, is no longer a major problem.

In nineteenth-century Over-the-Rhine, stores, churches, saloons, and beer gardens lay near at hand. Shopkeepers often lived above, behind, or next to their shops. Residents, observe Carl M. Becker and William H. Daily, lived "in a self-contained community. . . . Here the close-knit pattern of architectural forms compelled German-Americans to shop, work, play and pray together." The streets offered (and offer) a satisfying diversity of proportions: people to buildings, street width to building height, heights to widths, solids to voids, business scale to domestic scale, spires to "normal" building height. People related well, if perhaps unconsciously, to the low-scale buildings in warm, orange-colored brick. Only church spires broke the roofline. Beyond the buildings rose the encircling hills; above the hills, the sky. People walked amidst a jumble of narrow streets. Short blocks, often half the size of the already compact downtown blocks, linked streets. Alleys bisected the blocks, enhancing the intimate scale. East-west streets often jogged left or right; diagonal streets caused odd-angled intersections and houses. Both helped break the grid's monotony. Boundaries were (and are) clearly marked. Hills hemmed in Over-the-Rhine on the north and partially on the east; the canal (the "Rhine") delimited the district on the south and west.

Many American cities follow a well-established pattern. Downtown features a cluster of highrises, traversed or surrounded by freeways. Invariably, a wasteland develops on either side of the freeways. Inner-city neighborhoods decline or disappear. Gradually the affluent suburbs begin. Not so Cincinnati. It, too, has its downtown, its freeways, its affluent suburbs. America's century-long movement from inner city to outlying suburb, though slowed in recent decades, continues here as elsewhere. But inner-city neighborhoods of varying vitality still ring Cincinnati's downtown. In Paris and most other European (and South American) cities, the well-to-do live by choice in the center, the poor by necessity in distant suburbs. But in American cities the reverse is (usually) true: the well-to-do live in suburbs, the poor in or near downtown. It was not always so: once people of all economic levels lived in the center of American cities. In Europe, a historic inner-city neighborhood like Over-the-Rhine would thrive; in America, it declines, or stagnates, or, maybe, gets rescued.

Over-the-Rhine's housing stock tells us that the people who settled here, mostly foreign born, took pride in the neighborhood. They kept their homes immaculate, the streets clean. This is not what we shall see as we walk this tour. A house changes less than its sequence of inhabitants and their attitude toward their environment. Today some blocks appear in good condition; most do not. For still others it is hard to say. Housing stock, once excellent, is unevenly maintained. Perhaps Over-the-Rhine's National Register designation, which allows substantial tax credits to those who rehabilitate buildings within its bounds, will spur further restoration.

Over-the-Rhine's glory years were the later decades of the nineteenth century. Several factors account for the area's decline. Living patterns had been changing almost from the beginning. Many immigrants, having achieved prosperity, moved out; new immigrants took their places, eventually to leave themselves. Only in the twentieth century, after Cincinnati ceased absorbing the major waves of European immigration flowing over the American continent, did Over-the-Rhine begin its long decline to inner-city slum. This is one factor. Another is World War I, which made Germans and things German unpopular. A third is the Volstead Act (i.e., Prohibition), which in 1920 shut down Over-the-Rhine's saloons and beer gardens, a chief source of its prosperity. A fourth factor is the automobile. In 1919 Americans owned 6,000,000 automobiles, in 1929, 23,000,000. The automobile's dramatic rise in popularity in the 1920s permitted people to wander at will. The suburban brick house, the dream of many Over-the-Rhine residents as of Americans generally, became a reality easier to achieve. The neighborhood lost its cohesiveness; after World War I the term "Over-the-Rhine" was less frequently heard. The 1943 WPA guide to Cincinnati refers to Over-the-Rhine as the "Central Parkway Area" and devotes to it only one of its twenty-five tours. After World War II urban dilapidation increased, and crime rates soared. Over-the-Rhine became known as "the Upper Basin" or the "upper half of downtown." To all these designations it answers, but to none so well as Over-the-Rhine.

Prosperous cities, now as in past times, function as magnets for people in less prosperous areas. For successive waves of immigrants Over-the-Rhine served as a port of entry. By the 1890s the well-to-do had largely abandoned Cincinnati's Basin; by 1900 the middle class had also begun to depart, first by tram, then by automobile. The German influence in Over-the-Rhine peaked in the early years of the twentieth century. After World War II black and white migrants from the economically depressed South settled here because of the Cincinnati area's job opportunities. More blacks moved to Over-the-Rhine in the late 1950s and 1960s when I-75's construction leveled great chunks of the West End. Although German and other European immigrants shaped Over-the-Rhine's architecture in the nineteenth century, in the late twentieth century it is a largely black and Appalachian slum.

The new immigrants were poor. They remain poor. They live in Over-the-Rhine not from choice but from economic necessity. Some do not appear adapted for, or interested in, urban life. Once Over-the-Rhine served as a staging ground for upward mobility. Today it harbors the poor, the elderly, the down-and-out, and the homeless. Many people here have neither the economic resources, educational training, or work skills to get out. Unlike previous residents, they will not go away unless compelled. Plans for the area that do not include them court failure. But let the present inhabitants feel pride in their neighborhood and the process of gradual dilapidation might reverse itself. Here and there it has. Over-the-Rhine has the potential for poor and affluent, white and black, old-established and relative newcomer, to come together in a showcase neighborhood.

In recent decades Over-the-Rhine's future has occasioned much debate. Local groups have disagreed among themselves: some wanted new development and low-income housing preserved, others thought high-income development the answer. The issue boiled down to whether the city should bolster Over-the-Rhine's economic base *or* renovate its housing stock. It pitted shopkeepers against the poor. The factions involved agreed only to disagree. But in spring 1986, after a decade of controversy, Over-the-Rhine's feuding groups came together on a $10 million, five-year plan that received city council support. The 1.3 million dollars appropriated the first year called for rehabilitating 300 housing units, a streetscape program, and improved lighting in the Findlay Market and Vine St. business districts. Eventually the city hopes to reverse Over-the-Rhine's population decline.

To me, the greatest enigma about Cincinnati is why what should be its most cherished neighborhood has been for so long, by its citizens and by the city government, its most neglected. Potentially, Over-the-Rhine could assume the importance in Cincinnati's urban life that the French Quarter has in New Orleans's or Greenwich Village in Manhattan's. Like them, it is an architectural cornucopia a stone's throw from center city. Nearer home, Columbus's German Village, a smaller area, far less impressive architecturally, has in recent decades undergone a stunning transformation into a prime inner-city residential neighborhood. Savannah and Charleston have taken strong steps to preserve their historic districts as human-scaled, pedestrian-oriented areas. Such districts are not only sources of urban pride, but are major social and economic resources. Over-the-Rhine, in addition to its historic and architectural value, has a much greater sense of neighborhood than most bedroom communities. Preserving and revitalizing it should be a main goal of the city. Unfortunately, it has not been. Street maintenance and trash collection are a civic disgrace. Filth abounds. As the head of the Over-the-Rhine Chamber of Commerce once put it: "Most people just don't think of Over-the-Rhine as a neighborhood. It's another planet."

The long-term prognosis is not promising. The city lacks funds, or desire, or both, to make a major commitment to Over-the-Rhine's future. Large private investors have thus far shied away. The district's population slowly spirals downward, and historic buildings fall down or are bulldozed as I write and you read. But if this potential Cinderella could attract a Prince Charming sensitive to its special needs, it might again become, as it earlier was, one of Cincinnati's most vital neighborhoods. Neighborhoods, after all, are not disposable commodities. Perhaps the "homesteading" that has worked reasonably well in Baltimore—that is, the city purchasing and then allowing people to buy abandoned shells for a nominal sum on promise of restoration—could be more vigorously pursued. Homesteading has been tried here and there in the city but only on a limited scale.

Although the area we shall walk through is rundown, moribund it is not. Its streets support diverse life. Numerous storefronts are indeed boarded up but the chief commercial streets—Vine, Main, less so Race—support, as they have for over a century, varied enterprises, whether old established firms that cater to a city-wide clientele or small shops providing the local populace with needed goods and services. Over-the-Rhine still retains considerable population and economic vitality.

Esthetically, Over-the-Rhine was, and often still remains, a dream. Walking its streets allows us to experience what is meant by diversity within harmony, human scale, the use of texture and warmth in building materials, and the pleasure provided by architectural detail. Look around and touches of beauty appear everywhere: a window box bursting with blooms, a newly painted façade, a tiny garden glimpsed down an exterior hallway, an unaltered cast-iron storefront, two kids playing stickball in an alley. We shall find it exciting just to wander through the streets and alleys, following our intuition, enjoying spatial sequences that constantly surprise. If we look up, we discover streets climbing at preposterous angles, steps that disappear in greenery, buildings that exist in crazy visual relationships to one another—some even appearing to emerge out of the roofs of those below. Irregular in shape, their windows peering blankly out upon the city, these hillside houses form an ingenious architectural pattern against the green hills. Over-the-Rhine may be untidy and dilapidated but it is not visually dull. I have found its streets safe enough during daylight hours. To the curious it offers a cornucopia of pleasures. To experience Cincinnati without exploring it is to experience a diminished thing.

We begin our tour on the median of **Central Parkway** and Vine St. Under us once flowed the Miami and Erie Canal. As a living urban way, Cincinnati's widest boulevard strikes me as a flop, grandiose boulevard-mongering at its worst, or nearly. Fortunately, this city, compared to most others, has few such boulevards. But a failed urban way was not the original intent. In 1906 the Cincinnati Park Board asked George Kessler, a leading landscape architect who had laid out Kansas City's fine park system, to prepare a similar plan for Cincinnati. The 1907 Kessler plan included as well an ambitious program of civic improvements. One was for a central multilaned artery to connect downtown with residential and commercial districts to the west and north. This artery would have allées of trees and a median of benches, fountains, balustrades, and lighting. It would recall a Parisian boulevard or, nearer home, Boston's Commonwealth Avenue.

Central Parkway, completed in 1928, indeed became a grand boulevard. It replaced the canal and the subway excavated—and now abandoned—in its bed. But nothing else happened. Most new construction occurred elsewhere, then stopped with the Depression. Each succeeding decade saw Central Parkway become less central. Today, for almost all of its length, it is a dreary thoroughfare. Most buildings on it go back to canal days; the little new construction is undistinguished. Rarely do we see people walking along its sidewalks. Photographs from as late as the 1950s show a grassed median with a walkway down the center, streetlights, fountains, and trees. Though twelve tall gaslights remain, most others have vanished to provide additional traffic lanes that rarely appear needed. No less than the canal it replaced, Central Parkway serves as an "edge" or border to demarcate Over-the-Rhine. It also serves as a barrier. Many Cincinnatians who work downtown rarely venture across it.

Although by 1919 the canal was an eyesore, we may regret—at least with hindsight—its disappearance. Open water is almost always pleasing. Amsterdam, Copenhagen, Groningen, Bruges, Venice, the area around London's Regents Canal, allow us to discover the possibilities for urban pleasure offered by cities with canals. Water makes for diverse cityscapes and visual richness. Picturesque craft, scenic walks, unexpected vistas, views up and down the canal from the bridges—all are enhanced by the magical presence of water. Most American canals have been filled in or converted to roadways. Unlike canals in Europe, their scenic and recreational possibilities, both for summer and winter, have rarely been tapped. Now they cannot be. Even if by the twentieth century Cincinnati's canal lacked commercial viability, spruced up it could have provided a spectacular urban amenity far greater than the gardens proposed, but never fully implemented, for Central Parkway.

Across from the Kroger Building a huge **mural of Cincinnatus** fills the north wall of the Cincinnatus Building, formerly the Brotherhood Building (1923). This Renaissance Revival structure, named originally after the Brotherhood of Railway Clerks, was renamed in 1983. That year Kroger, to celebrate its centennial, commissioned New York-based Richard Haas to do this mural. Haas's murals have enlivened a number of Manhattan's dead corners. Here his work depicts a setting of illusionary architecture: a Baroque staircase, upon which stands a triumphant Cincinnatus, leads up to a Pantheon-like dome. The scene, though, is out of character: Cincinnatus was a humble man. This *capriccio,* the most complex of Cincinnati's wall paintings, makes clever use of perspective and trompe l'oeil. Find the real windows, the real doors. Where does the real cornice leave off, the painted one begin?

Vine St., to which we now turn, slices Cincinnati in two. It traverses Over-the-Rhine's heart. Never was Vine livelier than in the nineteenth century's last decades. During the 1890s, in the two miles between the Ohio River and McMillan St., the street boasted no less than 113 drinking establishments. At that time there existed two Vine streets: one, American in flavor, reached from 4th St. to the canal; the other, Teutonic, stretched from the canal to McMillan at the top of the hill. It is the lower half of this second Vine St., once Cincinnati's main tourist attraction, that we shall walk along and recreate in our imaginations. You would cross the canal, enter a beer garden, and slowly sip your lager while listening to a German band. The oom-pah-pah of the music booms forth amidst the clack of man-sized mugs. Burghers fondle handlebar moustaches as they discuss Bismarck's savvy leadership of the now-united *Vaterland.* It is these distractions, sponsored by the large German population and available on Sunday no less than on weekdays, that set Cincinnati apart from other American cities. It led to Cincinnati's designation, from the 1870s, as the "Paris of America." A fun-loving city it was then (somewhat less so today), with its theaters, legitimate and burlesque, its old world restaurants and beer gardens, its bowling alleys and shooting galleries, its gambling dens, its houses of prostitution and its assorted fleshpots, but also, beginning in that decade, a city that took its musical and artistic life very seriously indeed.

In 1893, when annual per capita consumption of beer in America averaged sixteen gallons, Cincinnatians drank forty. Cincinnati, in fact, led American cities in beer consumption. One Dr. Walcker imbibed his daily quota of five gallons of lager; brewery workers regularly put away forty, fifty, even sixty glasses a day. Order a five-cent beer and you got sausage and bread as a lagniappe. Saloons and beer gardens constituted Vine St.'s leading enterprises. If many contemporaries affectionately recalled Over-the-Rhine as the embodiment of German *gemütlichkeit,* others

Vine St., 1890s, southwest corner of 5th St. Over a two-mile stretch of Vine once clustered 113 drinking establishments. With each glass patrons could claim a *Wienerwurst*. Numerous street signs enlivened the nineteenth-century urban scene. Courtesy of the Cincinnati Historical Society.

regarded it as a haven for vice, corruption, and violence. The reality falls in between. Although the *gemütlichkeit* of the beer gardens certainly existed, the core of the neighborhood consisted of frugal, hard-working immigrants, Germans chiefly but by no means exclusively, seeking to achieve a better life for themselves and their families, even to get out into the newly accessible suburbs. But Vine St. did dispense alcohol in abundance. In 1901, when the temperance crusader Carrie Nation toured the street, axe ready in hand to shatter bar windows, she expressed awe, so the story goes, at the near-solid phalanx of saloons and beer gardens. Asked why she had not broken any windows, she replied, "I would have dropped from exhaustion before I had gone a block."

Aficionados of **street furniture** will delight in Over-the-Rhine: cast-iron fronts (often with the manufacturer's plate still on them), plaques of metal, marble, or encaustic tile in the sidewalk, lampposts and merchants' signs. Even when we are hardly conscious of it, such street furniture helps shape our impression of the cityscape. It entertains us visually and, read aright, it can teach us much regarding the city's history. For half a century after 1850 most Cincinnati storefronts were made of cast iron. A few are in stone. Wood fronts, rarer still, also exist. Cast-iron fronts give themselves away by rust patches; when in doubt, apply a small magnet. Often we can read on them the manufacturer's name: J. F. Krieger, Columbia, Wm. Schumacher, Edwards, L. Schreiber & Sons. Two still in business are B. J. Rowekamp and the Stewart Iron Works.

1109 Vine is the A. P. Hauck Co. Building. This Queen Anne structure long housed Doerr's, a popular restaurant and bakery, founded in 1890. If we look closely at the cast-iron front, we discern on it the manufacturer's plate with the name "The L. Schreiber Sons Co. Cin. O." The adjacent 1111, Italianate, has an even more elaborate cast-iron front with rope-turned columns and Corinthian pilasters. Look up as well as down. 1115 Vine, five stories and Queen Anne, has a spectacular metal cornice topped by an urn. Such cornices are quite literally the crowning glories of Over-the-Rhine's late nineteenth-century commercial architecture. Splendid specimens abound throughout the district. Further along at **1127–29 Vine** we come upon a stately Beaux Arts structure designed by the Hannaford firm. Its imposing (metal) columns indicate it originally housed a bank, in this case the German National Bank, once a key Over-the-Rhine institution. Then it became Otto Printing. In 1988 it underwent conversion into a 130-seat auditorium. Ensemble Theatre of Cincinnati, the city's other equity house, presents here new and seldom-produced plays.

America's decision in April 1917 to enter World War I on the Allied side fundamentally altered the nature of **German-American life** in Cincinnati and elsewhere. Overnight, or nearly, things German were stigmatized. Frankfurters became hot dogs, sauerkraut "Liberty Cabbage." The German National Bank, like many other German organizations, altered its name, emerging as the Lincoln National Bank. German street names also underwent a sea change: Bismarck became Montreal; Berlin, Woodward; Hannover, Yukon; Bremen, Republic; Hamburg, Stonewall; Erkenbrecher, Albany (eventually becoming Erkenbrecher again). German St. even became English St. Schiller and Goethe remained, however. Signboards in German disappeared. Families anglicized their names; prominent Germans were harassed, dismissed from their posts, censured, and sometimes interned. In 1918 the Public Library relegated its fine German collection to the sub-basement. Cincinnati's precarious German theater—Germans spoke of it as their *Schmerzenskind*—did not revive for years. Several German-language newspapers folded. The *Volksblatt*, Cincinnati's first German-American newspaper, on the scene since 1836, did not survive the war. If German was still spoken in the home, rarely was it heard outside.

Cincinnati had achieved a nationally acclaimed German language instructional program in its public schools, but as anti-German sentiment mounted during the first years of the war it became a target. In July 1918 the State of Ohio dismissed teachers of German from the public schools. In May of the next year the state forbade the studying of German in any school below the eighth grade. Although the U.S. Supreme Court declared this law unconstitutional in June 1923, by then the damage was done: bilingualism, in effect in Cincinnati since 1840, was dead—and a dead issue. Not until 1975 was German reintroduced in one of the city's elementary schools.

Of American cities, Cincinnati, St. Louis, and Milwaukee were probably the most Germanic. Of the three, Cincinnati became a German city earlier and retained its German characteristics longer. All the German states, including the Free City of Lübeck, stationed consuls here. Robert Heuck, who grew up in a German-speaking household at the turn of the last century, recalls the older Over-the-Rhine:

> Here the German immigrant would stay with his friends or relations until he found a job, and a home of his own. In this area German was the common language; for instance, I spoke German before I spoke English. Churches, the denomination of which was familiar to the German, abounded in this area. Services were held in German. Turner Halls, Saengerbunds and Fests, literary clubs and social clubs of all types were organized. There were four German newspapers published in Cincinnati at that time, and there were German banks, German doctors, German lawyers, German merchants whose clerks spoke German and understood the German's needs. There were stores such as Alms & Doepke's, Hanke's, Siefert's, Japp's and Esberger's, among others. There were German restaurants that served food familiar to his palate: wine and, of course, beer to his taste.

The typical German was bilingual, even to the extent of using both languages in the same sentence. Few traces of this bilingualism remain. One that does I find charming. When a Cincinnatian does not understand something, he or she says "please"—the English equivalent of the German *bitte*.

In the 1890s twenty-three saloons graced Vine St. between 12th and 13th streets. Here also were a number of the city's leading entertainment meccas. At 1221 Vine, now a parking lot, stood from 1860 to 1872 the *Loewengarten,* or Lion Garden, which offered music by German masters. It was succeeded by the **Coliseum,** a glorified saloon with a stage. Here the famed marksman Frank Frayne, in exhibitions of shooting prowess, often in conjunction with his wife, regularly demonstrated his skill. Performing in *Sly Slocum* in 1882, Frayne would shoot an apple off her head. He faced away from her, balanced a rifle on his shoulder, and lined the apple up in a mirror. For protection his wife wore a steel band under a kerchief. One night, in haste, she forgot the band, Frayne's aim was low, and he shot her between the eyes. In the ensuing uproar Frayne barely escaped with his life. In 1882 Heuck's Opera House followed the Coliseum. It offered, not the classical repertory, but blood-and-thunder melodramas like *Darkest Russia, Blue Jeans* (which had the heroine tied to a sawmill conveyor belt), *Tillie, the Sewing Machine Girl,* and *Davy Crockett* with Jim Jeffries.

On the northwest corner of 13th and Vine Streets stood—and still stands in part, minus its open cupola—the **People's Theater** (1875), which began as Heuck's Theater. The lobby and saloon remain; the auditorium has been razed. Both the People's Theater and Heuck's Opera House were the progeny of Hubert Heuck. Here performed such showmen-entrepreneurs as "Wild Bill" Hickok and William F. "Buffalo Bill" Cody. During the latter's week-long run Heuck's sold eighty-four kegs of beer. Very much a *Volkstheater,* People's was in its day Cincinnati's most popular burlesque house. *Burlesque* did not mean girly shows; rather, it lived up to its dictionary definition of lighthearted satire on serious plays and revues. All this excitement had begun to wane before World War I. The war, closely followed by Prohibition, further doused Vine's high spirits.

Architecturally, Vine St. retains a good deal of interest. Its buildings illustrate a full range of late nineteenth-century eclectic styles. 1313, erected in 1885 in a Renaissance Revival style, is the former **Cosmopolitan Hall.** This magnificent building became at the turn of the century a community entertainment center, where Germans and other immigrants met and danced. The Kirby (no. 1331), with "1885" on its façade, is an attractive red-brick Queen Anne apartment building. The pediment of the adjoining structure, the Loewenstein Building, sports a splendid lion. *Löwe* is German for lion, *Stein* means stone, but this beast is of metal.

Behind 1410 Vine's picturesque Renaissance façade was once Henry **Wielert's Pavilion** (1873). The best known and perhaps the most stylish of Cincinnati's beer gardens, Wielert's marked the end of the central Vine St. entertainment district, as Doerr's on Central Parkway marked the beginning. At one time seventeen beer halls stood in between, among them Kissell's, Schickling's, and Hildebrand's. A large saloon occupied Wielert's first floor. George Cox, Cincinnati's Republican "boss," held court at a round table, or *Stammtisch,* permanently reserved for him. Behind was a garden, covered but open at the sides, lined with busts of Goethe and Schiller, Beethoven and Schubert, Mozart and Mendelssohn. Henry Farny's famous sketch depicts the garden pullulating with life and conviviality. As many as 1500 might attend a special concert given by Michael Brand's orchestra, a picked group of forty to fifty musicians that in 1895 became the nucleus of the Cincinnati Symphony. The garden backed against the Central Turner Hall on Walnut St., where in the 1880s and 1890s local political groups met. Runners hotfooted it to Cox with the latest developments. Closed at Prohibition, Wielert's has undergone several transformations. For a time it functioned as the Gildehaus Funeral home; now it houses the "Living Word Love Center."

Liberty St., to which we have arrived, is Over-the-Rhine's major east-west artery. From 1802 until 1849, when the city annexed the land from Liberty to where the Western Hills viaduct now is, it served as Cincinnati's northern boundary. The land was known as "Northern Liberties." It earned its name: beyond it officials could not enforce city ordinances. Those who wished to drink, gamble, or break Cincinnati's severe Sunday "blue laws" simply stepped across the line. By 1840 this area, though still largely occupied by vegetable gardens, began to be built upon.

Few churches dared locate on Vine St. But across Liberty, glistening in its orange and yellow glazed brick, stands **St. Francis Seraph** (1859). James McLaughlin, later architect of Shillito's and the Cincinnati Art Museum, designed this building—one of his more unusual concoctions—for a group of Franciscans from Austria. The glazed brick façade dates from 1925. I wonder if the individual behind this color scheme hadn't visited Rome and there admired the Trinità dei Monti (Trinity of the Mountains), the seventeenth-century church that culminates the vista up the Spanish Steps. Trinità dei Monti's contours, no less than its orange and yellow coloration (paint on stucco), make it an irresistible parallel to St. Francis. This church, with its turrets and round-arched windows, is ostensibly Romanesque; the yellow brick pilasters hint at Greek Revival. The pyramidal spires are set at 90-degree angles to their bases. Adjoining St. Francis was Cincinnati's first Catholic cemetery. When larger cemeteries opened up elsewhere, the parish deposited unclaimed bodies in the crypt, where fragments of gravestones from before 1858 line the walls of one chamber.

On this site, a wall plaque informs us, stood the diocese's first Catholic church. In 1819 Irish river men erected here a simple frame structure, fifty-five feet by thirty, and dedicated it as St. Patrick's. Although most accounts state that anti-Catholic prejudice forced the congregation to build outside the city limits, John H. Lamott, writing the Cincinnati archdiocese's official history in 1921, dismisses this as unlikely, arguing, conversely, that the site's central location, as convenient to Catholics living outside the city as within, made it a good choice. Cincinnati's Catholics, with their limited financial means, could not at first afford higher-priced property within the city. In 1822 the congregation moved its frame church to Sycamore St. near 6th St., where St. Francis Xavier now stands.

At this point, if the need for sustenance is upon you, I recommend either Stenger's Cafe or Grammer's Restaurant. Stenger's is at 1720 Vine, two short blocks further north; Grammer's is one block east, on the corner of Walnut and Liberty Streets. A visit to either will afford insight into the Over-the-Rhine of yesteryear. Stenger's, a workingman's saloon from the 1930s, serves good basic food at bargain prices; Grammer's, in business since 1872, offers somewhat more elegant fare. If you decide for Stenger's, we will soon afterwards pass Grammer's; if for Grammer's, we can take Stenger's in on the next tour. The following three paragraphs assume that the choice is Stenger's.

Stenger's Cafe offers German staples: mettwurst, bratwurst ("metts" and "brats" in local parlance), white beans, potato pancakes, and what must be Cincinnati's most ample open-faced roast beef sandwich. Every day it takes in fifty pounds of beef and nineteen of ham. The original Stenger's began nearby, on Dunlap St. in 1893 but, like saloons everywhere, closed at Prohibition; in 1934 John Stenger, Jr., opened at this location. Leo Sundermann, his son-in-law, runs the place today, assisted by family members and Cincinnati's most cheerful waitress, "DeeDee" Yeary. Inside, we move back two generations in time: lincrusta walls, pressed metal ceiling, overhead fans, bentwood chairs. Ranged along the bar, an engaging mix of patrons' faces constitute a cross section of Cincinnati.

Although their primary purpose was to sell beer, saloons had important other functions. Beyond Stenger's bar is the "Annex," the sitting room once found in so many Over-the-Rhine neighborhood saloons. In such rooms, patrons formed partnerships, swapped real estate, discussed legal, political, family, and neighborhood problems, held professional consultations, and organized *Bauvereine*, or building associations, the ubiquitous savings and loan associations that made home ownership possible. In the volatile and fluid world of immigrant Over-the-Rhine, Zane Miller has written, "the flourishing of German voluntary associations represented not an expression of ethnic cohesion, unit[y] and order, but rather efforts to fabricate a sense of community." These efforts were largely successful. Here musical, literary,

People's Garden, Over-the-Rhine. As residents cultivate their plots, empty lots are transformed into gardens.

and social clubs also met, and here card players dealt innumerable hands. Around the saloon revolved the daily life of Over-the-Rhine. The saloon fulfilled, as Stephen Z. Starr has pointed out, "all the functions of a neighborhood club house and civic center."

Opposite Stenger's, at 1725 Vine, is the five-bay **Kauffman Building.** Renaissance Revival in style, it was erected as an apartment house (and an investment) by the John Kauffman Brewery. "1879," on the left cornice (partially destroyed in a 1988 fire), is the date of erection; "1863," on the right, is the year the brewery moved to Vine St., a block or so south, from Deer Creek valley. The central cartouche honors G. F. Eichenlaub, Kauffman's partner and father-in-law. He arrived in Cincinnati in 1832, walking from New York in fifteen weeks. A block behind Stenger's, on Back St., is Over-the-Rhine's People's Garden. The street gave its name to the bestselling novel *Back Street* (1931), by Cincinnati-born Fannie Hurst.

We return south down Vine St. 1622, the Romanesque Revival structure with a sign saying "Schuermann," served as the Kauffman Brewery's malt house. "1886" indicates the date of completion; "1856," the date of the main building (the brew house, once located to the north and now a parking lot), is also the year the brewery was founded. Note the hops in relief as part of the molding below the second-story windows. The older building directly behind, now occupied by Husman Potato Chips, also formed part of the Kauffman complex.

If you have not detoured to Stenger's, continue east along Liberty St. North on Walnut St., at 1610, is the simple Romanesque Revival Walnut Street **Baptist**

Church (1866). It began as the *Baptisten Kirche,* Over-the-Rhine's single German Baptist congregation, one that grew out of the Dunkards, or "Dunkers," a sect of German Baptist brethren, who originally arrived in Pennsylvania in 1719. Dunkards were in Benjamin Stites's party that settled Columbia, a few miles upriver from Cincinnati, in November 1788. The name derives from their belief in baptism by total immersion. After World War I the German Baptists joined their American brethren. Further north, where Walnut intersects with McMicken Ave., we sight a circular concrete structure (1973): the successor to Wesley Chapel that once stood at 5th and Sycamore streets, a site now occupied by the Procter & Gamble garden.

Grammer's Restaurant, on the southeast corner of Walnut and Liberty streets, is one of Over-the-Rhine's few active establishments that recalls its German past. Founded in 1872 by a German-born baker, Anton Grammer, it too shared in the district's turn-of-the-century prosperity. The original building was on Vine; the present quarters date only from 1911, the year of Anton Grammer's death. The structure adjoining (1436 Walnut), part of Grammer's since 1966, went up in the 1880s; an attractive lyre motif graces its cast-iron balcony. Grammer's long played a vital role in Cincinnati's German life. Until 1911 members of the German Bakers' Singing Society met here. After World War I the German Literary Club gathered upstairs. In 1984 Jim Tarbell, owner of Arnold's on 8th St., purchased the restaurant.

Within, Grammer's decor remains Teutonic in an indelibly American way. Photographs of the original Grammer's greet us as we enter. The bar is of burled mahogany; decorating the walls are stained glass and ancient steins. The ornamental stamped metal ceiling, typical of work done by several turn-of-the-century companies, was produced by the Edwards Manufacturing Co., whose former building behind the Taft Museum we looked at in chapter 5. The cut and leaded glass in the door facing Walnut St., reputedly from Germany, was more likely made locally. Originally the front room was for diners, the middle contained billiard tables, and the back, or sitting, room, was for regulars. Murals of the late 1940s, in the style of a German *Wirtstube,* depict castles, green hills, a river far below: scenes along the Rhine that, after a few glasses, no doubt become scenes along the Ohio at Cincinnati.

South down Walnut, on the west side of the street where a parking lot is now, stood until 1974 the Central Turner Hall (1859). Founded at Friedrich Hecker's instigation in October 1848, the Cincinnati *Turnverein,* or **Turner Society,** is the nation's oldest. The first *Turnhalle,* or Turner Hall, dates from 1850. The Turners began as an athletic club, their motto, *Mens sana in corpore sano* ("a sound mind in a sound body"). So Juvenal, and so the Turners. For years Central Turner Hall served as a focal point for gymnastics, fencing, and wrestling. Nor was mind forgotten. The Hall housed a German-language theater and a concert room. Later, it became a hub for social activities and local politics, usually of a liberal bent. Across the lot and very much worth a look we make out the gingerbread wooden portico—where the band played—of Wielert's Pavilion, "Boss" Cox's hangout. Thus were power and pleasure linked in turn-of-the-century Cincinnati.

We walk along Liberty to Main St., then north on Main to Schiller St. Beyond the intersection is the neo-Tudor **Rothenberg School** (1913). Neo-Tudor or Tudor

Revival (the style spawned a number of variant names) was popular for academic buildings between 1890 and 1930, presumably because it recalled the medieval universities and the revival of learning. The entrance facing north has elaborate terra cotta decoration. At the top of the right pinnacle sits a boy, cross-legged, reading a book. Opposite, a little girl paints a ball—perhaps an allusion to Rookwood? Atop the building's western tower sit two lackadaisical elves.

Main St. deadends at Mulberry. Where the steps begin was the base station of the old **Mount Auburn,** or Main St., **inclined railway** or "incline." 850 feet long, it deposited people at the top of the hill, 312 feet above, where Jackson Hill Park is now. George A. Smith and James Doherty formed the Cincinnati Inclined Plane Railway Company in 1871 and, after many physical and legal difficulties, constructed the incline. The earliest of Cincinnati's five inclines, the Mount Auburn opened on May 12, 1872, two years after the Monongahela incline in Pittsburgh, the nation's first—and still functioning—incline. A pair of seventy horsepower engines operated two huge cable-winding drums to raise one platform up the hill while the other descended. Although the ride took only one and one-half minutes, it was expensive. A bus from downtown to the incline station cost five cents, the incline itself another nickel, and at the top it was five cents more for the horsecar to take you further. But within a month 600 passengers a day were using Smith's incline; by the end of the first year it had carried more than a million. It made Mount Auburn readily accessible from the Basin in a few minutes. Before, it had taken horsedrawn omnibuses an hour or more to wend their way slowly up the Sycamore St. hill. A very speculative scheme when first announced, the Mount Auburn incline led to the erection of inclines elsewhere in the city. In 1878 Smith rebuilt the cars with open platforms to haul horsecars. On October 15, 1889, the most serious accident in the history of the city's inclines occurred: a clutch failed on street car #29 and it plummeted to the bottom and crashed, killing six of seven passengers. The Mount Auburn incline ceased operations in 1898, the first to close as it had been the first to open.

We return to Liberty and look south down **Main St.** The west side of the street offers a fine late nineteenth-century streetscape. Several buildings date themselves. That on the southwest corner, transitional between Italianate and Queen Anne, went up (as the pressed metal cornice tells us) in 1888. Italianate influences include heavy brackets, wrought-iron balconies, and stone quoins; Queen Anne elements include finials on the cornice and a gable topped by a globe, decorative serrated brick panels, belt courses that form continuous bands with the window sills, and, on the second floor, slightly arched window trim. At 1419 Main St. August Willich, Prussian-born Civil War general, lived for several years after the war. Now part of Ball Furniture, the two ground-level Gothic arches indicate that within was once a church. At 1411, we come upon a Queen Anne building with another splendid cornice, this one surmounted by corner urns flanking a dateplate reading "1885." For the next decade Queen Anne flourished in Cincinnati. Brick pilasters, corbeling, decorative terra cotta panels, and keyboard lintels, i.e., alternating light and dark bricks as on a piano keyboard, mark the façade. At ground level is a relatively unaltered Schreiber cast-iron storefront.

We turn left on **Orchard St.** This east-west cross street is residential (as distinct from the wider north-south streets, which are usually commercial, at least at ground level). Several residents on Orchard owned businesses on Main. One block long, the street offers unpretentious Greek Revival and early Italianate residences. 215 Orchard, one of its several restored houses, has a delicate basement grille; a swan floats in the fanlight. On the north side, the church (1859) has a later tower that culminates in turrets with intricate corbeling. Trees, recently planted (and maintained) by property owners, validate Orchard's name. Utterly unspectacular, at least at first glance, Orchard yet feels comfortable. A few people have cared and have worked together. Their efforts have borne fruit. With decent attention, other residential streets in Over-the-Rhine could also blossom.

The **Salem United Church of Christ,** at Liberty and Sycamore streets, began in 1856 as the Salem Evangelical and Reformed Church. *Salem* is Hebrew for peace. We read on the façade one of Over-the-Rhine's few remaining German inscriptions: "Deutsch evangelisch reformi[e]rte Salem's Kirche." Only the odd inscription in stone evidences the origin of over a third of Cincinnati's population. Most inscriptions vanished during the violent anti-German campaign of 1917–1919. This German Gothic building dates from 1867. Plain and severe in appearance, it has an austere orange-red brick façade. The nave, only three bays long, accentuates the church's verticality: Salem for the size of its plot could be Cincinnati's tallest church. Narrow pointed arched windows, token buttresses, and an octagonal spire all lead up to the church's focal point: a gilded **Angel Gabriel** in full flight.

Crosses do not usually sit atop German Protestant churches. Philippus (seen in the next chapter) has a raised hand pointing heavenwards. St. Peter's Evangelical, formerly at Main St. and McMicken Ave. in front of the Rothenberg School, had a gilded rooster to remind Peter of his lack of faith: thrice the cock crowed, thrice Peter denied his Lord. The Salem Church's angel, brass over wood and twelve feet long, warns us of the Day of Judgment. Gabriel has an interesting story behind him. The congregation that commissioned Gabriel could not decide whether it wanted him flying sideways or standing up. Sideways was undignified, standing up contrary to nature. Besides, standing up, Gabriel could not serve as a weathervane. So evenly matched were the opposing forces within the congregation that Gabriel ended up— in the basement. There he languished, then disappeared, only to turn up atop a deserted Mormon church in Nauvoo, Illinois. Gabriel returned (by rail) to Cincinnati, where he, or rather his 1960s replacement, now flies sideways, on his stomach, evidently "at top speed," observes Alvin Harlow, who tells the story, "as one must who is announcing the end of the world."

Since 1977 the congregation has sponsored an active community program, Gabriel's Corner, with contemporary and socially relevant plays, art exhibits, crafts fairs, workshops, and community cultural events.

Across Liberty St. lies **Liberty Hill,** sometimes known as Prospect Hill. Though Liberty Hill actually falls within the boundaries of Mount Auburn (chapter 9), we visit it now. A natural flow of buildings, recalling the hill towns of Germany and Italy, hugs the steep hillside. Italianate and Greek Revival brick houses predominate. Great American Broadcasting Co., the massive modern brick-and-glass

building, bestrides the hill like a medieval castle. Figuring out means to get up
Liberty Hill occupied Cincinnatians for half a century.

About 1850 **horsedrawn omnibuses** began carrying passengers up the hill.
From downtown to the top of Mount Auburn took as much as two hours because the
horses needed to be rested on the hill and more of them hitched up. The trip cost
fifteen cents, a considerable expense when many workers earned less than a dollar a
day. Main streets were paved with limestone blocks or rough cobbles. Bus rides
were slow and bumpy. Unpaved streets were often impassible in wet weather; if the
roadway iced over, service was suspended entirely. An obvious improvement was to
lay rails, though streetcars on rails still had to be drawn by horses; 1859 marked
their first appearance on Cincinnati's streets. In 1864 the Mount Auburn Street Railroad put down tracks up Liberty Hill to Highland, then along Ringgold St., north
on Josephine St., and on to Auburn Ave. Though improved, travel by horsedrawn
streetcars on rails was still slow and cramped. Horses were expensive to care for;
they lasted only a few years because of the grueling work; an epidemic in November
1872 caused many horses and mules to sicken and die. The large number of horses
in the nineteenth-century city also deposited tons of manure on the streets, daily
about three gallons of urine and twenty pounds of manure per animal. Still, the
horsedrawn streetcar was the first effective urban transportation. We have become
so accustomed to cheap public transportation in our cities that we forget what a
revolution it caused in getting around. The next stage in the conquest of Liberty Hill
occurred with the development in 1872 of the Mount Auburn incline. Opposite
Salem Church we may have noticed a low building. It served as a streetcar depot, or
car barn, at first for the incline.

In 1888–1889 the **Mount Auburn Cable Railway** Company began operations
over a four-mile route. Also charging fifteen cents for the ride, it pulled cars up the
hill via a continuously moving underground cable. Invented in San Francisco in
1873, the cable car was a welcome advance. That city's steepest hills were now
safely attainable. The whirr of the underground cables, the clang of the cars as they
stop at each level cross street, continue to give a distinct aural dimension to San
Francisco's urban life. Except there, however, cable car companies usually had a
short life. The Mount Auburn Cable Railway lasted only fourteen years. In 1888,
the year it began operations, the first electric trolley was successfully tested in Richmond, Virginia, and in the 1890s American cities benefited from the rapid development of electric rapid transit. After 1902 Mount Auburn was served by trolley, and
by 1912 Cincinnati had 212 miles of track. The last trolley ran in 1951. Today
diesel-powered Queen City Metro buses mount Liberty Hill.

Sycamore St. marks Liberty Hill's western boundary. The **John Walker
House,** on the northeast corner with Liberty, is a fine Greek Revival townhouse
(1847). Walker, a native of Scotland, was one of the few Cincinnati brewers not
German. The portico, in part concealed behind a later Italianate storefront, added
by Walker's nephews in 1861, appears intact. It originally housed an apothecary.
The adjoining Queen Anne house retains its roof finial: a rare survivor. Further
along, 1618 Sycamore has massive stone window molds on the second story; the

wrought-iron metal railing features an unusual geometrical pattern. We turn right on Milton St. and head uphill.

Hill dwellers have restored a number of townhouses and small apartment buildings on Milton. Steep steps lead up to 322–326, attractive Second Empire town houses. 334–336, the **"Vogeler,"** has a lively frieze of beribboned festoons and wreaths, repainted in cheerful period colors. Note the etched glass on the entrance fanlight and sidelights. Terraced gardens contribute to the overall effect of stateliness.

Milton St., a steady climb, offers through alleys and over houses splendid panoramas. Just before Cumber St., a view opens up of the Procter & Gamble Towers, St. Paul's golden cupola, and the old *Times-Star* Building. In the right foreground below is the former First District Public School, now condominiums. Behind, down Milton, stretches Over-the-Rhine. Until about 1960 a white haze caused by Basin industry and pollution often obscured the view. At the now marked intersection with Young St., viable stairs lead up to Boal St., the next parallel street to Milton. We contemplate but do not climb them.

"Level roads don't suit me," exclaimed the poet Byron, traversing flat Belgium on May 1, 1816; "it must be up hill or down." Hilly Cincinnati might have suited him. (Three years earlier, after *Childe Harold* had taken the literary world by storm, he had expressed delight "to be redde on the banks of the Ohio"—at Cincinnati, presumably.) As Byron suggests, hills (like rivers) offer parallels to human life. They suit certain temperaments more than others. "Landscape has an especial influence on those who inhabit it . . . in spiritual and psychic ways," writes John K. Howat. "The look and feel of a land communicates not easily described messages to those who are sensitive enough to receive them." The **hills** of Cincinnati may suit those who like images of striving and ascent—*ad astra per ardua*—more than those who do not. Conversely, being walled in by hillsides may foster inward-looking sentiments.

Some people count seven hills, some seventy. Cincinnati may have more hills and valleys than any other city in the United States. Actually, geologists tell us that the city's hills are not really hills at all. We notice that they are all about the same height. That is because Cincinnati is actually a city of valleys eroded thousands of years ago to form the uplifted peneplain. The elevated projections of land called hills are merely isolated remnants of the old plateau. They are hillsides rather than hills. No matter, for the hillsides look like hills and—when we climb them—feel like hills. Hills are more than backdrops for the cityscape or orientation points; climbing one of them brings home in basic ways their reality.

San Francisco is another city of hills. Slightly higher and usually less steep than Cincinnati's, San Francisco's hills are laced with streets lined with houses and telephone poles. The grid is maintained unmercifully. Instead of following the graceful contours of the hills, the streets march up, down, and across with rarely deviating symmetry and provide a rollercoaster ride. Although the architecture on the San Francisco hills is often appealing, we sense that humanity has powerfully exerted its will upon the natural environment. In Cincinnati the steepness of the hills means that few streets can directly climb them. Houses cluster at their base and at their summits, but appear less frequently in between. The slopes have usually been left to nature. The hills also break the city up into manageable units; we have no sense of endless space or artificial dividing lines as we do in a prairie city like Chicago. Rather, we sense that our environment will forever be hemming us in or preparing us for a vista. What San Francisco's hill streets lack most are trees. Not so Cincinnati, whose hills have trees, are more curvilinear, and look more natural. The rolling expanses of green bring the gentle rhythms of the country into the city. Hills tell us where we are by constantly updating our perspectives on the city. They heighten our sense of place by making us aware not only of the buildings and sights around us but by allowing us to see distant ones.

The sense of the undiscovered, even the call of the wild, remains ever present in Cincinnati. We find the undiscovered in the city's streets, its buildings, its alleys, its steps leading who knows where. But we find it also in the city's hills. They serve as unofficial nature preserves and, to a degree, as parks, though parks that few use. Climbing them can pose difficulties because more often than not the stairs connecting the Basin with the hilltops have fallen into disrepair. Caroline Williams, author of evocative pen-and-pencil sketches of Cincinnati scenes, once recalled a newspaper story about "a Cincinnati boy who climbed the side of a cliff behind his home and then found that he could go no farther up the hill and could not return down the slope. A woman went to his rescue . . . a man went to hers . . . and finally a fire company brought its long ladders and returned them all to the street." The most famous horror story involving a Cincinnati hill is, however, told by Mrs. Trollope, who one summer day climbed the slope behind her cottage (then in the country but now in what is Over-the-Rhine). She wandered about, submitted indignantly to assaults by the abundant insect life, and was left prostrate by the heat. On the way back, she lost her bearings completely and descended the wrong hill, to discover she still had three miles to go before arriving at her cottage. Once, walking on Boal St., a companion and I decided to experience the Cincinnati hills at first hand, so at a likely spot we headed in and began climbing. The terrain was rough, but, even with street shoes, not impossible. The feeling was eerie, however. Unable to see beyond the canopy of green, we felt ourselves surrounded by a great forest. Thoughts of Mrs. Trollope's ordeal came to mind. Yet we also knew that less than a hundred yards in any direction lay the city. Eventually we made it to the top, found an asphalt path, and followed it. When we came out on Walker St. in Mount Auburn, we finally knew where we were. (We traverse this same path in chapter 10.) Nothing has made me appreciate Cincinnati's hills more than having scaled one of them.

One reason why Milton, Boal, and others of Cincinnati's terraced streets lack housing in places is that the hills are made up of soft, geologically unstable shale, limestone, and clay. From an environmental point of view, many hillside buildings in the past have been inappropriately designed. Hamilton County, Ohio, which comprises the Cincinnati area, outspends every other county in the United States in per capita cost from landslide damage. The city has accorded the hills a measure of protection. A zoning ordinance has set up an "environmental quality district" to protect natural phenomena including geological strata, significant scenic views, and vegetation. In 1985 the Hillside Trust, a local land conservation group dedicated to preserving Cincinnati's heritage of hills, sponsored a national competition for ten units of housing to be built on Boal St. on land owned by the Trust. The competition was held in order to call attention to the problem of hillside housing. The designs had to show sensitivity to the hill site. The Trust hopes that the houses built—none has been as of this writing—will become models for the subsequent development of Cincinnati's hills.

We proceed up Milton St. Four identical but variously painted Greek Revival two-story row houses (nos. 533–539) are set back sufficiently to have gardens in front. On Highland Ave. we turn right. Below is Goat Hill. Across I-71 we see the fantasy Elsinore Tower. To the right, the former Holy Cross monastery crowns Mount Adams; to the left, the campanile and dome of the Art Museum come into view. Jutting above the horizon on the far left, barely visible in summer, is the Hannaford-designed Water Tower.

Where Highland Ave. intersects Liberty Hill stands the **Pendleton house** (1870). Second Empire in style, with a bracketed cornice and a mansard roof pierced by dormers, it is painted, very unhistorically, white and blue. It occupies the most dramatic site in the city. It signals the entrance to Liberty Hill from Highland; it also culminates the vista up Liberty Hill. Beautifully set on the hillcrest, seemingly suspended in space, the Pendleton house is visible from downtown and Mount Adams. At night, floodlit, it glows. Cincinnatians have long valued it as a visual landmark.

The Pendleton house gets its name from "Gentleman George" Pendleton (1825–1889). Representing Cincinnati's First District during the Civil War, he spoke out boldly against the war. In 1864 he was the Democratic vice-presidential candidate and, from 1879 to 1885, a U.S. senator. Subsequently, he served as U.S. minister to Germany. Pendleton married the former Alice Key, whose father, Francis Scott Key, had composed "The Star Spangled Banner," not yet the national anthem. A believer in fair practices within government, he sponsored during his senate term the Pendleton Civil Service Act (1883). It provided for the creation of the Civil Service Commission, the establishment of a classified service among certain groups of federal workers, and for competitive examinations to fill positions that fell within its purview. Quite possibly drafted in this house, the Pendleton Act gained its sponsor national prominence. It remains in force to this day.

As we walk down Liberty Hill, one beautifully restored house after another comes into view. We catch glimpses of the city below. Near the bottom, 412 Liberty Hill (1867) looks like an old schoolhouse, and formerly was the **"First District Public School,"** one of a number of closed inner-city schools. An eclectic composition, Italianate with a central Gothic gable, the building was designed by William Walter, architect of the Covenant-First Presbyterian Church (chapter 2) at Elm and 8th streets. A textbook example of adaptive re-use, it was converted into condominiums in the 1970s.

We cross Liberty St. and descend the steps to Broadway, which temporarily deadends here. The seven houses on Broadway's west side, numbers 1341–1353,

Over-the-Rhine panorama. The photograph, taken from Mount Adams, captures the nineteenth-century city of spires and towers. Right to left, we make out the tower of St. Paul's Church, the steeple of Old St. Mary's, and the vast Music Hall with the twin spires of its central façade. Behind Music Hall, across the Millcreek Valley, is Union Terminal. Courtesy of J. Miles Wolf.

are mostly Italianate. 1349 has unusual hood molds, with clustered columns and acorn drops, and a cornice no less unusual. 1341 and 1343 are twins: one is painted, one not.

To the west a **skyscape** of steeples punctuates the skyline. They tower head and shoulders above the three- and four-story buildings of Over-the-Rhine. Vertical steeples balance horizontal rooflines. Again we have a sense of the nineteenth-century city, without the haze and with its skyline of spires holding its own, unintimidated by modern skyscrapers. St. Mary's white steeple commands the center, City Hall's massive tower the left flank, Music Hall's great central gable the right. These skyscrapers of an earlier era ministered to the city's religious, civic, and musical needs. Their prominence indicates what buildings Cincinnati's citizens wished to accent visually. In few other American cities can we savor so fully and so often an earlier cityscape.

The east side of Broadway from Liberty St. to 13th St. displays an urban landscape that defies urbanity. Instead, it appears semirural. Houses have front lawns, large trees, gardens. **1342 Broadway** (1834) is Federal. Note the smaller scale, windows with simple lintels, the fanlight, and along the south side an attractive two-story veranda, an 1860 addition. Owned by Samuel Birdsall, an early Cincinnati

Over-the-Rhine garden. This secluded garden adjoins the
Boss House at 1324 Broadway. The Ionic columns came
from the estate of Cincinnati Symphony conductor Thomas
Schippers.

pharmacist, the house once was in the country. Moving here in 1840, Birdsall and
his wife lived in this house for nearly fifty years. And Birdsall was no more than a
ten-minute walk from his pharmacy at 5th and Main—as we are from Fountain
Square!

At **1324 Broadway** (1852) lived after the Civil War Christian Boss, owner of
the Gambrinus Stock Company Brewery, at 12th and Sycamore streets and in operation from 1867 to 1922. Gambrinus, a mythical king of Flanders or Brabant, allegedly brewed the first beer. He survives—understandably—in many national
folklores. Actually, beer goes back at least as far as the Sumerians. Beer recipes are
the oldest we have. One, on a Sumerian tablet written in cuneiform that dates from
1800 B.C., appears as part of a hymn to the goddess Ninkasi. We can even think of
beer as a cornerstone of civilization, for historians have argued that one reason ancient man turned from hunting to farming was to raise grain for beer. Most statues
we see around town honor the officially acclaimed. The less heralded are often more
interesting and arguably more important. A statue to Gambrinus or even to Ninkasi,

to stand alongside that of Cincinnatus at Sawyer Point, would call attention to another of the city's traditions—and give an appropriate new companion to the flying pigs.

The Boss house retains Greek Revival lines under its Renaissance Revival limestone façade. Above its side door juts a fine wrought-iron entry canopy. Houses all along this stretch of Broadway display cast-iron railings in varying patterns. The Boss house, like several others between Broadway and Sycamore, has a stunning "hidden garden." It would be pleasant to think that Over-the-Rhine might become as well known for its gardens as Boston's Beacon Hill or New Orleans's French Quarter.

A large Renaissance Revival building (1910) dominates Broadway's west side: the former Woodward High School. Since 1973 it has housed the **School for the Creative and Performing Arts,** which offers academically strong programs for artistically gifted teenagers. Huge double brackets support the massive cornice. Gustav W. Drach, the architect, also designed the Textile Building on 4th St., and we sense kinship between the two structures in their ponderousness and prominent detailing. The land and money that William Woodward had earlier donated allowed the creation in 1831, two years before he died, of Woodward Free Grammar School, in effect, a private high school and, from 1835 to 1851, a "college." (The distinction between high school and college was not as clearly defined then as now.) In the latter year Woodward was attached to the Cincinnati public school system. William McGuffey taught here for two years, his brother Alexander for thirty. Joseph Ray, mathematics teacher and principal from 1851 to 1855, prepared a series of textbooks, including an *Eclectic Arithmetic* (1837; 10th ed., 1839), that revolutionized math teaching in public schools and, like the McGuffey *Readers,* became classic texts. The present building, for which William Howard Taft (class of 1874) spoke at the dedication, is the fourth on the site. It retains its colorful Rookwood water fountains within. A plaque in the driveway marks the burial place of Woodward and his wife, Abigail Cutter Woodward, once his ward. A commemorative statue, once here, now stands before the new Woodward High School on Reading Road and Seymour Ave. In the cartouche over the doorway we discern a large "W," on the stained-glass window "WHS."

We turn left (east) at 13th St., then left again on **Spring St.** Spring, like Broadway, deadends in steps at Liberty St. It has townhouses, gardens, and at 1311 a pottery—the kiln is visible from the street. The atmosphere is even more rural than on Broadway. 1316 (ca. 1850), with double chimneys, is an exquisite vernacular Greek Revival townhouse. On Spring's west side are several former carriage houses, 1337 for example, that formerly served the Broadway mansions.

At 13th and Spring streets we come upon one of the city's former **bathhouses.** Still evident are its separate entrances for men and women. The building now serves a church congregation. Over-the-Rhine houses did not originally have interior plumbing. Privies were usually in outhouses at the back of the property. Even as late as 1940, many houses still had outside toilets. In the nineteenth century if you wanted a bath, you washed yourself in a tub or went to a bathhouse or, if well-off, to a hotel. Julius Fleischmann, mayor from 1900 to 1905, advocated the building of public bathhouses. The first opened in 1904. For a nickel, customers received a towel and soap, hot and cold water, and thirty minutes in their choice of tub or shower.

We walk to the corner of 13th and Pendleton streets. Eastwards, rising toward Mount Adams, stretches a splendid streetscape of three- and four-story Italianate rowhouses. On the south side hardly a break occurs in the orange-red brick façades. The hill's slope gives the cornice line a stepped effect. We walk along 13th, noting the variety of façade detailing. Look behind for visual drama: 13th appears to run into the tower of Old St. Mary's. At the other end of the street, we turn right on Reading Road, then walk back down 12th St. Jones & Speer, the architectural firm responsible for remodeling a number of the city's older firehouses, themselves occupy a converted firehouse ("Fire Co 42"), built in 1905 by Harry Hake, near the Reading Road end. The firm is responsible, too, for restoring St. Paul's, at 12th and Spring streets, whose golden cupola, sighted earlier from Liberty Hill, now towers above us.

St. Paul's (1850) has simple lines, tall round-arched windows, and classic dentil and egg-and-dart moldings. Doric pilasters support an unbroken entablature; the windows reflect Greek Revival or Renaissance influence. Quatrefoils on the carved doors and transoms supply a Gothic touch. In its design, St. Paul's resembles the almost contemporaneous St. Mary's, which we shall pass shortly. Its architect was Seneca Palmer, the man responsible for Mrs. Trollope's Bazaar. Step back into Pendleton Square, the postmodern plaza/playground before the church, to get a proper sense of the façade's harmonious proportions. A fire in 1899 left standing only the church walls and stained-glass windows. The present tower dates from that year. Samuel Hannaford and Sons replaced the earlier Gothic steeple (itself a replacement) with a neo-Baroque design that, rather surprisingly, culminates the symmetrical façade perfectly. On the steeple a German inscription reads "restauri[e]rt nach dem Brande" ("restored after the fire"). St. Paul's golden cupola, visible from Liberty Hill and many points in the Basin, serves the city as an important visual image.

St. Paul's forms part of a complex of buildings put up at various times after 1850 that includes a girls' school, a boys' school, a convent, and a rectory. The Renaissance Revival girls' school, adjoining the church, dates from 1908.

We enter St. Paul's through the courtyard. The interior, like the exterior, has been exactingly restored. As the neighborhood deteriorated after World War II, the parish dwindled to minuscule size. The Archdiocese deconsecrated St. Paul's in 1974, the same year it received National Register designation. Subsequently it stood empty; then in 1981 the I. T. Verdin Co. bought it, along with its former buildings. Verdin is a Cincinnati company known since 1842 for its carillons, bells, and public clocks. Recently it set up its corporate headquarters here. Verdin has installed new clocks and bells in St. Paul's tower. Since 1983 the interior has functioned as a mart, the only one of its kind in the country, selling church-related products. Adaptive reuse at its most imaginative! Open to the public during normal business hours, the mart has brought new activity to this depressed area.

The **interior** dazzles. The elaborate trusswork, designed for the exhibits by Ken Jones of Jones & Speer, creates divisions yet scarcely obstructs our view of walls, windows, and ceiling. Pineapples, a symbol of hospitality, hang from the elaborately coffered ceiling. Recessed lighting illumines the rosettes within the coffers. Like many other nineteenth-century churches, the furnishing and decorative elaboration of St. Paul's was an ongoing process that stretched into the twentieth century's early decades. The apse murals, for example, date from 1925. From the balcony we obtain closeups of the stained glass windows. That nearest on the right represents the wedding feast at Cana. Made by F. X. Zettler of the Royal Institute of Bavarian Glass Painting in Munich, it won first prize at the 1893 Columbian Exposition in Chicago. Its companion across the nave, also by Zettler, depicts the Ascension. Cincinnati retains a fine but little-known heritage of stained glass—from England and France as well as Germany, as well as much domestically made glass—in its churches, its older residences, and in the mausoleums of its cemeteries.

"St. Paulus Schule," on Pendleton St. behind St. Paul's, is the **former boys' school.** Founded in 1862, it was added to in 1887, again in 1894. An eclectic composition, it mixes Renaissance Revival window molds (on different floors segmental, pedimented, and rounded), Eastlake detail, Queen Anne inset panels, and overall High Victorian detail. Stone stringcourses (the horizontal bands) link the windows and help unify the façade. The historically accurate Victorian color scheme lovingly picks out the façade detail. Don't miss the exuberantly corbelled chimneys. The building now functions as the Pendleton Square Design Center. Next door is St. John's Convent.

Across the street is another **Pendleton house,** also recently restored. This one was erected by Nathaniel Greene Pendleton at Reading Road and Broadway around 1803 and reassembled brick by brick at this location in 1848. George Pendleton was born here in 1825. Eventually "Gentleman George" abandoned the low-lying Basin for the hillside domain we passed earlier. The house has been much enlarged. This area is known as Pendleton. Defined by Sycamore St., Liberty St., and Reading Road, it split off in 1987 from Over-the-Rhine to become Cincinnati's newest official neighborhood.

We proceed three blocks west along 12th St. **Olde Sycamore Square**—five immaculately restored buildings on Sycamore St.'s east side—will delight the urban voyeur. I. T. Verdin Co. designed the elegant sidewalk clock. This streetscape suggests the possibilities that exist for restoration elsewhere in Over-the-Rhine. The **Queen City Diner,** on Sycamore's west side, once an authentic Mountainview Dining Car, constructed in 1955, long functioned as a real diner. Entering the American mainstream in the 1920s and 1930s, diners reached a peak in popularity just before and after World War II, in New England especially. Diners never caught on to the same degree in the Midwest, West, or South. Often done in the popular streamlined moderne Art Deco variety and using new materials like stainless steel and formica, diners dazzled a generation. Waitresses called you "hon"; the owner was often a Greek. In the late 1950s diners began a long downhill slide. Few are around today. If older buildings often gain from being contrasted to new, a newer building like this one gains from being set near a group of older structures. Brought here in 1984 from Massillon, Ohio, this diner was redone in an exuberant postmodern rendering of Art Deco: neon piping, banners, shiny black plastic seats, chrome everywhere. It offers, not "diner fare," but a trendy upscale menu.

We continue west along 12th to Main. Main St. here presents a harmonious late nineteenth-century streetscape comparable to that we glimpsed earlier looking south from Liberty St. Before 1897, cross streets west of Main had numbers; east of Main, names. 12th St. was once Abigail (after Abigail Cutter Woodward). We can still read "Abigail" cut in stone on the northeast corner. 13th was Woodward; 14th, Webster. The city, to simplify matters, decided to continue the numbers east of Main. For the first century of Cincinnati's history Main St. divided east from west. Subsequently, as downtown shifted west, Vine became the dividing street. Also, before 1897 houses were numbered consecutively from the river, odd on one side, even on the other; 521–523 Walnut, the address of L. Schreiber and Sons, for example, was not off Fountain Square, but near Liberty St. The address of Wielert's, now 1410 Vine, was originally 514 and 516 Vine. Then in 1891 a city ordinance decreed that houses be numbered in relation to their cross street, e.g., 1400 Vine would be on the 14th St. block, etc. This explains the seemingly odd numbering we discover on some older Over-the-Rhine buildings.

The four buildings south of 12th down Main St.'s east side have undergone restoration. They are part of a general refurbishment that is slowly marching up Main to Central Parkway. The bronze-and-glass shop front of 1140 gleams. Across the street, at 1221–1223 Main, is Mary Magdalen House, which serves the homeless. Here they can shower, wash their clothes, and perhaps renew their spirit. St. Mary's Garden, adjoining, is a pleasant oasis. On the sidewalk tiles before the entrance to 1225–1227 we read "Keyer." Until 1983 a huge pipe, arguably Cincinnati's most picturesque street sign, hung above the store. Rescued, it now hangs in the Folk Arts gallery of the Cincinnati Art Museum. 1231 Main still has its wooden front. Across the street on the next block, 1302 (1930) once held Buckeye Savings and Loan. Its portico sports a classical pediment with Egyptian lotus-leaf capitals: Art Deco, zany as usual. 1306–1308 is a former Good Fellows Hall (1852), a German fraternal organization.

At 13th and Clay streets is **Old St. Mary's,** Cincinnati's largest and most venerable Catholic church. The "Old" was added in 1904 when St. Mary's in Hyde Park was erected. Originally (as we read on the façade) "St. Marien Kirche," Old St. Mary's was built to serve the rapidly swelling German community settling north of downtown. The parish was founded by Johann Martin Henni, a Swiss-born priest who established the Milwaukee diocese shortly afterwards. Even though the Irish controlled the city's Roman Catholic hierarchy, Archbishop Purcell willingly allowed each nationality its own priests and parishes. Whereas St. Peter's was oriented toward Cincinnati's Irish population, St. Mary's was built for its German. It was the city's second German-speaking Catholic parish. Begun on Ascension Day 1841, the church building was dedicated on July 3, 1842. Franz Ignatz Erd, a German, was the architect. Old St. Mary's still serves immigrants to Over-the-Rhine by offering masses in Spanish as well as in English, German, and Latin.

In the nineteenth century **cholera** epidemics sporadically swept over American and European cities. Outbreaks in Cincinnati had occurred in 1832, 1833, and 1834. The city suffered a particularly virulent epidemic in 1849. Over-the-Rhine, with its high population density, was particularly hard hit by the dreaded disease whose cause and control were still unknown. Like most nineteenth-century urban parishes, St. Mary's lost many members. Of the 4114 who died from cholera in Cincinnati from May through August 1849, 796 were parishioners of St. Mary's. In July alone priests officiated at 345 funerals.

St. Mary's original dimensions were 66 feet by 142 feet (the length was extended in 1865 to 190 feet). Plain Doric pilasters lead to an unbroken entablature. Round windows are not unusual in an essentially Greek Revival structure. The steeple rises 170 feet. The quatrefoils are, as on St. Paul's, a Gothic touch. Legend, perhaps supported by fact, has the octagonal spire built around a tree trunk taken from the surrounding woods. The spire rests on an octagonal base, which springs from the square tower; this is called a *broach spire*. In it is the city's oldest public timepiece. I. T. Verdin installed the original clockwork and bells. Church clocks once served as a public utility. Well into the nineteenth century a pocket watch was an heirloom; wristwatches did not come into common use much before 1910. Few workers could afford one so church clocks served, more than they do now, as public timepieces.

The adjoining church school (1843), Greek Revival and severe, now houses the St. John Social Service Center. Founded in 1936, it provides counselling, clothing, household goods, and (across the street at the restored 124 E. 13th) emergency food. Along with Mary Magdalen House on Main St., it is part of the parish's service to the largely non-Catholic community. The parish house (1845), tucked in between the church and the school, is also Greek Revival. The Stewart Manufacturing Co. of Covington made the elegant wrought-iron balconies, a maze of curlecues. By 1875 the Cincinnati area had hundreds of firms engaged in the manufacturing of iron products. The lacelike iron work we admire in New Orleans largely derives from Ohio Valley foundries, chiefly Cincinnati's. The city, we remember, ranked in 1860 as the nation's third largest industrial center, surpassed only by New York and Philadelphia.

The **interior** of St. Mary's is quite wonderful. Harmonious, subdued, well maintained, it has hardly changed since the nineteenth century. Like that of St. Paul's, it is an open space uninterrupted by columns. Inscribed at the base of the stained-glass windows, imported from Bavaria, are the donors' names. In 1890 the ceiling was coved and painted. Under the high altar repose the alleged remains, brought from the Roman catacombs, of St. Martura, a third-century matron who died for her faith. Above the high altar hangs a large painting, actually one of three, each reflecting a different event in the life of Mary. The paintings, from Germany, hang on tracks and are moved by ropes and pulleys. They change with the church seasons. In the balcony loft the curious will find huge pipes: *disjectra membra* from Music Hall's organ.

We leave St. Mary's and proceed south down Clay St. 1207 and 1209 Clay are two Italianate rowhouses erected after the Civil War. We may have wondered why Over-the-Rhine dwellings are often so narrow. In the nineteenth century the city taxed householders by the width of their frontage. Some houses, on plots eighty feet deep, have only a twelve-foot frontage. The cast-iron fence, enclosing the small courtyard or area, kept out passing horses, cattle, sheep, and of course pigs. Cast-iron fences also invite passers-by to look in but keep out. These houses have doors to one side, but many houses we have passed—including 1208 across the street—

have an open alleyway instead. Often the houses are L-shaped, with the base of the L along the front lot line. The open space by the long side allows a small courtyard.

L. Schreiber & Sons made the cast-iron fronts of the two buildings on the southwest corner of 12th and Clay streets. From Clay we walk along 12th to Walnut St. Embedded in the pavement on the south side is a marble tablet that reads "Martin Eichhorn." Appropriately, Eichhorn, in business at this location after 1882, made monuments out of marble. On the southeast corner of 12th and Walnut is the Gobrecht Building (1884). "Piano key" window molds, along with the corbeling and inset terra cotta and brick panels, identify the Gobrecht as Queen Anne. It too has a Schreiber front. We seem here to have arrived in Schreiber country.

Opposite is the **Germania Building** (1877), one of Over-the-Rhine's architectural treasures. The stone façade, wondrously ornamental, was designed by Johann Bast. It combines Italian Renaissance window decoration with incised Eastlake hairline detail. Italianate double scrolled brackets support the huge pressed metal cornice, a later addition. L. Schreiber did the cast-iron shop front and also the cornice. The effect of this building is altogether Teutonic. In a second-floor niche stands Germania herself, sculpted by Leopold Fettweis. Germania, symbolizing German *Kultur* and the German spirit, was, in the widest sense, a humanist. Below her feet we discover a palette (art), books (learning), a telescope (astronomy), a capital (architecture), and flora (nature); atop them all sits a globe. In 1917, with America's entry into World War I, "Germania" hastened to metamorphose into "Columbia." "E Pluribus Unum" appeared on her cape.

The Germania was long associated with **Heinrich Arminius Rattermann,** who in 1858 cofounded (as the gable panel once stated) the *Deutsche Gegenseitige Versicherungs-Gesellschaft von Cincinnati,* or German Mutual Fire Insurance Co. Its purpose was to insure the property of his fellow German immigrants. Unlike the inscriptions on the Salem Church and Old St. Mary's, this one failed to survive World War I, at which time (1918) the company became Hamilton Mutual, under which name it continues. The Germania Building served as company headquarters. Rattermann's income from this business permitted him to pursue his loves of music, literature, and history. An avid Germanophile, he wrote opera librettos in German, helped found the North American *Saengerbund,* organized several music festivals, and edited *Der Deutsche Pionier* (1874–1885), a monthly journal that appeared from 1869 to 1887 and in which subsequent historians have found a mine of information about German-American history and culture. A nationally known author and historian, Rattermann is Cincinnati's most important German-American man of letters.

Above the former 12th St. entrance (now a window) Apollo drives four horses. They pull the chariot of the sun across the heavens. Apollo, Greek god of music and poetry as well as of the sun, symbolizes the diversity of Rattermann's interests. In the twentieth century, buildings with Germania and Apollo do not often come our way. More's the pity, for though such sculpture may not be high art, neither is it *kitsch.* Buildings like the Germania were meant to be "read" and studied, much as we read and study a book. Educative as well as decorative, Germania and Apollo derive from an era in which people viewed the humanities and commerce, not as being in opposition to each other, but as complementary.

Germania Building. Built in 1877 for the German Mutual
Fire Insurance Company, the Germania is one of the many
buildings in Over-the-Rhine that recalls the once-prevalent
Teutonic presence. During World War I the goddess Germania on the façade metamorphosed into Columbia.

We proceed south down Walnut St. to the Central Parkway median to get a good
view of the **Ohio Mechanics Institute Building.** Founded in 1829, it was the first
technical school west of the Alleghenies. Mechanics institutes, a nineteenth-century
phenomenon, are products of the Enlightenment belief that knowledge realizes human potential. The first mechanics institute was probably founded in Glasgow in
1800; one opened in London in 1824, backed by Henry Brougham; and two years
later Josiah Holbrook set out influential recommendations for adult education in
America. Established across the land, these "mechanics institutes" or "lyceums"
offered scientific and "useful" knowledge to many who had not had or could not
afford a formal education.

During the nineteenth century the Ohio Mechanics Institute, through its lectures, its library, and its courses in such subjects as drawing, mathematics, and
engineering, played an important supportive role in the city's industrial growth.
Miles Greenwood, instrumental in establishing Cincinnati's professional fire department, backed it staunchly and served as its president from 1847 to 1854. Fittingly,

the present building occupies the site of Greenwood's Eagle Iron Works. Until 1898 classes were held at night. This structure (1909), designed by Harvey E. Hannaford, elder son of Samuel, in a Tudor Revival style, is, in effect, a larger version of the Rothenberg School seen earlier on this tour and, like it, has distinctive Flemish bond brickwork. In the twentieth century the Institute has pioneered in technical courses. In 1958 it became the Ohio College of Applied Science, in 1969 a division of the University of Cincinnati. In the summer of 1989 it moved to the former Edgecliff College campus in Walnut Hills. The year before, state funding was secured to transform this building into an arts complex. Current plans call for it to house the Cincinnati Ballet, the American Theater Organ Society, and (perhaps) the Contemporary Arts Center.

Along Walnut St. we see the marquee of the **Emery Auditorium.** In 1908 Mary M. Emery donated $500,000 for the auditorium, built from 1910 to 1912 as a memorial to her husband, Thomas J. Emery. With 2200 seats and excellent acoustics, it served the Cincinnati Symphony as home from 1912 to 1936. Mary Emery thought the orchestra would feel more comfortable playing in an auditorium less awesome than Music Hall's. She went on to become the most generous of the Ohio Mechanics Institute's many benefactors, contributing to it steadily until her death in 1927.

The Emery auditorium is one of four remaining theater-style concert halls in the country. The Emery is in good company. The other three comparable auditoriums are Carnegie Hall (1891), Chicago's Orchestra Hall (1904), and Detroit's Orchestra Hall (1919). All four were influenced in their design by Adler and Sullivan's Auditorium Theater (1889) in Chicago. Three at this writing are regularly used for orchestral performances; the Emery is not. Of the four, the Emery is the only one in which all seats face forward for a full view of the stage. The Emery's "mighty Wurlitzer," salvaged in 1969 from the Albee Theater on Fountain Square and the only theater pipe organ in the area, was rededicated here in 1977. It gets good use before and during programs (nostalgia films from Hollywood's Golden Days) sponsored by the Ohio Valley Chapter of the American Theatre Organ Society.

Across Walnut St. is the **American Building** (1927). One of the city's first Art Deco office buildings, it was erected in the hope, or belief, that Central Parkway, completed the following year, would become a major boulevard. That did not happen. Not until the Kroger Building, catty-corner from it, went up in 1960 did Central Parkway gain another significant structure. The American Building's heavy mass tapers to setbacks on the sides; higher up balconies appear. The huge arched romanesque entrance on Central has amusing stonework of human faces, animals, and muscular, bellicose dwarfs. On the painted lobby ceiling cavort medieval dragons and griffins.

To return to Fountain Square, we walk down Walnut to 5th St., then west one block. If energy remains for the second Over-the-Rhine tour, it begins two blocks west at Central Parkway and Race St.

OVER-THE-RHINE II

1. Cincinnati Automobile Club
2. First Lutheran Church
3. Washington Park
4. Nast Methodist Church
5. St. Paul's Church
6. Prince of Peace Lutheran Church
7. Findlay Market
8. Over-the-Rhine Community Center
9. Philippus Church
10. Former Christian Moerlein Brewery
11. Former Jackson Brewery
12. Former Clyffside Brewery
13. John Hauck House
14. Bloom Middle School
15. Hualpa Apartments
16. Hauck Brewery Site
17. Former Windisch-Mulhauser Brewery
18. Elm St. Health Center
19. Music Hall
20. Hamilton County Memorial Building
21. Apostolic Bethlehem Temple (St. John's Church)
22. Pipe Fitters Union
23. Crosley Telecommunications Center
24. Central Police Station
25. Betts House
26. Jewish Cemetery (Bene Israel)
27. YMCA

8

Over-the-Rhine II

THIS tour takes us through Over-the-Rhine's western half. We will look at Washington Park, the historic churches on Race St., the still-vital Findlay Market, and the former breweries that before Prohibition kept saloons on Vine St. overflowing. We detour into the West End to see the magnificent mansions on Dayton St. before returning along Elm St., where our main stops will be Music Hall, Cincinnati's most imposing Victorian edifice, and Memorial Hall. A second (optional) excursion takes us again into the West End, where in the Betts-Longworth Historic District we come upon a cluster of nineteenth-century buildings, several undergoing restoration, that have the promise of becoming a showcase of urban renewal.

We stand on the northwest corner of Central Parkway and Race St. Catty-cornered across Central Parkway, in beige and salmon brick, is the **Cincinnati Automobile Club** (1904). Once a Cincinnati Bell telephone exchange, it was designed by Hake and Kuck in an Italian Renaissance style with windows set in two-story arches. The modern extension (1984), simple in its design, maintains the older building's scale and color. We proceed north up Race past a fine sequence of two- and three-story commercial buildings (ca. 1860–1930) in a wide range of styles. Most are occupied; several have recently been restored. One that has not been is the penultimate building before 12th St., an attractive mid-nineteenth century Renaissance Revival townhouse. It has an unusual recessed center bay, a stone balcony, and much subtly incised architectural ornamentation. That the stone ornament was cut by a machine gives it a brittle, cast-iron quality. Cast-iron storefronts were often sanded and painted to look like stone; here the stone is cut to look like metal. This style—actually more an influence—draws upon Greek elements and is called neo-Grec. It stresses angularity. Often door and window lintels have acroteria protruding at the ends. Neo-Grec derives from developments introduced by France's Ecole des Beaux Arts. It was most popular in America from 1875 to 1881.

Race St., unlike Vine, is a street of churches. The **First English Lutheran Church** (1894) chose to conduct its services in English, not German: thus the name. The original congregation goes back to 1842. The massing of this building recalls the Romanesque churches of Auvergne. Designed by Charles Crapsey & W. R.

Brown, First Lutheran is an eclectic composition: Gothic details set off the red sandstone Romanesque tower, 130 feet high and capped by copper pinnacles with crockets. A magnificent Gothic window with perpendicular tracery punctuates the façade. Gothic, too, is the insistent use of the quatrefoil, or four-lobed flower, motif.

On the corner Klinckhamer Apartments occupies the site of the Park Brewery, operated here by Joseph Niehaus and Heinrich Klinckhamer from 1861 to 1896. In 1890 Park was one of Cincinnati's twenty-six breweries.

Washington Park, on our left between 12th St. and the Washington Park School on 14th, is older than most of the buildings surrounding it. Before the city acquired the land for park purposes between 1855 and 1863, it held within its confines four cemeteries serving Episcopalian, United Methodist, Evangelical (Lutheran), and Presbyterian congregations. The majestic Victorian pillars facing Race St., comparable to those before the Taft Museum, once marked the main entrance. Many bodies originally here were reburied in the newly opened Spring Grove Cemetery. Parks in the Basin were, at mid-century, few and far between. They still are. Then as now Basin land was valuable. Washington Park, according to D. J. Kenny's 1875 guide to Cincinnati, was a needed "breathing spot" for those who had to endure "the smoke-laden atmosphere of a great city." In 1958 a school and playground complex, replacing houses, mutilated the park's north end. It already seems in worse shape than buildings a hundred years older on adjoining streets.

Nast Trinity Methodist Church, at 1310 Race, presents a symmetrical, archaeologically correct, Romanesque façade of rock-faced masonry and finely detailed terra cotta. As in many other German Protestant churches, the meeting hall is on the ground floor, the sanctuary on the second. The German inscription above the left-hand door informs us that the congregation's original church went up in 1842; "1880" above the right-hand door dates this building, designed by the Hannaford firm. The congregation (as the inscription over the front door indicates) goes back to 1835. The name of Wilhelm Nast (1807–1899) is indelibly associated with it. Throughout his long life Nast worked with untiring zeal to make German immigrants into teetotaling Sabbatarians and to propagate his faith. He founded in 1839 and for half a century edited *Der Christliche Apologete,* a high-quality family weekly that became German Methodism's leading organ in the United States. It ceased publication only in 1941.

At the northwest corner of 14th and Race streets we see a multistoried wooden veranda. **Verandas** are a distinctive architectural feature of Over-the-Rhine. They first appeared in India. As our word bungalow derives from Indian *bangla,* meaning house "in the Bengal style," so veranda, another word from India, derives from Hindi *varanda.* Verandas caught on quickly in the American South, where they offered plantation owners both shade and exterior walkways. During the summer Over-the-Rhine houses, especially those with western or southern exposures, became unbearably hot. Triple brick façades held heat all night, and occupants sweltered within for days on end. People with verandas sat on them and enjoyed what breezes came by. On hot summer nights verandas became good places to sleep. They had another practical use, as well. Many Over-the-Rhine buildings lacked internal staircases, so the verandas' wooden steps often provided the only way to get from floor to floor. Now chiefly used to hang wash, Over-the-Rhine's verandas are rarely properly maintained. More's the pity, for they are an integral part of the district's architectural heritage.

Along 14th St., at the intersection with Pleasant St., we encounter another vestige of that heritage. The Greek Revival building (with added Italianate decoration) has a rare wooden storefront. Many buildings like this one had a first-floor shop above which lived the owner and his family.

At 15th and Race streets we come upon **St. Paul's Church**, formerly German Evangelical, or Lutheran. Below "1850" on the façade we read the Schilleresque message, "Wahrheit, Tugend, Freiheit," i.e., truth, virtue, freedom. Here, the words imply, was professed no emotional credo, but one that smacked of ethical imperatives. The congregation came from northern Germany. The façade replicates a temple front. An unbroken entablature marks it; simple Doric pilasters define the clock tower. Gothic arches enliven Greek Revival severity in this massively proportioned edifice. The church never had a steeple. To help pay off building costs the congregation rented space to a drugstore, which remains to this day. Adjacent to the church is a Renaissance Revival townhouse. Above the molds on the first floor windows four ferocious-looking dolphins stand guard; from the second-story sill heads of humans, animals, and birds stare down. The builder obviously wished to have a bit of fun. These grotesques recall those atop columns in European cathedrals.

Just before Liberty St. we encounter the Gothic façade of **Prince of Peace Lutheran Church** (1871), formerly Concordia Lutheran. Stone (recently cleaned of paint) against red brick makes for a lively façade. Gothic became the favored mode for ecclesiastical buildings after 1850. The church's steeple appears to lean backward. (Given the building's state of repair, we may be grateful it does not lean forward!) Andrew Erkenbrecher, who founded the Cincinnati Zoo, was the congregation's best-known member. In 1950 it moved to Clifton.

Race St., like Vine, offers a cornucopia of nineteenth-century urban architecture: domestic, commercial, and ecclesiastical. Whereas Prince of Peace is Gothic, St. Paul's combines Greek Revival with Gothic; Nast Lutheran and First Lutheran mix Romanesque with Gothic. Over-the-Rhine's residential buildings are usually Greek Revival or Italianate, commercial buildings usually Renaissance Revival, Italianate, or Queen Anne. Verandas, we recall, derive from India. Unlike most previous periods, Victorian America no less than Victorian England worked not in one, but in many, architectural styles. There were losses, to be sure. No single style, to the regret of some Victorians, puts its stamp on the period. But the rewards, as Donald J. Olsen has pointed out, "were considerable: for giving up the possibility of a genuinely original style, the Victorians gained the freedom to move with pleasure and assurance among all styles that human ingenuity had ever devised. Esthetically the Victorian became not merely a citizen of the world but a citizen of all times past." Olsen even finds appealing, as I do, "the vices of an architecture that gloried in excess."

We cross Liberty St. and continue north along Race. If it is a Wednesday, Friday, or Saturday, we shall encounter unexpected bustle. Cars occupy every available space; people have arms full of food. We soon discover why: **Findlay Market**.

Findlay Market is Over-the-Rhine's heart. Try to take this tour on a market day, for then the area reveals an animation it otherwise lacks. On market days Findlay Market is the only section of Over-the-Rhine where we can still gain a sense of thronging life, of the human compression, even congestion, that formerly made Cincinnati one of the most densely populated cities in North America.

The tract of land bounded by Liberty, Vine, and Elm streets and, on the north, by the "Hamilton Road" (now McMicken Ave.) was known as "Northern Liberties" or "Findlay's Woods," after its owner since 1833, General James Findlay. In 1849 the city annexed the entire area north of Liberty St. In 1852 Findlay's heirs gave a parcel of the General's land to the city for a market. The first market house, completed in 1855, was an open shed. Meat and vegetables hung on hooks exposed to dust and pollution. A 1902 remodeling enclosed the market and installed refrigeration.

Like most older American cities, Cincinnati once had numerous outdoor markets, large and small. Urban renewal and "progress" gradually mowed down all the others. Findlay's location in a rundown neighborhood did not augur well for its survival. But in the early 1970s the city skillfully restored the decaying market building. It retains, in part, its original cast-iron columns. Painted in playful colors, Findlay Market puts to shame the ersatz "festival markets," i.e., disguised shopping centers, that in the 1980s cropped up around the country, such as those in Toledo (which closed in 1990) and in Lexington. Not a standardized nonplace, Findlay is the authentic article, the area's closest thing to a European shopping experience. It offers not gourmet fare or boutique goods but basic foods. People from all over the city come here to buy more than to look. But it is a good place to look, too. And to smell and touch, even to find a bargain. Both market house and square belong to the city, which leases the stalls inside and the booths outside. Particularly on a Saturday morning, when many people do their weekly shopping, Findlay Market teems with activity. It may be more popular now than ever before. An esthetic and human experience as well as a culinary one, Findlay Market brings back bygone days. The vivid displays of color, the friendly crowds, the sounds no less than the sights, easily lure us to spend time maundering within. Spilling over into adjoining streets, Findlay Market manages to deliver qualities of animation and spontaneity to the urban scene that, with the best will in the world, few professional planners can achieve. The market fosters human communion, people talking, bumping into each other, looking, buying, having fun. On display is the vitality of the city.

Outdoors, vendors sell fruit, vegetables, and, in fair weather, flowers; indoors, meat, sausage, poultry, fish, eggs, bread, imported cheeses, and "sour goods" (pickles, horseradish, relish). The vegetable stands and carts remind us of an earlier time when they frequented the streets, when vegetables were not packaged in cellophane, when daily shopping included exchanges of conversation and news. We roll back the years, step inside, and make our way along the packed aisle. Too narrow to accommodate easily the press of eager shoppers, it forces us to flow with the crowd. It also allows us to visualize both sides of the aisle at once. In Quincy Market (1826) of Boston's Fanueuil Hall complex the main walkway is only eleven feet wide. Here it is seven. The narrowness is a virtue. Many names above the stalls—

Findlay Market. This colorful market, offering a medley of meats and cheeses, fruits and vegetables, remains a main focal point in Over-the-Rhine. Courtesy of J. Miles Wolf.

Wassler, Luken, Mueller, Erkerlein, Trefzger, Rothhaas, Vielhauer, Geiger—are Teutonic in origin. The same families have operated market stands for several generations. We may even hear a little German spoken. As we move along we succumb to a mélange of mouthwatering aromas. We savor, in imagination at least, every kind of sausage conceivable, sniff still warm homemade bread, and at Silverglade's, here since 1921 and still family run, drool over exotic cheeses, among them a *fromage de chèvre* that I find nowhere else in the city.

Since 1921 the Findlay Market Association, a group of civic-minded merchants, have sponsored an **Opening Day parade** that marks the start of the baseball season. In the early years of the Red Stockings many fans who watched the team at nearby Crosley Field lived in Over-the-Rhine. As professional baseball's oldest team, the Reds have the right to open the season at home. Earlier it was the custom for the first game of each season to be played here on a Monday, while the rest of baseball had to settle for a lowly Tuesday. Today the parade marches from Findlay Market to Riverfront Stadium, as formerly it marched to Crosley Field at Findlay St. and Western Ave. Upon arrival the parade goes around the field before presenting the Reds, as a good luck token, their official flag for the year. In Cincinnati Opening Day is an unofficial holiday.

Virtually every nineteenth-century urban architectural style puts in an appearance in the buildings around Findlay Market. Visible north up Elm St. against a hill is a fortress-like structure with "Cinti. Metal Blast" boldly written upon it. This is the former Jackson Brewery. Globe Furniture, on the corner of Elm and Elder streets, has also built an attractive modern showroom further west on Elder. We go a short stretch south along Elm. The first five buildings on the right are, respectively, Renaissance Revival with neo-Grec elements, Greek Revival, Italianate, Renaissance Revival again, and Queen Anne. None is exactly in a pure state. We turn left up the first alley—the now visible official name is Globe Alley—and walk east toward Race St. Streets and alleys in nineteenth-century Cincinnati, when not paved with brick (as here), were paved with cobblestones or cut stones. At the first intersection, we note a curved, somewhat battered stone projecting from the building's base. It once protected the soft brick from being damaged by vehicles that cut the corner too closely. We continue to mid-block, then head south into the metered parking area. The city planned to put in a multilevel garage here but, fortunately, never has. From the parking lot we walk back to Race St.

The arched entrance before us serves as a gateway to the **Over-the-Rhine Community Center** (1971). Taking up most of the block, this complex offers interesting juxtapositions of old and new. It consists of a Senior Services Center, a Parent-Child Center, and a Recreation Center. Older structures have been refurbished and repainted; the infill buildings, two or three stories high, sympathetically maintain Over-the-Rhine's human scale and street line. The whole was designed by Indianapolis architect Evans Woollen, who, wishing to avoid the devastation associated with many urban renewal projects, mercifully left as many existing structures as possible.The idea, here developed with considerable sensitivity, was to realize an architecture particular to the place for which it was built. We may walk through the complex. Children play in its open spaces. Above them looms the steeple of the former St. John's Church. When the church was built in 1845, the steeple was placed, unusually, to the right of the altar. The church faced south, its main façade on Green St. Although both St. John's and its church school were torn down in 1972, the steeple remains, beckoning to a congregation that no longer exists. It reminds us, as does the occasional solitary Wren steeple in the City of London, of other times and ways of life.

At this point, if hunger pangs are upon you, consider Stenger's Cafe, at 1720 Vine, one short block away; or, a little farther, Grammer's Restaurant at Walnut and Liberty streets. Otherwise, we continue walking north up Race.

Philippus Church (1890) terminates the vista. The golden finger atop its steeple, pointing skywards, admonishes us to heavenly thoughts. The façade, brick with stone trim, has unity, good proportions, a marked vertical thrust, even a certain vivacity. It begins with a simple gabled portal, moves upward with decorative corbelling that turns into machicolations, then rises to pinnacles. Recessed pointed arched windows flank the lower tower, itself punctuated by a rose window; three small arched windows are sandwiched between rectangular panels of carved stone. The broach spire, an octagonal spire resting on a square base, culminates in the upraised finger. The sanctuary, as usual in German Protestant churches, is on the second floor. The congregation of Philippus, one of the last to use German exclusively for services, only adopted English in 1921.

Steps up the hillside may tempt us to explore Fairview. Instead, we walk west along McMicken Ave. At the intersection with Elm St., the **Bellevue incline** mounted the hill. It functioned from 1876 to 1926. Originally limited to foot passengers, the incline was rebuilt in 1890 to accommodate vehicles and streetcars. Unlike Bible-reading Americans, Over-the-Rhine's German burghers liked a relaxed "Continental" Sunday. "The contrast between the lower-class German section and the English," wrote a German traveler, Franz von Löher, in 1855, "is especially apparent on Sunday. In the English, everything is quiet; while in the German, people crowd into beerhalls and coffeehouses on nearby hills." No city in America was more alive on Sunday than Cincinnati.

Bellevue House, erected at the top of the incline in the late 1870s, provided music, drink, food, good company—and a sweeping view of the Basin. The hilltops could be as much as fifteen degrees cooler than the dusty city below. James W. McLaughlin designed Bellevue House. It was patronized by a clientele reputedly less discriminating than that of the other incline houses. In 1888 Ohio passed a Sunday "closing law" for drinking establishments; in the early 1890s, as the Temperance movement gained strength, the state began to enforce it. Sunday had been the busiest day. Now, like the other establishments atop Cincinnati's inclines, Bellevue House closed and, in 1901, it burned.

We are now in the heart of brewery country. South down Elm St., a complex of buildings once formed the **Christian Moerlein Brewery**. Occupying three city blocks in its heyday, it is still largely intact. Moerlein, with Adam Dillmann as his partner, then Conrad Windisch, started a brewery in 1853; by the 1880s, now sole owner, he had the city's largest, and the only one with a national reputation. By the 1890s it put out 350,000 barrels annually of its brands, "National Export," "Barbarossa," and "Old Jug Lager" or "Krug-Bier." At 1910 Elm stands the former Moerlein barrel factory (1862). Its architectural style derives from the *Rundbogenstil,* or "round-arched style," appropriately a style of Germanic origin that first appeared in this country in 1846 or 1847, brought over by German immigré architects.

Brewery architecture is a fascinating subject onto itself. Often the buildings were flamboyant affairs. Those erected in the 1850s and 1860s, influenced by Germany's *Rundbogenstil* of the 1830s and 1840s, display Romanesque Revival characteristics. These include decorative brick cornices with corbelling, recessed round arches dividing walls into bays, bull's-eye windows above round-arched windows, and an arcaded ground floor. Another example of this style, not on this tour but within walking distance, is the former Bellevue Brewery at 603 West McMicken. On the building before us barrel ends appear to protrude above the ground floor. Until the 1880s breweries shipped their beer exclusively in barrels; thus cooperage played an important part of any brewery operation. For the many smaller breweries that did not make their own barrels it was an important Cincinnati industry. At 1916 Elm is the former Moerlein bottling plant (1895), Renaissance Revival. Bottling beer only began in the mid-1870s. No statue ever adorned the statuary niche, or alcove, of this building. Such a niche often reserves space for a statue that isn't there, or may never have existed: a joke of sorts, like the empty chair at a dinner party. The bottling plant's hard brick was produced thirty years after the barrel factory's soft brick. The Moerlein brewery folded after the onset of Prohibition. The

Christian Moerlein Brewery, early 1900s. Cincinnati's largest brewery went out of business in 1920 with the arrival of Prohibition. The building with the smokestacks is the Moerlein brew house (1868). It was erected in the round-arched Romanesque style that derives from the German *Rundbogenstil*. Although the brew house no longer exists, most of the other Moerlein buildings still stand. In the 1980s Hudepohl, a local brewery, revived the name with its Christian Moerlein beer. Visible at the extreme left is the Bellevue incline, which functioned from 1876 to 1926. The mansarded building to its right is McMicken Hall, the location of the University of Cincinnati before it moved to its hilltop campus. Courtesy of the Cincinnati Historical Society.

A. Nash Co., until 1942 a leading manufacturer of custom-tailored clothes for men, succeeded it; now the K-D Lamp Co. occupies the former bottling plant.

On Henry St. is the old Moerlein ice house (1876), now Apex Furniture. The basement, four stories deep and as large as many a high school auditorium, kept the lager cool in the days before refrigeration. The actual brew house (1868), on the northeast corner of Henry and Elm streets, was razed in 1947. 2017 Elm was once the Moerlein home, before the migration in 1882 to 2407 Ohio Ave. on Fairview hill above, the latter within easy reach of the brewery via the Bellevue incline. At 2019 Elm is Moerlein's former office (1873), with a fine stone façade made to look like cast iron: the neo-Grec influence again. 2023, Greek Revival and also part of the complex, probably dates from mid-century. The star-tie rods, inserted between the floor joists, prevent the building from bowing out.

Up the hill fronting on Mohawk St., just past the intersection of Elm St. and McMicken Ave., is the former **Jackson Brewery** (1860), Romanesque Revival. We have already sighted this building—"Cinti. Metal Blast" visible on the pediment—from Findlay Market. The brothers Kleiner, Meinrad, and Fridolin (wonderful names!), refugees from the 1848 revolution, bought the brewery in 1854. In 1873 they sold it to George Weber, who led it to bankruptcy in 1887. Reincorporated, the brewery made a comeback in the 1890s with Jackson Pure Old Lager. After Prohibition, it reopened under the name of Squibb-Pattison, then became Jackson again.

We continue west along McMicken Ave. This area has been known since the early nineteenth century as Mohawk. In the late 1820s Frances Trollope lived on the corner of McMicken (then, and to 1870, Hamilton Road) and Dunlap St. One of Mohawk's earliest residents, Mrs. Trollope remains its—and the city's—most notorious. Her eldest son Thomas recalled her country cottage as a "roomy bright-looking house, built of wood, and all white with the exception of the green Venetian blinds."

Before Stonewall St. we pause in front of the red-brick warehouse at 246 West McMicken. It once housed the Cincinnati brewery that has undoubtedly undergone the most changes in name. It began in 1842 as the Klotter Brewing Co., founded by George Klotter; three years later Klotter took as partner Johann Georg Sohn. After Klotter withdrew in 1867, the business became the John G. Sohn Brewery, then in 1900 the William S. Sohn Brewing Co., and in 1907, five years after the younger Sohn's death, it took the name Mohawk. **Clyffside** after 1933, it brewed the popular Felsenbrau, which translates loosely as "brewed in the cliffs" (or rather stored in hillside tunnels). In 1945 Clyffside merged with Red Top, which had a colorful history in the 1950s before going out of business in 1958. It was John G. Sohn who put up this Queen Anne brew house; he had his house (since razed) next door. Discernible on the façade above "1887" is a six-sided star, in Jewish tradition the Star of David. The star might appear to indicate a synagogue; actually, brewers often put it on their barrels to symbolize purity. Above the entrance, surrounding three barrel ends, are two charming terra cotta putti as well as a shovel and sifter, tools used for the barley from which beer is made. The building to our left, now stucco coated, goes back to the 1840s. The Jackson and Sohn breweries, as well as several others, had large underground tunnels, thirty-five feet wide, with walls nearly three feet thick, that burrowed 200 feet into the hillside and remained a steady 53 degrees. Before the days of mechanical refrigeration these tunnels kept the lager cool.

Beer made Cincinnati famous before it did Milwaukee. The city's first brewers were English. David Embree opened a brewery by 1811. In 1848 Cincinnati had eleven breweries, in 1860 thirty-six, at which time it had become America's third largest brewing city. By then Germans dominated the industry. In the 1830s Gabriel Sedlmayr in Munich and Anton Dreher in Vienna had developed the process for making lager beer, a lighter, less alcoholic, sweeter brew. Immigrant Germans brought it to Cincinnati. Lager requires low temperatures and used large quantities of ice. It also requires a fairly lengthy period of rest, or "lagering" in a cool place. (*Lager,* a German word first codified in an English dictionary in 1854, means "warehouse.") Lager displaced English beer and proved the key to Teutonic control of the industry. The ice needed to keep the lager cool came from lakes and ponds and, in Cincinnati's case, the canal. But the supply was uncertain and, at five to seven dollars per ton, expensive. In the late 1870s refrigeration machines, capable of producing ice year round for $1.50 per ton, came on the market, once again changing the nature of the brewing industry.

In 1919, the year enough states ratified the Eighteenth Amendment (**Prohibition**), the city still had twenty-six breweries. Ohio as a whole voted to become dry, but not Hamilton County (Cincinnati and environs), where the vote ran a lopsided 76,000 against to 20,000 for. The Volstead Act, which went into effect in January 1920, put many breweries and saloons out of business. The breweries either switched to nonalcoholic beverages or folded; the saloons sold other liquids, led a clandestine existence, or closed. "Prohibition deprived German social life of an essential element," Don Heinrich Tolzmann, a historian of Cincinnati's Germanic culture, has pointed out; "gone were the family beer gardens, sitting room and nickel beer which had brought people together in the community." After the Twenty-first amendment repealed Prohibition in 1933, the local industry came back, but with new names and less vigor. The city's three largest breweries—Moerlein, Windisch-Muhlhauser, and Hauck—did not survive Prohibition. Today, a single brewery—Hudepohl-Schoenling—remains in Cincinnati.

Just past Stonewall St., the Italianate apartment building (on McMicken's south side) has attractive stone window and door molds. The Imperial movie house, on McMicken Ave. facing Mohawk Pl., has a 1930s Art Deco façade. We go left on Mohawk, cross Central Parkway—thinking of the Miami and Erie Canal here until 1919—and enter the part of the West End known as Brighton. Mohawk Pl. metamorphoses into Linn St. The West End was formerly one of Cincinnati's most vital neighborhoods. Enough of its original fabric of a hundred years ago survives to give us a vivid sense of earlier urban life. In the grass-covered triangle, a romanesque arch announces the Dayton Street Historic District. A delight for crawling children, the arch came from the demolished York Street Police Station.

Dayton St. should come as a surprise. The square pillars capped with finials (once they guarded the entrance to the Jergens mansion in Cumminsville) formally announce the city's single finest residential ensemble. Cincinnati boasts many superb mansions but nothing quite like the sequence here. In the 1860s and 1870s a number of wealthy manufacturers and brewers, chiefly of German origin, made Dayton St. their home. The street became Cincinnati's version of New York's Fifth Avenue. But the Queen City's commercial barons built no spectacular chateaux; instead, they put up sturdy brick mansions, set them close together, and sometimes added a stone façade later. In the 1870s and 1880s Dayton St. compared in elegance to Chicago's Prairie Avenue. But whereas few grand residences now remain on the Chicago thoroughfare—or on New York's Fifth Avenue—most built on Dayton still stand. Dayton St. was the last major residential development in the Basin before the horse cars, inclines, cable cars, and electric trolleys precipitated the flight to the hilltops. In these decades Over-the-Rhine and the West End acquired their greatest population. Dayton St. once pulsed with life.

With the twentieth century the street entered a slow decline. Many mansions were divided into apartments. The 1943 WPA guide to Cincinnati gave Dayton St. a mere half-page. "The buildings are there yet," sighed Alvin Harlow in *The Serene Cincinnatians* (1951), "melancholy mementos of a vanished world." Indeed, Day-

812 Dayton St. This 1870 house was home to John Hauck, one of Cincinnati's major nineteenth-century brewers. Hauck added the sandstone façade in 1882, the year after he bought the house from George W. Skaats. Hauck was one of several wealthy Cincinnati merchants who lived on Dayton Street in the decades after the Civil War. The house is now owned by Historic Southwest Ohio.

ton St. seems frozen in time. But neglect often serves as the handmaiden of preservation. Those who owned or lived in the mansions-*cum*-apartments lacked funds, or interest, to make major structural alterations. In recent decades Dayton St. has enjoyed a quiet Renaissance. The wealthy patricians who built on it will not return, but in their stead have come urban pioneers, white and black alike, who in restoring the old mansions have made a commitment to revitalizing a long-stagnant neighborhood. Along with its neighboring streets, Dayton offers the genuine urban pleasure of walking in a neighborhood that gives signs of coming back.

We begin our tour with 812 Dayton. Known today as the **John Hauck house**, it was erected in 1870 by George W. Skaats. Hauck acquired the house in 1881, and the next year added the stone façade. The most popular new mode for domestic architecture at this time was the Renaissance palazzo style, initiated in the 1830s in England by Sir Charles Barry. We saw a good example of it earlier in the Fechheimer mansion facing Piatt Park. The palazzo-type façade on the Hauck house, boldly if coarsely handled, gives it a somewhat ponderous air. Interior shutters (reproductions) cover the front windows: they kept (and keep) light out in summer, heat in in winter. The Hauck mansion, like other residences on the street, retains its carriage house. Now owned by Historic Southwest Ohio, the house has had its ground-floor family rooms restored to an approximation of their 1870s appearance. As yet unrestored bedrooms occupy the floor above; servants would have lived in third-floor rooms. Eventually a full museum restoration of the entire house is envisioned, with the upstairs bedrooms returned to their original state.

Downstairs rooms afford interesting glimpses into the life of a wealthy Cincinnati patrician in the post-Civil War decades. A Diana in bronze on the newel of the entrance staircase greets us. We are escorted through the formal parlor, with its portraits of John and Katherine Hauck; the music room; the dining room with its exquisite fireplace of Italian marble; and the informal parlor. Fine craftsmanship is everywhere evident in the period furniture, including original Hauck family pieces, hand-grained doors, intricate brass hinges and knobs, parquet floors, hall tiles, carved wood and marble mantels, and painted ceilings, both freehand and stencilled in classical and floral designs. In Victorian times coal-burning fireplaces (later furnaces), along with the smell of gas lighting, encouraged high-ceilinged rooms. Not until the 1880s, when electric lighting and the incandescent gas-mantle came in, did low ceilings—and coziness—become feasible. The house celebrates a Victorian Christmas, with antique decorations and ornaments on the Christmas tree. Available at the Hauck house are pamphlets detailing walking tours in Over-the-Rhine. One describes the mansions, including this one, on the Linn to Baymiller block of Dayton St.

Johann, or John, Hauck came to America from Bergzabern in the Palatinate in 1852, aged twenty-three. In Cincinnati he began by working for his uncle George Herancourt, a leading brewer. In 1858, after marrying the daughter of the proprietor of the Lafayette Brewery, he succeeded his father-in-law as brewmaster. In 1863, in partnership with John U. Windisch, he opened his own brewery, which enjoyed an immediate success. In 1879 Hauck bought out Windisch and formed the John Hauck Brewery Company. His "Golden Eagle" lager found especial favor in Cincinnati. Within the city's German community brewers enjoyed great respect. Hauck concerned himself with civic affairs, and in the 1880s he rescued the Cincinnati Zoological Society, then undergoing one of its periodic financial crises, by purchasing its grounds and leasing them back when the Society had again become solvent. Hauck's Brewery, fronting the Miami and Erie Canal on Central Ave., stood a block away from his house. Living on Dayton he could keep in close touch with its operations.

The Dayton St. townhouses, particularly those on the street's north side, are grander than those in Over-the-Rhine, but underneath the stone façades (and visible on side façades) is the familiar orange-red brick. The houses date from 1860–1890; in style, most are Italianate or Renaissance Revival. Because Dayton St. constituted prime real estate, lot size was strictly limited. Northside houses have lots forty-nine feet wide; southside houses, thirty-two. The buildings look better when viewed at an angle rather than *en face*. Good perspectives require trips back and forth across the street.

808 Dayton is the Thomas Gaussen house (ca. 1868). The orange-red brick sets off the full Italianate, or Florentine, hood molds. **816 Dayton,** which John Hauck purchased in 1890 for his daughter, Mrs. Emilie I. Heine, is two-thirds the size of

his own house. Here the coupled, or paired, window molds of the Hauck house are separated. 816 has spectacular bevelled glass but lacks the quoins that define the edges of 812. Beyond the outer entrance we discern recessed doors. (Except during its hours of opening, the recessed doors of the Hauck house remain invisible.) Most Dayton St. houses had two sets of doors; they provided both insulation and protection. Across the street is 813, the three-story **Ferdinand Karrmann house** (ca. 1860), one of the few stone-fronted houses on Dayton's southside and one with neo-Grec touches. Delicate grilles are positioned over the basement windows; coal for the furnace would have come through one of them. (809 still has its coal delivered thus.) Karrmann, well known as a bookbinder, also served as treasurer to Heinrich Rattermann's German Mutual Fire Insurance Co.

The four-bay asymmetrical composition at 818 has its entrance off center. We hardly notice the asymmetry because the right bay's paired windows balance, to a degree, the left's full windows. The floriated capitals display fruits and vegetables; otherwise the stone decoration is restrained. **824 Dayton,** a kind of Germanic Italianate with Rococo Revival curlicues, is one of the block's two stars. Its façade—with a recessed center bay, ground-level balconies, and an elaborate pedimented doorway—is extremely sophisticated in design. Quoins define the two side bays. The façade has few vertical joints; some sandstone blocks may be ten feet long.

824's eroding cast-iron railing appears original; 818's, too immaculate, appears not. Note that each railing has a slightly different pattern. Indeed, Dayton St. from one end to another offers a cornucopia of cast-iron designs. Equally varied are the stone gate posts. 830's railing, finest of all, is in a sophisticated Greek Revival water leaf pattern. Though Dayton St. was for a time Cincinnati's "Millionaire's Row," it was also a main thoroughfare between the canal and Millcreek pork-packing plants. Such elegant railings were not purely decorative; they also kept out the pigs driven daily through the streets.

830 (1851), the finest townhouse on Dayton St., is also one of the most sophisticated Greek Revival designs in the country. The mansion is attributed on solid grounds to Isaiah Rogers, the nationally known architect who designed Cincinnati's famed Burnet House (chapter 4). It is known as the **Hatch house**, after George Hatch, owner of a soap and candle factory and, from 1861 to 1863, mayor of Cincinnati. Hatch left the city in the latter year, run out of town, some say, for openly Confederate sympathies. The façade achieves an impeccable balance between horizontal and vertical. It has a half-recessed octagonal entrance with niches on either side. Fluted Corinthian columns stand guard, behind which are square pillars. Double pilasters define the façade, instead of quoins as on 824. The capitals, like those on St. Peter-in-Chains downtown, derive from the Tower of the Winds in Athens as illustrated in Stuart and Revett's *Antiquities of Athens* (4 volumes, 1762 to 1816)—*the* Bible for serious architects like Rogers working in the Greek Revival style. On either side of the entrance is a full two-story bow window. The double-bow or swell front, common in England and especially common in Brighton, first appeared in Federal guise on Boston's Beacon Hill about 1805. This is the only house I know of in Cincinnati that has one, and it looks quite grand. The *porte cochère,* or coach door, on the left-hand side is a later addition repor-

830 Dayton St. This sophisticated Greek Revival design was executed by Isaiah Rogers, one of America's premier architects at midcentury. The double bow front, an English fashion via Boston, may well be unique in Cincinnati.

tedly by James W. McLaughlin. It allowed people to come and go regardless of the weather.

838 Dayton was long the home of General Andrew Hickenlooper. President from 1877 to 1902 of the Cincinnati Gas, Light and Coke Co. (now CG&E), the general also served a term as Ohio's lieutenant governor. The house features contrasting bands of stone: one pecked, one smoothly dressed. 842, the home of John Hauck's son Louis, has a doorway of radiating stones, called *voussoirs*. Louis occasionally had as his guest here the famous (and massively proportioned) German contralto Ernestine Schumann-Heink, a regular at May festivals before World War I. (A stagehand, observing her trying to squeeze through a narrow passageway, suggested she try to ease herself through sideways, to which came the withering riposte, "Young man, mit mir der ist no sideways.") 846 has over its entrance a finely carved stone balcony, large frieze windows, and the block's only limestone façade. (The others are of sandstone.) Here lived Joseph Earnshaw, an English-born surveyor who, along with his father Thomas, worked on the original design of Spring Grove Cemetery. 850, the brick corner house, offers fine carving in stone. Adding a mansard roof kept this Renaissance Revival house stylistically up to date. Note the

lyre motif on the roof cresting. Across Dayton is the attractive 847, one half of a double house. Its elaborate cast-iron side porch recalls New Orleans's French Quarter.

West of Baymiller St., the mansions on Dayton are more modest. Fewer have undergone restoration. It is well worth walking to the end of Dayton St. Appropriately located amidst Renaissance Revival and Italianate mansions, **Bloom Middle School** (1915) is itself in an Italian Renaissance style. Particularly fine are the elaborate tile and terra cotta entrances. The school was named after Lafayette Bloom, long principal of another school on nearby Winchell Ave. Fairview hill, its topmost houses boldly silhouetted against the sky, looms to the north. In 1843 hundreds of Cincinnatians donned white and marched up the hill to await the end of the world. They were among thousands nationwide who subscribed to the preachings of William Miller, a farmer turned Baptist preacher, who was convinced that the second coming of Christ was imminent. Twice, on April 23, 1843, and again on March 22, 1844, his followers waited patiently atop Fairview hill for the world to end. Nothing happened, however, and Millerism, like so many other millennial sects, faded into oblivion.

932, built in 1859, was in the 1860s and 1870s the home of John Taylor, who ran one of Brighton's oldest grocery firms. Now the building serves the **Community Church**. Its longtime pastor, **Maurice McCrackin,** became one of the most effective advocates against the displacement of the West End's poor through gentrification.

What can a city do with the West End and other depressed historic neighborhoods like it? Some advocate gentrification as the best hope; others point out that gentrification displaces the poor. Do nothing and the neighborhood disintegrates further; keep the present inhabitants and it remains depressed; gentrify and you force them to move elsewhere. McCrackin argues that people, not façades, should be the primary concern. The city should safeguard the rights of the area's longtime residents. In response to the threat of uprooting through gentrification, McCrackin and others formed the Community Land Corporation in 1980. Having purchased houses on Dayton and adjoining streets, the Corporation holds the land for the common good through a community land trust. Apartments or houses (but not land) are sold on suitable terms to longtime area residents; what the Corporation provides is in effect home ownership for low- and moderate-income families, hitherto at the mercy of landlords. This policy ensures that the West End retains not only racial balance but a population of different economic levels. Other local organizations pursuing policies somewhat comparable to the Community Land Corporation, but usually renovating and renting rather than selling, include Sign of the Cross (1979), Owning the Realty (1982), Tender Mercies (1985), Mary Magdalen House (1988), and the Miami Purchase Association, which since 1979 has focused its efforts on the West End.

939, unusual for Dayton St., is a Queen Anne intruder. Among much architectural detail, note the piano key window molds capped by a white keystone. A single red tile effectively sets off each side of the pediment dormer. On the next block, the neo-Tudor **Heberle Elementary School** (1929) is named after Joseph Heberle. A man of little education himself, Heberle campaigned arduously so that Cincinnati children from poor families would have free school texts. Little gentrification appears to have taken place in Dayton's Freeman-to-Colerain and Colerain-to-Winchell blocks. 1015's stone façade, smudged Renaissance Revival, dates from the 1870s or early 1880s, a period that witnessed the last stage of the mid-century Renaissance Revival. Note the stonework's linear neo-Grec decoration. On the next block, 1113 Dayton has an unusual pediment oriel, with three windows and a balcony. That the roof retains its finial—few survive this long—and virtually intact cresting makes a big difference in the way we perceive the house. 1123, three bays wide, is a particularly fine example of Italianate Victorian. I-75's hum has become louder as we have proceeded down the street. Erect a sound barrier to screen out the interstate's roar and this stretch of Dayton might again become one of Cincinnati's most stunning urban landscapes.

We return to the intersection with Colerain Ave. If we were to walk north on Colerain (toward Fairview hill) four blocks to Harrison Ave., we would come to **Brighton's Corner**, the onetime commercial heart of Brighton. Brighton was conveniently near the stockyards; the Brighton House, once on the northwest corner and long a Cincinnati landmark, was a popular hotel with cattle- and pig-raisers. Throughout most of the nineteenth and well into the twentieth century, Brighton functioned as one of Cincinnati's major commercial and transportation centers. Four lines of the city's horsedrawn street railway served it during the 1860s and 1870s. "The Brighton of today is a revelation," wrote Max Mosler in his 1902 history of the district; "it is now the undisputed industrial bee-hive of the Great Queen City of the West." Mosler was president of the Brighton German National Bank, whose splendid building (1898), having replaced the old Brighton House, still stands. Once a buzz of activity, Brighton's Corner is now a very quiet place, in fact hardly a place at all. As an embodiment of urban desolation, it is profoundly affecting to contemplate. Central Parkway sideswiped Brighton in the late 1920s; as a transportation artery the Parkway has, in its turn, yielded primacy to the interstate. The result is that now almost no traffic flows through Brighton. Population is scant, commerce virtually nil. Mosler's bank, since the Depression a branch of Central Trust, limped along until 1978. Sam Luel, son of Eastern European Jews who survived the Holocaust and after World War II opened a grocery in Brighton, restored the building as a memorial to them.

Instead of walking north to Brighton's Corner, however, we continue one block further east on Dayton St., then turn south down Freeman Ave. Alleys—some hardly wider than a car, often with grass peeping through the paving bricks—bifurcate major streets. The temptation to wander at will up and down the alleys amidst cityscapes of intimate scale we shall resist for now. The **Hualpa**, at Freeman and York, a Queen Anne apartment house, has fine corbeling above its much-altered façade. Wooden or, more probably, cast-iron balconies have been filled in with brick; still visible are the cast-iron supports for vanished storefronts. 1820 Freeman, Victorian Italianate, has good carved floral stonework in its entrance spandrels. The full window molds differ at each level. The area railing, with both cast- and wrought-iron elements, is crowned by a classical palmette, or palm leaf, motif. At Hulbert and Freeman we come upon the former First German Reformed Church (1889), an asymmetrical Gothic composition of rock-faced masonry. Avery Row, opposite, comprises four miniature two-story townhouses, Greek Revival in form, Italianate in detailing. "Avery Row" and "1861" are visible on a fifth. More obviously Italianate, it rises a full three stories.

440 Findlay St., around the corner, is a symmetrical five-bay Italianate mansion. Its arched stone window molds, no less than its gate posts, are particularly fine. Note the staccato effect of the chiseled alternating and diagonal lines on the quoins, a frequent pattern on Cincinnati mansions of a certain level of opulence. The wider the mansion, the more it looks like an Italian *palazzo*. We go up the alley alongside the house to York St. 930 York, once a Bell telephone district office, subsequently became a factory in which, on July 24, 1951, an accident occurred that caused the building to become radioactive. Not until 1988 did a cleanup begin. We walk east along York. On the north side we go past five two-story midnineteenth century houses. The last is the Convent of St. Dominic. Its window fanlights have turn-of-the-century metalwork; the cast-iron railing of its wooden porch looks like fine wicker-work. At 910–912 York opened in 1989 the city's first wheelchair housing facility for elderly citizens; run by EPIC (Elderly Persons in Community), a nonprofit organization, it provides assisted living for the elderly poor of the West End and Over-the-Rhine.

At the intersection with Baymiller St. is the York Street M. E. (Methodist Episcopal) Church, on whose gable we read "A.D. 1866." We go north a half block to **Naeher St.** Naeher, an alley, provides a picturesque back entrance to the Dayton St. mansions. Up and down Naeher are the former carriage houses, or stables, the same structure often serving both purposes. Some have been restored, most not, a few converted into small apartments. Naeher has the potential, at least in this mind's eye, to metamorphose into an English mews. We return down Baymiller to York St. and turn left (eastward). 836 York is Queen Anne, whereas 834 features an unusual Flemish Renaissance pediment. Both houses have a single pressed metal bow window on the ground floor, a wrought-iron fence, and a tiled mansard roof. Their identical rear façades indicate that the same builder probably put up both of them.

We arrive at Linn St. **Popeye's**, its red-and-orange design a startling architectural contrast to the surrounding nineteenth-century brick houses, serves excellent Cajun food, including red beans and rice and mouthwatering biscuits. A New Orleans franchise, this is its only Cincinnati location. York, along which we continue, offers several picturesquely painted Greek Revival houses. At number 538 a woman's head, a ground-floor terra cotta window voussoir, peers toward us. 510 York, once the home of Heinrich Rattermann and long a mecca for the city's German-American intellectuals, looks ready to fall down. Just in from the northeast corner of York and John streets is the former **ice house** of the **Hauck Brewery**. The brewery, torn down in 1957, sat on the massive stone foundations visible beyond the ice house. Around the corner, the commercial building (ca. 1890) with large arches at 1761 Central Ave. also once formed part of the brewery. "Red Top," a successor brewery, appears affixed over "Hauck." Cincinnati Time now occupies the structure.

Central Avenue was for nearly a century the West End's main commercial thoroughfare. It began as the original route out of Cincinnati, going via Brighton's Corner to Ludlow's Station, later Cumminsville, now Northside. Its lower stretch, between the Miami and Erie Canal and the Ohio River, was a major north-south artery. Route 2 of the Cincinnati Street Railway Co., serving Brighton after 1859, ran along Central. But as early as the mid-1880s Central had begun to become tawdry. With its one hundred saloons, it ranked just after Vine St.'s one hundred and thirty-eight. Today the street is virtually derelict.

We jog to the right, then to the left, and continue on Charlotte St. to Central *Parkway* (the former Miami and Erie Canal). South one block, then turn left on Findlay, right on Elm. At **1819 Elm** the intact cast-iron shop front, designed by "Cincinnati Architectural Iron Works," once housed a bank, for under the paint we discern "The Guarantee Deposit Co." This is the first of a string of scarcely altered cast-iron storefronts that stretch to the corner of Elder St. That across the street at 1810–1812 Elm, by L. Schreiber & Sons, has rope columns and composite capitals. As we walk toward Findlay Market, we again encounter people with full shopping bags. Now that we are entering the home stretch of this long tour, this is the time to make purchases.

We continue past the Market down Elm St. The Queen Anne apartment house at 1710 has an elaborate pressed metal cornice, topped by a finial-*cum*-ball, still spectacular though badly rusted. Once the building housed the "ware rooms" of C. Grosse Furniture. Established in 1870, the firm moved to this building in 1885. "596" under the name indicates the number before Cincinnati renumbered its streets in 1897. I. G. Grimm, of 13 McMicken Ave., made the cast-iron front.

At Liberty St., we walk west one block to Central Parkway. Beneath us lie the tubes for Cincinnati's never-completed subway. We stand above a large station, converted in the 1960s into a fallout shelter and underground city hall. Opposite, we see a huge Romanesque Revival structure (1866) that looks like an impregnable fortress. Obviously, we have found another ex-brewery. The gable's corbelled brickwork, along with the oculi and the round-arched windows, are hallmarks of the *Rundbogenstil* characteristic of Cincinnati's mid-nineteenth century brewery architecture. This building housed the **Windisch-Muhlhauser Brewery**. Underneath it are extensive cellars. Founded in 1866 by Conrad Windisch and Gottlieb and Henry Muhlhauser, the brewery reorganized in 1882 as the Lion Brewery (a name adopted after its best-known brew). A decade later, it ranked, after Christian Moerlein, Cincinnati's second largest brewery, with production at 175,000 barrels yearly. It was among the first, in 1882, to adopt the new ice machines to keep beer cool. Windisch-Muhlhauser closed finally in 1922. Otto Burger and Sons occupied the plant after 1934 before, in turn, closing in 1973. Another large building (1888), south of the main structure, served as the new brewhouse. After the new building went up, the 1866 building became the malthouse. In 1985 the 1888 building was torn down.

North up Central Parkway, the low-lying complex of buildings on the west side houses the Schoenling Brewery. It opened after Prohibition. In 1986 Schoenling merged with Cincinnati's other remaining brewery, Hudepohl, founded in 1885, to become the **Hudepohl-Schoenling Brewing Co.** Schoenling sells Little Kings Cream Ale; its market is national. Hudepohl offers Hudy Lite, Hudy Gold, and Hudy 14K (reintroduced in 1988); a top-of-the-line beer, Christian Moerlein, resurrected in 1981 the name of the city's largest and most famous brewery. In 1983 this new Moerlein became the first American beer to pass Germany's ancient purity law, the *Reinheitsgebot*. Established in the 1490s, this law (still in force) decrees that beer sold in Germany may only contain four basic ingredients: water, yeast, malt, and hops. Although Hudepohl has no plans to export Moerlein to Germany, it hopes to gain a national market for it here.

We return along Liberty St. to Elm and proceed south. The **Elm Street Health Center** (1896), once (as we read on the façade) the "Sixth District" elementary school, provides health care for neighborhood residents. Neo-Baroque in conception, nervous and vital in its syncopated movement, this building is one of a number of Cincinnati's older schoolhouses that has found new use. Stone bands traverse the façade; vermiculated voussoirs surround the entrance. Pillars, presumably once part of the school gates, sprout in the small garden area amidst ginkos. Across the street at 1514–1516 Elm, the Fulda (ca. 1910) comes with an inner court. When Cincinnati's apartment houses find their historian, the Fulda's plan will form part of the story. Opposite is the Samuel W. Bell Home for the Sightless, a nearly windowless modern brick structure. The shed roofs, wandering in several directions at once, emulate those of Charles Moore's Sea Ranch condominiums in California. A more successful emulation is "The Cloisters" on Mount Adams. From 15th to 14th streets, on Elm's east side, are nine houses, a number Italianate, several at least (including that on the corner of 14th) Greek Revival. Together, they compose a typical north-south Over-the-Rhine streetscape. Opposite the corner house is the excellent gourmet restaurant Bacchus.

Music Hall's imposing presence dominates the next stretch of Elm St. Completed in 1878, the building ranks as Samuel Hannaford's masterpiece, the chief jewel in Cincinnati's Victorian crown. Immediately, it owes something to Ware and Van Brunt's design for Memorial Hall, Harvard, which also has two towers framing a central entrance. More distantly, it draws inspiration, as Montgomery Schuyler has conjectured, from the High Victorian Gothic Midland Hotel built by Sir Gilbert Scott in front of London's St. Pancras station. Schuyler rated Music Hall a "real composition"; he admired "its comparative quietude in a style in which . . . keeping quiet was the most difficult thing for a designer to do." The building's only flaw, Schuyler thought, was that it lacked "detachment and foreground." Because Cincinnati's compact blocks and dense population made Basin land extremely valuable, Music Hall had to be erected close to the street line. Thus we cannot easily gain a full perspective on its vast 372-foot façade.

"*Ah, voilà quelque chose!*" said the Frenchman upon first sighting Harvard's gargantuan Memorial Hall. "There is something!" Memorial Hall is big. Music Hall is bigger still. It looms before us like some great antediluvian beast: huge, ungainly, riveting. Contemplation of this massive structure cheers the soul. The soaring pinnacles prompt us to aspire to the promised land—of music! We observe the influ-

Music Hall. Cincinnati's temple to music (1878) was designed by Samuel Hannaford. Wings on either side of the central façade (not shown in this photograph) stretch the building's length to 372 feet. The largest hall in the United States regularly used for classical music concerts, it is currently home to the Cincinnati Symphony, the Cincinnati Pops, the annual May Festival, the Cincinnati Ballet, and the Summer Opera.

ence of the *Rundbogenstil,* the "round-arched style." Yet the design is more neo-Gothic than neo-Romanesque. In scale, height, and effect, the building is unmistakably Gothic, High Victorian Gothic at that, the elaborate polychromatic Gothic that (influenced by John Ruskin's writings) gained popularity in America after the Civil War. Gothic is superimposed over Romanesque in the three central arches; encompassing them, a huge Gothic arch frames a rose window. Visible on the gable of the central arch is an interlaced "1877." Towers capped by finials flank this central portal. The powerful, fragmented façade with its restless brickwork culminates in a peaked roof of broad planes and gables. Although the roofline has lost its cresting, its turrets, and some of its finials, it still presents a dynamic silhouette. Destined to crown the apex of the central block was a statue of the Genius of Music that, though it appears in several well-known lithographs, apparently was never set in place.

Music Hall works in detail as well as overall. The façade, busy and rhythmic, stepping in and out as it marches along, produces lively patterns of light and shadow. All kinds of arches—pointed, round, segmented—put in appearances. Façade detail, copious and well crafted, intrigues the eye. We discover, peeking out amidst the stonework, woodwinds, flutes, violins, lyres, French horns, even birds in song. On the south hall we come upon sunflowers, on the north, machinery and architects' tools. The richness of the Victorian building, according to Ada Louise Huxtable, "is a complex system of symbols and meanings, of visual devices and sensuous effects that may have titillated a nouveau riche culture, but that also formed an ex-tremely sophisticated and skillful, erudite and brilliant, highly manneristic nine-teenth century building art." Structures like Music Hall, long belittled, have begun to gain recognition as good architecture. I will go further: Music Hall verges on great architecture. Few American cities have a building devoted to music that com-pares with it. Unlike New York's Lincoln Center or Washington's Kennedy Center, centers for the arts set off from the surrounding city, Music Hall stands in the middle of a colorful, historic neighborhood, an integral part of the urban fabric. The new cultural centers often remain empty and dead all day. When performances begin and end, monumental traffic jams ensue. Lincoln Center and the Kennedy Center rival Music Hall neither visually nor urbanistically.

We tend to think of Cincinnati's golden age as coincidental with the steamboat era that reached its peak before the Civil War. After the war, Chicago and St. Louis, more centrally located on the rail network, passed the Queen City in population. But Cincinnati's slower growth should not obscure the enormous outburst of energy and civic pride that characterized it in the 1870s. The Cincinnati Southern Railroad, projected in 1869 and linking Cincinnati to Chattanooga by 1880, was intended to recapture southern markets lost during the Civil War. In 1870 Eden Park opened. The next year saw the dedication of the Tyler Davidson Fountain. In 1873 the old Cincinnati College became the nation's first municipal university, in 1874 the lavish Second Empire post office was begun downtown, and in 1875 the zoo opened its doors and Hebrew Union College became America's first rabbinical seminary. In 1877 John Shillito built his huge emporium at Race and 7th streets, in 1878 George Ward Nichols helped establish the Cincinnati College of Music, and in 1880 Maria Longworth Nichols, capitalizing on the growing interest in art ceramics, founded Rookwood Pottery. The decade also witnessed the movement that led to the estab-lishment in 1881 of the Cincinnati Art Museum. Many of these 1870s cultural or-ganizations prosper to this day.

"The vital force of any city," wrote the Countess of Chambrun, née Clara Long-worth, more than half a century ago, resides less in its size than "in the continuity of its values and traditions. It resides even more especially still in the will of her citizens to collaborate for her best interests and see to it that material progress keeps pace with intellectual aspiration." These words remain as true today as when they were written. For the most part, Cincinnatians have collaborated to support a diver-sity of cultural institutions. In the shaping of a city's cultural life, size of metropol-itan area, though important, is not absolutely crucial. By demographic standards a moderately sized city, culturally Cincinnati, with its long-established and vital mu-sical and artistic traditions, feels like a small big city. Its dimensions are readily encompassable, unlike those of New York or even Boston. And Cincinnati has, and by and large supports financially if not always by actual attendance, big-city cultural institutions.

Appreciation of **music** was natural for Cincinnati with its rich European cul-ture. By the 1870s its musical life had long flourished. A half century earlier, not Germans alone but English, Welsh, and Swiss had organized musical societies. In 1848 German choral organizations from Cincinnati, Louisville, and Madison, Indiana, held a *Sängerfest*, or "festival of song." (The custom derived from German *Sängerfeste* held to celebrate the ripening of the grapes.) That year the German *Sängerbund* of North America was formed here. Programs expanded in the 1850s and 1860s with Germans taking the most prominent role. In 1867 the *Sängerfest* chorus had grown to nearly 2000 voices. Not only local groups but visiting ensembles added vitality to the musical scene. Several times, beginning at the *Sängerfest* in 1869, Theodore Thomas, America's preeminent conductor, brought his New York orchestra here to give concerts. Thomas recalled in his autobiography that Cincinnati "ranked second only to New York, Boston, or Philadelphia, in musical achievement." In 1870 the city put up Saengerfest Hall, a 5000-seat wooden building with a tin roof, to house the *Sängerfeste* as well as the industrial expositions that the city had begun that year. Designed as a temporary structure, it occupied the present site of Music Hall.

In 1872 Maria Longworth Nichols conceived of the first May Festival and proposed Thomas as musical director. Held the next year, the Festival enjoyed a resounding success. By 1875 both the industrial expositions and the May Festival had outgrown Saengerfest Hall. That year, during intermission at the Festival's opening night, torrential rains drummed on Saengerfest Hall's tin roof. Maestro Thomas waited patiently more than half an hour to begin again. Clearly it was time the city had a hall commensurate with its musical ambitions. Enter Reuben R. Springer, a leading Cincinnati businessman and longtime philanthropist, who had made his fortune before the Civil War in the riverboat and commission business and had subsequently increased it through solid investments in railroads and real estate. Springer offered $125,000 to build a majestic new hall if other citizens would match this sum. They did, and construction began in late 1876. Springer averted a crisis by adding another $50,000, again as part of a matching gift. In all, he paid over $250,000 of the building's total cost of nearly $450,000. Erected within a year, Music Hall had its grand opening in time for the 1878 May Festival.

A decade before Adler and Sullivan's Auditorium Theater (1889) in Chicago, Music Hall was intended as a multipurpose structure. Between 1870 and 1888 Cincinnati sponsored a series of annual or biennial expositions to promote the city's manufactures. Fourteen in all, each drawing up to half a million persons, they no doubt indirectly fostered the city's cultural institutions. 1879 marked the first exposition to be held in Music Hall; over a thousand exhibits vied with six giant elephants, courtesy of P. T. Barnum, for spectators' attention. For the last and biggest of these fairs, the 1888 Centennial Exposition of the Ohio Valley and Central States, both Music Hall and its two wings were crammed with displays, crowd-pleasing no less than commercial. Horticultural Hall, erected in Washington Park, was joined to Music Hall by a bridge across Elm St. Machinery Hall, 1250 feet long, was erected behind Music Hall over the nearly defunct Miami and Erie Canal; visitors glided along the turgid waters of the canal in gondolas imported from Venice.

Music Hall's central block contains the auditorium. Carriage lanes originally separated Music Hall from wings to north and south, both completed in 1879. (The lane separating the north wing remains partially visible from Elm St.) The south wing, once a two-level exhibit hall, now contains, at ground level, offices for the

Cincinnati Symphony, May Festival, Summer Opera, Cincinnati Ballet, and, on the second level, a large ballroom. As the Topper Club in the era of Dixieland jazz, this ballroom endeared itself to a generation of Cincinnatians. The north wing, also originally an exhibit hall, subsequently functioned as an arena for basketball, wrestling, boxing, and for equine events. It now holds an almost stage-sized rehearsal hall and a two-level storage area large enough to keep sets for forty operas.

Even if classical music is not your passion, the **interior** of Music Hall is not to be missed. It is fully as grand as the exterior. A concert here provides an architectural as well as a musical experience. The marble tiles of the foyer are in a checkerboard. The gazebo before us dispenses champagne and wine. Three chandeliers hang above our heads. Concertgoers peer down from above the balustraded railing of the elliptical balcony. The first impression is one of space. Despite the crowd, we rarely feel congested in Music Hall's public areas. The foyer and corridors have a vastness about them suggestive of a bygone era. Their expansive design may owe something to Charles Garnier's contemporaneous Paris Opéra (1875), equally vast and far more flamboyant. Even at intermissions when the corridors are thronged with people and humming with talk we retain our initial impression of space.

At the back of the foyer statues or other memorials honor major contributors to Cincinnati's musical tradition. "Aiken" at the far right commemorates Charles Aiken, first supervisor of music of the Cincinnati public schools, a remarkable man who instilled a love of music in the city's schoolchildren and rallied them to contribute $3000 for the erection of Music Hall. Many children he coached went on to perform here. A lifesized Reuben Springer, sculpted by Preston Powers, Hiram's son, stands to the left of the main entrance. Against Springer's wish, the auditorium was named after him. A genuinely modest man, he also objected to this statue and refused to attend its unveiling in 1882. A 1970 plaque honors J. Ralph Corbett, whom we may thank for Music Hall's present appearance, and for much else in Cincinnati's musical and cultural life. A bust commemorates Max Rudolph, the Cincinnati Symphony's music director in the 1960s. Next, Theodore Thomas stands behind the podium in Clement Barnhorn's larger-than-lifesize bronze. Theodore Thomas led the first sixteen May Festivals beginning in 1873 and ending in 1904. This statue was unveiled at the first concert of the 1910 Festival; President Taft delivered the dedicatory address. To Thomas's right, a half-length bust honors Stephen Foster. Though Foster died in 1864 and thus never saw Music Hall, he spent four impressionable years in Cincinnati and made an incalculable contribution to American musical life.

We go through the glass doors into the right stair hall. Here we find relics from Cincinnati's past. The huge pier mirror, 5 feet wide and 13 feet tall, once adorned the Burnet House at 3rd and Vine streets, demolished in 1926.

By the stairs hang two **wooden panels** from Music Hall's organ. When completed in 1878 the Hood & Hastings organ was the largest in the United States. In an age when bigness was regarded as innately good, it quickly became a focus of civic pride. The organ screen, of cherry and sixty feet high by fifty feet wide, was consciously intended to be a major work of woodcarving art. It was hand carved, the designs based on natural forms, from September 1877 to May 1878, by over one hundred students of the McMicken School of Design (soon to become the Art Acad-

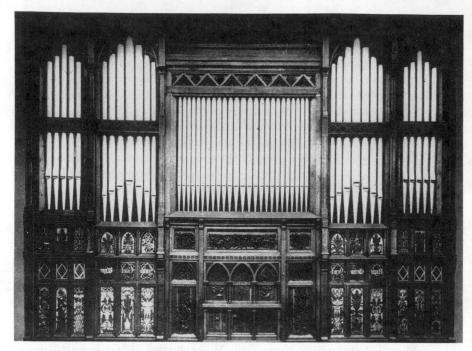

Music Hall organ. The organ screen was carved in cherry in the 1870s by Cincinnati's leading woodcarvers Benn Pitman, Henry Lindley Fry, his son William Henry Fry, William
Henry's daughter Laura Fry, and their students. It was the most ambitious project ever attempted by Cincinnati's thriving woodcarving movement, which achieved national renown.
Once the largest organ in the United States, it was removed when the stage was enlarged in
1969. The screen was dismantled and auctioned off. Courtesy of the Cincinnati Historical
Society.

emy) under the supervision of Benn Pitman, Henry Lindley Fry, and his son, William Henry Fry. Pitman and his students completed the greater portion of the screen,
including ten of the fifteen panels dedicated to individual composers; the Frys and
their students carved the other five panels, as well as the towers and the ornament in
between. Laura Fry, William Henry's daughter, designed nine of the floral panels
and carved one. This decorative collaboration was the most ambitious project ever
attempted by the thriving Cincinnati woodcarving movement. In its day the organ
screen was hailed as a major example of the woodcarver's art in America. Originally, it stood at the back of the stage area and was visible at all times. Concertgoers
appreciated its presence, and for aspiring woodcarvers it was an unfailing source of
inspiration. But, like most nineteenth-century art works, the organ screen suffered
a decline in critical esteem during the long decades of reaction against Victorian
taste. Unfortunately, when Music Hall began a major modernization in 1969, the
organ was dismantled and—in an extraordinary act of vandalism—the screen was
broken up and most of its panels were auctioned off.

In addition to the two panels before us, a number of the composer panels have been placed on the wall of the orchestra pit. They are thus visible—to members of the orchestra—during opera and ballet performances. Bits of the actual organ are, I gather, still in Music Hall's attic; some organ pipes are stashed in the tower of Old St. Mary's. Three panels of the honeysuckle frieze decorated and carved by William Henry Fry have found their way to the Cincinnati Historical Society. Since 1969 the climate in regard to the American Aesthetic movement of the 1870s and 1880s— and to art objects made in Cincinnati—has changed remarkably. In the Metropolitan Museum of Art's major 1986 exhibit of the Aesthetic movement, art objects made in Cincinnati—including a number of pieces stemming from its native woodcarving movement—took up an entire room. The published catalogue, *In Pursuit of Beauty: Americans and the Aesthetic Movement* (1986), referred to Music Hall's organ screen as "the magnum opus of the wood-carving movement." Arguably the single most important collaborative work of art ever achieved in Cincinnati, the organ screen has met an ignominious end. Few who use the stairs even notice the remaining panels.

The sense of space we have experienced in Music Hall's foyer and corridors hardly prepares us for the vastness of the auditorium. With 3632 seats it is the largest facility regularly used for orchestral performances in America. It is larger than New York's Carnegie Hall, Philadelphia's Academy of Music, Cleveland's Severance Hall, Boston's Symphony Hall, or Chicago's Orchestra Hall. Both the Auditorium Theater in Chicago and the opera house of Manhattan's Lincoln Center are larger, but the first is no longer used for orchestral performances and the second is limited to opera. Music Hall is big because when it was built many Cincinnatians believed that their city, even though surpassed by Chicago and St. Louis as the Midwest's largest, would still rank among the greatest in the nation, and could still become a center for music. In Music Hall Cincinnati has one of the most impressive musical performance facilities of any American city.

Thanks to the generosity of the Corbett Foundation, funded by Patricia and J. Ralph Corbett, Music Hall's interior was extensively remodelled between 1969 and 1973. Before this, the previous major renovation of the interior had occurred in 1895–1896. Cincinnatians wanted to produce opera, which required an orchestra pit and elaborate stage facilities. The orchestra platform was brought forward, to enhance the sound, and the wooden walls were plastered over. Hannaford, the original architect, supervised the work. The restoration of 1969–1973, the hall's fourth, provided a hydraulic orchestra platform, air conditioning, and escalators. The awkward mauve light clusters in front of Music Hall, reminiscent of a turn-of-the-century Parisian boulevard, as well as the modern signposts fronting the street, date from 1985. Two years later another renovation began, this one intended chiefly to enhance the Hall's already fine acoustic qualities.

The **auditorium** is vaguely neo-Baroque. Ivory and gilt curvilinear designs work within a rectilinear framework. A huge coffered proscenium arch delimits the stage area. Two balconies hover above the orchestra. Above them is a beam-and-coffered ceiling—such beams and such coffers! The chandelier, from Czechoslovakia, leads the eye up to a shallow saucer dome; garlands of flowers and fruit encircle

Arthur Conrad Thomas's 1905 mural, *The Allegory of the Arts* (1905). Somewhat reminiscent of Tiepolo and other Rococo masters, it depicts Music, Science, History, and Literature paying court to Zeus. After having savored the building outside and in, prepare to savor the music. The acoustics are as fine as the architecture, so fine indeed that Eugène Ysaye, violinist and maestro of the Orchestra after World War I, rated them finer even than Carnegie Hall's, "absolutely the most perfect in the country."

Founded in 1895, the **Cincinnati Symphony** is America's fifth oldest orchestra. In 1895–1896 forty-eight musicians under the baton of Frank von der Stucken, born in Texas but trained in Germany and Dean of the Cincinnati College of Music, presented ten pairs of concerts. Over the years the symphony has built up an extensive repertoire and reputation. Under a series of major conductors it has become one of America's best, if still largely underrated, orchestras. In 1909 the young Leopold Stokowski, only twenty-seven and little experienced as a conductor, began his tumultuous three-year association with it. But it was Fritz Reiner, music director from 1922 to 1931, succeeding Ysaye, who moved it to the front rank. Reiner is remembered for his ability to turn lackluster orchestras into first-rate ensembles. What he did in the 1950s with the Chicago Symphony he had done in the 1920s with the Cincinnati Symphony. He also introduced Cincinnati audiences to the work of such modern composers as Bela Bartok. Eugene Goossens, Max Rudolph, Thomas Schippers, and Michael Gielen have maintained the orchestra's reputation. Presently the symphony is under the baton of Jesús López-Cobos, who, when appointed, was also music director of the Berlin Opera, principal guest conductor of the London Philharmonic, and director of the Spanish National Orchestra. Guest conductors have included Richard Strauss, d'Indy, Respighi, Stravinsky, Milhaud, Monteux, Koussevitsky, and Toscanini. The orchestra has presented a number of American premieres, among them Mahler's *Fifth Symphony* and Strauss's *Alpine Symphony,* the latter in 1916, no easy feat with American involvement in World War I looming. More recently, it has commissioned two of Aaron Copland's most celebrated works, *Fanfare for the Common Man* and *Lincoln Portrait.* In 1966 the orchestra was the first American orchestra to go on a world tour. Its first two seasons were at Pike's Opera House; from 1897 to 1912 and since 1936 Music Hall has served as its home. Here the orchestra plays a twenty-four week season, beginning in September and ending early in May. Music Hall also hosts the Cincinnati Pops created in 1977 and led by Erich Kunzel, its inaugural director. In 1984, with the opening of Riverbend ten miles upriver (which we shall visit in chapter 13), the Cincinnati Symphony Orchestra has acquired a summer venue as distinctive as Music Hall.

Since 1873 Cincinnatians have revelled in the orgy of choral music known as the May Music Festival, now simply the **May Festival.** Its establishment was one of the major milestones in the musical history of this country. The oldest continuous musical event of its kind in a major American city, it was once America's leading music festival and still ranks among its best. The May Festivals were the outcome not only of the *Sängerfeste* but of English-speaking choral societies going back to 1819. Maria Longworth Nichols, subsequently the founder of Rookwood Pottery, was the inspiring force, assisted by the organizational skills of her husband, George Ward Nichols, behind the first Festival. Theodore Thomas directed it, to immense acclaim, as he did the second in 1875. The third May Festival, the first in Music Hall, took place in 1878. Robert Vitz, the chronicler of Cincinnati's nineteenth-century cultural scene, cites the critic for the New York *Tribune* who hailed it as "the greatest festival of art that America has ever beheld."

1878 also saw the founding, with Thomas as director, of the **Cincinnati College of Music.** Nichols, the school's president, vowed to make Cincinnati "the musical center of the United States." Had the city, after all, not persuaded the great **Theodore Thomas** to abandon New York to head its new College of Music? Luring the country's top conductor away from New York was regarded as a civic coup. "Cincinnati danced hornpipes over the capture of Theodore Thomas," wrote the Albany *Journal.* A cartoon in *Puck* (October 9, 1878) showed Thomas conducting before an audience of well-bred swine. The caption read, "From the Metropolis to the Porkopolis." Eighteen months later, however, Thomas resigned after a dispute with Nichols over what direction the college should take, he arguing for selective admissions and high standards, Nichols wishing the college to show a profit. This unfortunate outcome Thomas's biographer, George P. Upton, deems one of the great disappointments of Thomas's career.

Thomas's resignation in no way alienated him from the May Festival Board or from his love for Cincinnati's musical life. He continued at the helm of the Festivals, which were a boon to his career, their programs a joy to prepare and execute. Thomas's widow thought that "in the end the Cincinnati Musical Festival standards far surpassed those of Europe, and they became the most perfect concerts of their class in the world." In 1880 six hundred singers sang Beethoven's *Missa Solemnis,* possibly in its first American performance, so well that critics lauded the chorus the best in the country. After having conducted every performance himself since 1873, Thomas brought his sixteenth and last Festival in 1904 to a rousing close with Beethoven's *Ninth Symphony.*

The early May Festivals had brought together choral groups, accompanied by local and visiting orchestras, every two years (with an occasional three-year interval). In 1967 the festival became an annual event. On Friday and Saturday evening of the last two weekends in May, the symphony performs major choral works, some old favorites, some rarely heard, works that cannot easily be performed during the regular season. In recent years, Covington's Basilica of the Assumption has hosted a fifth performance. The May Festival Chorus, a trained group of up to two hundred strong drawn from an impressive reservoir of local singing talent, accompanies the orchestra. James Conlon, an American currently director of the Rotterdam Philharmonic, has directed the May Festivals since 1979.

The Cincinnati **Summer Opera,** founded in 1920, is, after New York's Metropolitan, America's second-oldest company. Among the pioneer experiments in summer opera, it was known for five decades as the Zoo Opera. Performances took place at an open-air pavilion at the Cincinnati Zoo, whose denizens often gave singers a run for their money. Visiting divas found themselves in duets with tigers or accompanied by a chorus of monkeys; a claque of ducks cruising the nearby lake quacked approval at inappropriate moments; Sherrill Milnes once inhaled a swarm of gnats. In the 1920s radio station WLW carried the operas; during the 1930s NBC broadcast them coast to coast. Fausto Cleva served as music director for nearly thirty years and was succeeded in 1963 by James de Blasis. Since 1972 performances have taken place in the now air-conditioned Music Hall. The **Cincinnati Ballet,** organized in 1970, performs dance throughout the year at Music Hall. With the orchestra's regular season, the May Festival, the Summer Opera, the Ballet, the symphony's outdoor concerts in city parks and now at Riverbend, music lovers can enjoy live classical music in Cincinnati most weekends in the year. Euterpe, Muse of Music, truly smiles upon the Queen City.

Leaving Music Hall, we walk along the edge of **Washington Park**. The statue to the right of the Elm St. entrance honors **Friedrich Hecker.** An enthusiast for German nationalism, Hecker fought to establish a republic in the 1848 revolution. When the revolution failed, Hecker, along with thousands of other "48ers," emigrated to the United States. 20,000 Germans greeted him upon his arrival in New York on October 5, 1848. Later that month, passing through Cincinnati, he instigated the founding of the nation's first Turner Society. In 1860 Hecker gave support to the 9th Ohio Volunteer Regiment, composed exclusively of Cincinnati's Germans, largely Turners, and known as *Die Neuner* (the 9th). Engraved on the plinth of his monument are, appropriately, "1848" and "1861." The German words translate, "By word and deed [he fought] for the people's freedom in his old and new native lands."

The statue to the left honors Col. **Robert M. McCook,** commander of *Die Neuner.* McCook, of Irish descent but speaking German, was the law partner of Judge Johann B. Stallo, a noted German jurist and leader of Cincinnati's German community. Stallo and McCook raised a full regiment of veterans in three days; most men in it had already served in Europe. McCook shared command with the Prussian August Willich, a former military officer, who as the regiment's adjutant drilled it fiercely and made it into an efficient fighting unit. Brought to Cincinnati by Stallo in 1858, Willich was a Communist whom Marx rejected as too visionary, labelling him a "spiritual Communist" and "the knight of the noble conviction." For two and one-half years Willich edited the Cincinnati *Republikaner.* His radical views on economics and society must have made lively reading among the Queen City's German community during the tense years before the Civil War. After a stint with *Die Neuner,* Willich became commander of his own regiment, the Thirty-second Indiana volunteers, in August 1861. *Die Neuner,* under McCook's leadership, took part in the siege of Corinth, and in the battles of Perryville, Chickamauga, Chattanooga, Lookout Mountain, and Missionary Ridge. McCook died in action in August 1862. Members of his old regiment had this monument erected in 1878; Leopold Fettweis did the bust, as five years later he did Hecker's.

A vital community once centered around Washington Park. In summer bands played German waltzes and Sousa marches under the raised octagonal gazebo/bandstand (1912) that replaced the original pond. "1861," engraved on the boulder just north of the gazebo, indicates the year the park was dedicated. Once thought to be a meteorite, the boulder came no further than from the Little Miami River. In Washington Park the Germans first held their annual *Schützenfest,* an all-day celebration of civic pride. In 1888 Horticultural Hall for Cincinnati's Centennial Exposition went up here.

The Hamilton County Memorial Building (1908), erected for Grand Army of the Republic and Spanish-American War veterans, is known as **Memorial Hall.** Designed by Hannaford and Sons, it is the finest of Cincinnati's few Beaux Arts buildings. This style, named after Paris's Ecole des Beaux Arts, was brought home by American architects who had studied at that once greatly influential school. After about 1900 the Beaux Arts style gained wide acceptance in America for public structures. Typical features include a symmetrical façade, monumental stairs, paired columns, large round-arched window openings, and statuary, often freestanding. Topping the columns here are pioneers, and soldiers and sailors from the Revolution through the Spanish-American War. Keystone figures are of Mars, the Roman god of war. This building is beautifully balanced, horizontals and verticals in equilibrium. Another of Cincinnati's Beaux Arts structures is the former German National Bank Building at 4th and Vine streets. But whereas the bank façade is cool and classical, Memorial Hall's is energetic and dynamic. The period interior includes a virtually unaltered 600-seat auditorium, the smallest of Cincinnati's major theaters. Both building and auditorium deserve a loving restoration and are now likely to get it. Most recently used by the Cincinnati Commission on the Arts, Memorial Hall was leased in 1988 to the Miami Purchase Association, founded in 1964 and the area's chief preservation organization, which will renovate the structure and use it as its headquarters.

South of Memorial Hall, six houses create an attractive late nineteenth-century streetscape. 1209 Elm St., an eclectic composition, sports a French Renaissance (or François Iᵉʳ) gable astride its mansard roof. It recalls, *in parvo,* the Chateau of Chambord in the Loire Valley. Classical designs of urns, fruits and flowers, acanthus leaves and palmettes, adorn the projecting stone bay. Discernible on the frieze of 1215 Elm, High Victorian Italianate merging into Queen Anne, is "1887"; the façade offers a pedimented cornice and attractive corbelling. This sequence of houses, gradually undergoing restoration, ranks among Cincinnati's most stunning.

St. John's Church (1868; "1867" on the façade is optimistic), at 12th and Elm, once housed Cincinnati's oldest German Protestant congregation. Originally of German Lutherans and Swiss followers of Zwingli, it went back to 1814. Later, St. Johannes Kirche became (as we read in the Victorian fanlight) "St. John's Unitarian." A modern building on Resor Ave. in Clifton now houses the congregation. A drugstore installed here in the 1880s lasted until at least the 1950s. In 1946, as Over-the-Rhine began to lose its German population, St. John's became a Church of God. Now it belongs to the Apostolic Bethlehem Temple Church. Its façade is uncompromisingly Gothic: pointed windows, pinnacles, gables, machicolation, even corner buttresses. The tower once supported a wooden spire, removed after storm damage in 1916. Around the corner, down 12th St., is the Drop-Inn Center. Here since the mid-1970s, it shelters, feeds, and counsels between 130 and 200 indigent men per night. The new addition went up in 1989.

This has already been a very long tour. If fatigued, you may want to skip the final portion, chiefly the fascinating Betts-Longworth Historic District, or leave it for another day. If so, simply continue down Elm St. to Central Parkway, where the tour ends. If stamina remains, however, we retrace our steps to Grant St. (just past Memorial Hall) and turn left to Central Parkway. The three-story building (1927) on the east side, Classical Revival with Flemish bond brickwork and earth-colored terra cotta trim, now houses the Pipe Fitters Union. But the façade decoration tells another tale. Verdi and Wagner appear on the roundels facing Central, Mendelssohn and Mozart on those on the side façades; and Beethoven and Bach, peering down from the entrance spandrels, occupy the place of honor. Terra cotta putti above the entrance play musical instruments. Are they in training to become pipefitters?

Actually, we are standing in front of the former administration building of the Cincinnati College of Music, of whose four-building complex only this one remains. Originally lodged in Music Hall, the College of Music later moved to a building south of the Hall (now a parking lot). A few years before, in 1867, Clara Baur had founded a Conservatory of Music, modelled after that in Stuttgart. Both the College and the Conservatory prospered. In 1955 they merged and, in 1962, as the College-Conservatory of Music, became part of the University of Cincinnati.

The Corbett Walkway crosses Central Parkway. We ascend it from the Music Hall side and walk out under its plexiglas shield to the middle. Ahead is the **Crosley Telecommunications Center** (1976), which houses WCET (channel 48), Ohio's first educational television station. It began broadcasting in 1954 from the former Dexter Hall (now the Corbett Tower) in Music Hall. WGUC (90.9 fm), Greater Cincinnati's main classical music radio station, began broadcasting on September 21, 1960. Within is also an art gallery and the Gray History of Wireless Museum, the latter of particular interest to radio buffs for its replica of Powel Crosley's broadcasting studio of the 1920s.

If we look south, we see the gabled Convention Center straddling Elm St.; to its right is City Hall. Looking north up Central Parkway, we sight St. Monica's campanile atop Fairview hill. Below, on Central Parkway we sight on the right a row of beige-and-cream townhouses containing an emporium for architectural antiques. The broad planes of Music Hall's energetic roofline engage the eye as they soar skyward. The asphalt shingles retain somewhat the pattern and color of the original slates; the original cupolas are gone. Still, how like an actual cathedral apse is this rear façade!

If we look down at the median strip below us, we discover one of the city's streetlights topped with a yellow-gold bonnet. With its projecting point it resembles a German World War I helmet. Being from New York City, I am struck by how easy it would be to vandalize these short, quaint-looking lights. Traffic engineers indicate that streetlight vandalism in Cincinnati is not a problem, however. In all my walks around the city, though I have seen a goodly number of bonnets askew, I have yet, somewhat to my amazement, to come upon one broken. Similarly with the city's equally quaint, locally made Murdoch water fountains: they appear unexpectedly in the city and they invariably function, winter and summer. And public phone booths actually have phone books in them. I have not seen one in a Manhattan phone booth since the early 1960s. Until recently, the fire alarm pillar boxes, painted a festive red, yellow, and black, were well maintained, but lost their red alarms after the installation of a 911 system. Minor matters, you may say, but are they really? At the least they indicate a certain respect for civic amenities.

We continue across the walkway past the gazebo. Below, a series of contiguous circular courtyards (1977) makes for an interesting urban space, an exercise in geometry. This little amphitheater, apparently destined for a broad range of activities, is pleasant to contemplate but in my experience little used. Down the ramp we go to find ourselves on Ezzard Charles Drive, named after the hard-luck heavyweight champion born nearby. Charles beat his idol Joe Louis for the title in 1949. Once across Central Parkway, we are again in the West End. Opposite is the yellow-brick **Central Police Station** (1955; 1969). Cincinnati's force has long enjoyed a reputation for excellence. For cities its size it remains one of the safest in the United States regarding numbers of major crimes committed. Its crime rate is well below the national average. To my knowledge, it has no organized crime, no organized gambling, no houses of prostitution. Mystery fans will be delighted, however, to learn that in fiction Cincinnati *does* serve as a venue for extraordinary criminal intrigue. Jonathan Valin, with a series of Harry Stoner mysteries, and A. M. Pyle, with Detective Cesar Franck, have set their tales of murder and mayhem here. Pyle's Franck has his desk in this building; Valin's Stoner often drops by to consult with Detective Al Foster. But Franck and Stoner have not met.

We walk west to Central Avenue, *not* Central Parkway: an awkward conjunction of names, particularly since neither is now central. Robert A. Taft High School (1951) stands on the street's north side, Queen City Vocational Center on its south. The latter facility was intended to become the focus of an eventual complex designed for residential, commercial, and public uses—a complex that has not yet come off. A pedestrian bridge crosses Ezzard Charles Drive. Ezzard Charles is one of Cincinnati's few thoroughfares with visual closure. It begins and ends with a focal point. Behind us stands Music Hall's apse-like rear façade; ahead looms Union Terminal's majestic half dome. Since the avenue bends slightly, we see both landmarks only from the bend.

West down either side of Ezzard Charles Drive stretch low-rise federal housing projects: to the south **Lincoln Court** (1941–1942), originally mostly for blacks; to the north **Laurel Homes** (1936–1938; 1940), originally mostly for whites. Both were in their day among the nation's largest urban renewal projects. Laurel Homes impressed Harlan Hatcher in *The Buckeye Country* (1940) as "bright and clean and hopeful areas in grim neighborhoods, like exotic flowers in a swamp of muck." Would we so regard these complexes today? After four decades the buildings are still inhabited. That is something. Unlike Pruitt-Igoe in St. Louis, thirty-three eleven-story slabs built in 1954 but dynamited (after extensive tenant vandalization) by the city sixteen years later and unlike countless other projects in shambles elsewhere, Lincoln Court and Laurel Homes appear to provide decent basic housing.

Five units underwent modernization in 1979–1981. And there is certainly less debris about than elsewhere in the West End and Over-the-Rhine. After World War II, planners abandoned low-scale buildings such as these for highrise towers like those in Pruitt-Igoe. Invariably, they were statements of mediocre architecture no less than of social failure. Fortunately, Cincinnati has few such highrise projects. The buildings before us keep the human scale evident in Over-the-Rhine and the West End.

As we continue west along Ezzard Charles, we pass a group of Italianate row houses, all but one deserted and boarded up. This is the most visible side of the **Betts-Longworth Historic District,** part of a larger area known as Queensgate II. Queensgate II comprises the section of the West End that stretches north from City Hall at 8th and Plum to Ezzard Charles Drive. The West End Task Force, formed in 1966, evolved a plan for the extensive revitalization of Queensgate II. Proposed housing was in part destined for low and moderate income tenants. But after a few initial successes work stopped when the federal government reduced funds available to cities.

Betts-Longworth was an early subdivision. Five blocks long and two blocks wide, it is bounded on the north by Ezzard Charles, on the south by Court St., on the east by Central Avenue, and on the west by John and Mound streets. The district is named after William Betts, whose two-story Federal farmhouse (1804) still stands at 416 Clark St., and Nicholas Longworth, who owned much land here. Within Betts-Longworth are, in varying degrees of dilapidation, a number of attractive Greek Revival, Italianate, and Queen Anne buildings. Rehabilitation plans, bandied about for two decades, appear to be becoming a reality. The city has since installed new sidewalks and planted trees. Betts-Longworth, rich in history and in architecture, may again make its contribution to Cincinnati's urban vitality. A. M. Pyle in his novel *Murder Moves In* (1986) nicely renders the tensions felt by older inhabitants when newcomers move in to restore the old houses.

We turn left on John St., left again on Hopkins St. This stunning keyhole-shaped street offers a virtually intact nineteenth-century streetscape. Frederick Alms purchased 420 Hopkins in 1873. We return to John. One block further south, fronting Clark St., is the Gothic St. Luke's Baptist Church. Once a major crosstown feeder to the West End, to Union Terminal and Crosley Field, Clark is now a very quiet street. Named after Elizabeth Clark Betts, William Betts's mother, it retains some splendid houses, mostly Italianate. 419 is, however, Greek Revival, 416 (the Betts house) Federal. Tiny windows and dollhouse proportions mark the **Betts House** as from an earlier age. Only the two-story brick front section is original; the house has had numerous additions, several of which remain. It is canted three and one-half degrees in relation to other buildings on Clark, a tipoff that it went up before the area was gridded in 1815. When it was built in 1804, Cincinnati's population hardly topped 1000. Fields, meadows, and truck gardens once surrounded Betts's farmhouse; north stretched a grassy area known to contemporaries as "Texas." Betts himself ran a brickyard and worked his 111-acre farm. In 1819, when Cincinnati officially became a city, only ten households were located in this part of town. Although the Betts-Longworth district lay within city limits, intensive settle-

William Betts house. The front portion of this tiny Federal house on Clark St. dates from 1804, making it the oldest brick house in the city. William Betts ran a brickyard and worked a 111-acre farm. The once-rural area north of here was commonly known as "Texas."

ment did not begin here until the late 1830s and early 1840s. Betts's descendants, in the area until 1878, helped develop the neighborhood.

One of Cincinnati's longest surviving buildings, the oldest in the city standing in its original position, the Betts house finally received a loving owner who in 1990 completed a restoration that converted it into two apartments. Otherwise, this city, which has too few house museums, might have undertaken to use the building to give latter-day Cincinnatians an idea of what early nineteenth-century urban life was like. Opposite, 427 Clark, an Italianate townhouse, has sophisticated neo-Grec detailing. James Gamble, cofounder of Procter & Gamble, took a leasehold on 422 Clark in 1859 and purchased the house in 1889. William F. Doepke moved in across the street, at 421 Clark, in 1873. It is pleasant to think of him setting off to work in the morning with his partner, Frederick Alms, who had moved to Hopkins St. the same year. Houses on Clark are set off from the sidewalk by raised front yards. Several have undergone tasteful restoration. The Flemish Renaissance commercial block/apartment building (ca. 1880) on the northwest corner of Clark and Central Ave. has stepped corgy gables and a corner turret. The ground level held—and may

Jewish cemetery. Founded in 1821, the cemetery was deactivated in 1849. Many of the forty-two weathered gravestones have inscriptions in Hebrew. Rebecca and Joseph Maas, whose headstones are in the foreground, died within two days of each other in 1849, victims of the cholera epidemic.

again hold—shops. Once a bustling commercial thoroughfare, Central Ave., originally "Western Row," by the 1930s had become lined with pawn shops, cheap restaurants, saloons, and dubious nightclubs. We may still discern on the brick walls of surviving structures traces of such long-departed establishments.

At Chestnut St., a block south on Central Ave., we come upon what is probably the oldest **Jewish cemetery** west of the Alleghenies. In 1821 two of Cincinnati's six practicing Jews paid Nicholas Longworth $75 for this 40- by 40-foot lot. Maintained by Bene Israel, the city's first Jewish congregation, the cemetery received interments until 1849 when, as a result of the cholera epidemic, it was closed. Many of the forty-two weathered gravestones have inscriptions in Hebrew. The strip fronting Central Ave., acquired in 1838, was never used for burials, and in 1873 three shops were built on it. The brick wall and iron gate were added at this time. The removal of the 1870s shops gives the cemetery greater visibility; the former Rosen's Dry Goods Store adjoins the property. Most downtown graveyards were later relocated to hilltops or beyond; this is the only one to have remained in its original location. The West End, though supporting a substantial Jewish population by century's end, was not a Jewish neighborhood during the time of the cemetery's use.

We turn down Chestnut. 420–426 and 432–434 Chestnut are Italianate vernacular; 428–430, similar in design but one story higher, has rounded rather than square hood molds. Left on John St., south a block, then back up Elizabeth St. to Central Avenue. A left to Charles St. deposits us on Central Parkway.

On the median at Central Parkway we cannot miss the bright red, plough-shaped sculpture, *Aggravation of Space* (1980) by a French sculptor, Jean Boutillis. At Central Parkway and Elm St. stands the main **YMCA** (1918), Italian Renaissance in style. Two-story arched windows, with metal spandrels in between, are set within an elaborate pattern of brickwork. Horizontal and vertical bands alternate. The building settles down as it rises. The ubiquitous lions peer down from its elaborate cornice. Like the previous tour, we end this one on Central Parkway, a block from where we began, and standing next to a building paid for in part by Mary Emery.

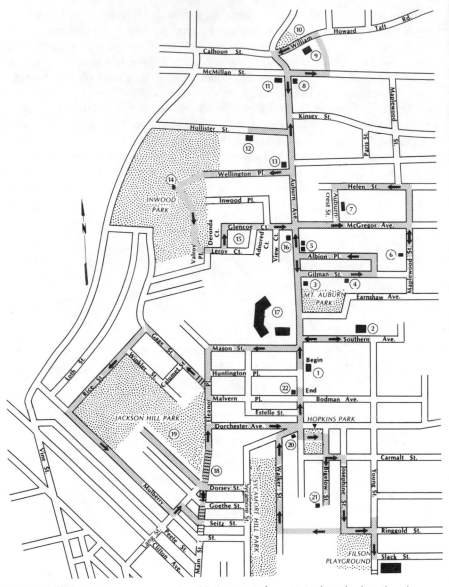

MOUNT AUBURN

1. William Howard Taft Historic Site
2. Taft School
3. Mount Auburn Firehouse
4. Jacob D. Cox House
5. Philip and Thornton Hinkle Houses
6. Swiss Chalet (2225 Maplewood)
7. Gorham A. Worth House
8. Holy Name Rectory
   (Eugene Zimmerman House)
9. Mount Auburn Presbyterian Church
10. Corryville Triangle Park
11. Mount Auburn United Methodist Church
12. Episcopal Church of Our Savior
13. Graveson House
14. Friedrich Ludwig Jahn Cenotaph
15. Glencoe
16. Sunny Side
    (William Howard Doane House)
17. Christ Hospital
18. Site of Mount Auburn Incline
19. Jackson Hill Park
20. Henry Martin House
21. James Keys House
22. Riddle-Phillips House

9

Mount Auburn

"SWEET Auburn, loveliest village of the plain," sighed Oliver Goldsmith in *The Deserted Village* (1770). In 1837 (the story goes) a Mrs. Summer, a Bostonian visiting her daughter here, put up a sign at the corner of Liberty and Sycamore streets pointing up the hill, "Mt. Auburn, 1 Mile." Cincinnati's suburb incarnated more than the rural tranquility of Goldsmith's immensely popular poem. Mrs. Summer no doubt recalled Mount Auburn Cemetery in Cambridge, Massachusetts, founded six years before as the nation's first garden, or rural, cemetery. Goldsmith's line fits Cambridge's cemetery. It works less well for a Cincinnati hilltop. Yet, though Mount Auburn is now more an urban enclave than a village, it retains something of its earlier idyllic character of *rus in urbe*.

We begin our tour at 2038 Auburn Ave., the William Howard Taft National Historic Site. The Taft house stands just past the crest of the hill where Sycamore metamorphoses into Auburn. Bus number 53 brings us here from downtown in a few minutes. If we wish to walk in Clifton later in the same day, it will take us there also.

Auburn Ave. itself is a ridge street, what geologists call a hogback. On it we stand above the surrounding landscape. Although architecturally rich, Mount Auburn's interest lies as much in its unexpected vistas, its uneven terrain that takes us up and down, its seemingly forgotten parks. To the south is Liberty Hill, explored in the first Over-the-Rhine chapter; to the east are streets with excellent housing stock dating from 1870–1910; to the west is lower Mount Auburn, a half-forgotten area, built-up earlier and, like Liberty Hill, geographically more a part of Over-the-Rhine. In this walk we can follow Mount Auburn's most characteristic architectural style, the Tuscan villa, in all its phases, from its beginnings as an essentially Greek Revival cube in the 1840s and 1850s to the elaborately towered mansions of the 1870s. An architectural style, like a culture, develops over a period of time (in the Midwest usually a few years after the East coast); it never completely emerges at once. Intermixed throughout Mount Auburn are a medley of Gothic, Romanesque, Second Empire, Queen Anne, and neo-Georgian structures, even a few Swiss chalets and the occasional Tudor Revival.

"I was charmed by the appearance of Cincinnati and its adjoining suburb, Mt. Auburn," wrote Charles Dickens in 1842, on the occasion of his first American sojourn. Dickens liked little that he saw in the New World. Of American cities besides Cincinnati, only Boston received his commendation. At the time of his visit about fifty families lived on Mount Auburn. James Keys had built the first house in 1819, at the end of what is now Bigelow St. People referred to the site as Keys's Hill; others wished to call it "Montesano," Italian for Mountain of Health. More families joined Keys, and the isolated houses became a small community. Mount Auburn gradually became the largest independent village in the Cincinnati environs. In 1849, the year of the great cholera epidemic, the city annexed it.

People moved to Mount Auburn because of its location, convenient to downtown. Plots of land offered views to east, south, and west. For several decades the village remained purely suburban, green, still country. "One range of hills succeeds another," wrote Sidney Maxwell in *The Suburbs of Cincinnati* (1870), "so that there is scarcely a limit to the beautiful locations for suburban homes." Those who lived on Mount Auburn's salubrious heights after midcentury included the Tafts; General E. F. Noyes, governor of Ohio and ambassador to France; General Jacob D. Cox, governor, congressman, and president of the University of Cincinnati; Matthew Addy, the Canadian who started the iron foundry works in the town downriver that bears his name, Addyston; Alexander McGuffey, William's brother and himself author of the fifth McGuffey's *Reader;* and William Howard Doane, entrepreneur, inventor, hymn writer, and collector of older musical instruments. Whereas the Haucks clustered on Dayton St. and the Geiers and Moerleins moved to Ohio Ave., west of Vine St., the Tafts, Hinkles, Doanes, mostly families of English and Scottish descent, often via New England, settled on Auburn Ave.

People also moved to Mount Auburn because they found the Basin increasingly crowded and polluted. Cincinnati early spawned an enveloping industrial haze. "The soft coal spreads such a dust," Louise Taft lamented in the 1850s, "that everything is black with it. It is worse in the city than on the hill." Soft, or bituminous coal, universally used for industrial and residential purposes, produced this polluted air. Smoke reducing ordinances carried little clout. Compared with the Basin, Mount Auburn offered fresher and cleaner air. In the nineteenth century it also registered as much as fifteen degrees cooler. Today, with tighter air controls, we hardly notice a difference.

After 1872, the year the Mount Auburn incline opened, settlement rapidly increased. Once virtually isolated and still rural in atmosphere, Mount Auburn became more a part of the city. Its eastern slopes gradually filled with fine houses. Well into the twentieth century the suburb remained a bastion of gentility. After World War II, dispossessed blacks from the West End settled in Mount Auburn. By the 1960s the neighborhood had become a haven for drug addicts; heroin sales were made openly in neighborhood parks and on street corners. The police did nothing because the community put no pressure on them to get the drug pushers out. Finally, as part of an overall campaign to improve Mount Auburn, a group of citizens, led by a black activist, Carl B. Westmoreland, Jr., decided to go after the pushers. And they succeeded. Among the city's forty-odd neighborhoods Mount Auburn's crime rate fell from third highest to twenty-third. In 1967 its residents set up their own development corporation, designed both to renovate the neighborhood's houses and to integrate it economically by bringing in middle-income whites and blacks. Since then Mount Auburn has slowly come back. Today it defies easy summary. Factory hand and physician, black and white coexist together: a coexistence that constitutes one of Cincinnati's largely unheralded success stories.

Despite its demographic changes Mount Auburn retains much of its nineteenth-century housing stock, as fine as that anywhere else in the city. No longer owned by the original families, its grand mansions now house medical, legal, or other professional offices; a few underwent conversion into apartments. In 1973 a cooperative effort among longtime white residents, newly arrived blacks, and preservationists gained the Auburn Avenue Historic District listing on the National Register of Historic Places. Auburn Ave. became the most visible symbol of the neighborhood's efforts to revive itself. But in 1981 the Cincinnati city council, by not designating Auburn Ave. a local historic district, failed to protect it. Without local listing, National Register status does not impede the destruction of historic buildings. And since 1973 a number have come down. Fortunately, if belatedly, the council in January 1988 reversed itself and approved local designation. Auburn Ave. is still an imposing sight. With this protection it is now a less endangered one.

Our tour begins at the **William Howard Taft National Historic Site.** Its importance is less architectural than historic. On September 15, 1857, William Howard Taft, twenty-seventh president (1909–1913), subsequently Chief Justice of the Supreme Court (1921–1930), was born here. The National Park Service has restored the house to its appearance in Taft's boyhood. Three rooms—the double-parlor, the library or study, and the nursery—were opened to the public in September 1988.

Taft is Cincinnati's best-known name. The family has sired a roster of individuals eminent in the law and, invariably as Republicans, in state and national politics. **Alphonso** (1810–1891), the patriarch and perhaps the most interesting of all the Tafts, came from an old Vermont family. Arriving in Cincinnati in 1838, he developed a successful law practice, and later became a superior court judge (1865–1871). "Taft, grave, thoughtful, with solid, not brilliant parts," James Wickes Taylor wrote of him in 1844, "and commanding business, and establishing reputation, by his sterling qualities of head and heart." Unafraid of controversy, he forbade in 1869 the reading of the Bible and the singing of hymns in public schools—a decision that probably cost him his chance, in 1875 and 1879, to become governor. He was a man of vision as well as of principle. An 1850 lecture on "Cincinnati and Her Rail-Roads" argued for this relatively new form of transportation at a time when the city's business interests were still enamored with the Ohio River and the Miami and Erie Canal. Summoned to national office in 1876, Taft helped shore up, as Secretary of War and Attorney General, the waning integrity of President Grant's administration. From 1882 to 1884 he served as minister to the Austro-Hungarian Empire; after 1884, to Russia. Alphonso married in 1841 Fanny Phelps, a fellow New Englander, with whom he had five children. The eldest was Charles Phelps Taft (1843–1929) whose home now contains the Taft Museum. Fanny died in 1852, and the next year Alphonso married another New England woman, Louise Torrey.

William Howard Taft was born of this second union in 1857. Growing up on

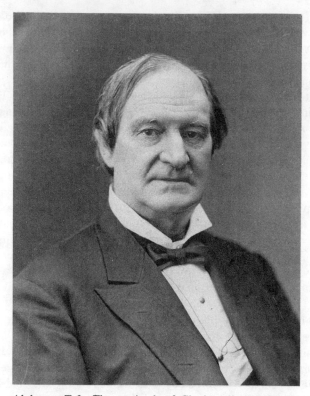

Alphonso Taft. The patriarch of Cincinnati's best-known
family, Alphonso Taft (1810–1891) came from Vermont in
1838 to try his fortunes in semifrontier Ohio. Cincinnati
was until the Civil War the largest and most prosperous city
in the trans-Appalachian West. Here Taft established a successful law practice. In 1876 he became briefly Secretary
of War under U. S. Grant and in the 1880s served as minister to the Austro-Hungarian empire and to Russia. His son
by his first marriage to Fanny Phelps was Charles Phelps
Taft, whose home is now the Taft Museum; among Alphonso's children by his second marriage, to Louise Torrey, was
William Howard Taft, president of the United States from
1908 to 1912. Courtesy of the Cincinnati Historical Society.

Mount Auburn, he went to the local elementary school, to Woodward High School,
and, like most male Tafts, to Yale. Subsequently, he took a degree from Cincinnati
Law School. He decided to devote his life to public service. For someone of his
education and background, given the corrupt state of American politics, it was an
unusual decision. Taft held a succession of local and state offices, among them,
assistant prosecutor (1881–1882) and assistant solicitor (1885–1887) for Hamilton
County, and judge of the Ohio Supreme Court (1887–1890). In 1886 he married

Helen Herron of Cincinnati. To him, like his father, the national scene also beckoned. From 1890 to 1892 he was solicitor general of the United States; afterwards, he served eight years as a judge of the U.S. circuit court of appeals. In 1901 he was appointed governor-general of the Philippines, and in 1904 he entered Theodore Roosevelt's cabinet as Secretary of War. When in 1908 Roosevelt chose not to run again for president, the Republicans nominated Taft, who defeated the Democratic candidate, William Jennings Bryan. "I am going to be honest with myself," Taft wrote then; "I cannot be spectacular." Although few historians disagree with his prediction, Taft did successfully enforce antitrust measures against the monopolies and actually secured more convictions than had Roosevelt. A conservationist like Roosevelt, he continued Roosevelt's progressive policies by withdrawing oil lands from public sale and by purchasing vast areas of Appalachian forest. In 1910 he became the first president to open the baseball season by throwing out the first ball. Pauline Wayne, the family cow, was the last bovine to graze on the White House lawn. Big for his age even as a boy—his school chums nicknamed him "Big Lub"— Taft grew to 336 pounds during his term in office and, in a celebrated incident, once got himself stuck in the White House bathtub. In 1912, after the Republicans renominated Taft, disaffected Republicans formed the Bull Moose Party and put up Roosevelt. With the Republican vote split, the nation elected Woodrow Wilson. Taft's first and last love was, however, the law. In 1921 President Harding appointed him Chief Justice, a position he was temperamentally more fitted for than the presidency. Happier on the bench than in the political arena, Taft served with distinction as Chief Justice until shortly before his death in 1930. In the presidency a self-admitted "fish out of water," as Chief Justice he was finally, as he had guessed years earlier, "entirely at home."

The Taft line continues to prosper in Cincinnati and elsewhere. Robert A. Taft (1889–1953), eldest son of William Howard, became a Republican senator from Ohio and eventually, as "Mr. Republican," leader of the party's conservative wing. The Taft-Hartley Act of 1947, which limited the power of labor unions, bears his name. In 1952 he narrowly lost the Republican nomination for president to Dwight Eisenhower. Charles Phelps Taft II (1897–1983), another of William Howard's children, worked in myriad ways as leader of the Charter Party, as mayor and as a sixteen-term councilman, for the well-being of his native city. A figure of national significance, Charles Phelps Taft became in 1947 the first layman to become president of the World Council of Churches. Taft largesse and Taft competence continue. Jane Taft Ingalls and Louise Taft Semple have contributed generously to the Taft Museum and to the Cincinnati Art Museum. Robert Taft and Robert A. Taft II, among other Tafts, maintain the family interest in the law and in Republican politics.

2038 Auburn was built around 1840 in the Greek Revival style. In 1851 Alphonso Taft bought the house and 1.82 acres of land for $10,000 and the next year added the back ell, doubling the house's size. Seven years later he put the still-standing stone wall around the property. Curved Italianate touches, such as the scalloped crenellations above the portico and on the roof fringe, date from this time.

Taft House, ca. 1867. The young William Howard Taft, born in 1857, sits on the stone post by the driveway. The Greek Revival house, built about 1840, has been restored to its 1860s condition. In 1988 the National Park Service opened it to the public. Courtesy of the Cincinnati Historical Society.

These visitations of the picturesque mollify Greek Revival severity. The north entrance, looking like an embryo pagoda, hints at Chinese influence. With its squarish appearance, observation platform, open grounds, and distinctive wall, the house became a Mount Auburn landmark. Greek Revival structures favored white; the present yellow with burgundy (or sienna) lintels and ledges, the shutters hunter green, accentuate the house's vaguely exotic air. The colors are historically accurate for the Italianate style in the 1860s. Thanks to the restoration, the observation platform, or "widow's walk," again has its cast-iron railing. The house remained in the family until 1899. In 1962 interested parties organized the William Howard Taft Memorial Association to preserve it; in 1969 the house passed to the National Park Service.

In the double-parlor, portraits of Alphonso and Louise look down upon us. What looks like rosewood Rococo Revival furniture is actually walnut grained to look like rosewood. The furniture is authentic for the time if not for the family. In fact, the only original family piece may be the desk in the library; some of the books, including the inevitable set of Walter Scott, belonged to Alphonso Taft. The wallpapers, copies of originals, and the applied woodgraining evoke a mid-Victorian American interior. The nursery gives insights into how a middle-class household of this time managed its children. It includes a crib and a bed in which two of the boys slept; the lucky nurse would have managed on the uncomfortable trundle bed. Alphonso's Wooten desk, from his downtown law office, dominates the room that follows. It and the upstairs rooms open to the public offer displays that record the Tafts' history as it intertwined with the nation's.

Upon exiting, we proceed down Southern Ave. Like other side streets east of Auburn Ave., Southern retains considerable architectural and historic interest. Numbers 220 and 224, mansard roofed, are Second Empire. Asbestos cement shingle siding, popular in the 1930s and 1940s, presumably cloaks wooden façades. Across the street five Queen Anne rowhouses (ca. 1885) masquerade as one building: the drab paint, landlord olive, hides fine decorative brickwork including piano key moldings. On the left stands the Queen Anne style **William Howard Taft School** (1890), finding new use as a Montessori Learning Center and as the Mount Auburn Health Center. The original schoolhouse on this site, a four-room brick structure of 1854, young Taft attended from 1862 to 1870. Prominently noted on the school's façade are the names of the building committee. Such a practice, highly unusual today, appears to indicate a greater responsibility toward local schools than many people now feel. Further down Southern stood for years the gabled house of Alexander McGuffey, William's younger brother, a sight frequently shown nineteenth-century visitors to Mount Auburn. Professor at Woodward High School and, as mentioned, author of the fifth McGuffey's *Reader*, he died here in 1896. We can look over the trees at the engaging roofline of the Cincinnati Art Museum: a further reminder, if needed, of how much green space remains in central Cincinnati. We retrace our steps to Auburn Ave.

2112 Auburn is asymmetrical Richardsonian Romanesque. Twin wall dormers balance the façade, itself capped by a pyramidal hipped roof. Stained glass appears in first- and second-floor windows. Paired dwarf columns of polished granite set off the entrance; the capitals have acanthus-leaf decoration. Projecting from the north façade is an oriel window with a decorative base and stained-glass transoms. Our examples of Richardsonian Romanesque thus far have been commercial. City Hall and the Krippendorf Building on Sycamore St. are progeny of Richardson's single Cincinnati building, the Chamber of Commerce. 2112, though in brick (Richardson usually worked in stone), is one of its residential offspring. Originally the dark red brick would have been unpainted. 2112's emphasis is largely vertical, unlike Richardson's own buildings, which hug the ground.

One block north, at 2142, is the former **Mount Auburn Firehouse,** now a "Guest Haus" for Christ Hospital across the street. Three small windows extend across the original entrance, now blocked off. Through it once clattered horse drawn fire engines. The tower's semicircular horseshoe window echoes the shape of the front door. A Moorish touch perhaps, or, more likely, homage to the horses that drew the old fire wagons until World War I.

We detour down Gilman St. The "Linden," a Romanesque Revival apartment building on the southeastern corner, has fine wrought-iron work adorning its entrance on Gilman. Where the half arch is was once the coal shute. 241–243 Gilman, the **Jacob D. Cox house** (ca. 1880), is High Victorian Italianate. With its falling-down porch and gutted interior, it is beyond saving. But it would make a perfect haunted house. Brigadier General in the Civil War, Republican governor of Ohio from 1866 to 1868, Secretary of the Interior under Grant, Cox also served as congressman, dean of the Cincinnati Law School, and for two years as the University of Cincinnati's president. He lived here from 1883 to 1897. Opposite, 238 retains a hint of Italianate lines; the adjoining 244, despite additions including a mansard roof, began life as a Greek Revival cube. We turn left on Albion Place, several houses on which repay serious looking, and follow it back to Auburn Ave.

Both **2210** and **2212 Auburn,** with their mansard roofs and elaborate dormers, are Second Empire in style. A father and son, Philip and Thornton M. Hinkle, put them up in 1874. 2110 may have begun as a brick cottage, with the upper story added later. On Albion Place, just before Auburn, we may have noticed its attractive carriage house. The decorative work on the metal hood molds, painted to resemble stone, is identical on both dwellings. Philip, who lived in 2210, manufactured portable wooden houses of his own design in kits. He shipped them by steamboat or along the expanding railroad lines to Iowa, Kansas, Nebraska, Texas, and the South. By the end of the century, customers could have purchased prefabricated houses from Sears Roebuck and Montgomery Ward. Thornton, owner of 2112, became a well-known lawyer.

We continue north along Auburn Ave., then turn down McGregor Ave. 222 McGregor (1870), set well back from the street, is an Italianate clapboard house

Swiss chalet, 2225 Maplewood Ave. Designed by Lucian Plympton, this is a fine example of one of America's rarer architectural styles. Cincinnati has a number of Swiss chalets dating from the 1890s.

Gorham A. Worth house. The central section of this Federal house (1819) grew wings about 1860. Gorham A. Worth was cashier of the Cincinnati branch of the Second Bank of the United States, a poet, and a witty memorialist of his time in Cincinnati.

whose multicolored roof slates form an unusual pattern. 224, severely geometrical, has a splendid round-arched entrance. Its roof retains two finials and most of its cresting. A magnificent red oak shades the front yard. 227 and 229 McGregor, two three-story Greco-Italianate rowhouses built as one unit, differ chiefly in cornice and in additions.

Further along, 268 McGregor, with a curving and indented bargeboard and a balcony, heralds the city's largest collection of **Swiss chalets,** a style popular in 1890s Cincinnati. We turn south (right) along Maplewood St., where at 2225 we come upon Mount Auburn's most accomplished Swiss chalet, designed by Lucian Plympton for Charles F. Hurm in 1894. Plympton, a Chicago architect who went to Switzerland to learn the style, also did the city's finest Swiss chalet at 2214 Upland Place in Walnut Hills. Swiss chalets usually have two and one-half stories, low-pitched roofs, shingles in a scale pattern, and extremely wide eaves supported by decorative brackets. The wood siding is often elaborately carved and painted. "O Herr behüt diess Hüttlein," Swiss German in Gothic script, translates as "God, watch over this little house." A handsomely carved wooden balcony thrusts out from 2225's south side. 2212 and 2207 Maplewood also reflect, in their porch, gable, and scaled shingles, Swiss chalet influence. We reverse our steps on Maplewood, cross McGregor, turn left (uphill) on Helen St., before turning left again on Auburncrest St.

Occupying the east side of Auburncrest is the **Gorham A. Worth house** (1819). It is one of Cincinnati's finest residences. Federal in style, it may be the oldest frame house in the city, predating by less than a year the Taft house on Lytle

Park. Inasmuch as the conveyance made to Worth is dated May 6, 1818, a year earlier than the date usually assigned to James Keys's house, Worth's dwelling may also have predated Keys's as Mount Auburn's first. Note—if you can see past the breakfront of white pines masking the façade—the exquisite tracery of the elliptical fanlight. The pyramidal mansard-roofed wings (ca. 1860), though stylistically out of tune with the original Federal building, balance the house nicely. Worth, cashier of the Cincinnati branch of the Second Bank of the United States, was also a frontier poet, subsequently a witty memorialist of Cincinnati. He built this house as a country residence. A later owner, Robert McGregor (who gave his name to the adjoining street), is one of the many who, tradition says, hosted here in 1860 "Baron Renfrew," i.e., the nineteen-year-old Prince of Wales, "Bertie," forty-one years later to be Edward VII. The Prince allegedly proclaimed McGregor's daughter Helen (who gave *her* name to another nearby street) "the prettiest girl in America." The Prince's approbation, as the WPA guide observes, "put Helen in a select class that was enlarged only when the Prince went on to other cities."

Back up McGregor we go to Auburn Ave. On the block between McGregor Ave. and McCormick Place stood until 1986 an oddly symmetrical Italianate mansion (1870), with a massive projecting tower, put up by Cincinnati-born A. Howard Hinkle, no relation to Philip and Thornton down the block. The mansion was designed by A. C. Nash, best known in the Cincinnati area by his still-standing courthouse (1884) for Newport, Kentucky, and was built by Isaac Graveson. Hinkle, after a modest beginning as a bookbinder, eventually rose to become managing director of the American Book Company. Planned Parenthood's Margaret Sanger Center last occupied the house. Arsonists struck on December 30, 1985. Six months later the building, judged irreparable, was torn down: one of at least ten losses the Mount Auburn Historic District has suffered since 1973. The **Elizabeth Campbell Center** (1987), erected in its place and named after one of the city's pioneering woman doctors, now houses the offices of Planned Parenthood. This postmodern concoction ties in to Auburn Avenue's Italianate and Second Empire structures via its height, orange-red brick, stone banding, Italianate hood molds on second-story windows, and huge oculi (round windows) at either end. Even the mansard roof nods toward Second Empire.

The rowhouse, compact and economical, is one of the most admirable urban housing types ever devised. At 2356–2362 Auburn we come upon four restored **Italianate rowhouses** (1876), put up by Philip Hinkle. Rowhouses, always more frequent along the Eastern seaboard than inland, were one solution to the rising urban congestion of the nineteenth century. As the nation's economy boomed in the last quarter of that century, more and more Americans yearned for a single-family detached dwelling on its own plot of land. Only in recent years have rowhouses, now usually marketed as condominiums or "townhouses," come back in popularity. Cincinnati once had a number of sequences of older rowhouses. Few remain. These have been apartments since the 1920s. Each entrance formerly indicated a separate dwelling. Doorway and window molds, similar in the four, are made of pressed metal, as are the cornice and brackets. Though by mid-Victorian times iron had gained a measure of respect in construction, metal ornamentation was often disguised to resemble a traditional building material, usually stone, sometimes wood, by painting it. Don't miss the delightful cherubs, now badly eroded, on 2358's newel.

2404 and 2406 Auburn are turn-of-the-century Georgian, or Colonial, Revival. The 1876 Centennial Exhibition in Philadelphia introduced the idea of a distinctly American architecture into the national consciousness. Two houses designed in the late 1870s by Charles Follen McKim, later of McKim, Mead, and White, initiated the **Colonial Revival** movement. Colonial Revival is only loosely based on colonial architecture; as a style, rather than seeking to create accurate historical replicas, it used selected elements in a contemporary manner. The World's Columbian Exposition in Chicago in 1893 propelled Colonial Revival into widespread popularity. The style also developed in reaction to an increasingly industrial America. Examples of Colonial Revival, uncommon before the 1890s, appear with increasing frequency through the 1920s. Invariably much larger than the colonial houses from which they sought inspiration, Colonial Revival mansions were often grand but as often grandiloquent. The restoration of Williamsburg begun by John D. Rockefeller in 1926 further enhanced Colonial Revival's aura as a national style. Architects continue to draw upon its motifs. By providing Americans with a sense of security, stability, and roots, Colonial Revival has become by far the longest lasting of the Revival styles.

2404 Auburn was the home of Dr. Elizabeth Campbell. Below the central roof dormer we find a Palladian "window" that sports a fanlike "fanlight" in wood, miniature Corinthian columns, and dentils that echo the portico's and the cornice's larger dentils. 2406, built later, has a pedimented portico with fluted Doric columns and an elliptical fanlight over the front door. Understated quoins in brick, a characteristic Georgian feature, add a note of elegance.

Where Holy Name Church now stands once stood the Matthew Addy house, an Italianate mansion that Kenny's 1875 guide to Cincinnati singled out as one of Mount Auburn's beauty spots. Addy, a Canadian who immigrated to Cincinnati in 1857, became one of the city's leading industrialists. As the South developed its iron industry after the Civil War, he encouraged southern entrepreneurs to think of Cincinnati as their natural market. Downriver at Addyston, named after him, he established the Addyston Pipe & Steel Company in 1889.

2448, set well back on the hill, dominates the corner of Auburn Ave. and East McMillan St. It now serves as Holy Name's rectory. Ellmore Cunningham, who built this mansion in 1859, sold it around 1880 to **Eugene Zimmerman.** Zimmerman had one of those spectacular nineteenth-century careers that leaves us lesser folk of the twentieth gaping. Born in Vicksburg in 1845, he joined the Union Navy and, in 1863, at age eighteen, became a steamboat captain. That year he took part in the Union siege of his old hometown. After the war he started a lumber mill in the Queen City; later he became president of the Cincinnati, Hamilton, & Dayton Railroad. In 1896, to celebrate his daughter Helena's debut into society, Zimmerman had this house extensively remodeled. An Italianate mansion metamorphosed into a Georgian Revival, with ground-floor Palladian windows, two-story Ionic pilasters, and a redesigned entrance (the addition cuts off its right tip). In 1900

Helena, no doubt betraying the energy of the family genes, eloped with the Duke of Manchester, a noted turn-of-the-century *roué*.

East on McMillan St., six Italianate row houses descend the hill. Cement stoops are new, but the decoration, mansard roofs, two-story oriel windows, and recessed entries are original. Across the street, Cincinnati Dental Services has imaginatively remodelled in a postmodern idiom the former Holy Name Church School that closed in 1977. As we walk through the parking lot after 124 E. McMillan, we pass a stick-style carriage house, the roof with dormers and its original shingles, out of which rises a ventilation cupola. William Howard Taft Road, where we emerge, was cut through just before World War II. It now forms Mount Auburn's northern boundary. 125, probably 1850s, is Greek Revival-going-on-Italianate. The builder attempted, by adding brackets and window molds, to adapt a cubiform Greek Revival house to the increasingly popular Italianate style. Across the street, 130 and 132–134 (ca. 1885) form a group of contiguous Italianate rowhouses. Before the entrance to 130 is a heavy scrolled cast-iron bannister. We retrace our steps west along William Howard Taft to 108, Greek Revival. The style admits no curves, so 108's curved cornice must have arrived in mid-Victorian times. Brackets march rhythmically across it. The Federal Revival portico and fanlight appear to be early twentieth-century additions.

Mount Auburn Presbyterian Church (1890), the asymmetrical rock-faced structure across William Howard Taft Rd., replaced a functional wooden structure of 1869. Nineteenth-century congregations often began with limited resources. Henry E. Siter, the new church's architect, attempted here a Gothic rendering of Richardsonian Romanesque. Similarities in coloration, ornament, roof shape, and overall plan exist between this building and Richardson's Trinity Church, Boston (1877). Romanesque by weight and mass, the Mount Auburn church is yet, by its pointed windows and its decoration, Gothic. Terrifying griffins protrude from the tower. The interior, like that of most Cincinnati churches, is normally closed except for services. It well repays a visit. Golden oak walls complement glimmering stained glass. Tiffany did the two large windows; that at the back represents the Parable of the Sower. The high quality of the materials suggests the immense wealth once found in Mount Auburn.

Corryville Triangle Park lies across the street. On this site lived William Corry, whose farm once occupied much of Mount Auburn. From 1815 to 1819 Corry served as the "village" of Cincinnati's last mayor. Incorporated as a township in 1791, Cincinnati became a village in 1802, when it had a population of less than a thousand; and a city in 1819, when its population neared 10,000. North beyond Corry's home developed the independent hamlet of Corryville. Here Germans from Over-the-Rhine built small, trim homes. In 1870 Corryville merged with Cincinnati. Upper Vine St., now known as "University Village," retains an interesting cluster of nineteenth-century commercial buildings. East of Vine, in the area from Eden Ave. to Burnet Ave., once considered part of Mount Auburn, the curious stroller will come upon an abundance of nineteenth-century mansions. Looking north from Corryville Park we gain a sense of Cincinnati's "**Uptown**," a recent designation that takes in six Cincinnati neighborhoods: Corryville, Mount Auburn,

Walnut Hills (which begins about a half-mile to the east, on our right), Avondale (about a half-mile to the northeast), Clifton Heights—University Heights—Fairview (a somewhat amorphous area, including the largely residential hilltop neighborhoods to the south and west as well as the taller University of Cincinnati buildings we sight to our left), and Clifton (about a mile beyond the university buildings). "Uptown" encompasses, in addition to the residential neighborhoods and the university, the Cincinnati Zoo and ten of the city's hospitals.

A postmodern branch of the Cinco credit union (1986) stands on the southwest corner of Auburn Ave. and William Howard Taft Rd. Previously two massive wrought-iron water tanks, thirty-eight feet high and sixty in diameter, occupied the site. The city put in the first tank in 1869, then in 1871 installed a second to supply pressure for the new Tyler Davidson Fountain. New and larger tanks, looming over surrounding buildings, replaced these in 1894; in the 1970s the city tore down the complex. Across the street, the curving tower of the Auburndale Apartment Building addresses its corner site gracefully. An engaged urn interrupts the broken pediment of the entrance portico; the conspicuous shell motif to its right is Georgian Revival, via Rococo.

We return along Auburn. At the intersection with McMillan St. is the **Mount Auburn United Methodist Church** (1882). Early residents banded together to build the community's first church, an 1852 wooden frame building. That the first minister happened to be a Methodist determined the church's denomination. Until 1854, when the first schoolhouse on Southern Ave. was built, the church basement did duty as the community school. The present structure blends Gothic and Romanesque. Two engaged tourelles rise free above the symmetrical Gothic Revival façade; the dwarf columns below the central window are characteristically Romanesque Revival.

East McMillan St. and Auburn Ave. is an unassuming intersection, yet it suggests something of the city's architectural diversity. Within brief compass, we have a Gothic church (with Romanesque touches), the Italianate-*cum*-Georgian Revival house opposite, the mansarded rowhouses down McMillan, the turn-of-the-century Auburndale apartments, and the postmodern credit union of 1986. Not one of these buildings is outstanding, even particularly distinguished, but considered together they awaken the eye—and mind.

2421 Auburn is **Chateauesque** in massing, Romanesque in detail. Steeply pitched roofs, tall chimneys, pointed wall dormers (a dormer continuing the wall), round conical towers: these architectural elements derive loosely from French Renaissance chateaux along the Loire. The style, few examples of which exist in Cincinnati, is sometimes known in its American version as French Renaissance Revival or François Ier, after the colorful early sixteenth-century French monarch. Chateauesque became popular nationally in the 1890s for the mansions of the very rich. Often, in Newport and along Manhattan's Fifth Avenue, "Millionaire's Row," it was gigantesque as well. In 1895 Richard Morris Hunt completed for George W. Vanderbilt the granddaddy of Chateauesque extravaganzas, Biltmore House, near Asheville, North Carolina. By such standards 2421 is a modest cottage. Usually the walls of a Chateauesque mansion run smooth; those of 2421, however, are rusticated, a

Romanesque characteristic. Details, lovingly handled, are also mostly Romanesque. A stringcourse of acanthus leaves surrounds the conical tower. At the dormer's peak a face smiles down on us. On the south wall, the rounded bay window displays beveled glass; the most miniature of balconies surmounts it. Behind the mansion stands the original carriage house.

2411 Auburn is one of Mount Auburn's few cubiform Greek Revival houses not excessively gussied up with Italianate detailing, here limited to restrained hood molds. It was built in 1839 for John C. Wright, who six years before had founded with Timothy Walker the Cincinnati Law School. Among the characteristics of Greek Revival are simplicity of line and spareness of ornamentation. Plain Doric pilasters flank the recessed entrance. Metal stars, the end pieces of tie rods, protrude on both sides to prevent the walls from bowing out. The orange-red brick is particularly attractive. Above the door a **fire insurance mark,** dated "1839," depicts an early fire wagon. It identified the householder as one who subscribed to fire protection by a volunteer fire company. Such marks originated in London after the Great Fire of 1666; by 1752 Americans had adopted them. Before public fire departments came into being, householders depended on volunteer companies, which, in turn, often had ties to individual insurance firms. Firms appended a fire mark at a prominent place—it was good advertising—so that a volunteer company would know which buildings it insured. One company would not rush to save a burning house covered by another.

We walk down Hollister St. This quiet cross street, connecting Auburn Ave. with Vine St., was put through just after the Civil War. The brick wall on the right culminates in what looks like (but isn't) a dovecote. Through the trees emerges the splendid façade of **St. George's Church** (1873) in Fairview. Gothic in its soaring spires and rose window, St. George's reveals itself to be Romanesque in its decoration. The façade, an ecclesiastical variant of the *Rundbogenstil* we have observed in the former Moerlein and Windisch-Muhlhauser breweries, seems to have been modelled on St. George's Episcopal Church in New York (1848). The architect was Samuel Hannaford. Halfway down Hollister, the Episcopal Church of Our Savior has a wooden portico and stick style Gothic decoration. Roof slates form a complex geometrical pattern. Time appears to have forgotten Hollister's north side, with its charming clapboard and brick houses.

We go back to Auburn Ave. 2367 and 2365, the intricate woodwork of their porticos recalling the 1870s Eastlake style, are generically Queen Anne. 2365's roof gable hints at Flemish Renaissance; a splendid floral grille projects below its second-story window. Next door, 2355 is Italianate, though symmetrical bays suggest only partial emancipation from Greek Revival. Note the fully rounded, or Florentine, window molds and the incised keystones. Double brackets and severe quoins complete the composition. Among the immediate ancestors of such an urban *palazzo* are Sir Charles Barry's Travellers' Club (1829–32) and Reform Club (1841), both on Pall Mall, London, and both inspired by the High Renaissance.

2343 is Auburn Avenue's most spectacular Italian Villa. This "high style" mansion is one of the finest of its kind in America. On June 26, 1869, Isaac Graveson

St. George's Church. Photographed from Hollister Street in Mount Auburn, the splendid Romanesque façade of the church rises with Gothic verticality. It is an 1873 work of Samuel Hannaford.

paid $46,540 for two vacant lots on this corner, an indication of the high land values in Mount Auburn, and two years later he built this house. Graveson, an English immigrant who came to America in 1849 as a stonecutter, had become by this time one of Cincinnati's leading builders. In 1874 he sold this house to Mordecai Morris White for $83,000. A huge asymmetrical composition, this mansion (now known as **Graveson house**) flaunts on Auburn an extraordinary neo-Baroque entrance. Elaborate stonework surrounds the windows. On Wellington Place the tower boasts equally fine stone carving, as if Graveson wished to show to good advantage the skill of his stonecutters. White, the new owner, was born in North Carolina, the descendent of Quakers and the son of a plantation owner. He graduated from Earlham College in 1850 with a social conscience, for he returned to North Carolina, freed his slaves, and settled them in Indiana. A resident of Cincinnati after 1853, he started a wholesale grocery firm and in 1875, the year he moved into this house, became president of the Fourth National Bank. In 1861 he married Hannah Coffin and in 1911 the couple celebrated here, with an elegant party, their fiftieth wedding anniversary.

Along Wellington Place the attractive Tudor Revival building (1930) houses physicians' offices. The Cincinnati Orphan Asylum, chartered in 1833, stood here from 1861 to 1930. This new structure, first occupied by the orphanage, was a later commission of Samuel Hannaford & Sons. **Tudor Revival,** appearing in Cincinnati around the turn of the century, remained popular for more than three decades. Mount Auburn's architectural heyday had occurred earlier; thus, unlike Clifton, where we shall meet the style in abundance, the Mount boasts few examples. Tudor Revival, which comes in a variety of sizes and variants, mixes half timbering, brick, and stone; stucco often covers the area between the timbers. Tudor Revival structures usually have casement windows; stone carvings appear on the façade. The tower or roofline often culminates in a crenellated parapet, with the roof itself usually of slate. Horizontal, not vertical, is the emphasis: this building hugs the ground. Tudor Revival is a particularly good style for irregular terrain. The original cast- and wrought-iron fence surrounds the property; the original stone gateposts still stand on Auburn Ave.

Wellington Place retains its paving brick. 130, transitional Greek Revival, received at midcentury Italianate brackets and a veranda. 126, a much-modernized Gothic cottage, dates from circa 1837. It still has its cross gable with a pointed finial and pendant.

Wellington Place dead-ends in **Inwood Park.** Inwood Park began as "Shoenberger's Woods," named after George K. Shoenberger, who lived here before building "Scarlet Oaks" in Clifton after the Civil War. Though the house is long gone, its setting remains. A resort and garden followed; in 1904 the city purchased the property for a park. We go past the circular turnaround and down the steps. From both we may divine that the Shoenberger mansion was Italianate.

To the left, a rough-hewn granite **cenotaph** commemorates **Friedrich Ludwig Jahn.** In 1811, during the Napoleonic invasions, Jahn founded in Germany what later became the Turner Society. Through gymnastics, he believed, the *Turnverein* would not only make his oft-defeated compatriots more muscular but instill in them a fuller national consciousness. His aim was as much political as physical. Jahn wished to awaken in Germans a desire for democratic freedom. But after Napoleon's downfall reactionary governments came to power in Germany. In 1819 they banned the Turner Societies for over twenty years and imprisoned *Turnvater* Jahn. After the failure of the 1848 revolutions, those Germans who espoused democratic ideals increasingly found life in the Fatherland precarious. Many fled abroad. It was the "48er," Friedrich Hecker, who instigated the founding in Cincinnati in October 1848 of America's first Turner Society. Jahn's monument, unveiled in 1911, a century after the movement began, today lacks its bronze plaque. The still blooming leaves

Glencoe Place rowhouses. Rowhouses are rarely found in Cincinnati, but these—rehabilitated in the late 1960s—are now the center of a thriving community.

of the shattered oak, a typical Victorian funerary motif, symbolize renewal and rebirth.

Inwood Park, nearly seventeen acres, is scenic and rolling. A 1953 Parks Board publication described it as "a popular park." It mentioned "the artificial lake below, which is stocked with fish during the summer for children to try their hand at a fightin' bluegill or bass." In winter iceskaters pirouetted on its surface. Today the lake is dry, the park little used. Rarely do people walk in Inwood Park or through it or, for that matter, in most of Cincinnati's other parks. Saturdays the ballfield lies idle. But Inwood Park is at least pedestrian oriented. Paved walkways crisscross it. Near the Jahn monument one disappears mysteriously into the forest, another descends to Vine St., a third winds over to Hollister, still another heads south past the ballfield to Glencoe. All make pleasant strolls but we take the last, along the left field foul line. On the far side of the ballfield we descend the steps and turn left. We have arrived in **Glencoe.**

Sequences of two-bay rowhouses, with stoops and incised stonework, sweep sharply down the hill. Who would have expected this? We could be in Baltimore or Boston, cities that have retained more rowhouses than Cincinnati. With each house lower than the next, the rooflines evoke a lyrical stairlike rhythm, the beat repeated by windows, doors, and stoops. Residents crowd the streets in summertime. Even in colder seasons people mill about. With its high population density, Glencoe possesses genuine neighborhood spirit. Above this hillside nook looms Christ Hospital. Formerly Glencoe was known, from the cross that earlier crowned the hospital's cupola, as "Little Bethlehem." "On winter nights," observed the authors of the WPA guide, the poets of post-Depression Cincinnati, "when the steep hillside and the streets and homes of Little Bethlehem are snow-covered, the view of the cross from the streets far down in this valley distinctly resembles the familiar scene on Christmas cards."

We head up the hill toward Auburn Ave. On the right is a small children's park, "View Court." At the far end, incorporated into the rowhouses, is a Richardsonian Romanesque façade with a conical tower and a central gable, on which we read "Glencoe." The façade is all that is left of the hotel built here in 1899. The park offers a convenient place to sit and read the following two paragraphs.

Immigrant families spilling out of Over-the-Rhine originally occupied Glencoe's coldwater flats. According to Carl Westmoreland, "Glencoe, like Hell's Kitchen and Harlem in New York City, housed Cincinnati's German, Irish, Jews and blacks in dark, dank, poorly heated (if at all) overcrowded tenements." The immigrants suffered from exploitation, crime, and lack of fresh air and sunlight. By the mid-1960s few families still lived in Glencoe. A time of crisis had arrived. Community leaders—represented by the Mount Auburn Community Council, the Mount Auburn Good Housing Foundation, Glencoe's remaining families, and the City of Cincinnati—met to determine the neighborhood's future. Rather than bulldoze Glencoe, they decided to make it a place where people would be proud to live. The city used preservation techniques not only to retain Glencoe's architectural heritage but also to maintain its ethnic diversity. 106 large apartments give privacy, and pride, to the community's predominantly black residents. The city, with Bruce Goetzman as architect, created playgrounds, private courtyards, and passive open space. Although it tore down sections of the rowhouses, bricks from the demolished buildings screen parking lots. The demand for the apartments was overwhelming, and, as Westmoreland recalls, Glencoe "became the place to be rather than to be from." Much written-up, Glencoe has received national awards and international recognition.

Great credit for Glencoe's present health must go to **Westmoreland,** a neighborhood organizer who in 1966 helped found and long served as head of the Mount Auburn Good Housing Foundation. Instrumental both in getting the apartments renovated and in Mount Auburn's overall revitalization, Westmoreland explains Glencoe's achievement thus: "One would be hard pressed to duplicate this kind of attitude in traditional public housing because there is little sense of ownership, no sense of accomplishment, and little pride in living in an environment that others do not wish to live in."

We climb back up to Auburn Ave. The simple and spare Italianate villa (1850) on the corner predates Graveson house (no. 2433), one block north, by almost a quarter of a century. Deliberately asymmetrical, it retains, despite recent remodeling, good proportions, a square tower, and a bay with curved windows. On the left gate post we make out **"Sunny Side,"** on the right, the intertwined initials "WHD." Sunny Side was long the residence of **William Howard Doane,** who bought the house in 1879 from Jethro Mitchell. Doane was president of the J. A. Fay Co., makers of woodworking machinery. For his inventions he received the Order of the French Legion of Honor. He earned even greater renown with his hymn collections *Sabbath School Gems, Little Sunbeams, Silver Spray,* and *Songs of Devotion,* that included such favorites as "Tell Me the Old, Old Story" and "Jesus is Mine." Often Doane set music to the poetry of his blind cousin, Fanny J. Crosby, author in her own right of five thousand hymns, including "Rescue the Perishing" and "Safe in the Arms of Jesus." Over his lifetime he acquired a priceless collection of rare and ancient musical instruments. Doane donated this collection, his most enduring legacy, to the Cincinnati Art Museum, where, newly reinstalled in 1987, it ranks among the museum's treasures.

2209 Auburn, dating from about 1858, received in the 1870s a Second Empire mansard roof. Its first owner, Henry Powell, was the son of William Powell, founder of the William Powell Co., now the Powell Valve Company. In the nineteenth century the company, which produced brass pieces for plumbers, steam-fitters, and machinists, also made its share of the pressed metal decoration that we come upon everywhere in Cincinnati. Whereas the veranda pillars of this house are wood, the railings and much other ornamentation are pressed metal. Nineteenth-century homeowners often painted their metal decoration to resemble sandstone. With its elaborate central dormer and mansard roof, this house appears kin to the more ornate Phillip Hinkle mansion across the street.

The **Mount Auburn Baptist Church** (1884), like the Mount Auburn Presbyterian Church on William Howard Taft Rd., replaced an earlier wooden structure (1861). The building's massive lines, solid proportions, and rock-faced masonry reflect the contemporary enthusiasm for Richardsonian Romanesque. Like the Presbyterian Church, this one also draws elements from both Romanesque and Gothic. The tower's rounded Romanesque arch contrasts with its pointed Gothic entrance arch. Crapsey & Brown were the architects.

Christ Hospital's main building (1930), designed by Harry Hake, is a Georgian Revival highrise. A Williamsburg courthouse appears to rise above the roof balustrade. Cincinnatians have long regarded the tower, a glow of light on the night horizon, as a local landmark. Reasonably compatible is the newer wing on the left. The Medical Arts Building, nearer where we stand, complements both buildings. On this site once stood the Mount Auburn Young Ladies Institute, a well-regarded finishing school founded in 1856 by the Rev. E. A. Crawley. Anna Sinton (Taft) was a prized pupil. It boasted high academic standards no less than an up-to-date physical plant lit by gas and heated by steam. In 1889 James N. Gamble, of Procter & Gamble, endowed Christ Hospital downtown in one of the last of his many acts of philanthropy; four years later, moving here, it took over the school buildings.

Hospitals, like universities and other large organizations, tend to gobble up buildings and property around them. Good institutions themselves, they are usually less good for their neighborhoods. Until 1985 the **Johann B. Stallo** house stood at the northwest corner of Auburn Ave. and Mason St. Stallo, long a leader of Cincinnati's German community, was born in 1823 in Oldenburg, Germany. Coming to America in 1839, he studied at St. Xavier's College (now Xavier University) and subsequently taught German there. In 1849 he was admitted to the Cincinnati Bar. Later he became a judge. In 1885 Grover Cleveland appointed him minister to Italy, where he died in 1900. Stallo and Daniel Drake may well have had the finest intellects in nineteenth-century Cincinnati. No single discipline could hold this polymath. One of the Cincinnati Hegelians—the others were August Willich, Peter Kaufmann, and Moncure D. Conway—Stallo introduced the German philosopher's ideas into this country through his landmark study, *The General Principles of the Philosophy of Nature* (1848). His major work, *The Concepts and Theories of Modern Physics* (1881), earned him European no less than American renown. Stallo, according to the American intellectual historian, William H. Goetzmann, was "widely regarded as the most significant philosopher of science in nineteenth-century America."

We turn right down Mason. 111–131 Mason, an attractive sequence of gray stone rowhouses, have unfortunately lost their wooden porches and stoops. 103–109, built earlier, retain their gingerbread roof dormers; originally the corner tower would have risen higher. We turn left on Eleanor Place. The vehicles in Christ Hospital's new parking structure (1986) enjoy a splendid panorama over the city. On the northeast corner of Eleanor Place and Malvern Place, the attractive Elizabethan Revival apartment house (ca. 1880) culminates in an impressive squared dome. The façade's wall dormers rise in curved and stepped gables. Repair work in concrete on the corner bay simulates the façade's original rock-faced masonry.

For those who feel adventurous I recommend the following excursion through **lower Mount Auburn.** We descend the precipitous stairs off Eleanor Place between Huntington and Malvern, then wind along a tangle of less-travelled, but visually fascinating streets that stretch between Vine and Sycamore, before climbing back up to Jackson Hill Park. (Those who lack the half-hour or so this excursion takes may proceed directly to Jackson Hill Park, a hundred yards straight ahead, and pick up this tour on p. 285.)

Few Cincinnatians know lower Mount Auburn. Until I prepared this chapter I had rarely walked its streets. Cincinnati outgrew its Basin before the inclines and trams could provide convenient access to the hills. As Over-the-Rhine filled up, its inhabitants overflowed into these hillside pockets. The irregular terrain forces streets to abandon the grid and go their own ways. The crazy patchwork quilt of streets forms unusually shaped blocks; houses sprout in odd niches. "There is in any old city like ours," writes David McCord of Boston, "no end of undiscovered, secret places of enchantment equivalent to some of the simple but lost things of our own lost youth." Such were my feelings in discovering lower Mount Auburn for the first time. Today a rundown, sparsely populated neighborhood, lower Mount Auburn retains considerable architectural and visual interest. From its streets breathtaking views open up of the city below and of the bluffs above.

The stairs off Eleanor Place put us down on Gage St., which we descend, the bluffs on our right. We turn left on Rice St. Above us tower, now on our left, the bluffs of Jackson Hill Park. At the bottom of Rice, we go left again on Mulberry St. Rehabs and shells exist cheek-by-jowl. Spectacular vistas open up over the city. As Mulberry gradually becomes wider, abandoned buildings increase. Once Mulberry was at the center of a thriving community. Now litter afflicts the eye and offends the nose; bushes force us off the sidewalk, which in places vanishes. Today Mulberry St. cries out for more rehabilitation efforts and for infill housing. Why should it not again become one of Cincinnati's vital streets? We are traversing some of the finest urban terrain in the world—and it looks like a pigpen.

At the intersection with Lang St., we turn left (uphill) to Seitz St. Stairs at the bend lead down to Mulberry, where the Mount Auburn incline began, then to Main St., where we see the Rothenberg School. We, however, go up to Goethe St. Urban aficionados have restored several houses here. More steps, which we take, and we arrive at Dorsey St. These steps are officially closed, unofficially open. Locals use them all the time and we can too. Climbing them saves a long detour, via Sycamore and Dorchester, back to Jackson Hill Park.

Dorsey is the most spectacular of Cincinnati's terraced streets. If we walk east (toward Sycamore St.), we come upon a sequence of tiny, paired Second Empire rowhouses, numbers 211–219. Unlike the stone-fronted houses seen earlier on Mason, they have retained their wooden porticos. A century ago, workmen would have set off from them each morning down the hill to their jobs in the Basin. We walk west along Dorsey. It has even more restored houses than Goethe, almost all of them built against or into the hillside. Grand vistas open up over the Basin. We look at the city below as over a balcony. What would the comparable location in San Francisco, with comparable view, sell for?

The next set of closed-off steps will take us up to Jackson Hill Park. As we climb up the former roadbed of the Mount Auburn incline, a splendid view unfolds over the city, St. John's tower stands prominent and, further off, we discern the half-circle of Union Terminal. Its clock, minuscule at this distance, is actually sixteen feet across. We emerge, panting, on Eleanor Place. To our left lies Jackson Hill Park. Straight ahead, a hundred yards away, are the stairs we descended a short while ago. Our brief excursion is over.

Nearly 250 sets of **stairs** lie within Cincinnati's boundaries. They are the hills' pedestrian tramways, or inclines. But many, fallen into disrepair, the city has blocked off. The concrete treads are cracked or broken, overgrown with weeds, strewn with tree limbs, broken bottles, and litter. Maintenance on open stairs appears minimal or nonexistent. This should not be. The stairs promote pedestrianism and provide the urban resident with a sense of intimacy with the environment. When we climb a stairs, we do not know what we shall find at the top. Like following a curved path or river, the experience suggests the mystery of the unknown. When people can no longer use the stairs, the overall quality of their urban life declines. In the words of Carl Westmoreland: "What separates Cincinnati from other major cities are the steps, and they are essential. San Francisco has beautiful hills, but most access points are on private property. You never really get a good perspective of the hills, valleys and views unless you are in an expensive hotel or restaurant."

Mount Auburn incline, ca. 1880–1885. Built in 1872, the Mount Auburn incline rose 312 feet over its 850-foot length. It was the first of five such inclines, which provided the first effective means of transportation up the city's steep hills. The steps we climb in the Mount Auburn tour are set in the former incline railbed. Courtesy of the Cincinnati Historical Society.

Not so Cincinnati, or not quite. Along with the hilltop parks—Jackson Hill, Bellevue, Fairview—the stairs provide some of the best views. Close them and we find the urban experience diminished.

The inclines, observed D. J. Kenny in 1875, allow pedestrians convenient "starting points for a glorious walk on beautiful roads winding beneath noble trees and skirting green turf." Kenny continues: "Pedestrianism is now being indulged in more than ever before, and it is he alone who can see to the best advantage." Even though urbanites in this country no longer indulge in pedestrianism to the extent they did in Kenny's time, only by walking can we cover a city in depth and in detail.

Cincinnati's hills, along with the Ohio River, remain its topographical glory. I sometimes wonder whether native Cincinnatians sufficiently appreciate the beauty of the landscape around them, the difference it makes to have hills everywhere. Today, those who still value pedestrianism and enjoy exploring the city's hills face frustration at every turn. The hills are more difficult of access than they were a hundred years ago. Granted that in the age of the automobile fewer people walk about the city than before. Probably never again shall we see men and women with baskets descending the steps to shop at Findlay Market. But not everyone has an automobile available all the time; bus routes usually stick to major arteries. The stairs, by helping to crack the grid, create a more humane city. What we might see, if the city maintained them, is increased interaction between hilltops and Basin, ultimately more people inhabiting both. The result might be a more vital city.

The **Mount Auburn incline** (1872), whose roadbed we have just climbed, was a huge success. Immediately it was carrying 600 passengers a day; it remained busy at night and on weekends. Noting that people from other parts of town came to ride it for fun, the owner George Smith decided to build a public place of entertainment that overlooked the brow of the hill. Lookout House, as it was called, opened in autumn 1872. The Mount Auburn incline and **Lookout House** provided a model for the development of other Cincinnati hilltops. Within five years, inclines ascended Mount Adams, Price Hill, Bellevue Hill, and Fairview Heights. With them came the entertainment palaces: on Mount Adams, Highland House; in Fairview, Bellevue House; on Price Hill, the Price Hill House. (This last, initially nonalcoholic, gained Price Hill the dubious sobriquet of Buttermilk Mountain.) Only Fairview Heights lacked a hilltop house. Lookout House was a rectangular frame building, fifty feet wide by one hundred and fifty feet long, with a veranda and balcony, "Plain as a mud scow" in actuality, the house was touted by its hyperbolic manager, Frank Harff, as a magnificent pleasure palace. It contained a saloon, a theater, a concert hall, a restaurant, and a carnival. Harff knew that sustained popularity demanded variety, so he installed bowling alleys, produced fireworks displays, sponsored balloon ascents. An eighty-six piece German band and Swiss yodelers provided musical fare.

The incline houses competed fiercely for customers. In 1877 Harff had shipped by rail from the East, in a specially fitted boxcar, a dwarf white whale, nine feet long and weighing about seven hundred pounds. He exhibited it in a 168,000 gallon tank of salted water. But within a month the whale died. It underwent an "autopsy," which Lafcadio Hearn, ever the anatomist, wrote up for the *Commercial*. Undaunted, Harff had his whale embalmed. He assured the public that it would last another six months. Two days later the whale began to spoil. It had to be hauled off, and Harff spent the next week fumigating. But even dead his whale had drawn attention—and patrons—to Lookout House.

Jackson Hill Park occupies the site of the Lookout House. Few Cincinnatians, lamented the WPA guide in 1943, know about this park. Half a century later the situation has hardly changed. The panorama from Mount Adams to Fairview hill, sweeping 180 degrees, remains as fine as ever. We still have it pretty much to ourselves. Pieces of it we glimpsed in our walk in lower Mount Auburn; here we see it all, or would if the parks department cut back the scrub. To the east, we discern Mount Adams, with Highland Towers and the Rookwood Pottery buildings; to the south, rising above the grid, are Over-the-Rhine's spires and downtown's skyscrapers. Far in the distance the Ohio meanders in a lazy S-curve toward Constance, Kentucky. Across the Millcreek Valley lie the western hills. Fairview rises to the northwest. In Over-the-Rhine the church bells peal faint and distant; for Charles Lamb this sound was "the music nighest bordering upon heaven."

Before leaving Eleanor Place, we notice the sign for Excelsior St. The sign indicates good intentions: the city owns the land but never ran the street through. Although Excelsior goes nowhere, keep the name in mind: we shall encounter it below on Sycamore.

We proceed along Dorchester Ave. and arrive at the intersection where Sycamore St. and Auburn Ave. meet, marked by a mini-"flatiron" building. Across Auburn, the **Henry Martin house** (1870), number 1947, is a three-bay Italianate mansion with a mansard roof. Its brick is an attractive pastel beige. Double hood molds cap the front windows. Quoins delimit the corners. Architecture can be discussed in terms of corners, for the corner treatment, after the cornice on top, often constitutes the most sensitive part of a design. These quoins are chiselled, the lines reversed in alternate quoins; some quoins have been replaced, others are original. In 1888 Henry Martin built the Mount Auburn Cable Railway. It ran from downtown up Sycamore, along Dorchester Ave. past the still-standing cable house at Highland Ave., then down Highland. Martin, a pious Calvinist, chose to observe a workless sabbath, yet recognized that the public needed transportation on Sunday. Faithful to his religious beliefs, he resigned his position as president every Saturday night before midnight; Monday morning he resumed responsibilities. Martin's cable line was one of three cable railways, the others being on Vine St. and on Gilbert Ave. The other two gave up the ghost in 1898. Martin's lasted the longest, fourteen years, to 1902, before it too gave way to electric trams.

The land that comprises **Hopkins Park** was donated by L. C. Hopkins, dry goods merchant and Mount Auburn real estate developer, to the city in 1866 "on condition that it should . . . forever be kept free from buildings, and, within two years from the conveyance, should be tastefully laid out and planted with durable trees and shrubbery, and, besides, be inclosed with a substantial and neat iron rail fence." Such were Hopkins's provisos (as recorded in Sidney Maxwell's 1870 *Suburbs of Cincinnati*). We may judge for ourselves how well the city has kept faith. We walk across the park to Bigelow St., where at 1940–42 lived Edward F. Noyes, governor of Ohio from 1872 to 1874, later ambassador to France. Faced with "insulbrick," the aluminum siding of the 1940s, his house projects a forlorn air. Fronting the park to the south are massive 1880s row houses faced with gray rock-faced masonry. Waist-level tie rods emerge from the unit on Bigelow to our right. If you're wondering whether the rods go all the way through to Auburn Ave., they do!

We walk down Bigelow St. Until 1837 this area was known as Keys's Hill. **1905 Bigelow** (1819), James Keys's own house, is at the end of a private driveway and thus difficult to see. A stucco coating conceals all; tucked within is the original frame structure. "He was my nearest neighbor," recalled Gorham Worth of Keys. "We dwelt together upon the hills that overlooked the city from the north. What a beautiful spot was that on which his house stood." 1902 and 1906 Bigelow introduce us to the domestic architecture of **William Tinsley,** a major midwestern architect of the last century. 1902, a Gothic Revival cottage, was the architect's own house. It appears to have leapt, gingerbread barge board and all, from the pages of Andrew Jackson Downing's classic early Victorian treatise, *Cottage Residences* (1842). 1906, a modest Renaissance Revival, sports the same frieze tassel as its Gothic neighbor. In Clifton we shall encounter two of Tinsley's masterpieces: Calvary Episcopal Church and the Probasco house.

We return along Bigelow, go right down Carmalt St., and at Josephine St., turn right again. Facing the Filson Playground is a huge, graceless Italianate mansion, missing its tower and its veranda. Somewhere near here in August 1788 John Filson, the first surveyor of Cincinnati, looked out over the green valley and imagined the city-to-be. It was Filson, we remember, who named the fledgling settlement "Losantiville," then wisely disappeared into the forest. From Ringgold St. we glimpse across Deer Creek Valley the Art Museum. At the intersection of Young and Slack streets, the 1889 firehouse, rehabilitated into offices, has fine chiselled stonework. Like the Taft School on Southern Ave., the façade proudly displays the names of the commissioners responsible.

The well-landscaped modern building (1980) across the street houses **Great American Broadcasting Co.,** until 1987 Taft Broadcasting. Taft was appropriately located in the suburb that witnessed the flowering of the family fortunes in Cincinnati. By height, scale, and brick, the building blends nicely with its surroundings. Taft Broadcasting began in December 1939, though no one knew it then, when Hulbert Taft, Jr., convinced Hulbert, Sr., editor and publisher of the *Times-Star,* to buy radio station WKRC. In more recent decades, the company also became known for its amusement parks. It retained an interest in King's Island, twenty miles north of Cincinnati on I-71, and owned Coney Island, including Riverbend, the Cincinnati Symphony's summer home since 1984. When in 1987 American Financial Corporation, a Cincinnati holding company owned by Carl H. Lindner, Jr., acquired many of Taft Broadcasting's holdings, it split off the amusement parks except for Coney Island but kept television stations in Birmingham, Kansas City, Mo., Phoenix, and Tampa as well as local WKRC-TV.

Newly restored steps lead down from the end of Young to Boal St. The square base of pink granite on the left once supported an arch. The arch has a story behind it. Originally it formed part of the Hamilton County Courthouse destroyed in 1884 by fire. In the 1950s a wayward car knocked over the arch. Its left base remains; the rest has been stored. Taft Broadcasting once had plans to re-erect the arch. We retrace our steps and go up Young St. **God's Bible School and College,** founded in 1900, contemplates the sinful city below. The houses on Young's west side are now dormitories. 1803 is Renaissance Italianate; 1805–07, eclectic and geometric, reveals Queen Anne massing, shingle-style decoration, and Colonial Revival details; 1811 has popeyed hood molds. The Italianate mansion across the street has been overly restored.

From Ringgold an asphalt path meanders west through the woods. We came out at Walker St., which offers stunning views of Over-the-Rhine. Walker appears uncertain whether to live up to its scenic potential: some houses are redone, others not. We walk to the Sycamore St. end. Just past where Sycamore bends to the south Excelsior St. reappears. Never completed by the city, the street starts up the hill, then stops. Its other end we sighted on Eleanor Place. We now climb back to Auburn Ave.

Our final stop is 2021 Auburn, the **Riddle-Phillips house.** Beautifully set on what may be Mount Auburn's highest elevation, this mansion commands the surrounding landscape. Adam N. Riddle, prominent attorney and state legislator, built it in 1857; upon his death in 1870 it passed to Mrs. Thomas Phillips. After a variety of uses, it has been exquisitely restored by a firm of attorneys. Compared to later, more elaborate Italian villas, this one may appear simple and boxy, though with nice proportions. The tower or belvedere, usually the key element in an asymmetrical plan, is dead center on the south side. Up Auburn Ave. is visible the Taft house, where we began.

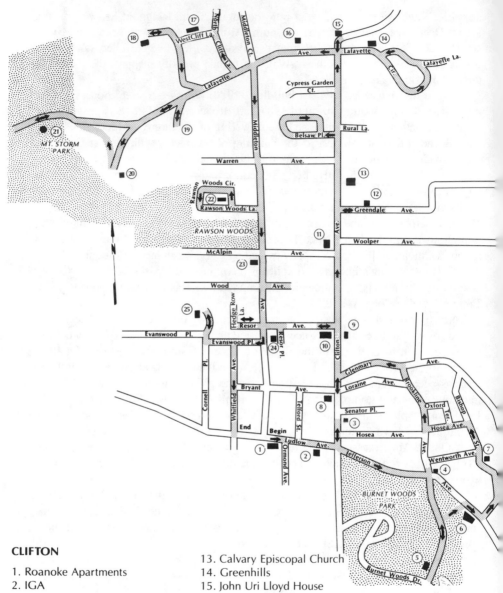

CLIFTON

1. Roanoke Apartments
2. IGA
3. Clifton United Methodist Church
4. Parkview (George B. Cox House)
5. Trailside Museum (Burnet Woods)
6. Parkside Apartments
7. Alexander Lewis House
8. United Presbyterian Church
9. Alfred T. Goshorn House
10. Church of the Annunciation
11. Clifton Public School
12. Greendale (William Resor House)

13. Calvary Episcopal Church
14. Greenhills
15. John Uri Lloyd House
16. Cincinnati Woman's Club
17. Oakwood (Probasco House)
18. Scarlet Oaks (Shoenberger House)
19. "Bishop's Place"
20. The Windings (Neff House)
21. Temple of Love
22. 1 Rawson Woods Circle (Boulter House)
23. 3655 Middleton
24. Battenberry
25. Reuben P. Resor House

10

Clifton

CLIFTON has never lacked admirers. "One of the garden-spots of America," D. J. Kenny called it in 1875, "known as widely as Cincinnati itself." Max Burgheim described it (in German) the same year as "the El Dorado of the aristocracy and the Mecca of all foreign visitors." In Clifton wealthy nineteenth-century Cincinnatians most fully realized the classical ideal of *rus in urbe,* "the country in the town." Twentieth-century observers have been no less kind. The Countess of Chambrun, *née* Clara Longworth (her exaggeration is perhaps thus pardonable), portrayed 1930s Clifton as "the most fabulously beautiful paradise of a suburb in America." After World War II, Clifton struck Alvin Harlow as the "most imperatorial" of all Cincinnati's suburbs, where "lawns were measured by acres and rooms by dozens in the pinnacled chateaux." Even today, Clifton constitutes one of the city's showplaces: rich in history, a wonderland of nineteenth- and early twentieth-century residential architecture. *Rus in urbe* has yielded gracefully to *urbs in horto* (the motto of Chicago!), "the town in the garden." For many Americans, the real *genius loci* of a city—the genius or spirit of a place, that is, the particular qualities that leave an abiding impression—lies in its residential neighborhoods. Clifton, with a *genius loci* definitely its own, will not disappoint.

We begin on Ludlow Ave., a block or two west of its intersection with Clifton Ave. Ludlow is named after Israel Ludlow, who after John Filson's death platted the Cincinnati-to-be. A number of bus routes from downtown (6th and Vine) serve Clifton. If we have taken the Mount Auburn tour earlier in the day, a number 53 bus from Auburn Ave. will bring us to Ludlow, where we get off at Middleton Ave. Clifton's boundaries are Dixmyth on the south, I-75 (following the bed of the Miami and Erie Canal) on the north, Central Parkway on the west, Ruther and Vine streets on the east.

Clifton's first dwellings were farmhouses. Until the early 1840s, the entire area, approximately 1200 acres, was divided among a dozen families. Then a few Cincinnati businessmen built summer residences. The first year-round houses date from later in the decade. In 1850 Clifton was incorporated as a village. Within a few years Cincinnati millionaires had begun to erect their "Castles on the Rhine" off Lafayette

291

Ave. Their presence gave Clifton its wider renown, and Cincinnati began to covet the increasingly prosperous village. After fighting off several attempts at annexation, Clifton finally succumbed to its larger neighbor in 1896, one year after the University of Cincinnati had moved to a site in nearby Burnet Woods. In the 1890s Good Samaritan Hospital established itself in Clifton, as did, a few years later, Hebrew Union College. Until annexation, Clifton had remained almost exclusively residential, a suburb of grand mansions and large estates. Annexation brought further settlement, often in the form of apartment dwellers. Between 1880 and 1910 population soared from about 1000 to 5540. Today about 9000 people call Clifton home. In recent decades the population, a mix of doctors, other professionals, professors, and students, has remained steady. Although most of Clifton's large estates have not survived intact, the twentieth century has been kind. Infill housing aside, the suburb's physical appearance has undergone few major changes. No industry, no slums, no gray areas scar its hills and dales. Even the gaslights, long a familiar presence on Clifton's streets, continue to shed their gentle glow.

For almost a century **Ludlow Ave.** has been Clifton's commercial heart. The business district gradually emerged here in the 1880s and 1890s to support the rapid population growth. Today the streetscape is usually animated: the number of people about indicates a prosperous neighborhood, as do the variety of commercial establishments: a hardware store, bakery, meat market, wine shop, two bookstores, shoe repair place, several restaurants including a natural foods emporium and Uno's pizza (of Chicago fame), a Graeter's, and, in converted storefronts, a branch of the Public Library. There are boutiques too, but not at the expense of utilitarian shops. Main St., U.S.A., if you like, yet tasteful, alive, and thriving. Several establishments have signboards on which Cliftonites leave messages indicating wants and needs.

Clifton Town Meeting, a local group founded in 1961, meets monthly to discuss community issues. (Its nostalgic name recalls the close-knit atmosphere associated with New England villages.) The group, which has no legal authority, is yet capable of exerting considerable political pressure to maintain its conception of Clifton. Recently it prevented Wendy's from establishing a fast-food franchise in the former Esquire Theater, which closed in 1983 while concerned citizens debated its future. (The owners finally caved in and donated the property to the city; in 1990 it again became a theater.) Walking about Clifton, we get a sense of a community both self-aware and self-confident, even a trifle smug in its sense of the rightness of its priorities.

Ludlow Ave., before it received its present name, was known as the old Cumminsville turnpike. If we followed Ludlow west down the hill, we would pass an old Jewish cemetery (founded in 1850) and end up in Cumminsville, the site of Ludlow's Station, a blockhouse built in 1790 to protect the Millcreek crossing. The next year Israel Ludlow laid out streets and built a mill. With the construction in the 1820s of the Miami and Erie Canal, Ludlow's Station grew in importance. The canal trade utilized its stores, hotels, and taverns. An assortment of ruffians populated the village, which became notorious for its brawls and which earned it the sobriquet of "Helltown." "Cumminsville," its name after 1838, honored David Cummins, a local farmer. The Cincinnati, Hamilton, & Dayton Railroad came through in 1851; from

Ludlow Ave., Clifton. The main commercial street of Clifton, Ludlow Ave. achieves its pleasant ambience through low-scale architecture and attractive shops. On the right is the Busy Bee restaurant, in the center is the newly restored Esquire Theater.

its position north of the tracks Cumminsville was sometimes known as "Northside," and that is the name we hear most frequently today. Northside is now cut off by the interstate as well as the tracks. The canal helped make the adjoining hills more easily accessible. Clifton's earliest ties were as much to Cumminsville, the social and economic center of the area, as to Cincinnati.

One of Clifton's numerous older apartment buildings, the Roanoke (359 Ludlow), at the southwest corner of Ormond and Ludlow avenues, is turn-of-the-century Georgian Revival, in plan a modified H. East along Ludlow (at 319), the postmodern façade of Keller's IGA Foodstore makes ironic use of classical forms. Three pediments divide the façade into five main elements that appear to step in and out: an entirely Palladian effect. Such a sequence of "little buildings" relates the IGA to its modest cousins on both sides of the street. The muted color scheme is also postmodern.

We arrive at the intersection of Ludlow and Clifton avenues. The first road through this area, built in 1795, ran from Ludlow's Station up present-day Ludlow Ave., and its extension, Jefferson Ave., to Cincinnati. William Irwin, who had bought the grist mill established by Israel Ludlow on the Millcreek, further opened up the Clifton area about 1814 when he put through a second road—Irwin's Mill Road, later Clifton Ave.—so that people could get to his mill. Here the two roads intersected. The **fire station** (1906), on the southwest corner, is one of several civic improvements that came about after Cincinnati annexed Clifton. Designed by Harry

Hake, who also did the Court St. station (now the Fire Museum), this is an exuberant building. Oversized *voussoirs* (the wedge-shaped stones around the windows) with huge keystones, an exaggerated play on Renaissance rustication, accentuate doorways and windows; a Vitruvian scroll beltcourse, separating the floors, flows along the façade. Across the street, at 302 Ludlow, we discern in the stonework the name "Meyer." Once this building housed Meyer's General Store, the chief emporium between downtown and Cumminsville. Catty-cornered from the fire station, a Flemish Revival structure houses the immensely popular local branch of Skyline Chili.

We walk north along Clifton Ave., past a phalanx of apartment houses, to the Methodist Episcopal Church (1892), now **Clifton United Methodist Church,** whose tower is visible from Ludlow. The building is Gothic, but non-soaring. Like the Mount Auburn Presbyterian Church, the church's heavy lines and massive, rough-hewn stonework indicate a debt to Richardsonian Romanesque. Quatrefoils hover over the Palladian window. The stained glass's prevailing blues are explained by its subject: Christ on the Sea of Galilee.

We return to Ludlow Ave. and proceed east along Jefferson. **260 E. Jefferson** (1902), now an apartment house, was once the Marburg Hotel. We can still make out the name high on the western façade. Georgian Revival like the Roanoke apartments, 260 has a more subtle decorative scheme. Note the wrought- and cast-iron grates before the French windows, the coupled and tripled columns, the two-story oriel windows, and, capping the pediment, a finial. On the third floor, the round-arched window displays fine stained glass. 248 Jefferson, vaguely Spanish Revival, has on its upper floor an art nouveau window: delicate stems support lavender irises. Further along is the **Enoch T. Carson lodge.** Entrance and windows indicate terra cotta's decorative possibilities. The building owes an overall debt to the Italian Renaissance, with Spanish Renaissance influence in its steps and lanterns. A compass appears in each roundel; masonic symbols peep out between the brackets underneath the cornice, among them the sun's rays (the sun rises in the East, where lives the Worshipful Master), Noah's ark (freemasons are known as sons of Noah), a beehive (emblem of industry), and an hourglass with wings (emblem of human life).

"Parkview" (1895), the George B. Cox house, across the intersection with Brookline Ave., is Chateauesque, that is, in the French Renaissance Revival style sometimes known as François Ier or Francis I. On Auburn Ave. we came upon a modest Chateauesque mansion that had Romanesque detailing including rough-cut rusticated walls. This house has the smooth-faced sandstone façade more typical of Chateauesque. It also has wall dormers pinnacled with balusters, a conical "candle snuffer" tower, and on the north side a *porte cochère*. Before the entrance sit two guardant lions, holding shields; they came a little later. George B. Cox, Cincinnati's "boss" from the mid-1880s until his retirement from politics in 1912, had Samuel Hannaford and Sons design Parkview. In 1938, after the death of Cox's wife Caroline, the house came into the possession of the Cincinnati Union Bethel. For a while it served as a woman's dormitory; since 1948 the local Pi Kappa Alpha fraternity has occupied it. Visible from the corner, on Wentworth Ave., is the **C. B. Russell house,** also by Hannaford, a freely adapted Richardsonian Romanesque mansion in rock-faced ashlar. As the Cox house is a study in plane and line, this house is a study in form and texture. Their plans must be similar: each has a wall dormer that faces west, and on each the tower projects at the salient point. The houses are obviously designed to be viewed in relation to one another. With its finial tilted, the onion dome of the Russell mansion looks like a Teutonic helmet askew.

We walk down the hill into **Burnet Woods**. Ducks quack on the picturesque artificial lake. Once it supported a flotilla of rowboats and pedal boats; a motor launch made the circuit; and in 1936 the Federal Theatre set up a floating stage for performances of Gilbert & Sullivan's *H.M.S. Pinafore*. Now the ducks have the lake to themselves. On the southern horizon, the spires of St. George's are barely visible above the treetops. The **Trailside Museum** (1940) is an attractive streamlined stone and wood lodge designed by Karl Freund that rusticizes Frank Lloyd Wright's prairie houses. The Museum presents a sampling of Cincinnati's geology, flora, and fauna.

Cincinnati has not done much with its parks in recent years. Burnet Woods, once the estate of Judge Jacob Burnet, was acquired by the city in 1872 and laid out by Adolph Strauch. It originally extended almost to McMillan St. Today Burnet Woods appears more desolate than most of the city's other parks. It lacks focus, a center. More people drive through it than walk in it. It was not always so. Old prints show pedestrians as well as carriages. The Groesbeck endowment, established in 1875, provided free music in the summer "for all time." But "all time" is no longer. The artificial lake (1875) should be the park's focal point but is not. We walk around it only with difficulty. Like other Cincinnati parks, Burnet Woods once maintained a network of trails. "Chipmunk Hollow Trail," for example, maundered from behind the Trailside Museum through the woods to the bandstand (where the concerts were given) near Clifton Ave. Although the 1943 Cincinnati guide speaks of Chipmunk Hollow Trail as "well-marked," anyone attempting to find, much less follow, this trail today will not get very far. A 1953 Cincinnati Parks booklet mentioned that the Trailside Museum received 25,000 visitors a year; and Philip D. Spiess, a Clifton historian, wrote in 1965 of the museum's "nationally-known nature program." But the city, facing a budget crisis that seriously undercut park funding, closed the Museum in 1981. Seven years later it reopened, staffed by volunteers. But it has never been open when I have come by. Burnet Woods has suffered greater indignities than neglect: the University of Cincinnati has thrice—in 1889, 1914, and 1950— lopped off segments, constituting more than half its original acreage, for campus expansion.

An asphalt path curls back up the hill to Jefferson Ave. We emerge alongside the **Parkside Apartments** (1895), a large shingle-style structure that looks like a turn-of-the-century Adirondacks lodge. It has a stone base, a clapboard first story, and shingles on the second. Delicate attenuated columns hold up balconies; wall dormers protrude above the cornice line; and seamed metal roofs cap the building's three façades on Jefferson, each of which faces a different direction. Outside of the East Coast, large shingle-style structures are rare: the Parkside is unique in Cincinnati.

Two nearby taverns once greeted thirsty Cliftonites returning along Jefferson from Cincinnati. The Brauneis Pavilion occupied the site of the Parkside Apartments; the Clifton House stood at the northeast corner of Jefferson Ave. and Bishop St. The area between Bishop and Clifton Ave., known as "the Hill Farm," was subdivided in 1851. For a time it became Clifton's population center. We turn down Bishop St. 3324–3322 Bishop, Queen Anne (1880) and virtually symmetrical, features a dominating wraparound veranda supported by spindles. Like the Parkside, diverse materials went into its construction: stone base, clapboards (and brick) on the first story, wooden shingles on the second. The pebble arrangement on the plaster pediment panel depicts flowers. The splendid soaring roofline, balanced by its chimneys, corbelling flaring outward, culminates in a magnificent iron weathervane. 3321, opposite, jostles the streetline: the house has a clapboard ground level, a shingled second story, a latticed pediment. A little leaf linden long shaded the south wall. Further along, 3360 Bishop began circa 1840 as the **Alexander Lewis house.** Here were entertained (it is said) Dickens, the Cary sisters, Grant, and William Howard Taft. The house has had numerous additions. The rear wing, originally Federal, is oldest; note the six-over-six windows. 3370 Bishop, hidden behind enormous yews, projects twin Swiss chalet gables.

3384 Bishop is Tudor Revival or Neo-Tudor or Jacobethan. The terms are virtually synonymous. In Clifton **Tudor Revival** began about 1910 and for several decades flourished mightily. More than any other twentieth-century domestic style, Tudor Revival suggests coziness and comfort, as much through the materials—timber, stone, stucco, slates—as through the manner in which the builder has juxtaposed them. Nineteenth-century estheticians thought that architectural beauty resulted from the "associations" a cultivated person felt in the presence of different historical styles. A Tudor-style villa, for example, evoked in the mind a vision of the half-timbered houses of "Merry Olde England" in the days of Elizabeth I. In its configurations it also relates to seventeenth-century Colonial houses. During the first third of the twentieth century Tudor Revival was the style of preference for Americans of Anglo-Saxon origin. In effect, it threw down the gauntlet of anglophile values to the teeming immigrant masses from southern and eastern Europe. Tudor Revival in America derives from the English architect Richard Norman Shaw. His "Arts and Crafts" buildings of the 1860s and 1870s inaugurated the British Queen Anne style, a direct progenitor, along with the English cottage, of American Tudor Revival. Tudor Revival houses are often superbly landscaped. Here junipers set off the curved fieldstone walkways. Deciduous trees (shag-bark hickory and beech) contrast with evergreens. Rocks circle the base of the trees, which, in turn, frame the house. We go left on Hosea Ave.

103 and 106 Hosea, opposite each other, reflect Swiss chalet influence. Both feature a dominant overhanging central gable. Huge wooden brackets support that of 103; on 106 we discover an acorn drop below the gable's point. The acorn motif once symbolized the new nation.

Gaslights line Hosea Ave., as they do many of Clifton's residential streets. They first appeared in 1812 in London's West End, where they caused a sensation. Primitive lighting systems had existed before, but essentially cities in earlier times were lit by no more than moonlight. In America gaslights were first introduced in

Baltimore in 1818. In all, Clifton has over 250 of Cincinnati's nearly 1200 remaining gaslights. Gaslight service began in 1875; the earliest lamppost I have found in Clifton with a year on it dates from 1892. Lampposts come in different styles; one common pattern has vines and tendrils creeping up the shaft. The lamps give off a soft light, particularly attractive in mist or light rain; some hum with a soft whir. A walk through Clifton in the evening can still evoke a nineteenth-century ambience. A few gaslights retain a metal circle on the side closest to a house: it prevents light from shining into bedrooms. The community has fought many a hard battle over the years to keep its gaslights.

We turn right down Brookline Ave. No. 3482, a huge Italianate confection set on a hill, is painted beige with putty-colored hood molds, both round arched and segmental. 164 Glenmary Ave. (1889), at the intersection, thinks of itself as an Elizabethan manor house. It has an interesting curved stick-style gazebo to which is attached a *porte cochère* with sleeping porch above. Further along, 218 (1890) sits well back from the street behind a knoll. The house achieves a strong vertical emphasis with high chimneys, a conical tower, and the triangles culminating in a pyramid.

Across Clifton Ave. is Immanuel Presbyterian, now **United Presbyterian Church.** The original rock-faced building fronting the street dates to 1883; the rear wing, rock faced also and including the tower, was rebuilt in 1926. Halfway up the tower, fieldstones surround a rosette window; a crenellated parapet tops the tower. The two parts blend together awkwardly.

Clifton Ave. and the streets running off it boast one of the finest concentrations of country villas in the United States. They come in most nineteenth- and early twentieth-century revival styles: Greek Revival, Italianate, Romanesque, Gothic, Flemish Revival, Chateauesque, Tudor, and Colonial. A style rarely appears in a "pure" example; more likely, we find combinations and variations. **"Eclectic,"** a catchall but useful word, defines many stylistic hybrids. We need not regard eclecticism negatively. At its worst, it unimaginatively copies and combines elements from the past; at its best, however, it puts them together in new and original ways. Architecture, wrote Sir Joshua Reynolds in 1786, affects "the imagination by means of association of ideas." For nineteenth-century architects, the more ideas evident in a building, it sometimes seems, the better was its architecture. Clifton Ave. began as a mud track to William Irwin's mill; eventually it became a country lane, then a treelined entry into a domain of the wealthy. Old photographs show elms arched over a narrower street. No more, for the city has widened the roadway and would—if not prevented by pressure from Clifton Town Meeting—widen it further.

Suburbanization began both nationally and in Cincinnati as a predominantly upperclass phenomenon. Americans then as now felt an inchoate longing for a more "natural" environment. This pattern not only followed English tradition, where the noble and wealthy retreated in summer to their country estates, but went back even further to the Italian tradition of *villeggiatura,* developed during the Renaissance, when the privileged of Rome, Venice, and Florence withdrew to their country estates for a summer of leisure. Like their European forebears, the wealthy in America acquired farmland beyond the city limits on which they built summer cottages. Enjoying country life, they enlarged or replaced the cottages with imposing year-round mansions. New owners vied with each other in landscaping their grounds. Country became suburb. "High moral qualities were assigned . . . to this supplementation of urban residence," writes Anselm Strauss; "summer in the country was a counter-weight to winter in the city." Wealthy Cincinnatians also wished, as Henry D. Shapiro and Zane L. Miller have observed, "to escape from the heat of city and to protect themselves and their families from the endemic and epidemic diseases, including Autumnal Fever and the dread Cholera." The persistent antiurban strain in American civilization has thus legitimate medical reasons as well as deep psychological roots. American cities were being abandoned even as they were being built.

We stop to look at **3540 Clifton Ave.** In 1888 James W. McLaughlin designed this rock-faced sandstone house, as much eclectic as Romanesque, for Colonel Alfred Traber Goshorn. Swirling decoration in incised stone surrounds the main entrance, over which extends a metal hood. A skylight caps the octagonal extension in which Goshorn placed his art collection. A huge Victorian urn adorns the lawn.

McLaughlin and Goshorn characterize Cincinnati's Victorian vitality: McLaughlin as one of its premier architects, Goshorn as one of its more colorful personalities. Each had fingers in numerous pies. **McLaughlin,** born here in 1834, studied architecture with James Keys Wilson, architect of the Wise Temple. Although he designed many residences, McLaughlin remains best known for his public and commercial commissions: St. Francis Seraph (1859), Shillito's, now Lazarus (1877), the old Hamilton County Courthouse (1887), the old Cincinnati Public Library (1869), and the original buildings of the Cincinnati Art Museum (1886) and Art Academy (1887). Not coincidentally, Goshorn, the director of the last two institutions, gave him the commission for his new home.

Goshorn was a Cincinnati industrialist who with his two brothers ran the Anchor White Lead Co., which made the white lead used for white paint; subsequently, it merged with the National Lead Company. So exceptional were his organizational skills that in the 1870s Cincinnati's business leaders picked him to head several of the city's industrial expositions. Success here attracted national attention: Goshorn was chosen to direct the 1876 Centennial Exhibition in Philadelphia, at which he did such an outstanding job that he received decorations from fourteen nations including a knighthood from Queen Victoria. The honor may have gone to his head. Cincinnati's only knight strutted about Clifton sporting mutton-chop whiskers, expensive white vests, a gold-headed cane, and a top hat. On formal occasions his chest blazed with stars and medals, from the Royal Swedish and Norwegian Order of the Pole Star to the Imperial Japanese Order of the Rising Sun of the Meiji. The WPA guide ferreted out the following bit of gossip: "It is said that his family name was originally Goosehorn and that a local paper once ran a story headed with an allusion to this change in name: 'Goose by name and goose by nature, but Gosh by legislature.'" Sir Alfred had the distinction of introducing to Cincinnati, notes Philip Spiess, "the Eastern Seaboard custom of eating pie with a fork." A more substantial distinction was his long tenure as first director of the Cincinnati Art Museum.

The hexastyle (six-columned) front of the **Church of the Annunciation** (1931), across the street, makes it look like a classical temple. The attenuated Ionic columns give the building a narrow aspect. Note the roofline *anthemions,* i.e., decorations based on the honeysuckle or palmette leaf, and in the center the acroterion. Above the side door on Resor Ave., a stone bas relief depicts an apparently composite bird, part eagle, part flamingo. More likely it is a pelican feeding her chicks, a Christian icon for Christ sacrificing Himself for His flock. The nursing pelican on the Central Trust Tower façade (chapter 4) is more lifelike. On Resor's other side stands **St. John's Unitarian Church.** Its congregation spun off in the nineteenth century from a German Lutheran parish at Elm and 12th streets. The front addition of St. John's is simple and highly symbolic: it includes three projecting vertical window slits that admit sunlight only at the year's equinoxes. We return to Clifton Ave. and continue walking northwards.

Before the drive to Clifton Elementary School we come upon imposing wrought-iron gates. The lotus pattern has vague art nouveau echoes. In the 1870s Alexander McDonald, starch manufacturer, oil magnate, banker, and philanthropist erected here a splendid thirty-five room mansion, "Dalvay," that, according to the Countess de Chambrun, outclassed all other Clifton mansions in size and luxury. It was bought in 1920 by George K. Balch, who put up the gates; in 1961 the city tore the mansion down for the school. To the east a splendid view opens up over the trees.

McAlpin Ave., previously Central Ave., was run through in the 1850s. Across it is **Clifton Public School** (1906), Renaissance Revival. The architect is E. H. Dornette. A cupola crowns the school's squared dome. The buff-brick façade, in five sections, steps in and out, with the two wings stepping out furthest. This building replaced the Resor Academy (1870), erected through the generosity of William Resor, which itself had replaced an earlier school. For a time this intersection became the de facto village center. But Cliftonites, wishing to retain the village's residential character, prevented a central business district from growing up here. Behind the school is the modern Clifton Community Center (1977), compatible with it in brick color and in its red-tiled roof.

Before Clifton School stands the **Probasco Fountain** (1887), designed by Samuel Hannaford, a simple granite creation crowned by a bronze toadstool. "Thirsty and ye gave me drink" the inscription reads. "Me" may have been Henry Probasco's horse. Rumor has it that the quadruped drank deeply at the Tyler Davidson Fountain; by the time it reached Clifton, where its owner lived, its thirst needed further quenching. So Probasco, who provided the Tyler Davidson Fountain downtown, donated the second fountain. A charming story, well told by Philip Spiess, but unlikely. Note the troughs for dogs. With the widening of Clifton Ave. the fountain abuts the street rather too closely.

Just after Clifton School, somewhat in the distance, appears an **Italianate mansion** (ca. 1867), difficult to see except when the leaves have fallen. Painted beige and olive green, it blends with nature's colors. In *The Architecture of Country Houses* (1850) Andrew Jackson Downing, nineteenth-century propagandist for rural living, advocated natural colors for Italianate houses: tan, gray, brown, taupe, the colors of stone. Trim would have been of a slightly different hue. Today most Italianate houses are painted a most unhistoric white, a color Downing deemed too "glaring" and conspicuous "in contrast to the soft green of foliage." He disliked white on pictorial grounds because it clashed rather than harmonized with the landscape. A house, according to Downing, "must nestle in, grow out of the soil." White houses could not do this. White, the color of marble, is historically correct for Greek Revival, where it reflects the neoclassical desire to imitate stone buildings in wood, but not correct for most other Revival styles.

"Intense sensitivity to the landscape was a pervasive motif of the aesthetic life of nineteenth-century America," Jane B. Davies has pointed out. "Expressed in literature and in the work of the Hudson River school of painters, it was also evidenced by a greatly increased interest in landscape gardening." By midcentury Downing had established the principles of the asymmetrical, picturesque house set within a landscape designed for it. His writings popularized ideas about landscape that Frederick Law Olmsted subsequently put into practice in his park plans. Downing's ideas were taken up at midcentury by an expanding middle class of merchants and entrepreneurs. He and his followers educated them to a more sophisticated taste in landscape than has prevailed at any time since in this country. In *Homes of the New World* the Swedish author Fredrika Bremer, visiting America in 1850, observed: "Nobody, whether he be rich or poor, builds a house or lays out a garden without consulting Downing's works."

Downing sought to harmonize architectural styles with the landscape. House and landscape existed, for him, in a symbiotic relationship. Following eighteenth-century and Romantic esthetic theory, he distinguished sharply between the "picturesque" and the "beautiful." The picturesque, taking inspiration from the dark, brooding canvases of Salvator Rosa, was marked (in the words of George B. Tatum) "by irregularity, abruptly broken contours, and by rough and irregular shapes." The beautiful, harking back to the landscapes of Claude Lorrain and Poussin, displayed (Tatum again) "a preponderance of gently flowing lines, roundness and regularity, balance and symmetry, perfection and repose." Given Clifton's undulating topography, it was Downing's concept of the beautiful that held primary appeal here. In his view, the Italian or Tuscan villa, which he considered a "direct offspring of Grecian art," was the proper architectural companion to the beautiful in landscape gardening. Downing and other mid-nineteenth-century theorists wished to recreate in America an older conception of a house as essentially a country residence established and maintained by a person of means and discriminating taste.

As early as the first century B.C. wealthy Romans built country houses outside their cities. Toward the end of the fourteenth century it became the fashion for wealthy Florentines to retreat to villas in the Tuscan hills and there engage in learned conversation. American villas recall Renaissance villas. Although the Italian villa as recreated in America retained classical details, it allowed an irregular floor plan that suited the utilitarian demands of mid-nineteenth century American households.

Even more beautifully sited, at the end of a long curving drive, is **3767 Clifton Ave.** (ca. 1870) next door, another Italian villa. Acquired by Joseph Rawson in 1876, it long maintained on its grounds Clifton's last surviving farm and farmhouse (the latter best seen from McAlpin Ave.). The tower bull's-eye windows play off against those on the roof. Paired brackets support the cornice. The ground-floor

3767 Clifton Avenue. This splendid Italian villa of the late 1860s, bought by Joseph Rawson in 1876, is set back from the road and reached via a winding drive.

windows are round arched; those above, segmental. Like the Italian villa we have just passed, this one is asymmetrical, irregular in massing, though less rich in color and texture. In its varied shapes and fractured surfaces, it appears to identify with the landscape. But the landscape was also meant to identify with the house.

The Rawson villa and its neighbor to the south embody Downing's ideas regarding the beautiful. Both are set back from the road and reached by a winding drive. Originally they would have been freestanding, without shrubbery or trees blocking a view of their lines. They depended on discreet landscaping to set them off. The idea of the villa, after all, gives special significance to the garden. In his *Remarks on Forest Scenery* (1791) William Gilpin, the eighteenth-century chronicler of the picturesque, had discussed trees as esthetic objects. Echoing this discussion, Downing in his *Treatise on the Theory and Practice of Landscape Gardening* (1841) divided trees into two groups: round-headed ones were beautiful; pointed ones, picturesque. Trees and shrubs—and urns—should be set singly and in groups at designated places on the grounds to achieve the effect desired.

The Rawson house and its neighbor also suggest Clifton's scale in the decades after the Civil War. Most properties came with ten to thirty or more acres. However impressive we may find Clifton's mansions yet unseen, we must remember that they have lost the ample grounds that once surrounded them as well as the landscaping that set them off—and the drama that both grounds and landscaping supplied. Whether we are contemplating a country house, a highrise, or a public building we should not ignore the relationship of architecture to landscape. With regard to country houses, in most cases—certainly in Clifton—where the house has not greatly changed, the setting has been altered almost beyond recognition. These two Italianate houses, situated in their spacious grounds, form an exceptionally well-preserved composition.

We turn down Greendale Ave., opposite, to number 254, **"Greendale,"** which gave its name to the street it eventually fronted. Replacing a summer cottage dating to 1843, Greendale was originally built about 1848 as a Greek Revival cube by William Resor, whose Phoenix Foundry made a variety of iron products. One of the first Cincinnati businessmen to settle in Clifton, Resor prided himself on his well-kept grounds, which Sidney Maxwell spoke of in 1870 as the "crowning beauty of his premises." In the flowery Victorian manner, Maxwell rhapsodized over "the long and graceful drive . . . ; the noble forest trees; numerous and rare evergreens, and the broad lawn, covered with the richest tapestry of nature's loom, and interspersed with the choicest flowers and plants." All combined to "captivate the spectator at once." About the time Maxwell wrote, Greendale metamorphosed, with a mansard roof, to Second Empire. Its roof cresting, along with the hexagonal roof slates, remains intact. The wraparound veranda with its attractive circular corner gazebo, supported by cast-iron columns (and once glassed), dates from this time. Updated again in 1885, the house was reoriented in 1893 to face Greendale Ave., newly cut through.

232 Greendale, a few doors down, dates to about 1910. Hall and Burroughs, a local firm, designed this house. With its stucco exterior, broad eaves, narrow vertical rectangular windows (those on the ground floor with their original mullions), and overall angularity, 232 recalls Frank Lloyd Wright's Prairie houses. The pent eave, reminiscent of eighteenth-century Georgian architecture, accentuates the horizontal emphasis. We return to Clifton Ave., turn right, and continue northwards.

Calvary Episcopal Church, despite the "1867" visible above the entrance, was not dedicated until January 1868. William Tinsley, whose work we encountered in Mount Auburn, designed this asymmetrical church in Early English Gothic. It was built by Isaac Graveson. Calvary bears a familial resemblance to Tinsley's earlier Christ Church (1862) on Monument Circle, Indianapolis. Henry Probasco and George K. Shoenberger, whose mansions we shall come upon soon, helped finance Calvary. The spire is of freestone, not the less durable slate; its pattern suggests clapboarding. Spangled with trefoils and quatrefoils, the spire sends the eye soaring skywards. Each of the church's gables has a bull's eye within a trefoil. The west window drew its inspiration from the "Five Sisters," a thirteenth-century window in the north transept of York Cathedral. Tinsley twice signed the building with his W and T monogram: on a corbel in the interior and at the end of the right-hand boss (below the stained glass window) on the exterior of the south transept. Samuel Hannaford and Sons designed the parish house (1925) behind.

3779 Clifton, combining stone with half timbering and stucco, is a superb example of Tudor Revival. The façade steps in and out; the massive chimney, set on a diagonal, has fine carved stonework; a Tudor arch surmounts the double door; and small casement windows with diamond glazing (mullions on a diagonal grid) peek out at irregular intervals. Capping the entire composition is a variegated, many-gabled slate roof. The design is free flowing, yet integrated. The architect made this house look low and earthbound by deemphasizing the walls. In places the gables descend so low they appear to join the foundation. Tudor Revival's stress on the horizontal is contemporaneous with Frank Lloyd Wright's comparable stress in his Prairie houses. Indeed, Wright did a few Tudor Revival houses in the 1890s, and his Prairie houses feature Tudor elements. A ground-hugging house like 3779 also recalls, in its contours and solidity (though not in size), cottages in England's Cotswolds.

As so often with Tudor Revival, the landscaping is shaped to rise in gentle undulations. Here it is masterfully done. The planting of shrubs around the foundations of houses began in late Victorian times. The Italian villas we have just seen would have been left (as they remain) freestanding, though they would have had ornamental plantings near the house and on the lawns. Here the eye curls up the hill, to variegated shrubbery, out of which, with an air of the inevitable, rises the house.

We continue north on Clifton Ave. The cottage just before **Belsaw Place** has an unusual brick pattern. Rows of headers alternate with rows of stretchers, the latter almost twice as high as the headers: an effect curious and pleasant. A tour of Belsaw Place, a Tudor Revival enclave, allows us to sample the style in all sizes, shapes, and combinations. The two most opulent designs crown the hill.

3842, on the opposite side of Clifton, sports a handsome three-sided jigsaw porch or **veranda.** It is the house's salient architectural feature. Without a veranda, A. J. Downing stated categorically in *The Architecture of Country Houses,* "no country house is tolerable in the United States." Seldom found in England, the veranda seemed to Downing "indispensable" in America's warmer climate. The veranda also went a step further than the bay or oriel window in uniting the house's interior with external nature. With the addition of awnings or shades one had a well-protected outdoor living space. Herman Melville was an admirer of verandas, which, like many of his contemporaries in this country, he called "piazzas." For him they somehow combined "the coziness of in-doors with the freedom of out-doors."

The next house along, 3850 Clifton (ca. 1860), reveals behind the trees massive stone chimneys. 3858, from the turn of the century, displays at least three different kinds of shingles along with a sharply raking gable. Two eyebrow windows (with fanlike decoration no less!) peer out from the roof. Next, 3874, with the square tower, is probably Clifton's oldest standing dwelling. **Robert Buchanan,** who bought forty-three acres here from Nicholas Longworth, built this summer cottage in 1843. Buchanan (1797–1879), a cousin of the President, began as a "produce and commission merchant," went into cotton manufacturing, invested in steamboats, and became president of the Commercial Bank. He presided over the Western Academy of Natural Science until its merger in 1871 with the Cincinnati Society of Natural History. As a hobby he experimented with grapes and strawberries. His *Culture of the Grape and Wine Making* (1850) went through several editions; Longworth contributed an appendix containing "directions for the cultivation of the strawberry." In 1843 Buchanan organized the Cincinnati Horticultural Society. The year following he was the guiding force behind the establishment of Spring Grove Cemetery. Subsequently, in collaboration with Adolph Strauch, he made it a showcase for the picturesque. For several decades the Horticultural Society exerted considerable influence in shaping the suburban Cincinnati landscape, as a Philadelphia correspondent testified in the 1860s: "As a center for correct taste in rural architecture, landscape gardening, and the various arts that are associated with suburban and rural life, Cincinnati is a long way in advance of Philadelphia, New York or Boston, and all chiefly owing to the importance which the leading men of the city, years ago, attached to the operation of a live horticultural society." Varied and challenging were the occupations and interests that Cincinnati, the most dynamic young city of the trans-Appalachian West, could offer an energetic man like Robert Buchanan in the pre-Civil War decades!

"Brightside" (no. 3892), at the corner of Clifton Ave. and Layfayette Circle, is in style circa 1900 Georgian Revival. A semicircular portico sets off two-story paired Ionic pilasters; the semicircular attic window echoes the portico and the huge oriel window below it. Adamesque decoration of garlands, swags, and sunburst motifs abounds. Quoins firmly anchor this somewhat busy exterior.

We turn right into Lafayette Circle. Robert Buchanan also put number 230, **"Greenhills"** (ca. 1848), on his estate. Originally a Greek Revival cube, Greenhills became an Italian villa twenty years later. The main entrance once faced west; the present main entrance was a side door. A bull's-eye window pierces the projecting gable. Metal cresting is set around the mansard roof, the circular openings of which echo those in the hood molds as well as the bull's eye. A tower balances the composition. Buchanan, an ardent horticulturist, sensitively landscaped the grounds. From his verandas the prospect opened out, as Sidney Maxwell observed in 1870, "upon the extensive and elegant improvements of Clifton, Mt. Auburn, and Avondale"; to the north he looked over "the Millcreek Valley, with its varied spectacle of village and farm, cultivated fields and distant forest-covered hill." Though Maxwell does not specify Spring Grove Cemetery, it would have provided Buchanan, president of its board of directors for thirty-five years, with his favorite view.

The Georgian Revival structure (1915) at the top of Layfayette Circle formerly housed the Abbe Meteorology Observatory. In 1868 Dr. Cleveland Abbe came to Cincinnati to direct the Mount Adams Astronomical Observatory, where he was soon focusing his energy more on forecasting weather than on charting the stars. In 1869 Abbe issued the first regular weather bulletins in the United States. The next year he left Cincinnati for Washington to become head of the newly established U.S. Weather Bureau.

Standing on one of Clifton's highest points, we proceed (right) around Lafayette Circle. To the south, east, and north the land drops off precipitously. Houses date from the first half of this century; no two alike, yet they work as an ensemble. Opposite number 150, down Lafayette Lane, Cincinnati's chief cluster of low, flat-

Dupee house (1959), Lafayette Lane. This is one of a cluster built after World War II in a secluded, wooded area of Clifton. Such houses are meant to be unobtrusive—to be seen in a natural environment, not on rectangular suburban lots. Buried in the shade in summer, they blend into nature.

roofed, rectangular **Modern Movement houses** from the 1950s and 1960s lies hidden in the forest. Wooden walls and large expanses of glass relate inside to outside. We are meant to view the scene, not from the outside looking in, but from the inside looking out. Frank Lloyd Wright conceived of a house not as an intrusion upon the landscape but as an integral part of it. These residences are meant to be unobtrusive, to be seen in a natural environment, not on rectangular suburban lots. In summer, buried in shade, they blend into nature.

We return to Clifton Ave. To the north looms the huge Romanesque Revival **John Uri Lloyd house.** Commanding the crest of the hill, it gives a resounding climax to the avenue. Designed about 1885 by James W. McLaughlin, this mansion of rock-faced sandstone loosely adapts Richardsonian Romanesque forms. On the left, the slate roof sweeps dramatically down past a roof dormer; below it, two red granite columns set off the deliberately off-center entrance. On the right, a round-arched window balances the entrance porch. In between, a conical tower perches on half of an octagonal base; though not centered, the tower gives the house the effect of symmetrical asymmetry. Projecting from the east façade is a second-story enclosed sleeping porch. McLaughlin built this house for Solomon P. Kenyon, a coal baron. After 1908 it was owned by John Uri Lloyd, pharmacist, scientist, teacher, book collector, author not only of scholarly works but of widely popular novels, among them, *Stringtown on the Pike* and *Warwick of the Knobs,* that depict rural life in turn-of-the-century northern Kentucky.

Clifton Ave., this section of it known earlier as Crescent, meanders down the hill. At the bottom was Mummert's Basin, part of the Miami and Erie Canal, where

John Uri Lloyd house. Prominently set at the highest point of Clifton Avenue, this Roman-esque "castle" (ca. 1885) is seen by all before they descend to the Millcreek Valley. James McLaughlin, one of the city's important nineteenth-century architects, designed this house. It was later purchased by Lloyd, a noted pharmacologist and author, and founder of the Lloyd Library.

canalmen could turn around or store their boats. It became a favorite swimming hole for Clifton youths. On the other side of the canal and the Millcreek, the Cincinnati, Hamilton, & Dayton Railroad began operations in 1851. Its coming eased commu-nications to Cincinnati and made Clifton an even more desirable place for city busi-nessmen to live. They descended the hill to Winton Place, or went down Ludlow Ave. to Knowlton's Corner in Cumminsville, to catch trains into the city. (The Win-ton Place Depot survives, not on its original site, but in Sharon Woods Village north of Cincinnati.) A commuter as well as a through line, the CH&D followed the curve of the Millcreek Valley and opened up for suburban settlement communities such as Glendale further north.

We retrace our steps and turn in on **Lafayette Ave.** The land here once formed part of "The Clifton Farm," a 510-acre property owned in the 1830s by Charles S. Clarkson. During the 1837 Depression Clarkson mortgaged his land to the Lafayette Bank, which in 1842 foreclosed and subdivided it. In 1844 the Bank, to make indi-vidual lots more saleable, ran Lafayette Ave. through the center of the tract. Lafa-yette became home to Cincinnati's wealthiest. After 1870, observe Henry D. Shapiro and Zane L. Miller, the colossal mansions off Lafayette, rather than the older houses along Clifton Ave., came to symbolize the suburb. Architecturally, Greek Revival and Italianate gave way to Romanesque and Gothic. Though the early houses are imposing, Shapiro and Miller note, "only the homes begun in the late 1850s and completed in the 1860s truly strive for the monumental." "Pretentious and consciously baronial," they were designed to be seen, to awe the city. This is particularly evident in the site selection. Whereas the earlier Italianate houses are set midway up a slope, the later Gothic and Romanesque castles dominate a summit. Downing had argued against imitating English manor houses; America was a republic, he insisted, and its houses had to reflect republican constraint and lack of ostentation. But the conspicuous materialism of the Gilded Age that succeeded the Civil War made such idealism less fashionable.

Several of these castles still stand. One that no longer does is "Sunflower Place," the home of George W. McAlpin, one of the founders of the department store on 4th St. that still bears his name. It stood on the north side of Lafayette Ave., the site now occupied by the **Cincinnati Woman's Club** (1967). Decoration is sparse on this undernourished Georgian Revival structure. Single keystones decorate the brick voussoirs. Whatever energy Georgian Revival lacked as a style by this time, the Woman's Club does convey a certain serenity. The landscaping, a vast, gently rolling lawn with trees placed at designated intervals, reinforces the serenity. Energy, however, characterizes the Woman's Club itself, which goes back to 1894 and which over the decades has actively worked for Cincinnati's good.

Across the street stands a Tudor Revival house with fraternal twin gables: one with chimney within, one with chimney without. In 1888 Lucian Plympton, better known for his Swiss chalets, designed **341 Lafayette,** opposite the Woman's Club entrance, in a more or less Queen Anne style. It is utterly asymmetrical, with a veranda resting on plump columns, out of which rises a splendid squat circular tower capped by a finial. Next, number 363, Tudor Revival and superb, dates from 1914. Arthur Heun of Chicago was the architect. The house has a pronounced, beautifully modulated horizontal emphasis. A vastly oversized English Cotswold cottage, it appears to emerge out of its hillock. Four interlocking roofs on the left, each higher than that previous, accentuate the house's horizontal movement. They are balanced on the right by a five-part arcade; the final arch stretches out nearly twice as wide as the four previous. But landscaping, so essential for Tudor Revival, is here inadequate. We continue along Lafayette, then turn in (right) on North Cliff Lane, from which a vista opens over the Millcreek Valley. North Cliff Lane curls left and becomes West Cliff Lane, which is dominated by number 430, the **Probasco house.**

William Tinsley, architect of Calvary Episcopal, designed this splendid mansion for Henry Probasco. Isaac Graveson provided the stone and was the builder. Probasco chose Tinsley over Isaiah Rogers as his architect, persuading him to leave Indianapolis for Cincinnati. Erected from 1859 to 1866 in a modified Norman Romanesque Revival design, the house, known as "Oakwood," is Tinsley's only Romanesque design. It is a resounding success. Oakwood remains Gothic, however, in its original massing and in its overall plan, which owes something to A. J. Davis's Hudson River villas. Tinsley may have been the first architect, working locally, to unite in a private house limestone and sandstone. He set sandstone blocks, beige and golden tan, within limestone borders. Other Cincinnati architects subsequently

Probasco house. Here lived the donor of the Tyler Davidson Fountain, Henry Probasco. A major midwestern architect, William Tinsley, designed this mansion, completed in 1866 and one of Cincinnati's grandest, in an essentially Norman Romanesque style. Originally the house sat in thirty acres of landscaped grounds.

adopted this practice. Floral and geometric designs characteristic of Romanesque stonework surround Oakwood's front entrance. The foliated frieze above the bay window becomes a first-story balcony. On the gable we barely make out the initials "HP" and "JA" (for Henry Probasco and his wife Julia Amanda) and the date "1860." Also visible is a "T" over a "W," William Tinsley's monogram. A concave octagonal roof caps the round tower, which culminates in an elaborate weathervane.

This is a very long house. Circulation within is on a cruciform plan. Among the ground-floor rooms are a French drawing room, a German sitting room, and an English paneled library with ceiling frescoes usually attributed to Francis Pedretti. Pedretti, who had worked with Isaiah Rogers on New York's Astor House, came to Cincinnati with Rogers to decorate the Burnet House. He is considered the first significant decorator to have worked in the trans-Appalachian West. Henry Lindley Fry and William Henry Fry, leaders along with Benn Pitman of Cincinnati's impressive woodcarving community, spent three years carving the monumental staircase. With its elaborate geometric and floral motifs, no two balusters alike, it is an extraordinary example of the Cincinnati school of American woodcarving. Second-floor rooms radiate off a skylighted central octagon with a minstrel's gallery. To the left is the service wing, added after 1872, itself the size of many a house. Probasco knew he would never have to look upon an industrial area. Oakwood, like other mansions north of Lafayette Ave., faces the green vales of Spring Grove Cemetery. This house is one of America's great suburban villas. Though hemmed in by infill housing, it is in a superb state of preservation.

Born in 1820, **Henry Probasco** came at age fifteen to Cincinnati, where he obtained a job as clerk in the Tyler Davidson Co., a leading hardware firm and major supplier of tools to Cincinnati's metalworks industry. By 1840 Probasco, now married to Davidson's half-sister Julia, had become a partner; by 1846 the company had become the city's largest hardware concern. After Davidson's death in 1865, Probasco sold the company (it became Lowry, Perin, and Co.) and, at age forty-six, retired to devote his time to travel, to building one of the Midwest's finest libraries, and to developing his artistic collections. Nineteenth-century sculptures on Oakwood's grounds included August Kiss's *Amazon,* in bronze; Chauncey B. Ives's *Sans Souci,* in marble; and other major pieces by the then famous. Books included a hundred copies of editions of the Bible, some in vellum, others in foreign languages; illuminated medieval manuscripts; rare editions of Shakespeare, including a First Folio; Aldines and Elzevirs, books issued by the famous Renaissance publishers; and, among the incunabula, a 1481 folio Dante; as well as the Elephant Folio of Audubon's *Birds.* In 1873 Probasco issued a *Catalogue* of his collection.

But the 1880s brought financial reverses to Probasco, and in 1887 he was forced to dispose of his fine art collection, the premier collection of its day in Cincinnati, at auction in New York. In 1890 his extensive library and incunabula collection, also sold at auction, became the nucleus of Chicago's Newberry Library, established three years before and heavily endowed. The Newberry bought the books through the agency of Robert Clarke, Cincinnati's leading publisher and bookseller, and of William Frederick Poole, former librarian of the Cincinnati Public Library, editor of the classic Poole's *Index,* and now the Newberry's head. A third auction, of marble statuary, ceramics, and furniture, took place in 1899. Probasco died in 1902, in modest circumstances.

Oakwood's grounds, originally thirty acres, were once a thing of beauty. Years of labor, recalled Sidney Maxwell in 1870, went to achieve "the present perfect state, with the gentle slopes, the gradual rise and fall of the surface. . . . Deep ravines have been filled, elevations cut down, and inequalities reconciled." Probasco had a conservatory and a rosarium with four thousand roses. He cultivated "shade and ornamental trees," native and foreign; he even had "a valuable collection of evergreens, gathered from various countries of the globe. The Pyrenees, the Himalayas and the Rocky Mountains have each made their contribution."

Clifton's undulant **topography** replicates, in little, that of Cincinnati. The land's configuration, Maxwell thought, made it "admirably adapted to country seats." Perched on eminences, Clifton's houses looked across at each other. A hundred years ago, Clifton was not a little like today's Indian Hill, the exclusive residential area that developed east of Cincinnati in the 1920s and 1930s. The size of the estates in Indian Hill makes the houses difficult to see; "Peterloon," the only one open to the public, occupies 1200 acres, the acreage of all of Clifton. Similarly, the

Shoenberger house. Completed in 1871 for $750,000, Scarlet Oaks, as the house is also known, was probably the most expensive building erected until then in Cincinnati. James Keys Wilson, architect of the Wise Temple downtown, designed this huge Gothic castle for George K. Schoenberger.

former size of the Clifton estates—few under ten acres, many thirty and forty, one seventy-three—made its mansions a more elusive sight than today. Landscaping, consciously presented, was also more easily visible. Early guides to Cincinnati comment on Clifton's lawns, shrubs, greenhouses, plantings, the diversity of trees, foreign, native, deciduous, evergreen. "Within the village proper," said Mayor Hosea in 1870, "the gentle slope, the softly undulating lawn, the tasty cottage and the imposing villa, with every variety of shrub, plant, flower and evergreen, distinguish [Clifton] as one of the most delightful suburban spots in the country."

We walk to the end of West Cliff Lane, cross on the path, and turn right. We have entered the grounds of the Scarlet Oaks-Bethesda Retirement Community. Attached to the far end of Scarlet Oaks Manor (1960), the long building in muted orange brick, is a huge Gothic "castle," **"Scarlet Oaks"** (1871). Designed for

George Krug Shoenberger by James Keys Wilson, Scarlet Oaks was in its day, with fifty-one rooms, Cincinnati's largest, most lavish mansion. The exterior is of limestone, trimmed in freestone. "1867," the year construction began, appears on the east gable. Unlike the Probasco house, the thrust of Scarlet Oaks is more vertical than horizontal. Largely Gothic in style, this building soars. Pinnacles with crockets, pointed windows, castellated turrets, tall, narrow chimneys: all elements rise to the tower. From there the octagonal tourelle carries the eye to the top of the flèche, eighty feet above ground. Scarlet Oaks demanded to be, and was, landscaped in what Downing called the picturesque mode. Such landscaping, by choosing pointed evergreens, for example, would have emphasized the building's height, irregularity, boldness, and strength.

Shoenberger, born in 1808, came to Cincinnati in 1834 from Pittsburgh to open a branch of his father's ironworks. The branch did well. Shoenberger first resided downtown, then moved to a splendid Italianate mansion, "Inwood" (where now is Inwood Park), in Mount Auburn. Responding to the Civil War call for arms, he prospered hugely. An even grander house in Clifton befitted his dignity. For it Shoenberger selected the highest, most visible, point of the forty-seven acre tract he had bought. Begun in 1867, Scarlet Oaks was completed within four years.

Today Scarlet Oaks is attached to an architecturally unsympathetic complex. It also loses by being deprived of the landscaping that would have enhanced its natural setting. A hundred years ago a visitor, following the long drive curling in to the house from Lafayette Ave., a lake on one side, would have experienced a sequence of carefully designed, gradually unfolding views. That from the house itself, described by D. J. Kenny, was beyond compare. "The great avenue in the distance crowded with pleasure-seekers; the beautiful cemetery of Spring Grove, with its lines of stately monuments; the numerous railroad tracks, and the trains themselves looking but small in the distance, all compose a landscape rarely to be surpassed."

Trains, for Sidney Maxwell as for Kenny, lent the nineteenth-century landscape "additional interest." Few regarded them as an intrusion upon nature. Between 1830 and 1860 the nation put down thirty thousand miles of track. They not only transformed the landscape but provoked considerable debate in mid-nineteenth century America. Most communities welcomed the railroad without reservation; many people even thought it made the scene more picturesque. But not Nathaniel Hawthorne, who felt "a torment" when he saw protruding upon the natural scene "the great, high, ugly embankment of the rail-road." And not James Fenimore Cooper, who lashed out at the "fiery trains" whose passage disrupted rural life. Thoreau was characteristically ambivalent: he both inveighed against and was awed by the "devilish Iron Horse" with its breath of fire and "ear-rending neigh." Walt Whitman, however, exulted wholeheartedly in the sound of "locomotives rushing and roaring, and the shrill steam-whistle. I hear the echoes reverberate through the grandest scenery in the world." In short, the railroad—the technological wonder of the age—epitomized the conflict between retreating nature and encroaching civilization. The view from Scarlet Oaks is characteristic of what Leo Marx has identified as the **"middle landscape,"** that is, a landscape that mixes technology and the beauties of nature. In this conception, the railroad is less an intrusion than a proper part of the scene. Such "middle landscapes" occupy intermediate ground between country and city, nature and civilization. Today our response to the scene—with trucks audible below and perhaps a plane above—may be closer to Kenny and Maxwell than to Hawthorne and Cooper. No great matter, for in this particular "middle landscape" few trains run.

No less dramatic was the view of Scarlet Oaks from the Millcreek Valley below. The ground on which the house stands falls sharply to the south, west, and north. With its tower at the salient point of the spur, it dominates the scene. Scarlet Oaks gives the impression of a castle on the Rhine. If descending Colerain Ave. in winter, look up and, there it is, high on its hill, spire piercing the sky.

Kenny terms Scarlet Oaks's architecture French domestic Gothic; the National Register calls it Chateauesque, presumably because it anticipates the grandiose Biltmore House, outside Asheville, North Carolina. The house harks back to "Woodburn," the Gothic mansion (ca. 1855) that Wilson had designed earlier for John Baker at 1887 Madison Road in East Walnut Hills. For Patrick A. Snadon Scarlet Oaks, vaguely ecclesiastical in its appearance, deftly melds German, French and English sources into a new "synthetic Gothic." Like Tudor Revival a half century later, Gothic was usually a style for the wealthy. Renaissance details mix with the prevailing Gothic in a way that recalls French Renaissance chateaux. To fashion the stone and woodwork Shoenberger brought artisans from Europe. In the end Scarlet Oaks cost him $750,000, a huge sum then, particularly when we remember that a decade later the gargantuan Music Hall came in well under $500,000. "What I admire here," Samuel Johnson boomed before Iverary Castle in Scotland, "is the total defiance of expense." We may feel the same before Scarlet Oaks. Shoenberger died in 1892, his second wife some years later. Unlike many large houses, this one did not become a problem upon the death of its original owners. In 1908 Ernest H. Huenefeld purchased the mansion and presented it the next year to the German Methodist Church and Bethesda Hospital, for use as a sanatorium. In 1919 Scarlet Oaks became a home for the retired. Residents no longer live in the mansion.

If we apply at Scarlet Oaks *Manor,* it may be possible to visit the mansion's interior. We do better to call ahead and arrange for a resident to give a guided tour. Much within remains as it was a hundred years ago. The main hall has a cathedral ceiling, with elaborate, hand-carved paneling and original stencilling. On one side, the living and dining rooms lead off; on the other, the chapel and library. Materials and workmanship, inside and out, are of exemplary quality. Bats—a symbol of good luck, happiness, and long life in Oriental folklore and art if not in Western— decorate wainscotting and walls. The four panels of Thomas Cole's major allegorical work *The Voyage of Life* once hung in the chapel, formerly Shoenberger's art gallery. Arguably the masterpiece of this Hudson River School artist, they had been acquired by Shoenberger before 1845 and almost immediately began to influence landscape painting in Cincinnati. Rediscovered in 1962, *The Voyage of Life* has hung since 1971 in the National Gallery in Washington.

We follow the entrance road down the hill to Lafayette Ave., where we turn right. The dormitory-like building is **Lafayette Hall** (1919), originally the Bethesda home's first annex and renovated in 1987 as apartments for use by residents.

Across Lafayette an unnamed street wanders up the hill. At the hill's highest point—it may be the highest point in Clifton—stands an asymmetrical mansion (no. 429), vaguely Romanesque, vaguely Chateauesque, called **"Bishop's Place."** A tall, slate-capped conical tower shoots up from a basically horizontal composition. The façade stone has a weathered air. Gargoyles project outwards, finials and chimneys upwards. Above the first floor bay window two griffins stand guard. "1881" is discernible on the four corners of a panel on the west façade, but the house was not completed until 1885. At the rear is a wooden *porche cochère*. James McLaughlin designed this house; Truman Handy, a prominent builder, built it for himself but died before moving in. Not until the late 1960s was Bishop's Place surrounded by infill housing.

We return to Lafayette Ave. and continue west. Number 439, on our left, is early twentieth-century Colonial Revival; Corinthian columns support its two-story portico. Number 515, the Second Empire mansion (1865) next door, has a mansard roof with segmental and round-arched dormer windows. The picturesque concave tower retains its cresting. The awkward extension on the west side dates from 1920.

Before entering Mount Storm Park, we cast a glance to the north. In winter, visible above the trees after the leaves have fallen, are Scarlet Oaks's *flèche* and Oakwood's tower. A century ago, these mansions would have stood by themselves. Twentieth-century infill housing deprives them of the natural setting once so much a part of the architectural effect intended. For generations reared on Sir Walter Scott's *Waverley* novels, enormously popular in nineteenth-century America, the sight of a tower-crowned hilltop gave beholders a poetic thrill. Even now the sight of a spire and tower rising above the trees is magical. We could think we are in another century. Our illusion of being in the past continues when, a little further along Lafayette Ave., we take the turn to the left and discover a castle in the forest. The first time I saw **"The Windings,"** as the castle is called, was in the gathering twilight of a winter day. One or two lights were on; a few snowflakes drifted down. I felt I was approaching a medieval manor and for a moment imagined myself transported centuries back in time.

The Windings, the last in our tour of Clifton's spectacular cluster of nineteenth-century villas, was completed in 1869. Said to be modelled after England's Kenilworth Castle, the house was designed by Thomas Sargent for William Clifford Neff. In its design, as Patrick Snadon has pointed out to me, The Windings is based on "Rockport," a mansion designed by the English architect, Gervase Wheeler, and published in A. A. Turner's *Villas on the Hudson* (1860). The Windings's floor plan is exactly Rockport's, except that Sargent has moved it ninety degrees. Swiss wood carvers reportedly labored for three years on the hand-wrought oak and black walnut mantels, panels, doors, and staircase. Neff, a pork packer, no doubt savored the aroma of the Millcreek pork-packing factories wafting upwind to his demesne. Reputedly he so overspent himself on his house that he could not afford to live in it and in 1876 sold it to the Sisters of the Sacred Heart. It eventually housed Sacred Heart Academy, a girls' preparatory school. Neff's castle stopped with the four-story tower. As the school grew, additions became necessary. The chapel, designed by Hannaford, was dedicated in 1887. Sacred Heart Academy closed in 1970. The

Windings, which retains much of its former elegance within, has recently undergone conversion into condominiums. Other units have been built on the grounds.

"Edgewood," another grand mansion, once stood on the level area adjacent to Lafayette Ave. It was George Shoenberger's wedding gift to his granddaughter, who married Max Fleischmann. Max and his brother Charles, immigrants from Hungary, opened a plant at Riverside, downriver from Cincinnati, where they produced a superior dry yeast for baking. At the 1876 Philadelphia Centennial Exhibition their Vienna Café scored a popular success. Edgewood, subsequently a dormitory for Sacred Heart Academy, was torn down in 1983.

We continue along Lafayette to **Mount Storm Park.** The name derives from the storms that rapidly moved up the Millcreek Valley. Here from 1846–1852 Robert Bonner Bowler built an elegant Renaissance Revival mansion, "Mount Storm." A native of Providence, Rhode Island, Bowler went west as a young man. Before the Civil War he made a fortune in the dry goods business; later, diversifying his interests, he became president of the Kentucky Central Railroad. From his property he could look down upon the railroad yards of the Millcreek Valley.

Today only the **Temple of Love,** the coach house, and part of the estate's fencing remain of Bowler's Mount Storm. The hill gradually rises to the temple. Silhouetted against the trees and the sky, it focuses the landscape. Eight fluted metal Corinthian columns support its gadrooned dome; an urn serves as finial. Swans, rosettes, and acanthus leaves circle the frieze. The Temple of Love, in form a Greek tholos, ultimately derives from the Choragic monument to Lysicrates in Athens. Its ancestors include the vestal temples of Rome and Tivoli; more directly, it descends from the Temple of Love in the grounds of Versailles, inaugurated by Marie Antoinette at a fête for Louis XVI. Originally, Marie Antoinette's temple enclosed Bouchardon's symbolic statue of Venus. Bowler's temple, virtually an exact copy of that at Versailles, never had a statue.

Adolph Strauch may have designed the temple. He certainly was responsible for the grounds. Born in Silesia in 1822, Strauch began as a gardener in the Hapsburg imperial gardens of Schönbrunn and Laxenburg. He also worked for Prince Hermann von Pückler-Muskau on his estate in Muskau in Silesia. Later Strauch travelled throughout Europe and visited England. In 1851 he came to America and the next year, having by accident missed a train connection to Buffalo, found himself with a day in Cincinnati. It was, for him and for this city, a fortunate mishap. In London, at the Great Exhibition of 1851, he had met Bowler, who invited him to look him up if ever he should find himself in Cincinnati. Strauch did and worked for Bowler from 1852 to 1854. He also landscaped the estates of other Cliftonites, among them, Buchanan, Probasco, Shoenberger, and Neff. Strauch, according to Blanche Linden-Ward, designed "their estates to create the impression of a single property. . . . Eliminating fences and other visible property lines, Strauch sculpted sweeping lawns punctuated by carefully placed bosks of trees framing palatial homes and defining distant vistas. The plan gave the suburb a unified design on an unprecedented scale." Clifton began to take on the appearance of an English or European park. In 1854 Strauch became landscape gardener, subsequently superintendent, of Spring Grove Cemetery, where he gained international renown for his

Temple of Love, Mount Storm Park. The temple is the chief surviving structure on what was once the estate of Robert Bonner Bowler. It ultimately derives its form from the Greek *tholos* via the vestal temples in Rome and Tivoli and, perhaps even more, from the Temple of Love on the grounds of Versailles.

picturesque landscaping. The cemetery, still much as he laid it out, remains his most enduring monument.

Bowler's Temple of Love did not have a statue in it because, unlike Marie Antoinette's, it stands above a reservoir that supplied water to ten greenhouses. With seventy-three acres, Bowler could indulge his love of horticulture. His conservatories and gardens became well known throughout the Middle West. He had greenhouses for palms, orchids, roses, banana trees, as well as for exotic flowers and herbs culled from both hemispheres. Mount Storm also had gardens, orchards, a waterfall, and a lake on which swam black and white swans. Bowler's grounds, recalls Kenny, were "covered with English and Norway pines, besides maple, willow, English elm, Tartarian maple, and varieties of the linden." One hundred feet west of the Temple, two blocked-off entrances lead to a small cave, once probably a root cellar. On snowy days in winter the young and not-so-young find the hill excellent sledding. Visible at the bottom is Bowler's former coach house, now a private residence. Today, though only a few of the rare trees remain on the grounds, the hill still descends in a sequence of rolling lawns. With its hill, its lawns, and its Temple of Love, Mount Storm presents a **"picturesque"** scene, picturesque in the sense of looking "like a picture." The implication is vague but pleasant. As noted, "picturesque" also refers to a school of nineteenth-century American landscape design, and Mount Storm is picturesque in this sense too.

This American school derived from the writings in England of William Gilpin and Uvedale Price, with the latter's *Essay on the Picturesque* of 1794 being the most significant statement. Humphrey Repton popularized the picturesque in England, both in his practice as a landscape architect and through his writings, in the decades subsequent, as did John Claudius Loudon, a contemporary of Andrew Jackson Downing in America, whose notions regarding the picturesque and the beautiful we looked at earlier in this walk. Although accurately described by one writer as "an aesthetic concept of bewildering contentiousness," the picturesque in landscape usually includes variety, intricacy, irregularity, movement (or the illusion of it), and roughness. The picturesque is related to, indeed derives from, earlier thinking by Edmund Burke, whose *Philosophical Enquiry into the Origin of Our Ideas of the Sublime and Beautiful* (1757) established these concepts in esthetic discourse. The "sublime" does not concern us here since sublime landscapes—for example, the Alps or Niagara—do not occur in the Cincinnati area and in any case cannot be recreated by man. The "beautiful" also looks back to Lancelot "Capability" Brown, the famous English landscape architect who was Burke's contemporary and who "improved" many estates including Stowe and Blenheim. In landscape design the beautiful includes broad meadows or greenswards, set off by low hills, lakes, and groups of trees. It stresses unity, proportion, and harmony; it induces a sense of repose. Strauch's mode of landscaping, like Frederick Law Olmsted's, favors the beautiful but includes elements of the picturesque. In their artful recreation and shaping of nature Strauch and Olmsted blend together both elements harmoniously.

Some half-dozen environments in Cincinnati still reflect formal picturesque and beautiful principles of landscape design, most of which predate the founding of the city. These formally picturesque environments include Clifton, Spring Grove Cemetery, Eden Park, the Cincinnati Zoo, and the outlying village of Glendale. We have visited or shall visit all of them. Adolph Strauch had a hand in the design of everyone but Glendale, which was laid out the year before he arrived in Cincinnati. Mount Storm Park and Burnet Woods are the best surviving bits of Strauch's work in Clifton. Spring Grove Cemetery still reflects to an amazing degree his notions about landscape as do, though to a lesser extent, the zoo and Eden Park. Strauch is for the Cincinnati area what Olmsted is for the nation. As the federal government has decided to protect and restore Olmsted-designed landscapes, so the city of Cincinnati might consider doing the same for Strauch's. He is, after all, also a figure of national stature and influence, particularly, as we shall see when visiting Spring

Grove Cemetery, in landscape design for cemeteries. The picturesque he favored is a particularly apt style for Cincinnati since it both complements and enhances the naturally irregular and variegated landscape of much of the city, notably the part of it bordering the Ohio River with curving hills on either side of the winding watery path.

Bowler and his wife, the former Susan Pendleton (sister of George), delighted in entertaining bigwigs, including Emperor Dom Pedro of Brazil and, in September 1860, the Prince of Wales. Impressed by Cincinnati's suburbs, the prince declared tactfully that he had "seen none finer in all the world." Clifton he called the "Eden of the Cincinnati aristocracy." It reminded him, he said, of England—as well it might, landscaped as it was to look like an English park. In July 1864 Bowler met a premature death when his carriage went out of control on the steep Sycamore St. hill. In 1911 Alice Bowler, his son's widow, sold Mount Storm to the city of Cincinnati. Although the city razed the house in 1917, this step preserved the grounds from commercial or residential development. Now Mount Storm provides Clifton's northwest end with a park that complements Burnet Woods on the southeast.

From the park shelterhouse (1936) a sweeping panorama opens up over the Millcreek Valley. The Western hills delimit the horizon. I-74 rides off to Indiana; I-75 winds underneath us around the Millcreek Valley. Below and to the left is Cincinnati Technical College, its stadium prominently visible. Far to the left, we make out several buildings on the University of Cincinnati campus. Crosley Hall (1968), with its oversized cornice, is in the gruff New Brutalistic mode. Also visible are St. George's twin spires and McMicken Hall's steeple.

We retrace our steps along Lafayette Ave. and turn right on Middleton Ave. Ahead of us is Good Samaritan Hospital; further off, the tower of Hughes High School. Tudor Revival, in different sizes, shapes, forms, and combinations of materials, dominates this stretch of Middleton. If tired, we barrel on directly to Ludlow Ave.; if energy remains, we digress to left and right.

Our first digression is to the right into Rawson Woods Lane. Frank Lloyd Wright designed **1 Rawson Woods Circle** for Cedric G. Boulter in 1954. It is a horizontal composition built of concrete blocks and Douglas fir (stained Taliesin red), with vertical window panels and a flat roof. Wright designed everything, including the light fixtures and furniture. Even in winter the house is (purposely) difficult to see. Wright also designed two other houses in the Cincinnati outskirts, one in Amberley Village and another in Indian Hill. We proceed counterclockwise around Rawson Woods Circle. On the right, two modern houses in the International Style's boxy two-story version date from the 1930s. They reflect in their sharp angles Bauhaus influence. Decoration is sparse. These houses are worth looking at, both for their own sakes and because Cincinnati has few such. Number 6, the work of the local firm of Potter, Tyler, and Martin, went up in 1934. Number 20's red door provides a lively touch of color. Aside from this flurry of modernism, Tudor and Colonial Revival predominate here. South-facing houses overlook **Rawson Woods,** a 10.66-acre L-shaped nature preserve that acts as a third greenspace between Mount Storm and Burnet Woods. Acquired by the city from the Rawson estate in 1923 and 1928, it is closed to the public. From the numerous bird feeders

6 Rawson Woods Circle. This house, designed by the local firm of Potter, Tyler, and Martin in 1934, is one of the Cincinnati area's few International style, or Modern Movement, houses.

visible on this tour Clifton must be a birdwatcher's paradise. We continue south up Middleton Ave.

At McAlpin Ave. begins the built-up section of Clifton. Cut through in the 1850s, the street served as Clifton's informal dividing line: large lots and opulent residences to the north, smaller lots with modest, though still substantial, houses to the south. Clifton's population surged after its annexation by Cincinnati in 1896. **Apartment houses** sprang up along the streetcar routes that from 1888 ran, as buses still run, down Middleton Ave. Making almost total use of their lots, they are of course a concomitant of rising real estate prices. The denser housing helps make possible the animation we saw on Ludlow Ave. The turn-of-the-century Georgian Revival apartment house at 3655 Middleton is typical. It has recessed balconies and decorative bowed wrought-iron railings. An upper unit here, generous in size and with views in several directions, strikes me as the ne plus ultra of urban-suburban apartment living.

We walk left to the end of Wood Ave. to admire the fine wrought- and cast-iron gates marking the back property line of Clifton Elementary School. We passed the front gates earlier on Clifton Ave. These strike me as finer. Note the Balch family's intertwined "B." Nearby stands the boarded-up coach house for Alexander Mc-Donald's "Dalvay." We return to Clifton Ave.

We turn left on Resor Ave. Young skateboarders find the gentle slope of the street ideal. 356 has its Georgian Revival embellishments—porch pediment, porch cornice line, and side entrance—gaily painted in rainbow colors reminiscent of San Francisco townhouses. Above the side entrance the multicolored window completes the festive note. Across the street, number 3, or 3553, Resor Place is a huge wooden Italianate confection painted gray with white trim. On this site stood **"Battenberry,"** a large cottage built circa 1846 by Reuben P. Resor for his mother. About 1860 this mansion was constructed completely around the cottage. The mansard roof, presumably added later, indicates kinship to Second Empire. A bull's-eye window, looking like a ship's porthole, pierces three sides of the tower. Upper-story window molding meshes into the cornice line. The house exudes angles: façades, different on every side, step forward and backward. Like the Lafayette Ave. mansions, the Resor house originally sat on a much larger plot. Encircled by infill housing in the 1920s, it is difficult to put into perspective. The house actually faces north, with our closest view, however, being from Resor Place. Resor Ave. once served as the main entrance into the Resor compound. The original homestead, from the 1840s, stood on the site of St. John's Unitarian Church.

We return to Middleton Ave. and continue west up Resor Ave. to Hedge Row Lane. The houses on this charming street snuggle against the hill; those rising behind are on Cornell Place. The hedgerow, not a traditional English hedgerow, is a vigorous, unpretentious thicket of **Osage orange** trees that, most likely, date from the middle of the last century. Osage orange originally grew only on the banks of the Osage River in Arkansas. Jonathan Turner, an enterprising Yankee, introduced this thorny plant to the Midwest to serve farmers as inexpensive fencing. Osage orange enjoyed enormous popularity for several decades after 1840. (Barbed wire did not come upon the scene until 1873.) Osage orange could spread to a width of 20 feet or more and grow to a height of 30 feet. The first fence around Spring Grove Cemetery, in place by 1857, consisted of Osage orange trees.

Until quite recently, we could have climbed the hill and stood in front of **Reuben P. Resor's mansion** on Cornell Place. But to get to it now we must return to Middleton, turn right, then right again on Evanswood Place. Cornell Place curls off to the right and we curl with it.

The huge asymmetrical mansion (3515 and 3519) before us, built by Reuben P. Resor about 1846, is Gothic in its massing, Italianate in its round-arched windows. The octagonal tower, with its blind windows, is also Gothic, as are the gable-end finials and the quatrefoils. Often the round-arched windows come in threes, with the central window slightly higher. The second-floor windows next to the tower have label moldings, sometimes called a shouldered architrave. This Resor house passed through various hands and for a time became the Clifton School for Young Ladies, "Miss Ely's School." Now stuccoed over, it has undergone conversion into apartments. Formerly, like the mansions on Lafayette Ave., the Resor house dominated extensive grounds, in this case forty acres. It was reached by a long drive (later Resor Ave.) from Clifton Ave. The broad verandas commanded a view of the Millcreek Valley; from the garret apartment a magnificent view unfolds over the forested expanses of Clifton.

From this point we return to Ludlow Ave. via Whitfield Ave. The third house on the right (no. 3475), with its crenellated balconies, combines Flemish with Tudor Revival. Note the decorative shield on the rounded central gable. At Ludlow we turn left and soon find ourselves in the commercial heart of Clifton.

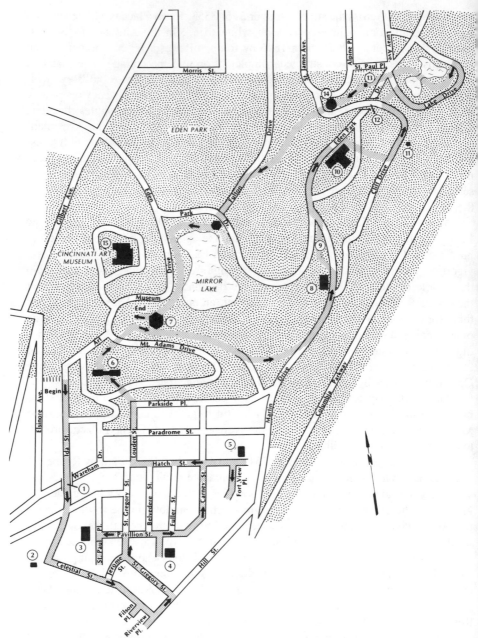

MOUNT ADAMS

1. Ida Street Bridge
2. Rookwood Pottery
3. Former Holy Cross Monastery
4. Church of the Immaculate Conception
5. The Cloisters
6. Playhouse in the Park
7. Murray Seasongood Pavilion
8. Pumping Station
9. Deupree Memorial Gazebo
10. Krohn Conservatory
11. Ohio River (Navigation) Monument
12. Melan Arch Bridge
13. Vietnam Memorial
14. Water Tower
15. Cincinnati Art Museum

11

Mount Adams

WALKING from downtown to Mount Adams is difficult. Because of the expressways in between, you may find it easier to take a taxi or the number 49 bus, or drive. City officials have talked for years about an aerial tramway to connect Mount Adams with downtown but no tramway has yet appeared. If you decide to walk, proceed to Central Parkway, which curves north into Reading Road. Follow Reading Road to Elsinore Place (the bridge over the expressways), cross Gilbert Ave. and go right, up Elsinore Ave. On the far side of the bridge, you will front **Elsinore Tower** (1883), a Norman Romanesque Revival minicastle designed by Charles Hannaford. Hannaford based his design upon a stage set A. G. Moore, superintendent of the Cincinnati Water Works, saw in a production of *Hamlet*. This extravagant yet very appealing building began as a valve house for the Cincinnati Waterworks. It was also intended to be a main entrance into Eden Park. Steps behind lead up to the Cincinnati Art Museum. But no longer is it a valve house or much used as an entrance. A short distance along Elsinore Ave., a second set of steps climbs the hill. Climb them and they will leave you, breathless, at the northern end of Ida St.: this is the beginning of our tour.

Looming above downtown, **Mount Adams** is perched on the most prominent of the city's hills. It constitutes an island within the larger archipelago of hills that is Cincinnati. Bluffs cut Mount Adams off on the west and south; Eden Park surrounds it on the north. As seen from downtown or the river, Mount Adams approximates a triangle, stablest of geometric forms. Atop the hill, the campanile of the former monastery juts into the sky. Mount Adams possesses its own particular charm. It may remind you of a Rhine village or a Tuscan hilltown or your favorite San Francisco hilltop. If it does not have the architectural distinction or historical associations of, say, Boston's Beacon Hill, it boasts an incomparably more dramatic site.

As well as physical harmony, Mount Adams possesses visual unity: a unity of scale rather than of style. Except for Highland Towers, the tall apartment building, the structures on Mount Adams are modest. Its houses, despite the variety of archi-

Mount Adams, from Carew Tower. The Church of the Immaculate Conception (Immaculata) stands against the sky. Courtesy of J. Miles Wolf.

tectural modes, make for (as Donlyn Lyndon has said of Boston) "a rich, sculpted, and episodic order." Here the whole is definitely greater than the parts, interesting as are the parts. Culturally, Mount Adams stakes a legitimate claim to be Cincinnati's artistic heart, its Montmartre. In Eden Park we find the Playhouse in the Park, the Cincinnati Art Museum, the Art Academy, and the Krohn Conservatory. The Mount complements these cultural institutions with restaurants, outdoor cafes, artists' studios, old houses, and narrow streets. In brief, it provides the most pleasant of urban ambiences.

Mount Adams began as Mount Ida. This modest hill derived its earlier name, not from the legendary mountain above Troy, the abode of the gods in Homer's *Iliad,* but from Ida Martin, a washerwoman, the laundress for Fort Washington, who reputedly lived in one of the huge old sycamores then common. Fairy tales can originate in the New World as well as in the Old. In 1843 Cincinnatians renamed Mount Ida in honor of former president John Quincy Adams.

After 1830 Nicholas Longworth covered much of Mount Adams with vineyards, which prospered until the Civil War. In addition, Mount Adams supported limestone quarries. A number of early inhabitants were stonecutters and carters. Old prints suggest that not only was the Mount eighty to a hundred feet higher than now but that it had a different configuration. In this regard Cincinnati has suffered less than Boston, where all but one of the hills have been reduced or eliminated since the Revolution, trundled down in carts as landfill or used for building foundations. In 1867 James Parton described Mount Adams as "an almost precipitous hill . . . which has been dug into, and pared down, until it has about as much beauty as an immense heap of gravel." He also indicated why few had settled on it. "Around the base of this unsightly mountain are slaughter-houses and breweries, incensing it with black smoke, and extensive pens filled with the living material of barrelled pork."

In 1843 Longworth gave four valuable acres on Mount Adams for an astronomical observatory. Its presence sparked development. Other concerns, including an iron foundry and a wooden shoe factory, joined the limestone quarries. Harrison P. Diehl's fireworks factory moved here in 1849. Diehl put in a park and an observation tower, and made a grand display. His Pyrotechnic Garden, popularly known as "the Pyro," flourished in spite, or perhaps because, of the inevitable explosions and mishaps. After midcentury, German and Irish immigrants began to settle on the slopes near riverfront factories and adjoining the vineyards. Workingmen erected modest houses on the 25- by 100-foot lots. Unlike Mount Auburn and Clifton, patrician enclaves, Mount Adams was always a working-class community. It had, at least until recent years, no ostentatious houses. During the Civil War, because of the hill's vantage point over the Ohio and comparative inaccessibility, cannons were set up here but were never fired. In 1873 the Passionist Fathers took over the Observatory building; in 1891 Rookwood Pottery went up near the site of the fireworks factory, which had moved to Reading Road in 1885. By the mid-twentieth century, as Americans elsewhere abandoned inner-city residential neighborhoods, Mount Adams remained a working-class, largely Catholic neighborhood, its residents chiefly of Irish and German descent, with a few Italians and, occupying houses in Lower Mount Adams, on Baum and Kilgour, a number of Appalachians. Americans have often ignored the advantages of magnificent natural sites, and for decades prosperous Cincinnatians ignored Mount Adams.

In 1960 an enterprising firm called Towne Properties began to buy and refurbish the old brick and frame houses on St. Gregory St. Already in the late 1950s a few middle- and upper-income professionals had taken up residence on Mount Adams. Renovation—sometimes sympathetic, sometimes not—has continued ever since. The wealthy and trendy have discovered Mount Adams, as they have Montmartre and Greenwich Village and other picturesque spots of the world. Some might say they have already taken it over. Condos and townhouses have sprouted on virtually every available parcel of hillside. With real estate prices here higher than anywhere in the city, Mount Adams has become an upscale neighborhood. We wander through streets lined with working-class homes but only those few still with insulbrick or asbestos siding will have blue-collar workers in them. The jazzier-looking ones, remodelled with decks and repainted in carousel colors, do not. At once very old and very young, this urban village of less than 1600 inhabitants offers most of the amenities of life—except a place to park. Whether as former blue collar or as present upper middle-class enclave, Mount Adams retains a strong sense of identity.

We begin on **Ida St.** Viewed from the sidewalk, its dwellings present a sober and sedate demeanor; viewed from below, they present modernistic, glass-filled nether sides. Polluted air long hung heavy over the Basin; steamboats filled the Ohio River with black smoke. Ida, with its street-facing buildings, demonstrates the nineteenth-century Cincinnatian's indifference to views.

The renovated townhouses and rowhouses offer a nice mix, mostly in vernacular examples, of architectural styles: Gothic Revival-*cum*-Swiss chalet, Renaissance Revival, Italianate, Second Empire, Queen Anne, even a sort of Bauhaus. Number 1281, Renaissance Revival, offers fine brick and carved stone window moldings. 1269–1275 are Queen Anne rowhouses; the raised wooden porches unify, and render the building intimate. Color is provided by piano-key brick lintels and the serrated, multicolored bricks beneath the cornice line. The nineteenth-century façade is, as so often on Mount Adams, deceptive: the contemporary recessed extension on the right indicates that within modernity has triumphed. 1261–67, Italianate rowhouses, have unusual sawtoothed lintels that form part of the stone beltcourses. 1255 is an imaginative modernization of an older house. The red-painted stucco harmonizes with the older red brick. 1251, adjoining, is imitation Bauhaus. 1243, a colorful Swiss chalet, may have begun existence as a Gothic cottage. New and redone buildings blend in reasonably well with older structures.

901–927 Paradrome (ca. 1885), at the intersection, is a five-part composition unified by its three pediments. A slate mansard roof covers the intermediate sections. On the corner, newer brick infill indicates a store once occupied the premises. Ward, Fitzpatrick & Co. did the cast-iron front. We shall come upon other ex-storefronts. Before World War II Mount Adams had far more neighborhood enterprises than it does now. Further along Ida, the modest **Pilgrim Chapel** (1890), so named because it was a preaching station of the Presbyterian Church, was—and is—upper Mount Adams's only Protestant church. Evenings it is open for use by other religious groups. The hill's two Catholic parishes helped raise funds for its erection. The Chapel makes use of simple geometrical forms: circles, semicircles, and rectangles. Beltcourses of rock-faced masonry, catching the sun's light, become smaller as they rise. The projecting central bay, with its belfry or bell cote, alleviates a basically triangular composition.

The **Ida Street Bridge** (1931), one of the city's first Art Deco bridges, replaced a wood-and-steel trestle structure erected in 1882 by the Mount Adams Inclined Plane Railway Co. That first bridge gave Mount Adams its only access from Cincinnati not excessively steep. Six pillars support the new span, their vertical lines echoed by those of the balustrade. Unusual for its time was the viaduct's built-in lighting. Below, the city stretches before us. Clearly visible on Liberty Hill, to our right, is the white cupola of Christ Hospital. Nearer in, we discern the Chinese-box, red-and-black Great American Broadcasting building and, below it, the white Pendleton house. Before us, Central Parkway recedes into the distance. Music Hall is to its right, Union Terminal appears to be just behind it. Dominating the foreground are St. Paul's golden cupola and Old St. Mary's spire. On the far left appears the elongated posterior of the former *Post* and *Times-Star* Building. During our walks in downtown and along the Ohio River we have often experienced Mount Adams visually. Now we stand on it, looking down instead of up, and we discover that the perspectives it offers upon the city are even more spectacular.

Above us, exquisitely set, looms the former Holy Cross Monastery. At the far end of the viaduct Monastery St. drops down sharply to the valley. About 1793 the Reverend James Kemper, pioneer Presbyterian preacher, put down here with the aid of his three sons the first crude log, or "corduroy," roadway in order to move his family through what is now Eden Park and settle in today's Walnut Hills, named after his farm. (Kemper's log cabin, still extant, we may see in Sharon Woods Village.) Monastery's name reflects its longtime destination; previously, it was Observatory Road. Even though by 1800 two other roads—East Court St., now Wareham Drive, and "the Road to the Hill," now Hill St.—had also been put through, in the early nineteenth century Monastery St. offered the chief way up Mount Adams. The steep grades indicate why people settled Mount Adams later than they did areas of Cincinnati further from downtown.

A sign announces **Rookwood Pottery.** Its architect was H. Neill Wilson of Pittsfield, Massachusetts. The half timbering with stucco infill, along with the fanlike pattern, may reflect Arts and Crafts influence; the bare gables and the tendency toward banded windows certainly do. Arts and Crafts was an offshoot of the Gothic Revival; a tower projecting out over the hill, visible in old prints but since gone, made the composition look even more picturesque. The building's horizontal emphasis may indicate Japanese influence, an influence also on Rookwood ware. Circular chimneys announce the former kilns within. The factory, combining workrooms, decorating studios, and a salesroom, was designed in the spirit of William Morris's ideal workplace. Rookwood's handsome wrought-iron gates came from the Hamilton County Courthouse destroyed during the 1884 riots. Feeding rooks, one beakless, crown the gateposts. The gateposts lack a third rook though feet remain. Rooks reappear on stained-glass dormer windows. An I. T. Verdin clock stands before the entrance.

Mrs. **Maria Longworth Nichols** had worked as a potter for several years when in 1880 her father, Joseph Longworth, bought her an abandoned schoolhouse on Eastern Avenue to establish her own pottery. She named it "Rookwood" after the family's suburban estate in East Walnut Hills. It derived its name, she said, because of the large numbers of crows that inhabited "an old dead elm tree." The name is reassuringly similar in sound to the classic Wedgwood. *Rookwood* is also the name of a once-popular novel by W. H. Ainsworth. Maria Nichols ruled her pottery, financially and artistically, until 1883 when she hired William Watts Taylor as general manager. In 1885 her husband George Ward Nichols died, and the next year she married Bellamy Storer. In 1890 she turned control of the pottery over to Taylor. That year Rookwood, seeking larger quarters, purchased the property adjacent to the Mount Adams incline. Construction proceeded in three stages. The original portion (1891) is to the south nearest the river; above its main entrance appears the Rookwood Pottery mark, a reversed "RP." In 1899 the central section was added. The third and last addition, which since 1976 has housed a restaurant, dates from 1903–1904.

Rookwood Pottery developed a familial relationship with its neighbors, the Art Museum, the Art Academy, and the Sterling Cut Glass Co., all within easy walking distance of one another. Many Rookwood decorators graduated from the Art Academy; W. W. Taylor, Rookwood's president, served as one of the Museum's trustees; Joseph Henry Gest, the Museum's director, became Rookwood's president after Taylor's death in 1913. For several decades economic prosperity went hand in hand with growing critical acclaim. By the late 1920s, however, the commercialization

Maria Longworth Nichols Storer. A fervent amateur potter, she founded Rookwood Pottery in 1880 and guided its destiny during its formative years, relinquishing control to W. W. Taylor in 1890. Courtesy of the Cincinnati Historical Society.

and mass production of pottery cut into the market for Rookwood's handmade ware. The Depression and World War II drastically reduced its business. After successive owners, the Herschede Company bought the troubled enterprise in 1959 and the next year moved Rookwood's operations to Starkville, Mississippi. In 1967 Rookwood ceased all production.

    Within the restaurant's interior the ambience is informal. Ductwork and rafters are exposed. Massive iron bands bind the brick kilns. Blown-up photographs of Rookwood's potters at work decorate the walls. Glass vitrines display Rookwood ware with the artists indicated. Chair backs feature rooks, and we may dine inside

Workers at Rookwood. Every piece created at Rookwood was unique. The pottery provided creative opportunity for female as well as male workers. Courtesy of the Cincinnati Historical Society.

the kilns. Rookwood's hamburgers rank among the city's best. They are named, not after the potters, however, but after prominent "burghers" of the city: William McGuffey, Stephen Foster, Henry Farny, John Shillito, Andrew Erkenbrecher, even Ida herself. Those not up to pronouncing "Erkenbrecherburger" might try a Porkopolis or Hearnburner Chili (after Lafcadio Hearn).

Between Rookwood Pottery and Highland Towers, the apartment building, formerly stood the main structure of the **Mount Adams incline.** Completed in 1876, four years after that on Mount Auburn, the Mount Adams incline's 945 feet of track rose 260 feet from Lock St. It bridged Kilgour, Baum, and Oregon streets; from below we can still make out the stone supports marching up the hill. In 1879–1880 and in 1891 the incline was rebuilt, first to carry the Cincinnati Street Railway's horsedrawn cars, then to accommodate electric lines. Passengers now could continue their journeys from downtown without disembarking at the bottom and reembarking at the top. The streetcars of the old Zoo-Eden route ran over the Ida St. trestle bridge, down Ida, still Mount Adams's only level street, around the east side of the Art Museum, over the upper level of a double-decked viaduct (demolished in

Mount Adams incline. Streetcars of the Zoo-Eden line (route 49) ascend and descend the incline. Its 945 feet of track rose 260 feet. The Rookwood Pottery complex (1891–1904) is at top left; at top right is the Sterling Glass Company (1902), which replaced the Highland House. Sterling Glass was in turn replaced by Highland Towers in 1964. Many of the houses in this photograph are gone, though some of the incline's original supports remain embedded in the hillside. Courtesy of the Cincinnati Historical Society.

1949) that spanned the Gilbert Ave. entrance to Eden Park, then proceeded up Gilbert. A familiar and much-loved landmark, the Mount Adams incline lasted until 1948, the longest to survive of Cincinnati's inclines.

In March 1986 the Ohio legislature appropriated four million dollars for Cincinnati to build an aerial tramway linking Mount Adams with the proposed entertainment district north of 6th St. downtown. Gondola-like cars would traverse nearly 3000 feet in just under four minutes. The tramway would also serve the city as a visual icon. But questions about its economic viability persist, and at this writing the project is on hold.

Highland House (1876) formerly adjoined the Mount Adams incline. Its architect was George W. Rapp. Built to capitalize upon the phenomenal success of Mount Auburn's Lookout House, Highland House was a much grander structure than its rival and enjoyed an even more phenomenal success. In 1878 the management lured the exuberant Fred Harff, "mein Host" at Lookout House, to Highland House. Although Harff did not bring a white whale with him, he otherwise kept things hopping. With bowling facilities, dining rooms, a concert hall, a theater, a beer garden,

Streetcar on Mount Adams incline. After 1891 the incline was able to handle electric street-cars. Passengers could continue their journeys from downtown without disembarking at the bottom and reembarking at the top. From the incline they enjoyed spectacular views over downtown. The longest to survive of the city's five inclines, the Mount Adams lasted until 1948. Courtesy of the Cincinnati Historical Society.

and adjacent picnic grounds, Highland House could handle as many as 8000 guests at one time. A pavilion on the east side was built in 1877 in time for the arrival of Theodore Thomas, who from August 20th to September 10th led his famous orchestra for twenty-three concerts here. Throngs crowded the pavilion, which seated 1400, and the esplanade, which accommodated 4000 more. Average attendance at the concerts topped 4000. Nor did audiences consist solely of Cincinnatians; special railroad excursions brought in music lovers from out of town. In 1879 Thomas's orchestra played, with comparable success, another twenty-six concerts, and returned again for a week in 1881. Highland House was a regular stop on the Thomas highway, as his annual tours came to be called. Subsequently, however, the level of entertainment at Highland House declined. Politicians, followed by the "sporting gentry," patronized the establishment. The House's reputation suffered, and by the 1890s, as one Victorian commentator archly observed, "sordidness [had] replaced the sparkle and vivaciousness of the past. Even the police were occasionally unable to preserve decorum." In sum, Highland House had become a rough-and-tumble place. Stricter enforcement of Ohio's Sunday no-drinking laws forced it to close in 1895. The Sterling Cut Glass Co. (1902) replaced Highland House on this site.

Highland Towers (1964), in turn, replaced Sterling Glass, which moved to

Highland House. Designed by George W. Rapp in 1876, Highland House was easily the largest and most spectacular of the resorts erected at the tops of the inclines. The incline station is at the far left. Highland House and the surrounding grounds could handle as many as 8000 patrons. Courtesy of the Cincinnati Historical Society.

Hyde Park. This twenty-three story structure extends almost as far down as up. The "ground" floor is the tenth. The Ugly Highrise in Mount Adams's Victorian pond, Highland Towers should never have been—"an abuse of light," E. Pope Coleman called it. Location, height, scale: all, in my view, are wrong. Mount Adams's most prominent site, its prow, required a structure that would work with, not disrupt, the hill's visual harmony. This one looks more like a project than the upscale apartment house it is. What provides a view for tenants provides an eyesore for others.

We start downhill on Celestial St. Frame houses along Celestial and adjoining streets went up after the Civil War. Not grand mansions but working-class dwellings, they are set closely together because space was (and is) valuable. Parking remains a problem, in part because houses here lack driveways or service alleys. Workingmen could not afford a horse or carriage. Today, these closely packed houses suggest urban intimacy. Tidy gardens, often behind decorative iron fences, heighten the intimacy. In summer, window boxes overflowing with blooms brighten façades; trees shade the sidewalks. Such modest amenities give Mount Adams an Old World charm. Urban density, we feel, can be a very good thing.

1051 Celestial, a modest stucco-over-brick cottage, has traditionally been identified as the residence of **Charles Francis Hall.** Now largely forgotten, Hall (1821–1871) was in his day America's foremost arctic explorer and author of *Life with the Esquimaux* (1864) and the posthumous *Narrative of the Second Arctic Expedition*

(1879). Although recent research has failed to link Hall conclusively with this house, it seems likely that he resided on Mount Adams. Like many in his generation, Hall was fascinated by Sir John Franklin's famous expedition that had set out from England in 1845 to find a northwest passage. Years went by without news. For more than a decade Franklin's fate aroused intense speculation in England and America. By 1857 hope had virtually ended in England. Not so with Hall. Convinced that survivors might still be alive, Hall twice in the 1860s launched Arctic expeditions. To toughen himself against the cold he spent, according to one account, the winter of 1859 living in a tent on Mount Adams's southern hillside. His final expedition, in 1871, financed by the federal government, aimed to reach the North Pole. It didn't, though his ship *Polaris* attained the farthest point north of any vessel to that time. Hall died in Greenland under suspicious circumstances—he had received toxic amounts of arsenic during the last two weeks of his life—and was buried there. For Henry Howe, Ohio's chronicler, there was "no greater hero in all Arctic history." Of Hall's Arctic ventures, General Adolphus W. Greely, himself a polar explorer of note, claimed that "with similar limited resources no man has surpassed Charles Francis Hall."

We turn in on Filson Place, named after John Filson, Cincinnati's original surveyor. Numbers 2, 4, 6, and 8 Filson Place, circa 1885, are four interconnected Second Empire rowhouses, several originally occupied by Rookwood artists; mansard roofs allow a second story. Further along Celestial, another cul de sac, Riverview Place, mixes tiny nineteenth-century houses, contemporary condos, and a white Modern Movement creation (1983), with a cylindrical tower prominently visible from below.

We turn left on Hill St. Concrete steps, one of a number of viable stairs allowing interaction between Mount Adams residents and flatland foreigners, between *haute ville* and *basse ville,* disappear down the hill. Those with a few minutes to spare and stout legs (for the return!) might consider descending them. At the bottom a walkway to the right leads to the streets—Kilgour, Baum, Oregon—of **lower Mount Adams,** itself an interesting area to explore. These streets were built up before those on the hill above. We continue straight down more stairs, however, and cross Columbia Parkway on a pedestrian overpass, then wind further down the hill on an asphalt path that eventually drops us off on Martin Drive. Paths like this one allowed early Mount Adams workers easy access to riverfront factories.

Until recently a huge rusticated arched gate of white stone guarded the entrance on Martin Drive. On either side of the arch stretched massive battered walls. They probably contained the reservoir of 1853, once here. With the Front Street Pumping Station opposite us riverwards, there had been reservoirs here or nearby since the early nineteenth century. The arched gate may also have formed part of the waterworks. Behind it was an impressive oval esplanade, also of stone, but covered with vines, undergrowth, and graffiti. Resembling a ruined garden of the Italian Renaissance, this complex, the most Piranesian spot in all Cincinnati, disappeared in 1990.

Back at the top of the hill, just beyond the steps, the perforated metal tube serves as a sewer vent pipe. Where Hill St. intersects with St. Gregory St. is a

Martin St. arch. Through this magnificent, rusticated portal
hardy pedestrians began the ascent from Martin Drive to
Mount Adams. The arch was demolished in 1990 for
Adams Landing.

squarish stuccoed stone house (no. 1002), circa 1850, with a two-story wooden
portico. One of the oldest buildings on Mount Adams, it is an attractive vernacular
example of the Greek Revival style.

We turn up St. Gregory, the Mount Adams street most reminiscent of Montmartre. As the Sacré Coeur looms above the houses on Montmartre, so the Church
of the Immaculate Conception looms above those on St. Gregory. Be sure to peek
down the alleys separating them, and into the tiny courtyards. People here live in
close proximity. Decks protrude from every available wall surface. A visitor from
outer space might well conclude that a race of sunworshippers dwells in Mount
Adams. Inclined streets also offer distinct visual advantages; as foreground buildings and distant prospects are juxtaposed, architecture and topography work happily
together. Towne Properties, the firm that first began to restore the area, still owns

many buildings. Its plaque is a familiar sight. Jerome St., to our left, retains its brick paving and granite curbs. No. 1011, set off by two Russian olive trees and exquisitely landscaped, was built in 1965 by a Japanese-American couple on Japanese lines. Opposite and above, the postmodern townhouses (1987), each with a different façade, retain the scale of surrounding buildings. We go back to St. Gregory St. and continue uphill. Boutiques and restaurants here can and do have, like Francis Macomber in Ernest Hemingway's tale, a "short, happy life."

It is easy to get lost on Mount Adams. First-time visitors find it difficult to orient themselves within the apparently crazy-quilt pattern of streets. The streets themselves vary in length and width; most go up or down; many are one way, which tends to confuse car traffic; several bend, which adds visual interest but confuses further. Such diversity, however, enhances the neighborhood's intimate pedestrian scale. It is unlikely you will take this tour without asking, or being asked, for directions at least once. Actually, Mount Adams's streets do compose a grid of sorts but the hill's contours break it up and the constant up-and-down makes us lose consciousness of it. Even frequent visitors to Mount Adams get lost quite easily (and happily) within its small compass. Appropriate here is a French verb *flâner* that means "to hang around, stroll, walk from place to place with no purpose other than looking and enjoying." Mount Adams is a good place in which to *flâner*, to poke about and enjoy the street scene, the buildings, the vistas. I recall E. M. Forster's recommendation that "the best way of seeing" Alexandria's Turkish quarter "is to wander aimlessly about." It is good counsel, and we may apply it to Mount Adams. As with earlier tours, I provide an itinerary, but if the mood strikes you, feel free to become a *flâneur* and wander aimlessly about on your own. The Mount is most walkable. At every turn it rewards the pedestrian with serendipitous moments.

We go left at Pavillion St. up to St. Paul Place. Fronting us is the disused **Holy Cross Church,** or Church of the Passionist Fathers (1895), designed by Louis Piket. Its Renaissance Revival façade would not look out of place in Florence. The geometrical forms—circles, semicircles, rectangles, triangles—recall the Renaissance's fascination with mathematical relationships in art and architecture. The face and heart of Christ, symbols of the Passionist Fathers, appear on the façade. Angel faces look down from the springing points of the blind arches. Within, unrestored as of this writing, a huge barrel vault culminates in an apse balanced by niches. Beneath was (and is) a grotto, dedicated in 1898 to Our Lady of Lourdes. In 1970 the parish merged with that of Immaculate Conception, on the other side of Mount Adams, and in 1974 the church was deconsecrated. The community formed a nonprofit corporation to hold it until a sympathetic developer was found. This was Towne Properties, which in 1978 bought both it and the adjoining **Holy Cross Monastery.**

The monastery and church form an attractive ensemble that, visible from afar, dominates the hilltop. The orange-brick structure (1901) directly before us, also designed by Piket, now houses offices. It is attached to another building that, its façade yet uncleaned, appears older but is not; it was scheduled to become an executive-style inn. From St. Paul Place only its 130-foot tall campanile, the brick still a dark brown, is visible. As the campanile rises, fenestration increases from one to three. Borrowing forms and details from Romanesque as well as Renaissance, this campanile is one of Cincinnati's handsomest.

The **Cincinnati Observatory** previously occupied the site of the monastery. In 1841–1842 **Ormsby McKnight Mitchel,** a dynamic speaker, gave a hugely popular series of lectures on astronomy before Cincinnati's Society for the Diffusion of Useful Knowledge. The lectures sparked a sudden enthusiasm for astronomy in Cincinnati. Many Americans at this time thought that telescopes would enable them to discover the underlying principles of the universe. Nicholas Longworth promptly donated four acres on Mount Adams for an observatory. In late 1842 the Society, having raised $7,500 in $25.00 subscriptions, authorized Mitchel to procure a suitable telescope. "The monies for the telescope and construction of the observatory were raised by public subscription," Stephen Goldfarb has observed, "making this the first astronomical institution of its size to be built without royal or governmental patronage." Mitchel, who never did anything by halves, went to Munich where he commissioned an 11-inch Merz and Mahler refracting telescope. The largest in the United States in its day, the Cincinnati telescope was second in size only to that at the Royal Observatory at Pultova, Russia.

Mitchel persuaded John Quincy Adams, our sixth president and subsequently a longtime member of the House of Representatives, to speak at the dedication of the Observatory's cornerstone on November 9, 1843. Adams had an interest in science generally and in astronomy particularly. Twenty years before, during his presidential term of office, he had been keenly disappointed when Congress failed to establish a national observatory. Now seventy-six years old, Adams, "Old Man Eloquence," made the long journey west by train (to Buffalo), steamer (to Cleveland), canal boat (to Columbus), and stagecoach (to Cincinnati). Because of a torrential downpour he delivered his oration not at the observatory site but downtown at the Wesley Chapel. Astronomical observatories were, for Adams, "Lighthouses in the Sky." After he finished his oration, the audience voted by acclamation to change Mount Ida's name to Mount Adams. But funds to build the Observatory came in slowly. Mitchel, who designed the building himself, pitched in alongside the workmen. In 1845 the Observatory, eighty feet long by thirty wide, became usable; its roof could be rolled back to permit observation. Mitchel went on to serve as the Observatory's first director. He made at least one significant discovery: that the red star, Antares—*alpha* in the constellation of Scorpio—had a small green companion. Commissioned a major general in the Civil War, he died of yellow fever in 1862.

During Mitchel's tenure the Observatory faced one financial crisis after another. In addition, Mount Adams became increasingly affected by Basin smog. Smoke from hundreds of factory chimneys obscured the sky even on clear nights. In 1872 the Cincinnati Astronomical Society, which owned the Observatory, surrendered its property and jurisdiction to the newly founded University of Cincinnati. The next year the Observatory moved to quarters on Mount Lookout, on land donated by John C. Kilgour, who also gave $10,000 for a building. In 1904 a new Observatory was built near the first and a second 16-inch telescope installed. The Observatory remains active. Like others of the city's nineteenth-century institutions, it continues to contribute to the public good. Most Thursday evenings the University's Physics department offers guided tours with opportunities for viewing the stars.

Our story is not complete. In 1868 the Cincinnati Astronomical Society had brought in, belatedly to replace Mitchel, **Dr. Cleveland Abbe.** Realizing the impossibility of making useful contributions to astronomy on the Mount Adams site, Abbe obtained funding from the Cincinnati Chamber of Commerce to establish a fledgling weather bureau. With the cooperation of the Western Union Telegraph Company, he received telegraphed reports of meteorological data from around the country and on September 1, 1869, he began to issue daily weather bulletins. Subscribers were charged a small fee for the service, which quickly became popular. Advance warnings of storms and sudden changes of temperature could save merchants and farmers from large losses. Local pork-packers, for example, found it useful to know when a warm spell was coming, for it might force them to halt slaughtering. When in 1870 the federal government established the United States Weather Bureau as an adjunct of the Army Signal Service, it appointed Abbe chief meteorologist. He left Cincinnati to begin a long and distinguished career in Washington. In addition to weather forecasts, Abbe is responsible for instituting time zones, originally for the benefit of the railroads, across the country. The Cincinnati Observatory thus gave, indirectly at least, the nation its **Weather Bureau.** In his journal for June 1871 Ralph Waldo Emerson listed among the new scientific wonders of the age: "Add now, the daily predictions of the weather for the next twenty-four hours for North America, by the Observatory at Washington."

At the far (south) end of St. Paul Place, numbers 1034–1040, "Monastery Point," are Georgian Revival rowhouses. Or are they? Amazingly, when glimpsed earlier from Jerome below, these Janus-faced houses appeared postmodern. We present a bold postmodern face to the world, they seem to say, but you enter through the traditional and reassuringly familiar Georgian Revival portal. At the other end of St. Paul Place, at 1033 Monastery St., was the **Hessler Studio of Dancing.** Here native Cincinnatian Doris Day, née Kappelhoff, honed her dancing skills. From her home she took four streetcars to reach Hessler's. Hessler's was the third dance school she had attended and the one, she recalled in her autobiography, that she "fell in love with." It taught "Ballet—Toe—Tap—Acrobatic Dancing." Hessler's recognized her as a prize pupil and sent her to perform all over the city. One night when she was thirteen, a train hit an automobile in which she was a passenger: her career as a dancer was over. Barely twenty, Doris Day left for Hollywood as a singer.

We return down Pavillion St. At the intersection with St. Gregory St. we look north (left) down the street at the former **Mount Adams Public School** (1895). For decades Mount Adams school children had to walk down to schools in the Basin. In 1885 the school board found temporary quarters on the hill, and ten years later it put up this Queen Anne building. H. E. Siter, who designed a number of the city's other contemporaneous public schools, was the architect. The names of the building committee are blazoned on the façade. The school's most prominent features are its wide gables and steeply pitched hipped roof. Note the delicate Tudor arches etched in the beltcourse above the second story. Like the contemporaneous Mount Auburn school, this one has found appropriate reuse: since 1979 as classrooms for the Art Academy. Across the street, closer to us, was Holy Cross School. Now a new commercial complex (1988), on the whole compatible in scale, brick, and cornice line with the older buildings, fills the site.

Mount Adams offers meals for every taste and pocketbook. Nearby pubs and restaurants cater to diverse clienteles. Longworth's, visible from the corner, was formerly Fire Co. No. 15, the last horsedrawn operation in the city when it closed in 1922. The building dates from 1887. We now continue along Pavillion and turn right on Guido St.

The **Church of the Immaculate Conception** (1859), or (as it is more usually called) Immaculata, dominates the crest of Mount Adams. Visible from up and down the Ohio River, this Gothic structure of local gray limestone possesses utter simplicity of line. On December 8, 1854, Pope Pius IX affirmed the dogma of the Immaculate Conception; in 1858 Our Lady at Lourdes identified Herself as the Immaculate Conception; that year Archbishop Purcell, the prelate responsible for St. Peter's Cathedral downtown, donated the land; and in 1860 this church, designed by Anthony and Louis Piket, was dedicated.

In June 1871 it came under the direction of the Passionist Fathers. Father Guido Matessi, for whom Guido St. is named, was the first superior. The church rectory served as their first midwest home. In 1873 Father Guido established Holy Cross Retreat in the now-disused Observatory. It housed the Passionist Fathers until the new monastery buildings went up in 1901. On the Observatory property Father Guido also had built a second parish church of wood to serve English-speaking Catholics, mostly from Ireland, who had settled on Mount Adams. Immaculata was then given over to German speakers. The wooden church yielded in 1895 to the brick church we admired earlier. Since consolidation with Holy Cross in 1970, this parish is known as Holy Cross/Immaculata. Both parish schools closed in the 1970s.

Immaculata has been since 1860 the goal of an annual Good Friday Pilgrimage, and two years later was designated a pilgrimage shrine for Catholics who wish to honor the Virgin Mary. An hour before midnight on Holy Thursday pilgrims gather at the bottom of the steps on St. Gregory below. They await the first moment of Good Friday. At midnight the ascent begins and continues for twenty-four hours until the early minutes of Holy Saturday. The devout say a prayer on each step as they inch their way toward the summit. This Good Friday custom has led to Immaculata's second name as the "Church of the Steps." Some have trekked up these steps for forty, fifty, even sixty years.

Immaculata is usually open. We enter through the side door. The interior, without columns, is less austere than the exterior. The altar is of carved wood. From 1862 to 1870 Johann Schmitt, Frank Duveneck's teacher, painted the brightly colored apse murals. We gain the terrace in front of the church.

Mount Adams's quaint houses supply the foreground for still another dramatic **prospect.** The broad views that fascinated Frederick Law Olmsted and which he strove so hard to shape—think of those from Lookout Hill in Brooklyn's Prospect

Park, from Belvedere Castle in Manhattan's Central Park, and from Schoolmaster Hill in Boston's Franklin Park—Cincinnati enjoys as a natural blessing of terrain. The city has, if that were possible, a surfeit of prospects. Here, over picturesque gables and chimney-pots, we look out on the city. Before us the Ohio River makes a great double curve. Cradled in one of its loops are the towers of downtown Cincinnati. Across the Ohio lie the soft-toned, forested Kentucky hills, green fading into blue, blue into gray, line beyond line. After the buildings and the hills the landscape flattens out. We sense the vast spaciousness that lies beyond, a spaciousness that is the fundamental fact of the American landscape.

Why do we enjoy such views? I have often wondered. The appreciation of scenery is, after all, in the history of Western culture, though not of Eastern, a relatively new phenonemon. Petrarch's ascent of Mont Ventoux in the fourteenth century constitutes a turning point. Although Renaissance painters had included mountains as background, not until the eighteenth century did people begin seriously to think about and appreciate mountain scenery. Our modern habit of viewing the landscape from a hill or mountain has its roots in the eighteenth-century English landscape tradition, in the prospect poems inspired by it, and in the concept of the picturesque.

One reason we enjoy the view from Immaculata may be that to command a scene from above offers us delight and the illusion of control. Delight in that the perspective pleases, the illusion of control in that we feel we "understand" what we see before us. "Distance," said the poet Thomas Campbell, "lends enchantment to the view." Human beings, according to Tony Hiss, have an innate preference in landscape for prospect. Hiss defines *prospect* as a place from which we have "a long, sweeping vista—a place where viewing is unhindered and we can take in information from miles around." Samuel Johnson had earlier defined *prospect* in his *Dictionary* as a "view delineated; a picturesque representation of a landscape." We can agree with both Hiss and Johnson. Our liking for prospect may even have, as René Dubos has conjectured, a biological origin. From the heights ancient man could sight potential enemies before he himself was sighted. The view from above made survival more likely. Today, however, our experience of prospect is primarily esthetic. There is of course no certain way to enjoy scenery. You know it is right when it stirs the emotions.

Along with the Hudson River painters, the American Transcendentalists—exemplified by Emerson and Thoreau—best understood what prospect meant. In "Nature" (1836) Emerson, influenced perhaps by the eighteenth-century English essayist Joseph Addison, identified "a property in the horizon" that belonged to "no man but he whose eye can integrate all the parts." This property is free and open to all with eyes to see. For Addison, one of the first theorists of the picturesque, "a spacious Horizon is an Image of Liberty, where the eye has Room to range abroad, to expatiate at large on the Immensity of its Views, and to lose it self amidst the Variety of Objects that offer themselves to its Observation." In sum, a vista offers us the illusion of freedom.

Our capacity for perception enables us to experience many different kinds of pleasure. Thanks to the creative power of the human eye, Emerson writes, "the primary forms, as the sky, the mountain, the tree, the animal, give us a delight *in and for themselves.*" The pleasure we experience arises "from outline, color, motion, and grouping." For Emerson man had a primary need to enjoy prospects. "The health of the eye seems to demand a horizon," he continues; "we are never tired, so long as we can see far enough." Sight here begins to approach insight. In *Walden* (1854) Thoreau, citing Krishna in Hindu mythology, insisted that without a wide perspective human happiness remained illusory: "There are none happy in the world but beings who enjoy freely a vast horizon." For William Carney, "the contrast is between the unstructured space beyond and the stable, firm earth below."

Elevation enables one to see, evaluate, and respond to what is going on below. Just as Cincinnati's river is not too wide, so its hills are neither too high nor too precipitous. Again, the human scale seems right: from the river bank, we could see people on the far shore; from this hill, we can see people below. From neither vantage point need we feel overly distanced from the surrounding life. Enjoying the prospect from Mount Adams, we stand above the city and its people, but we also sense that they are near and that we are a part of both. We can also enjoy the scene as theater. Below, boats chug up and down the river, people walk in the streets and riverside parks, automobiles move along roads and cross bridges. This activity takes place within a context of the river, the hills, the movement of the clouds above, the feel of the wind on our faces.

On cloudy days we watch from Mount Adams the play of light and color on the Ohio River as it winds before us on its shimmering course. Water alters and tempers light. As the hours and seasons follow one another the Ohio is constantly changing its appearance. "A field of water," for Thoreau, "betrays the spirit that is in the air. It is continually receiving new life and motion from above. It is intermediate in its nature between land and sky." When Thoreau wrote he had Walden Pond in mind, but his words apply equally to any significant body of water that mirrors the changing sky. The Ohio's sinuous presence immeasurably enhances our pleasure in the prospects we enjoy from Mount Adams.

Below us the river, above us the sky. Cincinnati, a city of water and of hills, is also a city of light. From our vantage point high above the river we take in vast expanses of sky. For Emerson, the sky was "the daily bread of the eyes." Beholding it can be one of our greatest joys. We can be students of the sky and light as well as of the landscape and cityscape. Those who talk of the Midwest's dull scenery have not responded to its skies, its effects of atmosphere, its light. The fabled luminosity of Florence is intense and sharp, revealing objects uncompromisingly. We speak of the clarity of Tuscan light; in Raphael's paintings this pearly light, white shading into blue, defines the horizon. There is no *sfumato*, or haze: the horizon is etched absolutely. Or we recall the light of Paris and Ile de France, the ethereal transparency of its sky caught so well by the Impressionists. Light in Cincinnati, if less clear, can be no less evocative. Midsummer brings to the city a diaphanous haze in which heat appears to hang in the air. The hardwoods—and much of Cincinnati near the Ohio remains forest—add to the humidity of the air and thus to the viscosity of the light. To my mind, the landscape of the Ohio can be as beautiful as that of the Seine. But we are not used to thinking of it as beautiful. Whereas Monet, Pisarro, and Sisley have made us *see* the Seine, painters have not paid adequate homage to the Ohio's water, its hills and its sky. To capture the soft luminosity of the Cincinnati and Ohio landscape, in particular the aerial haze clothing its faraway hills, would require a poet's or a painter's sensitivity to place, a willingness to respond to the prospects that this city offers with such abundance.

Adams Landing, a large upscale housing development, began to rise below Mount Adams in 1990. It will stretch east from Bicentennial Commons, between Eastern Ave. and Columbia Parkway, to Kemper Lane. Adams Landing is scheduled to hold 1200 apartments and condominiums in six-story structures, with higher towers interspersed—how high has generated years of debate. No one denies that downtown needs additional residents, and few people now live in the area Adams Landing will occupy. But whatever the complex's final contours, it would be a pity if it detracted from Mount Adams itself. Its streets, its humanly scaled dwellings, its ambience constitute a precious and precarious resource. Mount Adams is irreplaceable. It belongs not only to residents but to those lured by the beauty of the site. Just as present legislation tends to protect buildings but not views of buildings, so views of and from hills also lack protection. The value of a view is not quantifiable. It may be esthetic, it may even be poetic or philosophical; it is certainly not tangible. Views are common properties to which everyone has a right. A real question also exists in regard to Mount Adams's stability, which Adams Landing may affect adversely. When I-71 was built in 1973 the side of the hill facing downtown caved in. Consequently, state and federal officials had to build a 1000-foot retaining wall, costing more than twenty-two million dollars, to shore up the fragile hillside.

We retrace our steps. Halfway to Pavillion St. a **pedestrian walkway** descends the hill. It winds behind terraces, restaurants, and gardens before debouching on St. Gregory St. Neighborhood walkways if maintained, as this one is, add a pleasurable dimension to urban life. Cincinnati cries out for an integrated network of walkways and steps to connect its hilltop neighborhoods with downtown. Like the steps, walkways allow pedestrians to establish an intimate relationship with the cityscape.

We turn right on Pavillion, then left on Carney St., a sharp descent, and walk down the hill. The Ohio River comes dramatically into view. At the far bend appears St. Rose's steeple. On the Kentucky side, directly across from us, is Bellevue's Church of the Sacred Heart (1893). Designed by Louis Piket, it has cream-colored brick and a bell tower of 1915 with a green copper dome. Since 1986 the church has been illuminated at night.

Carney St. drops sharply. Fewer houses here have undergone restoration than elsewhere on Mount Adams. At the bottom, we turn right on Hatch St., named for the pro-southern mayor, George Hatch, a soap and candle manufacturer who was also a Mount Adams developer. He was forced to leave Cincinnati in 1863. We may recall his splendid Greek Revival mansion, designed by Isaiah Rogers, at 830 Dayton St. The two-story houses on Hatch have the small frieze windows characteristic

Pedestrian walkway, Mount Adams. This walkway, connecting Guido and St. Gregory streets, allows glimpses into
gardens and back yards. It forms a part of the human-
scaled, pedestrian-oriented urban landscape of Mount
Adams.

of the Italianate style. Each house has a different lintel pattern. At Fort View Place
we turn right and walk to the end. Cannon here commanded the river in both directions during the Civil War. Steps descending to Hill St. form a vertical alley serving
three houses. Visible (and heard) below is Columbia Parkway.

We return to Hatch St. and continue downhill to the **Cloisters** (1972). This
group of wooden structures in polygonal shapes with shed roofs stands on piles
driven into the bedrock and supported by struts. The Cloisters does not endanger
Mount Adams's precarious, landslide-prone hillside. The complex is also virtually
earthquake-proof. Balconies are cantilevered out; window patterns vary. The metal
roofs, painted a soft orange, complement the wood, now weathered to an attractive
taupe: muted colors that reinforce the ensemble's understated effect. We may walk
into the complex to view the interior court. A less bucolic image of the Cloisters is
supplied by Jonathan Valin, the Cincinnati-based mystery writer, who sets several
gruesome scenes of *The Lime Pit* (1980) in "The Vicarage," unmistakably described
as "a gigantic redwood aviary propped on telephone poles."

The Cloisters. Balconies are cantilevered out from this residential complex (1972), designed by Hardy Holzman Pfeiffer. Writer Jonathan Valin described the Cloisters as "a gigantic redwood aviary propped on telephone poles."

Hugh Hardy & Associates (now Hardy Holzman Pfeiffer), an architectural firm of national distinction, designed the Cloisters. The shed roofs owe a debt to Charles Moore's Sea Ranch condominiums on the California coast. Moore's buildings, inspired by New England sheds and barns, themselves influenced numerous other slant-roofed residential complexes around the country. But the Cloisters's shed roofs also echo those in Over-the-Rhine and in Mount Adams itself, and help integrate the complex with the hill's other structures.

We return up Hatch St. To our right, a view opens up over Eden Park. 978 Hatch, once a one-story Victorian cottage topped with a mansard roof, has now become a twentieth-century International style mummy, wrapped so as to leave slits for eyes. Of the original building only the cornice peeps through. In both color and style, this is an unfortunate modernization. 973 Hatch retains its intact cast-iron front made by Rowekamp Bros., Ironworks, a firm that still exists.

Two well-known watering holes adjoin one another at the corner of Louden and Hatch streets: the Mount Adams Bar & Grill (938 Hatch) and, down the stairway and with a patio behind, the Blind Lemon (936). We turn right on Louden and cross Paradrome St. 1230–1236 Louden, a Queen Anne building with capped pyramidal towers and, in between, an infant pediment, now parades as "Bailiwick on the hill." Below the cornice we discover interesting corbelling, swags, serrated bricks, and rock-faced belt courses. The rear façade tells us that within all is modern.

Louden St. was previously known as Parallax St. Parallax is one of several Mount Adams streets that derived its name from Cincinnati's Astronomical Observatory. Another was Sidereal, appropriately enough an alley between Jerome and Ida streets. Although Parallax and Sidereal are no more, Celestial and Paradrome remain. In fact, Mount Adams's streets emanate a decidedly heavenly aura. In addition to the astronomical names, they memorialize a bevy of Christian saints: Paul, Jerome, and Gregory.

We have arrived at Eden Park. At the intersection of Louden St. and Parkside Place steps take us up to the **Cincinnati Playhouse in the Park.** This structure actually houses two buildings. The wing to the left contains the 223-seat Thompson Shelterhouse (1874; restored 1980), originally indeed a park shelterhouse and imaginatively remade into a small theater. That on the right holds the 629-seat Robert S. Marx Theater (1968). An atrium, the Marx Plaza (1980), connects the two theaters. Hardy Holzman Pfeiffer, architects of the Cloisters, designed both the Marx Theater and the Plaza. The firm, which specializes in redoing older structures and relating them to newer, achieved a decided success with the Playhouse complex.

Light and airy, the Playhouse lacks the traditional ornate embellishments— crystal chandeliers, gaudy tapestries, plush red velvet, excesses of gold and marble—that we associate with older theaters. Instead it offers a minimalist interior. In such a theater, presumably, the emphasis will fall on drama, not decor. Steps and floors consist of poured concrete, originally unpainted; ductwork is exposed; actors' dressing-room bulbs supplement natural, spot, and neon lighting. The floor-to-ceiling mirror presumably makes the audience more aware of itself, aware that it is, and will be, part of the show. White oak paneling in a 1987 remodeling covered the original tile wall (by Cambridge Tile) near the entrance to the Marx Theater. The tiles listed benefactors (and hinted at ornament); but the paneling added a welcome sense of warmth. The remodeling further lessened the high tech functionalism by removing the original fluorescent lighting. Overall, it softened the starkness of the structure. The picture window allows a fine view over Mount Adams, the Cloisters, and, across the unseen Ohio River, Bellevue's Sacred Heart Church. Anchoring the view on the far right is the monastery campanile. This view also relates the Playhouse to its park setting, which both encircles and complements it. The auditorium itself, shaped like an arc around a three-quarters thrust stage, has good sightlines and allows every member of the audience to be seated above the action.

The Playhouse in the Park launched its first season (in the Shelterhouse) in 1960 with Meyer Levin's *Compulsion.* Today, major productions, usually six a season and lasting three or four weeks, are staged in the Marx Theatre. In between, smaller-scaled productions, lasting two to three weeks, take place in the Shelterhouse. Plays here are more domestic in nature, require smaller casts, and, sometimes controversial, may appeal to more specialized audiences. In the Shelterhouse we sit only a few feet away from the stage in delightful intimacy with the actors.

If you should attend an evening performance, be sure to leave by the exit next to the Shelterhouse. The magical world conjured up by the play yields to the equally magical world of the city illuminated. The view in daylight allows us to pick out individual landmarks; the night view, equally riveting, lets us focus on the ensemble. After all, the lighting of cities after nightfall is a relatively new phenomenon in the history of urban life. It was first done at the Chicago Exposition of 1893; "The White City" was even more spectacular at night than during the day. Human beings, less in touch than ever with the rural night of stars and solitude, now experience the city as much by night as by day. Of Boston David McCord has written: "A fine city, like a good play, can be spoiled by bad lighting." Cincinnati has not been spoiled. In fact, it is more effectively lit than most cities I know. The Central Trust Tower, the Carew, Cincinnati Gas & Electric, and the Chiquita Center shine, amidst a fine supporting cast, distinctive and unmistakable at night. Since 1984 the Roebling Suspension Bridge, that jewel among the Cincinnati spans, has acquired its own tiara of lights.

If daylight still prevails, however, we continue our tour by going clockwise around the Playhouse. Jutting above the horizon is the campanile, in gray limestone, of the Cincinnati Art Museum. To its right is the red-brick Water Tower. To get to Mount Adams Drive we go down the concrete steps behind the Playhouse, casting as we do a backward glance at the Playhouse's parking garage (1990), designed to be unobtrusive yet gobbling up more of Eden Park's precious green space.

Detached on two or three sides from the surrounding community, Cincinnati's hilltop parks command the scene in splendid isolation. They appear to be designed more for vehicles, carriages originally, than for pedestrians. People drive to, around, and through them. The occasional jogger does his or her rounds, but except on sunny days few people walk or sit in the parks. Footpaths appear to be afterthoughts. Although it is just possible to walk through **Eden Park** without getting run over, competing with the cars takes a bit of practice. And to walk from, say, the Playhouse in the Park to the Krohn Conservatory, a relatively short distance as the crow flies, requires knowledge of the park's topography, its footpaths—and a determined effort of will.

Eden Park opened on July 1, 1870. Nicholas Longworth had named his vineyard "the Garden of Eden," and the park took the name over. Longworth's attempts to interest Cincinnati in acquiring park land date back to 1818. In 1846 he tried to persuade the city to buy a portion of his Mount Adams property. But the city consistently rebuffed his efforts. Land he offered the city at $1400 an acre in 1846 was, a decade later, worth $10,000 to $14,000 an acre. But when in 1865 Cincinnati found itself obliged to enlarge its waterworks, city engineers discovered that a tract owned by Longworth's heirs would make an ideal site for reservoirs. Practical motives for Eden park thus preceded esthetic. In 1866 the city authorized the land's purchase, part outright, the rest on favorable lease, with an option to buy. Subsequently, it made other purchases until it had over two hundred acres.

Trees, shrubs, and grass replaced the Longworth vineyards. Adolph Strauch, the noted landscape architect who had established a national reputation designing Spring Grove Cemetery, was instrumental in shaping Eden Park. As superintendent of the Board of Park Commissioners from 1871, Strauch fought to keep Eden Park

Eden Park scene, early twentieth century. Eden Park, like most American parks, was used more in earlier periods than it is now. Here we see a Sunday scene, with men in straw hats and women in summer bonnets. Horsedrawn carriages still greatly outnumber automobiles. Courtesy of the Cincinnati Historical Society.

a naturalistic retreat. Roadways he conceded were necessary; otherwise he preferred that manmade structures not encroach upon the park's beauty. Until the Mount Adams incline opened in 1876, however, Eden Park was accessible chiefly to those possessed of a horse or carriage. The leisured class liked to drive through parks—at the relaxed pace of the era—and liked to enjoy the scenery. Thus roads are at the most scenic spots and offer the best vistas. In the Eden Park of today this still holds true. Signs once admonished those pedestrians who did scale the heights not to trespass on the grass. The idea was that the urban poor would find being in a park an uplifting experience, but they had to behave themselves.

     While travelling in England Frederick Law Olmsted had liked the way park designers used animals to embellish the scene, so he included a deer paddock, a centuries-old symbol of gentility, in Manhattan's Central Park, Brooklyn's Prospect Park, and Chicago's Washington Park. Central Park also had until 1934 a sheep meadow. Grazing animals complemented the picturesque landscape, functioning as a grace note within the natural scene. Following Olmsted's lead, Strauch established a deer preserve in Eden Park. The look he desired was, like Olmsted's for Central Park, an idealized version of a natural setting: rolling lawns, clumps of trees strategically placed, the presence of water. Central Park, Olmsted boasted, was a "creation." He thought of it as a work of art and himself as an artist. He was also a humanist and a humanitarian. "The main object and justification" of Central Park, he wrote, "is simply to produce a certain influence in the minds of the people and to make a life in the city healthier and happier." Like Central Park, Eden Park was a carefully contrived and almost completely manmade landscape. It too aspired to make "a life in the city healthier and happier."

Eden Park subsequently became a key element in Cincinnati's greenbelt. In 1906 the city invited George E. Kessler, a disciple of Olmsted's and a landscape architect well known in his own right for designing the Kansas City park system, to submit a plan for the expansion of Cincinnati's parks. Kessler's scheme for Cincinnati, published the next year, went even further than his already ambitious Kansas City plan. It recommended that Cincinnati take advantage of its natural topography to develop hillside parks that made use of the vistas over the Basin and the Ohio River. Broad treelined boulevards would link the hilltops from Fairview to Eden Park, then march east to where Alms Park is now, and west to Mount Echo and beyond. Similarly, a treelined boulevard would have linked Burnet Woods and Eden Park.

Kessler's scheme, August Heckscher has observed in *Open Spaces: The Life of American Cities* (1977), kept

> a perfect balance between the squares and malls of the central business district and the parks of outer residential areas; between movement and stability; between neighborhood and metropolis. The open space system possesses an integrity and harmony that make it a true work of art, surpassing in scale and complexity anything previously proposed for an American city.

For Heckscher, the Kessler plan "represents the culmination of traditional park planning. In effect, it turns the whole city into a park, with open spaces defining and giving form to the business and residential sections." Kessler's grandiose scheme, truly breathtaking in its imagination and scope, would have given Cincinnati the finest park system in the country. Unfortunately, only the drive through Eden Park and its extension, now called Victory Parkway, were realized. Not for decades were Central Parkway and Columbia Parkway, both envisaged in the Kessler plan, completed.

By the later nineteenth century the picturesque vision had faded. Landscape design in this century lacks figures of the stature of Olmsted, Strauch, and Kessler. It often appears to have lost its way. After 1890 the playground movement gained many adherents in this country as abroad. Hard upon it came pressure to place sports fields in the parks. The prevalent philosophy behind park design now is that a park should embody multiple uses reflecting the diverse recreational needs of the population. Bicentennial Commons is an example of this philosophy and, on its own terms, an extremely successful one. It pays attention to landscape as well as provides facilities to keep people occupied. But for lovers of the picturesque there remains Eden Park, 183 acres of it. It will not disappoint.

Halfway down the slope is the **Murray Seasongood Pavilion** (1960). Music has been made on or near this site since 1872. The Seasongood Pavilion replaced the Schmidlapp Bandstand, a tile-roofed structure that itself replaced in 1914 a small wooden shelterhouse. The shelterhouse was the first structure to be built in

Eden Park, the first of many to compromise Strauch's vision of a natural environment untrammeled by human works. In 1892 Jacob Schmidlapp gave the city $50,000, the income to provide music for the public in Eden Park; a previous gift for the same sum by William Groesbeck had funded concerts in Burnet Woods. During the hot summer months bands played Old World classics. The Seasongood Pavilion, a gift from his sister, Martha S. Stern, commemorates one man's dedication to the cause of good government. Seasongood was instrumental in forcing through the city's charter in 1924 and subsequently became the city's first reform mayor. His efforts helped end nearly forty years of rule in Cincinnati by "Boss" Cox and his henchmen. The lines on the right side of the stage, from Wordsworth's sonnet sequence *The River Duddon,* affirm that a man's generous deeds survive his death. The Pavilion stage, now used for graduation exercises as well as for concerts, frames Mirror Lake and the Kentucky hills beyond. Above, on Mount Adams Drive, occurs the annual observance in mid-summer of "A Day in Eden." This festival includes music, performances, and balloon rides. For it the park's cultural institutions feature special exhibitions and tours.

The paths on either side of the Pavilion join below in a service road. On the far side of **Mirror Lake** (1965), the shallow reflecting pond, is the gazebo (1904). It is perfectly placed as an eye-catcher and a viewpoint. Visible above the trees is the Water Tower (1894). A reservoir has been here since 1878; previously a quarry occupied the site. The city covered over the reservoir, which now exists below Mirror Lake. A jet stream fountain (1987) shoots water sixty feet into the air. Beyond and below was a second reservoir, actually the first completed (1872). Work on this double-basin reservoir began in 1866. The advantage of having two was that when one needed draining, the other remained in service. The contours of both reservoirs followed Eden Park Drive. Locals now use the massive retaining wall of the lower reservoir, only partially demolished, to hone their mountaineering skills. The contractor who undertook the demolition thought that within was earth, not more stone; the city eventually had to let him out of the contract. As many an English country estate of the eighteenth century has a grotto or temple to set off the landscape, so now Eden Park has its own picturesque "ruin." On top of the retaining wall for the lower reservoir was a carriageway named for David Baker Pass, president of the Board of Public Works and the chief official behind the reservoir project. One of the carriageway's columns with Pass's name on it remains embedded in the hillside.

We follow the service road down the hill. On October 6, 1927, **George Remus** committed here one of the most publicized murders in Cincinnati history. In 1919, after the Volstead Act was passed and Prohibition became the law of the land, Remus and his wife Imogene moved to Cincinnati. Very quickly he made the city one of the bootleg capitals of America. In his third year of operation Remus grossed 25 million dollars and had a fabulous fifty-room mansion built on Price Hill. At the height of its activity, his empire employed 3,000 people and he had in hand 3,000,000 gallons of contraband liquor. But in 1922 the Justice Department caught up with the "King of the Bootleggers" and two years later sent him off to the federal penitentiary in Atlanta. Imogene subsequently took as her lover Franklin Adge, the special agent who had broken the case for the Justice Department. Upon exiting

Gazebo, Eden Park. The gazebo, painted a colorful green and yellow, replaced a thatched-roof spring house in 1904. The tiny onion dome, capped by a finial, hints of the East. The gazebo is meant to catch the eye, and it does.

from prison, Remus caught up with her here and shot her. Public sympathy was strangely with him. Artfully pleading "transitory maniacal insanity," Remus was judged not guilty and was sentenced to Lima State Hospital for the Criminal Insane. Five months later, having declared Remus sane, the state of Ohio set him free.

On our right, the Cloisters steps rhythmically down the hillside. From here we see how well the complex works within its site and with Mount Adams's older structures. We go left down the embankment toward the machicolated reservoir wall. At the base it is forty-eight and a half feet thick; earth infill has half-buried the massive limestone blocks of the arches.

Before us is the Romanesque Revival **Pumping Station,** now disused. On the façade we make out "Cincinnati Waterworks": in the spandrels below the name, "1889"; above it, our old friend, *Juncta Juvant,* i.e., "Strength through Union." Below *Juncta Juvant* we discern a scale, a sword, and a caduceus. Three concentric inset arches delimit the main entrance; floral decoration appears in the spandrels and pediment. Stone quoins delimit the windows, and the building culminates in deep corbelled machicolations. Near the top of the chimney animal heads—griffins it would seem from the wings—peer down upon us.

The Cincinnati Water Company, organized in 1817, began two years later to provide water for the bustling young community. Pumped from the Ohio River, first by horse power, later by steam engine, the water was raised into reservoirs and by gravity piped through wooden mains to consumers. Occasionally mains become clogged by such marine fauna as, according to one report, "eels, a 16-inch catfish, and an 18-inch salamander." In 1839 the water company, now controlling nineteen miles of wooden mains and three-and-a-half miles of iron pipes, came under city ownership. Decade after decade demand continued to outrun supply. The city intended that the Eden Park reservoirs provide for the area north of 4th St. In 1908 it abandoned the Front Street Pumping Station (whose ruins we saw in Bicentennial Commons) and moved the Water Works about eight miles upstream to California, Ohio. The city's Main Pumping Station (1907) is about two miles upriver.

We walk uphill across the lawn to an asphalt path, which we follow through a landscaped area. The path goes by the Deupree Memorial Gazebo (1982). If it is summer, a birdbath stands opposite; if winter, it has metamorphosed into a bird feeder. In spring we experience here an explosion of spider magnolias. Visible ahead is the **Krohn Conservatory** (1933). Actually the third structure on this site, it replaced a municipal greenhouse of 1894, itself a replacement for the building that went up after the 1879 Cincinnati Exposition. Named for Irwin M. Krohn, long a member of the Board of Park Commissioners, the Conservatory houses plants from around the world.

Large iron-and-glass structures are a nineteenth-century phenomenon. Although the first arose in 1833 in the Paris botanical gardens and Kew Gardens outside London had its Great Palm House by 1848, unquestionably the best-known was Joseph Paxton's gigantic Crystal Palace (1851), set up in London's Hyde Park to house the Great Exhibition. Glass technology, like bridge engineering—for example, that for Cincinnati's Roebling Bridge—constitutes one of the major contributions that nineteenth-century engineering made to architecture.

The Krohn Conservatory is Cincinnati's horticultural showcase. The casual visitor will find it pleasant to while away an hour or so here; the passionate horticulturalist will of course want to linger. Regular displays include palms, ferns, tropical plants, cacti, and orchids. In the vestibule *Bougainvillea spectabilis*, from Brazil, hangs above our heads. The entrance hall rises forty-five feet. Looking up, we feel an exultant sense of light, air, and space. We are facing the Palm House, which besides palms contains banana and rubber trees. Goldfish swim in the stream below. Plant motifs adorn the Art Deco railing metalwork. We traverse a tropical rain forest along a curved path. At the far end we may pass underneath the waterfall via a grottolike tunnel or cross the Japanese-style bridge.

The left-hand wing houses tropical plants; high humidity and warm temperatures make themselves felt. Going counterclockwise, we find here several important economic plants: pomegranate, cacao, guava, and, at the center, severely pruned, a tall papaya tree. Opposite the papaya is a chauvier fig tree, the Conservatory's oldest specimen.

The Floral Display House, to our right upon entering, features changing displays. Invariably they draw the largest crowds. Krohn, one of the country's few conservatories that still puts on seasonal shows, presents six annually: pre-spring, Easter, Mother's Day, summer, fall chrysanthemum, and Christmas. Around the walls of the Floral Display House are citrus trees bearing oranges, tangerines, giant Ponderosa lemons and grapefruit. The orange tree on the left is the Conservatory's second oldest specimen. Off this wing is an impressive collection of cacti. Above the orchid display at the far end, possibly the Conservatory's loveliest spot, ranges the huge *Monstera deliciosa,* better known from the shape of its leaves as the Swiss Cheese plant. Once I saw a nearly full-grown kitten asleep atop it. Sometimes open is a small outdoor wing with a trellis of ironwood, which leads to a charming fountain of a boy holding an apple. As you leave the building don't miss the glassed exhibit case of insect-eating plants.

During the Christmas season the Krohn presents a full-sized Nativity scene, with stable, crêche, statues, and live sheep and cows. Originally displayed in 1939 in Lytle Park downtown, the Nativity scene migrated to the Conservatory's front lawn in 1960. In early spring a host of daffodils blooms on the hillside opposite. Plantings in Cincinnati's parks are staggered: flowers and shrubs bloom during the entire growing season. The Parks department puts out a brochure indicating what flowers may be found when and where.

We turn right, go around the building, and cross the parking lot. Carl Kern, who did work both at Spring Grove Cemetery and at the Cincinnati Zoo, executed the rocky landscape behind the Conservatory. At the top of the stairs (Cliff Drive) go left to the Upper Overlook. A granite obelisk—the **Ohio River,** or **Navigation Monument** (1929)—stands at the hill's highest point. Below us the river makes a lazy S curve. Dayton, Ky. lies behind its flood wall; marinas dot the shoreline. The Ohio River Monument commemorates the achievement of the Army Corps of Engineers, which in the 1920s built fifty locks and wicket dams along the length of the Ohio. From Pittsburgh to Cairo, Illinois, a distance of 981 miles, the river was "canalized" to a minimum depth of nine feet. No longer would low water in summer interrupt river traffic. On the plaque are canoes, flatboats, and steamboats representing a palimpsest of river scenes from the seventeenth century to the twentieth. Note the imaginative rendering of the Carew Tower, begun in 1929 but not yet completed. The foreground Indian salutes this river activity: given what the white man's coming meant for him, it is a gentle response. At the dedication, President Hoover, an ex-engineer, declared: "What the river has lost in romance, it has gained in tonnage." That is undeniable. But towboats and barges, however efficient as carriers, lack the picturesque grace of steamboats.

We walk along the sidewalk toward the Water Tower. To the right, just before the bridge, a path with steps leads downward. The path drops us off on Eden Park Drive next to one of the eagles flanking both approaches to the **Melan Arch Bridge.** The eagles came from the Chamber of Commerce building at Vine and 4th streets that burned in 1911. Built in 1895 by the Melan Arch Construction Co. of New York and named for its designer, Josef Melan, this bridge is one of America's earliest steel-reinforced, poured concrete spans. Prior honors in the use of concrete go,

Vista over the Ohio River, from Eden Park. This view, from Twin Lakes overlook, may be the finest of the many splendid river views from Eden Park. The photograph looks east, upstream, toward a majestic "S" bend. The line midway up the hill is Columbia Parkway. St. Rose's Church and the city's Main Pumping Station are just left of center.

of course, to the Romans and the Mayans. Built by an Austrian engineer, Frederick von Emperger, the Melan Arch Bridge preceded by less than a decade downtown's pioneering concrete highrise, the Ingalls Building.

We walk along the Lower Overlook in front of the Twin Lakes, created in 1891 on the site of the quarry that had supplied limestone for the reservoir's retaining walls. We enjoy the last and possibly the finest in our series of **vistas** over the Ohio River and the Kentucky hills. This section of Eden Park forms a symphony of curves, another lovely exercise in the picturesque. We return by crossing the footbridge separating the ponds, which are joined by an artificial waterfall. These ponds, like that in Mount Auburn's Inwood Park, were created for iceskating. Iceskating, long popular in Holland, was little practiced in America until it caught on in Central Park in 1858. It quickly became a favorite winter pastime, immortalized in Currier & Ives prints. Iceskating must have once had more devotees than it does now, for when I have walked by in winter the ponds have been drained. The picturesque "comfort station" and concession stand are of stone, with metal shutters and shingle roofs. The restrooms are among the few in Cincinnati parks that remain open. Public restrooms are an indication of how civilized a city is (at least in the amenities), and on this count it pains me to say that Cincinnati, like most American cities, does not come off well—at least in comparison to British and European cities. Nearby, the *Capitoline Wolf* nurses two infants, Romulus and Remus. The wolf came to Cincinnati in 1931, a gift from the city of Rome. "Anno X" on the plaque refers to the tenth year of Mussolini's Fascist regime. The Etruscan original of this statue stands on Rome's Capitoline Hill. Presumably Cincinnati rated its copy because of its name, indirectly derived from the Roman general Cincinnatus. Long before even that worthy's time, Romulus, so the legend goes, grew up to found Rome, named after him. The two infants of the original (actually Renaissance additions) transform the wolf's bellicosity to a fiercely protective attitude toward her human babes.

On the greensward across Victory Parkway stands Cincinnati's **Vietnam Memorial.** Mounted on a marble base, a lifesize bronze, traditional in style, depicts two battle-weary foot soldiers. Their poses suggest human suffering and human endurance more than heroism. This monument, by local sculptor Ken Bradford, invites comparison with the representational group of three infantrymen placed near Washington's Vietnam Memorial in 1983, following the heated controversy over Maya Ying Lin's abstract 1982 design of polished black granite panels that had won the original competition. Cincinnati's veterans themselves chose Bradford's design.

The circular **Water Tower** (1894) has loomed over us ever since we entered Eden Park. Visible from many parts of the city, it has long remained a favorite visual icon for Cincinnatians. Designed by the Hannaford firm as a castle keep, or *donjon,* the 172-foot tower, originally a pressure tank, sits on a massive ashlar base. The droplet to the left of the entrance designates the structure as an American Water Landmark. Note the huge brackets below the brick-and-stone crenellated parapet. Bewinged gargoyles, cousins to the griffins we admired on the Pumping Station, adorn the elevator shaft, once crowned with a turret. Formerly the tower afforded visitors (as the 1904 Baedeker guide noted) splendid views over the city, the Ohio River, and the Kentucky Highlands. Disused since 1912, the tower is no longer open to the public.

Down the hill on the right we come upon a curved stone wall known as **"Authors' Memorial Grove."** On April 30, 1882, Cincinnati's first Arbor Day, and the first in the United States, local schoolchildren placed stone markers before thirty-six trees planted to commemorate American authors, both local and national. Arbor Day, adopted by many civic improvement societies in the late nineteenth century, was once a widely recognized holiday. Local authors commemorated here included Alice and Phoebe Cary and Harriet Beecher Stowe; national figures included such giants as Poe, Hawthorne, Longfellow, and Emerson, who died during the very hour the delegation from Hughes High School planted a tree in his honor. The park badly needed trees, for throughout most of Cincinnati's history its hills have been bare. In 1980 the battered markers that had survived nearly a century were placed here.

We return to the ridge and walk down to **"Presidents' Grove."** Markers at the bases of trees identify presidents. Jackson gets a scarlet oak, Grant a red oak. For some curious reason George Washington gets, not a cherry tree, but a white oak. Later presidents have chosen their trees, e.g., Jimmy Carter picked a loblolly pine. Nearby, Richard Nixon's tree has mysteriously vanished.

A blacktop path to the right curls steeply downhill to a paved area. Ahead is the **gazebo,** painted a colorful green and yellow. Replacing a thatched-roof spring house, the gazebo originally provided a view over the upper reservoir. Each of its

Water tower, Eden Park. This structure (1894), designed by the Hannaford firm in the style of a castle keep or *donjon,* has not been used since 1912. Visible from many places, the water tower has long been a favorite icon for Cincinnatians.

eight sides has two scalloped arches supported by cast-iron columns with decorated capitals. The red-tile octagonal roof culminates in an onion dome, crowned by a finial; it hints of the East. The spring here, once thought to have medicinal value, was closed in 1912 by the City Board of Health as unsanitary. We go right, following the path around the reservoir, and up past the Seasongood Pavilion. Ida St. lies beyond. The large building on the hill to our right houses the Cincinnati Art Museum, the largest of Eden Park's manmade incursions and the subject of our next tour.

The Cincinnati Art Museum. Photo by Ron Forth, 1986. Courtesy of the Cincinnati Art Museum.

12

Cincinnati Art Museum

C ITIES without museums are diminished things. Museums tell us much about the state of a city's cultural life; they are, in effect, the custodians of its cultural integrity. Museums reflect a city's development, its history, its tastes, its values, and what it has thought (and thinks) important culturally. For a city its size, Cincinnati has splendid museums, for which it can—and does—feel deserved pride. I grew up within a few blocks of New York's Metropolitan Museum of Art and often stopped by on free afternoons after school. I scampered through its vast spaces and cavernous galleries, then half-deserted on weekdays, gaping at the treasures around me, felt more than understood. Images and impressions from those visits remain with me to this day. A museum can be one of the institutions that shapes a person's life. The Metropolitan helped to shape mine, and I suspect that for many Cincinnatians the Art Museum has helped to shape theirs.

The **Cincinnati Art Museum** contains impressive collections of art from many civilizations and schools. Its holdings span more than fifty centuries and range from Egyptian to modern works. Visitors find themselves constantly surprised not only by individual works but by the collection's overall quality. Although the Art Museum, unlike the Metropolitan, does not overwhelm one with masterpieces, what it lacks in large collections, it makes up in balance. Its smaller size allows us a more easily encompassable experience. The holdings of seventeenth-century Spanish and eighteenth-century British painting are outstanding; the Far Eastern and Islamic holdings are both select and resplendent; the extensive collections of older musical instruments and African art, both subjects incorporated into the museum's holdings at early dates, are unusual for a general art museum. And for a few artists—Gainsborough, Corot, Hiram Powers, Frank Duveneck, Rouault—we can look at a number of major works.

In 1870 Boston, Washington, and New York founded museums of art. The 1870s, fertile for so much of Cincinnati's cultural life, witnessed not only the first May Festival and the building of Music Hall but also the movement that led to the Art Museum. There had been earlier attempts. In 1828 Frederick Eckstein had made a serious attempt at schooling frontier taste by founding an Academy of Fine Arts;

355

for a few years after 1838 a Cincinnati Academy of Fine Arts struggled along; and in 1854 the energetic Sarah Worthington King Peter established the Ladies Academy of Fine Arts. Though it disbanded in 1864, it left behind the important legacy of involving Cincinnati women in the arts. In the Women's Pavilion at the 1876 Centennial Exhibition in Philadelphia, Cincinnati women had a room of their own, where their art ceramics and carved wooden furniture attracted widespread attention. The next year, Elizabeth Perry, heir to Sarah Peter's vision, organized the Women's Art Museum Association, a group of public-spirited women dedicated to establishing a permanent art institution in Cincinnati. They proposed as model for the new museum London's Victoria and Albert (then called the South Kensington Museum), which specialized in the decorative and applied arts. The new museum, they believed, should have practical as well as esthetic value.

What turned vision into reality was Charles West's offer in 1880 to give $150,000 toward a museum building, providing the community matched this gift. One month later, it had surpassed it. In 1881 the Cincinnati Art Museum Association, the successor to the Women's Art Museum Association, acquired its first objects. The next year the city provided the museum with nearly twenty acres in Eden Park, and West announced a second gift of $150,000 for endowment. Alfred T. Goshorn, who had headed the Centennial Exhibition in Philadelphia, was chosen as first director. James McLaughlin was hired as architect, and work began on a building in the Richardsonian Romanesque style, which was dedicated in 1886. Though now surrounded by later additions and difficult to see, the museum's original structure still stands. The neighboring **Art Academy**—also designed by McLaughlin, also Romanesque—was completed the next year. Old photographs show the two buildings standing somewhat apart, the academy behind and left of the museum (they are now physically connected to one another).

The drive to the museum through Eden Park, with its spectacular views over the Ohio River and the Kentucky hills, is itself exhilarating. (If walking from downtown, follow the directions for Mount Adams to Elsinore Tower, then climb the steps behind the tower.) Four massive Doric columns topped by a pediment indicate the main entrance. To its right, the raised temple porch with Ionic columns derives from the Temple of Athena Nike on the Acropolis in Athens. Before it stands Jacques Lipchitz's oversized bust (1960) of Robert A. Taft. From here the museum appears to be a turn-of-the-century Beaux Arts building. But in approaching the museum complex we may have noticed a modern façade, then a Romanesque façade. Behind the modern resided until recently the Cincinnati Historical Society; behind the Romanesque still resides the Art Academy. The academy began in 1869 as the McMicken School of Drawing and Design. In 1871 it became the School of Design of the University of Cincinnati and in 1884, subsequent to a generous gift of $370,000 from Joseph Longworth, it was transferred from the University to the Cincinnati Museum Association. In 1887 it emerged as the Art Academy of Cincinnati. "The Special Aim of this School," the initial catalogue stated, "is not merely the study of Painting and Sculpture, but also the improvement of the industrial arts." The academy fostered the extraordinary efflorescence of painting, ceramics, and woodcarving that took place in Cincinnati at the end of the nineteenth century. By

1900, and for several decades afterwards, it ranked among the best schools of its kind in the country.

Like other older American museums, Cincinnati's is built in a mix of styles that offers a short course in the city's taste for monumental architecture, a course we shall largely forgo for now in order to contemplate the treasures within. Suffice it to say here that the Doric portico before us concludes the Schmidlapp wing (1907), designed by Daniel Burnham Associates. Jacob Schmidlapp, who had earlier chosen Burnham to put up his skyscraper at 4th and Walnut streets, chose the Burnham firm to design the wing in honor of his daughter. Since the end of World War II it has served as the museum's main entrance. Six other additions have followed the Schmidlapp wing: the Ropes wing (1910), the Hanna, Emery, and French wings (1930), the Alms wing (1937), and the Adams-Emery wing (1964). We shall more easily contemplate the evolution of the museum complex from the garden within than from here.

What sets the Cincinnati Art Museum apart from most other major museums I know is its distinctive local accent. More than many cities its size, Cincinnati has nourished diverse forms of art. During the last three decades of the nineteenth century the city became a major contributor to the national arts scene, traditionally dominated by the East Coast, and also became a significant artistic center in its own right. Its achievement includes paintings by artists who were born or trained here, or who lived here, among them Frank Duveneck and Henry Farny; hand-decorated ceramics from the Rookwood Pottery, America's chief art pottery; hand-carved wooden furniture by, or made under the direction of, Benn Pitman, Henry Lindley Fry, and William Henry Fry; and, in the twentieth century, paintings and Rookwood compositions from the city's hotels. Several picturesque street signs even turn up in the Folk Arts room. Works in all these modes justify local pride, and at its best this art has more than parochial or regional significance. Out of the cityscapes we have walked through, and the buildings we have looked at, came the paintings, ceramics, and furniture we shall see. By honing our sense of Cincinnati as a place, they give depth to our portrait of the city.

Unfortunately, the museum's presentation of Cincinnati's artistic heritage makes it difficult to gain an overall sense of its development or significance. Paintings by local artists are tucked away in small rooms behind glass doors on the far side of the American collections; the few pieces of Cincinnati-made furniture on display are scattered about, and the Rookwood ceramics are placed in a gallery that most visitors use as a hallway. A comprehensive, coherent presentation would do much to establish the city's legitimate claim that during the nineteenth century it ranked as the major art center in the trans-Appalachian West. To the visitor, these works of Cincinnati art may remain largely unknown. Equally, they may be among a visit's pleasant surprises.

No one can take in a collection such as this at a single visit. As with any intense experience, the effort of concentration becomes after a time too great. "These wonders," Keats said upon viewing the Elgin Marbles, bring about "a most dizzy pain." The mind may experience, as Keats's did, almost unbearable fullness. Afterwards, it may be left with only vague memories, the chief of which may be fatigue. But the contemplation of great art, as Keats implies, can also be exhilarating and profoundly moving. It challenges us to respond to the towering achievements of human creativity. Cumulatively, a visit to a good museum enables us to experience, in outline form at least, the sweep of human history.

Those who prefer to savor the museum gradually may wish to break up this tour, perhaps by looking at one floor one day, the other on a second occasion. But since many people on an initial visit like to glance at least once at "everything," I take you on a serendipitous stroll through nearly all the galleries. I rarely linger over individual objects, and I do not always indicate the museum's best-known works. No tour should entirely preempt the sense of surprise that a museum, no less than a city, offers. The best result this chapter could have is to compel you to make repeated visits, to devise your own tours. Eventually you may find yourself returning to look hard at only one or two sections, then perhaps at only one or two objects.

Gallery displays often change. Familiar works disappear, replaced by others that, unfamiliar at first, become familiar in their turn. Museums are always moving objects (and collections) about, renovating galleries, planning exhibitions. (Beginning in January 1991 a large portion of the museum underwent a major renovation designed to restore its interior spaces to their original grandeur. The renovation is scheduled to take nearly two years.) Because of this I usually do not indicate the precise location of a work in a gallery; it may vary from the time I write this chapter and the time you read it. One visit will barely probe the collection's depth. Like other major repositories, the museum repays repeated visits. Art historians and museum buffs will go through the galleries in their own way and at their own pace. For them, this chapter will indicate the nature of the holdings and suggest how they may find what interests them. Others may use the chapter as an introduction to the collection, still others as a gallery-by-gallery tour.

A few words about layout. Like other large complexes built over decades, the Cincinnati Art Museum may at first appear daunting. The floor plan is intricate; rooms are of different size and shape; decors vary. View the layout as a challenge, one that forces you to establish visual landmarks as you go along. The gallery plan has been described as "meandering" but also as "comfortable." In short, it is not unlike the city itself. A comfortable layout can foster a sense of intimacy and here we often have the impression that we are less in a public gallery than in a private home. The experience usually remains intimate in another sense: even on weekend afternoons great fleets of people do not usually clog the galleries. Thus we may view art objects in the tranquillity necessary for appreciation. Paintings are hung sufficiently apart that we have room in which to contemplate them. Like Cincinnati itself, the Art Museum has more to offer us than its individual works of art. What we find depends, as in our walks around the city, upon how much energy we bring to the endeavor, how hard we are willing to look, how eagerly we care to respond to what our eyes see.

First-floor galleries contain Egyptian, Greek, Etruscan, and Roman antiquities; historic musical instruments; tribal arts; medieval artifacts; decorative arts, which include American, English, and French period rooms; and Near East, Islamic, and

Far East holdings. European and American paintings occupy the second floor. Since many visitors will find them of primary interest, we begin there. By and large we can follow the schools sequentially, and that is a blessing. Unlike some other museums whose donors have insisted their benefactions be kept together, this museum has integrated its major gifts into the collection. Thus the museum has benefited from its donors without having them impose overly their vision of art on the collection or on the way it is presented. Before climbing the stairs be sure to pick up a floor plan at the reception desk. You will often refer to it.

Italian school (**gallery 65**). This gallery contains paintings from the Italian Renaissance, with a few subsequent. Botticelli's *Judith with the Head of Holofernes,* a radiant composition in blues and oranges, depicts the biblical heroine who insinuated herself into the arms of the Assyrian general Holofernes, then slew him as he slept off a drunken stupor. Judith strides homewards; her insouciant smile gives nothing away. Another, more polished version of this episode hangs in the Uffizi. On the reverse of the Cincinnati panel, the couchant deer and monkeys constitute Botticelli's only known work without humans. Bronzino often painted *Eleanora,* wife of Cosimo de' Medici. A formal portrait, it is concerned with pose and courtly bearing. It was among the collection of forty-six Old Master paintings that Mary M. Emery bequeathed to the museum in 1927. This collection, the most important ever left to the museum, also includes works by Cranach, Titian, ter Borch, Hals, and van Cleve.

Carracci's oval *Clytie* presents a flower-child vainly resisting the urgings of Cupid. A mortal spurned by Apollo, Clytie slowly wasted away. In pity the gods changed her into a sunflower—she holds one in her right hand—who then might always gaze in hopeless love toward the sun. Mantegna's *Esther and Mordecai,* one of the museum's great treasures, depicts the Old Testament heroine consulting with the sage Mordecai about a Persian edict that decreed the massacre of the Jews. Mantegna here attempts stone-like sculptural forms and paints them in a monochromatic color scheme (black, white, and gray) known as *en grisaille.* Greco-Roman statues were then believed unpainted, and Mantegna had them in mind painting this picture. To accentuate the monumental appearance of the figures he makes us look up at them. In Botticini's *Virgin and Child* the Virgin's illumined face is somber, her child's uncertain, as if He had foreknowledge of His fate. The landscape is ethereal; foreground, midground, and background are exquisitely delineated. The round form (called a *tondo,* from Italian *rotondo,* "round") increases the illusion of depth.

Although Titian did other portraits of the Holy Roman Emperor *Philip II,* they derive from this full-scale sketch, known as a *modello,* for which Mrs. Emery in 1914 paid $315,000, then an extraordinary sum. Titian kept this painting in his studio as a model for his later court portraits of the Emperor. He depicts Philip wearing the Order of the Golden Fleece, the oldest and most prestigious of the medieval chivalric orders. Tintoretto's *Portrait of a Venetian Doge,* newly restored, glows. In a frame behind the doge is his villa on the Brenta to which he would have escaped for the summer. Stage curtains and dramatic spotlighting mark Guercino's *Mars with Cupid* as a Baroque composition, one that reaches beyond the picture

Andrea Mantegna, *Esther and Mordecai*. This painting depicts the Old Testament heroine consulting with the sage
Mordecai about a Persian edict that decreed the massacre of
the Jews. Few paintings by Mantegna exist in the United
States; Cincinnati is fortunate to have this one. Courtesy of
the Cincinnati Art Museum.

frame. The implied presence is that of Venus, toward whom, in a now-lost pendant,
Mars looks longingly. Tiepolo was a Venetian who spent his last years at the Hapsburg court in Madrid, where he did *San Carlos Borromeo*. Meant to be viewed from
below, this painting once formed part of a grand altarpiece. Borromeo, patron saint
of seminaries, appropriately finds a home in this city once filled with seminaries and
religious institutions.

Walnut wainscotting and a brocaded silk wallcloth nicely set off the artworks,
refuting twentieth-century notions that art is best seen against a neutral background.
Most artworks were intended for rooms that were anything but neutral. We experience the paintings in this gallery in a sympathetic and complementary environment.
Appropriate pieces of period furniture, artworks in their own right, also complement the paintings. We find here a painted Renaissance *cassone* and two late
eighteenth-century chairs from Genoa. The elaborate frames were also often designed specifically for the paintings they enclose.

Spanish paintings (**galleries 66, 67**). The gigantic Tendilla *retablo,* or altarpiece (ca. 1550–1555), dominates gallery 66. This room was created to resemble
the hall of a neoclassical Spanish palace. The retablo, named after the Count Ten-

dilla who commissioned it, is a richly carved architectural composition. The thirteen panels facing us, a collaborative work from the studio of Jan Sanders van Hemessen with Caterina van Hemessen, depict stories from the Old and New Testaments that few at that time could read. Center panels represent the life of Christ, side panels Old Testament scenes. Only on Sundays and church holidays was the retablo opened; other days communicants gazed at the Annunciation, done *en grisaille*, to which the Old Testament had pointed. Now that the retablo is always open, we have to supply the drama ourselves. If you've ever wondered how the serpent offered Eve the apple, the panel at the top left shows you—in his mouth. In sacrificing Isaac (right-hand panel) Abraham, in apparently swiveling his head 180 degrees, performs an anatomical miracle.

Murillo's endearing *St. Thomas of Villaneuva as a Child Dividing his Clothes among Beggar Boys* spotlights the future saint, known for his generosity and charity. Whereas the beggar boys remain in the shade, St. Thomas occupies the light. Murillo, by making his subject a child, virtually created a new genre. Velázquez depicts *Philip IV,* less politically ambitious than Titian's Philip II, as a patron of the arts. He has the long face and projecting lower lip characteristic of the Spanish Hapsburgs. Alonso Cano in *St. John the Baptist* has wonderfully drawn the Lamb of God; appropriately, for it, not the epicene St. John, is the painting's subject. In El Greco's *Christ on the Cross with View of Toledo* Christ dominates an unearthly landscape.

Gallery 67. The earliest frescoes from the Ermita (Hermitage) de San Baudelio date from the twelfth century, others from the fourteenth and fifteenth centuries. The artists are unknown. A pilgrimage church built when the Moslems still controlled Spain, the Ermita remains, but since the 1920s its frescoes have gone to Boston, Indianapolis, The Cloisters, and to Cincinnati. The museum has recreated the original setting, which allows you to get a sense of a painted Romanesque interior. No one has quite figured out what an ibis is doing over the main altar. The falconer is probably the donor who paid for the murals. He rides a white ass, a most unknightly steed, perhaps in deference to the humble mount on which Jesus entered Jerusalem. Yet his glance in its insouciance rivals Botticelli's Judith's. In the nearby *Annunciation* Juan de Flandres modelled both Gabriel and the Virgin upon an idealized but recognizably red-haired Isabella of Castile.

Flemish, Dutch, German, and French schools (**galleries 68, 69**). Flanders, occupying present-day Belgium and northern France, long had a vigorous cultural life. Its artistic traditions culminated in the gigantic figure of Rubens (1577–1640). Like Titian's *Philip II,* Rubens's *Samson and Delilah* is a sketch, or *modello,* for a larger painting, now in the National Gallery, London. Rubens employed in his studio a small army of assistants who had a particular specialty; for example, one did foliage, another clouds, a third animals, a fourth drapery. Often in a reputed "Rubens" the artist has done only the face. But this exquisite *modello* is entirely his. Rubens seized the culminating moment in the story, when the Philistines snip away Samson's strength-giving hair. Might slumbers in that arm. Skin tones are brilliantly modulated. The chiaroscuro lighting and asymmetrical composition, figures massed unevenly to left and right, create high drama. Delilah's expression is hard to fathom: does it indicate ambivalence about what is happening?

Portrait of a Dutch Family is Frans Hals's only known small-scale portrait. The family members chose old-fashioned attire to link themselves with the tradition they lacked. The diagonal format, no less than the sure brushwork, gives vitality to the composition. Flowers and fruit often carry symbolic meaning in paintings of this time; for example, the foreground roses may indicate the transience of love, the clinging vines, fidelity. As so often in Hals, the countenances of his subjects border on rascality. Hals worked fast, for low fees, and required few sittings. This painting was done in part by his studio assistants. In Cuyp's *River Landscape with Bagpipe Player* a pastoral morning light bathes the cows, birds cross the vast sky, and a squat boy watches the man playing. The shattered beech in the foreground of Ruisdael's *River Landscape with Castle on a High Cliff* serves as a *repoussoir*, that is, it leads the viewer's eye into the picture. The river is utterly still. The ghostly sheep appear transfixed by the bridge boards. The beech may symbolize life's brevity, its "vanity" (*vanitas*) in the biblical sense; the river its course, the sheep its transience. The gradations of blue in the crisp winter sky of van der Neer's fine *Winter Landscape* give the illusion of intense cold. The Taft Museum holds a sunny landscape by this painter, but winter scenes were his specialty. "All shod with steel we hissed across the ice," writes Wordsworth in *The Prelude* of his ephiphanic experience. The Dutch burghers seem more concerned with diurnal consequences.

Dutch artists specialized in genre scenes. Gerard ter Borch's *A Music Lesson* is equally a lesson in courtship. The young man's admiring eyes have trouble following the score. The Dutch had a relaxed attitude toward lovemaking and enjoyed poking fun at the folly of romance. Hair styles help date this picture to the 1670s. Particularly remarkable is ter Borch's ability to render the sheen of satin. Secular in subject, such a painting as this would have hung in a private house.

Van Dyck powerfully depicts *A Member of the Spinola Family*. Linked by his armor to the virile military tradition of the Middle Ages, Spinola reaches out from the picture plane with his baton. It indicates his rank as an infantry commander—and his power. Van Dyck uses diagonals, characteristic of Baroque art, to embody Spinola's dynamic character. Tensions are held masterfully in equilibrium. Spinola looks beyond us; his sidewise gaze and uncombed hair indicate indifference to the audience. Ironically, for so proud a man he has not been precisely identified. *Portrait of a Young Girl Holding a Medal,* long attributed to Rembrandt, is now thought to be by one of the master's students. It remains nonetheless an affecting study. Reaching out, the woman tries to show the medal, or miniature. Unlike the formal portraits by Titian or Bronzino, or Van Dyck's Spinola, she wants to relate to us. The artist probes a psychological state. Van Miereveld, also a student of psychology, sensitively renders the features of his seventy-two year old Dutch burgher, *Arent Jacobsz van der Graeff*. The two faces in Abraham Bloemaert's *Liberation of Saint Peter* reveal effects of light that recall Caravaggio, while crisscrossing diagonals accentuate the drama.

Gallery 69 focuses on Flemish art and on French painting to 1800. The tones of Claude's *Artist Studying from Nature* are as warm as van der Neer's were cold. This is Wordsworthian "light that never was, on land or sea." When the museum acquired

Anonymous Netherlandish, *Portrait of a Woman*. A stark, introspective work, this portrait was formerly attributed to Adriaen Ysenbrandt. Courtesy of the Cincinnati Art Museum.

Vouet's *The Toilet of Venus* in 1974 from the demolished Sinton Hotel downtown, it was not known to be a Vouet and Venus was prudently clothed. After a cleaning in which the drapery was scaled off, she appears before us in all her Baroque voluptuousness. Boucher's *Washerwoman,* superbly contrived, reflects the gilded Rococo world of mid-eighteenth-century France. Its aristocracy longed, or professed to long, for a pastoral existence. A few years after Boucher painted this work Marie Antoinette, bored with stately Versailles, began to play shepherdess in *le Petit Trianon.* Fragonard's *The Letter,* as well as countless epistolary novels and intrigues, testifies to the eighteenth century's delight in letter writing. Fragonard painted the woman with measured brushstrokes, her dress more loosely. Both the Boucher and the Fragonard derive from a 1946 bequest by Mary Hanna of Italian, Dutch, French, and British masters that splendidly complements Mary Emery's collection.

Flemish paintings include portraits of *Francis I* and *Eleanor* of France, husband and wife, done by studio assistants of Joos van Cleve, as well as a charming *Madonna and Child* that may be authentically his. What could be more simple, more direct, more powerful than the *Portrait of a Woman* formerly attributed to Adriaen

Ysenbrandt and now "anonymous Netherlandish"? Hans Memling's *St. Stephen* and *St. Christopher* are wing panels; the center panel is elsewhere. Memling depicts the saints with gentle realism; St. Stephen, contemplating a stone, anticipates his martyrdom, visible in the far distance, as is St. Christopher's. The foreground flowers are recognizably accurate. Lucas Cranach the Elder renders *St. Helena,* mother of Constantine the Great, holding the (presumably true) cross she discovered during her celebrated pilgrimage to Jerusalem. Herri Met de Bles's superb *Landscape with the Offering of Isaac* reveals him to be a stylistic ancestor of Breughel. He is one of the first painters to value landscape as an end in itself.

Gainsborough and the British school (**galleries 71–73**). The museum's outstanding Gainsborough collection includes two major landscapes and a bevy of portraits. One portrait, *Mrs. Philip Thicknesse,* is an incontestable masterpiece. As a portraitist Gainsborough worked in the tradition of Van Dyck, himself influenced by Rubens. His bold, clear brushwork may go back even to Titian; such a style, David Piper observes, has an "almost liquid urgency."

Thomas Gainsborough came to Bath in 1759, invited by his friend Philip Thicknesse, to paint the aristocrats who came to take the waters and to socialize. There in 1760 he painted Ann Ford, about to become Mrs. Thicknesse. Unlike other English artists, Gainsborough embraced the swirling lines and curves of French rococo. "No other painter," claims Piper, "had thus caught the essence of silks and lace in motion." The fluttering brushstrokes may owe something to Gainsborough's apprenticeship to an engraver. The idea of Mrs. Thicknesse's informal pose comes from Van Dyck, though its relaxed nature marks a departure. Gainsborough must have known her well to depict her *en déshabillé.* A keen musician like his subject, he has her sit *contrapposto,* cittern in hand. The bass viol, or *viol da gamba,* in the background may have been his own. Gainsborough unifies his composition by the diagonal lines of the drapery, the rug, and the pose. Setting off the diagonals are the vertical lines of the bass viol on one side, the table leg on the other. Mrs. Thicknesse appears poised and stylish; her regard radiates confidence. Like El Greco and later Sargent, Gainsborough thought of ideal beauty in terms of elongation. Needless to say, Mrs. Thicknesse liked her portrait.

No other Gainsborough portrait here quite matches this tour de force. The *Earl of Warwick,* aristocratic male elegance incarnate, holds the plans for the state dining room of Warwick Castle; on the table lie engineering and architectural instruments. But the Earl himself is not, as Matthew Arnold a century later said of Americans, "interesting."

Gainsborough painted portraits for a living. At heart he preferred landscapes. The tiny *Gypsy Scene*—done at age thirteen or thereabouts!—reveals Dutch influence, Ruisdael particularly. The confident brushwork indicates an artist who already seems mature. The two large-scale landscapes, *The Cottage Door* and *Returning from Market,* compare with the best of Constable and Turner. To draw the trees, obviously not true to nature, Gainsborough used broccoli stalks as models. The scene, with the thatched roof and the simply clad peasants, is picturesque, and Gainsborough helped familiarize the English with the picturesque ideal. *Returning*

Thomas Gainsborough, *Mrs. Philip Thicknesse*. A major Gainsborough work, and one of the Museum's most beguiling paintings. A keen musician like his subject, Gainsborough has her sit, *contrapposto*, cittern in hand. The bass viol, or *viol da gamba*, in the background may have been his own. Ann Thicknesse was an essayist and a novelist as well as a musician. Her *Sketches of the Lives and Writings of the Ladies of France* (3 vols., 1778) went through several editions and is still worth perusing. Courtesy of the Cincinnati Art Museum.

from Market, lighter and more consciously graceful than *The Cottage Door*, reveals Rococo influence. Landscape painting in the eighteenth century occupied a lowly niche; only still life ranked lower. Whereas Gainsborough's milords would have hung portraits in the large salon of their country houses and given history paintings pride of place in the gallery, they would have relegated landscapes to the boudoir. A century later, with the triumph of the Impressionists, this hierarchy was reversed.

William Hogarth's *Southwark Fair* (gallery 72) contains many moral messages, the chief of which is that virtue is rewarded, vice punished. Hogarth is the one major English artist of his time to depict the people of England and contemporary social customs. He popularized his paintings through engravings, which usually have greater detail as well as differences in detail. (Downstairs, the eighteenth-century English room displays his series *The Four Times of the Day.*) Hogarth loved drama, and *Southwark Fair* (1733) depicts life's impromptu dramas as well as actual stage performances. A woman hawker touts the fair. When the stage collapses under a group performing *The Fall of Bajazet,* drama becomes life: Hogarth's point. Several contemporaries appear in unflattering guise. "The face is the index of the mind," Hogarth claimed, and he does not appear to have rated his fellows highly. A show-cloth of a wooden horse disgorging soldiers announces *The Siege of Troy.* Southwark Fair, an annual event, took place south of the Thames, opposite London Bridge. So rowdy did it become that the City of London banned it in 1763. Hogarth did far fewer paintings than engravings. Cincinnati is fortunate to have one of them.

More than any other painter, Sir Joshua Reynolds incarnates the dazzling British school of portraiture that flourished from the mid-eighteenth century until the death of Lawrence in 1830. He wanted to paint like the Old Masters and sought the "Grand Style," based upon Italian High Renaissance figure and history painting. More intellectual than his contemporary and rival Gainsborough, Reynolds painted smoothly, in contrast to Gainsborough's feathery touch. *Boy with Grapes* is Italian in color, pose, and sensibility. *Viscount Pulteney* appears cold and unfeeling, his face callow, his mouth weak; it is no surprise to learn that he was a wastrel and gambler. The flesh hues are unnaturally white because the carmine in the paint has faded. In absolute contrast to the dissolute viscount is sweetly smiling *Miss Ridge.*

Henry Raeburn, a generation younger than Gainsborough and Reynolds, became known as the "Scottish Reynolds." The girls in *The Elphinstone Children* are in Empire dress; their hair, tufted in front, is done *à la guillotine.* A diagonal line (surveyor's tripod?) unifies the composition. The brilliant light is that seen after a storm. Obsessed by light, Raeburn (according to Piper) "was capable of almost hallucinating visions"; his "sitters seem almost to float, translucent and aerial, in reflected light and shadow." *Sir James Gordon* (gallery 71) dazzles in its autumnal colors. *The Leslie Boy* (gallery 73), Raeburn's stepson, was a shy, charming lad, who, sad to say, drowned a month after this picture was painted.

Works by Romney, Lawrence, Hoppner, and Constable also hang about us. Romney's vacant-eyed ladies rarely stay in mind. His *Countess of Sutherland* (gallery 72), though a beauty, lacks feeling: she is calendar art, art of surface virtuosity. The problem lies more with the painter than with his sitters, whom he cannot endow with character or substance. *Mrs. Corbet and Daughter* are, in effect, two beautiful dresses. Like Raeburn, Sir Thomas Lawrence was of the next generation. A child prodigy, painter at twenty-one of Queen Charlotte, the youngest full member in the history of the Royal Academy, Lawrence became the most brilliant portraitist of Regency England and the darling of fashionable society. His *Master Tucker* (gallery 73) is a charmer, but *Mrs. Frances Gregg and Her Son* are more naturally posed. Her unillusioned glance contrasts with the abstracted expression of the intensely blue-eyed moppet. This painting possesses an unsettling, brooding quality. Even a master can have an off day, however: *Lady Beauchamp* has her torso out of line, foreshortened, the proportions all wrong. John Hoppner's *Master Meyrick* and *Lady Alicia* pose a puzzle: which is the boy, which the girl? Guess before you look at the captions. Constable had a lasting influence on the Barbizon School, so well represented in Cincinnati, but only *Waterloo Bridge,* a favorite subject, hangs here.

Period pieces of furniture adorn the British rooms. In the Gainsborough gallery, an early eighteenth-century settee, in effect three chairs put together, has cabriole legs and vase-shaped splats. On the splats are Oriental scenes, or European imaginings of what the Orient looked like, done in "Japanning," a Western version of Japanese lacquer work. The settee is mostly curves; even the seat rises. It forms a bridge between the rectilinear William and Mary chairs in the Dutch gallery and the elegant side table, circa 1720, in gilt gesso on wood, that stands in front of the Hogarth, the latter an incongruous but perhaps ironic juxtaposition. Most unusual are the pedestals, circa 1820, in the style of Thomas Hope. Hope went beyond the Neoclassicism of the Adam brothers. The lions' heads reflect Egyptian influence. Ebonized and marbleized, these pedestals are actually of wood. The vases in jasper, 1880s copies of the famous Portland vase, are Adamesque in inspiration. (Another copy of the original, which is a deep blue, we shall discover downstairs in gallery 25, the British Decorative Arts.)

Benjamin West's huge *Ophelia and Laertes* is the museum's best-known history painting. It hangs in the British galleries because West, an American, spent most of his life in England. The British have had a long tradition of importing their painters. Copley preceded West; a century later, Sargent followed him. Reynolds took West up in London, where he quickly made a name for himself. At Reynolds's death in 1792 West succeeded him as the Royal Academy's second president. That year he painted *Ophelia and Laertes*. The eighteenth century valued history painting above all other kinds. Alberti's classic *Della Pittura* (1436) had proclaimed its preeminence; Reynolds confirmed it in his famous *Discourses* (1769–1790). *Ophelia and Laertes* focuses on the moment in *Hamlet* when the returning Laertes discovers that his sister Ophelia has gone mad because she thinks Hamlet has rejected her. The costumes are contemporary, the facial gestures timeless: Claudius upset, Gertrude grimly pensive, Laertes heaven-storming, Ophelia wild-eyed. The gestures reflect the exaggerated acting techniques of the eighteenth-century stage.

Part of the fun in exploring a museum is to look at the acquisition dates on the captions. Doing so gives us a sense of how the collection has developed over the years. *Ophelia and Laertes* was acquired by Nicholas Longworth sometime before 1835, when the distinguished British traveler Harriet Martineau noted, in the course of a party at his home, "West's preposterous picture of Ophelia, the sight of which amazed me after all I had heard of it." Presumably it had floated down the Ohio, like Longworth himself, by flatboat. To find it in Cincinnati understandably amazed Harriet Martineau. (Some years ago I was equally amazed to discover, immured in Mount St. Mary's Seminary in the Cincinnati suburb of Mount Washington, a historical painting equally spectacular, Benjamin Robert Haydon's *Christ's Entry into*

Jerusalem.) West's painting hung in the music room of Longworth's house. In 1882 his son Joseph gave it to the museum and it has been on view ever since.

American painting **(galleries 74–81).** The American galleries succeed the British. If English artists idealized their subjects, New World artists did not. Before the Civil War American artists, it used to be said, painted by "the light of distant skies"—chiefly English and Italian. John Singleton Copley's portrait of the tight-lipped merchant, *Thomas Greene,* refutes this view. Character stands revealed. Copley, only twenty when he painted Greene, was an accomplished master at fifteen. The light, coming from the upper left, brings out the sheen of the table cloth; it makes the chair glow, the silver knee-buckle sparkle. The ship in the background presumably indicates Greene's occupation, or interest. Copley's exact detail and psychological penetration appear more Dutch than English. Would Reynolds have included the wig powder on Greene's shoulder? Greene's no-nonsense regard draws us back to him again and again. Across the room, Charles Willson Peale suggests, by straightforward expression and simple dress, the integrity of *Francis Bailey* and *His Wife.* Nearby, John Hesseltius's foppish *Philip Francis* smirks in the direction of Charles P. Polk's simpering *William Woods,* a tea merchant by the invoice in his hand: my candidates for the two ugliest faces in the museum.

In gallery 75 hang William Dunlap's portraits of *Moses Judah and His Wife,* the former Rebecca Gratz; two Gilbert Stuarts, one of the *Rev. Joseph Stevens Buckminster,* the other, inevitably, of *George Washington;* and Thomas Sully's assured portrait of *William Alston,* obviously influenced by Lawrence. The next gallery (76) has Matthew Jouett's luminous portrait of *Mrs. Jouett* and Eastman Johnson's *Edmund Dexter,* who in 1842 entertained Dickens at his house on 4th and Broadway. (In Spring Grove Cemetery we shall admire Dexter's High Gothic mausoleum.) George Caleb Bingham's *Order #11* captures a dramatic incident on the Kansas-Missouri border during the Civil War. Issued in 1863, Order #11 decreed martial law and, in effect, a scorched earth policy; houses concealing suspected Confederates were ordered burned. Bingham, then state treasurer of Missouri, bitterly opposed the decree. A man lies shot on the ground. Smoke from burning houses rises in the distance. Whereas Bingham in his most famous painting, *Fur Trappers on the Missouri,* now in the Metropolitan, captures the hazy white light of early morning, here by placing his personages on a stage and spotlighting them he achieves accusatory intensity.

Interesting as portraitists and depictors of the social scene, American artists achieved even greater success in landscape. Paintings by the Hudson River school, the first distinctively American school in theme and approach, hang in these rooms. In *View Across Frenchman's Bay from Mt. Desert Island, after a Squall* (gallery 75), a rare seascape by Thomas Cole, the school's founder, a tiny ship scuds before the oncoming storm that may overtake it before it reaches port. Humanity is helpless, Cole implies, before sublime natural forces. The eagle in the left foreground—comparable to Tennyson's "Nature red in tooth and claw" in the contemporaneous *In Memoriam*—symbolizes the indifferent cruelty of the natural world toward man. Asher B. Durand's *The American Wilderness* (gallery 76), a late work, presents

John Singleton Copley, *Thomas Greene*. Greene's no-nonsense character stands revealed in this realistic early work by an American master. Copley, only twenty when he painted Greene, draws upon Dutch realism no less than upon English polish. The ship in the background presumably indicates Greene's occupation as merchant. Courtesy of the Cincinnati Art Museum.

infinite vistas lying beyond an unkempt foreground. Pantheism, the belief that God is present in His work, permeated nineteenth-century Western thought. By revealing the divine immanent in landscape, the landscape painter like Durand became a teacher of moral truths. Frederic Edwin Church's *Falls of the Tequendama* (gallery 77), in Ecuador, attempts the religious sublime. The largest of the paintings from Church's first South American trip, it depicts a scene the artist had made a special journey to visit. The falls are 670 feet high. Perched on the limb to the left is a huge and gaudy macaw; below it, we discover the artist's name and the date. The wide angle of vision in Church's panoramic art, here vertical instead of the more usual horizontal, astonished contemporaries. Bierstadt's *Bow River Valley, Canadian Rockies* appears less finished than many of his larger canvases. Other Hudson River artists represented include George Inness and Jervis McEntee. Ralph Blakelock's *Moonlit Lake,* ominous and foreboding, offers a less confident, more poignant vision of the American forest than Durand's.

William Harnett artfully arranged the contents of his haunting still life, *The Last Rose of Summer* (gallery 77), in a classic pyramid, with three-dimensional reality. Winslow Homer's genre scene, *A Sunday Morning in Virginia*, renders a black family reading the Bible. Thomas Eakins's *Archbishop William Henry Elder* of Cincinnati (gallery 78) is in a meditative mood. Painted when the archbishop was eighty-four, this picture demonstrates Eakins's psychological acuteness. Colors are appropriately muted and somber; the archbishop's eyes, though alert, are tired. He appears to ponder the life beyond.

Andrew Wyeth's *Portrait of Henry Teel* (gallery 79) is another powerful study of solitude. Teel looks out of the window of a sparsely furnished room. His mental life is as impoverished as his physical surroundings. Teel has suffered and endured, but has not understood why. If he expects revelation, it will not come. The sun's rays enter but shed more light on the floor more than they do on Henry Teel. Critics consider Wyeth a realist—we may discern affinities with Eakins—but this scene approaches surrealism. Hans Hofmann's *Toward Crepuscule* (1963), in gallery 82, throws at us squares and rectangles in an exuberant palette of green, red, and orange. Violent brushstrokes express emotion no less than does color.

Few find the ladies in Grant Wood's *Daughters of Revolution* (gallery 80) sympathetic. In 1932 Wood became embroiled in a controversy with the Iowa chapter of the Daughters of the American Revolution. The Daughters did not want a stained glass window designed by Wood, but made in Germany, for the Cedar Rapids Veterans Memorial Gallery. The ladies objected to the German manufacture. To make his point about misguided patriotism Wood put Emmanuel Leutze's *Washington Crossing the Delaware,* an American icon that was painted by a German, in the background and surrounded his frame with stars: nice juxtapositions to his most unrevolutionary ladies. While Wood is considered a Regionalist, Edward Hopper is not. *Street Scene, Gloucester* is poignant in its vacancy. Hopper uses America's vernacular architecture to comment on loss and alienation in modern society. His paintings have a timeless quality. Silence is everywhere. The distinctive towers of Our Lady of Good Voyage Church, built by Portuguese fishermen, are visible in the distance. A petulant *Patience Serious* represents Cincinnati-born Robert Henri, a traditional artist with untraditional ideas. Important in his own right, Henri served as a role model and theorist for a group of painters, The Eight, who became the Ashcan School.

Gallery 81 contains a sampling of American Impressionism. Most American Impressionists studied in France. Upon returning to the United States, they created an Impressionism different from the French. Whereas the flickering light of French Impressionism breaks down the subject's identity, making it secondary to that light, paintings by Americans are more solid in mass, more spatial in composition. Subject matter, whether figure or landscape, retains its substance. Brilliant, fragmenting light dominates the picture plane of the French Impressionists; not so the American. In *Pont Royal, Paris* Childe Hassam, in character with other American Impressionists, stresses tangible forms. No Impressionist, John Singer Sargent, like them, works to establish a mood. His *Two Girls Fishing* stops a moment in time. *Italian Girl with Fan* (gallery 78), Experience to the two girls' Innocence, displays im-

Grant Wood, *Daughters of Revolution.* After *American Gothic,* this is Wood's best-known painting, and an unusual instance of satire in his art. In 1932 Wood became embroiled in a controversy with the Iowa chapter of the Daughters of the American Revolution. The Daughters did not want a stained-glass window designed by Wood, but made in Germany, for the Cedar Rapids Veterans Memorial Gallery. To make his point about misguided patriotism, Wood put Emmanuel Leutze's *Washington Crossing the Delaware,* an American icon painted by a German, in the background and surrounded his frame with stars. Courtesy of the Cincinnati Art Museum.

mense assurance. The petulant mouth, mocking yet distant, seems to say, *"je m'en fout"*—"I don't give a damn." Note the careful modeling of face and arm; elsewhere, bravura brushstrokes prevail. To elongate his proud Venetian, Gigia Viani, Sargent draws a "line" from tip of toe to top of canvas.

Cincinnati artists **(galleries 83–87).** Pass through the glass door from gallery 78 into gallery 83. During the nineteenth century Cincinnati became the major art center west of the Alleghenies. A number of artists with ties to the city—of birth, training, or residence—achieved national distinction. Many, however, left Cincinnati. They did not find what they needed here, and often they did not come back. One Cincinnati artist who did come back, Frank Duveneck, is an undisputed master, both as a painter and as a teacher of painters. Duveneck, Duncanson, Farny we have already encountered at the Taft Museum; here we come upon them again, in greater depth, along with John Twachtman, Edward Potthast, Miner Kellogg, William L. Sonntag, Worthington Whittredge, Elizabeth Nourse, and, in sculpture, Hiram Powers (gallery 41). Like American artists elsewhere, they made their most distinctive contribution in landscape, submitting in turn to the influence of the Hudson River school, the Barbizon painters, and the Impressionists.

Beach scenes were Edward Potthast's favorite subject. A blaze of light illumines the women's blouses in his *Sailing Party.* But the painting is about them, not the light. Paler in its color tones is John Twachtman's *Springtime.* Both he and Potthast were born in Cincinnati, and both were among the "Duveneck boys" who studied with the master here and in Europe. Twachtman admired the Impressionists but also submitted to the subdued palette of the French academic artist, Bastien Lepage, even more to Japanese woodblock prints. Some consider him the finest American Impressionist.

The museum bought Joseph Sharp's *Harvest Dance* in 1894, the year the artist painted it, and has kept it continuously on view. Like Caleb Bingham, Charles T. Webber addressed himself to an historical subject. *The Underground Railroad* represents Levi Coffin, a Cincinnatian and Quaker who was unofficial "president" of the underground railroad, receiving a group of fugitive slaves. He sits on the wagon; Catherine Coffin, his wife, is in the center, and Hannah Haydock, a noted abolitionist, is at the far left. The blacks are actual people Webber sketched on a trip South. One of the most vivid characterizations of the underground railroad, Webber's painting was exhibited at the Columbian Exposition in Chicago in 1893, where thousands viewed it. Recent historians of slavery, however, argue that it perpetuates a stereotype: valiant Quakers watching over helpless, grateful slaves. In reality, more often than not, blacks helped blacks.

Gallery 84 is devoted to Henry F. Farny. Long an illustrator for *Harper's Weekly,* Farny spent most of his life in Cincinnati. He was also a painter of note, who often went west to study and paint the diurnal activities of the nomadic Plains Indians. By these works he is best known today. *The Truce,* with its monocled traveler who looks like Teddy Roosevelt (but is actually Farny's friend, the Cincinnati newspaperman Edward Flynn), *Renegade Apaches,* and *Indian Elk Hunting* all depict the tension in the land as the pioneers settled the trans-Mississippi West. The Sioux, one of several tribes that adopted Farny, called him "Wasitcha," or "white face maker chief." Under the signature of many of Farny's Indian paintings we discover this name represented by a circle with a dot in the middle. Farny's gouaches have a luminosity the oils sometimes lack. Not all his work focuses on the West. In *The Silent Guest* (1878) Farny utilizes a somber color scheme (influenced by Duveneck and the Munich school) to capture an older man asleep by his glass, a regular at one of Cincinnati's beer gardens. Like Sharp's *Harvest Dance,* this painting has also been on view uninterruptedly since its acquisition.

Gallery 85 features the work of Frank Duveneck. Space allows the museum to show only a fraction of its holdings, the largest anywhere. Even in his native city it is difficult to explore Duveneck's talent in depth. As in the Farny gallery, paintings rotate frequently. Born in Covington, Duveneck went in 1869 to Munich, which had replaced Düsseldorf as the major German art center. There he studied the Old Masters—Rembrandt, Hals, Velázquez, Goya—and responded to their thick paint surfaces and dark backgrounds. These artists had a strong interest in psychological portraiture, and portraiture became Duveneck's major mode of expression. Among contemporaries, he found inspiration in Manet, in Courbet, and in Courbet's German follower, Wilhelm Leibl. At this time Duveneck possessed a dark, glowing palette, known as the "Munich manner," and a freely brushed realistic style. From 1878 to 1888 he lived in Italy, where his palette lightened and his paint surfaces became smoother. In 1890 he returned to teach at the Art Academy and in 1905 became its director. He was a splendid, inspiring teacher at all stages of his career. At his death in 1919 he left the museum a major collection of his own paintings as well as many that his students had given him.

Henry James praised Duveneck's work for its "vigor, frankness, and comprehensive simplicity"; for Sargent, he was "the greatest talent of the brush in this generation." *Whistling Boy,* his best-known painting here, renders a Munich street urchin. He appears related to the ragamuffin in the Taft's larger-scaled *Cobbler's Apprentice.* Even the poses are similar. Duveneck's free brushwork, along with his frequent echoes of the Old Masters, made him widely popular. In conception and subject matter, *Whistling Boy* recalls Hals; in color scheme, Manet. When shown in Boston in 1873, it established Duveneck's reputation.

Several paintings by Robert Duncanson, the mulatto artist who called Cincinnati home most of his life, hang in gallery 86. Usually on display is *Blue Hole, Little Miami River,* possibly Duncanson's masterpiece. It marks an advance over the murals in the foyer of the Taft Museum. Less dramatic than they, this somber work pays attention to detail—the texture of the rock formations, the muted sheen of the water—yet Duncanson suffuses the scene with poetry. The almost primeval landscape, in John Bryan State Park near Yellow Springs, Ohio, has hardly changed; even now, the Little Miami, which empties into the Ohio east of Cincinnati, remains a scenic, virtually unspoiled stream. Duncanson's 1858 *Portrait of Nicholas Longworth,* his sometime benefactor, I find, if not completely successful, at least oddly appealing. A note pinned to Longworth's suit cuff reminds him of the day's chores and appointments: a homely touch, true to life, comparable to Copley's painting in Thomas Greene's wig powder. The Catawba grapes drooping over the table hint at Longworth's viticultural interests. Duncanson captures his shrewd eyes and nononsense mouth. However, the brooding Ohio Valley sky in the background indicates Duncanson's real interest and strength.

In the same gallery hang two presidential portraits by Miner Kellogg: one a wizened *Andrew Jackson,* the other a dandified *Martin Van Buren.* They contrast presidential styles. Nearby is Audubon's *Robert Best,* first director of Cincinnati's Western Museum, who comes across as an insensitive clod. This painting makes one glad Audubon achieved subsequent fame with birds. William L. Sonntag toured Europe with Duncanson in 1853; the sober hues of his *Landscape* will recall Duncanson's palette. A greater talent than either Sonntag or Duncanson, Worthington Whittredge is represented here by two fine landscapes: *The Mill* and, in the adjoining gallery 87, *The Aqueducts of the Campagna.*

A splendid painter again receiving merited recognition is Elizabeth Nourse, whose style drew upon both Impressionism and Realism. Usually one painting by her hangs in gallery 87. *Peasant Women of Borst* owes something to Millet, more to Gauguin. Purchased in 1892, it was the first painting by a major woman artist to enter the museum's collection. *Venetian Lace Makers* by Cincinnati-trained Robert Blum depicts an unusual urban setting. The elegantly dressed girls recall Sargent.

Also in this gallery is a chest of drawers beautifully carved by Agnes Pitman. Under the tutelage of her father, the charismatic Benn Pitman, a native woodcarving tradition developed after 1873 within the McMicken School of Drawing and Design. Pitman, brother of Isaac, the inventor of a popular form of shorthand, had come from England to Cincinnati in 1852 to promote his brother's method. Imbued with Ruskin's esthetic ideals, he stressed simplicity and originality of design. Pitman taught a generation of Cincinnati women how to express themselves in wood, and for several decades the city enjoyed an outstanding reputation for its artistic woodcarving. The artifacts created are now recognized as a major achievement within the American Arts and Crafts movement. Pitman was abetted in his efforts by two other emigrants from England, Henry Lindley Fry and his son, William Henry Fry. Along with many other woodcarvers, the elder Fry had worked on the new Houses of Parliament and afterwards, in ecclesiastical Gothic, under Gilbert Scott in Westminster Abbey. The younger Fry (once described by Murray Seasongood as "a swarthy craftsman who wore a gold ring in one ear") fathered Laura Fry, also a leading woodcarver. The Frys, who decorated Joseph Longworth's "Rookwood" and Henry Probasco's "Oakwood," gave private lessons in woodcarving. The Pitmans and the Frys maintained allegiance not only to Ruskin but also to Ruskin's disciples, William Morris and Charles Eastlake. (Chapter 8 contains a discussion of the fate of their major collaboration, the Music Hall organ.) In keeping with Eastlake's tenets, Cincinnati's carved furniture was solid (no veneers), stained, and not varnished. Carvers favored local woods such as cherry and walnut; decoration emphasized natural forms and indigenous flora. The movement flourished through the 1920s.

Agnes Pitman not only designed this chest of drawers, including the drawer pulls and escutcheons, she carved the chest herself, cast the hardware in bronze, nickel plated it and then blackened it to complement the stained walnut. Local flora representing the months from April through September she rendered in a romantically natural manner. "Some who see this carving," observed the Cincinnati *Commercial* of September 16, 1875, "consider the sides of the chest of drawers even more beautiful than the front." Only two pieces of the Cincinnati carved furniture shown at the 1876 Centennial in Philadelphia are known to exist today. This is one of them.

Nineteenth-century French painting (galleries 101–104). We begin with the arch rivals, Delacroix and Ingres. Delacroix's *Medea Slaying the Children of Jason*, versions of which also exist at Lille and in the Louvre, presents a wild-eyed but resolute Medea preparing to kill her tearful children. Note the theatrical lighting: we look up as if before a stage. The personages form a triangle, traditionally the most stable of compositional frames (think of Raphael's madonnas or the Botticini *Virgin and Child* contemplated earlier); but Delacroix, by moving the triangle to one side, unbalances it—and us. Ingres depicts the musician Cherubini, in his day ranked Beethoven's equal, holding hand to head: *Il Penseroso,* man thinking.

Like the Taft, the Cincinnati Art Museum has superb holdings of the Barbizon school. A number of these artists actually lived in Barbizon, a village near Fontainebleau. *Plein-air* painting, or painting out of doors, had occasionally occurred before the mid-nineteenth century, by Constable for one, but the Barbizon artists preferred it to working in the studio. Daubigny achieved prominence in 1853 with

The Pond of Gylieu. Paintings by him suggest peace and a sense of reverie. In a harmony of blues and greens, he depicts waterbirds, the limpidity of the water, even the luminous air, rinsed and cleaned. Daubigny returned to this subject again and again: an 1876 version hangs in the Metropolitan, and between 1858 and 1877 he painted five others. Even before Monet's exercises in serial landscape—haystacks, cathedral façades, islands (we shall see one shortly)—Daubigny returned again and again to the same scene for inspiration. But to my mind no later version of the pond of Gylieu recaptures the freshness of this first rendering.

The dab of red (a well-known hallmark) in Corot's *Le Tournant de la Seine à Port Marly* sets off an otherwise muted palette. His *Ruins of the Chateau of Pierrefonds* renders the castle before Viollet-le-Duc's extensive restoration after 1857. This work enables us to study the evolution of Corot's style. Originally a work of the 1830s, it was repainted thirty years later. Corot reworked the foreground figures in his sketchy later manner; he may never have seen the rebuilt chateau. Corot's *Don Quixote*, a favorite subject of Daumier and later of Picasso, encapsulates the episode of Cardenio, who tries vainly to escape the oncoming Don. Art historians have speculated that Daumier, on a visit to Corot, painted the Don and Sancho onto the unfinished canvas. Nearby, the faceless laborer in Millet's *Going to Work* proudly carries his pitchfork; his wife, basket over her head, stands strong in support. Together, they embody Millet's central, quasi-religious belief in the dignity of hard work. Common humanity, he tells us, has a grandeur all its own.

Art historians often type Daumier and Courbet (gallery 102) as realists, yet their work seems equally imbued with Romanticism. Daumier, known for his lithographs satirizing middle-class foibles and political corruption, painted few canvases, finished fewer. Most date from the 1860s during a three-year sabbatical from journalism. *Orchestra Stalls* is unfinished only in the sense of certain of Michelangelo's sculptures: the artist stopped when he had said what he wished to say. Courbet, born in Ormans, often painted the dark forests and looming chalk cliffs of eastern France: witness *A Gorge in the Jura* and *The Forest in Winter. Sunset, Vevay* captures a scene in nearby Switzerland on the Lake of Geneva.

Academic art **(gallery 103).** Bouguereau's *Girl Eating Porridge* is coy, sentimental, very appealing. His paintings with their careful detail and impeccable finish, brushwork carefully concealed, fitted well amidst the elegant clutter of High Victorian decors. Immensely popular in his day, Bouguereau fell into disregard as the Impressionist star rose. But Renoir, for one, admired his nudes tremendously. Today, without need to take sides, we may enjoy Academicians like Bouguereau no less than Impressionists like Renoir. Louis Majorelle's tea table, circa 1900, an exquisite Art Nouveau piece, uses the woodgrain as part of its decoration of curves and natural forms. In Karl F. Lessing's *Landscape* our bird's-eye point of view, high over the virtually treeless plain, affords us a tremendous sense of space. The monk in the foreground suggests both Lessing's religious vision and the littleness of man. After Lessing's death in 1880, Joseph Longworth purchased from his estate a number of paintings as well as 900 drawings and gave them to this museum, where they remain—unseen. Anton Mauve's *Shepherd and Sheep* may look familiar: the Taft has a larger, brighter version of this subject, one to which the artist returned frequently. In both versions, the sheep appear to go in the direction that we face the painting. The small-scale bronze model of the Tyler Davidson Fountain was sent to Henry Probasco for display in the library of Oakwood. It reveals major differences, as well as numerous changes of detail, from the executed work on Fountain Square. The four figures around the basin are not carefree boys, nor on Fountain Square does a praying youth accompany the man imploring rain. Here the *Genius of Water* appears to stand on a pineapple.

Impressionists and Post-Impressionists (**gallery 104**). Impressionism became popular after World War I, *after* the major Cincinnati art patrons had formed their collections. Thus the museum has few Impressionist paintings; the Taft, we remember, has none. In 1985 it acquired its first Monet, the seascape *Rocks at Port [de] Goulphar* (1886). This painting of Belle-Isle off the Brittany coast, part of a sequence, represents one of Monet's early forays into serial landscape. Sisley's *Bougival* reveals Barbizon influence but also a bright Impressionist palette. He suggests the details; our eyes shape them. At his death Degas left his *Ballerina* unfinished in his studio. This bronze cast was made then. Yellow and blue tones surround the pink face of Renoir's tiny *Girl with Bonnet*. Through shape, color, pattern, Renoir renders not only what he sees but how he *feels*.

Post-Impressionist artists represented here include Cézanne and Van Gogh. Cézanne's early *Still Life with Bread and Eggs* (1865) reflects Manet's dark palette. Even the knife is black. In the Baroque seventeenth century, still life took on new importance, but it was not until a century later that French still life painting achieved in Chardin its first great master. Of him Marcel Proust, no mean observer of life himself, once wrote: "Until I saw Chardin's paintings I never realized how much beauty lay around me in my parents' house, in the half-cleared table, in the corner of a tablecloth left awry, in the knife beside the empty oyster-shell." Philip R. Adams has well described Cézanne's *Still Life with Bread and Eggs* as "a pre-Impressionist work by the greatest of Post-Impressionists." The painting is nicely positioned next to Manet's *Women at the Races,* possibly a fragment of a lost painting. More overtly Impressionist is the lighter palette of Cézanne's *Still Life in Blue with Lemon*. Gone are the blacks. Sometimes on display in gallery 64 (prints and drawings) is Cézanne's late great watercolor, *The Bridge at Trois-Sautets,* done shortly before he died in 1906. It reveals Cézanne moving beyond Post-Impressionism. These three works, considered sequentially, enable us to glimpse Cézanne's evolution as a painter over forty years. Both the Cézanne paintings came to the museum from the collection of Mary E. Johnson, third of the Marys to whom this museum owes so much. She also bequeathed to it works by Van Gogh, Matisse, Picasso, Chagall, and Rouault.

The somber tones of Van Gogh's *Head of a Peasant Woman* indicate that, like Cézanne, he too submitted to Manet's overpowering influence. In the later *Undergrowth with Two Figures* Van Gogh applied the brushstrokes with fierce intensity: globs of paint are pressed onto the canvas with the palette knife. The wildflowers leap up at you. In 1885 Van Gogh insisted that artists had to "paint things not as they are . . . but as they feel them." Intense color henceforth becomes the norm in painting. Whereas Bouguereau's polished surface appears to eliminate the painter, Van Gogh's violent brushstrokes insist upon his presence. This canvas signs itself. Blue suggests infinity, yellow the sun. But the two figures? In letters of June 1890 to his brother Theo, Van Gogh described this enigmatic scene. A month later he killed himself.

Modern art (**galleries 96, 99, 105–107**). Picasso's first truly Cubist work, *Les Demoiselles d'Avignon* in New York's Museum of Modern Art, dates from 1907. His *Still Life with Glass and Lemon* of 1910 here reflects his continuing enthusiasm for Cubism. Pictorial space, John Russell has well observed, "changed its character at the same time as the physicists were revising our notions of physical space": an interesting coincidence, if coincidence it is. The monumental *Head of a Woman* (1922), from Picasso's neoclassical period, nods toward representational art. The 1937 *Still Life* (gallery 106), a series of interlocking triangles, relates in its composition to the famous *Guernica,* begun on May 1, immediately after Picasso completed this painting. Note the precise date of *Still Life:* "30 Avril XXXVII."

Matisse's *The Gray Hat* appears virtually representational, but in *Rumanian Blouse* he works in line: the woman has but a few wisps of hair. Charlie Brown would have liked her. Jawlensky in *Seated Woman* (1911) expresses himself through color. Color, in John Russell's words, is "energy made visible." Date is important here. For almost two decades pale pastel shades had reigned supreme. Then in 1909 Diaghilev's Ballets Russes exploded upon the Parisian scene. The bold flat colors of his decors effected a revolution. A riot of barbaric hues—purple, jade and emerald green, scarlet, garish oranges—became the rage. Jawlensky adopted these colors for *Seated Woman.* So did Franz Marc for *The Red Horses,* a triangle of caracoling horses. Both Jawlensky and Marc wished to reinvigorate painting by harking back to primitive, demotic, even demonic modes of expression. Modigliani is a more subdued colorist. Influenced by African tribal masks, he draws elongated oval faces. Eyes in *Girl with Bangs* and *Portrait of Max Jacob* become gray-blue smudges, though in *Woman with Red Necklace* the pupils are visible.

Of twentieth-century European artists, Georges Rouault is the best represented in Cincinnati. Compare his stunning *Christ in Profile* to *The Clowns* and *Wounded Clown.* Rouault's clowns, a favorite subject, are as sad faced as Christ, for Rouault saw clowns as avatars or prototypes of Him. A deeply religious man, he served an apprenticeship to a stained-glass maker. Later, he built up his glazes to give his canvases the illusion of stained glass. Another feast of color is Chagall's *The Red Rooster.* It floats in space. Above it floats a blue-faced man, the artist perhaps. A green-faced man watches from behind a tree while a donkey plays a violin. Perhaps the man would like to play too. We enter a fairy world of fantasy: gravity and reality are suspended. The effect is surrealistic, dreamlike, a reminder that Chagall often recreated the landscapes of his dreams. Younger people respond particularly to this painting, but it is by no means solely for them.

Gallery 99. Joan Miró's huge curved mural, the largest painting ever executed by the artist, once hung in the Terrace Hilton downtown. Strange goofy creatures wander about; on the right, a Snoopy-like dog's head looks up. New combinations of figures arise each time you contemplate this surrealistic composition. The mood is whimsical; the bonbon colors, particularly the cerulean blue, enchant the eye. Asked for an explanation, Miró stated that his shapeless, amoeba-like forms, some with holes in them, represent the patterns and figures of nature. This mode, called biomorphic abstraction, originated with the Swiss artist Hans (or Jean) Arp. It influenced the sculptors Constantine Brancusi and Henry Moore. In time, the forms of biomorphic abstraction sifted down into popular art, affecting the shape of swimming pools and dining tables.

Alexander Calder's *Twenty Leaves and an Apple* (1946) is larger, monochromic, and a year older than his mobile at the Contemporary Arts Center. It once hung in the Terrace Hilton's main lobby. Calder frequented Miró's studio, and perhaps we may find parallels between Miró's lines and Calder's forms. Saul Steinberg's large-scale *Mural of Cincinnati*, the third of the works that the Terrace Hilton gave to the museum, has long been "in restoration." Too bad, for in it Steinberg indicates his liking for the whimsical, the offbeat, and the decorated aspects of Cincinnati's cityscape. *Brown, Orange, Blue on Maroon* by Mark Rothko (gallery 96, behind the Miró), another Abstract Expressionist, is more subdued. Its sensitive color modulation creates quiet vibrations. Rothko insisted on the lowest lighting levels whenever he exhibited. A late painting such as this one benefits from low light.

The modern galleries include a number of paintings and sculptures from the 1970s and 1980s. The RSM Company has given the museum its collection of recent art in an unusual arrangement that calls for the museum to sell a portion of it at regular intervals, with the funds used to purchase new works by emerging artists. In this way, the museum will observe the intent behind the collection: always to present the cutting edge of contemporary work. In the process Cincinnatians keep up with the latest movements in art virtually as they occur.

Prints, drawings, and photographs (**galleries 64, 98, 108–110**). Temporary exhibits often fill galleries 98 and 108–110, but gallery 64 (overlooking the main entrance) displays a miniscule, ever-rotating sampling of the museum's holdings. These were greatly augmented in 1942 when Herbert Greer French left the museum his superb collection of eight hundred Old Master and nineteenth-century European prints. One half of gallery 64 displays works from the fifteenth to the eighteenth centuries by, among others, Durer, Rubens, Rembrandt, Claude, Hogarth, Gainsborough, Piranesi, and Goya; the other half, prints, drawings, and photographs by modern masters, including Daumier, Degas, Toulouse-Lautrec, Braque, Cézanne, and, among the photographers, Julia Margaret Cameron and Ansel Adams.

We have come full circle, so we descend the stairs to begin exploring the first-floor galleries. If, as is probable, you are hungry at this point, the museum's **Terrace Court Restaurant** is excellent. Its hours of opening are listed on the floor plan brochure. To get to the restaurant, traverse the Greek and Roman galleries, go through the glass doors, and take the stairs on the left one flight down.

On the walls of the Terrace Court hang four *Rookwood panels* (1907), designed by John Dee Wareham and representing the Four Seasons, from Cincinnati's demolished Sinton Hotel. We shall see Rookwood ware in abundance in gallery 35 but the panels here are the first examples of Rookwood put to architectural use. Since originally they adorned the Sinton's Grand Café, fittingly they again hang in a restaurant. Rookwood tiles went on to grace a number of other buildings erected in Cincinnati and across the country. In Cincinnati we find them on the façades of the Gidding-Jenny and Dixie Terminal buildings on 4th St., the former Baldwin Piano building on Gilbert Ave. below Mount Adams, and at either end of the Carew Tower arcade. Floors, walls, ceiling, and booths of the tearoom in Union Terminal are composed of Rookwood tiles. Elsewhere we find them in the Rathskeller of Louisville's Seelbach Hotel, in Baltimore's Pennsylvania Station, and, beneath the grime of New York's IRT subway, in the Wall and Fulton St. stations, the 23rd and 86th St. east side stations, probably also in the 77th and 96th St. stations.

The restaurant's outside "court" has tables interspersed amidst modern sculptures. From this pleasant patio you look up at the Romanesque façade of the Alms wing (1937). Its construction required the reopening, at enormous expense, of an Indiana quarry to find stone that matched the museum's original building. On warm days I find this courtyard an oasis of calm, one of the most restoring places I know.

Egyptian, Greek, Etruscan, and Roman art **(galleries 2–8).** These galleries, leading directly off the entrance vestibule, display artifacts from the ancient world. The columns within echo the columns without. The prowling lion (ca. 350 B.C.), of Pentelic marble, the same marble used for the Parthenon, once formed part of a funerary monument. Long exposure to the elements has caused its worn look. The caption is on the reverse side, a reminder of the time when visitors entered the Schmidlapp wing from the other end.

Egyptian art. The small Egyptian collection (galleries 2–3) contains a brightly painted mummy case (663–332 B.C.). Two predynastic vases from Abydos, 5000 to 6000 years old, appear contemporary in color and finish. Next to them is a lotus-shaped cup in an eye-catching turquoise glaze. In gallery 3 a bas relief depicts a noblewoman with stylized hair sniffing a lotus. The body is mostly in frontal profile, the face in side profile. Already a division of labor has occurred: one person prepared the wall, another sculpted, a third painted.

Greek, Roman, and Etruscan art. The female folded arm figurine, Cycladic and dating from the third millennium B.C., is as old as Greek art can get. Stylized, the left arm above the right, it is an unusually large example. Probably a votive figurine, it was once, like most Greek sculpture, gaudily painted. Picasso in his Cubist phase learned from such "primitive" figurines. A circus performer wearing winged boots holds up lions, who in turn support the stylized bronze votive mirror (sixth century B.C.). From the Archaic period, it echoes Egyptian forms. The slender Etruscan warrior (sixth century B.C.), dressed (so to speak) for battle though lacking spear and shield, presumably frightened enemies by his huge stride and crested helmet. He has his modern counterpart in Giacometti's sculptures. The spirited bronze Roman bull with the spectacular curled tail gazes longingly toward the marble heifer. Probably a cult figure for Apis, the sacred bull worshipped in Memphis, this bull is of uncertain date. For a time he served as a fountain—with some

Roman bull. This high-spirited creature with spectacular curled tail was probably a cult figure for Apis, the sacred bull worshipped in Memphis, Egypt. Courtesy of the Cincinnati Art Museum.

damage to his hide. Probably the standing male figure (second century B.C.) is Asklepios, Greek god of medicine. He reveals a considerable difference from the circus performer holding the mirror. Idealized, he stands naturally, in *contrapposto*, with body curved and weight largely shifted to one leg.

If the Egyptians stylized and the Greeks idealized man, the Romans rendered him realistically. Experts date the sculptured *Portrait of a Young Nobleman* by hair mode to the reign of Septimus Severus (190–205 A.D.). *Portrait of a Noblewoman* depicts a member of the court. Her plaited hair tied behind is in the fashion set by the Empress Julia Domna.

The realistic heifer (first century A.D.), found in the ruins of a Roman villa, presumably derives from Myron's famed fifth-century B.C. bronze. Like "the heifer lowing to the skies" in Keats's "Ode on a Grecian Urn," it suggests the timelessness of art. The majestic marble *loutrophoros* (gallery 5) depicts a grave scene. From the loutrophorus was poured the bridal bath; its use here signifies the death of an unmarried person. The young warrior bids farewell to his seated father and to life. Father and son clasp hands in a gesture of exquisite tenderness. The soldier behind the young man probably died in battle. On the mosaic frieze above our heads, from Ostia, Rome's seaport, arabesques entwine a charging dog, a prancing bull, and a chariot drawn by yoked deer. Cupid serves as charioteer.

In gallery 6 the *amphora* attributed to the (anonymous) Swing painter (590 B.C.) depicts Hercules slaying the Egyptian king Busiris. Busiris practiced human sacrifice, choosing victims from foreigners visiting his country. Hercules, clad only in the skin of the Nemean lion, tosses Egyptians about; one somersaults over his shoulder. Our knowledge of early Greek painting derives largely from surviving pottery. This amphora is in the black figure style—black figures on the naturally red clay—in which the figures have pointed noses and toes. Black-figured pottery yielded in the sixth century B.C. to red-figured vessels (red figures against a black background), a technique that afforded greater flexibility in drawing. In the lip cup by Tleson (gallery 7) we discover a realistic rooster and hen. This large shallow bowl is a paradigm of Cincinnati's Basin. In the same case a *kylix* depicts the death of Orpheus. Three fragments from a white-ground calyx *krater,* a very rare type, incompletely preserve five individuals clad in polychrome clothing. The scene depicts the meeting of Helen and Paris. These fragments are considered the finest piece in the Museum's collection.

Mithras Slaying a Bull dominates the oval gallery 8. This powerful high relief sculpture came from one of Mithraism's underground sanctuaries. One survives in Rome, another in London. Mithraism, deriving from Zoroastrianism, gained special popularity in the army. In the first centuries A.D. it spread throughout the Roman Empire to become a major rival cult to Christianity. But the Mithraic religion did not allow women communicants and gradually died out. Here Mithras slays the sacrificial bull while a snake and crustacean suck his life-giving blood. Helios, the sun god, watches impassively; Luna, the moon, is missing. The work's strong diagonals give it tremendous kinetic energy.

The Nabataeans (**galleries 8, 11–12**). The Art Museum's collection of Nabataean antiquities, acquired in 1939, is the only such outside of Jordan. One of the most remarkable peoples of history, the Nabataeans created an empire that covered much of present-day Israel, Jordan, Syria, and Saudi Arabia. They reached their apogee during and following the first century B.C. but weakened under pressure from the Romans, who annexed their kingdom in 106 A.D. No civilization has surpassed their achievements in water engineering and agriculture. Nelson Glueck, archaeologist and later president of Hebrew Union College, excavated in 1937–1938 the hilltop temple of Khirbet Tannur, southwest of the Dead Sea in modern Jordan. Zeus-Hadad, chief god of the Nabataeans, dominates gallery 12. He combines features of the Greek god, Zeus, and of the Semitic god, Hadad. His craggy head was deliberately made larger than his body. Once he held a thunderbolt in his left hand, in his right probably a scepter. Even mutilated, he radiates authority.

Medieval art (**galleries 9–10, left of the oval room**). Here we come upon armor, weapons (chiefly polearms), reliquaries, carvings in wood, and grotesque stone capitals of humans, fabulous beasts, and plant life. On the capital from Toulouse, the men may be pilgrims, for Toulouse lay on the pilgrimage route to the shrine of St. James at Santiago de Compostela. If the proportions seem strange, in a church the columns would have stood higher than they do here. On another capital two men hang on to each other's hair as they fight with clubs; two others fight with swords and shields. These combats may symbolize the conflict between good and evil. In the center, the Virgin announces to her cousin Elizabeth that she is pregnant. Grotesque figures are found on still other capitals. Crushed by his load, his foot gnawed by a dragon (look for the teeth), the *Man with Dragon* appears decidedly unhappy. Perhaps Victor Hugo had in mind such an anguished figure for the hunchback Quasimodo in *Notre-Dame de Paris*.

The Gothic *Donor of the Hospice of Salins* manages to be both realistic and ideal. The seventeenth-century wax *Portrait of a Lady of the Court* appears almost contemporary, and timeless in its jaded sensuality. The tomb effigy of Don Sanchez Saiz Carillo, circa 1250–1275, possesses heroic proportions and a dignified mien. Long before El Greco, Spanish artists elongated the human figure. Don Sancho still sports his crusader's cap. Like other funerary statues of the time, the hands are crossed; but Don Sancho, as a good Christian knight, should lie with his head facing east, toward Jerusalem. The flowing robes of the late fourteenth-century *Virgin and Child,* from Siena and also elongated, are of luxurious pattern and design. This graceful figure, standing *contrapposto,* reflects the transition from austere Gothic to sensuous Renaissance. The Romanesque *Virgin* (twelfth century) from Toulouse, stiff and stylized, faces us frontally. She gazes into space; her expression, like the eyes painted on the Egyptian mummy case seen earlier, seeks the eternal.

Musical instruments **(galleries 15–17, beyond the oval room).** In 1914 and 1919 William Howard Doane donated his extensive collection of rare historic musical instruments from all over the world to the museum. The collection has become, with additions, one of the best outside New York's Metropolitan. The instruments are often themselves works of art, and were intended as such. The dark walls and low lighting in these galleries protect delicate wood finishes and inlay. The instruments, glowing in their display cases, seem almost to generate their own light. We see a bronze Roman *buccina,* a kind of horn from the first century A.D., an Indian *gourd,* a Burmese *harp,* and a broadnecked Indian *sitar* from which protrude peacock feathers. The Amati family originally perfected in their modern forms the violin, viola, and cello. On view is a priceless Amati *viola* of 1619. A music-loving member of the Medici family may have ordered this instrument, for it appears to bear the Medici crown. The *oboe d'amore* is signed by Jakob Denner ("I." = "J.": "J" was not then in use). What the Amatis were to violins the Denners, contemporaries of Johann Sebastian Bach, were to oboes. Close your eyes and imagine the sensuous-sounding *cittern,* sometimes on display, being strummed by Gainsborough's Mrs. Thicknesse upstairs. It is appropriate that this display of humanity's musical heritage should be in a city that itself has such strong musical traditions.

Decorative arts **(galleries 19–42).** The galleries past the glass doors contain a comprehensive presentation of Rookwood pottery, displays of American costume, and rooms recreated from American, English, and French houses.

In the 1870s Cincinnati women played a major role not only in founding this museum and in carving wooden furniture but also in the development of art ceramics. In 1874 Benn Pitman, who had begun classes in woodcarving at the McMicken

School of Design the year before, also began teaching china painting, initially to his woodworking students, largely women. In the mid-1870s and for several decades afterwards the achievements of Cincinnati's art pottery and carved furniture often went hand in hand. Like the carved furniture, Rookwood garnered national acclaim and constituted a major force in the American Arts and Crafts movement.

The ceramics work of two women in particular, Mary Louise McLaughlin and Maria Longworth Nichols, stands out. McLaughlin, sister of the architect James McLaughlin, made in the late 1870s notable experiments in underglaze decoration. She has rightfully been called "the pioneer of china painting in America." In 1880 Maria Longworth Nichols (after 1886 Mrs. Bellamy Storer) founded Rookwood Pottery. Four years before, at the Centennial Exhibition of 1876 in Philadelphia, Mrs. Nichols had reacted strongly to "the wonderful beauty of the Japanese exhibit. It was there," she recalled, "that I first felt a desire to have a place of my own where things could be made." That place was Rookwood, which began in an abandoned schoolhouse on Eastern Avenue, but in 1891 moved to the still-standing buildings on Mount Adams. Blessed with a group of inventive designers, many female and often trained under Benn Pitman, Rookwood experienced a surge of creativity in the next two or three decades. Though most of its decorative techniques originated in England and France, the designs on its wares derive largely from Japanese art, prints especially, or Japanese art as interpreted by French *Japoniste* artists like Emile Gallé, whose shapes Rookwood designers often copied.

The exhibit cases in gallery 35 begin at the left with pre-Rookwood pottery of the 1870s and move forward chronologically. The first cases include several pieces from the Cincinnati room of the Women's Pavilion of the 1876 Centennial Exhibition along with works by Mary Louise McLaughlin. Her "Cincinnati Faience," as she called her underglaze slip painting, was eventually adopted at Rookwood. Further down the hall is her largest effort, the "Ali Baba" vase, more than three feet high, a prodigious accomplishment by virtue of size alone.

The Rookwood cases rightly focus on the pottery's greatest period, from 1880 to 1910. Some early pieces are eye catching. They include a small 1884 vase by Mrs. Nichols that illustrates the famed "Tiger Eye" glaze. A vase of 1885, in "Cameo Bisque" by Albert R. Valentien, depicts an oriental blowfish against a bluish white blackground. Also his is a plaque in "Standard" glaze depicting an ear of dried corn. In the same case, an 1893 vase features a band of storks set against a deep rust background. It is by Kataro Shirayamadani, a Japanese artist ("Sherry" to his friends) who began work at Rookwood in 1887 and stayed with the firm, except for 1915–1925, until 1948. *Trinity of Dragons: Earth, Fire, and Water* may be his masterpiece. Unlike dragons in Western art, Japanese and Chinese dragons embody the spirit of change and thus represent life itself.

Rookwood designers kept abreast of technical developments, experimented constantly, and created new glazes and designs. After 1900 Rookwood replaced its "Standard" glaze with "Vellum." Rookwood won its first major international recognition when the judges at the 1889 Paris *Exposition Universelle* awarded its wares a Gold Medal. That award was the first of many, at home and abroad. Gradually, Rookwood gained a reputation as the Tiffany of art ceramics. "No ceramic establishment which has existed in the United States," wrote E. A. Barker in 1893, "has come nearer fulfilling the requirements of a distinctive American institution than the Rookwood Pottery."

Historic American rooms **(galleries 26–28, 33, 39, 41, 42).** This section of the museum is its most labyrinthine. Finding your way from room to room may become confusing. Gallery 41, for example, around the corner from the Rookwood exhibit, is sometimes reached through gallery 36, other times through galleries 39 and 40. It recreates a "Carpenter Classic" Federal hall from two Kilgour houses in Cincinnati. "Carpenter Classic" means that the builder has translated the stone architectural elements into wood. Sculptures by Hiram Powers, America's most important nineteenth-century sculptor, fill the room.

Born in Vermont, Powers came to Cincinnati in 1819 and resided in the city for fifteen years. Here he designed wax effigies and automata, including grotesque monsters for a long-running exhibit, *The Infernal Regions,* in Joseph Dorfeuille's Western Museum, ancestor of the present Museum of Natural History. From wax models to marble was the next step. Powers greatly impressed Nicholas Longworth, who sent him to study, first in Washington in 1834, then after 1837 in Florence. In Florence he became famous, and there he remained until his death in 1873. Powers adhered to the Neoclassical canons of Canova and Thorwaldsen, which stressed a smooth finish. Sculpture overshadowed painting in mid-nineteenth century America, and Powers's Greek and Roman gods achieved enormous popularity in an age that valued the classical ideal in its institutions and architecture.

The Greek Slave (1843), Powers's best-known work, represents a Christian girl, depicted nude. It became the most celebrated artwork of its day. Powers drew his inspiration from the Greek War of Independence against the Turks; presumably the demure slave is being eyed by lustful Turks. Exhibited in 1847–1848 along the East Coast and in Cincinnati, the sculpture caused a sensation with its sentimental eroticism. Puritans objected violently to the nudity, not least in Cincinnati. Miner Kellogg, impressario of the triumphal tour, informed Powers that "the ladies here are rather more modest than anywhere else." In addition, proslavery forces found the subject offensive. Displayed at the Crystal Palace Exhibition in 1851, *The Greek Slave* established Powers's European renown. Although Cincinnati only has a discreet bust of *The Greek Slave* (the original is in the Corcoran Gallery, Washington), *Eve Disconsolate,* another very circumspect nude, gives us an idea of Powers's skill in full-figured composition. The serpent is at her feet; on the pedestal we discern the initials "H. P." and "N. L.," the latter Nicholas Longworth, who commissioned the work. If Powers found his greatest satisfaction in creating ideal works like *The Greek Slave* and *Eve Disconsolate,* his real contribution lies in his busts of statesmen, men of letters, lawyers, and businessmen. Works both ideal and real are on display. The real often shades into the ideal: Powers's bust of *Nicholas Longworth* makes that cagey entrepreneur appear more heroic, more like an ancient Roman, than does Duncanson's portrait upstairs. In the twentieth century, as part of the reaction against Victorian literalness, Powers's reputation went into eclipse. Recent decades have witnessed a more balanced attitude toward his work.

Gallery 42, off the Kilgour hall, contains an early nineteenth-century room from Charleston, South Carolina. On display are several different kinds of "Chippendale" chairs. Most of the furnishings come from Philadelphia, then the center of American craftsmanship, and New England. In the adjoining Folk Arts room (gallery 40) we pass beneath a ship's figurehead, no mermaid but a bekilted Scotsman. Hanging from one corner is a huge tin pipe. This unusual street sign hung until 1983 before the Keyer Pipe House at 1225–1227 Main St., passed near the end of our first Over-the-Rhine tour. Gallery 39 features a Carpenter Classic Greek Revival doorway and fine iron work, with anthemions and running-scroll motifs, both circa 1830 and from the Oliver Spencer house, once on the southern slope of Mount Adams.

From here we retrace our steps to the Rookwood exhibit (gallery 35), then enter through a low doorway on the right, opposite the "Ali Baba" vase, the recreated rooms from the Cary house (galleries 29–32). The dining room, parlor, and bedroom are painted in period colors and refurbished in the style of 1816–1860. In the parlor, the secretary-bookcase (1830s), in bird's-eye maple, is a documented Cincinnati piece. Samuel Best of this city made the tall clock between 1802 and 1818. The museum has collected costume since its founding, and gallery 34 exhibits it in installations that change several times a year. The Victorian drawing room (gallery 33), made up from the Groesbeck mansion (1870) and other vanished Cincinnati houses, represents High Victorian decor, including fine examples of rosewood Rococo Revival furniture. The room is of the same period as those we have seen in the John Hauck house on Dayton St. and the William Howard Taft birthplace on Auburn Ave. We walk back along gallery 35, then enter the early nineteenth-century ballroom (gallery 28), painted a sage green, taken from "Soldier's Joy," a still-standing Federal mansion along the upper Rappahannock in Virginia. American craftsmen had not yet come up to English standards; thus the woodcarving here is simpler than in comparable English work. Some upper pieces are plaster simulating wood. The chest-on-chest and high chest, both from mid-eighteenth century Philadelphia, exemplify the best American craftsmanship of the period.

***English rooms* (galleries 26, 27).** The Jacobean room (26) includes furniture from the time of James I (1603–1625). The chimneypiece of Bath limestone, made sometime between 1611 and 1630, probably in 1626, came from Montecute House in Bristol. It was once painted, though now we can only guess at the color scheme. The *Five Senses,* stolid-faced females probably more decorative than symbolic, surround the family coat of arms. English furniture of this period, invariably oak, features rectilinear design with shallow carving. Note the bulbous urns on the cupboard and bed; on both cupboard and chest we make out the *guilloche* pattern of interlocking curves.

The eighteenth-century English room, circa 1730, derives from a town house in Grosvenor Square in London's fashionable West End. Every element in this carved and painted wood-panelled room, symmetrical though with Rococo flourishes from France, was done with close attention to detail. The Rococo influence appears notably in the exquisite carving on the door surrounds and mantel of drapery, tassels, and scrolls. The running wave pattern on the chair rail, or *dado,* is called a *Vitruvian scroll*. Apple green is the room's original color. The furniture, now no longer oak but mahogany, reflects Dutch influence. Upholstery, here a cherry-red damask, began to be used in the eighteenth century. Note the cabriole legs of the chairs, the shallow carving of the knees, the upturned scrolls on the feet. Four hand-colored engravings by Hogarth—*Morning, Noon, Evening, Night*—adorn the side walls. One William Frankland holds forth in the overmantel; behind his left shoulder, ghostlike, looms a bust of the regicide, Oliver Cromwell. Cromwell, needless to say, had not been popular after the restoration of the Stuarts in 1660. Bitter memories of the Civil War and the Protectorate left his name at a low ebb for nearly two centuries. For Frankland to identify himself openly with Cromwell's Puritan faith and republican politics took courage.

British decorative arts (gallery 25). This long, very narrow room contains a choice collection of furniture, silver, and ceramics from the late seventeenth to the early twentieth century. We begin at the far end with the spectacular linden surround attributed to that greatest of decorative wood carvers, Grinling Gibbons. He frequently signed his work with peapods, here visible to the left of the central section. Contemporaneous with it is the Mortlake tapestry, based on a Raphael cartoon in London's Victoria and Albert Museum. Opposite the pair of gilt eagle consoles hangs a looking glass with *verre églomisé* borders. The Wedgwood display focuses on regency pieces. The nineteenth century's architectural eclecticism, exhilarating but confusing, finds reflection in the decorative arts. Worcester, Doulton, Mintons, and Royal Crown Derby are represented chiefly by High Victorian work. Several examples have lacelike designs of unbelievable intricacy; others reflect the Japanese mode that swept the West after 1870. From the captions we discover that the museum acquired many Victorian ceramics in the 1880s. Dusted off after decades in storage, they again dazzle in their detail and in their coloration. Architectural in conception is the magnificent breakfront secretary bookcase, circa 1790, made in London. Inlays of lighter and darker colored woods define the drawers. Designed in the style of a China cupboard, this bookcase doubles as a desk.

French rooms (galleries 21–24). Outstanding are the four seventeenth- and eighteenth-century French rooms. Past the Grinling Gibbons surround is the tiny Henry IV study, or *studiolo*, circa 1610, possibly unique in this country. On the woodwork are Italian Mannerist paintings based on Tasso's *Aminta* (1583). The other three French rooms, spanning the eighteenth century, reflect movements in taste and artistic expression during the reigns of Louis XV and XVI. We view them slightly out of chronological order. The first is a Louis XV painted room, circa 1750, full of *singeries* and *chinoiseries,* fantasy designs based on monkeys (*singes*) and "Chinese" designs, both mid-eighteenth century enthusiasms. The next room, a Louis XV salon from Paris, moves us back a generation in time to about 1720. It is in the French Régence style, transitional between the monumental rectilinear style of Louis XIV and the playful curvilinear Rococo style of midcentury that we have just seen. The wood panels, or *boiseries,* intricately sculpted with flowers, were designed by a Flemish wood carver, Jacques Verberckt. They were originally painted; the museum hopes to repaint them when funds permit. Among the luxurious *ébenisterie* of French eighteenth-century master craftsmen is a *bureau plat,* possibly a late work designed by André Charles Boulle, Louis XIV's famous cabinet maker, and a *commode* rich in inlay and ormolu by Jean-Pierre Latz.

Four Beauvais tapestries (1778–1780) in the adjacent room depict the *douceur de vivre* of prerevolutionary France. They deserve our scrutiny. The "ACC" on three of them stands for André Charlemagne Charron, the workmaster at Beauvais at this time; "DM" on the fourth is for de Menou, his successor. Louis XVI gave the tapestries to Louis Benigne de Bertier de Sauvigny upon the marriage of one of his daughters. Formal gardens overgrown with foliage, a frequent background to Rococo art, suggest a never-never land of pleasure. But the family's later history is tragic. De Sauvigny and his father-in-law were among the Revolution's first victims. On July 22, 1789, a week after the Bastille fell, a mob summarily executed them. When de Sauvigny's eldest son Antoine—depicted holding a telescope on the second tapestry, *The Education of the Children*—saw the heads of his father and grandfather paraded through the streets of Paris, he went mad. The final French interior is a Louis XVI salon, circa 1785. With its rectilinear painted and gilded *boiseries,* it is stylistically the purest of the rooms. Symmetry returns with the neoclassical style though Rococo touches persist in the garlands over the mirrors. At the far end the oval *table de fantasie,* by Charles Topino, has marquetry *chinoiseries* on the shelf, top, and sides; even the front drawers do not break the continuity of the inlaid landscape. Behind us hang two small idealized scenes of Roman ruins by Hubert Robert.

Tribal arts **(galleries 13, 14).** In 1988 an expanded display of tribal arts, sensuously lit and presented in a postmodern decor, opened in these galleries. The museum has splendid collections of American Indian and African art, of which it can show few examples at any one time. In 1890, when it acquired the Steckelmann collection of African art, the museum may have been the first American institution to collect African objects as art rather than merely as ethnography. Primitive art began to be appreciated after 1900. Picasso, Modigliani, and other Western artists drew upon its forms for inspiration; in music Stravinsky evoked elemental forces of nature in *The Rite of Spring.* The female figure from Lumbo, Gabon, is an important example of classic African art. The engaging Duala canoe is an extremely rare item. Indian artifacts from the Ohio valley, long a center of archaeological research, include the *Waverly tablet* from the Adena culture, 800 B.C. to 200 A.D. The birdstone above it, from the Early Woodland period (4000–1000 B.C.), is a marvel of spare design.

Far Eastern art **(galleries 18, 48–54).** Gallery 18, off gallery 14, focuses on the China export trade. The eighteenth-century English settee in the Gainsborough gallery or Topino's *table de fantasie* in the Louis XVI room behind us reveals Western imaginings of the Orient. These "westernized" eighteenth- and nineteenth-century pieces made in China for the European and American markets allow us glimpses of how the Orient imagined the West. Some Chinese designs could pass as Western, others immediately give themselves away as oriental.

After World War II the museum made a conscious and sustained effort to build up its holdings of Near and Far Eastern art. These collections now rank among its greatest strengths. In 1982 all the Far and Near East rooms were attractively redone; mahogany exhibit cases and muted lighting were installed. By providing an ambience of understated elegance, the galleries show the art objects—which change frequently—to good advantage. Gallery 54, devoted to Japan, displays several screens: among them are the rather crowded *Gathering of the Thirty-six Poets* by Tami Buncho (early nineteenth century) and the more austere *Three Pigeons on a Maple Branch and Sparrow on Bamboo* by Watanabe Seitei (late nineteenth century). A silk *uchikake*, or over-kimono, is decorated with birds, leaves, and flowers. On the hanging scroll, done with a calligrapher's brush, the popeyed sage Daruma stares at us. The Japanese, like the Chinese, rated calligraphy equal in importance to painting. Daruma is the legendary founder of Ch'an, or in the Japanese, Zen, Buddhism. It is said that during one of his meditations Daruma fell asleep. When he awoke he was so chagrined that to assure against such a transgression happening again he cut out his eyelids. From the earth where the eyelashes dropped grew the tea plant, the leaves of which could banish sleep.

If a breath of fresh air beckons, the doorway between gallery 54 and 53 leads to the **Sculpture Court,** established in 1931 and redesigned by Henry Fletcher Kenney in the 1940s. We stand on the raised flagstone terrace and look toward a shallow, green-tiled reflecting pool. Pebbled walks and shrubs connect the two. The formal design gives the Sculpture Court a classical serenity. Contributing to the serenity are (on the left and before us) the Emery and Hanna wings, both Roman Revival (1930), designed by the Cincinnati firm of Garber & Woodward. Burnham's Greek Revival Schmidlapp wing is on our right; behind us is the Ropes Wing (1910) and the campanile of the 1886 building. Joyful females by Harriet Whitney Frishmuth limber up; light and airy, their movements belie the solidity of bronze. Saint-Gaudens's *Amor Caritas* offers a more sedate accompaniment.

The three Chinese rooms (galleries 51–53) constitute one of the museum's high points. Two cases in gallery 53 exhibit bronzes from the Shang dynasty (ca. 1750–1045 B.C.). Made for offerings of food and wine to ancestral spirits, the ritual bronzes of patriarchal China are the earliest of the great Chinese arts. In quality of detail and craftsmanship they have never been surpassed, in China or elsewhere. Six other cases offer a short history of 4000 years of Chinese ceramics, from neolithic times through the reign of K'ang Hsi (1662–1722 A.D.). We begin with earthenware from Kansu province. The T'ang dynasty horse, in *san ts'ai*, three-color glaze (blue and yellow, with touches of green), once formed part of a lord's tomb. The horse looms over two handmaidens who await their lord's bidding in the afterlife. All three figures have an unsophisticated charm and vigor. Nearby is a creamy-white glazed plate with floral decoration (Sung dynasty, twelfth century) of extraordinary delicacy. In the standing case are K'ang Hsi porcelains, including a bowl in what the Chinese surely did not call *café-au-lait* glaze. They closely guarded the secret of their hard-glazed porcelain, invented, most probably, in the Sui dynasty (581–618). Not until more than a millennium later, in 1709, did the Dresden potter Johann Böttger succeed in making true porcelain in Europe. In the wall cabinet the large box in carved cinnabar lacquer, lent to the museum in 1887 and presumably not to be returned, depicts "the gathering at the orchid pavilion."

The dragons on the dragon coat (gallery 52) symbolize life. Unlike Western

Ceremonial vessel, Shang Dynasty (China), bronze. The
finely incised decoration of bronzes of the Shang dynasty
(ca. 1750–1045 B.C.) has never been surpassed. Courtesy
of the Cincinnati Art Museum.

dragons, the dragon in the Chinese cosmology is benevolent, the genesis of strength
and goodness. Among the handscrolls, the earliest from the twelfth century, and
hanging scrolls (fourteenth to sixteenth centuries) are several of high distinction.
The *Four Sages of Shang-Shan,* or Mount Shang, by Ma Yüan (Southern Sung,
early thirteenth century), is one of the summits of Chinese painting. Except for this
scroll and another in Shanghai, Ma Yüan's other known paintings—there are only
five in all—are on silk. Paper allowed the artist greater freedom of touch. The observation of nature in *The Four Sages* is especially fine. We are meant to "read"
Chinese paintings, like Chinese script, from right to left. On the other side of the
case, Chu Ta's *Birds and Lotus Pond* is done in a freer style. The birds appear poised
in limitless space. The Chinese word for "landscape" (*shan-shui*) literally means
"mountains" (*shan*) and "water" (*shui*), the essential components of all Chinese garden and landscape scenes. No less are hills and water the essential components of
our Cincinnati prospects. The great Chinese landscapes have an uncanny ability to
take us out of ourselves; to many they are a source of spiritual refreshment and
solace. On the scrolls the red squares, called *chops,* indicate owners. The black

pictographs are elucidatory comments by the artist about his painting; he uses them to shed light on his purpose or basic idea, or to help the onlooker understand more clearly his intentions.

The core of the museum's masterpieces of Chinese sculpture (gallery 51) date from the sixth century A.D. In the *Votive Stela with Buddhist Trinity* (522 A.D.) the Buddha is depicted in high relief, the two Bodhisattvas in lesser relief. The Buddha attained Nirvana; his disciples, the Bodhisattvas, could have attained Buddha-hood but instead stayed behind in a lesser state to aid mortals in this life. The Buddha sits crosslegged in the lotus position: his right hand makes, or would make if it were there, the gesture of assurance; his left rests in the position of charity. *Asparas*, celestial musicians and goddesses, dance on either side of the incense burner above the Buddha's head. The sculptured forms in high relief work effectively against the background of tightly incised linear design. Off to the left, the standing Bodhisattvas with sweet, withdrawn smiles wear elaborate headdress. Bodhisattvas are often depicted in the raiment and jewelry of an Indian prince. The Buddha, who scorned both luxury and asceticism, eschewed such garb and ornament. In gallery 51 is also a polychromed wooden Bodhisattva, a Kuan-yin, the goddess of mercy, the comforter, ever popular because she carried the assurance of special purity. She rests in the position of royal ease, one arm negligently on a raised knee. Originally all these figures would have been in temples.

Gallery 50, devoted to South Asia, offers different national conceptions of Buddha as well as intimations of his presence. For several hundred years artists did not represent the Buddha. Early conceptions tried to suggest his eternal nature; only gradually did he take on national characteristics. On the Buddhist relief from India, Buddha's hard-to-find footprints on the footstool below the empty throne suggest that he was once there; the circular cushion with a curving swastika on the throne itself may symbolize his universal presence. The many-armed *Shiva* is the same Shiva who appears, in a stylized Art Deco relief, above the 5th St. entrance to the Netherland Plaza Hotel. Shiva, the great teacher, the force of life, is both preserver and destroyer. He dances on the back of an evil spirit, the dwarf Muyalaka, who personifies human ignorance. The drum he holds in his upper right hand represents the sounds and rhythm of life. It sets the tempo of his dance. As long as Shiva dances, the world lives; when he tires and rests, the sacred fire he holds in his upper left hand will destroy it. Here, fortunately, he is in perpetual motion, yet still. In the adjacent gallery 49 is a seventeenth-century Jain shrine. Jainism is another of the philosophical religions stemming from India. The carving, of extraordinary finesse, depicts humans, elephants, monkeys, and decorative forms. Here too the shrine's throne is empty. Placed before the shrine are a pair of gray-green marble columns, done a millenium earlier, that derive from a Hindu temple. Two bands of minutely carved ornament circle the shafts.

Gallery 48 displays a sampling of the museum's treasures from Mughal India. Islam, firmly established in northern India by the eleventh century A.D., reached its artistic climax during the Mughal, or Moghul, dynasty that reigned from the early sixteenth to the mid-eighteenth century. Inspired by Persian art, the Mughals practiced miniature painting that came to rival the masterpieces of Persia. The opaque watercolors—colorful scenes from the daily life of the wealthy and powerful—possess incredible detail. *Akbar Listening to a Courtier,* an acknowledged masterpiece, includes a number of convincingly realistic likenesses. In a corner case, an ivory powder flask, in the form of an antelope, is carved with great delicacy.

Islamic art (**galleries 44–47**). Among the museum's distinguished collection of Islamic art is a sixteenth-century "fragment" (it fills a large wall) of a Herat medallion rug. By its fine weave, complex design, and rich colors, this rug is a significant work in the history of textiles.

Off gallery 46, the tiny room from Damascus (1711 A.D.) came from the Andrew N. Jergens mansion (1890s), formerly in Cumminsville, demolished in 1968. In the decades before and after 1900 there arose among the wealthy a fad for exotic rooms, predominantly Japanese, Moorish, or Indian. Jergens bought this room in 1932 while traveling in Syria; it is one of only two such rooms in American public collections. Clad in appropriate dress, Jergens would invite his guests to take their coffee within. The Arabic inscriptions insist that hospitality be warm. The walnut walls are painted, gilded, and lacquered. Once our eyes have gotten used to the half darkness, we can begin to pick out detail. Stay a while and visions from the *Arabian Nights* rise around you. I find this room the city's most magical small interior.

The *mihrab* (gallery 45), or prayer niche oriented toward Mecca, dates from the late fifteenth or early sixteenth century. The glazed ceramic tiles represent arabesques; bits of brown and mustard set off the dominant turquoises, cobalts, and greens, favored colors of Islamic artists, "cool" colors, the color of the water that was so precious in the desert. The design, continuous and unending, suggests God's infinitude. The manuscript pages, like the miniature paintings from Mughal India that derive from them, reveal exquisite detail. Such decorative virtuosity reminds us that for a millennium Islam possessed a more advanced culture than the Christian West. Two somewhat atypical manuscript pages (which rotate frequently) are *A Young Man Playing the Flute* and the incredible *Starving Horse.*

Ancient Near Eastern art (**gallery 43**). This is one of the museum's major collections. One treasure, behind the turquoise seated lion, is the golden libation bowl of Darius the Great, king of Persia from 522 to 485 B.C. The alabaster *Kneeling Figure Bound with Serpents* (2600–2400 B.C.) is one of the earliest Sumerian artifacts. Two large fish are suspended around the man's neck; two serpents appear to embrace him. The iconography remains obscure, to me at least, but he seems to be in a lot of trouble. The *Bowl with a Frieze of Lions Hunting Bulls* (722–626 B.C.) the museum speaks of in one of its publications as "the largest and most elaborately decorated rock crystal vessel yet known in ancient Near Eastern art." It is one of the rare objects from the daily life of Assyria to survive. The stylized *Relief of a Winged Genius* (Assyrian, 870 B.C.) depicts a strong, powerful individual. On his left, the exquisite *Relief of an Attendant* shows a man carrying a full wineskin. On the other side of the doorway, stucco ibexes nibble on fruit.

We have returned to the main entrance hall. If you are hungry, the Terrace Court Restaurant downstairs awaits; if souvenirs beckon, the museum has a book and gift shop.

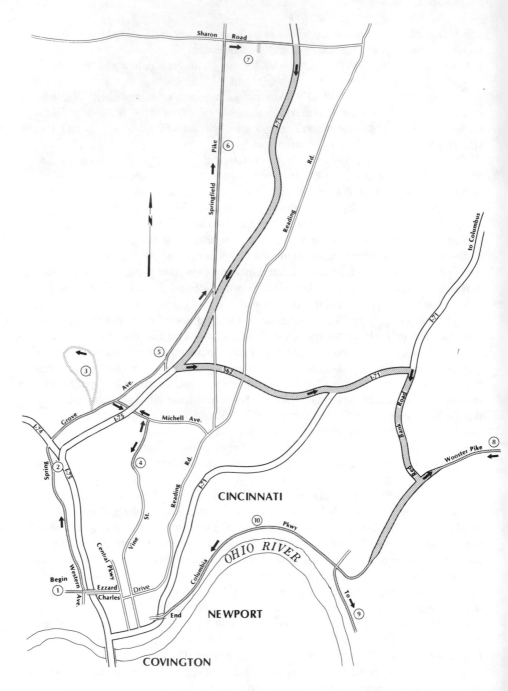

A DRIVING TOUR

1. Union Terminal
2. Cincinnati Workhouse
3. Spring Grove Cemetery
4. Cincinnati Zoo
5. Procter & Gamble
   (Ivorydale)

6. Wyoming
7. Glendale
8. Mariemont
9. Riverbend
10. Columbia Parkway

A Driving Tour

Union Terminal—Cincinnati Workhouse—Spring Grove Cemetery—
Cincinnati Zoo—Procter & Gamble—Glendale—Mariemont—
Riverbend—Columbia Parkway

DESPITE the title, this is a tour of walks. You do have to drive, however, to get from place to place. The tour *can,* I suppose, be accomplished in one very long day, at least if you drive around the suburbs and skip the zoo. Ideally, each stop might form the goal of a morning's or an afternoon's excursion. If you fancy zoos, for example, Cincinnati's is excellent and going through it could take much of a day. Short-term visitors to the city will not have the time to cover this chapter in such a leisurely way, however, so for the sake of convenience I have discussed the locations sequentially. Although I necessarily leave out much, I hope to give an impression of outer Cincinnati's wealth of architecture, the beauty of its suburban landscapes, and the considerable historic interest that lies behind both. Rather than attempt to include everything, I have, as with previous tours, preferred to discuss only a few places, these few, however, in some detail.

You can drive much of this tour on the interstates; however, with a few exceptions I keep you on Cincinnati's older roads. The interstates get you there faster but the older roads allow you to see more. Whether by interstate or by secondary roads, Cincinnati is an easy city in which to get around. Unlike larger cities, for example Los Angeles or Chicago, in Cincinnati you don't *have* to take the freeways. When you do, they are rarely clogged, as they are so often elsewhere. I-275 (completed in 1979), the lengthy ring road that circles Cincinnati and northern Kentucky, has in places stimulated development but elsewhere passes through what appears to be primeval forest. In many ways Cincinnati offers the best of both urban and suburban: a vital central core ringed by easily reached suburbs.

Union Terminal

We begin at **Union Terminal** (1933), accessible from I-75 or from downtown via Central Parkway and Ezzard Charles Drive. The terminal, located in the Millcreek

Union Terminal. Completed in 1933, Union Terminal was the city's main train station until it closed in 1972. This Art Moderne masterpiece reopened in the autumn of 1990 as the Museum Center, housing the Museum of Natural History and the Cincinnati Historical Society. The gigantic half-rotunda within provides one of Cincinnati's most breathtaking public spaces and contains spectacular murals by Winold Reiss. Courtesy of J. Miles Wolf.

Valley, is called "Union" because it combined all seven of Cincinnati's railroad lines and five separate terminals into one. Before 1920 few such terminals existed in America or England. Though people had talked of a union terminal in Cincinnati since the Civil War, the difficulties involved seemed insuperable. Its construction thus represented a bold venture in city planning. The site, chosen to maximize the possibilities for axial arrangement of railroad track, covered 287 acres on which twenty-two buildings were erected and ninety-four miles of track laid. At $41,700,000, the terminal complex remains the most expensive ever built. Visible from I-75 and several hilltops, Union Terminal is one of the city's most prominent visual landmarks.

The *baroque,* according to the Penguin *Dictionary of Architecture,* is "characterized by . . . expansive, curvaceous forms, a sense of mass, a delight in large-scale and sweeping vistas, and a preference for spatially complex compositions." This definition fits Union Terminal perfectly. Built during 1929–1933, the terminal is baroque in its curvilinear forms, its scale, its compositional complexity, and in the sense of grandeur it conveys. Beautifully set, it competes with nothing around it. Space is organized to carry the viewer to a central focus. The long *allées,* once more spectacularly landscaped than now, lead to the huge semicircular arch that concludes Cincinnati's grandest axis. Until 1973 the train concourse axis behind coincided with, and continued, the plaza axis. As with Renaissance and Baroque palaces, form and space are used here to considerable effect. The plaza is designed less for human use, less to create a people-oriented space like Fountain Square (which retains strong formal qualities), than to awe. Union Terminal's "arms" embrace you, invite you within, much as Bernini's colonnade does for St. Peter's in Rome. From the esplanade fountains water, always a magical element in a landscape, tumbles down its welcome.

Certain kinds of buildings fulfill symbolic roles that go beyond their functional tasks. For a century, the railroad station served as a city's chief entrance door. It provided many who came to the city with their first impressions. A railroad station can express "the nobility of the city," Paul Goldberger has observed in regard to Manhattan's demolished Penn Station, "and hence of the people within it, a kind of shared grandeur." Like Penn Station, Union Terminal was designed to overwhelm arriving passengers, to make them aware that they had arrived at an important place. Its gigantic arch serves, in effect, as a monumental city gate. Though Penn Station is no more and Union Terminal no longer Cincinnati's gateway, the terminal itself fortunately remains. We may still appreciate the imaginative grandeur of its conception.

Union Terminal is Cincinnati's best example of Art Moderne. Art Moderne, a derivative of Art Deco, is not to be confused with Modern Movement, or International style, architecture. As opposed to Art Deco's more flamboyant zigzags, for example, in Manhattan's Chrysler Building, Art Moderne uses simplified classical forms. With the streamlining of automobiles and airplanes, rounded forms gradually supplanted the rectilinear lines of Art Deco. Exterior and interior decoration in Union Terminal is austere; a compromise is effected between traditionalism and modernity. With its arch, its dome, its extended "arms," the design of Union Terminal is basically curvilinear. The façade, of limestone with stainless steel trim, looks enormous. It *is* enormous. Bas reliefs (by Maxfield Keck) of a muscular female and male, the latter in Captain Marvel headgear, symbolize Commerce and Transportation, or, more generally, movement, speed, and power. Such large-scaled detailing accentuates the terminal's public presence. The gigantic clock reminded incoming passengers to hurry; once it also served as a neighborhood landmark.

Union Terminal's architects were Alfred Fellheimer and Stewart Wagner. (Their names appear on the building's dedication stone.) Fellheimer was at this time probably America's leading designer of large train stations. The partners placed the overall supervision of the terminal design in the hands of a talented younger member of the firm, Hungarian-born Roland Anthony Wank. Wank, who had a strong interest in modern functionalism, later became the TVA's first architect. Subsequently he designed the planned community of Greenhills, Ohio, north of Cincinnati. In 1930 Paul Philippe Cret, architect of the Pan American Union (1907) and the Folger Library (1931), was brought in to advise on exterior ornament. Cret, whose own style was evolving at this time from neoclassical to Art Deco, played a major role in determining Union Terminal's ultimate Art Moderne appearance.

The terminal's façade drew inspiration, Jayne Merkel has pointed out, from Eliel Saarinen's Helsinki Central Station (1910–1914). It displays a large, stylized arch flanked by two enormous figures. Fellheimer visited the Helsinki station in 1927, the year his firm began work on Buffalo's New York Central Terminal, where a huge arch also dominates the façade. Even more than the Helsinki and Buffalo terminals, however, Union Terminal's arch recalls the two gigantic arches of King's Cross Station, London (1851). Its arches Fellheimer singled out (in a 1952 article) as being "of strongly modern construction and appearance." In its functional circulation, Cincinnati's terminal has significant affinities with New York's Grand Central Station. Grand Central was built by the St. Paul, Minnesota, firm of Reed and Stem in collaboration with Warren and Wetmore of New York. Fellheimer and Wagner, Reed and Stem's successors, handled pedestrian and vehicular circulation no less masterfully in Union Terminal than their predecessors had in Grand Central. In essence, Union Terminal possesses an *infundibuliform,* or "funnel-shaped," form, or rather a half funnel-shaped form that is, Fellheimer wrote in 1933, "placed on its side and guid[es] the traveler unmistakably to and from the point of contact with the train service." Once within we shall study this circulation pattern. No station subsequent to Union Terminal rivals the intrinsic excellence of its form and plan.

Contemporaneous with the Carew Tower/Netherland Plaza complex, Union Terminal went up during Cincinnati's late 1920s building boom. Believing a purely classical design inappropriate, Fellheimer and Wagner deliberately broke with the past. But no less does Union Terminal, as Carl Condit has pointed out, bring to a close the traditional Beaux Arts concepts of monumentalism and civic art. "The last grand gesture in the old tradition," Condit calls Union Terminal, "yet the first to be executed in the modern style."

The terminal was designed to handle 216 trains a day, 108 incoming, 108 outgoing. "It could have accommodated 420 trains per day," Condit believes, "nearly double the number for which it was theoretically designed." But through 1945 the terminal averaged only 128 trains per weekday. No one could regard the facility as taxed. Only during the war years, 1942 to 1945, did it run at full capacity. Even as it went up, Americans in increasing numbers were choosing to travel by car. After World War II railroad activity continued to wane. The last passenger train left Union Terminal on October 28, 1972. Shortly afterwards, the Southern Railway, which had bought the terminal, demolished the train concourse. The single daily passenger train serving Cincinnati (Amtrak's Cardinal, on the Washington-Chicago run) used the tiny Amtrak station on River Road, a mile or two southwest, until 1991, when service resumed at Union Terminal.

In 1975 the city bought the terminal for three million dollars. In 1978 it leased it to a Columbus developer, who turned it into an urban shopping mall. Opened in 1980, the mall never quite caught on. The number of stores, from an initial forty, had declined by 1983 to three. On May 6, 1986, Cincinnatians passed a levy that would raise 41.7 million dollars, exactly the sum the terminal complex had cost originally, to convert the building into a **Museum Center.** The Cincinnati Historical Society Museum and Library now occupies the southern half, the Museum of Natural History the northern. The Historical Society plans reconstructions of the Public Landing and of city streets at various periods in Cincinnati's history. The Natural History Museum will have a spectacular Ice Age exhibit, the size of a football field, that will include a glacier complete with a waterfall and lifesized models of the huge animals that once roamed the Ohio Valley. It will also have a Children's Discovery

Center. The terminal's rotunda will remain public space. An OMNIMAX theater now occupies the former entrance to the train concourse. The Museum Center opened in stages, beginning in November 1990, just as this book went to press. With most permanent exhibits not yet in place, I have limited the following discussion to the terminal's interior public spaces.

As we enter the terminal, the first glimpse of the rotunda takes our breath away. Nothing on the relatively austere exterior prepares us for the sense of space, the explosion of color. Larger than we might expect from the exterior, this freestanding half dome was—and is—the largest ever built in the Western hemisphere. The span across is 185 feet, the height 106 feet. The half dome reflects sound. Kids position themselves by the water fountain at one end and whisper to friends at the other.

Two **murals** of glass tile mosaic, measuring twenty-five feet high by one hundred and five feet wide, dominate this grandiose space. They constitute the largest assemblage of secular mosaics in the United States. Each begins on the far side with pioneer times and ends in the middle with the present. The future—the entrance to the train concourse—remains open to the imagination. We may walk under and into it. "Read" from outside to inside, the murals work on several different planes and symbolic levels. Monumental foreground figures are realistic; the midground functions as an intermediate stage between realism and abstraction; the upper background offers an abstract, futuristic vision. Initially, the murals may strike us as cluttered; actually, they are extremely subtle works of art, people's art if you wish, yet sophisticated in technique, composition, and symbolism. Like the public sculpture we have seen, the murals repay contemplation, as much for the ideas they embody as for the esthetic pleasure they give.

Winold Reiss designed the murals. Unknown craftsmen working for the Ravenna Mosaic Co., then based in New York, executed and installed them under Reiss's supervision. Born in Karlsruhe in 1886, Reiss attended art schools in Munich. Like George Grosz and other Germans of his generation, he became fascinated by Indians as a boy by reading Karl May's German-language westerns and James Fenimore Cooper's famous *Leatherstocking Tales*. In New York after 1913, Reiss learned much from the great Indian collection of the American Museum of Natural History. In the 1920s and 1930s he spent summers in Browning, Montana, sketching the Blackfeet. His use of primary colors in depicting Indians, blacks, and other minorities recalls Fauvism and German Expressionism. Reiss also became a well-known *ensemblier* of large public interiors: hotels, restaurants, and theaters.

The left-hand mural celebrates the epic of America. In the foreground, civilization advances, from the proud Indian to the hardy pioneer, to the railroad engineer, to construction workers. In the midground, under the steel frame, we make out locomotives, early steamboats, ferryboats, and an ocean liner. In the background we follow the history of American transportation from the Indian's dog travois (top left) to a 1930s dirigible hovering over a futuristic city. Below is a New York harbor scene: ocean liners navigate the Hudson, not the Ohio.

The mural is a stunning, enormously complex composition. Individual figures, extraordinarily detailed, are well worth studying with binoculars. Even a fingernail may consist of half a dozen tesserae. Color combinations appear much more vividly close up than at a distance. Look hard, for example, at the pioneer's shirt or pants or at any of the faces. Reiss used models for most, perhaps all, of his portraits. The blond-headed pioneer Reiss based on his brother Hans; his nineteen-year-old son Tjark served as model for two other portraits. The Indians he based on actual Indians he had sketched in Montana. Turtle, Middle Rider, and Chewing Blackbone are on the left. The number of "minorities" in these mosaics—Indians, blacks, women, and children—indicates the artist's respect for America's varied citizens. Our greatest asset, in Reiss's view, was ethnic and cultural diversity. The human figures tower over the environment. Reflecting his humanistic and egalitarian message, they embody a faith in the dignity and worth of all peoples.

The right-hand mural focuses on Cincinnati. Man dominates the foreground. We begin (on the far right) with the scout and the soldier in the days of Fort Washington. Pioneers yield to farmers and laborers. The black roustabouts and riverboat captain symbolize the picturesque river age. The strong, confident blacks do not lack self esteem. We then move to the builders of the future Cincinnati. In the midground we see the city's early settlement, rural scenes, climaxed by another vision of tomorrow's city. At the Public Landing we make out, among several boats that have played a role in Cincinnati's history, the fabled *Island Queen*. Clearly discernible are the Carew and the Central Trust; behind them loom structures yet unbuilt, even a "skywalk" of sorts. Do the Roman arches allude to Cincinnatus? The upper background, totally Art Deco, begins with steamboats, which advance in design, and ends with airplanes winging their way over futuristic Cincinnati. Reiss's color range exploits the light-reflecting qualities of the mosaics, which can look dramatically different at different times of day or year, even from our position in the rotunda. In certain lights the foreground figures appear to recede as the background comes to the fore: an uncanny effect.

The human figures, along with the lower half of the composition, are in mosaic; the background is "silhouette mosaic," that is, individual tesserae outline the design while painted stucco fills in the areas in between. Originally the murals were to have been oils on canvas. Mosaics were chosen, however, because in a railroad terminal they are more easily kept clean and would always present a bright, colorful image. Public murals throve in the 1930s. Cities commissioned them to dramatize civic greatness or to imply political progress. "Optimistic portrayals of stylized heroic workers in local agricultural or industrial activities," Eva Weber has written, "represented . . . aspirations of continuity, stability and perseverance through hard work."

The rotunda's present color scheme is close to the original cheerful colors. It may even be Union Terminal's most futuristic feature. Reiss chose a warm palette of yellows, oranges, and browns. Bands from pale yellow to bright orange surround at irregular intervals a central arc of silver. These brilliant colors are meant to startle. They startled when the terminal opened in March 1933, and they startle today. The terminal's decorative scheme was not only innovative, it was also cheaper than the original neoclassical plan, abandoned not only for artistic reasons but because of cost. Begun the year the stock market collapsed, Union Terminal came to completion during the Depression. But cost was not the only factor. Henry M. Waite, the

Union Terminal mosaic. This scene from Winold Reiss's sweeping panorama within the terminal rotunda depicts a riverboat captain addressing a dockhand. Courtesy of J. Miles Wolf.

terminal's chief engineer, wrote: "We tried to build something new, fresh and joyous. . . . We decided that the Terminal, which leads into all parts of the world, should be as bright and gay as the flowers and birds of the open country. And when we tried the bright colors the effect was joyous and stimulating."

Of modern railroad stations, Union Terminal had the most elaborate and imaginative provision for pedestrian and vehicular traffic. Arriving passengers entered the terminal via the north wing, which had separate channels for cabs, cars, and buses (trolleys were never used). The city envisioned a tie-in with its projected but never completed subway. Passengers walked up the curving ramp, purchased a ticket at one of the counters, and proceeded to the train concourse. Passenger "pathways," permanently marked on the rotunda floors in gray, red, and tan terrazzo, are one further element in the magnificently executed circulatory scheme. Debarking passengers, reversing the sequence, would have entered the rotunda, descended the south ramp, and taken a bus or taxi to the city.

Transit passengers, or anyone else, would have benefitted from the terminal's variety of services. They could pick up a newspaper, browse in the drugstore, shop for clothing or toys, see a newsreel, have a soda, snack at the lunch counter, or enjoy a sit-down meal in the dining room. They could also get a haircut, have their shoes shined, or take a shower. In addition, the terminal contained a cafeteria, three private dining rooms separated by folding doors (the rooms doubled as conference rooms), a second soda fountain, a tearoom (entirely made up of Rookwood tiles), bookstore, bakery, beauty parlor, first-aid station, and Western Union. During World War II the tearoom served as a USO room. It is now a UDF ice cream parlor. A tiny Art Deco theater, supplied during the summer with cooled air and still intact, showed newsreels for "between trains" time. Union Terminal, designed as a genuine people's palace, had all the characteristics of a mini-city. It lacked only living accommodations. The contemporaneous Carew Tower-Netherland Plaza constituted another such mini-city.

The former checking lobby beyond the rotunda has two other mosaic murals. That on the right shows Henry M. Waite, the terminal's engineer, holding a blueprint of the station. To his left are Murray Seasongood, mayor of Cincinnati, and Colonel C. O. Sherrill, the city manager. To his right is George Dent Crabbs, who devoted years to unifying the station facilities of Cincinnati's seven railroads. The left-hand mosaic shows the completed station. Left to right are C. A. Dykstra, city manager at the time of completion; H. S. Worcester, Cincinnati Union Terminal president; and Mayor Russell Wilson. These men wrought well.

415 feet beyond the terminal's present end, where the OMNIMAX theater is now, stretched the train concourse. Off it ran eight subsidiary concourses, each 1600 feet long with fifteen public and two private tracks. Seventy-eight feet across, thirty-seven feet high, the train concourse also functioned as a waiting room. It too housed mosaic murals, fifteen in all. Each twenty feet square, they depicted the city's industries. Before the concourse was demolished in 1973, the Miami Purchase Association, a local preservation group, helped raise money to remove these murals to the Greater Cincinnati airport, where all but one have been attractively reinstalled.

Upon leaving Union Terminal, we go right on Western Ave., right on Gest St., and right again on Dalton St., which takes us underneath the terminal. At Bank St. Dalton becomes Spring Grove Ave. We are traversing the **Millcreek Valley,** industrial Cincinnati's former, and still throbbing, heart, a winding twenty-mile corridor that stretches from the Ohio River to the Hamilton County line and beyond. Spring Grove Ave. was owned originally, from Harrison Ave. out to Carthage, by Ethan Bates and Richard Hopple. Laid out in 1855 and soon known as "The Avenue," this pleasant rural drive commenced at the Brighton House and wound up the Millcreek Valley. "The lands west of the Avenue, after leaving Brighton," wrote an anonymous reporter for the Cincinnati *Commercial* in 1866, "are a succession of gardens and hot-houses." Until after the Civil War the Millcreek Valley's truck farms supplied the city with vegetables. Before 1873, when the city bought it, Spring Grove Ave. was a toll road. Graded, macadamized, and lined with paved gutters, this "broad and beautiful" road, was by the 1870s a hundred feet wide. Lined with "magnificent trees," it offered one of Cincinnati's most celebrated drives. Under its giant elms young bloods raced their horses; on summer afternoons the town beaux and belles paraded in their carriages.

Gradually the Millcreek Valley became the center for pork-packing and for the city's heavy industry. The bus ride along a later Spring Grove Ave., George M. Henzel recalled in the teens of this century, "passed a lot of nice smelling businesses, and a few not so nice smelling. . . . To fully enjoy the ride, the windows had to be open. First there was Streitman's Factory and the smell of the cookies baking. Next, Jergens Soap Co., and the odor of perfumed soaps and lotions. Soon you approached the Stock Yards and you pinched your nose to prevent your stomach from doing nip-ups. If you got your fingers off of your nose just in time, you caught the smell of Kahn's American Beauty Hams. Another mile or so and you were passing through Ivorydale, named for Procter and Gamble's Ivory Soap. The smells here were not the same as those back at Jergens, inasmuch as P & G made a lot of products, the odor of which spread over all of Ivorydale. All of this for a nickel." With the arrival of the factories, Spring Grove's rural character disappeared. Although industry here has declined since World War II, it remains significant. At the northern end of the Millcreek corridor, in Evendale, is General Electric's aircraft engines division, the area's largest employer. In between, dozens of large and small manufacturers, historically the backbone of the Greater Cincinnati economy, turn out goods of every description. Although the area's 1,740,000 inhabitants leave it now twenty-third in population among American metropolitan areas, Cincinnati ranks thirteenth in the value of its manufacturing shipments. With its central location and easy access to interstates, the Millcreek Valley remains ideal for manufacturing. Unfortunately it has little undeveloped land. The sites already occupied are often too small or too expensive to justify the demolition of existing structures for new development.

The **factory** is the first new building type of the modern world inaugurated by the French and Industrial Revolutions. In its basic form the early nineteenth-century factory was a narrow rectangular block several stories high. Since power (steam usually) was transmitted by a system of shafts, gears, and leather belts that extended to the top floor, equipment had to be as close to the power source as possible. Thus the desirability of multistoried structures. Multistoried factories lasted throughout the century. Many of those built on Spring Grove Ave. still stand; new ones have also gone up. The older constructions can be grand affairs, with the ample fenestration needed in the days before electric lighting. Turn-of-the-century buildings appear to be all windows. The older factories keep the street line and often adjoin each other. Designed for the streetcar era, they lack parking. Twentieth-century factories emphasize linear production flow on a single level. With electricity replacing steam, the need for the shafts, gears, and belts disappeared. The newer factories move objects more efficiently horizontally by forklifts or similar vehicles than vertically by elevators. Thus the newer buildings are wide-spreading structures, invariably one story high, climate and light controlled with few or no windows, and inevitably include parking.

Industrial architecture is an acquired taste, but well worth the acquisition. Spring Grove Ave. allows us an excellent opportunity to take in the evolution of Cincinnati's factory architecture for over a century, and a fascinating lot of structures we shall see. Our route traverses the crowded southern end of the Millcreek corridor. We soon go under the 3300-foot long Art Deco Western Hills Viaduct (1932) built across the trainyards as part of the Union Terminal complex. The central arch spans the Millcreek. On the left, adjoining each other, are the Wm. Powell Co. (1846; this building, 1893), now **Powell Valve,** and the **Andrew Jergens Co.** (1882; these buildings, 1894–1936).

We go under the Hopple Street Viaduct. Soon afterwards, on the left, is **Kahn's** (1882; these buildings, 1928—), still the producers of "America's Beauty Meats" and Cincinnati's sole remaining on-site meat-packing company. We are now in the former heart of the stockyard district, which moved here more than a century ago from the Deer Creek Valley on downtown's east side. Before Chicago surpassed it as America's meat-packing center, Cincinnati had well earned its nickname of "Porkopolis." Every week 14,000 hogs ride their last mile down Spring Grove. Kahn's, now Ohio's largest meat packer, slaughters over 700,000 annually, more than in the 1850s when Cincinnati was the nation's pig capital. At Alabama Ave., just past Kahn's entrance, we turn right and proceed one block to Colerain Ave., where we turn left and stop in front of the park.

The Cincinnati Workhouse

Before us stands, or stood, the **Cincinnati Workhouse** (1869), formally (in bureaucratese) the Community Correctional Institute (CCI). With the park as foreground, we have sufficient perspective to take in this Brobdingnagian structure. Corner towers, with machicolations and corbelling, anchor the five-part, symmetrical 510-foot long front; a cupola crowns the mansarded center section. The proportions are huge. "An edifice needs length to be splendid," wrote Charles Eusebius, Prince of Liechtenstein; "the longer the better." Though no Versailles or Schönbrunn, in Cincinnati the workhouse is surpassed in length only by several of the riverfront warehouses. Designed by Samuel Hannaford and Edwin Anderson, it combines Romanesque Revival forms with Second Empire grandiloquence. Not unlike a gigantic crenellated brewery, the workhouse would have made a mead hall worthy of Beowulf himself. Originally a "Work House," the workhouse was conceived as a place for rehabilitation as well as for incarceration. And, like Music Hall and the original Fountain Sq. and the public schools of the 1880s and 1890s, it was a public place, part of the civic endeavor, a place meant to be seen and admired, a place in which both the city and the community took pride. The park before us was once carefully landscaped. A century ago, communities vied to have buildings like the workhouse; now they vie *not* to have them.

Cincinnati Workhouse. The Workhouse, as its name implies, was conceived as a place for rehabilitation as well as incarceration. Designed by Samuel Hannaford, who built Music Hall, this imposing structure (1869) was demolished beginning in November 1990.

Inside are three tiers of tiny, poorly lighted cells. Plumbing is virtually nonexistent. Long ago the workhouse outgrew its purpose as a holding station for petty criminals. Periodically, the city talked about closing the facility; in fact, it did close from 1920 to 1927. In 1981 the city turned it over to Hamilton County, which in 1985 opened a new $60 million "Justice Center" downtown intended to replace it. But the Justice Center rapidly became overcrowded, so a wing of the workhouse remained (in 1990) in use. But the building's days were numbered. The persistent report of the workhouse's imminent decease became a reality in November 1990 when this great building, designed by the city's major architect, began to fall before the wrecker's ball. If the preservation of Union Terminal represents one of Cincinnati's shining successes in adaptive re-use of a historic structure, the demolition of the Cincinnati Workhouse—a building equally worthy of preservation—ranks as one of its abject failures.

Monumental structures enable us to get our bearings in a city. The workhouse, like Union Terminal, serves Cincinnati as an architectural focal point. If its looming presence astounds us from here, it startles motorists whizzing by on I-75 even more. It elicits a pleasant "there it is" long before we know *what* it is. More people have asked me to identify it for them than any other Cincinnati building. By virtue of its size, its fortresslike contours, and its coats of (now badly flaking) white paint, the workhouse is, in effect, the city's Neuschwanstein.

We return to Spring Grove Ave. and continue north. Spring Grove curls eastward. To our left lies Cumminsville, "Ludlow's Station" when founded in 1790, now **"Northside."** Hard hit by the 1937 flood, when water flowed through second-story windows, Northside has slowly come back. It offers much of historical and architectural interest. Here Andrew Jergens lived in an "Anglo-Norman" Romanesque castle, since demolished. To the right loom the Clifton hills. From Spring Grove Ave. we can make out, in winter at least, the towers of George K. Shoenberger and Henry Probasco's "castles." Soon Spring Grove Cemetery comes up on our left. We turn in at the main gate and park in the lot to the right.

Spring Grove Cemetery

Cemeteries are known by the personages they keep. **Spring Grove Cemetery** is no exception. Here lie many of Cincinnati's great: its pioneers, the Symmes family, John Filson, John and Daniel Gano; its early great men, Daniel Drake, Nicholas Longworth, Ormsby McKnight Mitchel, General William H. Lytle, Salmon Chase, Henry Probasco, James Gamble, William Procter, Levi Coffin, Miles Greenwood, John Hauck; its merchant barons, H. and S. Pogue, George W. McAlpin, and John Shillito; its notorious civic leader, George Barnsdale "Boss" Cox; its artists, among them Henry Farny; its mavericks, Frances Wright and Powel Crosley, Jr.; even its baseball stars, including Miller Huggins, the Yankees's fiery manager during the Babe Ruth years. Although William Howard Taft lies in Arlington and Robert A. in Indian Hill, Alphonso, the patriarch, as well as most other family members, are buried here. Visiting Spring Grove allows us to pay our respects to the men and women who over two centuries have made Cincinnati.

With 782 acres Spring Grove is the largest private nonprofit, nonsectarian cemetery in the country. 170,000 people lie buried here. Only 425 acres are developed, the remainder managed as productive woodland. With its fourteen lakes, thirty-five miles of road, and more than 850 labeled species of trees, Spring Grove can claim to be Cincinnati's finest park. Certainly it is its best kept. It is also a museum without walls, at least a sculpture garden without walls. Eminent sculptors, European and American, have designed a number of its monuments. A walk through its grounds reveals a century and a half of changing attitudes toward art, architecture, and landscape. It reveals also, as Blanche Linden-Ward has well said, "changing notions about life, death, nature, family, and community." In addition to being a cemetery, an arboretum, and a sculpture garden, Spring Grove is also a bird sanctuary, a park with scenic vistas, a place of instruction and meditation, and (since 1979) a National Historic Landmark. Originally intended as a cemetery and a horticultural showcase, Spring Grove remains today, in all sense, a refuge. It is arguably the most beautiful of all American cemeteries.

"Curved lines," Daniel Drake once remarked, "symbolize the country, straight lines the city." Although a checkerboard neatness characterized the street pattern of western towns like Cincinnati, curves controlled the design of the new cemeteries, west and east. Curves, as Ian Nairn once observed, do not in themselves possess a special virtue. They are not intrinsically better than a grid. The Levittowns are as curved as you like. But curves can enhance our pleasure in life, and Cincinnati, in defiance of its street grid, is a curvaceous city, nowhere more so than in its major cemetery.

The mid-nineteenth century witnessed the founding of most of America's major cemeteries. Mount Auburn in Cambridge, Massachusetts, not only gave its name to a Cincinnati suburb but effected a breakthrough in cemetery design. Laid out in 1831, Mount Auburn owed, in its turn, a debt to Paris's Père Lachaise, founded in 1804. Mount Auburn was parklike with meandering drives, naturalistic pools, and secluded groves; mausoleums, instead of standing out on flat ground, were built into the slopes of hills. Mount Auburn, as David Schuyler has noted, conveyed what Olmsted deemed the cardinal precept of cemetery design: "the respect paid by the community of the living to the community of the dead." It soon ranked as one of the major points of interest in the Boston area. By 1848, noted A. J. Downing, it was receiving over 60,000 visitors a year.

Until the early nineteenth century people viewed graveyards as unattractive necessities. In the eighteenth century a new attitude toward death gradually emerged, one that, as Philippe Ariès has pointed out, emphasized human mortality. Death became a subject of contemplation, of poetical reverie. Cramped urban cemeteries denied the dead a decent eternal home. But rural cemeteries, with their constant reminders of process, awakened the living to a finer sense of human mortality. Under Mount Auburn's influence "graveyard" and "burial ground" gave way to the more solacing "cemetery," which derives from a Greek word meaning "sleeping chamber." The Cambridge cemetery became the prototype of the American "rural cemetery" (the term then used, though "garden cemetery" might have been more apt). Its success led to the founding of Laurel Hill in Philadelphia in 1836, of Green-Wood in Brooklyn (then an independent city) in 1838, and, in 1845, of Spring Grove. By 1849, to cite Downing again, there was "scarcely a city of note in the whole country that has not its rural cemetery."

Cemeteries were the first planned countrylike green spaces within American cities. The major cemeteries were designed before the new picturesque city parks. Cemeteries, Alan Gowans has suggested, were in fact America's first suburbs. Certainly they pioneered curvilinear suburban layouts, as we shall see when we visit Glendale. A quarter century's prior experience of rural cemeteries prepared the way for Manhattan's Central Park (1858); similarly, by just that margin of time, does Spring Grove predate Cincinnati's first picturesque park, Eden Park (1870).

Before Spring Grove came into being, the Twelfth-Street Burial Ground, located where Washington Park is now, was the city's main graveyard. Twenty-three churches in the Basin also had burial grounds attached to them. Earlier public graveyards had succumbed before the rapidly expanding city. When Harriet Drake died in 1825, her husband Daniel, uneasy that her Twelfth-Street burial place might be temporary, pressed for a new cemetery well beyond the city limits. Cincinnati's professional and business elite also expressed concern over the lack of proper interment facilities. Most urban graveyards presented a crowded, unkempt appearance. Many people believed in miasmic theories of disease: decaying organic matter in graves emitted gases that endangered public health. Dickens reflects this belief in *Bleak House*. Cholera was another factor. Physicians no less than ordinary citizens feared that the urban graveyards played a role in the epidemics that in the 1830s and 1840s swept over Cincinnati. The city was also growing by leaps and bounds. Fed by a flood of German and Irish immigrants, it more than doubled its population in the 1840s, from 46,000 inhabitants in 1840 to 115,000 in 1850.

In 1843 interested citizens formed the Cincinnati Horticultural Society. Early the next year several of its members met to establish a Cemetery Association. Robert Buchanan took a crucial role in both organizations. Determined to establish a pastoral cemetery comparable to those near eastern cities, the Association purchased the 166-acre Garrard farm north of the Millcreek. It had the undulating topography suitable to create an idealized, naturalistic landscape; the site also preserved a wooded panorama to the north of Clifton, the new suburb where several members of the Cemetery Association lived, including Buchanan. On February 8th, 1845, the Association, after electing directors, chose Buchanan president. Spring Grove, its name suggested by the "numerous springs and ancient groves of trees," was consecrated on August 28, 1845.

Spring Grove's founding was part of the forward-looking, idealistic movement of Victorian America. The Cemetery Association professed lofty goals. "The improvement of our taste and habits in relation to our Cemeteries," stated the directors' report of 1857, "is a testimony of moral and mental progress as decided and impressive as is the enslavement of steam and electricity to our physical progress." The Association's intention "was to convert not only our souls to a brighter—holier belief, but to give our bodies a holier resting place, where brighter aspects are presented to the survivors." Here the living need not fear that urban expansion would force the moving of loved ones. The site chosen was beyond the city's anticipated growth. Unlike the earlier graveyards, Spring Grove would provide the dead with a permanent resting place.

John Notman, who had planned Philadelphia's Laurel Hill Cemetery, was called in to design Spring Grove. But his geometric plan, since lost, proved unsuitable to the undulating terrain. The cemetery board then turned to Howard Daniels, a local architect. Daniels, after a four-month trip to study other landscaped cemeteries, returned with a portfolio of drawings and ideas. Assisted by local surveyor Thomas Earnshaw, Daniels laid out Spring Grove in a picturesque design similar to Boston's Mount Auburn. He served for two years as the cemetery's first superintendent before leaving Ohio in 1850 to pursue a distinguished career as landscape architect in New York and Baltimore.

In 1854 Adolph Strauch became landscape gardener of Spring Grove and, in 1859, superintendent. After arriving in Cincinnati in 1852, the German-born Strauch had landscaped several Clifton estates, including that of Robert Bonner Bowler. He convinced Robert Buchanan to allow him to redesign Spring Grove in the picturesque mode. "Good taste," he wrote in 1857, "suggested that a rural Cemetery should partake more of the character of a cheerful park or garden, than of a common grave yard, where everything has a gloomy and dismal appearance, and every inch of ground is used for graves." Strauch built upon Howard Daniels's achievement, and it was primarily under his direction that Spring Grove was developed as a picturesque composition. In 1871 Strauch became superintendent of the city's park system as well and prepared plans for Burnet Woods and Eden Park, not all of which the city implemented.

With urban parks few and far between, nineteenth-century Americans flocked on fine spring or summer days to the new picturesque cemeteries. So attractive were they as sightseeing spots that guide books suggested routes and provided descriptions of major monuments. The cemetery was conceived both as a place to educate the populace and to inculcate morality. In looking at the monuments of those buried there, visitors gained spiritual elevation through pondering their collective achievements. Spring Grove, the 1857 report stated, was "a seminary of instruction." "The pious thoughts awakened" there "are aids in the education of the heart." "The lessons we may learn from the graves of our ancestors," the same document affirmed, "should not be neglected." Nor would the artistic education of visitors to cemeteries be neglected. Mount Auburn would become, claimed the *Boston Evening Transcript,* "as remarkable for the treasures of art collected there, as it now is for its scenery."

For funerary sculpture, Adolph Strauch looked to Egypt, to Greece and Rome, and to Etruria. "In modern days, also," he asked, "has it not been at the shrine of death that the highest efforts of the Michael Angelos, the Canovas, the Thorwaldsens, and only recently by our own eminent artist, H. Powers, have been elicited and exhibited?" "The tomb," he asserted, "has, in fact, been the great chronicler of taste throughout the world." Most memorials in Spring Grove reflect the forms and traditions of past civilizations. Like the banks and government buildings we have seen, cemeteries are bastions of tradition. The conservative designs, evocative of a sense of timeless permanence, offered people a sense of assurance and stability. The monuments also constitute a significant element in Cincinnati's architectural legacy and, like the city itself, they may be "read." Although we shall encounter symbols and forms that go back thousands of years, the memorials freely interpret them or utilize them in ways uniquely American. As we walk around Spring Grove we shall ponder differences in the shapes of the monuments; in the figures depicted; in the texture, appearance, and state of preservation of the material used; and in the symbolism of the design. For example, a ball on top of a monument symbolizes the soul, as does an urn.

"A scene of great natural beauty," Charles Weld wrote of Spring Grove in 1855, "contrasting strongly, but delightfully, in its hushed repose with the clamor and restlessness of the city." Nicholas A. Woods, who accompanied the Prince of Wales on his 1860 tour, found Spring Grove "exquisitely beautiful": "the hills are laid out in gardens, shrubberies, and ornamental lakes, where a living poetry of nature has been cultivated over graves and tombs"—upon which note Woods cites appropriate stanzas of poetry! In 1875 D. J. Kenny recorded that, exclusive of those attending funerals, 150,000 people visited the grounds. Today, with other parks and other distractions, the numbers are fewer. Modern monuments are also less interesting than those erected during the great age of American funerary art, roughly from 1850 to 1930. And many Americans avoid cemeteries, either because they have unhappy memories of them or because they fear death or because the rise of cremation obviates the need for visits. The result is a loss, a loss both personal and cultural. A "rural cemetery" like Spring Grove is a major esthetic and historic resource. It remains a place of great natural beauty, of instruction, of repose and contemplation.

Its monuments and landscapes deserve to be savored. Drive the following tour if you must, but I suggest strongly that you walk.

Opposite the parking lot is the new **Administration Center** (1983), an explosion of shed roofs designed by a Cincinnati firm, Architekton. The exterior lexan canopy continues within; interior spaces appear to flow outside. The building is exquisitely landscaped. Rounded shrubs set off exterior angularity. Available inside is a cemetery map, essential to keep your bearings in the curvilinear maze that is Spring Grove, and an excellent guide by Blanche Linden-Ward.

Two pavilions flank the entrance gateway. The larger (1863) is the former administration building; it contains a chapel, a reception room, and an office. The smaller (1867) is the former Carriage House, where visitors rested after the long ride from downtown or awaited transportation back. James Keys Wilson designed both buildings. The pattern of their stonework recalls that of the Shoenberger residence in Clifton, also designed by Wilson and visible across the valley. The former administration building is Norman Gothic; its tower has lost bits of the original stonework. Human faces peer down upon us. On the Carriage House, Gothic also but with a mansard roof, we look up at silently roaring lions.

Nearby is the **Norman Chapel** (1880), designed by Samuel Hannaford in the Romanesque style. Like the entrance pavilions, it is made of limestone blocks set within a sandstone border. The intricate geometric patterns, the flow of endless line, encircling the round-arched entrance are characteristic of the Romanesque style, itself indebted to the Byzantine, as are the differing capitals sitting atop the clustered or coupled columns. An intricate cast- and wrought-iron fence separates the Chapel from Spring Grove Ave.

Beyond the Chapel stretches a **Rose Garden.** A majestic sycamore as wide as it is tall, its branches seemingly suspended in space, towers over it. "What a thought that was when God first thought of a tree," wrote John Ruskin, no doubt with trees like this one in mind. Further off we sight a stand of evergreens. In winter especially the evergreens counterpoint the deciduous trees. Everywhere in this cemetery huge and rare species grace well-tended lawns. Fifteen of Hamilton County's twenty-one championship trees, i.e., the largest of their species in Ohio, are in Spring Grove. One yellowwood (in section 19) was recognized in 1988 as the nation's largest. 850 varieties of trees and shrubs, many not indigenous to the region, lie within the grounds. Many species are indicated; a granite marker identifies the championship trees. From the beginning Spring Grove's directors aspired to make the cemetery into an arboretum. They introduced plant materials in order to propagate new and varied species for the Cincinnati region. By thus aiding in the work of the Cincinnati Horticultural Society, many of whose directors were also on Spring Grove's board, the cemetery also served the community at large.

Trees are also used for artistic effect in the cemetery grounds. "A rural Cemetery without trees," wrote Strauch in 1857, "would be like a sandy desert without water." Already by that year Spring Grove boasted over two hundred species. Trees inspire in us, thought Strauch, a meditative mood: "the solemnizing influence of a deep forest has always been experienced and remarked"; the shape of trees "was probably the source of the Gothic style of Architecture." William Gilpin in *Remarks on Forest Scenery* (1791) evaluated species of trees for their esthetic qualities. Later, Frederick Law Olmsted arranged trees in his landscapes as part of a sequence of visual events that climaxed in stunning vistas. Like Gilpin and Olmsted, Strauch looked at trees, not so much as a botanist or gardener, but as a landscape artist. "A judicious location of avenues," he wrote, "the opening and closing of thickets, exhibiting the largest and finest specimens of trees, and the sudden transition from light to shade always produces a pleasing effect." Strategic planting of evergreens and deciduous trees was necessary to achieve such effects. On his arboreal palette Strauch used their forms and tints to create scenic effects. "By an artistic calculation, exercised in the employment of trees and of various colors and forms," he wrote in 1869, "nature always speaks a new and exciting language." Autumnal colors, for example, counteract "the monotonous appearance of a plantation of evergreens."

From the Rose Garden we return to the main avenue and go underneath the railroad overpass put up by the Cincinnati, Hamilton, & Dayton Railroad in 1850. The tracks, sensitively landscaped, are hardly noticed. The tunnel takes us into the cemetery proper. Once inside it, visual impressions diminish as gloom momentarily pervades. What will we find at the other end? An explosion of light, first of all. Then we see, for the first time, white monuments rising above the greensward.

To the left (section 20) an eagle sits atop a broken column. It holds in its beak a laurel garland, emblematic of the hero. This is the **Lytle monument,** commemorating General William H. Lytle, one of forty Civil War generals buried in Spring Grove. Lytle's stirring lyric "Anthony and Cleopatra" early earned him popular acclaim as a poet. In 1847 he enlisted in the Mexican War, later served in the Ohio legislature, and at the onset of the Civil War was commissioned colonel of the Tenth Ohio Volunteers, an Irish regiment from Cincinnati. Under the bronze high relief a single word carved in stone says it all: Chickamauga. There on September 20, 1863, leading his troops, General Lytle fell, aged thirty-six. The only son of a distinguished family, Lytle died unmarried. With his death the family name ceased. This monument dates from 1915; it replaces one corroded by acid rain. Like so many other monuments in Spring Grove, it commemorates not only an individual but members of his family. It also commemorates, as Blanche Linden-Ward perceptively points out, "family cohesion and is symptomatic of the 19th century view of death as an event in family and community history rather than merely in the 'life' of the deceased."

Just beyond the Lytle monument, columnar beeches set off the white marble **Broadwell sarcophagus.** It is modelled upon the tomb of Scipio, Roman Consul in 208 B.C., the original of which is now in the Vatican Museum. The beeches, Linden-Ward states, are placed in a manner to recall Jean-Jacques Rousseau's tomb on the Isle of Poplars in the park at Ermenonville, north of Paris. In his novel *Julie, ou la nouvelle Héloïse* (1761) Rousseau had so vividly described a picturesque *jardin anglais* that his last patron, the Marquis de Girardin, an enthusiastic reader of *Julie,* created such a garden at Ermenonville. In 1778 Rousseau died in it. His sarcophagus harks back, via Rome, to archaic Greek art; the poplars symbolize everlasting life. The Broadwell sarcophagus, both in its design and in its setting, is meant to recall a network of associations, modern (Rousseau) as well as classical (ancient Greece and Rome). Alert contemporaries would have grasped these associations. Modern visitors may need a little help.

Further along to the left, perfectly sited, is the **Fleischmann mausoleum** (1913), a miniature peristyled Doric temple. Standing in isolation and beautifully set as an eyecatcher, it is meant to recall the landscape of the "beautiful" and, in particular, the classical temples set in sylvan scenes that we enjoy in the paintings of Claude Lorrain. It may even echo the Pantheon at Stourhead, the famous eighteenth-century garden in England largely designed by Henry Hoare. Modelled upon the Parthenon in Athens, the Fleischmann mausoleum is the funerary equivalent to the Art Museum's Doric Schmidlapp wing (1907). Both drew their inspiration from the "White City," the 1893 Columbian Exposition in Chicago and the neoclassical ideals there espoused. Within the mausoleum a Tiffany window, in stunning amethyst, ruby, and aquamarine tones, depicts the Three Fates. Stained glass was very popular for mausoleum windows during the first three decades of the twentieth century. Mausoleums such as this derive ultimately from the extraordinary monument erected in 350 B.C. in Asia Minor for King Mausolus, a design Cass Gilbert freely adapted for the crown of the Central Trust Tower downtown.

We cross the stone bridge to **Strauch Island,** named after the man largely responsible for Spring Grove's appearance. In 1855 Strauch first began to drain and beautify the cemetery's lower reaches, then hardly more than a swamp and cow pasture. The necklace of lakes around us is his creation. "The limits of the water are never quite perceptible," Linden-Ward points out, "so the lakes seem much larger than they are." Even after repeated visits to Spring Grove, one would have great difficulty drawing the shapes of the larger lakes. The serpentine banks were also sculpted to look natural. No less shaped was the land itself. "The surface of the ground," wrote Strauch, "should be undulating rather than flat." But elaborate construction was necessary to give Spring Grove's grounds their "natural" appearance. Strauch rerouted roads to follow the land's contours. The undulating paths recall eighteenth-century English gardens. To achieve an uncluttered look he encouraged lot owners to authorize removal from their plots iron railing, lawn furniture, wooden fences and trellises, even hedgerows. Andrew Jackson Downing before him had deemed the common wooden fence "an abomination of which no person of taste could be guilty." Strauch also discouraged multiple monuments. "Too many monuments on one lot give it the appearance of a marble yard," he complained. Appropriately, he rests under a simple curved stone.

Strauch strove for the parklike naturalism of English estates like Stourhead and Stowe. In the 1850s Americans had not yet developed a taste for closely cropped lawns. Cemetery grass often reached up a foot or more, as the height of many older monument bases at Spring Grove attests. Strauch's reform of cemetery design, known as the "landscape lawn plan," attracted nationwide attention after the Civil War. Cemeteries elsewhere adopted it as a way of providing their grounds with a

Fleischmann mausoleum, Spring Grove Cemetery. Beautifully set at the edge of Geyser Lake, the mausoleum (1913),
a miniature Doric temple, is meant to recall the landscape
of the "beautiful" and, in particular, the classical temples
set in sylvan scenes in the paintings of Claude Lorrain.

parklike atmosphere. Strauch's sources included ancient Chinese landscape gardens, eighteenth-century English estates and their American descendants, the English picturesque tradition from Gilpin to Loudon, the widely influential *Cosmos*
(1850) of Alexander von Humboldt, even the theories of that most eccentric individual and brilliant landscape artist, Prince Hermann von Pückler-Muskau, for whom
Strauch had once worked. Embodying the beautiful in the open, undulating lawns
of its lower reaches and the picturesque in the uneven, wooded hills of its upper
reaches, Spring Grove became what Frederick Law Olmsted proclaimed it to be: the
best designed cemetery in America "from a landscape gardening point of view."

Egeria, Roman goddess associated with water and childbirth, looks out from
Strauch Island over Geyser Lake. The statue was a gift to Strauch. In *Childe Harold's Pilgrimage* Byron apostrophized Egeria as "a young Aurora of the air," "a
beautiful Thought," who imparted "the purity of Heaven to earthly joys." Her presence here is appropriate: Spring Grove celebrates life no less than death. Tree
branches sway in the breeze, leaves rustle, flowers nod, birds sing. (Birdwatchers
have identified more than two hundred species in Spring Grove.) On the ponds
swans and geese glide silently by. Fish, frogs, and turtles lurk within. Out of Geyser
Lake I have seen a fisherman pull good-sized bass. Ducks trailed by ducklings wad-
dle over the lawns. Chipmunks peek out from around tombs. Deer and fox wander
within Spring Grove's confines though we shall probably not see them. If the
weather is warm and the ground dry, lie down in the grass, look up—and listen.

Ducks quack, crows caw, birds chirp, insects hum; church bells peal faintly in the distance. We may even hear a passing train. Such a landscape stimulates the senses as much as it delights the eye. Being in Spring Grove conveys a sense of serenity. We feel, as Spring Grove's founders wished us to feel, that here we are part of an ongoing process, at one with nature and the universe around us.

From Strauch Island we return to the mainland. After passing the Sherlock sarcophagus, we cross a second rustic bridge. A **Union soldier** standing guard high on a plinth commemorates Cincinnatians who died during the Civil War. Commissioned from Randolph Rogers, a leading American sculptor, *The Soldier of the Line* was completed in Rome in 1864. The next year it was cast by Ferdinand von Miller at Munich's Royal Foundry, the same foundry that a few years later cast the Tyler Davidson Fountain. The flower beds around the base, notes Linden-Ward, are a concession to twentieth-century taste. Adolph Strauch would not have approved.

Cedar Lake serves as a backdrop for the **William A. Windisch mausoleum.** The stained glass window depicts the angel before Christ's tomb on Easter morning. He tells Mary Magdalene and Mary that their Savior has risen. Eastwards (section 22), in the mausoleum of 1865 marked **"Burnet,"** lies Judge Jacob Burnet, the early settler who helped shape Ohio's first constitution and for whom was named the famous Burnet House. On either side of the curved Baroque gable two putti lean against an urn. The mausoleum, set within the slope, fits unobtrusively into the natural scene. It is best viewed, reflected in the water, from across Cedar Lake. Like many Spring Grove mausoleums, its diminished scale makes it appear more distant than it is. Swamp cypress, their roots projecting from the water like "knees," rise up from the far shore. Nature and art appear to act in concert. On the adjoining knolls are graves of Civil War soldiers.

We curl north (following the broken green line) to section 24. Before us rise two gigantic elms. A plaque in front of the first commemorates Robert Buchanan, president of Spring Grove's directors from 1845 to 1879. From "Greenhills," his Clifton home, Buchanan could gaze upon the cemetery whose beauty he did so much to bring about. Climbing euonymus, looking like a gigantic bush, covers the base of the second elm.

At the westernmost tip of section 24 stands the towering **Nicholas Longworth obelisk,** the cemetery's largest when erected, that Hiram Powers designed for his friend and benefactor. Granite obelisks first appeared before temples to the gods in Egypt; later they found favor in Greece and Rome. Sections of many nineteenth-century American cemeteries look like obelisk forests. Egyptian obelisks have neither pedestal nor base; those here usually have both. Egypt surpassed "all other nations, either ancient or modern," wrote Strauch, "in the magnificence and grandeur of her monuments and tombs." Not all Americans agreed. Some deemed that Egyptian and classical monuments desecrated a Christian burial place. The broken column, for example, suggested to some Americans pagan ideas about the finality of death and appeared to deny the Christian belief in resurrection. We will see fewer crosses than we might expect. "Not until the 1870s," points out Kenneth T. Jackson, "with the popular revival of Gothic architecture, did many Protestants begin to accept the cross as a general emblem of Christian hope."

A spirited debate over funerary monuments arose in mid-nineteenth century America. In Spring Grove it was won by those, like Strauch, who believed the ancient monuments to be appropriate models. No other past civilization more than the Egyptian, they argued, had shown greater reverence for its dead. Egyptian funerary monuments embodied massiveness, strength, durability; they reached for the sublime. Obelisks, pointing heavenwards, symbolized hope. Cemetery monuments that drew upon Egyptian models not only evoked such historical associations but asserted the permanence of burial. In addition, Egypt was popularly thought to have been the first civilization; similarly, Europeans, having left the Old World, had been the first to colonize the New. How appropriate, then, for Americans to use obelisks—and other Egyptian (and classical) symbols—to commemorate their leading citizens.

We walk to the eight-sided former Interment Office, then continue north (uphill). The land we now traverse was the earliest used for burials because it was high and well drained. Roads here turn and twist, weaving through the terrain. "A curve of any kind is more beautiful than a right line," Ruskin declared in *Modern Painters II,* because "there are no lines nor surfaces of nature without curvature." Winding paths, we remember from our experience on the Ohio, also provide "mystery." We may even have an inborn preference for curved walkways where we cannot see our destination. We want to travel further, deeper, to resolve the mystery. The ever-changing contours and the varied landscaping give us the feeling that the grounds ramble on indefinitely. Here we are meant to give ourselves to the experience, to lose ourselves in the contemplation of nature and the monuments of man. Certainly there will come a moment in our tour of Spring Grove in which we will not know where we are.

Section 36 is on our right. A cross with lilies within, symbol of the Resurrection, marks the memorial to the Emery family that has played so significant a role in Cincinnati's development. John J. Emery put up the Carew Tower and Netherland Plaza; Mary M. Emery, his aunt, donated her Old Masters to the Art Museum. Her chief benefaction to Cincinnati, however, is the village of Mariemont, which we shall visit later.

Leaving the central avenue to our left, we continue right. On the left is section 45. Set back from the road, we discover on a gray stone plinth a smiling **sphinx** of blue marble. David B. Lawler, a prosperous businessman and one of Spring Grove's founders, had it erected in 1854 in memory of his parents, Matthew and Ann Lawler. The sphinx, like the obelisk, derives from Egypt. Does it express the doubts that Lawler, a freethinker, had regarding a future state? Its presence in Spring Grove caused a furor. Sidestepping the theological issue, Strauch defended the sphinx on esthetic grounds: it helped "relieve the monotony . . . caused by the too frequent recurrence of obelisks, columns, and Gothic pinnacles." Furthermore, said Strauch, "its colors, sober and sombre, suit the taste of some who complain of the too great prevalence of white marble in our Cemetery."

At the next intersection we take a hard left. To the left of the Kidd monument (section 46) stands a **Gothic ruin** memorializing Conrad Windisch, whose huge Romanesque brewery still stands at Liberty St. and Central Parkway. Stone ivy

Tomb of Conrad Windisch and Angel with trumpet, Spring Grove Cemetery. A shattered oak lies across the tomb's Gothic arch, above which we make out an hourglass with wings. Stone ivy climbs the wall. Beyond to the left a recumbent dog contemplates the tomb of its young master. Cemetery statuary of the period 1850–1930 is often of considerable artistic and symbolic interest. The angel here awaits the Last Judgment, when it will sound its trumpet to raise the dead.

climbs the tomb's wall. A shattered oak lies across the arch, above which we make out an hourglass with wings. How Teutonic the entire composition! It recalls the haunting paintings of Caspar David Friedrich, the great German Romantic artist who often depicted ruined chapels within a desolate landscape. Just beyond the Windisch monument a recumbent dog contemplates its master, William Coon Redman, whose short life of seven years, six months, and twenty-one days ended on March 7, 1834. More than a century of acid rain has eroded both dog and monument, as it has much else in Spring Grove.

We walk westward to the broken white line, then follow it, again uphill. Section 54 is on the right, then 65; section 53 is on the left. Before the ascent becomes rigorous, we sight (embedded in the hill at the lower end of section 79) an **Egyptian Revival mausoleum,** or mastaba, with slightly sloping walls, squat columns, and a cavetto cornice. Nearby, a massive section of petrified wood—presumably an American equivalent of the obelisk—commemorates the Robertson family. It conjures its own image of eternity. Across the road a stubby obelisk memorializes Alexander B. Latta, who claimed to have invented the first steam fire engine. Latta had wanted for his monument an iron portal of four Corinthian columns from which would have hung a miniature version of his fire engine. Strauch protested fiercely against what he considered a desecration of the grounds. Although Spring Grove's directors had earlier permitted David Lawler a sphinx, they balked at allowing Latta a fire engine.

We climb to the top of the hill. At the northern tip of section 97 an obelisk of

Quincy granite, erected in 1854, is the memorial to **Martin Baum,** early pioneer, entrepreneur, and builder of Belmont, now the Taft Museum. We descend via the gravel road, section 77 on our left. Where the gravel ends and pavement begins, we catch sight on the left of the modest **obelisk** commemorating Harriet and Daniel Drake. It is one of numerous monuments transferred to Spring Grove from the Twelfth-Street Burial Ground. "He who rests here," the inscription justly concludes, "was an early inhabitant and untiring friend of the city of Cincinnati with whose prosperity his fame is inseparably connected." Among Drake's claims upon our remembrance is his agitation for a permanent cemetery beyond the city limits. Nearby, another **obelisk** marks the burial place of Alexander McGuffey, who married Drake's daughter Elizabeth.

Prominently situated on the overlook is the red granite **George and Sarah Shoenberger sarcophagus.** We stand to its left, look toward Clifton to the southwest, and see the orange mass of Bethesda-Scarlet Oaks. Attached to it is the magnificent Shoenberger mansion, Scarlet Oaks. So distraught was Shoenberger by the loss of Sarah that he often retreated to the tower of his house to peer at her tomb through a telescope. On one occasion, rumor has it that the second Mrs. Shoenberger became so irritated that she locked her husband in the tower.

We walk back to the Drake obelisk and continue down the hill. At the southern tip of section 96 a draped urn crowns the Charles Davis mausoleum. Further down on the right, in section 95, a modest headstone announcing "A. O. Goshorn" commemorates the brother of the flamboyant director of Cincinnati's industrial expositions and later of the Art Museum, whose grand house we passed on Clifton Ave. We continue down the hill, curling right at the intersection. On the left, in section 53, a **stone oak** cut off in its prime memorializes the Patterson, Hering, and Zoeller families. Branches and ivy leaves represent children and grandchildren who died young. Death dates quickly follow birth dates, reminding us how astonishingly high infant mortality was in nineteenth-century America. The oak, an organic symbol, reminds us that death is a natural process. And not without its moment of comedy: at the rear, peeking out of a hollow branch, is a (stone) chipmunk!

On **Henry Knorr's tomb,** in section 75 (to the right), a young woman holds an hourglass in her left hand, a wreath in her right. We barely make out the eroded words: "A life spent well is crowned." Her voluptuousness is not unusual in nineteenth-century funerary art. In this walk we have seen (or will see) broken columns, shattered oaks, imploring angels, crestfallen damsels, winged cherubs, draped urns, classical temples, and recumbent goddesses. Baby angels, tiny lambs, leaves and broken branches represent children. These monuments have obvious symbolic import. Many in Victorian America believed this life to be but a brief prelude to the grave's eternity. Public displays over mourning, led by Queen Victoria's long grief over her Albert, were not only encouraged but expected. The selection, design, and placing of one's tombstone became a significant event in one's life. Nineteenth-century sculptors often derived a major portion of their income from funerary monuments. A cemetery like Spring Grove provides us with an outstanding opportunity to study their work.

We follow the road as it undulates downhill. Situated in section 31, on the right, is a cluster of older slate gravestones, some upright, some flat. They mark one of the Pioneer Lots purchased in 1858 by the city of Cincinnati to receive the remains, removed from the Twelfth-Street and other burial grounds, of the city's earliest settlers. For some it was the third interment. Below a simple slab lies Colonel Robert Elliott, an aide to "Mad" Anthony Wayne. He was killed by Indians in 1794. Buried in the city's first graveyard at 4th St. between Walnut and Main streets, Elliott was reinterred at Twelfth-Street before truly finding his last resting place in Spring Grove.

Beyond section 30, nicely set off by a Weeping European Beech, is the **Dexter mausoleum** (1869). Dominating Geyser Lake, it recalls in its overall form and soaring lines Paris's Sainte Chapelle. Though miniaturized, it is still an imposing structure. This High Victorian Gothic mausoleum in brown sandstone, designed by James Keys Wilson, memorializes Edmund Dexter. Dexter entertained Charles Dickens in 1842 at his splendid house at 4th St. and Broadway; his portrait we admired in the Art Museum. Pinnacles, crockets, flying buttresses here send the eye skywards; a steeple in the middle of the roof, depicted in early representations, would have accentuated even more the vertical emphasis. The mausoleum has also lost several pinnacles and crockets; the base pedestals at the front, flanking the steps, may have been designed to carry finials. Montgomery Schuyler, America's most distinguished architectural critic at the turn of the century, rated the mausoleum "a gem." "What specimen have we in America of as highly developed or as ornate Gothic in miniature which is more successful than this?" he asked. For Schuyler, it ranked with the best Gothic Revival architecture in England.

We bear right down the hill. On the left is the **Charles West memorial.** West, the major initial donor behind the Art Museum, reclines comfortably in an Eastlake armchair. Caryatids on the plinth represent the Liberal Arts, here defined as music, art, sculpture, and architecture. On the grass island at the road intersection, alumni of Hughes High School have erected a monument, with a contemplative maiden presiding within, to Thomas Hughes, whose benefaction led to the school's establishment. Across the drive (section 30), a monument of a recumbent woman, one bronze breast exposed, faces the East, pencil and slate in hand. This is the **Erkenbrecher monument,** commemorating Andrew Erkenbrecher, founder of the Cincinnati Zoo, our next stop. The German inscription, from one of Friedrich Rückert's *Kindertotenlieder,* speaks of life's reluctance to yield to death, yet insists that "Life only sees Death's dusky hand, / And not the shining cup it bears." On the far side of the pond, surmounted by a waterfall, rises a huge elm, already described by Strauch in 1869 as "venerable."

Further along is the temple to the "fighting McCooks," sixteen of whom fought in the Union army, four as generals. Colonel Robert, whose statue we saw in Washington Park, commanded the 9th Ohio Regiment, the German *Die Neuner.* The **McCook temple** is modelled after the Choragic Monument to Lysicrates in Athens. Where the road runs closest to Lake Mahketewah, the Indian name for "Millcreek," we sight on the opposite shore the red granite **sarcophagus** that Henry Probasco provided circa 1868 for his friend, Tyler Davidson. United in death as in life are Damon and Pythias. Probasco and his wife Julia, Davidson's half-sister, also lie

Dexter mausoleum. Designed by James Keys Wilson, this mausoleum (1869), in its overall form and soaring lines, is Paris's Sainte-Chapelle miniaturized. Probably Spring Grove's grandest monument, it badly needs restoration.

here. The huge white oak nearby commemorates Probasco's tenure on Spring Grove's board of directors. On the near shore, a plaque identifies the **Robinson mausoleum,** a miniature Gothic version, it would seem, of Paris's Moorish-Romanesque Sacré Coeur. Hope, Faith, and Charity, represented by three chaste damsels, lead the eye to Gabriel atop the dome, with his trumpet ready to herald a soul's arrival in heaven. Several generations of the family ran Robinson's Circus, a prominent Cincinnati institution active from 1824 to 1916, when the family sold it to the American Circus Corporation, later part of Ringling Bros. We walk eastward along the lake's southern bank and proceed under the railroad overpass back to the cemetery entrance.

Beautiful in all seasons and times of day, and in all weather, Spring Grove is especially resplendent in spring when magnolias, azaleas, crocuses, bluets, daffo-dils, jonquils, dogwoods, and forsythia bloom. If time allows and energy has not flagged, a drive to the cemetery's upper reaches will reward the seeker after scenic beauty. Along the northeast edge, facing Gray Road, a succession of spectacular flower beds produces an explosion of blooms. Further north, in section 135 is the *Megalith,* a pair of large upright sculptured stones. Diverse fossils are visibly embedded within them. From Stonehenge onwards many cultures have used megaliths or menhirs to suggest the mystery of their relationship with God. The adjoining section 134 contains a statue to John Chapman, "Johnny Appleseed," the legendary Swedenborgian missionary who crisscrossed the Midwest in frontier days planting apple orchards in Ohio and Indiana. A nearby overlook in section 132 provides a view over the cemetery.

Upon leaving, we turn left on Spring Grove Ave. Where it intersects with Winton Road once stood the Winton Place Railroad Station, now rebuilt in Sharon Woods Village. The station long served visitors to Chester Park, a popular amusement park founded in 1875, that in summer offered rides, vaudeville, and light opera. Its huge clubhouse surveyed a lake around which was a splendid boardwalk promenade. The Depression severely curtailed Chester Park's activities, and it closed in 1932.

If at this point hunger pangs have overtaken you, I recommend **Christos & Drivakis,** an excellent vegetarian restaurant that, since reopening in 1990, also includes nonvegetarian dishes. On the southwest corner of East Epworth and North Edgewood, it is easily reached by going north on Winton Road, then turning right onto East Epworth. From 1918 to 1978 three Greek immigrants—George Christos, his brother William, and John Drivakis—maintained here a fabled ice cream parlor. The restaurant, restored to its 1920s appearance, has a faintly Art Deco ambience: walnut paneling, mirrored booths, tables of etched vitrolite. Not your usual vegetarian place, where you exit with hunger pangs comparable to those with which you entered, Christos & Drivakis offers an international cuisine that included, and (we may hope) may again include, mouthwatering tofu cutlets and carob shakes.

We continue along Spring Grove Ave. If a visit to the Cincinnati Zoo forms part of the day's plans, we turn right off Spring Grove onto Mitchell Ave. We follow Mitchell under the railroad bridge and under I-75 until it intersects with Vine St. Where now flows interstate traffic once flowed, in an aqueduct over Mitchell, the Miami and Erie Canal. On Vine we turn right and stay on it until the second light (Forest Ave. on the left, Woolper St. on the right). We go left on Forest, and right on Dury St., which brings us to the zoo's main gate. If the zoo is not on the day's agenda, we continue along Spring Grove Ave. to the Procter & Gamble plant (p. 429).

The Cincinnati Zoo

Long one of the nation's best, the **Cincinnati Zoo** should not be missed. At barely sixty-four acres it is relatively compact. We can walk around it in half an hour, across it in minutes. The zoo's curvilinear layout, similar to Spring Grove's, may give you the impression that it is larger than it is; it will certainly cause you on occasion to lose your way. Older zoos like this one preserve in their layout a scale that vaster, more modern zoos lack. Yet, though small in physical size, the zoo maintains an impressive range of living creatures—some 750 species—in well-designed exhibit areas. Even a cursory visit demands a full morning or afternoon. Annual attendance in recent years has nudged the million-and-a-half mark, so a Sunday in summer is probably not the best time to go. The zoo deserves its popularity.

The Cincinnati Zoo opened on September 18, 1875. Of the major zoological gardens in America only Philadelphia's precedes it (by fourteen months) as the nation's oldest. The guiding force behind the zoo's founding was Andrew Erkenbrecher, miller, starch manufacturer, inventor, and first president of the telephone company. Interested in songbirds, Erkenbrecher had organized an Association for the Propagation of Rare Birds. Then in 1872, with Cincinnati reeling before an onslaught of caterpillars, Erkenbrecher counterattacked with a Society for the Acclimatization of Birds. The achievements of this latter organization rate a mixed review. On the down side, it imported and then let loose in southwestern Ohio several species of nonindigenous birds, of which, however, only "English" sparrows throve. But at a meeting on June 30, 1873, the Society formally raised the question of a zoological garden for Cincinnati. Two years later the zoo opened in its present location, then in rural Cincinnati, which it leased.

Theodore Findeisen, a German landscape designer, laid out the grounds, the building and exhibit sites, and the paths. Adolph Strauch, now superintendent of the city's park system as well as of Spring Grove, provided valuable advice and donated trees. Spring Grove itself provided the zoo with a model. The zoo's upper reaches—where are the pond, the lawn, and several of the still remaining great trees—embody Victorian ideas of the "beautiful" as we saw them in the lower reaches of Spring Grove cemetery. Findeisen's design for the zoo, David Ehrlinger has pointed out to me, "respected the natural topography and preserved existing trees." Walking the winding paths today we follow in effect the original design and experience bits of the original landscape. Gradually the zoo established itself. Setting it up in the mid 1870s represented a major financial undertaking, involving some $300,000, almost twice the expense for Philadelphia's zoo. Until New York's Bronx Zoo opened in 1899, the animal collection at Cincinnati was the largest in the country.

The original buildings were designed to suggest to visitors associations between wildlife and habitat. A buffalo house recalled the pioneers' log cabins, a camel house was tentlike in shape. No building, however, was completed by opening day in September 1875. Some animals were still stored in crates. The zoo had managed to acquire, from P. T. Barnum's Hippodrome and from Carl Hagenbeck in Hamburg, a substantial collection of creatures. It had lions, tigers, a puma and a leopard, monkeys and baboons, eleven bears, four llamas, a camel, two wallabies, and a kangaroo. It also had a selection of Erkenbrecher's imported songbirds, and an African elephant named Conqueror. When the zoo acquired Conqueror from a Dayton circus in 1875, his keeper, Sol A. Stephan, arrived with him. As Stephan was leaving to rejoin the circus, Conqueror, upset at being abandoned, let out a bellow, then crashed through his enclosure. Stephan, hurriedly recalled, agreed to stay on for "a few days." Days lengthened into weeks, Stephan resigned from the circus, then took over caring for other animals, became in 1886 the zoo's general manager, and in 1937, age eighty-eight, sixty-two years after first arriving, retired.

The zoo's early years, as Oliver M. Gale has wittily observed, "read like the Perils of Pauline." On at least three occasions it nearly foundered. In March 1885 John Hauck, the brewer, came to the rescue. He lent the zoo $135,000, gained title to the property, and granted the zoo a new, perpetual lease that allowed it to purchase its grounds at any time in the future. In 1898 the zoo, insolvent again, went into receivership. The next year the Cincinnati Zoological Company was formed, and in 1901 the Cincinnati Traction Company (the streetcar line) bought its stock. Owning the zoo was good for business: the zoo's main entrance was for decades at the intersection of Vine and Erkenbrecher, the streetcar's final stop on the popular Zoo-Eden line. The Traction Company ran the zoo until 1916. But when deficits mounted to over $50,000 a year, the company could no longer afford them. In October 1916 the city's resident angels, Mrs. Emery and Mrs. Taft, agreed to underwrite the zoo's deficits by becoming co-sponsors, in effect co-owners, of the zoo. This arrangement lasted until 1932 when, both ladies having died, the city purchased the zoo. It placed its operations under the Zoological Society of Cincinnati, a nonprofit corporation, that has run the zoo to this day.

In 1920, with the help of Charles Phelps Taft and Annie Sinton Taft, the Zoo Opera began. In its first seven-week season the company gave forty-two performances of eleven operas. The next year's schedule, thirteen operas and forty-five performances, enjoyed an even greater success. Cincinnati's Zoo Opera was among the pioneers in summer music seasons. For fifty-one seasons until 1972, when Music Hall was airconditioned, the Zoo Opera staged performances in a since-departed structure on the lawn. Many celebrated singers performed here. Broadcast over NBC in the 1930s, Cincinnati's Zoo Opera gained national attention. Zoo and opera interacted in unexpected ways; once, unrehearsed peacocks entered into a duet with the tenor. Some interaction was planned: during the Triumphal March in *Aïda* an elephant promenaded majestically across the stage. The zoo and the Summer Opera Association continue their collaboration at Music Hall. Performances of *Aïda* here now include not only an elephant but leopards, boas, even aardvarks.

Today, with the world's major zoos trying to become latter-day Noah's Arks, the Cincinnati Zoo has garnered national attention through an on-site breeding program of rare species. Its embryo transplants have greatly furthered the propagation of endangered species like the bongo. On a national level the zoo oversees the breeding program for the rare black rhinoceros, of which less than 3500 remain in the African wild. Since 1959 fourteen have been born at the zoo. The zoo now has a female Sumatran rhinoceros, smaller and rarer than the black rhinoceros, and hopes eventually to breed it. For its reproductive feats *Newsweek* once dubbed Cincinnati's the nation's "sexiest zoo."

Animals are not the only draw here. In my experience of the zoo, dating from the mid 1970s, it has steadily become a more attractive place. Since 1970 a master plan by the architectural firm of Glaser Associates has determined its development; a new plan came into effect in 1986. The 1970 plan led to a number of new and innovative animal exhibits. Further, plantings appropriate to the region from which the animals derive now complement buildings and enclosures. With over 2400 species (in 1990) of trees, flowers, and ornamental plants on its grounds, the zoo has become one of the nation's best landscaped parks. Few spaces in it do not engage the eye. The zoo, which began as an experimental garden as well as a zoo and which was intermittently maintained as a botanical garden, is again beautifully landscaped. In 1987 its horticultural achievements even gave rise to a new name: the Cincinnati Zoo *and* Botanical Garden.

Few people go to a zoo to look at its architecture. Fewer still associate architecture with zoos. We should do both, for the Cincinnati Zoo contains, in addition to unusual animals, unusual buildings and exhibit areas. Animal enclosures evolve no less than human ones. Zoos, like cities, are not accidents; they develop because of choices made over the years. Although in visiting a zoo the animals are our first interest, how we see them, how they are displayed, often conditions our impressions of them. To see animals in environments that seem to reveal their inner natures is a major pleasure of a zoo. Fortunately, it is a pleasure more frequent now than formerly. Zoo architecture and design constitute a subject unto itself. The Cincinnati Zoo's historic structures include the former Aviary (ca. 1875), now the Passenger Pigeon Memorial; the Monkey, now the Reptile, House (also ca. 1875); and the Herbivore or Elephant House (1905). All three, listed in the National Register, are notable for their functional design. Even more interesting are some of the newer structures and layouts. The buildings here are also smaller, less obtrusive, than in comparable zoos. No disconcerting megastructures, as at Boston's Franklin Park Zoo and Chicago's Brookfield, jut out from the landscape. The buildings here preserve a scale where neither humans nor animals are dwarfed. Zoos, like art museums and cities themselves, are always in a state of flux. Animals (or animal species) die, move on to other zoos, or are replaced. Plant species are no less transient. The constant change at the zoo challenges us to make each visit an adventure of discovery as well as a renewal of familiar pleasures.

After we have parked in the Penguin lot adjoining the main gate (acquiring a zoo map in the process), we wind our way through the "Jungle Jim" **entrance pavilion.** Rough-sawn board-and-batten siding and cedar shakes convey an appropriate "outdoors" image. The shed roofs are similar to those on the Cloisters in Mount Adams. Lush greenery hangs over the trellises. Squared logs define walkways; wooden stakes jut out from the ground. Conjuring up a safari-like atmosphere, these design motifs put us in a proper mood to contemplate exotic beasts and convey the sense of a world apart from the city. But this is not quite so. Situated on a plateau between Clifton and Avondale, the zoo permits glimpses of hills with houses on them. Its up-and-down topography reflects that of the city. As we walk around the grounds, we remain aware that we are not in some vast game preserve, twenty miles from downtown, but in the midst of, apart yet within, metropolitan Cincinnati. Exploring the zoo by following the map in a counterclockwise direction allows us to cover the main exhibits. We also avoid a steep climb at the end.

Directly opposite the main gate, the **Children's Zoo** (separate admission) contains more than cuddly domestic animals. On the right, carefree Magellanic penguins disport themselves; on the left, flamingoes stand immobile. The **Nursery** comes next. Once I came upon two white tiger cubs, progeny of Samantha and the irresistible Bhim, and watched a baby Chinese water deer struggle to walk. On another visit, two infant lowland gorillas, Rwanda and Mshangao (zoo officials try to pick names appropriate to the animals' homelands), frolicked in diapers. In the barnyard enclosure beyond we discover Vietnamese pot-bellied pigs, Zebu cattle from India, Merino sheep from Spain, alpacas from South America. Nearby, prairie dogs may or may not peer out of their burrows. Just beyond swim the walruses Bruiser and Aiutuk, gigantic creatures yet in water graceful as any seal.

We leave the Children's Zoo and continue downhill. The irregularly shaped **Walk-Through Bird Cage** (1962), made of unobtrusive steel mesh supported by I-beams, may be the most innovative of the several structures Carl A. Strauss & Associates, long Cincinnati's chief modernist firm, designed for the zoo. So well designed is the cage that it is easy to miss. Where does the wire mesh stop, the surrounding woods begin? We walk in a naturally simulated environment among the birds, tropical and domestic, who hop on the ground below the wooden walkway or fly above us.

The Art Deco **Bird House** (1936), formerly the reptile house, still holds a few amphibians and reptiles, including, to the right of the entrance, the ever-placid alligators. A glassed enclosure nearby houses a family of large Malay mouse deer. Mouse deer, it was discovered at New York's Bronx Zoo, are unhappy in large zoo cages. The tiny deer are far happier, and breed regularly, in cages no larger than a rabbit hutch. But the birds dominate here. At the far end rockhopper penguins cavort in the water or get fanned by polar blasts on land. In between, we must not miss the Tawny Frogmouth, from Australia, that by day looks like a stump, or the roadrunners from our own Southwest, invariably active, or the burrowing owls that swivel 180 degrees to eye us. Konrad Lorenz, the Nobel Prize-winning European ethnologist, once speculated (correctly) that human beings are attracted to animal faces that look like human babies: high forehead, small nose, large eyes, a generalized chubbiness. Such configurations, Lorenz conjectured, "release parental impulses." This theory helps to explain our positive response to round-faced burrowing owls, wide-eyed pampas cats, and chubby red pandas. Still, not everyone responds to animals in the same way. Here is Herman Melville on penguins: "neither fish, flesh, nor fowl . . . without exception the most ambiguous and least lovely creature yet discovered by man." John Ruskin, however, found penguins "the only comfort in life . . . one can't be angry when one looks at a Penguin."

Outside again, we pass the bears: Sloth (who feast on termites), Spectacled from South America, and polar. They live in naturalistic outdoor pens, or grottoes. A zoo's architecture, we realize, consists of more than buildings. The design of exhibits is equally important. Swiss-born and trained Carl Kern executed these lifelike settings in 1936. They were designed by Heinrich Hagenbeck, the elder son of the famous German zoo entrepreneur and architect, Carl Hagenbeck. Hagenbeck *père* developed in his Zoo Park (1907) in Stellingen, outside Hamburg, a revolutionary new approach to zoo exhibit design using free-view enclosures. Employing a concrete mix (gunite) to simulate naturalistic environments, Hagenbeck created an almost barless zoo. Unseen pits, somewhat comparable to the ha-has of English country estates, separate animals from humans. Working from designs by Heinrich Hagenbeck, Kern built in Cincinnati several of the earliest Hagenbeck-style environments in America. Barless animal enclosures not only separate the animals from edible visitors but give them, and us, a sense of their natural habitat. In these surroundings they feel comfortable and reproduce.

The hillside to our right will hold a Jungle Trails exhibit, with African and Asian primates and birds presented in naturalistic environments. We turn in (right) for **Big Cat Canyon,** a hilly, imaginatively designed outdoor enclosure. The white tigers bask in the sun. On one side a glazed wall of lexan and an electrified wire separate us from them; on the other, the height of the walkway. White tigers, paler than yellow tigers, have blue eyes and ash-gray stripes set within a creamy white background. They are not albinos. If the Cincinnati Zoo is known for one animal, it is the white tiger. The zoo owns the world's largest breeding colony of these exotic creatures. None has been sighted in the wild for years. Of the estimated one hundred and twenty-five in existence, the zoo had (by 1989) produced sixty-four. About ten remain here. Tigers in zoos are not unusual; white tigers are. They are also attendance boosters. Cubs in the mid-1980s went for $60,000; income from their sale aids other zoo programs. Bhim, a virile male, has sired an impressive number of the zoo's cubs, about half of them white, the rest a natural Bengal color. In zoo circles this irresistible feline has become known, justifiably, as "The Franchise."

The **Aquarium** (1950, remodelled 1968), another well-designed, unobtrusive

White tiger with cubs. White tigers have blue eyes and ash-gray stripes set within a creamy white background. They are a specialty of the Cincinnati Zoo, which owns the world's largest breeding colony of these exotic creatures.

building by Carl A. Strauss & Associates, presents both fresh- and saltwater exhibits. Of the freshwater, my favorite is "Amazon: The River Sea." The Amazon and its tributaries, I learned to my amazement, hold two-thirds of the world's fresh water. This realistic display recreates a jungle river habitat. Among its fish is the pacu, a larger but gentler (vegetarian) relative of the ferocious piranha; it munches on fruit that drops from overhanging trees. Like the bear grottoes, the "Amazon" exhibit is a carefully composed artifice, much of it fabricated from unnatural materials. Polyester resin was used for dirt banks and rocks, epoxy for tree trunks, silk for plants. The verisimilitude is startling. Of the saltwater exhibits, the Tide Pool is perhaps the least overtly spectacular. It recreates a maritime environment we often take for granted. We have to look for a while to realize how much life it contains.

Opposite the Aquarium is the four-acre **African Veldt** (1937), executed by Carl Kern from a design by Heinrich Hagenbeck. *Veldt,* Afrikaans for "field," usually refers to the grasslands southeast of the Sahara. The gunite *kopje,* or rock outcrop, conceals an indoor barn underneath it. The zoo's veldt permits animals to wander together freely in an environment that resembles their homeland. The Hagenbeck firm also designed the barless, moated lion and tiger grottoes (1934) north of the veldt.

We tour the veldt in a counterclockwise direction. On it or in the adjoining pens we see giant elands, the majestic greater kudus, Grant's zebras, and, identified by their lovely brown stripes, the rare bongos. The zoo has achieved its greatest success in breeding ungulates. **Embryo transfer,** or E. T., became a reality in 1983 when an eland calf was born to a surrogate mother of the same species. This event, the first nonsurgical E. T. in a nondomestic species, signalled a breakthrough. A main goal of this research was to use members of a common species like the eland as surrogate mothers for closely related but rarer species such as the bongo, of which only about seventy-five exist in American zoos. Bongos are also critically endangered in the wild, with native grasslands holding less than 1000. In 1984 the zoo successfully repeated the procedure, this time using an eland embryo preserved for one-and-a-half years in its "Frozen Zoo." That same year the zoo achieved an even more unusual embryo transfer: a female eland carried and gave birth to a bongo. This successful experiment, the first of its kind, bodes well for the future of endangered species. And in 1987 the zoo recorded the birth of a nonsurgically transferred gaur (an endangered species) to a holstein cow.

Leaving the veldt, we continue downhill past or through the Ape House before pausing before the outdoor rock formations on which scamper **Nubian ibexes.** Ibexes, we may remember, were the last creatures we saw—in stucco—in the Cincinnati Art Museum. This strikes me as one of the zoo's less successful enclosures, at least from the point of view of the ibexes. "Animals . . . should never be looked down upon," writes David Hancocks, author of *Animals and Architecture.* "Not only are there unwholesome psychological connotations in such a viewpoint, but it can be disturbing for an animal to have potentially dangerous enemies at such an unnatural vantage point, and it also encourages people to drop things, even if unintentionally."

Nubian ibex. This graceful ungulate scampers about upon a simulated rock formation.

In 1990 the adjoining special exhibit area featured the komodo dragon, a beast so rare—it lives on two islands in the Indonesian archipelago—that only one other American zoo had a specimen on display. **The Nocturnal House,** our next stop, reverses day and night. The creatures here, normally nocturnals, live within an eerie darkness. Once our eyes have adjusted, they contemplate a variety of creatures from barn owls to bats. My favorite is the aardvark, a friendly piglike beast with a spectacular snout and donkey-like ears, seemingly undisturbed by the giant fruit bats hovering over its head. Miss Tacoma, one of the zoo's aardvarks, became only the second captive specimen to rear her own children.

World of the Insect is the zoo's most unusual exhibit. If we dislike or fear insects, it may help us overcome our unease. Invertebrates comprise ninety percent of terrestial life yet zoos rarely do them justice. Only the Frankfurt and Tokyo zoos have comparable presentations. The exhibit here, which opened in 1978, now ranks among the zoo's most popular. Within we see a termite nest, diving beetles, irridescent green scarabs, and foot-long giant walkingsticks from Australia. Not all insects mentioned may still be around. Insects are more difficult to maintain than most other kinds of animals. But the varying exhibits in World of the Insect make a visit especially rewarding. Nor does every creature in it come from the insect world. Among those that don't (but which depend upon insects for food) are cactus wrens, archer fish, callimicos, and naked mole rats, the last named hairless, beady-eyed, and with big buck teeth. Some animals here are quite rare. The naked mole rats, for example, are only displayed elsewhere in the London Zoo. We go through the door into the Butterfly Rain Forest to find ourselves in the midst of ferns and trees; pacu and chocolate catfish swim about in the pond; hummingbirds hover in midair; and all around us flit, quite magically, multicolored butterflies. A wonderful experience!

The zoo's **Cat House** (1952, completely redone in 1985) contains a superb collection of felines of all sizes, more than we may have thought existed, from tiny rusty-spotted cats to large leopards. We observe the animals inside or out. Inside offers a sequence of beautifully designed exhibit areas, artworks in themselves. Instead of bars, we encounter sheets of glass, each a window into a piece of wild savanna, desert, or jungle. The jaguar prowls the ruins of a Mayan temple, a puma stalks the high country of the American West, a pampas cat wanders over a bit of Argentine grassland, a clouded leopard roams through an Indian forest made up of octopus-like trees.

Videos and graphics complement the animals. Eyeball-to-eyeball confrontations take place through the glass partitions. The cats do not blink. Yet, close as they are, the animals seem strangely distant. We do not smell or hear them. Glass protects them from contagious human diseases but also eliminates their smells and sounds; and to smell and hear wild animals may be nearly as important as seeing them. After all, we go to zoos to be outside. The animals here are camouflaged within fanciful replicas of their natural environments. To see them in a packaged atmosphere only makes an artificial experience even more artificial. It is as if the wild beasts in the magnificently realistic dioramas of New York's Museum of Natural History had come to life. But let us not quibble. We have before us a splendid feast of living cats. Here we encounter, at unsettling proximity, caracals with their pointed ears, ocelots, fishing cats, black-footed cats, jaguarundi, Pallas's cat, pampas cats, rusty-spotted cats (littlest of cats), marbled cats, and bobcats. Then come big cats: leopards, jaguars, servals, pumas, Siberian lynxes, clouded leopards, and snow leopards. Among the felines the zoo has also had its reproductive triumphs, including the first successful births in captivity of caracals, pampas cats, and sand cats.

Upon exiting, we turn right to the **Passenger Pigeon Memorial.** This pagoda-style structure, designed by James McLaughlin as part of the zoo's aviary, commemorates Martha, the last surviving passenger pigeon. Once America's most abundant bird, the passenger pigeon was also, with its slate-gray body and rose-breasted plumage, one of its most beautiful. Formerly flocks of up to a billion filled American skies. But Americans massacred these graceful birds indiscriminately. In *The Pioneers* (1823) James Fenimore Cooper graphically describes one such slaughter. Martha spent the last years of her life in this zoo. No mate was found for her and with her death in 1914 the species died. In 1918 here also died Incas, the last Carolina parakeet, our only native parrot. Extinction, as the World Wildlife Fund would say, is forever. The Memorial commemorates all species who have vanished through man's destructiveness.

The zoo has long been known for the successful breeding in captivity of its lowland gorillas. **Gorilla World** (1978) allows us to observe a group of them within a setting—caves, trees, waterfalls—close to their native rain forest. The sound of falling water fills our ears. Occupying an adjoining enclosure are the black-and-white colobus monkeys, enchanting creatures whose ways Gerald Durrell nicely renders in *Catch me a Colobus*.

On **Monkey Island** (1930, rebuilt 1985) live a troop of Japanese macaques, or snow monkeys, that stay outside the year round. Like the colobus, macaques groom each other, a practice that not only catches fleas but strengthens troop bonding. Turkomen markhor, goats with spectacular spiralling horns, share the island with the macaques. Nearby, the circular **Reptile House** (ca. 1875) may be the zoo's most eye-catching historic building. Tucked within a circle of composite columns are state-of-the-art exhibit areas illuminated in part by natural light, holding snakes, turtles, and lizards from all over the world. The Indian python slithers about with an eerie Hindu temple as backdrop. The radiated tortoises from Madagascar, born in 1987, may well outlive you. Crocodiles snooze in the center pit.

Beyond the Reptile House a bust of Andrew Erkenbrecher, the zoo's founder, sits within a brick niche. From here we may descend to **Wildlife Canyon,** which features unusual hoofed animals, including the extremely rare Sumatran rhino; warthogs; and babirusa, an appealing primitive pig from the island of Celites in Indonesia; as well as elands from Africa, bactrian camels from the Gobi desert, and wallaroos from Australia.

The **Elephant House** (1905, restored 1982), or Herbivora Building as it was long called, reflects Moghul or Moslem Indian architecture. Visible from the surrounding city, it sits on the zoo's highest point. Elzner & Anderson, the architects, designed a sequence of stately domes: it is as if the Taj Mahal had pupped. In the history of zoos exotic animals have generally had much greater exhibit value than endemic ones. To enhance that value, European zoos in the mid nineteenth century began keeping their exotic animals in imitation antique temples, mosques, Swiss chalets, tepees, log cabins, and so on. These older zoos were designed in what some have called the "atmosphere style." American zoos followed suit. Like the pagoda-esque aviary and the vaguely oriental Reptile House, the Elephant House with its picturesque domes conveys a sense of the exotic. By recalling the East it also recalls the homeland of the Asian elephants for whom the building was designed. Skylights and arched dome windows allow plenty of natural light. Elzner & Anderson, creators of the contemporaneous Ingalls Building on 4th St., the world's first concrete-frame skyscraper, pioneered here with ferro-concrete domes. The building houses a pair of black rhinos (Sababu is the growing baby), pigmy hippos, Malayan tapirs, Asian elephants, and Masai giraffes. The zoo's reproductive laurels are not new: in 1889 it recorded the Western Hemisphere's first giraffe birth.

In a forested enclosure or behind a screen of potted plants, we glimpse the zoo's rarest beast, a female okapi, one of only a few in America. Native to the dense tropical rain forests of Zaire (formerly the Congo), the shy okapi remained undiscovered until 1901. Its name means "forest horse." The okapi shares with its only relative, the giraffe, a similar shape of the head and slope of the back. An exceptionally beautiful creature, the okapi has a hazel coat, great fluid eyes, a stiff, giraffe-like walk, and, like the giraffe, a prehensile tongue. Okapis are often identified by

Elephant House. European zoos in the nineteenth century began keeping their exotic creatures in equally exotic buildings, and American zoos soon followed suit. Built in 1905 on the zoo's highest point, the Elephant House reflects Moghul, or Moslem Indian, architecture.

the configuration of the stripes on their hindquarters. Despite the stripes, the okapi is no relation of the zebra. Asengu, the zoo's okapi, taken in the wild, is considered crucial to replenish the bloodlines of okapis in captivity. She gave birth on December 12, 1989.

We proceed to **Gibbon Islands** (1973). The exotic-looking jungle gyms allow the gibbons and siamangs, when so inclined, to mount spectacular displays of acrobatics. Nearby, virtually at the zoo's center, are the red pandas. Are they related to raccoons, bears, or are they the giant panda's only living relative? Scientists are hard put to classify them. Red pandas have reddish-brown fur, white-tipped ears, black legs, and a long furry striped tail that usually extends straight out. Many people find them as cute as their bigger cousins. Nearby, rare Chinese plants—lacebark pines, Chinese sumacs, a Chinese prickly ash, and Chinese bamboos—complement the exhibit.

If we leave the zoo by the south auto exit, we pass Michael Bigger's monumental sculpture, *Helios Guardians* (1964). Cincinnati's first large-scale abstract sculpture, it remains one of its most interesting. Though beautifully set on its hillock, it

Red panda. With its reddish-brown fur, white-tipped ears, black legs, and a long furry striped tail usually extending straight out, the red panda never fails to attract visitors. In winter this panda may climb a tree, settle on a likely branch, and wrap its tail around itself like a scarf.

is noticed by few. Made of Cor-ten steel and twenty-four feet high, *Helios Guardians* is dedicated to Michael Grzimek. In 1959 Michael's zebra-striped airplane collided over the Serengeti with a griffon vulture and plummeted to earth. With his father Bernhard, Michael had coauthored a book, *Serengeti Shall Not Die* (1958), and prepared a film that brought the vast plains of Tanzania to the attention of Europeans and Americans only just awakening to the realization that human encroachment, rather than poaching, posed the chief threat to the animals of Africa. Bigger's sculpture appears to work on an abstract level. Does he wish us, as Richard N. Campen surmises, to conjure visions of six shield-bearing Greek hoplites guarding the sun god Helios? Or are they guarding the earth's vanishing species? Helios also watched over a herd of sacred cattle as he drove his horsedrawn chariot through the sky. Perhaps the sculpture symbolizes the spirit of the wild animals guarded by Helios—and by the zoo, Cincinnati's Helios, which has striven valiantly to preserve the animals of Africa.

Upon leaving the zoo bear right on Erkenbrecher to Vine St., then right again. Turn left on Mitchell Ave., right on Spring Grove Ave. Soon, as we cross a metal-truss bridge spanning the Millcreek, we glimpse a surrealistic industrial landscape: the Procter & Gamble complex. Shortly afterwards, we turn right into the visitors' parking across from the main entrance.

Procter & Gamble

Despite **Procter & Gamble's** prominence, Cincinnati is not a one-company town. P & G is not even the area's largest employer (General Electric is). The city's economy is diverse, with no one employer or industry dominating, a factor that has

Procter & Gamble factories. Designed by Solon Spencer Beman, the older buildings of the vast complex, known as Ivorydale, present a unity of appearance. The projecting tower of the central structure suggests, like the Hannaford-designed water tower in Eden Park, a medieval castle with its *donjon,* or keep. The long building to the right has red-brick window trim set within a limestone façade.

cushioned economic slumps. Several firms, P & G among them, offer public tours. These can be informative introductions not only to a company's products but also to its buildings. If you have called ahead and made a tour reservation, you will visit several departments within the vast complex. Tours vary, routes change, but in an hour and a half you will learn much about a company that claims that 97 percent of American households use its goods. Products made locally include Ivory, Camay, Joy, Dawn, Mr. Clean, Duncan Hines baking mixes, and Crisco.

Even if you do not go on a tour, take a few minutes to look at the buildings fronting Spring Grove Ave. Ground was broken for **"Ivorydale"** (the name of this vast complex) in 1885. The previous year a fire had broken out at P & G's Central Ave. plant. The company decided not to rebuild there but to establish a new and larger complex here. Ivorydale's architect was Solon Spencer Beman, best known as the planner of Pullman, George Pullman's company town in south Chicago. Until Pullman advised against it, Procter & Gamble had also planned a model town for employees. Instead, it decided upon a model factory. The original limestone buildings, well set back from the street, contrasted sharply with dingy contemporary factories. A broad lawn fronted the P & G complex; trees were planted and flowerbeds set, providing a pleasant atmosphere for work. Grounds and buildings are immaculately maintained. In 1979 the complex was nominated for listing as a National Historic Landmark. Yet the company, while professing that it had no plans to alter its historic buildings, fought the nomination. In 1980 it got Congress to include a rider on its historic preservation legislation that required the owner's approval before any property could be designated a historic landmark, thereby allowing P & G to veto such designation for Ivorydale.

Beman's work here reflects the romantic style of industrial architecture. The limestone-and-brick façades, substantial yet lively, present a unity of appearance. Beman's buildings stress solidity, mass, and dignity. He had an eye for beauty as well as for utility. The projecting tower of the central structure suggests, like the Hannaford-designed Water Tower in Eden Park, a medieval castle with its *donjon,* or keep. Particularly attractive is the long building to its right. Note the red-brick window trim set within the limestone façade. Windows still have their awnings (standard before air conditioning on commercial and industrial structures). On the rondels in the stepped gables we discern the controversial P & G logo (discussed in chapter 3). Further along to the right, set in an immaculate lawn of creeping bent, we come upon the Art Deco cenotaph of William Cooper Procter (1862–1934), active in company affairs from the 1880s, president from 1907–1930, and one of several descendants of the original partners who have provided the company with enlightened leadership. Employee contributions paid for this memorial.

In 1883 P & G offered a Saturday afternoon holiday without reduction in pay, then a radical step; in 1887 it introduced a pension and benefit plan, and in 1892 profit sharing, with the possibility of stock purchase. In 1923 Procter guaranteed employees forty-eight weeks of employment, with paid vacations. A few years later he acquiesced to requests for an eight-hour workday; workers received the same wages for eight hours they had received for ten. During the Depression the company never laid off a worker. Today Procter & Gamble maintains, on both sides of Spring Grove Ave., 213 buildings, in addition to plants in fifty cities in twenty-five states. Worldwide, in sixty different locations, the company employs 75,000 people, of which over 13,000 call Cincinnati home. A fascinating local mythology has attached itself to this very secretive, very conservative, immensely powerful corporation.

The name "Ivorydale" derives from Procter & Gamble's best-known product, **Ivory Soap.** Soap was not always a company mainstay. In 1879, the year the first batch of Ivory was ladled from a kettle, soap accounted for less than one-quarter of Procter & Gamble's income. More significant were candles and lard oil. Ivory was the turning point, and it came about through an accident. One day in 1879 an operator let his soap-mixing machine run through the lunch hour. The machine beat the soap into a lighter mix than usual, mixing air into the formula; the cakes went out on the market. Eventually P & G received an order for more of its "floating soap." The company was dumbfounded. It retraced the steps that led to the "error," then decided to produce the accidental soap on purpose, initially calling it by the prosaic name of "White Soap."

Without Harley Procter, grandson of the Procter founder and in charge of advertising, Ivory might have remained merely White Soap. One Sunday in church Harley heard this verse from Psalm 45: "All thy garments *smell* of myrrh, and aloes, *and* cassia, out of the ivory palaces." Thus Ivory Soap was born. The company first used Ivory as a trademark on July 18, 1879; three months later it sold the first cake. For several years Harley Procter focused on what he felt were Ivory's principal attractions: its purity ("99 and 44/100 % pure") and its multiple uses. He did not immediately grasp as a selling point the great value of the soap's floating quality. At a time when most ads stood only a few inches high, Harley took out full pages in popular magazines. He used well-known artists for illustrations and kept the text light, even humorous. In the end his ads revolutionized American advertising. Ivory went on to make Procter & Gamble's fortune.

We continue northeast on Spring Grove Ave., which merges into Vine St., then becomes Springfield Pike. Before reaching Glendale, we traverse a series of Millcreek Valley settlements: Elmwood Place, Hartwell, Carthage, Wyoming, Woodlawn. Each community developed within the context of the Millcreek Valley, whether as industrial area, worker housing, or residential suburb. Each has its own individuality and historic interest. Wyoming in summer earns its Indian name of "beautiful valley": planters around street signs overflow with blooms. As we approach Glendale, the main road (state routes 4 and 126) angles left. We continue straight ahead on route 747 north, however, now also called Congress Ave. Where it intersects with Sharon Road we turn right. About half a mile further, just before the railroad tracks, right again. The Glendale train station stands before us. We park in the village square.

Glendale

Suburbs are not new. American cities have been expanding virtually since they were established. Founding a suburb did not, at least initially, imply rejecting the city. Rather, suburbs allowed people a way to get, or to try to get, the best of both city and country, as we have already seen in Mount Auburn and Clifton. Before 1850 *suburb* referred to the outskirts of urban areas; after 1850 the word denoted a middle-class residential neighborhood. It also denoted a positive vision of urban and rural characteristics. Combining country and city became firmly established in American suburban planning. *"Rus mihi dulce sub urbe est,"* wrote Martial two millenia ago; "to me the country on the outskirts of the city is sweet." Most Americans agreed. Suburbs, instead of just growing like Topsy, began to be planned. A number of suburbs with curvilinear designs came into being. Even at the height of enthusiasm for the picturesque suburb, however, the grid remained predominant. Curvilinear plans were most often used in subdivisions designed for the gentry. Founded in 1851, **Glendale** is one of the earliest planned suburbs in America. It may well be the first with a curvilinear plan.

Like Spring Grove Cemetery's plan, which preceded it and the Cincinnati Zoo's, which followed it, Glendale's plan stems from the eighteenth-century *jardin anglais* and from Romantic theories of landscape that stressed curvilinear design. In

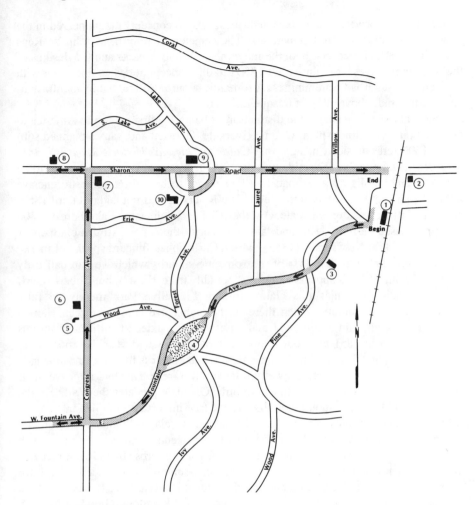

GLENDALE

1. Village Square and Train Station
2. Police Station
3. First Presbyterian Church
4. Floral Park
5. Church of the New Jerusalem
6. Lyceum
7. Grand Finale Restaurant
8. St. Gabriel Church
9. Town Hall
10. Christ Church

America, a few private estates excepted, these design concepts first appeared in the
1830s in the layout of rural cemeteries. The cemeteries, in turn, as John W. Reps
has pointed out, "influenced both the movement for public parks and the designs of
the parks themselves." Not until after 1850 did this concept of design find favor with
promoters of suburban communities. A romantic suburb was laid out in an informal,
naturalistic, and, above all, picturesque manner.

Several claimants vie for the distinction of being the first suburb in America to
be based on a curvilinear plan. One is Riverside, Olmsted and Vaux's planned suburb of 1600 acres outside Chicago. In *A Guide to Chicago's Historic Suburbs* (1981)
Ira J. Bach claimed that Riverside was the "first landscaped suburb connected to an
industrial metropolis by a railroad line and meant to be only a domestic enclave
rather than a complete urban settlement." But Riverside was not laid out until 1869,
nearly twenty years after Glendale. Another Chicago claimant is Lake Forest, 1400
acres purchased early in 1856 and laid out shortly thereafter. A third claimant is
Llewellyn Park in New Jersey (1853), which Christopher Tunnard speaks of in *The
City of Man* (1953) as "the first of the romantic suburbs which we can call truly
planned." John W. Reps appears to agree ("possibly the earliest"), but Robert A. M.
Stern emphatically denies this claim, finding Llewellyn Park merely "a fully
planned, ideal community." Then there is the eighty-five acre Evergreen Hamlet
outside Pittsburgh, laid out in 1851 and envisaged for sixteen families. Seven lots
were purchased in 1851 and four houses completed the next year. No more were
built, however, and four houses do not a suburb make. Nor is the plan curvilinear.

Riverside, Lake Forest, Llewellyn Park, Evergreen Hamlet: all have their
champions. As a planned, curvilinear suburb, Glendale predates them all. Yet the
distinction of being first should not obscure the true importance of Glendale and its
confrères. "These rare examples of residential parks," claims Tunnard, are "among
the most important American contributions to nineteenth century planning." Such
communities served as models for thousands of later suburbs. In 1976, in recognition of its distinction as the first known American suburb laid out according to topography, 392 acres of Glendale became a National Historic Site. If we regard the
zoo as a curvilinear residential suburb for the animal kingdom, Glendale we may
regard as a Spring Grove for the living.

That the Cincinnati, Hamilton, & Dayton Railroad's completion and Glendale's
founding occurred in the same year of 1851 is not coincidental. The year before, the
railroad had sought a right-of-way through Springdale, west of Glendale. The railroad wished to establish in Springdale a camp for railroad workers, largely immigrant Irish, to which residents objected vociferously. So the company shifted the
railroad a few miles east and set up its labor camp in what became Glendale.

On April 26, 1851, George Crawford and Henry Clark completed the purchase
of 600 acres from Edmund Glenn, John Riddle, and a few other local farmers.
Crawford and Clark foresaw that the nearly completed railroad provided excellent
possibilities for residential development. Later that year the Glendale Association,
thirty men who together had formed a joint stock company, in turn bought the 600
acres from Crawford and Clark. Edmund Glenn, whose farm had occupied part of

View of Glendale, ca. 1860. Glendale's distinctive curvilinear plan is clearly visible in this engraving. We are looking west. In the foreground are the railway tracks, with a train chugging along toward Cincinnati. The original station is just right of center. Sharon Avenue runs diagonally toward the central horizon. The larger buildings on its north side are of the Glendale Female College, actually a superior finishing school, here from 1854 to 1929. Courtesy of the Cincinnati Historical Society.

Glendale's site, gave his name to the putative village. Robert C. Phillips, described only as "a civil engineer from Cincinnati," laid out 200 of the 600 acres in lots of one to twenty acres. One would like to know more about this civil engineer. He was, perhaps without his ever realizing it, a pioneer urban planner. With its curving streets relating to topography, Phillips's plan was in advance of its time. But if Phillips was the surveyor in charge, the real author, at least spiritually, was Andrew Jackson Downing. Two articles by him in *The Horticulturalist*—"On the Improvements of Country Villages" (1849) and "Our Country Villages" (1850)—argue for a naturalistic approach to the cultivation of landscape. They read like a blueprint for Glendale.

Before 1851 a few residential parks had been laid out in England but none in America. The land Phillips platted was beautiful rolling country, traversed by two brooks and high enough that the Millcreek would not flood it. Phillips's plat used the hills to create a series of irregularly shaped lots and winding streets. Parks and a lake (drained in 1921) formed part of the overall design. The undulating plan, certainly an unusual arrangement for the gridlike Midwest, bemused many at the time and subsequently. "Glendale is laid out irregularly," commented Sidney Maxwell in 1870. "Whatever way the stranger takes, he is constantly impressed with the thought that he has made a mistake, and whatever point he attains is certain to be some one unlooked for."

The first house went up in 1852. Lots were sold to members of Cincinnati's professional and industrial elites. Judge Stanley Matthews was among the first to move out; later he was joined by Robert Clarke, the bookseller, and William Cooper Procter. The village was incorporated in 1855. Houses in the 200-acre platted area had to cost at least $1500. Glendale is thus one of the first suburbs in America, if not the first, to establish a minimum price for houses. The plat allotted each household up to five acres. Households had to be relatively self-contained, able to look after themselves. Meat or dairy products required sufficient pasture to keep cows. Glendale residents, Maxwell noted in 1870, "generally raise on their ample grounds all the [vegetables] that their wants demand." "The great advantage about Glendale," he concluded, "is, that it is a complete community." Glendale became, and to a degree remains, "a society itself." Even today it preserves its village-like quality. Glendale has not felt the need to overwhelm; its impact is understated.

Glendale in the twentieth century has grown very slowly. In 1900 its population was 1545; in 1930, 2360; in 1950, 2402; today (1990), about 2700. The 1942 village plan mandated a maximum village size of 3900; it preferred no more than 3000. Even this latter population may never be reached. Today, though many of the larger Glendale lots have been subdivided, the village's street layout remains virtually intact. The nineteenth-century houses also remain. They are in a diversity of Revival styles: Greek, Gothic, Italianate, Tuscan Villa, Romanesque, Georgian, and of course our old friend, Eclectic. Italianate perhaps predominates, though after the turn of the century many owners updated their houses with Colonial Revival modifications. Perpendicular rather than horizontal, Glendale houses often have full-length windows; most originally had a veranda in front. Descendants of the original owners often still live in them.

What sets Glendale apart is not so much its houses, interesting as they often are, but the ensemble. Individual houses take on added significance within the larger context. Glendale realizes our conception of a landscape formed by art. "There are no palatial mansions," wrote Maxwell in 1870, apparently in surprise, "no extensive lawns, no long sweeping graveled drives, such as the visitor sees in other suburbs." If we want to see what a picturesque, curvilinear nineteenth-century suburb looked like, we come to Glendale. Those who settled in Mount Auburn and Clifton entered an already laid-out community; Glendale was planned and settled at the same time. Those who moved here did not have to accommodate themselves to an existing street grid. They could embody within Glendale's plan their own ideas about houses and about picturesque landscape.

In addition to Glendale and Mariemont, our next stop, the Cincinnati area has a third historic planned community, Greenhills, Ohio. Lying on originally 6000 acres several miles due west of Glendale, Greenhills was one of three towns sponsored in the 1930s by the suburban resettlement division of the Federal Housing Administration. Intended for families of moderate income and designed by Roland Anthony Wank, the architect in charge of Union Terminal, Greenhills was completed in 1938. Not meant to incorporate full employment possibilities within its boundaries, it was, at least in principle, more a garden city than a self-sufficient community. Yet it had its schools, stores, and churches. If we visited Glendale,

Mariemont, and Greenhills in sequence, we would gain a good impression of American planning ideals as expressed in the 1850s, the 1920s, and the 1930s. We might even make one further stop. This would be at Forest Park, a 3700-acre planned community established by private developers in the mid-1950s, about thirteen miles north of downtown Cincinnati.

We begin our tour of Glendale at the village square. The **train station** (1880) is perfect in its proportions, straightforward in its detailing, picturesque yet functional. An earlier white frame structure, covered with honeysuckle and surrounded by a white picket fence, burned in 1879. The new station's roof overhang, supported by huge brackets, kept rain (and sun) off commuters. Simple, utilitarian, understated, this depôt is a good example of vernacular railroad architecture of its day.

The Cincinnati, Hamilton, & Dayton Railroad was not only crucial for Glendale's founding but also for its survival. A commuter as well as a through line, the C. H. & D. provided easy access to Cincinnati. Glendale lay near the extreme limit of practical commuting. Fifteen miles from downtown, the village was the terminus of the C. H. & D.'s commuter service. "Charge High & Damn Rough Ride," as

C. H. & D. railroad tracks and station, Glendale. The photograph was taken before 1880, when the present station was erected. From here inhabitants of Glendale set off on a fifteen-mile commute to downtown that took about forty-five minutes. Courtesy of the Cincinnati Historical Society.

oldtimers interpreted the line's initials, reminds us also that the railroad—and the community—was available only to the well-to-do. The first commuter train came through on September 18, 1851; soon there were fourteen a day. Residents walked or rode or were taken to the station, boarded the train for the forty-five minute ride into the depôt at 5th and Baymiller streets in Cincinnati's West End, and still had a good walk, or horse-car ride, to Fountain Square. Younger employees took the 7:20, seniors the 7:55, shoppers the 9:05 or 9:20. The total trip usually lasted about an hour and a quarter. Glendale Station long functioned as an informal community center. Each family had its regular place before it for its horse and carriage. Commuter service ceased in 1927, a victim to automobile competition. Today mostly freight trains use the tracks, now owned by CSX. The commuter rail lines had been the fundamental means of transportation for the nineteenth-century suburbs. The automobile altered the precondition for their existence. Mariemont, unlike Glendale, is a suburb of the automobile age.

Like most nineteenth-century suburbs, Glendale had its prosperous and less prosperous residents. In 1850 the C. H. & D. put up a labor camp to house the Irish laborers who built the railroad. Workers lived east of the tracks, gentry west. Some of the workers' houses still exist, though altered, across the tracks. After the railroad was finished, many workers remained. In the early days, Glendale's population consisted of them and the well-to-do who built the fine homes on the lots in Phillips's curvilinear plat. Glendale has not become an exclusive preserve of the gentry. It includes substantial working-class districts east of the tracks and both north and south of Sharon. Blacks, a quarter of the population, live chiefly in Glendale's northwest sector.

Though the trains stop no more, the **village square** has changed little over the past century. The median plantings are of seasonal flowers; in warm weather a modest fountain gurgles. A shingle oak towers over the fountain. Opposite the station is the **Willis-Dooley block** (1880). Replacing a wooden structure destroyed by fire, the Willis-Dooley block consists of two basic parts, the three-story "block" and a two-story wing. The fenestration of the three-story block differs at each level; the arched cornice gives the façade a vaguely palladian air. If the Willis-Dooley block looks familiar, it is because during the later nineteenth century many comparable "business blocks" of three, four, and five stories went up in small midwestern towns across the land. Such a block as this, J. B. Jackson has observed, "suggested in the arrangement of the floors the various functions for which it was suited: stores on the ground level, above that offices for lawyers and doctors, and on the third floor—a kind of *piano nobile* with tall windows—there was often a large space for an opera house, lodge hall, assembly room, or library." The third floor of the Willis-Dooley block housed the Masonic Hall, though only until 1887.

North of the station stands the **Iron Horse Inn,** formerly the Bracker Tavern (ca. 1854). The black image of "The Cincinnatian," a well-known nineteenth-century steam locomotive, decorates the wall. The food is excellent. A row of Bigtooth aspen lines the east side of the tracks. Across the intersection with Sharon Road, the two-story Italianate structure (1871) houses the tiny Glendale Museum, theoretically open from 1 to 4 P.M. on the first Sunday of each month but actually

Willis-Dooley block, Glendale. Replacing a wooden structure destroyed by fire, the Willis-Dooley block (1880) consists of two basic parts, the three-story "block" and a two-story wing. During the nineteenth century many comparable "business blocks" of three, four, and five stories went up in small midwestern towns across the land.

by appointment only. Now the **police station,** this building held until 1941 the mayor's office and council chambers.

Glendale is the only community I know of in the greater Cincinnati area where a walker may experience police harrassment. On two occasions in preparing this tour I was pulled over and questioned by the police, once politely, once less so. If you find unpleasant the prospect of being tailed by a police car, I suggest you stop by the station beforehand and identify yourself—or drive this segment of the tour.

From the village square we walk up East Fountain Ave. On the right, large trees shade the asymmetrical façade of number 160, a two-and-a-half story Tuscan villa. Built during the Civil War, it sits nicely on a rolling lawn some distance from the road. Opposite is the oval Van Cleve Park or "the Small Park." To the left is the **First Presbyterian Church complex.** The manse dates from 1891. The original church (1860), in the center, was Glendale's first. The buttresses, not in the original plan, were needed to support the sharply pitched roof. The second church (1873), Gothic Revival also, was designed by A. C. Nash. The tourelles are not identical twins; that on the left sports a more elaborately Gothic configuration. This building was entirely refurbished and restored in 1973. Together, the three structures form an attractive composition.

Gables cascade down 145 East Fountain (1932). This white brick-and-

120 E. Fountain Ave., Glendale. This unpretentious 1869 house is typical of those built in Glendale's early years. It sports an octagonal porch gazebo with fine spoolwork.

clapboard composition nestles into its site like the overgrown cottage it pretends it is. Two chestnuts shade the entrance, itself surmounted by an attractive Gothic switch-pane window. Across the street, 140 East Fountain (1855), a symmetrical Italianate cube, has paired windows with brick Florentine window molds; below the second-story windows, panels simulate a balcony balustrade. Originally, like many other Glendale houses, this one had a veranda in front. The wide-flung verandas of the nineteenth century were replaced by less elaborate millinery, or, more likely, removed altogether. But not always. Farther along, **120 East Fountain** (1869) sports an octagonal porch gazebo with fine spoolwork and a bead-and-rung frieze. A pale pink-and-white confection with a gazebo—if ever a house could force the dread words "How sweet!" from the most jaded of lips, this one could. Simple yet beguiling, this cotton-candy dollhouse is one of the Glendale houses we remember best.

On the left, 125 East Fountain (1854) was extensively remodelled after World War I in the neoclassical style. One of Glendale's larger mansions, it stands behind imposing gateposts and a lovely iron fence. In it lived Judge Stanley Matthews (1824–1889), U.S. Senator, Supreme Court justice, Glendale resident from 1854 and after the Civil War probably its most influential citizen. Number 95, further along on the left, is a low-lying, understated house (1858), neo-Federal in style. Palladio hovers behind this five-bay composition. With its balanced chimneys and seamed metal roof, number 95 may remind you of the Taft Museum downtown.

Its horizontal aspect contrasts with the vertical thrust of most of Glendale's other nineteenth-century houses. Here lived Charles Sawyer, Ambassador to Belgium, Secretary of Commerce under Truman (1948–1953), and a longtime Cincinnati benefactor whose generosity included an initial gift for Sawyer Point downtown.

Up on the hill, 80 East Fountain is one of Glendale's few Modern Movement houses. It appears to best advantage when seen from before the entrance to Floral Park. Zoning restrictions would prevent a modern house from being built in Glendale today.

Floral Park, more even that the village square, is Glendale's true heart. Popularly known as the "Big Park" it has remained essentially unchanged since 1851. There is nothing dramatic about Floral Park. Massive trees, to be sure, rise here, some a hundred or more years old, but otherwise the park contains no spectacular feature, offers no spectacular vista. But in its unobtrusive way this undulating, cared-for landscape provides a lesson in the romantic picturesque. The path before us curves; the park's lines curve; Glendale's streets curve; in fact, the entire village curves in response to the terrain. In Glendale as in Cincinnati we constantly go up or down. The flowing topography, unlike the flat terrain of Chicago's Riverside and Lake Forest, complements the curvilinear plan. The village, wrote Henry B. Teetor in 1882, looks like "an immense park." His words hold equally true today. Even Glendale's street names—Willow, Pine, Laurel, Ivy—convey (as Ted Eversole has pointed out) "the image of a pleasant, leafy, residential community." Such sylvan names were also favorites of the rural cemeteries. In summer a canopy of green envelops Glendale's houses. If architecture is your main interest, winter is the best time for a walk.

We follow the path through Floral Park. The scallop-shaped fountain in the center was given in memory of Charles Sawyer. In addition to quenching our thirst, the water refreshes park wildlife, among them, the unusual black squirrels (unusual at least for this area) imported long ago from northern Michigan. We emerge at the park's far end. James McLaughlin designed the lampposts with Welsbach burners, over a hundred in all, that encircle Floral Park and line most of Glendale's streets. On the base of the lamppost nearest us we make out "1893." Not all date from this time. One of Glendale's charming street signs, with the silhouetted bird and squirrel motif, stands near the lamppost. A. C. Denison, a Glendale resident, designed them in 1935.

We walk back along the park's north side. **70 East Fountain Ave.** stands on Glendale's highest point. When the parcels of land were distributed, the Glendale Association deemed this lot its "first choice." What appears to be a sawed-off Second Empire mansion dates from the early 1850s. The house looks incomplete because after World War II a fire destroyed the first story. The owners rebuilt the house as we now see it. Robert Clarke, who bought the house from Ezra Eliot in 1858, ran one of the major American publishing houses not located on the Eastern seaboard. A man who read books as well as sold them, Clarke had built onto his house the still-standing library, twenty-six feet by eighteen, with a twenty-foot domed ceiling. Into it he put his personal collection, 6000 volumes selected from forty years of handling and studying books. Clarke suffered from a problem common then as now to booklovers; already by 1870 his spacious library, Sidney Maxwell observed, was "quite too small."

We backtrack to 50 East Fountain. What appears to be an imposing neo-Colonial mansion began as a Greek Revival cube (ca. 1855). The portico of four square paneled columns was added later. Imitations or echoes of Mount Vernon's famous portico are common in Glendale. With its columns, the lawn rising to the house, the ironwork on the veranda and before the central window (an echo of New Orleans), and in summer the palms on the veranda, 50 East Fountain looks like a Southern plantation. The curved brackets below the cornice create wonderful shadows. Opposite, 55 East Fountain is Arts and Crafts in style. The second-story stucco exterior laced with stained wooden boards makes the house look like a domestic version of Mount Adams's Rookwood Pottery. We continue along East Fountain to Congress Ave. In spring wildflowers tapestry the rolling lawns.

780 Congress (ca. 1857), at the intersection of East Fountain and Congress avenues, commands the approach to Glendale. Its portico of paneled columns has earned the house its appellation of **"The Pillars."** Like many Glendale houses, it has undergone so many remodellings that we ascertain its original shape with difficulty. Most likely, early twentieth-century Colonial Revival was superimposed upon a Greek Revival frame, which, in this case, incorporated within its walls the original farmhouse of John Riddle, one of the area's pioneer farmers. Two couchant lions snooze in front of the main entrance on Congress Ave.

Owned by John Van Zandt—who reputedly served as Harriet Beecher Stowe's model for the character John Van Trompe in *Uncle Tom's Cabin*—780 Congress is traditionally thought to have served as a station along the Underground Railroad. Once tunnels connected the house to the huge pile across Congress at 25 West Fountain Ave. (next on our route) and to the gazebo at the back, perhaps also to other Glendale houses. Local lore has it that under Glendale there is a veritable catacomb of tunnels. Long since filled in, these underground passages hid escaping slaves. One July night in 1863 General John Hunt Morgan's Confederate raiders galloped, uninvited, through Glendale. Glendale residents hid their horses in the tunnels, or so we hear.

We cross Congress and walk to 25 West Fountain (1859). Built for Samuel Badger Allen, this huge Gothic Revival composition, asymmetrical yet balanced, looks like a country cousin to the Probasco house in Clifton. Gothic touches include the clustered chimneys, the stepped and pedimented gables and wall dormers, and the buttresses on the portico and right bay. Tudor arches appear above the windows. The blue limestone façade, with freestone trim, may antedate that of the Probasco house. We return to Congress Ave. and proceed north on Sharon Road.

The **Church of the New Jerusalem** (1861), Swedenborgian, is a superb example of vernacular Gothic ecclesiastical architecture. An asymmetrical board-and-batten composition designed by one Peter Mullett, the church survives virtually unaltered. This church's design probably emerged from *Upjohn's Rural Architecture* (1852), in which Richard Upjohn gave a plan for a small wooden Gothic Revival church with board-and-batten siding. This siding is the principal feature that distinguishes American rural Gothic churches from English. The boards and battens not

Church of the New Jerusalem, Glendale. This board-and-batten church (1861) is a superb example of vernacular Gothic ecclesiastical architecture. It houses the only Swedenborgian congregation in Cincinnati.

only animate the surface but give the design a lively verticality. Andrew Jackson Downing, aware of the esthetic qualities of board-and-batten siding, thought it "expresses the picturesque." The pointed gables over the double and triple windows echo those of the paired gables on the spire. All elements in the design—gables, spire, boards-and-battens, even the lines of the seamed metal roof—lead the eye upward. This diminutive structure soars.

Swedenborgianism derives from Emanuel Swedenborg (1688–1772), a Swedish mystic who believed himself the spokesman of a new revelation and whose writings exerted tremendous influence for over a century. Neither Protestant nor Catholic, Swedenborgianism, or (as it prefers to be known) the New Church, began in London in 1788. William Blake briefly fell under the spell of its doctrines. In America the faith gained extensive recognition for more than half a century. Ralph Waldo Emerson expressed awe before the vision of Swedenborg, whom he regarded as "the most imaginative of men"; although Emerson returned again and again to him in his writings, he could not accept Swedenborg's theology. One who could was William Cooper Howells, father of William Dean, who propagandized ardently for the new religion in Ohio. The first Swedenborgian congregation in Cincinnati dates from 1808 or before. The Glendale group is also one of the earliest west of the Appalachians. The most famous American Swedenborgian was John Chapman,

"Johnny Appleseed." When passing through southwestern Ohio in the early 1800s he worshipped with this congregation. Within the church's entrance hallway we see the bench (taken from an earlier building) on which he reputedly sat.

North of the church is the **Lyceum** (1891). Horizontal to the church's vertical, the Lyceum reflects Richardsonian Romanesque influence. The contrast, as much in materials as in style, pits the church's painted wood against the Lyceum's multitextured surfaces. These include rough-hewn stone quoins, brick walls, chiselled stonework, and the square squat columns framing the small windows.

Lyceums were public halls in which lectures were—and sometimes still are—given. In the nineteenth century they were an American phenomenon. The London Mechanics' Institute opened in January 1824. Two years later the first American lyceum, modelled upon the Mechanics' Institute, was founded. By 1828 there were a hundred. Lyceums, thought Josiah Holbrook, their main promoter, would help raise "the moral and intellectual taste of our countrymen." In *The Blithedale Romance* (1852) Hawthorne spoke of "those Lyceum-halls, of which almost every village has now its own." The lyceum movement continued strong into the 1870s. The word *lyceum* derives from the gymnasium near Athens where Aristotle taught. Americans, infatuated with the ideal of ancient Greece, hoped that lyceums would play a comparable role in developing American cultural life. Lyceums would be the cultural counterpart to the Greek Revival structures rising across the land.

Glendale's lyceum, very much a latecomer, was the brainchild of Robert Clarke. Clarke, who valued equally books and Glendale, founded this lyceum in 1882 and promptly presented it with a 5000-volume library. Early meetings were held in the Town Hall. But from the beginning Clarke had envisaged the Lyceum in its own building, with a library, a place to stage plays, to hold open forum discussions, and to allow different kinds of recreation. This building was completed in 1891. Today, if we judge from the activity on the tennis courts behind, the main emphasis appears to be recreation. *Mens sana in corpore sano,* or, more ruefully if you will, *O tempora, o mores!* If we look through the present doorway, we see the original round-arched entrance and, on the wall behind it, a photograph of Clarke.

Farther along is the Congress Avenue Public School (1900). Spanish Revival, it has an orange-tiled roof and an open tower. Additions date from 1928 and 1935.

We arrive at Glendale's main junction, Congress Ave. and Sharon Road. On the northeast corner, the three-bay Greek Revival house (ca. 1862) is known as **Corcoran's Corner,** after James Corcoran, an early owner. Opposite is a Victorian frame house (ca. 1875) painted slate blue with a pressed metal ceiling within made by the Edwards Manufacturing Co. Congress was formerly part of the main road from Cincinnati to Dayton, and from the early 1900s John J. Kelly had a saloon here. About 1930 Kelly built on an addition, from which his sisters Emma and Rose operated a small grocery. They also sold lollipops to the kids from the elementary school across the way and so, for over a generation, Kelly's became a candy shop legendary in Glendale annals. The sisters died in 1970, and in 1975 the **Grand Finale restaurant** opened here. Originally a creperie, the restaurant made its deservedly excellent reputation, as we might expect from the name, on its spectacular desserts. The chocolate cordial pie, a mousse-like concoction encased within a pecan crust, is a glutton's dream: one serving outlasts two persons. If the day is right, consider an alfresco lunch in the garden.

St. Gabriel Church (1907), a short distance west along Sharon, is a rock-faced Romanesque composition with an intriguing asymmetrical tower. A tiny spire, surmounted by a cross, peeps out of the crenellated tourelle. Few Romanesque buildings went up after the mid-1890s. Thus this church is *retardataire,* that is, a stylistic latecomer. Decorative plaques with curvilinear designs adorn the façade beltcourses. With many of the Irish railroad workers Catholic, St. Gabriel's parish was organized in 1858. Services were at first held in members' homes.

Preceding St. Gabriel is the parish house (1866), a three-bay Italianate structure. Four pairs of squared Tuscan columns support the porch. Behind it are floor-to-ceiling windows. The "garage" at the back has an interesting history. Episcopalians met in this frame structure in the 1860s. Having erected a new building, they sold it to St. Gabriel for $160.00—and $175.00 to move it. Ecumenicalism at a price! The building long served the parish as a classroom. Though the side facing us has two doors for vehicles cut in it, the front and far side have round-arched windows. From there it is still a pretty little church.

We return to Congress and continue east along Sharon. 56 E. Sharon (1870), on the north side, has chimneys encased by clapboards at either end. This small frame structure reminds us that not all Glendale houses were grand. Number 60 (ca. 1867), Second Empire, is unchanged except for the disappearance of its original veranda. The present (Eastlake) porch is, as often with Glendale porches, a later addition. This large dollhouse, four stories tall at the back, is higher than wide; the lowest story is below street level.

Glendale Town Hall (1875, with later additions) was designed by Samuel Hannaford as a Romanesque Tuscan villa. It houses an assortment of municipal services. Much be-plaqued, it reminds us that in Glendale an impressive roster of public-spirited citizens have actively involved themselves in the community. The Town Hall has a jerkinhead roof and, on both east and west façades, a spread-out Palladian window. Colored and patterned slates, original, accentuate the roof's huge planes. The well-proportioned octagonal chimneys act as a foil to the asymmetrically set tower.

Across the street, on Arbor Place, we see the base of the **Water Tower** (1892). When it collapsed in 1927, it caused a mighty, if temporary, inundation of Sharon Avenue. Old prints indicate an attractive turreted structure, not unlike that William Le Baron Jenney designed for Riverside, outside Chicago. Like Riverside's, Glendale's Water Tower was a distinctive local landmark. Half hidden between the tower's sandstone base and the War Memorial is a metal fountain (1894) donated by William A. Procter.

Christ Church, Glendale (1869), designed by Anderson & Hannaford, presents a full complement of Gothic accouterments, including pointed windows, gargoyles, and buttresses. Different-sized slates produce a pleasing roof pattern. Dominating the window facing us is Christ as Good Shepherd. The clock tower, a 1915 gift from the Procters, although impressive, appears out of scale for so small a building. From it the church clarion chimes "Happy Birthday" for any parishioner

Glendale Town Hall and Water Tower. The photograph
shows the Town Hall (1875) before modifications, with its
elaborate fretwork and pyramid-roofed tower intact. The
water tower (1892), foreground, exploded in 1927 and sent
water cascading down Sharon Ave. Today only the stone
base remains. Courtesy of the Cincinnati Historical Society.

celebrating an eightieth birthday. The bells also peal when a parishioner gives birth
to a baby. Boy babies get "Little Boy Blue," girls "Mary had a Little Lamb." This
charming practice once earned the church the dubious immortality of a mention in
Ripley's "Believe It or Not."

We return to Sharon and continue east. On our right at the intersection is 985
Laurel, which has undergone no less than five major remodellings. Even for Glendale it must hold some kind of record. The building started off in 1807 as a log
cabin, the Warwick house, one of the area's first dwellings, next became a twenty-
by forty-foot frame dwelling, then part of Edmund Glenn's brick farmhouse. The
present incarnation, a Queen Anne mansion with turrets, incorporates (so says the
plaque) the Glenn-Harkness-Keys house, 1835–1876, which in turn incorporates
the 1807 cabin. Broken up into six apartments since 1933, **Glen Gables** (as the
house is now known) presents a different appearance from every angle.

Harry Hake, Jr., designed 1025 Laurel (1939), the clapboard Georgian Revival house directly across Sharon. From 1854 to 1929 **Glendale Female College** occupied this site. "Not a serious case of sickness," Charles Cist remarked in 1859, had "occurred in the institution since its establishment." Cist alluded discreetly to the fact that the college—and Glendale—lay beyond the reach of the dreaded cholera. The most recent epidemic, from May through August 1849, had claimed over 4000 lives in Cincinnati. The college, actually a superior finishing school, boasted a distinguished roster of graduates.

140 East Sharon (1885), the Italianate mansion on the northeast corner opposite, is known as the DeCamp house. It remains virtually unaltered. Farther along, 160 East Sharon (1853), a five-bay Greek Revival structure with Italianate brackets, was built for Robert Crawford. Crawford, a member of the Glendale Association that commissioned the original plan, became in August 1855 the village's first mayor. 200 East Sharon (1858), much added on to, started out as a Tuscan villa. It has lost its tower, its brackets, and other Italianate details; it retains, however, its fine arched stone entrance with double doors. Nicholas Longworth purchased this lot, then sold it to Charles Spinning, who built the house. The mansion directly across Sharon (1869) was once owned by Florian Giauque, superintendent of Glendale School, later mayor. After Giauque's death, the new owner donated it for community use. Nicely set in a large grassy plot, it housed until 1987 a branch of the Public Library. Supporting the two-story veranda at the rear are unusual curved brick columns. We continue down Sharon past several unpretentious commercial buildings. Just before the railroad tracks, we turn right into the village square.

We leave Glendale by turning into East Fountain Ave., then immediately taking a right into Willow Ave. and another right onto Sharon Road. Follow Sharon east to I-75, where we get on the southbound ramp (direction: "Cincinnati"). To get to Mariemont we take, in large part, the interstate. Exit 7 ("Norwood") leads to state route 562, the Norwood Lateral Expressway. Here flowed, before glaciers changed its course, the Ohio River. Route 562 intersects with I-71, which we follow for a brief stretch north (direction: "Columbus"). We take exit 9 ("Fairfax/Red Bank Road"). After a mile or so along Red Bank Road, we turn left at the Colbank exit to route 50 (direction: "Cincinnati"), then almost immediately left again (direction: "Milford"). Route 50 East, Columbia Parkway, soon becomes Wooster Pike. A wooden sign, where a grass median bisects the road, announces "Village of Mariemont." Ignoring a subsequent sign for "Old Town Center," we continue along Wooster Pike. Soon we emerge from the forest at the present Mariemont town center, where we park.

Mariemont

Mariemont came about because of Mary M. Emery. We have already encountered her as the major benefactor of Christ Church's parish house on 4th St., of the Ohio Mechanics Institute's Emery auditorium and the YMCA on Central Parkway, and of the Cincinnati Art Museum. The greatest visionary among the wealthy American patronesses, Mrs. Emery was also the most retiring. For twenty years she gave steadily, shrewdly, and discreetly; her philanthropies extended not only to Cincin-

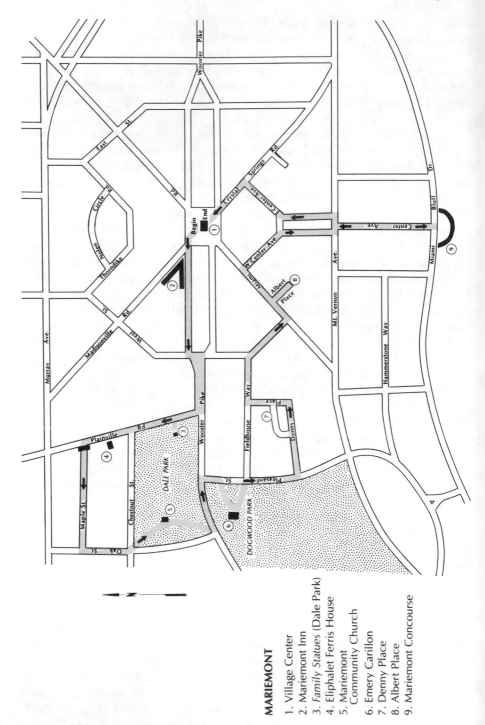

MARIEMONT

1. Village Center
2. Mariemont Inn
3. *Family Statues* (Dale Park)
4. Eliphalet Ferris House
5. Mariemont
   Community Church
6. Emery Carillon
7. Denny Place
8. Albert Place
9. Mariemont Concourse

nati but also to institutions, hospitals, charities, educational projects across the country, in Puerto Rico, even in Paris. After her husband Thomas J. Emery died in 1906, Mrs. Emery wished to establish a suitable living memorial to him. Though the original conception of a "model town" or "garden city" was probably Thomas Emery's, the accomplishment belongs to Mary Emery. Mariemont would be the most ambitious of her philanthropic endeavors, surpassing even the development of her art collection. Mariemont was the name of the Emery's Newport home, a name that may derive from Merry Mount, an early, half-pagan settlement near Boston, or, more appropriately, from Ma-re Mount, i.e., a place by the sea, Thomas Morton's name for this colony.

Preliminary planning for Mariemont took place before World War I. In charge was Charles J. Livingood, Mrs. Emery's right-hand man. An 1888 Harvard classmate of her son Sheldon, he was invited a few years after Sheldon's untimely death in 1890 to join the Emery firm. After Thomas Emery's death, Livingood managed both Mrs. Emery's business affairs and her civic benefactions. Beginning in 1913, Livingood's agents discreetly purchased parcels of land for the proposed community ten miles east of Cincinnati. Great secrecy was necessary, for rumors of all kinds were afloat. If the intended location of Mariemont had become known, land prices would have skyrocketed. Livingood used subterfuges, including having a Chicago-based real estate firm do the buying. In all, 423 acres were purchased. After the war Livingood called upon John Nolen, a noted landscape architect and an internationally recognized urban designer based in Cambridge, Massachusetts, to draw up the plan for Mariemont. Mariemont is Nolen's best-known and most successful design for a garden community.

In 1923 Mrs. Emery formed the Mariemont Company to supervise design and construction. The only shareholder, she provided several million dollars in financial support. Ground was broken on April 23 of that year, and shortly afterwards the chief public buildings and first residences went up. To design them Livingood selected twenty-six architects of distinction from Boston, New York, Philadelphia, and Cincinnati. Each was asked to emphasize his speciality in design but at the same time, in order to avoid inappropriate juxtapositions, to consider adjacent building groups. Charles F. Cellarius was the Mariemont Company's resident architect; Paul Philippe Cret, who influenced the design of Union Terminal, served as a consultant in 1927. When Mrs. Emery died that year, the bulk of her estate, some $25,000,000, went to form the Thomas J. Emery Memorial, the foundation she had created to carry on her philanthropic works. In 1931 the Memorial took over control of the Mariemont Company, which dissolved. The Memorial survives to this day.

Mariemont "is not designed for any special class of workers," stated the company brochure, "nor for workers solely." Not planned as a purely paternalistic (or, in this case, maternalistic) enterprise, Mariemont was to include all economic classes. In addition to individual dwellings, presumably for middle-class residents, the plan intended to provide working-class families with low-cost apartments and a healthful environment. But as early as 1923 construction costs drove rents far higher than anticipated. Thus from the beginning Mariemont developed as a middle-class enclave. By 1940 its population stood at 2760. The next year, in order to avoid the evil of annexation by Cincinnati, Mariemont was incorporated as a village. Construction, halted by the Depression, began anew after World War II. Architecturally, Mariemont is now quite a mix. In addition to the original variety of styles, it presents a number of post-1945 designs. Although houses come in different styles, sizes, and shapes, the community retains a certain visual unity. In 1979 Mariemont entered the National Register. When laid out, its population was expected to reach about 5,000, eventually to top out at 10,000. Even the lower figure has proven optimistic. The 1960 census gave the community 4120 inhabitants, its highest official count. Today Mariemont's residents, some 3300, inhabit one of Greater Cincinnati's most distinctive residential enclaves.

Mariemont, unlike Glendale, was planned as a relatively self-sufficient entity, a complete satellite town. Nolen designed Mariemont with the automobile in mind. The village, he pointed out, adjoined Madisonville and Fairfax and was close to the manufacturing suburbs of Oakley and Norwood. People would live near shopping areas and close to factories. The *New York Times* called it "a town for the motor age." Mariemont had its own elementary school, a high school, hospital, church, city hall, fire and police station, and (until 1954) its central heating plant. Unlike Glendale and Greenhills, it included an industrial zone, Westover, separated from residential areas by forest.

Mariemont was conceived as an American garden city. The idea of a garden city went back to England in 1898 when Ebenezer Howard published his *Garden Cities of To-morrow.* Howard advocated, as relief from the congested, unsanitary conditions of the late Victorian metropolis, the founding of new cities in the countryside, cities that would unite the energy and activity of the modern metropolis with the beauty and healthfulness of the country. Having spent as a young man ten years in America, Howard claimed to have gotten his ideas for the Garden City in the 1880s while looking at America's "wide open spaces." His new cities would have adequate housing, with industrial and residential districts strictly demarcated, and plenty of light and fresh air. Howard's ideas had tremendous appeal in England, where he helped found two model cities, Letchworth (1903) and Welwyn Garden City (1920). Both thrive today.

Under Howard's influence, American planners and architects designed a number of new towns and residential enclaves. Mariemont is contemporaneous with Sunnyside Gardens in Queens and Radburn in New Jersey, both designed by Clarence Stein and both among America's better-known garden cities. Often the new garden cities discarded the grid in favor of a curvilinear street pattern (as in Greenhills, Ohio), or, as in Mariemont's case, an essentially linear plan with transverse axes. Garden cities, many believed, would bring humanity, or that portion of it inhabiting them, into a new era of happiness and fulfillment. Utopia lay around the corner. "Town and country *must be married,*" Howard wrote, "and out of this joyous union will spring a new hope, a new life, and a new civilization." O brave new world! But in their heady optimism his words hardly yield to John Nolen's in his 1921 plan for Mariemont: "An Interpretation of Modern City Planning Principles to a Small Community to produce local Happiness. A National Exemplar." Indeed!

Mariemont's plan itself deserves our attention. We stand at the **village center** and face north toward the cinema marquee. To our left and right, we see divided roadways bridged by a turfed median. Four diagonal streets, intersecting theoretically at the midpoint of the village square, radiate outward. South of the square (beyond our direct vision) a wide north-south street leads to an overlook, Mariemont Concourse, on the lip of the bluffs. On this framework Nolen laid out a tree-lined network of streets, his plan a compromise between rectilinear grid and romantic curvilinearity. The plan's diagonals and transverse axes hark back to Baroque urban designs, as exemplified in Le Nôtre's gardens for Versailles or L'Enfant's plan for Washington. From above it approximates the design of the Union Jack, not inappropriately for a village that flaunts its echoes of Olde England.

A modest fountain splashes in the square. To the east stands a monument to Mrs. Emery; behind it stretches a beech wood traversed by footpaths. Trees, indeed, are everywhere. The sky is refreshingly uncluttered. Mariemont is one of the few American suburban communities in which, as in Europe, there are no utility poles and the attendant network of wires is underground. Except for through traffic on Wooster Pike the streets appear half deserted.

The Tudor Revival commercial buildings before us, half timbered and usually capped with slate roofs, lie low to the ground. Though undistinguished individually, they yet possess a basic unity of scale and style. The tiny business district contains, among other utilitarian establishments, a **Graeter's** (of ice cream fame), a pharmacy, and one of the area's few remaining neighborhood movie houses and the only one with a medieval marquee. To the west the **Mariemont Inn** (1929), now a Best Western, was designed by Zettel & Rapp of Cincinnati. The gray, green, and golden slates of its many-gabled roof blend harmoniously. An I. T. Verdin clock stands guard. We enter the Tudor Revival lobby. Oak wainscoting, massive columns with wide arches, exposed beams, festive banners descending from the ceiling: we are in a late medieval fortress. The **National Exemplar,** the in-house restaurant, is as exemplary as Mariemont itself: its blueberry pancakes rate as the city's best. On one of its rear walls a large-scale map reveals that the Inn's street axes were to have extended, quite grandly, twice their present length; an Elizabethan sunken garden, even a lawn for bowling, was to have occupied the space in between. Part of the era's fascination with Tudor Revival was its association with Shakespeare, with Walter Scott's historical romances, with the often dramatized rivalry between Elizabeth I and Mary, Queen of Scots, and with the movement to restore Sulgrave Manor, George Washington's ancestral home in England. But Mariemont did not quite become a Shakespearean village. The Depression, and the need for automobile parking, doomed the completion of its grandiose scheme.

We continue west along Wooster Pike, past the Tudor Kroger (1948), to Mariemont School (1939; addition, 1957), with a pedimented portico and a cupola. Across Plainville Road lies Dale Park. The *Family Statues* (1927) depict parents and grandparents doting upon their children. But do twentieth-century Americans wear bonnets and don sabots? Actually we are looking at French peasants. This statuary group, it says on the verso, derives from a Parisian original—but no origi-

Mariemont Inn. Designed by Zettel & Rapp of Cincinnati, the Mariemont Inn (1929) is Mariemont's most imposing building. It is in the Tudor Revival style, favored in the community in the 1920s.

nal was ever constructed. Further along Plainville Road (on the right) is the **Parish Center** (1930). Dedicated as a memorial to Thomas J. Emery, the Parish Center was originally known as the Recreation Building. George B. deGersdorff of New York was the architect of Mariemont's finest public building. The Mariemont Community Church purchased it in 1954. A complex composition, with a symmetrical tower asymmetrically set, the Parish Center works well as a whole. Contrasting materials—brick, stone, tile, stucco, wood—juxtapose colors and textures.

At 3915 Plainville Road stands the attractive **Eliphalet Ferris house** (1813). Federal in style and among Hamilton County's oldest buildings, it predates Mariemont by more than a century. The prolific Ferris family came from Connecticut and scattered over the Cincinnati area. This branch settled here in 1799. Nolen carefully fitted the house into the town plan. A plaque on the lawn tells us that on this spot on April 23, 1923, Mary M. Emery broke ground for Mariemont.

Ahead, across Murray Avenue in Madisonville, Plainville Road becomes a gallimaufry of wires, commercial signs, and billboards. With few or no zoning regulations, it is the typical strip street. We could be anywhere in America. But in Mariemont we are somewhere. As with Gertrude Stein's celebrated remark about Oakland, California, when you get to Plainville Road, there isn't any "there there"—that is, a sufficient complexity or richness of experience, a controlling vision to distinguish the place from others. It is a placeless place. But in Mariemont we do find a controlling vision. It is an environment informed by history. Mariemont reminds us that every townscape results from choices made and that alternatives exist if people wish them hard enough. The strip need not be.

A charming bow window above the arch between 3925 and 3927 Plainville Road indicates what is called the "honeymoon" apartment. The rowhouses (1925) up and down Plainville derive stylistically, via Philadelphia, from English eighteenth-century Georgian rowhouses: via Philadelphia, because a distinguished architect of that city, Edmund B. Gilchrist, designed them. Varying setbacks, irregular roof lines, and Flemish bond brickwork provide visual variety; a few houses have walled gardens. We go under the arch. To the left a Georgian Revival building with a Palladian window looks like a coach house but is actually an electrical substation.

Maple Street, appropriately treelined, consists of stucco-and-wood buildings, in style as much Arts and Crafts as Tudor Revival. All are different. Behind them runs a convenient service alley; garbage cans need not be set on the street. This section of Mariemont, known as the **Dale Park area,** was the first developed. Originally intended for lower-income tenants, the apartments filled up with middle-income tenants when unexpectedly high construction costs drove up rents. In 1924 the first families moved in. Mariemont, at its founding and for several decades afterwards, lay well into the country. Except for the Dale Park area, Denny Place, Albert Place, Sheldon Close, and a few commercial buildings, it was vacant land. Until World War II only Dale Park was fully developed.

At the first left, we sight the Dale Park Community Education Center (1925, with later additions), formerly the elementary school. It has a splendid neo-Georgian pedimented doorway and cupola. Next, the white windowless wooden building just before the intersection with Oak St., served for a year as a one-room schoolhouse until the completion of the Dale Park school. We turn left on Oak and note number 3914, a quaint half-timbered structure designed in 1924 by Charles F. Cellarius, which began life as Mariemont's combined fire and police station. The building had room for one fire truck, which exited through where is now the picture window. Glazed brick in various orange shades forms attractive diagonal patterns.

Once the intersection of Oak and Chestnut streets, now called the **"Old Town Center,"** functioned as Mariemont's commercial core. The shops with mullioned window panes originally supplied Dale Park residents with necessities. Shops still occupy the ground level; above are apartments. Mariemont thus offered (and offers) a wide variety of home types and living choices: single family, duplex, triplex, quadruplex, all the way to the apartment houses we see before us. The buildings, designed in 1925 by Ripley and LeBoutillier of Boston, play variations on Tudor Revival themes: slate roofs (originally at least), gables, casement windows, elaborate chimneys, limestone quoins reinforcing red brick walls (the Procter & Gamble plant had red brick within limestone), timber and stucco. The corner buildings have chamfered corners, that is, cut on a diagonal; other buildings step in and out to break the street line. Odd angles are everywhere; no two structures are alike. Landscaping is carefully integrated with architecture. On the village green a miniature fountain

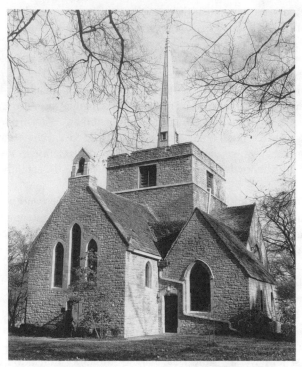

Mariemont Community Church. Built in an English Norman style, the church (1926) resembles but does not copy
that at Stoke Poges, outside London. It was the first structure begun in Mariemont. The architect was Louis E. Jallade of New York.

bubbles quietly. Mariemont's townscape, here at its best, reveals an understated
physical beauty and a quiet charm. This picturesque ensemble recreates the atmosphere of an English village.

Mariemont Community Church (1926), built in a simplified English Norman
style, resembles but does not copy the church at Stoke Poges, outside London, in
whose churchyard the poet Thomas Gray wrote his famous *Elegy*. Designed by
Louis E. Jallade of New York (with hints from Charles Livingood), the church was
the first structure begun in Mariemont. This charming but miniscule building is still
the community's only religious edifice, a situation I find puzzling, given Mary
Emery's own interest in religion and her exemplary support of Christ Church downtown. The stone shingles of the roof get smaller toward the top, making the building
appear higher than it is. The shingles look older than the walls and they are. While
traveling in England, Jallade heard that the stone roof on a tithe barn at Calcot, once
belonging to the Cistercian monks of Kingswood Abbey and dating from about
1300, had collapsed. Jallade had the Mariemont Company purchase the shingles to

reinstall here. The roof's sag, meant to indicate age, is deliberate. The skinny flèche, though modelled upon those on English country churches, looks out of place perched atop such a ground-hugging building. The hand-hewn beams of the interior trusswork came from an abandoned mill. Houses on Oak St. opposite derive from Elizabethan or Jacobean models. Their stone walls and half-timbered and stucco upper stories are meant to harmonize with the church's gray stone.

Behind Mariemont Church we come upon the disused **Ferris family cemetery.** Graves here date back to 1822. The church was intentionally sited adjacent to the cemetery, thus in setting as well as in form recapturing the scene of Gray's *Elegy.* Only lacking are "those rugged Elms, that Yew-tree's Shade." An obelisk commemorates Eliphalet Ferris (1784–1869), the long-lived patriarch whose house on Plainville Road we admired earlier. Like many of Cincinnati's early settlers, Eliphalet—wonderful name!—came from Connecticut. Nearby lie three of his children. The monument commemorates three others. Not one of the six lived past forty.

Below on Wooster Pike the Gothic stone-and-wood structure is a **lichgate.** The word derives from Old English *līc,* Middle English *lyche,* words for body. Pallbearers in earlier times set the bier down under the lichgate before entering the consecrated ground of the churchyard. The roof has stone shingles similar to the church's. Visitors to New York may remember the lichgate, on 29th Street between Fifth and Madison, before the Little Church around the Corner.

We walk up Wooster Pike toward the village center, then cross over and enter **Dogwood Park.** Below was once Mariemont's lagoon. The rustic stone boathouse, designed by Charles Cellarius, has a beautiful curved façade and within a stone fireplace. Boaters used the lagoon in summer, ice skaters in winter. Swans nested on the two-hundred foot long Serpentine Island. Silting caused the lagoon to be grassed over in the early 1960s.

Ahead stands the **Emery Carillon** (1929), designed by Harry Hake, *père et fils.* A single gothic arch dominates each façade; the limestone facing is in an ashlar pattern. Isabella F. Hopkins donated the Carillon in memory of her half-sister, Mary Emery. Its present complement of forty-nine bells ranges over four octaves and in weight from nineteen pounds to over two tons. Carilloneurs give concerts here throughout the year; in summer they take place on Sunday evenings at seven from Memorial Day through Labor Day.

Baseball diamonds and soccer fields occupy Dogwood Park's open spaces; to the west lies a stretch of forest. On its other side are further residential areas, as well as the present Mariemont Municipal Swimming Pool. Near it stood, circa 1450–1670 A.D., a large **Fort Ancient community,** with indications of earlier settlements going back 12,000 years. Between 1878 and 1911 Dr. Charles L. Metz, a Madisonville doctor with a passion for archaeology, collaborated with Professor Frederick Ward Putnam of Harvard University in excavating in the Mariemont area three village sites, ten mounds, and two circular earthworks. Near where the swimming pool is now he found more than 1200 Indian graves along with 1000 storage pots and many other artifacts. Thanks to Putnam, these domestic objects are now in Harvard's Peabody Museum, which after 1882 sponsored the excavations.

Beyond the swimming pool, past another stand of forest, is Mariemont's industrial sector, a forty-five acre tract between Wooster Pike and the railroad right-of-way. It was named Westover after the area in Newport where Mrs. Emery's house stood. The industrial sector had originally been intended for the low-lying land below the bluffs. But early in the planning for Mariemont it was wisely shifted to higher ground less vulnerable to flooding.

We walk south along Pleasant St. and turn left at **Denny Place,** an oval-shaped green on which rise dogwoods, firs, and elms. Two women architects, Lois Lilley Howe and Eleanor Manning of Boston, designed the attractive gabled houses in rough-cut stone. Their style recalls eighteenth-century Cotswold cottages.

We emerge on Fieldhouse Way. The modest brick-and-stucco houses here date from after World War II. The number of distinguished traditionalist architects involved in Mariemont and the different Revival styles they used manage to avoid the repetitiveness of design that we find in one-architect communities, for example, Beman's Pullman or Wank's Greenhills. But Mariemont's later houses benefit neither from the concern for architectural quality that shaped the community's earliest years nor from its idealistic thrust. These later houses, far less imaginative in design than those built in the 1920s, could have gone up in any other postwar American suburb.

We go right on West St., left on Miami Road. Far in the distance the village center fountain bubbles in the light. **Albert Place** (1925) is a charming cul-de-sac of brick two-family houses now painted white. Designed by Robert Rodes McGoodwin of Philadelphia, it was named, along with Sheldon Close, the parallel Tudor Revival cul-de-sac off East Center Ave., after one of Mrs. Emery's sons, both of whom died young. These cul-de-sacs are modelled upon the "closes" in English garden cities like Letchworth and Welwyn. Originally all the front porches on Albert Place were open. A picturesque service lane meanders behind the houses. Maples shade the brick sidewalks; well-tended lawns, ivy, flower beds, and flowering shrubs abound. In the early days the Mariemont Company handled all landscaping. Although individual owners long ago assumed responsibility, Mariemont's ensemble retains much of its initial harmony of appearance.

Instead of following Miami Road to the village center, we turn right on West Center Ave., which angles right, becomes Center Ave. and gains, then loses, a grass median. 3709 Center has a Japanese garden: smooth stones, gravel, plants, a lantern, even a buddha. Center leads to the **Mariemont Concourse,** an elliptical stone arbor (1925; 1964), which curves gracefully for 400 feet. Mature wisteria vines envelop the pergola. From here a view, splendid at all seasons and times of day, opens up over the Little Miami Valley. A hundred feet below us lie the Norfolk & Western tracks; beyond them, mostly out of sight in summer, flows the Little Miami River. Fields occupy the midground; wooded hills delimit the horizon. The scene is tranquil, understated, harmonious. Emerson said it most optimistically: "In the tranquil landscape, and especially in the distant line of the horizon, man beholds somewhat as beautiful as his own nature." We return along Center. East Center Ave. leads to Crystal Spring Road, which flows into the village square. Before resuming our

Mariemont Concourse. From this overlook, rebuilt in 1964, a fine view unfolds over the Little Miami Valley.

journey, we may wish to stop at Graeter's for a turtle sundae. We head back toward Cincinnati along Wooster Pike, which again becomes Columbia Parkway.

Riverbend

We have one more stop, an optional side trip to Riverbend, the spectacular open-air concert pavilion on the Ohio River. I recommend going to Riverbend only if you plan to attend a concert; otherwise, to visit the pavilion is difficult. Follow Columbia Parkway to Tusculum Ave. (the first light in about three miles). Turn left here to get to Riverbend. A right turn up Tusculum would take us past a dazzling sequence of late nineteenth-century frame houses painted in San Francisco colors; above is **Alms Park,** another of the city's hilltop enclaves and a stunning exercise in the picturesque. From the park's terraces we may enjoy spectacular views over the Ohio River and the Little Miami Valley. If not detouring to Alms Park or going to Riverbend, we continue along Columbia Parkway to downtown Cincinnati and pick up this tour on p. 462.

Tusculum deadends on Eastern Ave., where we go left. We are in the East End, a largely Appalachian area between Columbia Parkway and the Ohio that stretches

Tusculum Avenue rowhouses. With wooden frame houses done in vivid color schemes, Tusculum Avenue is the one place in Cincinnati that most closely resembles the streetscapes of "painted ladies" in San Francisco. This picturesque complex (1880) served as worker's dwellings before being transformed into condominiums in the 1980s.

about four miles east from downtown. Where Eastern Ave. begins to curl left, about half a mile along, we angle right down Airport Road. We come out opposite the main terminal of Lunken Airport. At this point we turn right on Wilmer Road. We are on the site of Columbia, the original settlement in the area, predating Cincinnati by a month and some days.

If we had gone left on Wilmer, we would have found, a hundred yards up the road, a **pioneer cemetery.** Originally the site of Columbia Baptist Church, the cemetery overlooked Columbia. The tall sandstone Corinthian column, rather weather-beaten now, was taken in 1885 from the old Post Office Building downtown and in 1889 re-erected at the top of the cemetery steps. The nearby bench made it here via the former garden of the College-Conservatory of Music and the Rose Scrapyard. Many of Columbia's first settlers are interred in this cemetery.

Founded by Major Benjamin J. Stites on November 18, 1788, **Columbia** was, after Marietta, the second permanent European settlement in the Northwest Territory. Stites bought 20,000 acres from John Cleves Symmes, who owned the land between the two Miamis. Columbia's city plan, dated December 3, 1788, and covering the present Lunken Airport, precedes Cincinnati's. The fertile fields, known from their one-time abundance of wild fowl as Turkey Bottom, enabled Columbia to become the granary for pioneers between the two Miamis. Like the third settlement in the area, North Bend (ten miles downriver from Cincinnati), the community grew slowly. Never more than a village, Columbia moved from here in 1815 to the base of Tusculum Hill. In 1873 it became part of Cincinnati.

Until 1947 **Lunken** was Cincinnati's commercial airport. It began after World

War I as a barnstorming facility. The Army Air Corps landed its planes here. In the 1920s Lunken attracted a number of flying companies, the best known being Embry-Riddle, which later became American Airlines. In 1927 Edmund H. Lunken donated 230 acres of land to the city, which then purchased an adjacent 870 acres and improved the site so that it could handle scheduled commercial flights. The new field was dedicated in September 1930. During the following decade Lunken became one of America's bigger municipal airports. But the flaw that doomed Columbia as a settlement also helped doom Lunken as an airport: the low-lying land flooded in high water. During the 1937 deluge, when Lunken lay under water for seventeen days, it gained the dubious sobriquet of "Sunken Lunken." Ringed by 300-foot hills, occasionally enveloped by mist from the two adjacent rivers, and without possibility of expansion, Lunken became increasingly less attractive as larger planes came upon the scene. The city, realizing it could no longer rely on the facility to serve the growing air traffic, began in 1943 to develop a new airport in northern Kentucky. Four years later Greater Cincinnati Airport opened. Lunken now mainly serves private planes and corporate jets. Its **terminal,** an Art Deco time capsule, is well worth a look. It retains its metalwork, linear styling, and William Harry Gothard's **WPA murals:** crude (perhaps intentionally crude) but powerful depictions of the Worker Depressed succeeded by the Worker Triumphant. The **Sky Galley Inn** within prepared the first meals served aboard a commercial airliner. It now offers, among other fare, a nonpareil taco salad.

We proceed past Lunken Terminal and turn left on Kellogg Road (route 52 East). The highway soon crosses the Little Miami River, one of America's loveliest streams, fortunately designated a Scenic River in 1969 and in 1971 included in the National Wild and Scenic River System. We continue along Kellogg Road for three more miles, then go under the I-275 bridge. To our right is **Coney Island,** Cincinnati's once-fabled amusement park. It began in the 1860s as Parker's Grove, an apple orchard frequented by picnickers; in 1886 it opened officially as "Ohio Grove, the Coney Island of the West." In the twentieth century Coney Island became less a place to have a quiet outing than a place to enjoy thrilling rides. Now, with King's Island Cincinnati's main amusement park, Coney Island has come full circle. It is again a place for a swim, a picnic, or dancing in Moonlight Gardens, a pleasant spot for the young, and the not-so-young, to wile away the hours.

If going to a Riverbend concert, we have a choice of parking areas. Closest to Riverbend is the huge lot between Coney Island and River Downs, the racetrack, but I recommend going in the first entrance (that just past the I-275 bridge). Doing so allows walking to **Riverbend** through the attractive Coney Island grounds or, even better, along the path adjacent to the Ohio River.

After entering Riverbend, we climb the stairs to the pergola, and gain, for the first time, a full view of the **pavilion** rising before us. The lawn, or berm, descends gently to the pavilion. Looking upon the scene, we experience a sense of spaciousness. Two huge erector-set, pyramidal towers frame an open-air shed roof, at whose apex is the stage. All the structural elements in Riverbend's design draw our eye to

Riverbend Pavilion. Two huge erector-set pyramidal towers frame an open-air shed roof. The summer home for the Cincinnati Symphony Orchestra, the Pavilion also is the scene for popular music concerts. In this early photograph the metal-panel statues are not all in place. Courtesy of J. Miles Wolf.

the stage. No one of them is insistent. Almost everything we see is functional, yet already the flags atop the towers and the statues above the roofline strike a note of fantasy.

Riverbend began to become a reality in 1982 when the Taft Broadcasting Company (now merged into Great American Broadcasting), which owns Coney Island, contributed fifteen acres for the building site and one million dollars. A private foundation contributed another million in the name of Hulbert Taft, Jr., Taft Broadcasting's founder; and the Corbett Foundation, which underwrote the renovation of Music Hall, gave two million more. A capital campaign raised additional funds. Riverbend's official name is the Hulbert Taft, Jr., Center for the Performing Arts; the structure before us is the J. Ralph Corbett Pavilion. Riverbend opened in 1984. It is the Cincinnati Symphony's summer home, and leading rock, pop, and country musicians also play here.

Michael Graves, paladin of postmodern architecture, designed Riverbend. While a student at the University of Cincinnati, Graves worked for six years in the office of Carl A. Strauss Associates and in creating Riverbend he collaborated enthusiastically with his former mentors, Carl A. Strauss and Ray Roush, Jr. A major factor in the pavilion's design was its location on a flood plain less than a hundred feet from the Ohio. The pavilion had to be resistant to flood damage, and easy to clean afterwards. In addition, the site, located on a bend on the river, invited a structure that would allow views not only of the stage but of the moving expanse of the Ohio framed by the Kentucky hills.

The pavilion deliberately echoes earlier structures. The twin towers, their shape influenced by Music Hall's, are also influenced by, and play off, the trusses of the I-275 bridge downriver. The metal flags recall those seen flying on a well-known 1879 lithograph of Music Hall. The roof's asphalt shingles appear in a stylized Greek key pattern, appropriately, for the Greek key originally symbolized flowing waves. The semicircular seating plan recalls the plan of a Greek amphitheater. The audience may view the landscape and the river to the left and right of the stage.

Tall **statues** grace the near end of the pavilion. If we look at the statues sideways we discover that they are actually two-dimensional metal panels, in effect, silhouettes of statues. Curiously asexual, Rubenesque in contour though not in sensual appeal, this octet of paired females represents the musical muses. Holding ancient-style instruments in hand, they strike varied, close-heeled *contrapposto* poses. Designed by Edward Schmidt in collaboration with Graves, the sixteen-foot high statues rest on three-foot bases. Trusses support them from behind. Their shape, when viewed frontally, recalls the caryatids holding up the Erechtheum's Porch of the Maidens on the Acropolis in Athens. They were inspired by eighteenth-century *grisaille* paintings (paintings done in black, white, and gray) that Graves saw in a Rococo church in Bavaria. (Mantegna's *Esther and Mordecai* in the Cincinnati Art Museum is an example of a *grisaille* painting from an earlier period.) Perhaps their noticeable solidity also echoes Teutonic *embonpoint* nearer at hand. In their position above the cornice line, the statues recall those above Palladio's villas and public buildings, even, as Jayne Merkel suggests, the composer's names we sometimes find on the façades of nineteenth-century symphony halls. Actually, the statues were originally to have been composers. But the Cincinnati Symphony board could not agree on *which* composers so as a compromise we have these figures of a more allegorical kind. It is just as well, for the pavilion was intended for popular as well as classical music.

The **pergola** curves gently over 660 feet. It is composed of pairs of burgundy-colored columns topped by a wooden trellis painted sky blue. Graves's color scheme derives from nature. Dark tones represent the earth, lighter shades the sky. Grave's pergola echoes that within Palladio's Teatro Olimpico (1585), an acknowledged "source" for Riverbend, but it also recalls those in the garden pavilions designed by Karl Friedrich Schinkel, the great German neoclassical architect, at Charlottenhof and for Schloss Glienicke. The wisteria entwining around the pergola columns relates it to the surrounding forest. Walking along the pergola, we may feel we are in a Renaissance garden looking upon a fairytale castle. Riverbend has a touch of Walt Disney to it; it is, after all, part of an amusement park. Like Mariemont, the complex radiates a sense of place. It tells you that you are not anywhere but in or near a particular place: in this instance, a certain Ohio River city that likes to put up buildings with pyramidal towers—and that perhaps takes itself, as Riverbend does not, a little too seriously. Graves's towers, a hallmark of his mature style, may well owe a debt to his long residence in Cincinnati during his young manhood. Riverbend gently spoofs the Queen City's numerous pyramidal structures.

We listen to the music seated in the acoustically excellent shed or stretched out on the grass berm under the open sky. The pavilion seats a little over 5000, the berm can accommodate 10,000 more. Food is available, and a picnic on the grass is delightful. Concertgoers may set up folding chairs or put down blankets. The lawns and trees offer a wonderful play of shifting greens that darken as dusk falls. We hear the susurrous rustle of the wind fingering the trees. The night air is as much a tonic to the ears as the music onstage. We catch glimpses of the Ohio, visible on either side of the stage, and we hear its sounds: the roar of speedboats, the solemn bass of towboat horns, the steady chug of the towboats themselves as their diesels strain to push the heavy cargoes along. Joyful squeals waft over from adjoining Coney Island. As night falls, a chorus of crickets and katydids—and whatever else feels in the mood—accompanies the music on stage. Sounds that might disturb in Music Hall hardly jar at Riverbend. We experience, in short, a musical alfresco. Concerts I have attended here have been unfailingly pleasant and relaxed.

From Riverbend we return to downtown Cincinnati via Kellogg Ave. At Stanley Ave. we turn right, go under the railroad bridge, and at the light head left onto Columbia Parkway. One block further, on the southwest corner of the intersection with Delta Ave., is the Precinct (1901). Long a police station, since 1981 a tony restaurant and night spot, the Precinct is known for its steaks and its attendant sports celebrities. Its building is a nifty example of adaptive re-use.

Columbia Parkway

At all times of day, in dawn mists or in fading twilight, beneath looming cloudbanks or under the bluest of Impressionist skies, **Columbia Parkway** from Delta to downtown remains Cincinnati's most cinematic automotive experience. At night, with lights punctuating the darkness, the experience takes on an eerie magic of its own. Even after countless trips, the beauty of this drive still has the power to catch me by the throat. Maneuvering in the narrow lanes and along the uneven roadbed may tax our concentration but at least we do not compete for space with trucks. When completed in 1938, Columbia Parkway functioned as Cincinnati's gateway from the East. It lies well beyond the reach of floods. The 1907 Kessler plan for Cincinnati's parks had argued for a parkway along the Ohio that could rival "in appearance and in value" Manhattan's Riverside Drive. Unlike that crowded thoroughfare, however, Columbia Parkway continues to provide a view. The landscape today does not appear too different from that fifty years ago. Columbia Parkway still affords, as Harlan Hatcher observed enthusiastically in 1940, "miles of unsurpassed views of the curving river and the Kentucky towns and hills."

Driving Columbia Parkway toward downtown we appear to be following a straight line. But suddenly, far to our left, the Cincinnati skyline comes into view. We are actually on a wide bend of the Ohio. The great sweeping curve of the river complements the vertical curves of the hills. Out of this undulating landscape, like the prow of some great ship, emerge the stable verticals of the city's skyline. They give downtown Cincinnati seen from afar the air of a midwestern San Gimignano. Ahead, the dramatic silhouette of Mount Adams and Immaculata juts against the sky. As we hurtle along the Parkway, the Carew appears to move to the right; soon it rises behind Mount Adams, in odd juxtaposition with the monastery's campanile,

Columbia Parkway and Mount Adams. The four-mile drive along Columbia Parkway from Delta Ave. to downtown Cincinnati is visually the most spectacular in all of Cincinnati. In this view, we are looking upriver. Courtesy of J. Miles Wolf.

then vanishes altogether. Just before Columbia Parkway intersects with Taft and Torrence avenues, we sight St. Rose's steeple. Earlier we saw it from the Ohio River and from Mount Adams; now it rises dramatically out of the shrubbery.

After the next intersection, where Kemper Drive leads to Eden Park, Columbia Parkway dips and rises. Suddenly we emerge from under the brow of Mount Adams. The downtown skyline, now startlingly close, lies before us. We again glimpse its overall shape. We respond to the highway's "kinesthetic" quality, the sense of motion the roadway conveys. The experience of driving possesses a drama of its own.

From Columbia Parkway we have a choice of three exits. We may continue straight until the parkway ends at 5th and Pike streets, near the Taft Museum. Or we may take the first exit, that for I-71 and I-75, which will put us on Fort Washington Way. Or we may opt for the next exit, the 6th Street/Downtown ramp that will deposit us on Broadway. I recommend the last since it will allow us to end our Cincinnati adventure with spectacular visual drama. For a few fleeting moments, as we ride this urban rollercoaster, we experience the city in a kind of metropolitan cinemascope. A widescreen epic unfolds in front of our car windshield, an epic all the more unusual because, like our experience of the city itself, it is real, repeatable, never twice the same, a challenge always there. At first the exit ramp appears to head away from the city. But then it swoops to the left, and for a moment it looks as if we will drive straight into the Procter & Gamble towers. At the last moment, however, the ramp swerves to the right and deposits us, breathless and invigorated, in the heart of downtown. We have completed our journey. We have observed Cincinnati's landscapes and architecture; we have thought about its history. But around the river's curves, along the city's streets, within its parks, up its hills, out in the historic suburbs, new urban adventures are waiting for you. In my end is your beginning.

Opening Times

This list provides opening times for primary tour items. For their locations, see the appropriate maps. The times given are accurate as this book went to press. If in doubt call ahead. Lobbies of public buildings are usually open during business hours. Unenclosed sections of the downtown skywalk system are open at all hours. Sections running through public buildings are closed Sundays but are open much of the rest of the time. Most church interiors are not open (thus not described in this book) except during hours of service. Church members are usually proud of their buildings and invariably have responded favorably to my requests for tours. The Cincinnati area code is 513. Admission fees are noted here, though amounts are not specified.

Chapter 1.

Carew Tower Observation Deck. Monday–Saturday, 10 A.M.–6 P.M.

Chapter 2.

St. Peter-in-Chains. Open during business hours during the week and on Saturdays.

Isaac M. Wise Temple. Tours by appointment (793-2556).

City Hall. Monday–Friday, 8 A.M.–4:30 P.M. Public tour Wednesday at 1 P.M.

Lloyd Library. Monday–Friday, 8:30 A.M.–4 P.M.

Fire Museum. Tuesday–Friday, 10 A.M.–4 P.M. Saturday and Sunday, noon–4 P.M. Closed Monday

Chapter 3.

Public Library. Monday–Friday, 9 A.M.–9 P.M. Saturday, 9 A.M.–6 P.M.

Ohio Book Store. Monday–Saturday, 9 A.M.–4:45 P.M.

Acres of Books. Monday–Saturday, 9 A.M.–5:30 P.M.

Chapter 4.

Mercantile Library. Monday–Friday, 9 A.M.–5:30 P.M.

Chapter 5.

The Taft Museum. Monday–Saturday, 10 A.M.–5 P.M., Sunday, 12 P.M.–5 P.M. Closed Thanksgiving, Christmas, New Year's Day. Voluntary contribution policy.

Chapter 6.

Mimosa. Saturday, Sunday, 1 P.M.–6 P.M. Expanded hours under consideration. Admission fee.

Chapter 7.

Stenger's. Monday–Thursday, 8 A.M.–5 P.M. Friday 8 A.M.–7 P.M. Saturday 8 A.M.–6 P.M.

Grammer's. Monday–Friday, lunch and dinner. Saturday, dinner only.

St. Paul's Church Mart. Monday–Friday, 9 A.M.– 5 P.M.

Chapter 8.

Findlay Market. Wednesday, 7 A.M.–1:30 P.M. Friday, 7 A.M.–6 P.M. Saturday, 7 A.M.–7 P.M. First Monday of each month, 7 A.M.–1:30 P.M.

John Hauck House. Tuesday, Thursday, Friday, 10 A.M.–4 P.M. Sunday, 12 A.M.–4 P.M. Admission fee.

Chapter 9.

William Howard Taft Memorial. Daily, 10 A.M.–4 P.M. Closed Thanksgiving, Christmas, New Year's Day.

Chapter 10.

Scarlet Oaks. House interior open by appointment. Call Scarlet Oaks-Bethesda Retirement Community (861-0400).

Chapter 11.

Rookwood Pottery. Daily, lunch and dinner.

Playhouse in the Park. The Atrium is open to the public before and during performances as well as during the day.

Krohn Conservatory. Monday–Saturday, 10 A.M.–5 P.M. Sunday, 10 A.M.–6 P.M. Easter Sunday, 7 A.M.–10 P.M. Easter week and Christmas, 10 A.M.–9 P.M.

Chapter 12.

Cincinnati Art Museum. Tuesday, Thursday, Saturday, 10 A.M.– 5 P.M. Wednesday, 10 A.M.– 9 P.M. Sunday, noon–5 P.M. Closed Monday. Admission fee (except Saturday).

Chapter 13.

Museum Center. Monday–Saturday, 9 A.M.–5 P.M. Sunday, 11 A.M.–6 P.M. Holidays, 9 A.M.–5 P.M. For ticket information, call 287-7000.

Spring Grove Cemetery. Daily, 8 A.M.–6 P.M.

Cincinnati Zoo. Summer hours, daily, 9 A.M.–8 P.M. (entrance closes at 6 P.M.). Winter hours, daily, 9 A.M.–6 P.M. (entrance closes at 5 P.M.). Admission fee.

Procter & Gamble. Monday–Saturday by appointment (983-1100).

Sky Galley Inn (Lunken Airport). Daily, lunch and dinner.

Coney Island. For information, call 232-8230.

Riverbend (232-6220). Open for evening performances in summer. Can be glimpsed with difficulty from Coney Island in season. Best enjoyed at a performance. Performance tickets are generally available through TicketMaster ticket outlets.

Bibliography

The bibliography lists many works I have drawn upon in writing this book. There have had to be, inevitably, many omissions. The publications of the Cincinnati Historical Society are a main source of Cincinnati lore and have proven invaluable to me. But to have listed individual articles in the *Queen City Heritage,* earlier known as the *Bulletin of the Cincinnati Historical Society,* earlier still as the *Bulletin of the Historical and Philosophical Society of Ohio,* would have unnecessarily extended the bibliography. Cincinnati is now more than 200 years old, and over that time has produced a flood of locally published writings. Although I have read as much as I could in this literature, by and large I have not listed individual items here, and I have not listed articles in the *Cincinnati Enquirer, Cincinnati Post, Cincinnati Magazine, Clifton Magazine,* and other local publications. In the *Enquirer* Owen Findsen regularly reviews the arts, and until 1989 Jayne Merkel reviewed new developments in architecture. Cincinnati is fortunate to have them both, and I have found their work invaluable.

Aaron, Daniel. "Cincinnati, 1818–1839; A Study of Attitudes in the Urban West." Ph.D. diss., Harvard University, 1943.

Altick, Richard D. *To Be in England.* New York: Norton, 1969.

American Landscape Architecture. Designers and Places. Edited by William H. Tishler. Washington, D.C.: The Preservation Press, 1989.

The American Renaissance 1876–1917. New York: The Brooklyn Museum, 1979. Distributed by Pantheon Books.

Andrews, Gregory E., and Ransom, David F. *Structures and Styles: Guided Tours of Hartford Architecture.* Hartford, Conn.: Connecticut Historical Society/Connecticut Architecture Foundation, 1988.

Angell, Roger. *Five Seasons. A Baseball Companion.* 1977; New York: Simon & Schuster, 1988. A Fireside Book.

Archer, John. "Country and City in the American Romantic Suburb." *Journal of the Society of Architectural Historians* 42 (May 1983): 139–56.

Architecture and Construction in Cincinnati: A Guide to Designers and Builders. Cincinnati: Architectural Foundation of Cincinnati, 1987.

Art Deco and the Cincinnati Union Terminal. Exhibition Catalogue. Cincinnati: Contemporary Arts Center, 1973.

Art Palace of the West. Cincinnati: Cincinnati Art Museum, 1981.

Bach, Ira. J. *A Guide to Chicago's Historic Suburbs*. Chicago and Athens, Ohio: Swallow Press/Ohio University Press, 1981.

Bach, Ira J., and Wolfson, Susan. *Chicago on Foot*. Chicago: Chicago Review Press, 1987.

Bachman, Ben. *Upstream: A Voyage on the Connecticut River*. Chester, Conn.: Globe Pequot Press, 1988.

Bacon, Mardges. *Ernest Flagg: Beaux-Arts Architect and Urban Reformer*. Cambridge, Mass.: MIT Press, 1986.

Baedeker, Karl. *The United States . . . A Handbook for Travelers*. 3d ed. Leipzig: Karl Baedeker, 1904.

Baldwin, Leland D. *The Keelboat Age in Western Waters*. Pittsburgh: University of Pittsburgh Press, 1941.

Bannister, Turpin C. "Bogardus Revisited; Part I: The Iron Fronts." *Journal of the Society of Architectural Historians* 15 (Dec. 1956): 12–22.

Barlow, Elizabeth. *Frederick Law Olmsted's New York*. New York: Praeger, 1972.

Barnard's Lincoln. Cincinnati: Stewart & Kidd Company, 1917.

Barnett, Jonathan. "A New Planning Process with Built-In Political Support." *Architectural Record* 139 (May 1966): 141–46.

Baron, Stanley W. *Brewed in America: A History of Beer and Ale in the United States*. Boston: Little, Brown, 1962.

Bender, Thomas. *Toward an Urban Vision: Ideas and Institutions in Nineteenth-Century America*. Lexington, Ky.: University Press of Kentucky, 1975.

Berry, Thomas Senior. *Western Prices before 1861: A Study of the Cincinnati Market*. Cambridge, Mass: Harvard University Press, 1943.

The Best of Cincinnati. Cincinnati: The Greater Cincinnati Chamber of Commerce, 1971.

Birmingham, Stephen. *The Golden Dream: Suburbia in the Seventies*. New York: Harper & Row, 1978.

———. *The Grandes Dames*. New York: Simon and Schuster, 1982.

Blair, Walter, and Meine, Franklin J. *Mike Fink: King of Mississippi Boatmen*. New York: Henry Holt, 1933.

———, eds. *Half-Horse, Half-Alligator: The Growth of the Mike Fink Legend*. Chicago: University of Chicago, 1956.

Blake, Peter. *The Master Builders: Le Corbusier, Mies van der Rohe, Frank Lloyd Wright*. 1960; New York: Norton, 1976.

Board, Helen. *Bertha Baur: A Woman of Note*. Philadelphia: Dorrance, 1971.

Bode, Carl. *The American Lyceum: Town Meeting of the Minds*. New York: Oxford University Press, 1956.

Boorstin, Daniel J. *The Americans: The Colonial Experience*. New York: Random House, 1958.

———. *The Americans: The National Experience*. New York: Random House, 1965.

———. *The Americans: The Democratic Experience*. New York: Random House, 1973.

Boris, Eileen. *Art and Labor: Ruskin, Morris, and The Craftsman Ideal in America*. Philadelphia: Temple University Press, 1986.

Boswell, James. *Life of Johnson.* 1791; London: Oxford University Press, 1953.

Bouton, Jim. *Ball Four.* New York and Cleveland: World, 1970.

[Bremer, Fredrika.] *America of the Fifties: Letters of Fredrika Bremer.* Selected and edited by Adolph B. Benson. New York: American-Scandinavian Foundation, 1924.

————. *The Homes of the New World: Impressions of America.* 3 vols. Translated by Mary Howitt. London: Chapman & Hall, 1853.

Brewing in Cincinnati 1885–1985. Cincinnati: Hudepohl Brewing Co., 1985.

Brooks, Gale. "Cincinnati '70: Birth and Rebirth." *AIA Journal* (Jan. 1971): 32–34.

Buckingham, James. *The Eastern and Western States of America.* 3 vols. London: Fisher, Son, & Co., 1842.

Burgheim, Max. *Cincinnati in Wort und Bild.* Cincinnati: Burgheim Publishing Co., 1891.

————. *Der Führer von Cincinnati.* Cincinnati: M. & R. Burgheim, 1875.

Burke, Mary Alice Heekin. *Elizabeth Nourse, 1859–1938: A Salon Career.* Washington, D.C.: Smithsonian Institution Press, 1983.

Burt, Nathaniel. *Palaces for the People: A Social History of the American Art Museum.* Boston: Little, Brown, 1977.

Busch, Moritz. *Travels Between the Hudson and the Mississippi 1851–1852.* Translated and edited by Norman H. Binger. Lexington, Ky.: University Press of Kentucky, 1971.

[Cameron, Elizabeth R.] *Cincinnati and the Arts: Past into Present.* Cincinnati: Junior League of Cincinnati, 1958.

Campen, Richard N. *Ohio: An Architectural Portrait.* Chagrin Falls, Ohio: West Summit Press, 1973.

————. *Outdoor Sculpture in Ohio.* Chagrin Falls, Ohio: West Summit Press, 1980.

Carrott, Richard G. *The Egyptian Revival: Its Sources, Monuments, and Meaning, 1808–1858.* Berkeley and Los Angeles: University of California Press, 1978.

Carter, Judge A. G. W. *The Old Court House: Reminiscences and Anecdotes of the Courts and Bar of Cincinnati.* Cincinnati: Peter G. Thomson, 1880.

Carter, Denny T. "Cincinnati and Its 19th-Century Artists." *American Art & Antiques* 2 (Sept.–Oct. 1979): 102–9.

————. *Henry Farny.* New York: Watson Guptill, 1978.

Cauffield, Joyce V. B., and Banfield, Carolyn E. *The River Book: Cincinnati and the Ohio.* Cincinnati: Program for Cincinnati, 1981.

The Centenary of the Cincinnati Observatory: November 5, 1943. Cincinnati: Historical and Philosophical Society of Ohio and the University of Cincinnati, 1944.

Chewning, John A. *Urban Walls: Cincinnati.* Cincinnati: Carl Solway Gallery, 1976.

Churchill, Winston. "Land of Corn and Lobsters." *Collier's,* 92 (August 5, 1933): 16–17, 45.

Cincinnati: A Guide to the Queen City and Its Neighbors. Cincinnati: The Wiesen-Hart Press, 1943.

Cincinnati Art Museum Handbook. Cincinnati: Cincinnati Art Museum, 1975.

The Cincinnati Cemetery of Spring Grove. Cincinnati: C. F. Bradley, 1857.

Cincinnati Historic Inventory. Cincinnati: Miami Purchase Association/City Planning Commission, 1978.

Cincinnati Historical Society Bulletin 39 (Spring 1981): 6–80. [special number on the Cincinnati Art Museum.]

Cincinnati in Bronze. Cincinnati: [n.p.], 1959.

Cincinnati Landmarks: A Bicentennial Exhibition. Cincinnati: Cincinnati Art Museum, 1976.

The Cincinnati Metropolitan Master Plan and the Official City Plan of the City of Cincinnati: Adopted November 22, 1948. Cincinnati: City Planning Commission, [1948].

Cincinnati, Ohio: "The Queen City." Cincinnati: Lemfee Publishing Co., 1926.

Cincinnati River Front: 1848. Cincinnati: South Ohio Savings Bank, n.d. [1960's].

Cincinnati Symphony Orchestra: A Tribute to Max Rudolph and Highlights of Its History. [Cincinnati: Cincinnati Symphony Orchestra, 1967.]

Cincinnati 2000 Plan: A Comprehensive Development Plan for Downtown. Appendix: Cincinnati 2000 Plan. Cincinnati: [City Planning Commission, 1982].

Cincinnati und sein Deutschtum. [By H. H. Fick.] Cincinnati: Queen City Publishing Co., 1901.

Cincinnati Union Terminal Dedication 1933. 1933; Cincinnati: [n.p., n.d.].

Cincinnati Zoo. Cincinnati: Cincinnati Zoo, 1986.

Cist, Charles. *Cincinnati in 1841.* Cincinnati: The Author, 1841.

———. *Sketches and Statistics of Cincinnati in 1851.* Cincinnati: Wm. H. Moore, 1851.

———. *Sketches and Statistics of Cincinnati in 1859.* [Cincinnati: n.p., 1859.]

Cities: The Forces That Shape Them. New York: Rizzoli, 1982.

Clark, Edna Maria. *Ohio Art and Authors.* Richmond, Va.: Garrett and Massie, 1932.

Clark, Kenneth. *The Other Half: A Self-Portrait.* New York: Harper & Row, 1977.

Clay, Grady. *Alleys: A Hidden Resource.* Louisville, Ky.: Cross Section Publishers, 1979.

Coffin, Levi. *Reminiscences of Levi Coffin.* 1876; New York: AMS Press, 1971.

Commemorative Booklet: Corporate Headquarters Building, Taft Broadcasting Company, April 1980. [Cincinnati: n.p., 1980.]

Condit, Carl W. *American Building.* Chicago: University of Chicago Press, 1968.

———. *The Chicago School of Architecture.* Chicago: University of Chicago Press, 1964.

———. *The Railroad and the City: A Technological and Urbanistic History of Cincinnati.* Columbus: Ohio State University Press, 1977.

Conway, Moncure Daniel. *Autobiography: Memories and Experiences.* 2 vols. Boston and New York: Houghton, Mifflin, 1904.

Coolidge, John. *Patrons and Architects: Designing Art Museums in the Twentieth Century.* Fort Worth, Texas: Amon Carter Musuem, 1989.

Coyle, William. *Ohio Authors and their Books . . . 1796–1950.* Cleveland and New York: World, 1962.

Craig, Lois, and the Staff of the Federal Architectural Project. *The Federal Presence: Architecture, Politics, and Symbols in United States Government Building.* Cambridge, Mass.: MIT, n.d.

Cronin, Vincent. *The Companion Guide to Paris.* New York: Harper & Row, 1963.

Curry, Jane. *The River's in My Blood.* Lincoln, Neb.: University of Nebraska Press, 1983.

Dannenbaum, Jed. *Drink and Disorder: Temperance Reform in Cincinnati from the Washington Revival to the WCTU.* Urbana and Chicago: University of Illinois Press, 1984.

Darnall, Margaretta J. "The American Cemetery and Picturesque Landscape. Bellefontaine Cemetery, St. Louis." *Winterthur Portfolio* 18 (1983): 249–69.

Davies, Jane B. "Llewellyn Park in West Orange, New Jersey." *Antiques* 107 (Jan. 1975): 142–58.

Day, Doris. See Hotchner, A. E.

De Chambrun, Clara Longworth. *Cincinnati: The Story of the Queen City.* New York: Scribner's, 1939.

———. *The Making of Nicholas Longworth: Annals of an American Family.* New York: Ray Long and Richard R. Smith, 1933.

Dicey, Edward. *Six Months in the Federal States.* 2 vols. London: Macmillan, 1863.

Dickens, Charles. *American Notes.* London: Chapman & Hall, 1842.

Downard, William L. *The Cincinnati Brewing Industry: A Social and Economic History.* Athens, Ohio: Ohio University Press, 1973.

Downing, Andrew Jackson. *The Architecture of Country Houses.* 1850; New York: Dover, 1969.

———. *Victorian Cottage Residences.* 1842; New York: Dover, 1981.

Drake, Daniel. *Natural and Statistical View, or Picture of Cincinnati. . . .* Cincinnati: Looker and Wallace, 1815.

Drury, John. *Historic Midwest Houses.* 1957; New York: Bonanza Books, n.d.

Dubos, René. *The Wooing of Earth.* London: Athlone, 1980.

Duffy, Edith. "A History of Cincinnati's Eden Park." M.A. thesis, University of Cincinnati, 1968.

Robert S. Duncanson: A Centennial Catalogue. Cincinnati: Cincinnati Art Museum, 1972.

Durant, John and Durant, Alice. *Pictorial History of American Ships.* New York: A. S. Barnes, 1953.

Early, James. *Romanticism and American Architecture.* New York: A. S. Barnes. 1965.

Easton, Loyd D. *Hegel's First American Followers: The Ohio Hegelians.* Athens, Ohio: Ohio University Press, 1966.

Ellis, Anita. "Cincinnati Art Furniture." *Antiques* 121 (April 1982): 934–41.

Engelhardt, Geo. W. *Cincinnati: The Queen City.* 1901; Cincinnati: Young & Klein, 1982.

Fairbanks, Robert B. *Making Better Citizens: Housing Reform and the Community Development Strategy in Cincinnati, 1890–1960.* Urbana and Chicago: University of Illinois Press, 1988.

Faran, Angeline Loveland. *Glendale, Ohio: 1855–1955.* Cincinnati: McDonald Printing Co., 1955.

Faust, Albert Bernhardt. *The German Element in the United States.* 2 vols. Boston and New York: Houghton Mifflin, 1909.

Fellheimer, Alfred. "Cincinnati Union Terminal." *Architectural Forum* 58 (June 1933): 453–78.

———. "Modern Railway Passenger Terminals." *Architectural Forum* 53 (December 1930): 655–94.

————. "Railroad Stations." In *Forms and Functions of Twentieth Century Architecture,* edited by Talbot Hamlin. 4 vols. 4:432–74. New York: Columbia University Press, 1952.

Favretti, Rudy T., and Favretti, Joy Putnam. *Landscapes and Gardens for Historic Buildings.* Nashville: American Association for State and Local History, 1978.

Ferebee, Ann. "Successful Cincinnati." *Design & Environment* (Winter 1972): 40–47.

Ferry, W. Hawkins. *The Buildings of Detroit: A History.* Detroit: Wayne State University Press, 1968.

Festschrift for the German-American Tricentennial Jubilee, Cincinnati, 1983. Edited by Don Heinrich Tolzmann. Cincinnati: Cincinnati Historical Society, 1982.

Fishman, Robert. *Bourgeois Utopias: The Rise and Fall of Suburbia.* New York: Basic Books, 1987.

Flint, Timothy. *Recollections of the Last Ten Years.* . . . Edited by George R. Brooks. 1826; Carbondale, Ill.: Southern Illinois University Press, 1968.

Foote, Glen R., comp. *Graphic History of Mt. Adams.* Souvenir commemorating the Dedication of the Mt. Adams Bridge. September 12, 1931.

Foote, John P. *The Schools of Cincinnati, and Its Vicinity.* 1855; New York: Arno Press and the New York Times, 1970.

Forbes, J. B. *Victorian Architect: The Life and Work of William Tinsley.* Bloomington, Ind.: Indiana University Press, 1953.

Ford, Henry A., and Ford, Kate B. *History of Cincinnati, Ohio.* Cleveland: L. A. Williams, 1881.

————. *History of Hamilton County, Ohio.* Cleveland: L. A. Williams, 1881.

Garland, Catherine A. *Nantucket Journeys: Exploring the Island, Its Architecture, And Its Past.* Camden, Maine: Down East Books, 1988.

Giglierano, Geoffrey J., Overmyer, Deborah A., with Propas, Frederick L. *The Bicentennial Guide to Greater Cincinnati: A Portrait of Two Hundred Years.* 2 vols. Cincinnati: Cincinnati Historical Society, 1988.

Girouard, Mark. *Cities and People: A Social and Architectural History.* New Haven: Yale University Press, 1985.

Glendale's Heritage. Glendale, Ohio: Glendale Heritage Preservation, 1976.

Goetzmann, William H. *The American Hegelians: An Intellectual Episode in the History of Western America.* New York: Alfred A. Knopf, 1973.

Goldberger, Paul. *On the Rise: Architectural Design in a Postmodern Age.* 1983; New York: Penguin Books, 1985.

————. *The Skyscraper.* New York: Alfred A. Knopf, 1981.

The Golden Age: Cincinnati Painters of the Nineteenth Century Represented in the Cincinnati Art Museum. Cincinnati: Cincinnati Art Museum, 1979.

Golden Jubilee Souvenir Cincinnati Music Hall 1878–1928. [Cincinnati: Cincinnati Music Hall Association, 1928.]

Goldfarb, Stephen. "Science and Democracy: A History of the Cincinnati Observatory, 1842–1872." *Ohio History* 78 (Summer 1969): 172–78.

Goss, Charles Frederick. *Cincinnati, the Queen City.* 4 vols. Chicago and Cincinnati: S. J. Clarke, 1912.

Gowans, Alan. *The Comfortable House: North American Suburban Architecture 1890–1930.* Cambridge, Mass.: MIT, 1986.

————. *Images of American Living: Four Centuries of Architecture and Furniture as Cultural Expression.* 1964; New York: Harper & Row, 1976. Icon Editions.

Graham, Phillip. *Showboats: The History of an American Tradition.* Austin, Tx.: University of Texas Press, 1951.

Green, Marilyn, and Bennett, Michael. *Cincinnati: A Pictorial History.* Norfolk, Va.: The Donning Co., 1986.

Greene, Letha C. *Long Live the Delta Queen.* New York: Hastings House, 1973.

Greve, Charles Theodore. *Centennial History of Cincinnati.* 2 vols. Chicago: Biographical Publishing Co., 1904.

Gruen, Victor. *The Heart of Our Cities. The Urban Crisis: Diagnosis and Cure.* London: Thames and Hudson, 1965.

Guide Book: The Cincinnati Zoo. Cincinnati: The Zoological Society of Cincinnati, 1942; rev., 1952, 1960.

Guide to the Collections of the Cincinnati Art Museum. [Cincinnati: Cincinnati Art Museum, n.d. (1950s?).]

[Haas, Richard.] *Richard Haas: An Architect of Illusion.* New York: Rizzoli, 1981.

Halprin, Lawrence. *Cities.* New York: Reinhold, 1963.

————. *Freeways.* New York: Reinhold, 1966.

Hamilton, Thomas. *Men and Manners in America.* 2 vols. 1833; New York: Augustus M. Kelley, 1968.

Hamlin, Talbot. *Greek Revival Architecture in America.* 1944; New York: Dover, 1964.

Hancocks, David. *Animals and Architecture.* New York: Praeger, 1971.

Harlow, Alvin. *Old Towpaths.* 1926; New York: Kennikat, 1954.

————. *The Serene Cincinnatians.* New York: Dutton, 1950.

Harris, Neil. *The Artist in American Society: The Formative Years, 1790–1860.* 1966; Chicago: University of Chicago Press, 1982. Phoenix Books.

Hart, Philip. *Orpheus in the New World: The Symphony Orchestra as an American Cultural Institution.* New York: W. W. Norton, 1973.

Hartegan, Lynda Roscoe, ed. *Sharing Traditions: Five Black Artists in Nineteenth Century America.* Washington, D.C.: Smithsonian Institution Press, 1985.

Hatcher, Harlan. *The Buckeye Country: A Pageant of Ohio.* 1940; New York: G. P. Putnam's Sons, 1947.

Havighurst, Walter. *Ohio: A Bicentennial History.* New York: Norton, 1976.

Hearn, Lafcadio. *An American Miscellany.* Collected by Albert Mordell. 2 vols. New York: Dodd, Mead, 1924.

————. *Children of the Levee.* Edited by O. W. Frost. Lexington, Ky.: University of Kentucky Press, 1957.

————. *Lafcadio Hearn: Selected Writings 1872–1877.* Edited by William S. Johnson. Indianapolis: Woodruff Publications, 1979.

————. *The Selected Writings of Lafcadio Hearn.* Edited by Henry Goodman. New York: Citadel Press, 1949.

Heckscher, August. *Open Spaces: The Life of American Cities.* New York: Harper & Row, 1977.

Hilton, George M. *The Cable Car in America.* Rev. ed. San Diego: Howell-North Books, 1982.

Hines, Philip R. *The Wines and Wineries of Ohio.* Franklin, Ohio: The Chronicle, 1973.

Hiss, Tony. *The Experience of Place.* New York: Alfred A. Knopf, 1990.

Historic Auburn Avenue. Cincinnati: Cincinnati Historical Society, 1982.

History of Cincinnati and Hamilton County, Ohio. Cincinnati: S. B. Nelson, 1894.

Holiday, Joseph E. *Calvary Episcopal Church, Cincinnati, Ohio: A History.* Cincinnati: Calvary Episcopal Church, 1967.

Hogarth, William. *The Analysis of Beauty.* Edited by Joseph Burke. 1753; Oxford: Clarendon, 1955.

Honour, Hugh. *The Companion Guide to Venice.* New York: Harper & Row, 1966.

Hotchner, A. E. *Doris Day: Her Own Story.* New York: William Morrow, 1976.

Hough, Michael. *Out of Place: Restoring Identity to the Regional Landscape.* New Haven and London: Yale University Press, 1990.

Houston, Matilda Charlotte (Jessie). *Hesperos; or, Travels in the West.* 2 vols. London: John W. Parker, 1850.

Howard, Ebenezer. *Garden Cities of To-Morrow.* Edited by F. J. Osborn. 1898; Cambridge, Mass.: MIT, 1965.

Howat, John K. *The Hudson River and Its Painters.* 1972; New York: American Legacy Press, 1983.

Howe, Henry. *Historical Collections of Ohio. . . .* Cincinnati: Derby, Bradley, 1848.

———. *Historical Collections of Ohio. . . .* 2 vols. 1888; Columbus: Henry Howe & Son, 1890, 1891.

Hurley, Daniel. *Cincinnati: The Queen City.* Cincinnati: Cincinnati Historical Society, 1982.

Huxtable, Ada Louise. *Architecture, Anyone? Cautionary Tales of the Building Art.* New York: Random House, 1986.

———. *Classic New York: Georgian Gentility to Greek Elegance.* New York: Doubleday, 1964. Anchor Books.

———. *Kicked a Building Lately?* New York: Quadrangle/New York Times, 1976.

———. *The Tall Building Artistically Reconsidered: The Search for a Skyscraper Style.* New York: Pantheon Books, 1984.

———. *Will They Ever Finish Bruckner Boulevard?* New York: Macmillan, 1971.

In Pursuit of Beauty: Americans and the Aesthetic Movement. New York: Metropolitan Museum of Art/Rizzoli, 1986.

Into a Second Century with Procter & Gamble. Cincinnati: Procter & Gamble, 1985.

Ivory Soap 1879–1954. Cincinnati: Procter & Gamble, 1954.

Jackson, John Brinckerhoff. *American Space: The Centennial Years, 1865–1976.* New York: Norton, 1972.

Jackson, Kenneth T., and Vergara, Camilo José. *Silent Cities. The Evolution of the American Cemetery.* New York: Princeton Architectural Press, 1990.

Jacobs, Jane. *The Death and Life of Great American Cities.* New York: Random House, 1961.

Jakle, John A. *Images of the Ohio Valley: A Historical Geography of Travel, 1740 to 1860.* New York: Oxford University Press, 1977.

Janson, H. W. *History of Art.* 2d ed. Englewood Cliffs, N.J.: Prentice-Hall, 1977.

Jenkins, Simon. *The Companion Guide to Outer London.* London: Collins, 1981.

Kaplan, Wendy. *"The Art That is Life": The Arts & Crafts Movement in America, 1875–1920.* Boston: Little, Brown, 1987.

Kaufmann, Edgar, Jr., editor. *The Rise of an American Architecture.* New York: Praeger, 1970.

Kenny, D. J. *Illustrated Cincinnati.* Cincinnati: Robert Clarke, 1875.

———. *Illustrated Guide to Cincinnati and the World's Columbian Exposition.* Cincinnati: Robert Clarke, 1893.

Kent, Cheryl. "Inside the Liveable City: The Atrium." *Inland Architect* 33 (Jan./Feb. 1989): 36–43.

[Kessler, George.] *A Park System for the City of Cincinnati.* Cincinnati: Park Commission, 1907.

Kidney, Walter C. *Historic Buildings of Ohio.* Pittsburgh: Ober Park Associates, 1972.

Kinkhead, Eugene. *Central Park, 1857–1995: The Birth, Decline, and Renewal of a National Treasure.* New York: W. W. Norton, 1990.

Kircher, Edwin J., Agranoff, Barbara, and Agranoff, Joseph. *Rookwood: The Golden Era of Art Pottery 1880–1929.* Cincinnati: n.p., 1969.

Knack, Ruth Eckdish. "Where Planning Counts." *Planning* 46 (Oct. 1980): 14–30.

Knox, Israel. *Rabbi in America: The Story of Isaac M. Wise.* Boston: Little, Brown, 1957.

Kostof, Spiro. *America by Design.* New York: Oxford University Press, 1987.

Kraemer, A. O. and Kraemer, G. A. *Kraemer's Picturesque Cincinnati.* 1898; Cincinnati: Ohio Book Store, n.d. [1985].

The Ladies, God Bless 'Em: The Women's Art Movement in Cincinnati in the Nineteenth Century. Cincinnati: Cincinnati Art Museum, 1976.

[Lakier, Aleksandr Borisovich.] *A Russian Looks at America: The Journal of Aleksandr Borisovich Lakier in 1857.* Translated and edited by Arnold Schrier and Joyce Story. Chicago: University of Chicago Press, 1979.

Lamott, John H. *History of the Archdiocese of Cincinnati 1821–1921.* New York and Cincinnati: Frederick Pustet, 1921.

Lancaster, Clay. *Architectural Follies in America.* Rutland, Vermont: Charles E. Tuttle, 1960.

Langsam, Walter C. *Cincinnati in Color.* New York: Hastings House, 1979.

Laycock, George and Ellen. *The Ohio Valley: Your Guide to America's Heartland.* Garden City, New York: Doubleday, 1983.

Leapman, Michael. *The Companion Guide to New York.* New York: Prentice-Hall, 1983.

Leonard, Lewis Alexander. *Greater Cincinnati and Its People.* 4 vols. New York and Chicago: Lewis Historical Pub. Co., 1927.

————. *Life of Alphonso Taft*. New York: Hawke, 1920.

Lewis, Sinclair. *Babbitt*. 1922; New York: New American Library, 1961.

Lief, Alfred. *"It Floats": The Story of Procter & Gamble*. New York: Rinehart, 1958.

Linden-Ward, Blanche. "Landscape as Art." *Dialogue* (Sept.–Oct. 1986): 22–25.

————. *Spring Grove Cemetery: A Self-Guided Walking Tour*. Cincinnati: Center for Neighborhood and Community Studies, 1985.

————, and Ward, Alan. "Spring Grove: The Role of the Rural Cemetery in American Landscape Design." *Landscape Architecture* 85 (Sept.–Oct. 1985): 126–31, 140.

Loomis, Chauncey C. *Weird & Tragic Shores: The Story of Charles Francis Hall, Explorer*. 1971; New York: Popular Library, n.d.

Ludwig, Charles. *Playmates of the Towpath*. 1929; Cincinnati: The Ohio Book Store, n.d. [1987].

Lynch, Kevin. *The Image of the City*. Cambridge, Mass.: MIT, 1960.

Lyndon, Donlyn. *The City Observed: Boston. A Guide to the Architecture of the Hub*. New York: Random House, 1982. Vintage Books.

McAlester, Virginia, and McAlester, Lee. *A Field Guide to American Houses*. New York: Alfred A. Knopf, 1984.

McAllister, Anna Shannon. *In Winter We Flourish: Life and Letters of Sarah Worthington King Peter 1800–1877*. New York: Longmans, Green, 1939.

McCord, David. *About Boston: Sight, Sound, Flavor and Inflection*. 1948; Boston: Little, Brown, 1973.

McCullough, David. *The Great Bridge*. New York: Simon and Schuster, 1972.

Mackay, Alexander. *The Western World: or, Travels in the United States in 1846–47*. 3 vols. London: Richard Bentley, 1849.

Mackay, Charles. *Life and Liberty in America*. New York: Harper & Brothers, 1859.

Madigan, Mary Jean Smith. "The Influence of Charles Locke Eastlake on American Furniture Manufacture, 1870–1890." In *Winterthur Portfolio* 10, edited by Ian M. G. Quimby, 1–22. Charlottesville, Va.: University Press of Virginia, 1975.

Mansfield, E. D. *Personal Memories . . . 1803–1843*. 1879; New York: Arno Press, 1970.

Mariemont: A Guide to Citizens & Property Owners. [Cincinnati: n.p., n.d. (1980s)].

Marryat, Captain Frederick. *A Diary in America, With Remarks on Its Institutions*. Edited by Sydney Jackman. 1839; New York: Alfred A. Knopf, 1962.

Martineau, Harriet. *Retrospect of Western Travel*. 3 vols. 1838; New York: Greenwood Press, 1969.

Marx, Leo. *The Machine in the Garden. Technology and the Pastoral Idea in America*. 1964; New York: Oxford University Press, 1967. A Galaxy Book.

The Mary E. Johnson Collection. Cincinnati: Cincinnati Art Museum, 1972.

Masson, Georgina. *The Companion Guide to Rome*. 1965; London: Fontana/Collins, 1974.

Masterpieces from the Cincinnati Art Museum. Cincinnati: Cincinnati Art Museum, 1984.

Maxwell, Sidney. *The Suburbs of Cincinnati*. 1870; New York: Arno Press, 1984.

Maxwell, Walter. "The Emery Estate." *Saxby's Magazine* 20 (Sept. 1909): 51–65.

Meeks, Carroll L. V. *The Railroad Station: An Architectural History.* New Haven: Yale University Press, 1956.

Merkel, Jayne. "Cincinnati." *Landscape Architecture* 75 (Sept./Oct. 1985): 118–25.

———. "Court Street Center, nee French Bauer Dairy Ice Cream Factory." *Inland Architect* 28 (July/Aug. 1984): 16–19.

———. "Dreaming in Deco: The Netherland Swings Again." *Inland Architect* 29 (Jan./Feb. 1985): 16–19.

———. *In Its Place: The Architecture of Carl Straus and Ray Roush.* Cincinnati: Contemporary Arts Center, 1984.

———. *Michael Graves and the Riverbend Music Center.* Cincinnati: Contemporary Arts Center, 1987.

———. "The Riverbend Music Center." *Cincinnati Arts* 1 (Fall/Winter 1988): 22–25, 117.

———, and Rudd, William J. *Drawn by Cincinnati: Architectural Drawings in the Collection of the Cincinnati Historical Society.* Cincinnati: Contemporary Arts Center, 1980.

Metzner, Henry. *A Brief History of the American Turnerbund.* Pittsburgh: National Executive Committee of the American Turnerbund, 1924.

Miller, Zane L. *Boss Cox's Cincinnati: Urban Politics in the Progressive Era.* 1968; Chicago: University of Chicago Press, 1980. Phoenix Edition.

———, and Jenkins, Thomas H., eds. *The Planning Partnership: Participants' Views of Urban Renewal.* Beverly Hills, Ca.: Sage Publications, 1982.

———, and Roth, George F. *Cincinnati's Music Hall.* Virginia Beach, Va.: Jordan & Co., 1978.

Moore, John Travers. *Cincinnati Parks.* Cincinnati: Cincinnati Park Board, 1953.

Morris, James (Jan). *The World of Venice.* New York: Pantheon Books, 1960.

Mosler, Max. *Historic Brighton.* Cincinnati: n.p., 1902.

Mulvey, Christopher. *Anglo-American Landscapes: A Study of Nineteenth-Century Anglo-American Travel Literature.* Cambridge, England: Cambridge University Press, 1983.

Munzer, Martha E., and Vogel, John, Jr. *New Towns: Building Cities from Scratch.* New York: Alfred A. Knopf, 1974.

Myers, Minor, Jr. *Liberty Without Anarchy: A History of the Society of Cincinnati.* Charlottesville, Va.: University Press of Virginia, 1983.

Nairn, Ian. *The American Landscape: A Critical View.* New York: Random House, 1965.

Neilson, Brian James. "Dialogue with the City: The Evolution of Baseball Parks." *Landscape* 29 (1986): 39–47.

Nelson, Paul David. *Anthony Wayne: Soldier of the Early Republic.* Bloomington, Ind.: Indiana University Press, 1985.

[Nevins, Allan, comp. and ed.] *American Social History as Recorded by British Travellers.* New York: Henry Holt, 1923.

Newcomb, Rexford. *Architecture of the Old Northwest Territory.* Chicago: University of Chicago Press, 1950.

Nolen, John. *New Towns for Old.* Boston: Marshall Jones, 1927.

O'Connor, Richard. *The German Americans: An Informal History.* Boston: Little, Brown, 1968.

The Official City Plan of Cincinnati, Ohio. Adopted by the City Planning Commission, 1925. Cincinnati: City Planning Commission [1925].

Olsen, Donald J. *The City as Work of Art: London—Paris—Vienna.* New York and London: Yale University Press, 1986.

———. *The Growth of Victorian London.* London: B. T. Batsford, 1976.

O'Rell, Max. *A Frenchman in America: Recollections of Men and Things.* New York: Cassell, 1891.

Orlemann, Clinton. Text by Hollis Stevenson. *Cincinnati: Paintings and Sketches.* Cincinnati: Orlemann Enterprises, 1986.

Over-the-Rhine Comprehensive Plan. Cincinnati: City Planning Department, 1984. Revised March 1985.

Parks, Warren Wright. *The Mariemont Story.* Cincinnati: Creative Writers & Publishers, 1967.

Parton, James. "Cincinnati." *The Atlantic Monthly* 20 (August 1867): 229–46.

Pastier, John. "The Business of Baseball." *Inland Architect* 33 (Jan./Feb. 1989): 56–62.

Peck, Herbert. *The Book of Rookwood Pottery.* New York: Crown, 1968.

Peirce, Donald C. "Mitchell and Rammelsberg: Cincinnati Furniture Manufacturers 1847–1881." *Winterthur Portfolio* 13 (1979): 209–79.

Perry, Dick, and Zink, Lawrence. *Fascinating Spirited Cincinnati.* Cincinnati: Cincinnati Chapter of the AIA, 1979.

———. *Not Just a Sound: The Story of WLW.* Englewood Cliffs, N.J.: Prentice-Hall, 1971.

Petty, Priscilla Hayes. *Under a Lucky Star: The Story of Frederick A. Hauck.* Cincinnati: Cincinnati Oral History Foundation, 1986.

Picturesque Cincinnati. Cincinnati: The John Shillito Co., 1883.

Pierson, William H., Jr. *American Buildings and Their Architects. Volume 2. Technology and the Picturesque: The Corporate and the Early Gothic Styles.* 1978; New York: Oxford University Press, 1986.

Pike, Martha V., and Armstrong, Janice Gray. *A Time to Mourn: Expressions of Grief in Nineteenth Century America.* Stony Brook, N.Y.: The Museums at Stony Brook, 1980.

Piper, David. *The Companion Guide to London.* 1964; London: Collins, 1981.

———. *Painting in England, 1500–1870: An Introduction.* London: The Book Society, 1960.

The Plan for Downtown Cincinnati. Cincinnati: City of Cincinnati, 1964.

Poole, William F. *The Tyler Davidson Fountain.* Cincinnati: Robert Clarke, 1872.

Procter & Gamble: The House that Ivory Built. Edited by the editors of *Advertising Age.* Lincolnwood, Ill.: NTC Business Books, 1988.

Quick, Michael. *An American Painter Abroad: Frank Duveneck's European Years.* Cincinnati: Cincinnati Art Museum, 1987.

Rasmussen, Steen Eiler. *London: The Unique City.* Rev. ed. 1934: Cambridge, Mass.: MIT, 1982.

Reps, John W. *The Making of Urban America: A History of City Planning in the United States.* Princeton: Princeton University Press, 1965.

————. *Town Planning in Frontier America*. Columbia, Mo.: University of Missouri Press, 1980.

Richards, Leonard L. *"Gentlemen of Property and Standing": Anti-Abolition Mobs in Jacksonian America*. New York: Oxford University Press, 1970.

Roe, George Mortimer, editor. *Cincinnati: The Queen City of the West*. Cincinnati: Cincinnati Times-Star Co., 1895.

Rogers, Millard F., Jr. *Favorite Paintings from the Cincinnati Art Museum*. New York: Abbeville Press, 1980.

————. *Spanish Paintings in the Cincinnati Art Museum*. Cincinnati: Cincinnati Art Museum, 1978.

Rose, Pete, and Kahn, Roger. *Pete Rose: My Story*. New York: Macmillan, 1989.

Ross, Ishbel. *An American Family: The Tafts—1678 to 1964*. Cleveland and New York: World, 1964.

Ross, Stephen J. *Workers on the Edge: Work, Leisure, and Politics in Industrializing Cincinnati, 1788–1890*. New York: Columbia University Press, 1985.

Ruggles, Alice McGuffey. *The Story of the McGuffeys*. New York: American Book Company, 1950.

Russell, Charles Edward. *The American Orchestra and Theodore Thomas*. 1927; Westport, Conn.: Greenwood Press, 1971.

Russell, John. *The Meanings of Modern Art*. New York: Harper & Row. 1981.

————. *Paris*. London: B. T. Batsford, 1960.

Sarna, Jonathan D., and Klein, Nancy H. *The Jews of Cincinnati*. Cincinnati: Center for Study of the American Jewish Experience, 1989.

Scannyhorn, Richard, and Steinle, John. *Stockades in the Wilderness: The Frontier Defenses and Settlements of Southwestern Ohio, 1788–1795*. Dayton, Ohio: Landfall Press, 1986.

Schabas, Ezra. *Theodore Thomas: America's Conductor and Builder of Orchestras, 1835–1905*. Urbana and Chicago: University of Chicago Press, 1989.

Scheiber, Harry N. *Ohio Canal Era: A Case Study of Government and the Economy, 1820–1861*. Athens, Ohio: Ohio University Press, 1969.

Scheller, William G. *The Hudson River Valley*. Helena, Mont.: American Geographic Publishing, 1988.

Schisgall, Oscar. *Eyes on Tomorrow: The Evolution of Procter & Gamble*. Chicago: J. G. Ferguson, 1981.

Schmitt, Peter J. *Back to Nature: The Arcadian Myth in Urban America*. New York: Oxford University Press, 1969.

Schuyler, David. *The New Urban Landscape: The Redefinition of City Form in Nineteenth-Century America*. Baltimore: Johns Hopkins University Press, 1986.

Schuyler, Montgomery. "The Buildings of Cincinnati." *Architectural Record* 23 (May 1908): 337–66.

Schweitzer, Fr. Aloys., and Gerbus, Henry. *The History and the Story of Findlay Market and the Over the Rhine Community Center*. Dedication Day, June 9, 1974. [Cincinnati: VIP offset, (1974).]

Scott, Mary Ann. *Dutch, Flemish, and German Paintings in the Cincinnati Art Museum: Fifteenth through Eighteenth Centuries*. Cincinnati: Cincinnati Art Museum, 1987.

Scully, Vincent J., Jr. *The Shingle Style and the Stick Style*. Rev. ed. New Haven and London: Yale University Press, 1955; 1971.

Sculpture Collection of the Cincinnati Art Museum. Cincinnati: Cincinnati Art Museum, 1970.

Sears, John F. *Sacred Places, American Tourist Attractions in the Nineteenth Century*. New York: Oxford University Press, 1989.

Sexton, P. M. *Mariemont: A Brief Chronicle of its Origin and Development*. Mariemont: n.p., 1966.

Shapiro, Henry D., and Miller, Zane L. *Clifton: Neighborhood and Community in an Urban Setting. A Brief History*. Cincinnati: The Laboratory in American Civilization, 1976.

Sheblessy, Sylvia Kleve. *100 Years of the Cincinnati May Festival*. Cincinnati: [n.p.], 1973.

Sikes, Jane E. *The Furniture Makers of Cincinnati 1790–1849*. Cincinnati: [n.p., n.d.].

Silverstein, Iola Hessler. *Cincinnati Then and Now*. Cincinnati: League of Women Voters, 1982.

——. *Hamilton County's Patchwork Quilt*. 1961; Cincinnati: University of Cincinnati Institute of Government Research, 1969.

Simons, Corinne Miller. *John Uri Lloyd: His Life and Works 1849–1936 with a History of the Lloyd Library*. Cincinnati: privately printed, 1972.

Sitte, Camillo. *The Birth of Modern City Planning*. Edited by George R. Collins and Christiane Crasemann Collins. New York: Rizzoli, 1986.

Smith, William C. *Queen City Yesterdays. Sketches of Cincinnati in the Eighties*. Crawfordsville, Ind.: R. E. Banta, 1959.

Sokolove, Michael Y. *Hustle: The Myth, Life, and Lies of Pete Rose*. New York: Simon and Schuster, 1990.

Sorkin, Michael. *Hardy Holzman Pfeiffer*. London: Granada, 1981.

Specter, David Kenneth. *Urban Spaces*. Greenwich, Conn.: New York Graphic Society, 1974.

Spiess, Philip D. *Sights and Scenes of Clifton: An Historical Tour*. Cincinnati: [n.p.], 1965.

Stannard, David E., editor. *Death in America*. Philadelphia: University of Pennsylvania Press, 1975.

Steffens, Joseph Lincoln. *The Struggle for Self-Government*. Edited by David W. Noble. 1906; New York and London: Johnson Reprint, 1968.

Steinmann, D. B. *The Builders of the Bridge: The Story of John Roebling and His Son*. New York: Harcourt, Brace, 1945.

Stephan, Sol. A. *Cincinnati Zoo Guide*. Cincinnati: Cincinnati Zoological Park Association, 1928.

Stern, Robert A. M. *The Anglo-American Suburb*. London: Architectural Design, 1981.

——. *Pride of Place: Building the American Dream*. Boston: Houghton Mifflin, 1986.

Stevens, George E. *The City of Cincinnati*. . . . Cincinnati: Geo. S. Blanchard & Co., 1869.

Stevens, Harry R. *The Ohio Bridge*. Cincinnati: The Roter Press, 1939.

Stevenson, Elizabeth. *Lafcadio Hearn.* New York: Macmillan, 1961.

[Strauch, Adolph.] *Spring Grove Cemetery: Its History and Improvements with Observations on Ancient and Modern Places of Sepulture.* Cincinnati: Robert Clarke, 1869.

Strauss, Anselm L. *Images of the American City.* New Brunswick, N.J.: Transaction Books, 1976.

Sullivan, Louis H. *Kindergarten Chats and Other Writings.* 1918; New York: Dover, 1979.

Sutton, Denys. "The Queen City of the West." *Apollo* 93 (April 1971): 4–8.

———. ed. [articles on collections in the Cincinnati Art Museum.] *Apollo* 93 (April 1971): 236–323.

Taft Museum Catalogue. Cincinnati: Cincinnati Institute of Fine Arts [1939; reissued 1958].

[Taft Museum.] *Apollo* 128, no. 322 (new series) (Dec. 1988): 389–412.

[Taft Museum.] *"Who was the Architect of the Taft Museum?" A Symposium June 11 and 12, 1987.* [Cincinnati: The Taft Museum, 1988].

Tanenhaus, Ruth Amdur. "Rookwood: A Cincinnati Art Pottery." *Art & Antiques* 3 (July/ Aug. 1980): 74–81.

Tatum, George B. "The Beautiful and the Picturesque." *American Quarterly* 3 (Spring 1951): 36–51.

Tauranac, John. *Essential New York.* New York: Holt, Rinehart, and Winston, 1979.

Taylor, James Wickes. *"A Choice Nook of Memory." The Diary of a Cincinnati Law Clerk 1842–1844.* Edited by James Taylor Dunn. Columbus: Ohio State Archaeological and Historical Society, 1950.

Teetor, Henry B. *The Past and Present of Mill Creek Valley.* Cincinnati: Cohen, 1882.

Tenkotte, Paul A. *A Heritage of Art and Faith: Downtown Covington Churches.* Covington, Ky.: Kenton County Historical Society, 1986.

Tenner, Armin. *Cincinnati Sonst und Jetzt.* Cincinnati: Mecklenburg & Rosenthal, 1878.

Thayer, Laura. *Cincinnati Old House Handbook.* Cincinnati: Department of City Planning/ Historic Conservation Office, 1984.

They Built a City: 150 Years of Industrial Development. Cincinnati: Cincinnati Post, 1938.

Thomas, Rose Fay. *Memoirs of Theodore Thomas.* New York: Moffat, Yard and Co., 1911.

Theodore Thomas: A Musical Autobiography. Edited by George P. Upton. 1905; New York: Da Capo Press, 1964.

Tolzmann, Don Heinrich. *The Cincinnati Germans after the Great War.* New York: Peter Lang, 1987.

———. *German-American Literature.* Metuchen, N.J.: Scarecrow, 1977.

———. *Spring Grove and its Creator: H. A. Rattermann's Biography of Adolph Strauch.* Edited by Don Heinrich Tolzmann. Cincinnati: The Ohio Book Store, 1988.

Tomkins, Calvin. *Merchants and Masterpieces: The Story of the Metropolitan Museum of Art.* New York: Dutton, 1970.

A Tour of Mariemont. Cincinnati: Mariemont Preservation Foundation, 1984.

Trapp, Kenneth R., ed. *Celebrate Cincinnati Art.* Cincinnati: Cincinnati Art Museum, 1981.

———. "Japanese Influence in early Rookwood Pottery." *Antiques* 103 (Jan. 1973): 193–97.

———. " 'To Beautify the Useful': Benn Pitman and the Women's Woodcarving Movement in Cincinnati in the Late 19th Century." In *Victorian Furniture,* edited by Kenneth Ames, 174–92. Philadelphia: Victorian Society, 1982.

Trillin, Calvin. "Eating in Cincinnati." In *The Norton Reader,* edited by Arthur M. Eastman et al., 601–6. 5th ed. New York: Norton, 1980.

Trollope, Frances. *Domestic Manners of the Americans.* Edited by Donald Smalley. 1832; New York: Alfred A. Knopf, 1949.

Trollope, Thomas Adolphus. *What I Remember.* Edited by Herbert van Thal. 1887; London: William Kimber, 1973.

Tucker, Louis L. *Cincinnati: A Students' Guide to Localized History.* New York: Teachers College Press, 1969.

———. "Cincinnati: Athens of the West." *Ohio History* 80 (1966): 11–25, 67–68.

Tunnard, Christopher. *The City of Man.* 1953; New York: Charles Scribner's Sons, 1970. 2d ed.

———, and Reed, Henry Hope. *American Skyline.* 1953; New York: New American Library, 1956.

The Tyler Davidson Fountain. Cincinnati: Robert Clarke, 1884.

Urban Open Spaces. New York: Rizzoli, 1979.

Venturi, Robert; Brown, Denise Scott; and Izenour, Steven. *Learning from Las Vegas.* 1972; Cambridge, Mass.: MIT, 1977. 2d ed.

Vexler, Robert I. *Cincinnati: A Chronological and Documentary History 1676–1970.* Dobbs Ferry, N.Y.: Oceana Publications, 1975.

The Village Plan, Glendale, Ohio. [Cincinnati?]: Village Planning Commission, [1944].

Vitz, Robert C. *The Queen and the Arts. Cultural Life in Nineteenth-Century Cincinnati.* Kent, Ohio: Kent State University Press, 1989.

Wade, Richard C. *The Urban Frontier: Pioneer Life in Early Pittsburgh, Cincinnati, Lexington, Louisville, and St. Louis.* 1959; Chicago: University of Chicago, 1976.

Wagner, Richard M., and Wright, Roy J. *Cincinnati Streetcars.* Cincinnati: Wagner Car Company, 1968, 1969 (nos. 1, 2, 3); Wyoming, Ohio: Trolley Talk, 1979, 1984 (nos. 8 and 9).

Walsh, Margaret. *The Rise of the Midwestern Meatpacking Industry.* Lexington, Ky.: University Press of Kentucky, 1982.

[Webb, Beatrice.] *Beatrice Webb's American Diary 1898.* Edited by David A. Shannon. Madison, Wis.: University of Wisconsin Press, 1963.

Weber, Eva. *Art Deco in America.* New York: Exeter, 1985.

White, John H. *Cincinnati Locomotive Builders 1845–1868.* Washington, D.C.: Smithsonian Institution, 1965.

White, Morton and Lucia. *The Intellectual Versus the City: From Thomas Jefferson to Frank Lloyd Wright.* 1962; New York: New American Library, 1964.

Whyte, William H. *City: Rediscovering the Center.* New York: Doubleday, 1988.

———. *The Social Life of Small Urban Spaces.* Washington, D.C.: The Conservation Foundation, 1980.

Williams, Caroline. *As Always—Cincinnati.* Burlington, Ky.: Penandhoe Press, 1951.

————. *Cincinnati Scenes.* 1962, 1968; Dayton, Ohio: Landfall Press, 1973.

————. *Cincinnati—Steeples, Streets, and Steps.* Burlington, Ky.: Penandhoe Press, 1963.

————. *The City on Seven Hills.* Cincinnati: Cincinnati Enquirer, 1938.

————. *Mirrored Landmarks of Cincinnati.* Cincinnati: Cincinnati Enquirer, 1939.

Wimberg, Robert J. *Cincinnati: Over-the-Rhine.* Cincinnati: Ohio Book Store, 1987.

————. *Cincinnati Breweries.* Cincinnati: Ohio Book Store, 1989.

Wischnitzer, Rachel. *Synagogue Architecture in the United States.* Philadelphia: Jewish Publication Society of America, 1955.

Wittke, Carl. *The German-Language Press in America.* Lexington, Ky.: University Press of Kentucky, 1957.

————, editor. *The History of the State of Ohio.* 6 vols. Columbus: Ohio State Archaeological and Historical Society, 1941–1944.

————. *Refugees of Revolution: The German Forty-Eighters in America.* Philadelphia: University of Pennsylvania Press, 1952.

————. *William Nast: Patriarch of German Methodism.* Detroit: Wayne State University Press, 1959.

Wolfe, Gerard R. *New York: A Guide to the Metropolis.* 1975; New York: McGraw-Hill, 1983.

Woods, Nicholas A. *The Prince of Wales in Canada and the United States.* London: Bradbury & Evans, 1861.

Wright, Robert A. "Monumental Details." *Inland Architect* 33 (March/April 1989): 64–69.

Wunder, John, ed. *Toward an Urban Ohio.* Columbus: Ohio State Historical Society, 1977.

INDEX

Numbers in italics signify important references; boldface numbers indicate illustrations.

485

Ohio State University Press

Text and jacket design by Hunter Graphics

Type set in ITC Times Roman
by Graphic Composition, Inc., Athens, GA.
Printed by Edwards Brothers, Inc., Ann Arbor, MI.

Times Roman was designed by Victor Lardent for
Stanley Morison, typographic adviser to *The Times* of London.
It was first used by *The Times* in 1932.